Deep Learning Architecture and Applications

Deep Learning Architecture and Applications

Editors

Xiang Zhang
Xiaoxiao Li

Basel • Beijing • Wuhan • Barcelona • Belgrade • Novi Sad • Cluj • Manchester

Editors
Xiang Zhang
Department of Computer Science, University of North Carolina at Charlotte
Charlotte, NC, USA

Xiaoxiao Li
Electrical and Computer Engineering Department, University of British Columbia
Vancouver, BC, Canada

Editorial Office
MDPI
St. Alban-Anlage 66
4052 Basel, Switzerland

This is a reprint of articles from the Special Issue published online in the open access journal *Algorithms* (ISSN 1999-4893) (available at: https://www.mdpi.com/journal/algorithms/special_issues/56U1X6P99B).

For citation purposes, cite each article independently as indicated on the article page online and as indicated below:

Lastname, A.A.; Lastname, B.B. Article Title. *Journal Name* **Year**, *Volume Number*, Page Range.

ISBN 978-3-0365-8830-8 (Hbk)
ISBN 978-3-0365-8831-5 (PDF)
doi.org/10.3390/books978-3-0365-8831-5

© 2023 by the authors. Articles in this book are Open Access and distributed under the Creative Commons Attribution (CC BY) license. The book as a whole is distributed by MDPI under the terms and conditions of the Creative Commons Attribution-NonCommercial-NoDerivs (CC BY-NC-ND) license.

Contents

About the Editors vii

Preface ix

János Hollósi, Áron Ballagi and Claudiu Radu Pozna
Simplified Routing Mechanism for Capsule Networks
Reprinted from: *Algorithms* 2023, *16*, 336, doi:10.3390/a16070336 1

Saidur R. Pavel and Yimin D. Zhang
Optimization of the Compressive Measurement Matrix in a Massive MIMO System Exploiting LSTM Networks
Reprinted from: *Algorithms* 2023, *16*, 261, doi:10.3390/a16060261 23

Shadab Anwar Shaikh, Harish Cherukuri and Taufiquar Khan
Recovering the Forcing Function in Systems with One Degree of Freedom Using ANN and Physics Information
Reprinted from: *Algorithms* 2023, *16*, 250, doi:10.3390/a16050250 39

Cesar Davila Hernandez, Jungseok Ho, Dongchul Kim and Abdoul Oubeidillah
Machine-Learning-Based Model for Hurricane Storm Surge Forecasting in the Lower Laguna Madre
Reprinted from: *Algorithms* 2023, *16*, 232, doi:10.3390/a16050232 53

Sebastian Bickel, Stefan Goetz and Sandro Wartzack
Detection of Plausibility and Error Reasons in Finite Element Simulations with Deep Learning Networks
Reprinted from: *Algorithms* 2023, *16*, 209, doi:10.3390/a16040209 71

Dominik Stallmann and Barbara Hammer
Unsupervised Cyclic Siamese Networks Automating Cell Imagery Analysis
Reprinted from: *Algorithms* 2023, *16*, 205, doi:10.3390/a16040205 89

Bradley Walters, Sandra Ortega-Martorell, Ivan Olier and Paulo J. G. Lisboa
How to Open a Black Box Classifier for Tabular Data
Reprinted from: *Algorithms* 2023, *16*, 181, doi:10.3390/a16040181 111

Daniela Galatro, Rosario Trigo-Ferre, Allana Nakashook-Zettler,
Vincenzo Costanzo-Alvarez, Melanie Jeffrey, Maria Jacome and et al.
Framework for Evaluating Potential Causes of Health Risk Factors Using Average Treatment Effect and Uplift Modelling
Reprinted from: *Algorithms* 2023, *16*, 166, doi:10.3390/a16030166 137

Lorenzo Arsini, Barbara Caccia, Andrea Ciardiello, Stefano Giagu and Carlo Mancini Terracciano
Nearest Neighbours Graph Variational AutoEncoder
Reprinted from: *Algorithms* 2023, *16*, 143, doi:10.3390/a16030143 151

Eran Shachar, Israel Cohen and Baruch Berdugo
Acoustic Echo Cancellation with the Normalized Sign-Error Least Mean Squares Algorithm and Deep Residual Echo Suppression
Reprinted from: *Algorithms* 2023, *16*, 137, doi:10.3390/a16030137 169

Steven Guan, Ko-Tsung Hsu and Parag V. Chitnis
Fourier Neural Operator Network for Fast Photoacoustic Wave Simulations
Reprinted from: *Algorithms* 2023, *16*, 124, doi:10.3390/a16020124 183

Olivier Pantalé
Development and Implementation of an ANN Based Flow Law for Numerical Simulations of Thermo-Mechanical Processes at High Temperatures in FEM Software
Reprinted from: *Algorithms* **2023**, *16*, 56, doi:10.3390/a16010056 201

Tahira Niazi, Teerath Das, Ghufran Ahmed, Syed Muhammad Waqas, Sumra Khan, Suleman Khan and et al.
Investigating Novice Developers' Code Commenting Trends Using Machine Learning Techniques
Reprinted from: *Algorithms* **2023**, *16*, 53, doi:10.3390/a16010053 223

Abouzar Choubineh, Jie Chen, David A. Wood, Frans Coenen and Fei Ma
Fourier Neural Operator for Fluid Flow in Small-Shape 2D Simulated Porous Media Dataset
Reprinted from: *Algorithms* **2023**, *16*, 24, doi:10.3390/a16010024 243

Taihao Han, Sai Akshay Ponduru, Arianit Reka, Jie Huang, Gaurav Sant and Aditya Kumar
Predicting Dissolution Kinetics of Tricalcium Silicate Using Deep Learning and Analytical Models
Reprinted from: *Algorithms* **2023**, *16*, 7, doi:10.3390/a16010007 257

Mihai-Alexandru Niculescu, Stefan Ruseti and Mihai Dascalu
RoSummary: Control Tokens for Romanian News Summarization
Reprinted from: *Algorithms* **2022**, *15*, 472, doi:10.3390/a15120472 273

Tuan-Vinh La, Minh-Son Dao, Duy-Dong Le, Kim-Phung Thai, Quoc-Hung Nguyen and Thuy-Kieu Phan-Thi
Leverage Boosting and Transformer on Text-Image Matching for Cheap Fakes Detection
Reprinted from: *Algorithms* **2022**, *15*, 423, doi:10.3390/a15110423 293

L. G. Divyanth, D. S. Guru, Peeyush Soni, Rajendra Machavaram, Mohammad Nadimi and Jitendra Paliwal
Image-to-Image Translation-Based Data Augmentation for Improving Crop/Weed Classification Models for Precision Agriculture Applications
Reprinted from: *Algorithms* **2022**, *15*, 401, doi:10.3390/a15110401 309

Alireza Namdari, Maryam Asad Samani and Tariq S. Durrani
Lithium-Ion Battery Prognostics through Reinforcement Learning Based on Entropy Measures
Reprinted from: *Algorithms* **2022**, *15*, 393, doi:10.3390/a15110393 327

Nikolaos-Ioannis Galanis, Panagiotis Vafiadis, Kostas-Gkouram Mirzaev and George A. Papakostas
Convolutional Neural Networks: A Roundup and Benchmark of Their Pooling Layer Variants
Reprinted from: *Algorithms* **2022**, *15*, 391, doi:10.3390/a15110391 345

Alireza Saberironaghi, Jing Ren and Moustafa El-Gindy
Defect Detection Methods for Industrial Products Using Deep Learning Techniques: A Review
Reprinted from: *Algorithms* **2023**, *16*, 95, doi:10.3390/a16020095 365

About the Editors

Xiang Zhang

Xiang Zhang is an Assistant Professor in the Department of Computer Science at the University of North Carolina (UNC) at Charlotte. Zhang is serving as director of the Charlotte Machine Learning Lab (CML), which boasts around 40 members, including esteemed professors and PhD candidates renowned for their expertise across diverse domains such as deep learning theory, computer vision, natural language processing, reinforcement learning, and time series analysis. Before joining UNC Charlotte, he was a postdoctoral fellow at Harvard University from March 2020 to July 2022. Zhang received his Ph.D. degree (in 2020) in Computer Science from the University of New South Wales (UNSW). His research interests lie in data mining and machine learning with applications in medical time series, brain–computer interfaces (BCIs), and pervasive healthcare. Zhang's research outcomes have been published in prestigious conferences (such as ICLR, NeurIPS, and KDD) and journals (like Nature Computational Science).

Xiaoxiao Li

Dr. Xiaoxiao Li is an Assistant Professor in the Electrical and Computer Engineering Department at the University of British Columbia (UBC), leading the Trusted and Efficient AI (TEA) Group, and an Adjunct Assistant Professor at the School of Medicine at Yale University. Dr. Li specializes in the interdisciplinary field of deep learning and biomedical data analysis. Her primary mission is to make AI more reliable, especially when it comes to sensitive areas like healthcare. At the TEA Group, they explore a wide range of topics from fundamental machine learning to more focused healthcare-driven AI solutions. The group delves into topics such as learning from multimodal and heterogeneous data, efficient AI models, federated learning, and creating AI models that not only perform tasks but can also be trustworthy. Some of their groundbreaking work includes AI-driven analysis of neuroimages, pathology slides, molecular and clinical notes. In essence, Dr. Li's work is all about bridging the world of advanced machine learning with the practical needs of the healthcare industry.

Preface

Amidst the ever-evolving realm of artificial intelligence, the emergence of deep learning stands as a transformative force, fundamentally reshaping how machines understand and process information. Yet, despite its prowess, deep learning techniques have predominantly focused on specific domains such as computer vision, language processing, and time series analysis, often overlooking the broader spectrum of vital real-world scenarios.

This reprint serves as a crystallization of this technological revolution, encompassing a compendium of advanced accomplishments in deep learning and their pertinent applications. Within these pages, readers embark on a comprehensive journey, delving into methodologies that span an expansive array of real-world contexts encompassing healthcare, finance, physics, and mechanics. This volume seeks to bridge the gap, bringing the prowess of deep learning to the forefront of diverse and critical domains.

Xiang Zhang and Xiaoxiao Li
Editors

Article

Simplified Routing Mechanism for Capsule Networks

János Hollósi [1,*], Áron Ballagi [2,*] and Claudiu Radu Pozna [2]

[1] Department of Informatics, Széchenyi István University, 9026 Győr, Hungary
[2] Department of Automation, Széchenyi István University, 9026 Győr, Hungary; pozna@sze.hu
* Correspondence: hollosi.janos@sze.hu (J.H.); ballagi@ga.sze.hu (Á.B.)

Abstract: Classifying digital images using neural networks is one of the most fundamental tasks within the field of artificial intelligence. For a long time, convolutional neural networks have proven to be the most efficient solution for processing visual data, such as classification, detection, or segmentation. The efficient operation of convolutional neural networks requires the use of data augmentation and a high number of feature maps to embed object transformations. Especially for large datasets, this approach is not very efficient. In 2017, Geoffrey Hinton and his research team introduced the theory of capsule networks. Capsule networks offer a solution to the problems of convolutional neural networks. In this approach, sufficient efficiency can be achieved without large-scale data augmentation. However, the training time for Hinton's capsule network is much longer than for convolutional neural networks. We have examined the capsule networks and propose a modification in the routing mechanism to speed up the algorithm. This could reduce the training time of capsule networks by almost half in some cases. Moreover, our solution achieves performance improvements in the field of image classification.

Keywords: convolutional neural network; capsule network; routing algorithm

1. Introduction

For processing visual data, convolutional neural networks (CNNs) are proving to be the best solutions nowadays. The most popular applications of convolutional neural networks in the field of image processing are image classification [1,2], object detection [3,4], semantic segmentation [5,6] and instance segmentation [7,8]. However, the biggest challenge of convolutional neural networks is their inability to recognize pose, texture and deformations of an object, caused by the pooling layers. Pooling layers are used in the feature maps. Where we can find several types of this layer: max pooling, min pooling, average pooling and sum pooling are the most common types of pooling layers [9]. Due to this layer, the efficiency of the convolutional neural network to recognize the same object in different input images under different conditions is high. At the same time, the size of the tensors is reduced due to the pooling layer, thus reducing the computational complexity of the network. In most cases, pooling layers are one of the best tools for feature extraction; however, they introduce spatial invariance in convolutional neural networks. Due to the nature of the pooling layer, a great amount of information is lost, which in some cases may even be important features in the image. To compensate for this, the convolutional neural network needs a substantial amount of training data where data augmentation is necessary.

Geoffrey Hinton and his research team introduced capsule network theory as an alternative to convolutional neural networks. Hinton et al. published the first paper in the field of capsule networks in 2011 [10], where the potential of the new theory is explained, but the solution for effective training it is not yet available. The next important milestone came in 2017, when Sabour et al. introduced the dynamic routing algorithm between capsule layers [11]. Thanks to this dynamic routing algorithm, the training and optimization of capsule-based networks can be performed efficiently. Finally, Hinton et al. published a matrix capsule-based approach in 2018 [12]. These are the three most important

results that the inventors of the theory have published in the field of capsule networks. The basic building block of convolutional neural networks is the neuron, while capsule networks are made up of so-called capsules. A capsule is a group of related neurons, where each neuron's output represents a different property of the same feature. Hence, the input and output of the capsule networks are both vectors (n-dimensional capsules), while the neural network works with scalar values (neurons). Instead of pooling layers, a dynamic routing algorithm was introduced in capsule networks. In this approach, the lower-level features (lower-level capsules) will only be sent to higher-level capsules that match its contents. This property makes capsule networks a more effective solution than convolutional neural networks in some use cases.

However, the training process for capsule networks can be much longer than for convolutional neural networks, where due to the high number of parameters, the memory requirements of the network can be much higher. Therefore, for complex datasets (e.g., large input images, high number of output classes), presently, capsule networks do not perform well yet. This is due to the complexity of the dynamic routing algorithm. For this reason, we have attempted to make modifications to the dynamic routing algorithm. Our primary aim was to reduce the time of the training process, and secondly to achieve a higher efficiency. In our method, we reduced the weight of the input capsule vector during the optimization in the routing process. We also proposed a parameterizable activation function interpreted in terms of vectors, based on the squash function. In this paper, we demonstrate the effectiveness of our proposed modified routing algorithm and compare it with other capsule network-based methods and convolutional neural network-based approaches.

This paper is structured as follows. In Section 2, we provide the theoretical background of the capsule network theory proposed by Hinton et al. [10] and Sabour et al. [11]. Section 3 clarifies our improved routing mechanism for capsule network and our parameterizable activation squash function. Section 4 describes the capsule network architecture used in this research. In Section 5, we present the datasets used to compare the dynamic routing algorithm and our proposed solution. Our results are summarized in Section 6, where we compare our improved routing solution with Sabour et al.'s method, and with some recently published neural network-based solutions. Finally, our conclusions based on our results are summarized in Section 7.

2. Theory of Capsule Network

The capsule network [10–12] (or CapsNet) is very similar to the classical neural network. The main difference is the basic building block. In the neural network, we use neurons, but in the capsule network, we can find capsules. Figures 1 and 2 show the main differences between the classical artificial neurons and the capsules.

A capsule is a group of neurons that perform a multitude of internal computation and encapsulate the results of the computations into an n-dimensional vector. This vector is the output of the capsule. The length of this output vector is the probability and the direction of the vector, indicating certain properties about the entity.

In a capsule-based network, we use routing-by-agreement, where the output vector of any capsule is sent to all higher-level capsules. Each capsule output is compared with the actual output of the higher-level capsules. Where the outputs match, the coupling coefficient between the two capsules are increased.

Let i be a lower-level capsule and j be a higher-level capsule. The prediction vector is calculated as follows:

$$\hat{u}_{(j|i)} = W_{ij} u_i \qquad (1)$$

where W_{ij} is a trainable weighting matrix and u_i is an output pose vector from the i-th capsule to the j-th capsule. The coupling coefficients are calculated with a simple SoftMax function, as follows:

$$c_{ij} = \frac{exp(b_{ij})}{\sum_k exp(b_{ik})} \qquad (2)$$

where b_{ij} is the log probability of capsule i coupled with capsule j, and it is initialized with zero values. The total input to capsule j is a weighted sum over the prediction vectors, calculated as follows:

$$s_j = \sum_i c_{ij} \hat{u}_{j|i} \qquad (3)$$

In capsule networks, we use the length of the output vector to represent the probability for the capsule. Therefore, we use a non-linear activation function, which is called the squashing function. The squashing function is the next:

$$v_j = squash(s_j) = \frac{\|s_j\|^2}{1 + \|s_j\|^2} \frac{s_j}{\|s_j\|} \qquad (4)$$

We can use the dynamic routing algorithm (by Sabour et al. [11]) to update the c_{ij} values in every iteration. In this case, the goal is to optimize the v_j vector. In the dynamic routing algorithm, the b_{ij} vector is updated in every iteration, as follows:

$$b_{ij} = b_{ij} + \hat{u}_{j|i} v_j \qquad (5)$$

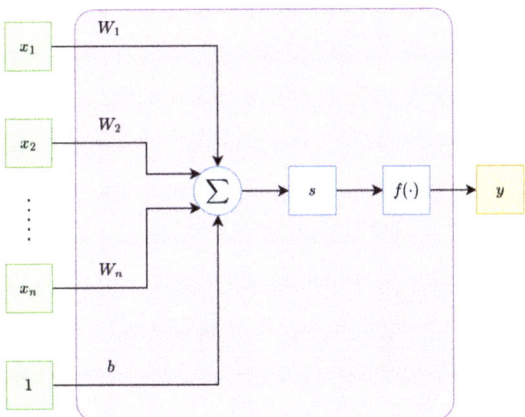

Figure 1. Typical structure of a neuron. (green: inputs, blue: operations, yellow: output, purple: neuron).

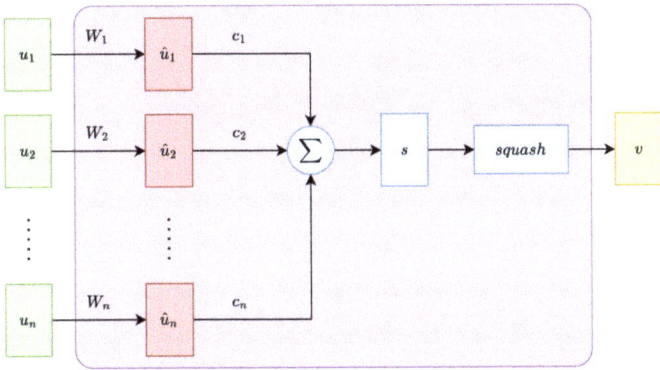

Figure 2. Typical structure of a capsule. (green: inputs, red: prediction vectors, blue: operations, yellow: output, purple: capsule).

3. Improved Routing Algorithm

Our experiments on capsule network theory have shown that the $\hat{u}_{(j|i)}$ input tensor in the dynamic routing algorithm has too large an impact on the output tensor and greatly increaes the processing time. When calculating the output vector v_j, the formula includes the input $\hat{u}_{(j|i)}$ twice:

$$v_j = \text{squash}\left(\sum_i \text{softmax}\left(b_{ij} + \hat{u}_{j|i} v_j\right) \hat{u}_{j|i}\right) \quad (6)$$

To improve the routing mechanism between lower-level and higher-level capsules, the following modifications to the routing algorithm are proposed:

$$v_j = \text{squash}\left(\sum_i \text{softmax}\left(b_{ij} + \sum_j \|v_j\|\right) \hat{u}_{j|i}\right) \quad (7)$$

Let

$$v_j = \begin{bmatrix} c_{11} & \cdots & c_{1m} \\ \vdots & \ddots & \vdots \\ c_{n1} & \cdots & c_{nm} \end{bmatrix} \quad (8)$$

where c_{kl} is the value of the l-th neuron of the k-th capsule. If v_j is an intermediate capsule layer, then n is the number of output capsules. If v_j is an output capsule layer, then n is the number of possible object categories.

Let

$$v_j = \begin{bmatrix} v_1 \\ v_2 \\ \vdots \\ v_n \end{bmatrix} \quad (9)$$

where $\forall x \in \{1, 2, \ldots, n\}$, let

$$v_x = \sqrt{\sum_{y=1}^{n} c_{xy}} \quad (10)$$

This minimal modification makes the routing algorithm simpler and faster to compute. Our other proposed change concerns the squashing function. In the last capsule layer, we use a modified squashing function, as follows:

$$squash_{our}(s) = \frac{s - e^{-\|s\|}s}{\|s\| + \varepsilon} \quad (11)$$

where ε is a fine-tuning parameter. Based on our experience, we used $\varepsilon = 1 \times 10^{-7}$ in this work. Figure 3 shows a simple example of our squash function in a one-dimensional case for different values of ε.

Figures 4 and 5 show a block diagram of the dynamic routing algorithm and our improved routing solution, where the main differences between the two methods are clearly visible.

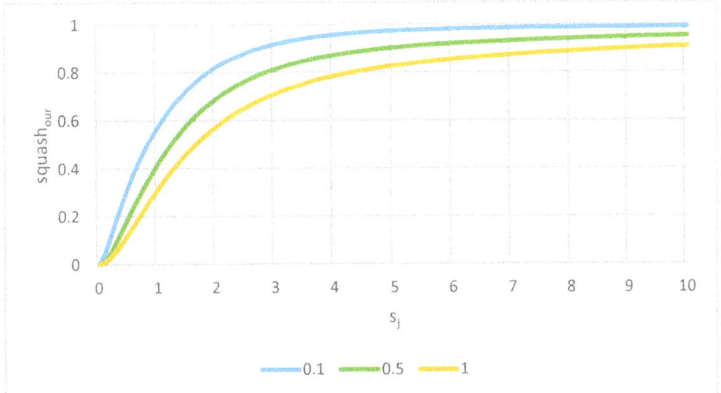

Figure 3. Our squash activation function with different ε values.

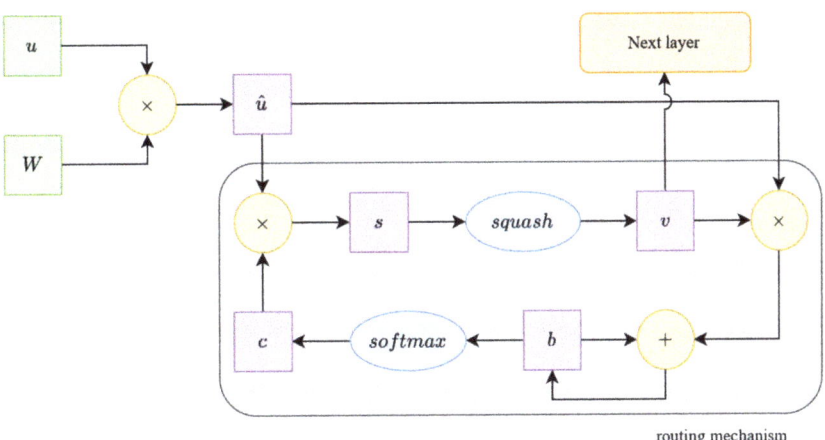

Figure 4. Block diagram of the dynamic routing algorithm by Sabour et al. [11]. (green: inputs, yellow: operations, blue: activations, purple: internal tensors).

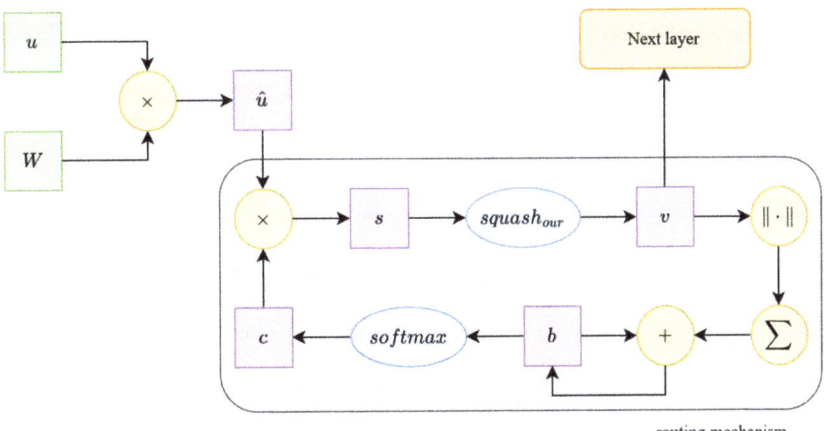

Figure 5. Block diagram of our proposed routing algorithm. (green: inputs, yellow: operations, blue: activations, purple: internal tensors).

4. Network Architecture

In this work, we have used the network architecture proposed by Sabour et al. [11] to compare our proposed routing mechanism with other optimization solutions in the field of capsule networks. This capsule network architecture is shown in Figure 6. The original paper used a fixed $32 \times 32 \times 1$-sized input tensor, because they only tested the network efficiency for the MNIST [13] dataset. In contrast, we trained and tested the capsule networks for six fundamentally different datasets in the field of image classification. In our work, the shape of the input layer varies depending on the dataset. We used the following input shapes: $28 \times 28 \times 1$, $48 \times 48 \times 1$ and $32 \times 32 \times 3$. After the input layer, the capsule network architecture consisted of three main components: the first is a convolutional layer, the next is the primary capsule layer, and the last one is the secondary capsule layer.

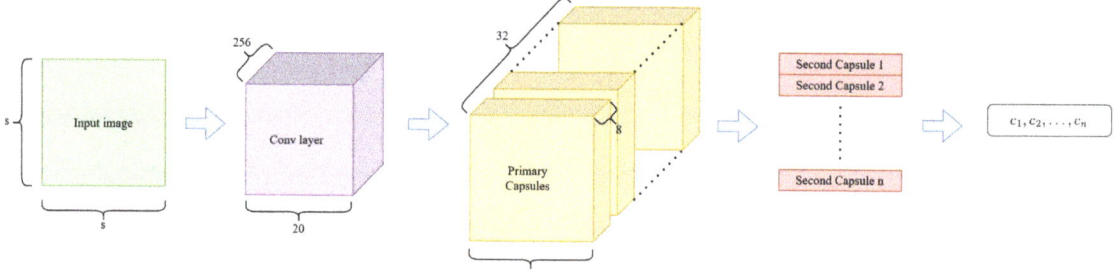

Figure 6. The capsule network architecture used in the research, based on work by Sabour et al. [11]. (green: input, purple: convolutional layer, yellow: primary capsule layer, red: secondary capsule layer, gray: prediction).

The convolution layer contains 256 convolution kernels of size 9×9 with a stride of 1, and a ReLU (rectified linear unit) [14] activation layer. This convolutional layer generates the main visual features based on intensities for the primary capsule layer.

The primary capsule block contains a convolutional layer, where both the input and the output are of the size 256. This capsule block also contains a squash layer. In this case, the original squash function (Equation (4)) is used for both implementations. The output of this block contains 32 capsules, where each capsule has 8 dimensions. This capsule block contains advanced features, which are passed onto the secondary capsule block.

The secondary capsule block has one capsule per class. As mentioned earlier, we worked with several different datasets, so the number of capsules in this capsule block varied, always according to the class number of the dataset: 5, 10 or 43. This capsule block contains the routing mechanism, which is responsible for determining the connection weights between the lower and higher capsules. Therefore, this capsule block represents the main difference between the solution of Sabour et al. and our presented method. In this block, we applied our proposed squash function (Equation (11)). The secondary capsule block contains a trainable matrix, called W (Equation (14)). The shape of the W matrix, for both solutions, is $pc \times n \times 16 \times 8$, where n is the number of output classes and pc depends on the input image shape as follows:

$$pc = \begin{cases} 32 \times 6 \times 6, & im_{size} = (28, 28) \\ 32 \times 8 \times 8, & im_{size} = (32, 32) \\ 32 \times 16 \times 16, & im_{size} = (48, 48) \end{cases} \quad (12)$$

where im_{size} is the size of the input image. The routing algorithm was run through $r = 3$ iterations in both cases. The output of this capsule block is a 16-dimensional vector per each class. This means that the block produces n 16-dimensional capsules, where n is the number of output classes. The length of the output capsules represents the probability values belonging to the given class.

5. Datasets

In this work, six different datasets were used. A classification task was performed for each dataset in our work. The datasets needed to have different levels of complexity. This allowed us to test as wide a range of datasets as possible. The selected datasets include grayscale and color images. The number of classes also varies, from 5 to 43. The size of the images is typically small, but here, again, we tried to experiment with different sizes. The datasets included a fixed background which had been used, as well as a variable color background which had been applied. Table 1 shows the main properties of the six datasets that we used in this research.

Table 1. Main properties of the datasets used.

Dataset	Image Size	Channels	Classes	Train Set	Test Set	Background
MNIST [13]	(28, 28)	1	10	60,000	10,000	false
F-MNIST [15]	(28, 28)	1	10	60,000	10,000	false
SmallNORB [16]	(48, 48)	1	5	48,600	48,600	true
CIFAR10 [17]	(32, 32)	3	10	50,000	10,000	true
SVHN [18]	(32, 32)	3	10	73,257	26,032	true
GTSRB [19]	(32, 32)	3	43	26,640	12,630	true

5.1. MNIST

The MNIST dataset (Modified National Institute of Standards and Technology dataset) is a large set of handwritten digits (from 0 to 9) that is one of the most widely used datasets in the field of image classification. The MNIST dataset contains 60,000 training images and 10,000 testing images, where every image is grayscale with a 28 pixel width and 28 pixel height. Figure 7 shows some samples from this dataset.

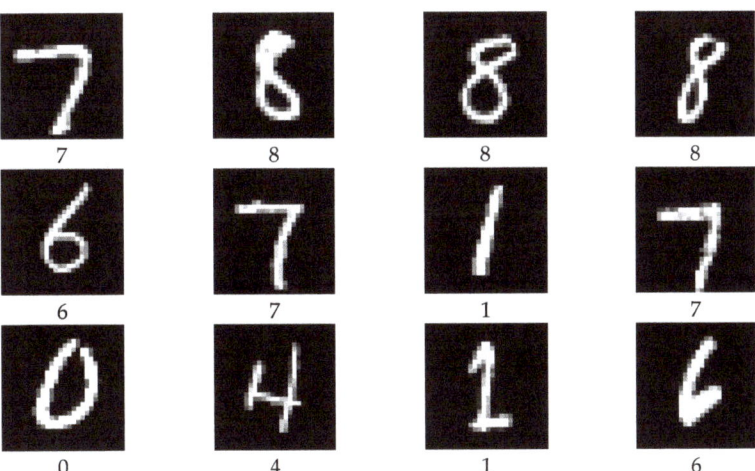

Figure 7. Sample data from MNIST dataset.

5.2. Fashion-MNIST

The Fashion-MNIST (or F-MNIST) dataset is very similar to the MNIST dataset. The main parameters are the same. It contains 60,000 training and 10,000 testing examples. Every sample is 28 pixels in width and 28 pixels in height, and a grayscale image where colors are inverted (an intensity value of 255 represents the darkest color). The Fashion-MINST dataset contains 10 fashion categories: t-shirt/top, trouser, pullover, dress, coat, sandal, shirt, sneaker, bag and ankle boot. Figure 8 shows some samples from this dataset.

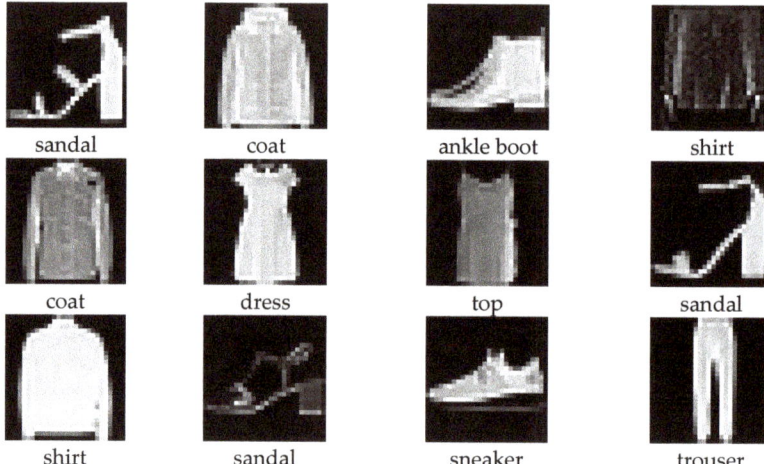

Figure 8. Sample data from Fashion-MNIST dataset.

5.3. SmallNORB

The SmallNORB dataset contains images of 3D objects. The specialty of this dataset is that the images were taken under several different lighting conditions and poses. This dataset contains images of toys belonging to five different categories: four-legged animals, human figures, airplanes, trucks and cars. The images were taken with two cameras under six lighting conditions, nine elevations and eighteen azimuths. All images are grayscale, with a size of 96 pixels in width by 96 pixels in height. However, in this work, we resized the images to 48×48 pixels. Figure 9 shows some samples from this dataset.

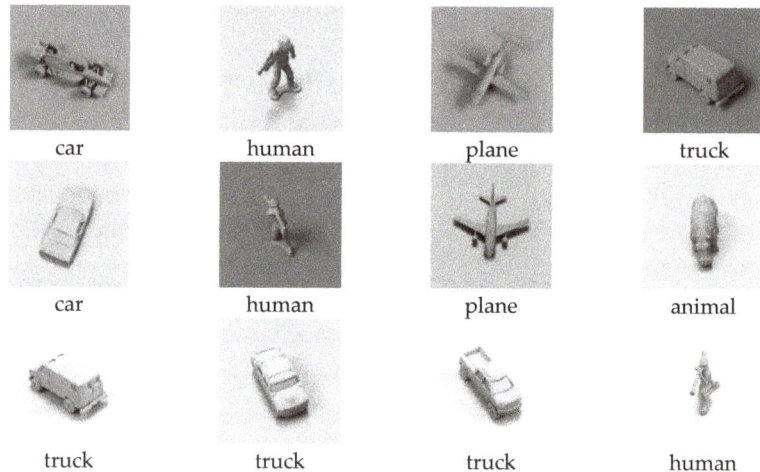

Figure 9. Sample data from SmallNORB dataset.

5.4. CIFAR10

The CIFAR10 (Canadian Institute for Advanced Research) dataset is one of the most widely used datasets in the field of machine learning-based image classification. This dataset is composed of 60,000 RGB colored images, where 50,000 images are the training samples and 10,000 images are the testing samples. Each image is 32 pixels wide and 32 pixels high. The object categories are the following: airplanes, cars, birds, cats, deer, dogs, frogs, horses, ships and trucks. Figure 10 shows some samples from this dataset.

Figure 10. Sample data from CIFAR10 dataset.

5.5. SVHN

The SVHN (Street View House Numbers) dataset contains small, cropped digits, like the MNIST dataset. However, the SVHN dataset is slightly more complex than the MNIST dataset. The SVHN is obtained from house numbers in Google Street View, where the background of the digits is not homogeneous and images may also include part of the adjacent digit. This property makes the SVHN dataset more difficult to classify than the MNIST dataset. The size of the images in this dataset is 32 pixels wide and 32 pixels high. The SVHN dataset contains 73,257 training samples and 26,032 testing samples. Figure 11 shows some samples from this dataset.

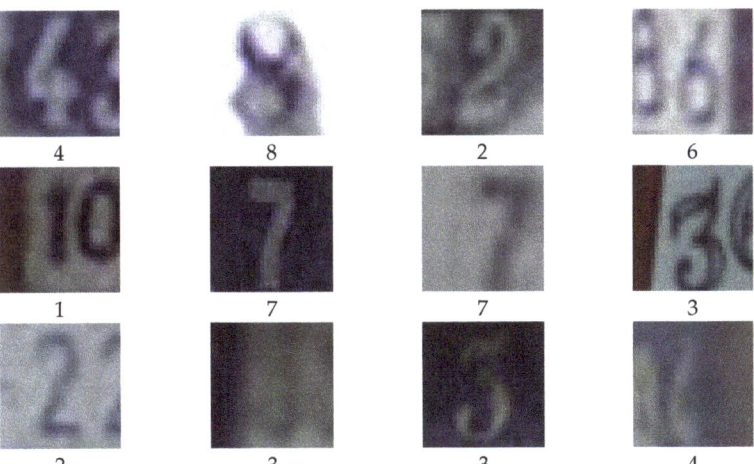

Figure 11. Sample data from SVHN dataset.

5.6. GTSRB

The GTSRB (German Traffic Sign Recognition Benchmark) dataset includes 43 classes of traffic signs. Each image contains one traffic sign with varying light conditions and rich backgrounds. Images are 32 pixels wide and 32 pixels high. The traffic sign classes are the following: speed limit {20, 30, 50, 60, 70, 80, 100, 120} km/h, end of speed limit (80 km/h), no passing, no passing for vehicles over 3.5 metric tons, right-of-way at the next intersection, priority road, yield, stop, no vehicles, vehicles over 3.5 metric tons prohibited, no entry, general caution, dangerous curve to the {left, right}, double curve, bumpy road, slippery road, road narrows on the right, road work, traffic signals, pedestrians, children crossing, bicycles crossing, beware of ice/snow, wild animals crossing, end of all speed and passing limits, turn {right, left} ahead, ahead only, go straight or {right, left}, keep {right, left}, roundabout mandatory, end of no passing and end of no passing by vehicles over 3.5 metric tons. Figure 12 shows some samples from this dataset.

Figure 12. Sample data from GTSRB dataset.

6. Results

In this work, the network architecture presented in Section 4 has been designed in three different ways and trained separately on the datasets presented in Section 5. The difference between the three networks is the routing algorithm used: the first is the original capsule network by Sabour et al., the second is our modified capsule network with some improvements, and the third is the efficient vector routing by Heinsen [20]. Capsule networks are trained separately on the six presented dataset. For the implementation, we used Python 3.9.16 [21] programming language with PyTorch 1.12.1 [22] machine learning framework and CUDA toolkit 11.6 platform. The capsule networks are trained on the Paperspace [23] online artificial intelligence platform with an Nvidia Quadro RTX4000 series graphical processing unit.

We trained all networks for 35 epochs with the Adam [24] optimizer algorithm where the train and test batch size are both 128. We also attempted to train the networks over many more epochs, but found that the difference between the three solutions does not change significantly after 35 epochs. In this study, we used 5×10^{-4} initial learning rate. In each epoch, we reduced the learning rate as follows:

$$lr_i = lr_{init} \times 0.97^i \tag{13}$$

where lr_{init} is the initial learning rate and lr_i is the learning rate in the i-th epoch. We used $\beta_1 = 0.9$ and $\beta_2 = 0.999$ hyperparameter values to control the exponential decay, and $\varepsilon = 1 \times 10^{-8}$ to prevent any division by zero in the implementation. In the training process, we used the same loss function as proposed by Sabour et al.

$$\mathcal{L} = T_k \times \max(0, m^+ - p)^2 + \lambda \times (1 - T_k) \times \max(0, p - m^-)^2 \tag{14}$$

where

$$T_k = \begin{cases} 1, & \text{if object of class } k \text{ present} \\ 0, & \text{otherwise} \end{cases} \qquad (15)$$

m^+, m^- and λ are hyperparameters. In the present work, we used the same values for these three hyperparameters as proposed by Sabour et al., in this case, $m^+ = 0.9$, $m^- = 0.1$ and $\lambda = 0.5$. The original study also used reconstruction in the training process; however, we did not apply this in our work. During training without reconstruction, the efficiency of the capsule network is reduced. In the long term, we want to translate our results in the field of capsule networks into real-world applications. In this respect, reconstruction of the input image is a rarely necessary step. Therefore, we explicitly investigated the ability of capsule networks without reconstruction.

Figures 13–18 show the accuracy of the training processes for the test sets of the six presented datasets with different numbers of routings. The value of r indicates the number of iterations which the routing algorithm has optimized the coefficients. Based on Sabour et al.'s experiment, the r = 3 is a good choice; however, we showed the efficiency with r = 1 and r = 10. This makes the difference more visible between the routing methods. As can be seen, for all six datasets, we have achieved efficiency gains compared to the two other capsule network solutions. The difference in efficiency between our and Sabour et al.'s solutions is minimal for about the first 10 epochs; however, after that, there is a noticeable difference in the learning curve. Although Heinsen's solution also proves to be effective in most cases; its performance is slightly lower than the other two solutions. It is also noticeable that changing the number of iterations has a much larger impact on Sabour et al.'s solution and that of Heinsen. Our proposed solution is less sensitive to the iteration value chosen during the optimization.

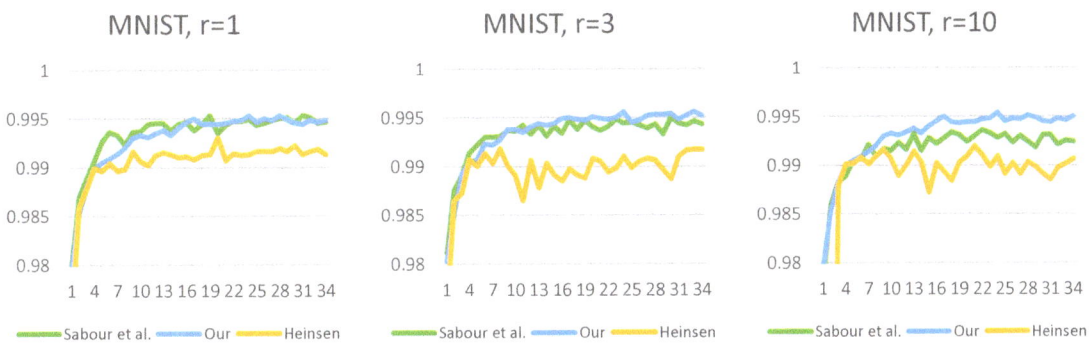

Figure 13. Classification test accuracy on MNIST dataset.

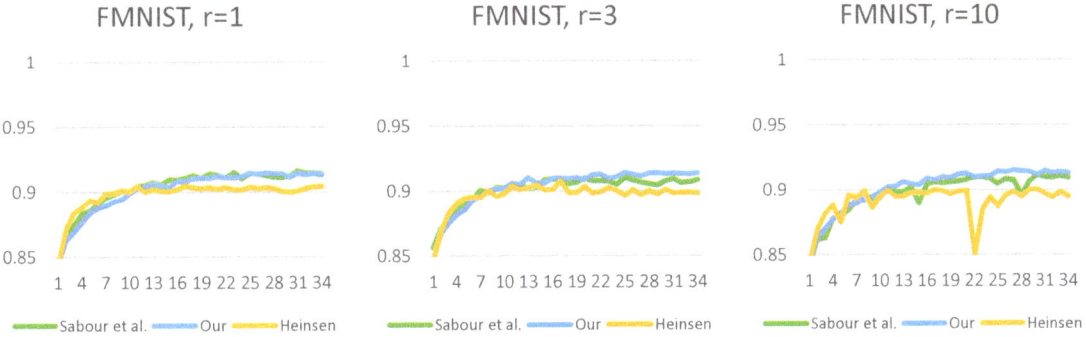

Figure 14. Classification test accuracy on Fashion-MNIST dataset.

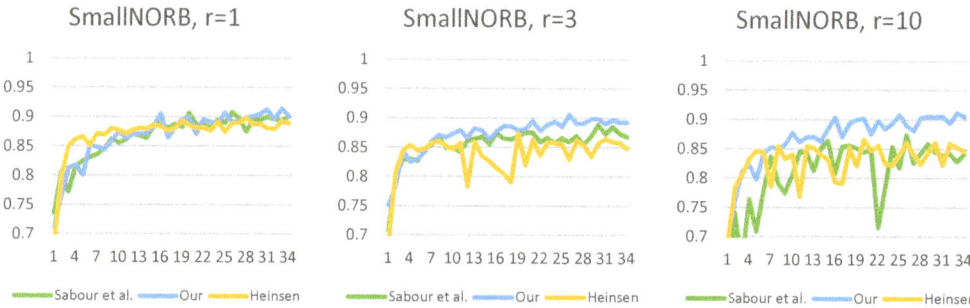

Figure 15. Classification test accuracy on SmallNORB dataset.

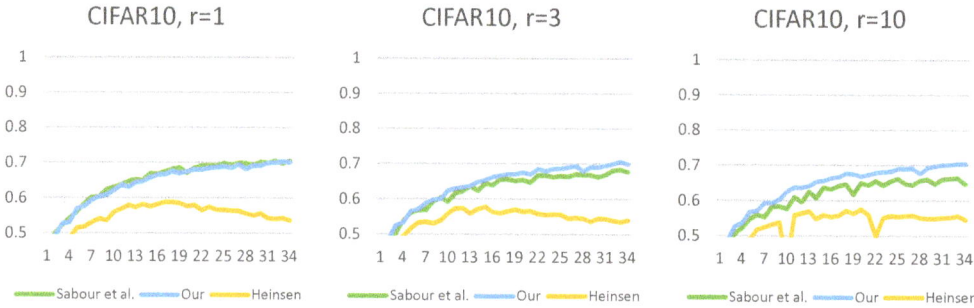

Figure 16. Classification test accuracy on CIFAR10 dataset.

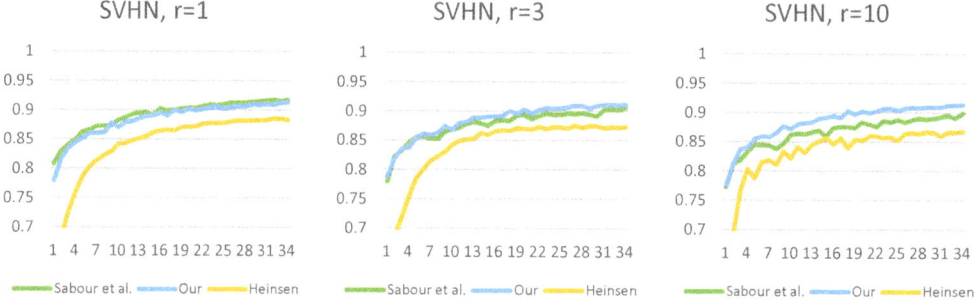

Figure 17. Classification test accuracy on SVHN dataset.

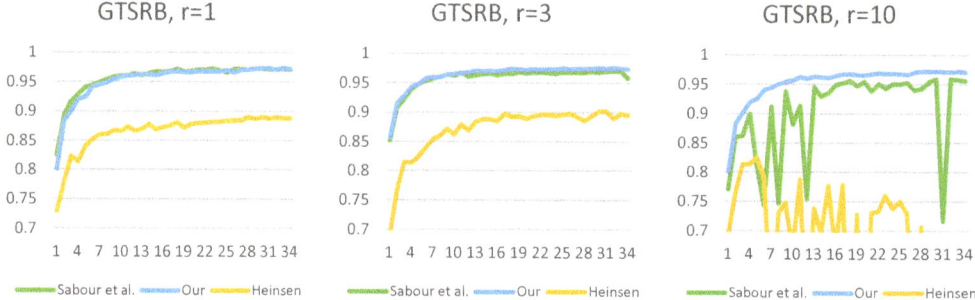

Figure 18. Classification test accuracy on GTSRB dataset.

Figures 19–24 show the test losses (Equation (14)) during the training processes with different numbers of routings. There is not much difference in the loss function, but it is noticeable that our solution is less noisy and converges more smoothly.

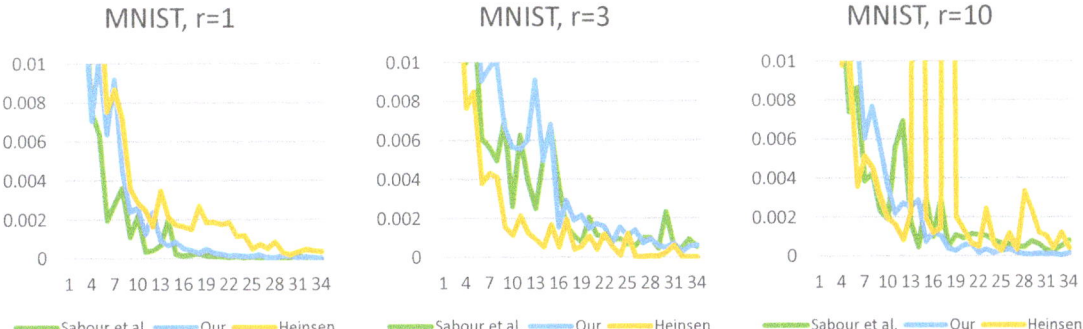

Figure 19. Classification test loss on MNIST dataset.

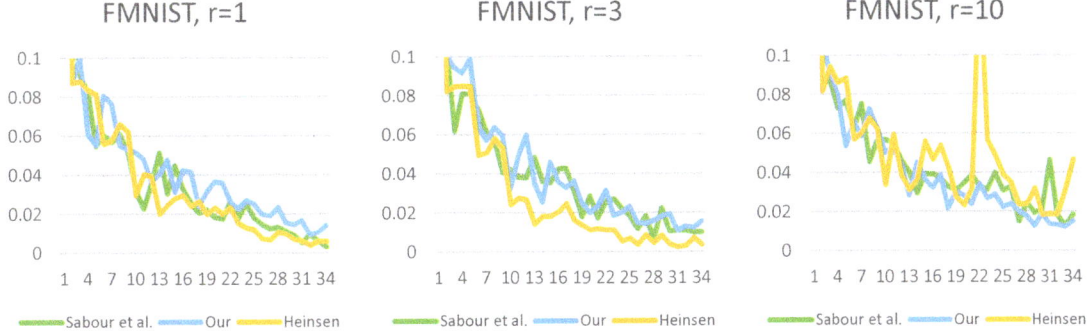

Figure 20. Classification test loss on Fashion-MNIST dataset.

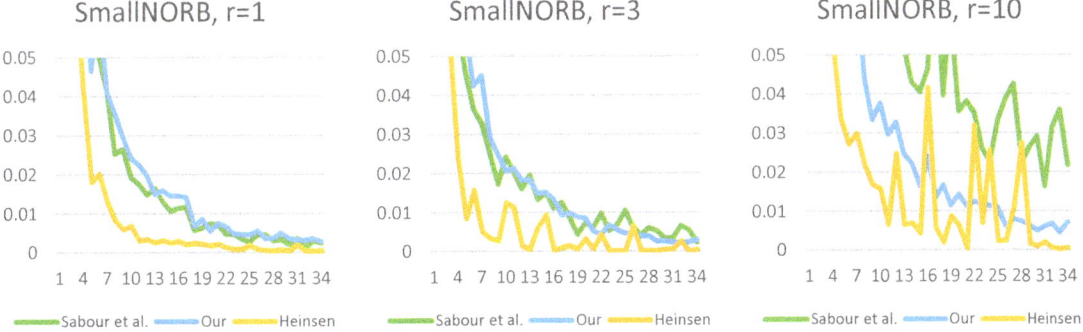

Figure 21. Classification test loss on SmallNORB dataset.

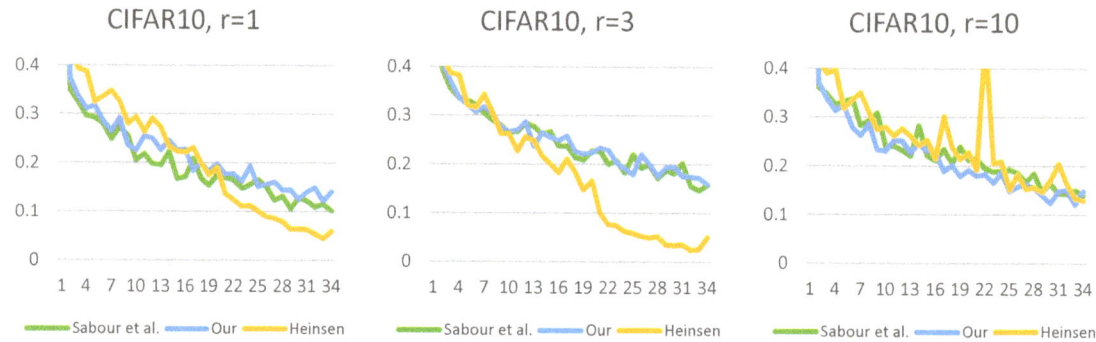

Figure 22. Classification test loss on CIFAR10 dataset.

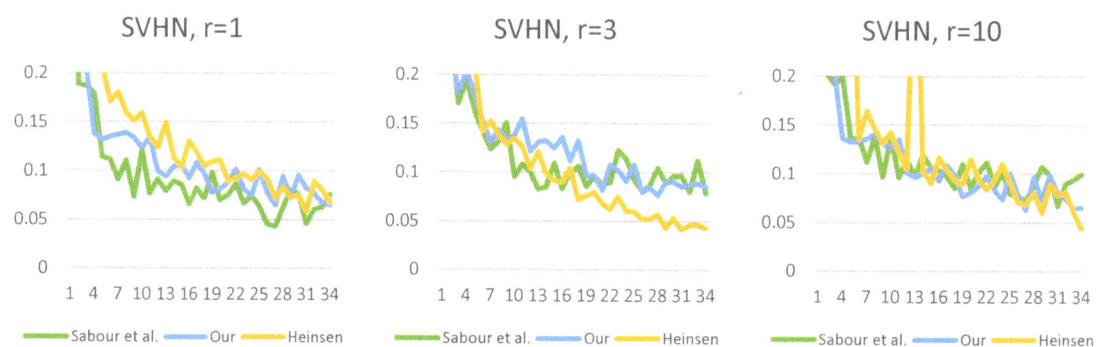

Figure 23. Classification test loss on SVHN dataset.

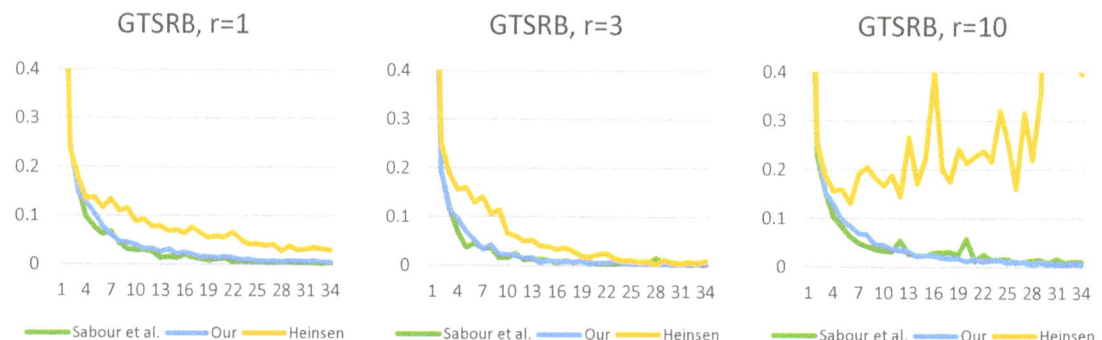

Figure 24. Classification test loss on GTSRB dataset.

Figure 25 shows the processing times for the three capsule-based networks. It can be seen that for all six datasets, the capsule network was faster with our proposed routing algorithm than with the dynamic routing algorithm introduced by Sabour et al. The smallest increase was achieved for the Fashion-MNIST and MNIST datasets, but this still represents an 18.60% and a 19.33% speedup. For more complex datasets, much higher speed increases were achieved. A running time reduction of 25.55% was achieved for SVHN and 26.54% for CIFAR10. The best results were observed for the SmallNORB and GTSRB datasets. For SmallNORB it was 35.28%, while for GTSRB, it was 48.30%. Compared to Heinsen's solution, our proposed algorithm performed worse, but the difference in efficiency between the two solutions is significant.

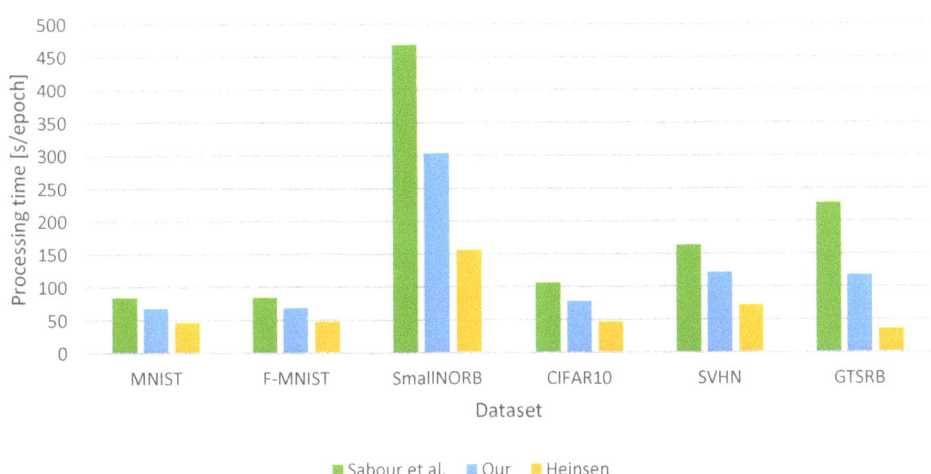

Figure 25. Comparison of training time on the same hardware (Nvidia Quadro RTX4000 series).

The test errors during the training process are shown in Table 2, where the capsule-based solutions were compared with the recently released neural network-based approaches. It can be clearly seen that our proposed modifications to the routing algorithm have led to efficiency gains. It is important to note that our capsule-based solution does not always approach the effectiveness of the state-of-the-art solutions, however, the capsule network used consists of only three layers with a very minimal number of parameters (<5.4 M). Its architecture is quite simple, but with further improvements, a higher efficiency can be achieved. Prior to this, we felt it necessary to improve the efficiency of the routing algorithm. Experience has shown that designing deep network architecture in the area of capsule networks is too resource-intensive. For this reason, it is necessary to increase the processing speed of the routing algorithm.

Table 2. Classification test errors on the different datasets, compared with other methods.

	MNIST	F-MNIST	S.NORB	CIFAR10	SVHN	GTSRB
Goyal et al. [25]	0.58%	-	-	10%	13.6%	9.29%
Taylor et al. [26]	2.09%	10.95%	-	-	-	-
Phaye et al. [27]	-	-	**5.57%**	-	-	-
Remerscheid et al. [28]	-	-	-	26.5%	-	-
Dupont et al. [29]	1.8%	-	-	39.4%	16.5%	-
Abad et al. [30]	0.6%	-	-	31.7%	-	-
Sabour et al. [11]	0.45%	**8.35%**	9.15%	29.36%	8.05%	2.67%
Heinsen [20]	0.7%	9.25%	10.18%	41.18%	11.36%	9.79%
Ours	**0.41%**	**8.35%**	8.54%	28.26%	**6.90%**	**2.22%**

Figure 26 shows the confusion matrices for the capsule network-based approaches in the case of the six datasets used. It can be seen that for simpler datasets, such as MNIST, the difference between the three optimization algorithms is minimal. For more complex datasets, the differences are more pronounced. Tables 3–8 show the efficiencies achieved by capsule networks for each class, separately. This table also shows that our proposed method is in most cases able to provide a more effective solution than the other solutions tested. However, there are cases where our solution falls short compared with solutions by Sabour et al. and Heinsen.

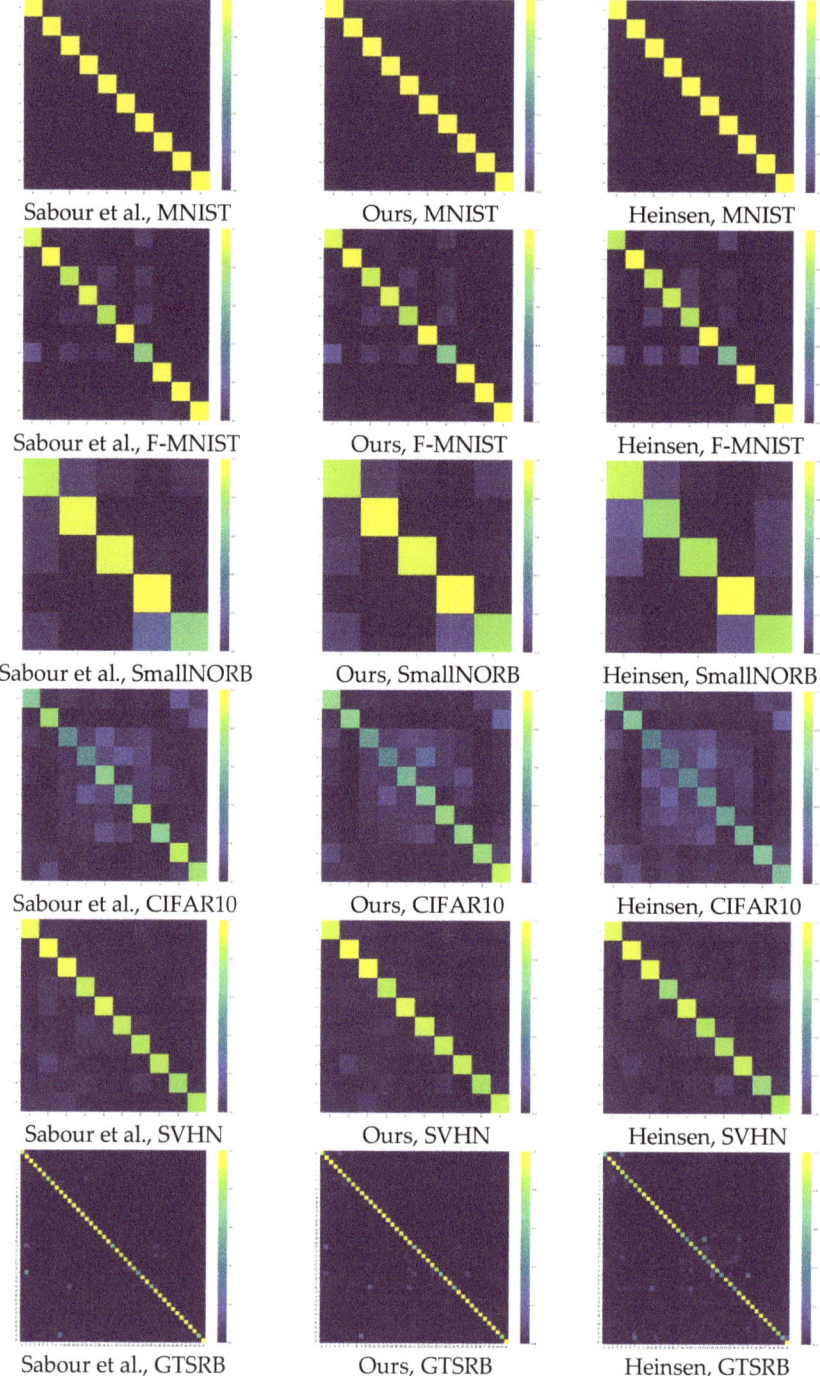

Figure 26. Confusion matrices for the capsule-based networks.

Table 3. Classification test accuracy by class for capsule networks on the MNIST dataset.

	Sabour et al. [11]	Ours	Heinsen [20]
0	0.9969	**0.9980**	**0.9980**
1	**0.9974**	**0.9974**	0.9965
2	0.9932	**0.9961**	0.9932
3	0.9941	**0.9950**	0.9941
4	0.9908	**0.9929**	0.9847
5	0.9933	0.9933	**0.9944**
6	0.9916	**0.9948**	0.9896
7	**0.9971**	0.9961	0.9893
8	0.9959	**0.9969**	0.9918
9	0.9891	**0.9921**	0.9851

Table 4. Classification test accuracy by class for capsule networks on the Fashion-MNIST dataset.

	Sabour et al. [11]	Ours	Heinsen [20]
T-shirt/top	0.8920	**0.9060**	0.8410
Trouser	0.9780	**0.9800**	0.9780
Pullover	0.8560	**0.8800**	0.8710
Dress	**0.9230**	0.9190	0.8900
Coat	0.8370	0.8390	**0.8400**
Sandal	**0.9810**	**0.9810**	0.9740
Shirt	**0.7320**	0.6770	0.6340
Sneaker	0.9790	0.9780	**0.9820**
Bag	**0.9840**	0.9820	0.9750
Ankle boot	0.9600	**0.9620**	0.9530

Table 5. Classification test accuracy by class for capsule networks on the CIFAR10 dataset.

	Sabour et al. [11]	Ours	Heinsen [20]
Airplane	0.6280	**0.7100**	0.6110
Automobile	**0.7780**	0.6810	0.6260
Bird	0.4630	**0.5180**	0.4230
Cat	**0.4660**	0.4440	0.3670
Deer	**0.6930**	0.5970	0.4340
Dog	0.5480	**0.6450**	0.5110
Frog	**0.8110**	0.7530	0.5380
Horse	0.6710	**0.7300**	0.5830
Ship	**0.8480**	0.7590	0.6260
Truck	0.7810	**0.8600**	0.5920

Table 6. Classification test accuracy by class for capsule networks on the SmallNORB dataset.

	Sabour et al. [11]	Ours	Heinsen [20]
Animal	0.8496	0.8645	**0.8681**
Human	0.9295	**0.9513**	0.7709
Plane	0.9206	**0.9210**	0.8175
Truck	**0.9958**	0.9932	0.9610
Car	0.7075	0.7973	**0.8192**

Table 7. Classification test accuracy by class for capsule networks on the GTSRB dataset.

	Sabour et al. [11]	Ours	Heinsen [20]
Speed limit 20 km/h	**0.8667**	0.8167	0.6500
Speed limit 30 km/h	0.9889	**0.9917**	0.9458
Speed limit 50 km/h	**0.9920**	0.9893	0.9707
Speed limit 60 km/h	**0.9889**	0.9756	0.9333
Speed limit 70 km/h	**0.9758**	**0.9758**	0.8727
Speed limit 80 km/h	0.9619	**0.9810**	0.8000
Speed limit 100 km/h	**0.8533**	**0.8533**	0.8067
Speed limit 120 km/h	**0.9133**	0.8822	0.8289
End of speed limit (80 km/h)	0.9444	**0.9511**	0.9000
No passing	0.9958	**1.0000**	0.9458
No passing for vehicles over 3.5 metric t	0.9924	**0.9955**	0.9697
Right-of-way at the next intersection	0.9619	**0.9714**	0.8929
Priority road	0.9812	**0.9884**	0.9087
Yield	**0.9972**	**0.9972**	0.9861
Stop	**1.0000**	**1.0000**	0.9630
No vehicles	**1.0000**	**1.0000**	0.9762
Vehicles over 3.5 metric tons prohibited	**0.9933**	**0.9933**	0.9533
No entry	**0.9972**	**0.9972**	0.8806
General caution	0.9385	**0.9410**	0.7231
Dangerous curve to the left	**1.0000**	**1.0000**	0.4833
Dangerous curve to the right	**0.9889**	**0.9889**	0.8889
Double curve	**0.7667**	0.7000	0.6778
Bumpy road	0.9833	**0.9917**	0.9083
Slippery road	**0.9467**	0.9267	0.6667
Road narrows on the right	**0.9444**	**0.9444**	0.5333
Road work	**0.9542**	0.9500	0.9438
Traffic signals	**0.8278**	0.8167	0.7833
Pedestrians	0.5000	**0.5667**	0.5000
Children crossing	**0.9933**	**0.9933**	0.9200
Bicycles crossing	**1.0000**	**1.0000**	0.9222
Beware of ice/snow	0.7667	**0.7733**	0.5000
Wild animals crossing	**0.9815**	0.9741	0.9074
End of all speed and passing limits	**1.0000**	**1.0000**	**1.0000**
Turn right ahead	**0.9952**	**0.9952**	0.9476
Turn left ahead	**0.9917**	**0.9917**	0.9833
Ahead only	0.9923	**0.9974**	0.9538
Go straight or right	**0.9750**	0.9667	0.9417
Go straight or left	**1.0000**	**1.0000**	0.9000
Keep right	0.9739	**0.9870**	0.9087
Keep left	**1.0000**	**1.0000**	0.8000
Roundabout mandatory	0.9667	**0.9778**	0.8000
End of no passing	**0.8000**	0.7667	0.5500
End of no passing by vehicles over 3.5 t	**0.9778**	**0.9778**	**0.9778**

Table 8. Classification test accuracy by class for capsule networks on the SVHN dataset.

	Sabour et al. [11]	Ours	Heinsen [20]
0	**0.9151**	0.8928	0.9002
1	**0.9686**	0.9547	0.9280
2	0.9393	**0.9549**	0.9152
3	**0.8636**	0.8550	0.7696
4	0.9080	**0.9164**	0.9045
5	0.8624	**0.8968**	0.8335
6	0.8402	**0.8720**	0.8255
7	0.8579	0.8742	**0.8757**
8	0.7861	**0.8193**	0.7657
9	0.8245	**0.8621**	0.8301

Table 9 summarizes the percentage of classes per dataset that were able to provide the best result for a given solution. From this approach as well, our solution performed the best. Only in the case of the GTSRB dataset was the method proposed by Sabour et al. more efficient. For the other five datasets, our proposed method was able to achieve the best accuracy for most classes. Tables 10–12 summarize the recall score, dice score and F1-score for the capsule-based implementations under study. It can be observed that, according to all three metrics, our proposed method performs the best. The solution by Sabour et al. performs better only for the Fashion-MNIST dataset, but there was no difference in accuracy of this dataset. The solution by Heinsen underperforms the other two solutions in the cases studied. It can also be seen that, where the method of Sabour et al. and our approach perform worse, the score of Heinsen's solution also decreases in a similar way.

Table 9. Best efficiency ratio per class for the presented capsule networks.

	MNIST	F-MNIST	SmallNORB	CIFAR10	SVHN	GTSRB
Sabour et al. [11]	15%	35%	**50%**	20%	30%	**51.94%**
Heinsen [20]	15%	20%	0%	**40%**	10%	0.77%
Ours	**70%**	**45%**	**50%**	**40%**	**60%**	47.29%

Table 10. Recall scores for the capsule networks.

	MNIST	F-MNIST	SmallNORB	CIFAR10	SVHN	GTSRB
Sabour et al. [11]	0.9939	**0.9159**	0.9056	0.6790	0.8958	0.9513
Heinsen [20]	0.9916	0.8937	0.8419	0.5311	0.8532	0.8304
Ours	**0.9948**	0.9124	**0.9138**	**0.6925**	**0.9012**	**0.9519**

Table 11. Dice scores for the capsule networks.

	MNIST	F-MNIST	SmallNORB	CIFAR10	SVHN	GTSRB
Sabour et al. [11]	0.9940	**0.9153**	0.9052	0.6748	0.9012	**0.9576**
Heinsen [20]	0.9916	0.8945	0.8419	0.5350	0.8546	0.8396
Ours	**0.9949**	0.9118	**0.9131**	**0.6882**	**0.9046**	**0.9576**

Table 12. F1-scores for the capsule networks.

	MNIST	F-MNIST	SmallNORB	CIFAR10	SVHN	GTSRB
Sabour et al. [11]	0.9940	**0.9159**	0.9056	0.6790	0.9084	0.9711
Heinsen [20]	0.9916	0.8937	0.8419	0.5311	0.8667	0.8920
Ours	**0.9949**	0.9124	**0.9138**	**0.6925**	**0.9122**	**0.9727**

7. Conclusions

Our work involved research in the field of capsule networks. We showed the main differences between classical convolutional neural networks and capsule networks, highlighting the new potential of capsule networks. We have shown that the dynamic routing algorithm for capsule networks is too complex and that the training time makes it difficult to build more deep and complex networks. At the same time, capsule networks can achieve very good efficiency, but their practical application is difficult due to the complexity of routing. Therefore, it is important to improve the optimization algorithm and introduce novel solutions.

We proposed a modified routing algorithm for capsule networks and a parameterizable activation function for capsules, based on the dynamic routing algorithm introduced by Sabour et al. In this approach, we aimed to reduce the computational complexity of the current dynamic routing algorithm. Thanks to our proposed routing algorithm and activation function, the training time can be reduced. In our work, we have shown its effectiveness on six different datasets, compared with neural network-based solutions and capsule-based solutions. As can be seen, the training time was reduced in all cases, by almost 30% on average. Even in the worst case, a speed increase of almost 20% was achieved. And in some cases, an increase in speed of almost 50% can be seen. Despite the increase in speed, the efficiency of the network has not decreased. For several different metrics, our proposed solution was compared with other capsule-based methods. As we have shown, our proposed approach can increase the efficiency of the routing mechanism. For all six datasets tested in this research, our solution provided the highest results in almost all cases.

In the future, we would like to perform further research on routing algorithms and capsule networks to be able to achieve even greater improvements. We would like to carry out more complex studies on larger datasets, compared with other solutions. We would like to further optimize our solution based on the test results. Our goal is to be able to provide an efficient and fast solution for more complex tasks, such as instance segmentation or reconstruction, in the field of capsule networks. This is necessary to create much deeper and more complex capsule networks, so it is important to address the issue of optimization. This will allow us to apply the theory of capsule networks to real practical applications with great efficiency.

Author Contributions: Conceptualization, J.H., Á.B. and C.R.P.; methodology, J.H., Á.B. and C.R.P.; software, J.H.; validation, J.H.; formal analysis, J.H.; investigation, J.H.; resources, J.H.; data curation, J.H.; writing—original draft preparation, J.H.; writing—review and editing, J.H.; visualization, J.H.; supervision, Á.B. and C.R.P.; project administration, J.H.; funding acquisition, J.H. and Á.B. All authors have read and agreed to the published version of the manuscript.

Funding: This research was funded by the European Union within the framework of the National Laboratory for Artificial Intelligence grant number RRF-2.3.1-21-2022-00004 and the APC was funded by RRF-2.3.1-21-2022-00004.

Data Availability Statement: Data sharing is not applicable.

Acknowledgments: The research was supported by the European Union within the framework of the National Laboratory for Artificial Intelligence (RRF-2.3.1-21-2022-00004).

Conflicts of Interest: The authors declare no conflict of interest.

References

1. Chen, X.; Liang, C.; Huang, D.; Real, E.; Wang, K.; Liu, Y.; Pham, H.; Dong, X.; Luong, T.; Hsieh, C.; et al. Symbolic Discovery of Optimization Algorithms. *arXiv* **2023**, arXiv:2302.06675.
2. Dosovitskiy, A.; Beyer, L.; Kolesnikov, A.; Weissenborn, D.; Zhai, X.; Unterthiner, T.; Dehghani, M.; Minderer, M.; Heigold, G.; Gelly, S.; et al. An Image is Worth 16x16 Words: Transformers for Image Recognition at Scale. In Proceedings of the International Conference on Learning Representations (ICLR), Vienna, Austria, 4 May 2021.
3. Wang, W.; Dai, J.; Chen, Z.; Huang, Z.; Li, Z.; Zhu, X.; Hu, X.; Lu, T.; Lu, L.; Li, H.; et al. InternImage: Exploring Large-Scale Vision Foundation Models with Deformable Convolutions. *arXiv* **2023**, arXiv:2211.05778.
4. Ghiasi, G.; Cui, Y.; Srinivas, A.; Qian, R.; Lin, T.; Cubuk, E.D.; Le, Q.V.; Zoph, B. Simple Copy-Paste is a Strong Data Augmentation Method for Instance Segmentation. In Proceedings of the Computer Vision and Pattern Recognition Conference (CVPR), online, 19–25 June 2021.
5. Su, W.; Zhu, X.; Tao, C.; Lu, L.; Li, B.; Huang, G.; Qiao, Y.; Wang, X.; Zhou, J.; Dai, J. Towards All-in-one Pre-training via Maximizing Multi-modal Mutual Information. *arXiv* **2022**, arXiv:2211.09807.
6. Yuan, Y.; Chen, X.; Chen, X.; Wang, J. Segmentation Transformer: Object-Contextual Representations for Semantic Segmentation. In Proceedings of the European Conference on Computer Vision (ECCV), Online, 23–28 August 2020.
7. Fang, Y.; Wang, W.; Xie, B.; Sun, Q.; Wu, L.; Wang, X.; Huang, T.; Wang, X.; Cao, Y. EVA: Exploring the Limits of Masked Visual Representation Learning at Scale. *arXiv* **2022**, arXiv:2211.07636.
8. Zhang, H.; Li, F.; Zou, X.; Liu, S.; Li, C.; Gao, J.; Yang, J.; Zhang, L. A Simple Framework for Open-Vocabulary Segmentation and Detection. *arXiv* **2023**, arXiv:2303.08131.
9. Zafar, A.; Aamir, M.; Mohd Nawi, N.; Arshad, A.; Riaz, S.; Alruban, A.; Dutta, A.K.; Almotairi, S. A Comparison of Pooling Methods for Convolutional Neural Networks. *Appl. Sci.* **2022**, *12*, 8643. [CrossRef]
10. Hinton, G.E.; Krizhevsky, A.; Wang, S.D. *Transforming Auto-Encoders. International Conference on Artificial Neural Networks*; Lecture Notes in Computer Science; Springer: Berlin/Heidelberg, Germany, 2011; Volume 6791, pp. 44–51.

11. Sabour, S.; Frosst, N.; Hinton, G.E. Dynamic Routing Between Capsules. In Proceedings of the 31st Conference on Neural Information Processing Systems (NIPS), Long Beach, CA, USA, 4–7 December 2017.
12. Hinton, G.E.; Sabour, S.; Frosst, N. Matrix capsules with EM routing. In Proceedings of the 6th International Conference on Learning Representations, Vancouver, BC, Canada, 30 April–3 May 2018.
13. LeCun, Y.; Cortes, C.; Burges, C.J.C. The MNIST Database of Handwritten Digits. 2012. Available online: http://yann.lecun.com/exdb/mnist/ (accessed on 9 April 2023).
14. Fukushima, K. Visual Feature Extraction by a Multilayered Network of Analog Threshold Elements. In *IEEE Transactions on Systems Science and Cybernetics, October 1969*; IEEE: Piscataway, NJ, USA, 1969; Volume 5, pp. 322–333.
15. Xiao, H.; Rasul, K.; Vollgraf, R. Fashion-MNIST: A Novel Image Dataset for Benchmarking Machine Learning Algorithms. *arXiv* **2017**, arXiv:1708.07747.
16. LeCun, Y.; Huang, F.J.; Bottou, L. Learning methods for generic object recognition with invariance to pose and lighting. In Proceedings of the IEEE Computer Society Conference on Computer Vision and Pattern Recognition (CVPR), Washington, DC, USA, 27 June–2 July 2004; pp. 97–104.
17. Krizhevsky, A. *Learning Multiple Layers of Features from Tiny Images*; Technical Report; University of Toronto: Toronto, ON, Canada, 2009.
18. Netzer, Y.; Wang, T.; Coates, A.; Bissacco, A.; Wu, B.; Ng, A.Y. Reading Digits in Natural Images with Unsupervised Feature Learning. In Proceedings of the 25th Conference on Neural Information Processing Systems, Granada, Spain, 12–17 December 2011.
19. Stallkamp, J.; Schlipsing, M.; Salmen, J.; Igel, C. The German traffic sign recognition benchmark: A multi-class classification competition. In Proceedings of the International Joint Conference on Neural Networks, San Jose, CA, USA, 31 July–5 August 2011; pp. 1453–1460.
20. Heinsen, F.A. An Algorithm for Routing Vectors in Sequences. *arXiv* **2022**, arXiv:2211.11754.
21. Rossum, V.G.; Fred, L.D. *Python 3 Reference Manual*; CreateSpace: Scotts Valley, CA, USA, 2009.
22. Paszke, A.; Gross, S.; Massa, F.; Lerer, A.; Bradbury, J.; Chanan, G.; Killeen, T.; Lin, Z.; Gimelshein, N.; Antiga, L.; et al. PyTorch: An Imperative Style, High-Performance Deep Learning Library. *Adv. Neural Inf. Process. Syst.* **2019**, *32*, 8024–8035.
23. Paperspace. Available online: https://www.paperspace.com/ (accessed on 9 April 2023).
24. Kingma, D.P.; Ba, J. Adam: A Method for Stochastic Optimization. *arXiv* **2017**, arXiv:1412.6980.
25. Goyal, P.; Duval, Q.; Seessel, I.; Caron, M.; Misra, I.; Sagun, L.; Joulin, A.; Bojanowski, P. Vision Models Are More Robust and Fair When Pretrained On Uncurated Images without Supervision. *arXiv* **2022**, arXiv:2202.08360. [CrossRef]
26. Taylor, L.; King, A.; Harper, N. Robust and Accelerated Single-Spike Spiking Neural Network Training with Applicability to Challenging Temporal Tasks. *arXiv* **2022**, arXiv:2205.15286. [CrossRef]
27. Phaye, S.S.R.; Sikka, A.; Dhall, A.; Bathula, D. Dense and Diverse Capsule Networks: Making the Capsules Learn Better. *arXiv* **2018**, arXiv:1805.04001. [CrossRef]
28. Remerscheid, N.W.; Ziller, A.; Rueckert, D.; Kaissis, G. SmoothNets: Optimizing CNN Architecture Design for Differentially Private Deep Learning. *arXiv* **2022**, arXiv:2205.04095. [CrossRef]
29. Dupont, E.; Doucet, A.; Teh, Y.W. Augmented Neural ODEs. In *Advances in Neural Information Processing Systems*; Curran Associates, Inc.: Red Hook, NY, USA, 2019; Volume 32.
30. Abad, G.; Ersoy, O.; Picek, S.; Urbieta, A. Sneaky Spikes: Uncovering Stealthy Backdoor Attacks in Spiking Neural Networks with Neuromorphic Data. *arXiv* **2023**, arXiv:2302.06279. [CrossRef]

Disclaimer/Publisher's Note: The statements, opinions and data contained in all publications are solely those of the individual author(s) and contributor(s) and not of MDPI and/or the editor(s). MDPI and/or the editor(s) disclaim responsibility for any injury to people or property resulting from any ideas, methods, instructions or products referred to in the content.

Article

Optimization of the Compressive Measurement Matrix in a Massive MIMO System Exploiting LSTM Networks

Saidur R. Pavel and Yimin D. Zhang *

Department of Electrical and Computer Engineering, Temple University, Philadelphia, PA 19122, USA
* Correspondence: ydzhang@temple.edu

Abstract: Massive multiple-input multiple-output (MIMO) technology, which is characterized by the use of a large number of antennas, is a key enabler for the next-generation wireless communication and beyond. Despite its potential for high performance, implementing a massive MIMO system presents numerous technical challenges, including the high hardware complexity, cost, and power consumption that result from the large number of antennas and the associated front-end circuits. One solution to these challenges is the use of hybrid beamforming, which divides the transceiving process into both analog and digital domains. To perform hybrid beamforming efficiently, it is necessary to optimize the analog beamformer, referred to as the compressive measurement matrix (CMM) here, that allows the projection of high-dimensional signals into a low-dimensional manifold. Classical approaches to optimizing the CMM, however, are computationally intensive and time consuming, limiting their usefulness for real-time processing. In this paper, we propose a deep learning based approach to optimizing the CMM using long short-term memory (LSTM) networks. This approach offers high accuracy with low complexity, making it a promising solution for the real-time implementation of massive MIMO systems.

Keywords: massive MIMO; hybrid beamforming; compressive measurement matrix; long short-term memory network

---

Citation: Pavel, S.R.; Zhang, Y.D. Optimization of the Compressive Measurement Matrix in a Massive MIMO System Exploiting LSTM Networks. *Algorithms* **2023**, *16*, 261. https://doi.org/10.3390/a16060261

Academic Editors: Xiang Zhang and Xiaoxiao Li

Received: 31 March 2023
Revised: 15 May 2023
Accepted: 18 May 2023
Published: 23 May 2023

Copyright: © 2023 by the authors. Licensee MDPI, Basel, Switzerland. This article is an open access article distributed under the terms and conditions of the Creative Commons Attribution (CC BY) license (https://creativecommons.org/licenses/by/4.0/).

1. Introduction

In recent years, the massive multiple input multiple output (MIMO) technology has emerged as a highly promising solution for modern wireless communication. With the growing demand for high-speed data transfer and low latency, the implementation of massive MIMO has become increasingly important, especially in millimeter wave (mmWave) communication, which is a crucial aspect for the future of 5G networks. The central idea behind massive MIMO is to equip base stations with a large number of antennas, which allows multiple users to be served at the same time in the same frequency band. This results in a significant increase in both capacity and spectral efficiency compared to traditional MIMO systems. The high number of antennas in a massive MIMO system enables it to provide much higher data rates than traditional MIMO systems [1–6]. As a result, the system is able to better utilize the available bandwidth and effectively mitigate the effects of fading and interference. In mmWave communication, massive MIMO systems address the problem of severe propagation attenuation and make efficient use of the signal bandwidth [7–9]. Additionally, massive MIMO is becoming increasingly popular in radar sensing due to its ability to enhance target detection and tracking accuracy, reduce false alarms, increase capacity, and improve coverage [10,11].

Despite the numerous benefits offered by massive MIMO systems, their practical implementation is a challenging endeavor. In a typical MIMO system, each antenna is equipped with its own radio frequency (RF) chain, composed of components, such as a band-pass filter, a low-noise amplifier, a mixer, a low-pass filter, and a high-resolution analog-to-digital converter (ADC). With the implementation of massive MIMO systems, the number of antennas and RF chains required at each base station is significantly increased, thereby leading to an increase in cost, complexity, and power consumption. To make the implementation of a massive MIMO system practical, one approach is to adopt the hybrid beamforming technique. Hybrid beamforming addresses this limitation by reducing the number of RF chains required in a massive MIMO system. It accomplishes this by splitting the beamforming process into two parts: a digital part and an analog part. In the analog part, the signals from multiple antennas are combined before they are passed through a reduced number of the RF chain. To achieve this effectively, a compressive measurement matrix (CMM), which projects the high-dimensional array received signal onto a low-dimensional signal considering the sparsity nature of the signals.

Numerous studies have investigated the design of beamformer and precoder matrices for MIMO systems [12–14]. The approach in [12] involves alternating optimization to optimize the transmit and receive beamformers using a minimum mean square error (MMSE) criterion between the received signal and the transmitted symbol vectors. Reference [13] considers the optimization of the precoder matrix based on the singular vectors of the channel matrix. In [14], a beamformer is optimized for MIMO-integrated sensing and communication (ISAC) scenarios, where the beamforming matrix is designed to achieve the desired radar beampattern, while maintaining a signal-to-interference-plus-noise ratio constraint for communication users. However, the aforementioned method requires knowledge of the signal directions of arrival (DOAs), which may not be available in many scenarios and is a parameter that needs to be estimated in our problem. Several papers have also explored compressive sampling-based DOA estimation techniques, such as [15,16]. In [15], a sparse localization framework for the MIMO radar is proposed by randomly placing transmitting and receiving antennas, and a random measurement matrix is used for target localization. Similarly, Ref. [16] develops a compressive sampling framework for 2D DOA and polarization estimation in mmWave polarized massive MIMO systems using a Gaussian measurement matrix. However, this type of random selection can lead to information loss and performance degradation as demonstrated in [17,18].

Information theory is another widely used framework for optimizing the CMM in massive MIMO systems. These principles of information theory provide a mathematical framework for quantifying the amount of information that can be transmitted over a communication channel. In [18,19], the CMM is optimized by maximizing the mutual information between the compressed measurement and the signal DOAs. This approach is based on considering the availability of a coarse prior distribution of the DOAs. By reducing the dimension of the received signal, the required number of front-end circuits is effectively reduced with minimal performance loss. Reference [20] extends this idea by developing a general compressive measurement scheme that combines the CMM and the sparse array. The framework can consider any arbitrary sparse array as the receive antennas and use the CMM to compress the dimension. As a result, it can effectively reduce both the number of physical antennas and the front-end circuits. They also optimize the CMM by maximizing the mutual information of the compressed measurements and DOA distribution, while considering the availability of the prior distribution of DOAs. In many practical cases, however, the required a priori distribution may not available. To address this issue, an iterative optimization approach is developed in [21]. Starting with no prior information on the DOA distribution, the CMM is optimized based on mutual information maximization and then used to estimate the DOA spectrum. The estimated normalized DOA spectrum is subsequently used as the prior information for the next iteration, thus iteratively improving the accuracy of the estimated DOA spectrum.

Optimizing the CMM in a sequential adaptive manner may lead to better performance compared to non-adaptive schemes [22,23]. However, using optimization techniques, such as projected gradient descent or simplified versions of projected coordinate descent, to obtain the desired CMM can be computationally expensive [24]. On the other hand, codebook-based methods, such as the hierarchical codebook developed in [23] and the hierarchical posterior matching (hiePM) strategy developed in [5], can reduce the computational burden. Nonetheless, the performance of codebook-based methods relies heavily on the quality of the codebooks and may be inferior to codebook-free approaches.

Recently, deep learning methods have emerged as a popular approach for effectively addressing complex optimization problems in various wireless communication and signal processing applications, including massive MIMO beamforming [25,26], intelligent reflecting surface [27,28], DOA estimation [29,30], and wireless channel estimation [31–33]. In a prior study [34], we developed a deep learning method for sequentially updating the CMM. Specifically, we trained a neural network without any prior information to obtain the optimized CMM, which was then used to update the posterior distribution of signal DOAs by leveraging the subsequent measurement. However, this approach faces two challenging issues. First, for each snapshot of the impinging signal, the CMM must be updated, the compressed measurement computed, and the posterior distribution updated. As such, it incurs high-computational costs, especially for updating the posterior distribution at each snapshot. Second, the posterior update relies on the accuracy of the estimated spatial spectrum, and any inaccuracies in this estimation can lead to performance degradation and slow convergence. Conversely, any inaccuracy or change in the posterior estimation will affect the spectrum estimation performance. In [35], LSTM neural networks are used in various communication system problems, including adaptive beamformer design for mmWave initial beam alignment applications. However, this study was limited to single-channel and single-user scenarios.

In this paper, we propose to exploit an LSTM network for sequentially designing the CMM matrix. LSTMs are a class of recurrent neural networks (RNNs) that are well suited for handling time-series and other sequential data due to their inherent architecture [36–42]. The previous work used a fully connected deep neural network (FCDNN), where the received signal in each time snapshot was treated independently. However, in real-world scenarios, adjacent time samples of the signal have strong correlations with each other. Therefore, we use an LSTM network to sequentially process data by retaining temporal dependencies between the input data points. Preserving time-dependent information enables more effective optimization of the CMM in each time snapshot, leading to faster convergence and better DOA estimation performance.

Notations: We use bold lower-case and upper-case letters to represent vectors and matrices, respectively. Particularly, we use I_N to denote the $N \times N$ identity matrix. $(\cdot)^T$ and $(\cdot)^H$ respectively represent the transpose and Hermitian operations of a matrix or vector. The notations $\oslash$ and $(\cdot)^{\textcircled{2}}$ are used to represent element-wise division and squaring, respectively. Additionally, $|\cdot|$ denotes the determinant operator. The operator $\mathbb{E}[\cdot]$ represents statistical expectation, whereas $\mathcal{R}(\cdot)$ and $\mathcal{I}(\cdot)$ respectively extract the real and imaginary parts of a complex entry. $\mathcal{C}^{M \times N}$ denotes the $M \times N$ complex space.

2. Signal Model
2.1. Array Signal Model

Consider D uncorrelated signals that impinge on a massive MIMO system equipped with N receive antennas from directions $\boldsymbol{\theta} = [\theta_1, \theta_2, \cdots \theta_D]^T$. The analog RF array received signal at time t is modeled as

$$
\begin{aligned}
\boldsymbol{x}^{\text{RF}}(t) &= \sum_{d=1}^{D} \boldsymbol{a}(\theta_D) s_d(t) e^{j\omega_c t} + \boldsymbol{n}(t) \\
&= \boldsymbol{A}(\boldsymbol{\theta}) \boldsymbol{s}(t) e^{j\omega_c t} + \boldsymbol{n}(t),
\end{aligned}
\tag{1}
$$

where $\boldsymbol{A}(\boldsymbol{\theta}) = [\boldsymbol{a}(\theta_1), \boldsymbol{a}(\theta_2), \cdots, \boldsymbol{a}(\theta_D)] \in \mathbb{C}^{N \times D}$ denotes the array manifold matrix whose dth column $\boldsymbol{a}(\theta_d) \in \mathbb{C}^N$ represents the steering vector of the dth user with DOA θ_d, $\boldsymbol{s}(t) = [s_1(t), s_2(t), \cdots, s_D(t)]^T \in \mathbb{C}^D$ represents the signal waveform vector, ω_c denotes the angular frequency of the carrier, and $\boldsymbol{n}(t) \sim \mathcal{CN}(\boldsymbol{0}, \sigma_n^2 \boldsymbol{I}_N)$ represents the zero-mean additive white Gaussian noise (AWGN) vector.

Figure 1 depicts the block diagram of the receiver antenna array of a massive MIMO system without performing compressed measurement. In this receiver array, each antenna is assigned with a dedicated front-end circuit, which converts the received analog RF signal to the digital base-band by performing down conversion and analog-to-digital conversion. However, dedicating a separate front-end circuit to each antenna in a massive MIMO system may be impractical, considering the hardware cost, power consumption, and computational complexity.

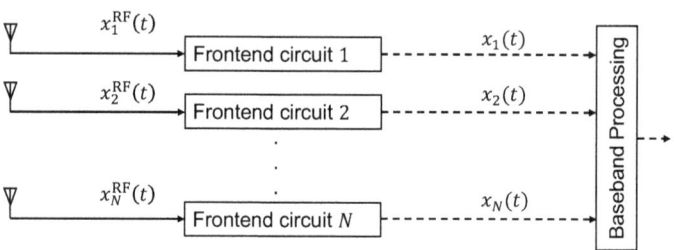

Figure 1. Block diagram of an antenna array without performing compression [18].

2.2. Compressive Array Signal Model

The number of antennas in a massive MIMO system is typically much higher than the number of users or targets. Consequently, the impinging signals can be considered sparse in the spatial (angular) domain. Such sparsity property allows us to design an optimal CMM that projects the array receive signal to a lower-dimensional manifold with no or negligible information loss. In this manner, the array receive signal can be compressed significantly in the analog domain as shown in Figure 2. As a result, the number of front-end circuits in the analog domain and the computation burden in the digital domain can be significantly reduced.

In this compressive sampling scheme, $M \ll N$ linear projections of the RF received signal $x^{\text{RF}}(t)$ are taken along the measurement kernels represented as row vectors $\boldsymbol{\phi}_m = [\phi_{m,1}, \phi_{m,2}, \cdots, \phi_{m,N}] \in \mathbb{C}^{1 \times N}$ with $m = 1, \cdots, M$. The mth compressed measurement of the RF received signal $y_m^{\text{RF}}(t)$ is the linear projection of the RF received signal $x^{\text{RF}}(t)$ in the mth measurement kernel $\boldsymbol{\phi}_m$, i.e.,

$$y_m^{\text{RF}}(t) = \left\langle \boldsymbol{\phi}_m, x^{\text{RF}}(t) \right\rangle = \sum_{n=1}^{N} \phi_{m,n} x_n^{\text{RF}}(t), \qquad (2)$$

where $x_n^{\text{RF}}(t)$ is the nth element of vector $x^{\text{RF}}(t)$.

Stacking all M measurement kernels forms the CMM $\boldsymbol{\Phi} = [\boldsymbol{\phi}_1^{\text{T}}, \boldsymbol{\phi}_2^{\text{T}}, \cdots, \boldsymbol{\phi}_M^{\text{T}}]^{\text{T}}$. Matrix $\boldsymbol{\Phi}$ is designed to be row orthonormal, i.e., $\boldsymbol{\Phi}\boldsymbol{\Phi}^{\text{H}} = \boldsymbol{I}_M$, to keep the noise power unchanged after applying the compression.

Denote $x(t)$ as the baseband signal corresponding to $x^{\text{RF}}(t)$. Note that vector $x(t)$ is not observed in the underlying system and is introduced solely for notational convenience. Then, the M compressed measurements in baseband yield $y(t) = [y_1(t), y_2(t), \cdots, y_M(t)]^{\text{T}} \in \mathbb{C}^M$, which is given as

$$y(t) = \boldsymbol{\Phi} x(t) = \boldsymbol{\Phi} A(\theta) s(t) + \boldsymbol{\Phi} n(t), \qquad (3)$$

where $\boldsymbol{\Phi} A(\theta) \in \mathbb{C}^{M \times D}$ represents the compressed array manifold with significantly reduced dimension compared to $A(\theta)$.

2.3. Probabilistic Signal Model

Consider signal DOA θ as a random variable with a probability density function (PDF) $f(\theta)$. In [18,19], it is assumed that coarse knowledge of $f(\theta)$ is available. In this case, according to the law of the total probability, the PDF of the compressed measurement vector y is expressed as

$$f(y) = \mathbb{E}_\theta\{f(y|\theta)\} = \int_{\theta \in \Theta} f(y|\theta)f(\theta)\mathrm{d}\theta, \tag{4}$$

where Θ is the angular region of the observations. We discretize the PDF $f(\theta)$ into K angular bins with an equal width of $\Delta\bar{\theta}$ so that the probability of the kth angular bin is approximated as probability mass function $p_k \approx f(\bar{\theta}_k)\Delta\bar{\theta}$ with $\sum_{k \in \mathcal{K}} p_k = 1$, where $\bar{\theta}_k$ is the nominal angle of the kth angular bin and $\mathcal{K} = \{1, 2, \cdots, K\}$. As a result, the PDF of y can be reformulated as

$$f(y) \approx \sum_{k \in \mathcal{K}} p_k f(y|\bar{\theta}_k). \tag{5}$$

That is, the PDF of y is approximated as a Gaussian mixture distribution consisting of K zero-mean Gaussian distributions $y|\bar{\theta}_k$. Considering a signal $s(t)$ impinging from the kth angular bin with a nominal DOA $\bar{\theta}_k$, the compressed measurement vector is given as

$$y|_{\theta=\bar{\theta}_k}(t) = \Phi(a(\bar{\theta}_k)s(t) + n(t)), \tag{6}$$

and the corresponding conditional PDF is

$$f(y|\bar{\theta}_k) = \frac{1}{\pi^M |C_{yy|\bar{\theta}_k}|} e^{-y^\mathrm{H} C_{yy|\bar{\theta}_k}^{-1} y}, \tag{7}$$

where

$$C_{yy|\bar{\theta}_k} = \Phi(\sigma_s^2 a(\bar{\theta}_k) a^\mathrm{H}(\bar{\theta}_k) + \sigma_n^2 I)\Phi^\mathrm{H} \tag{8}$$

is the covariance matrix of the compressed measurement vector $y|_{\theta=\bar{\theta}_k}(t)$ and σ_s^2 is the signal power. Additionally, define $C_{yy} = \Phi A(\theta) S A(\theta)^\mathrm{H} \Phi^\mathrm{H}$, as the covariance matrix of the compressed measurement with $S = \mathrm{diag}([\sigma_s^2, \sigma_s^2, \cdots])$ is the source covariance matrix.

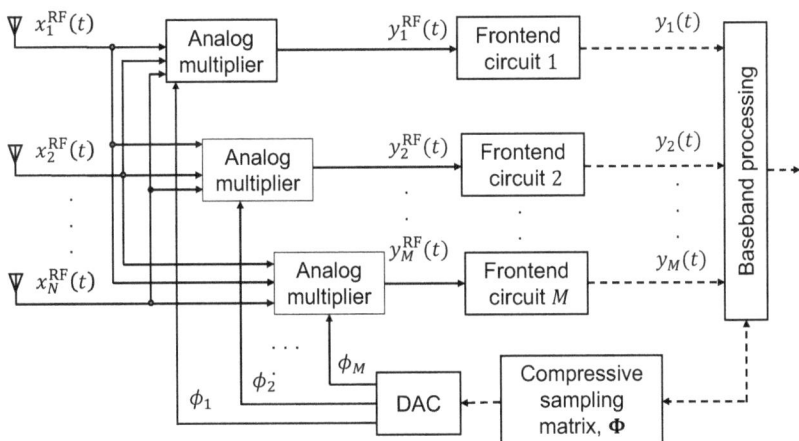

Figure 2. Block diagram of a compressive sampling antenna array [18].

3. Motivation for Using LSTM Network to Design the CMM

The objective of this paper is to design the beamforming matrix in a sequential manner. Specifically, we aim to optimize the CMM Φ at each time sample $t = 1, 2, \cdots, T$ in an adaptive manner such that the CMM Φ at time sample $t+1$ can be regarded as a function of all prior observations, denoted by $y(1:t)$ and $\Phi(1:t)$, i.e.,

$$\Phi(t+1) = \mathcal{F}(y(1:t), \Phi(1:t)), \qquad (9)$$

where $\mathcal{F}$ is a function that is exploited to map the past observations and past CMMs to design the next CMM.

However, the dimension of the past observations increases as the time index increases, rendering it impractical to optimize the CMM Φ using all prior observations. Therefore, a significant challenge of this sequential optimization process is to summarize all of the historical observations.

In [34], instead of using all past observations, the posterior distribution of signal DOA at time t is considered a sufficient statistic to design the CMM Φ at time $t+1$. However, this approach may be prone to robustness issues. For instance, if the posterior $p(\theta_k)$ for a signal containing the angular bin θ_k becomes small due to an estimation error during any time iteration, the error will propagate through the time iteration, resulting in inaccurate DOA estimation. Furthermore, in each time instant, it involves performing analog beamforming and spectrum estimation, which are computationally expensive, particularly for a large number of iterations. In addition, the paper uses a fully connected neural network, which does not well exploit the temporal correlation of the received data.

To address this issue, we propose an LSTM framework that can provide a tractable solution. LSTM is a type of recurrent neural network that can retain information over time in a variable known as the cell state. Moreover, to maintain the scalability of prior observation, LSTM incorporates a gate mechanism that controls which information to be discarded and which to be incorporated into the cell state, retaining only the relevant information from historical observations that are necessary for the given task.

Figure 3 illustrates a unit of the proposed LSTM framework at time t. At this time instant, the input to the deep learning unit comprises the current compressed measurement y_t and the cell and hidden states from the previous time samples, denoted as c_{t-1} and h_{t-1}, respectively. The LSTM unit has four gates, namely the forget gate (f_t), input gate (i_t), cell gate (g_t), and output gate (o_t), which respectively perform the following operations:

- Forget gate (f_t): This gate combines the current input $y(t)$ and the previous hidden state $h(t-1)$ to decide which information to forget and which to remember from previous cell state. The operation is given by

$$f_t = \sigma\left(W_f \left[y^T(t) \; h^T(t-1)\right]^T\right), \qquad (10)$$

where $\sigma(\cdot)$ denotes the sigmoid function, and W_f is a weight matrix corresponding to the forget gate.

- Input gate (i_t): This gate combines the current input $y(t)$ and the previous hidden state $h(t-1)$ to decide which information to store in the cell state. The operation is given by

$$i_t = \sigma\left(W_i \left[y^T(t) \; h^T(t-1)\right]^T\right), \qquad (11)$$

where W_i is a weight matrix corresponding to the input gate.

- Cell gate (g_t): This gate combines the current input $y(t)$ and the previous hidden state $h(t-1)$ to compute the actual representation that will go into the cell state. The operation is given by

$$g_t = \tanh\left(W_g \left[y^T(t) \; h^T(t-1)\right]^T\right), \qquad (12)$$

where $\tanh(\cdot)$ denotes the hyperbolic tangent function and W_g is a weight matrix corresponding to the cell gate.

- Output gate (o_t): This gate combines the current input $y(t)$ and the previous hidden state $h(t-1)$ to decide how much to weight the cell state information to generate the output of the LSTM cell, which is also denoted as hidden state h_t. The operation is given by

$$o_t = \sigma\left(W_o\left[y^T(t)\ h^T(t-1)\right]^T\right), \quad (13)$$

where W_o is a weight matrix corresponding to the output gate.

Finally, the cell state is updated according to

$$c_t = f_t c_{t-1} + i_t g_t, \quad (14)$$

which combines the amount of information from the previous cell state regulated by the forget gate and the amount of updated information. The output of the LSTM cell, i.e., the hidden state for time t, will be the filtered version of the current cell state regulated by the output gate, i.e.,

$$h_t = o_t \tanh(c_t) \quad (15)$$

The preservation of historical observations by the cell state c_t over time is evident from Equation (14). Additionally, the cell state does not exhibit growth as the time index increases; rather, it adaptively updates its information content. We, therefore, use the cell state information as a mapping of historical observations. At each time sample, these historical observations are exploited to optimize CMM Φ using another DNN. At the end of all time iterations, the minimum variance distortionless response (MVDR) spatial spectrum estimation method is employed to estimate the signal DOAs.

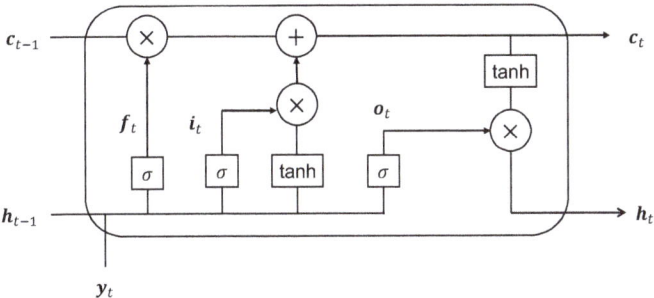

Figure 3. Proposed deep learning unit for time t.

4. Proposed LSTM Based Optimization of the CMM Φ

Figure 4 illustrates the end-to-end architecture of the proposed framework for realizing the equation presented in Equation (9). In the following subsections, we discuss the details of the proposed approach for the optimization of CMM Φ.

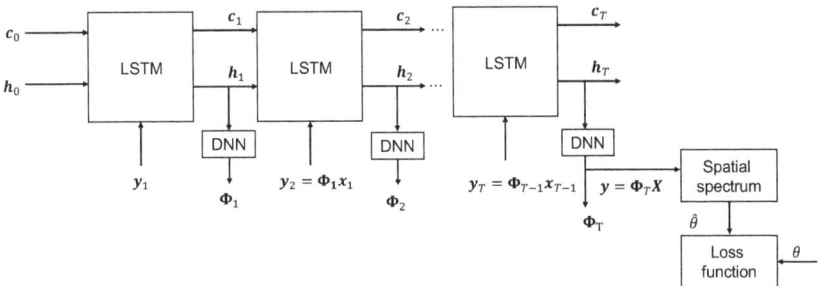

Figure 4. End-to-end deep learning framework for optimizing CMM Φ.

4.1. Data Pre-Processing

Using the array received signal vector at the massive MIMO $x(t) \in \mathcal{C}^N$ at time t, we form a tensor denoted by $X(t) \in \mathcal{C}^{B \times N \times 1}$ by concatenating the array received signal vectors for B different DOA scenarios. Collecting all time snapshots then produces the training tensor $X \in \mathcal{C}^{B \times N \times T}$. At the beginning, with a randomly initialized CMM Φ, we perform analog beamforming to obtain the compressed measurement tensor $Y(t) = \Phi(t-1)X(t)$ at time $t = 1$, where $Y(t) \in \mathcal{C}^{B \times M \times 1}$. Separating the real and imaginary parts of $Y(t)$, we concatenate them to form the input tensor $\hat{Y}(t)$ for the LSTM unit as illustrated in Figure 3.

4.2. Implementation Details of the Deep Learning Framework

The proposed deep learning framework comprises a series of LSTM units and FCDNNs. An LSTM unit summarizes the historical observations into a fixed-dimensional cell state vector $c(t-1)$, which serves as a sufficient statistic for optimizing the CMM in the subsequent time instance t. For a particular time snapshot t, the input tensor $\hat{Y}(t)$, along with the cell and hidden state tensors $C(t-1)$ and $H(t-1)$, serves as input to the LSTM unit. The tensors $C(t-1)$ and $H(t-1)$ are formed by concatenating the vectors $c(t-1)$ and $h(t-1)$ for all B scenarios and all layers of the LSTM network. Based on the gate mechanism described in Equations (10)–(15), the cell and hidden states are updated adaptively. We then employ an L-layer FCDNN to map the cell state information $C(t)$ to design the CMM $\Phi(t)$ at time instant t. The DNN output at time t is expressed as

$$\tilde{\Phi}(t) = \mathcal{A}_L(W_L \mathcal{A}_{L-1}(\cdots \mathcal{A}_1(W_1 G(t-1) + b_1) \cdots) + b_L), \tag{16}$$

where $W_l, b_l, \mathcal{A}_l$ are the weight, bias, and nonlinear activation function corresponding to the lth layer of the DNN, respectively. $\tilde{\Phi}(t)$ is the real valued representation of the complex valued CMM matrix at time t, i.e., $\tilde{\Phi}(t) = [\mathcal{R}(\Phi(t)) \; \mathcal{I}(\Phi(t))]$.

4.3. Post-Processing

We first reconstruct the complex valued $\Phi(t)$ from its real representation, where the real and imaginary parts of $\Phi(t)$ correspond to the left and right halves of $\tilde{\Phi}(t)$, respectively. The measurement kernels $\phi_m, m = 1, 2, \cdots, M$ are generally implemented using a series of phase shifters. Therefore, it is desirable for the CMM to satisfy a constant modulus constraint. In order to achieve this constraint, we set the activation function of the final layer as

$$\mathcal{A}_L(\mathcal{R}(\Phi)(t)) = \left[\mathcal{R}(\Phi) \oslash \sqrt{\mathcal{R}(\Phi)^{\textcircled{2}} + \mathcal{I}(\Phi)^{\textcircled{2}}}\right],$$
$$\mathcal{A}_L(\mathcal{I}(\Phi)(t)) = \left[\mathcal{I}(\Phi) \oslash \sqrt{\mathcal{R}(\Phi)^{\textcircled{2}} + \mathcal{I}(\Phi)^{\textcircled{2}}}\right]. \tag{17}$$

Subsequently, the obtained $\Phi(t)$, along with the updated $C(t)$ and $H(t)$, will be utilized to generate $\Phi(t+1)$, and this process will continue until the time snapshot $t = T$.

4.4. Loss Function and Back Propagation

In the underlying massive MIMO context, where the CMM Φ is optimized to enhance the accuracy of the DOA estimation, it is crucial to specify a suitable loss function that enables a comparison between the true DOAs and those estimated using the optimized Φ. Once the sequential updating of the CMM Φ is completed, the optimized Φ is used to find the compressed measurements $Y \in \mathcal{C}^{B \times M \times T}$ from the input tensor X as $Y = \Phi X$. Using these compressed measurements, we use the MVDR spectrum estimator to obtain the spatial spectrum. To do so, we first estimate the sample covariance matrix for the bth compressed measurement $Y_b \in \mathcal{C}^{M \times T}$ as

$$\hat{R}_{yb} = \frac{1}{T} Y_b Y_b^H \tag{18}$$

for $b = 1, 2, \cdots, B$. The MVDR spectrum is obtained as

$$\hat{p}_b(\theta) = \frac{a^H(\theta) \Phi^H(t) \Phi(t) a(\theta)}{a^H(\theta) \Phi^H(t) \hat{R}_{yb}^{-1}(t) \Phi(t) a(\theta)}. \tag{19}$$

We consider the DOA estimation problem as a multiclass classification problem, where in each angular bin, we make a binary decision whether a signal is present in the bin or not. To do so, we employ the binary cross entropy loss function between the estimated MVDR spectrum ($\hat{p}_b$) and the true DOA location (p_b) expressed as

$$\text{Loss} = -\frac{1}{B} \sum_{b=1}^{B} [p_b \log \hat{p}_b + (1 - p_b) \log(1 - \hat{p}_b)], \tag{20}$$

where B is the batch size of the training data.

5. Simulation Results

We consider a massive MIMO system consisting of $N = 50$ receive antennas arranged in a uniform linear fashion and separated by a half wavelength. We choose the compression ratio to be $N/M = 5$, which yields the dimension of the compressed measurement $M = 10$. The number of impinging sources in the massive MIMO system is considered between 1 and 9. The sources impinge from angular bins discretized by a $\Delta \bar{\theta} = 0.1°$ interval and within an angular range between $-90°$ and $90°$. As a result, there are 1801 components in the Gaussian mixture model. The number of snapshots is assumed to be $T = 100$.

We consider a 4-layer LSTM unit with 200 nodes in each layer, and a DNN with 3 layers and 500 nodes. The selection of the number of layers and nodes for both models is made to achieve a good balance between the predictability and generalization capability of the networks. A training dataset is created with 10,000 scenarios, each containing 1 to 9 sources randomly sampled from a uniform distribution ranging between $-90°$ and $90°$. The input signal-to-noise ratio (SNR) is randomly selected between 0 dB and 20 dB for each scenario. The test dataset consists of 1000 scenarios, which are generated using a similar approach.

We evaluate the performance of the proposed model against two related approaches as described in [21,34]. The non-neural network approach presented in [21] optimizes CMM Φ iteratively based on mutual information maximization, while the approach described in [34] uses an FCDNN to update the posterior distribution of the DOAs of the impinging signals. To compare these methods, we consider a test example with nine sources and their corresponding signal DOAs are $-55°$, $-48°$, $-44°$, $-20°$, $8°$, $20°$, $31°$, $41°$, and $45°$. Figure 5 shows the estimated spectra obtained from the methods where the input SNR is 5 dB. As demonstrated in this figure, the proposed method, depicted in (a), shows a cleaner spectrum compared to [21,34], as illustrated in (b) and (c), in a low SNR scenario. Figure 6 demonstrates the reduction in the loss function as the number of epochs increases. It is evident from the figure that the model converged well within the first 200 epochs.

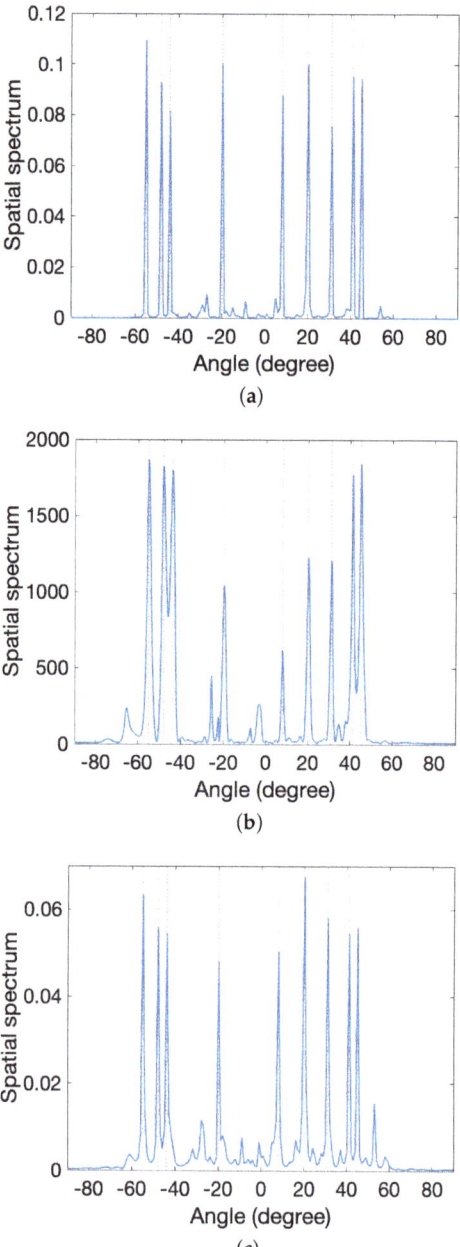

Figure 5. Comparison of the estimated spatial spectra. (**a**) Proposed method. (**b**) Method in [21]. (**c**) Method in [34].

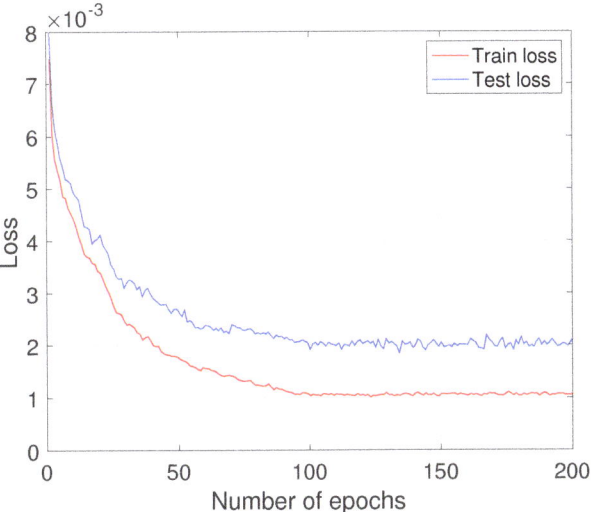

Figure 6. Loss vs. number of epochs.

In order to assess the methods' performance under different conditions, including varying input SNR levels, number of snapshots, and dimension of compressed measurement (number of front-end circuits), we compared their performance using the root mean squared error (RMSE), defined as

$$\text{RMSE} = \sqrt{\frac{1}{QD} \sum_{q=1}^{Q} \sum_{d=1}^{D} (\hat{\theta}_{q,d} - \theta_d)^2}, \quad (21)$$

where Q is the number of trials and $\hat{\theta}_{q,d}$ is the estimated DOA for the dth source of the qth Monte Carlo trial. In total, 1000 Monte Carlo trials are used to compute the RMSE values. Figure 7 presents the RMSE values with respect to input SNR, number of snapshots, and dimension of compressed measurement, and clearly shows that the proposed LSTM-based approach outperforms the other methods. Additionally, the Cramer–Rao bound (CRB) is included in Figure 7 for comparison.

To obtain the CRB, we first denote the unknown parameters in this problem, which include the signal DOAs and power of D sources as $\boldsymbol{\theta} = [\theta_1, \cdots, \theta_D]^T$ and $\boldsymbol{p} = [\sigma_1^2, \cdots, \sigma_D^2]^T$, respectively. We also define the noise power as σ_n^2, and $\boldsymbol{\omega} = [\omega_1, \cdots, \omega_D]^T$ as the spatial frequencies, where $\omega_d = \sin(\theta_d)/2$ is the spatial frequency of the dth source. Then, the unknown parameter vectors are grouped as $\boldsymbol{\psi} = [\boldsymbol{w}^T \ \boldsymbol{p}^T \ \sigma_n^2]^T$. Since we are interested in obtaining the CRB of the signal DOAs, we partitioned the unknown parameters as $\boldsymbol{\psi} = [\boldsymbol{w}^T | \boldsymbol{p}^T \ \sigma_n^2]^T$.

The CRB can be obtained as the inverse of the Fisher information matrix (FIM), which is defined as

$$[\boldsymbol{F}]_{u,v} = -\mathbb{E}\left[\frac{\partial^2 \ln p(\boldsymbol{y}|\boldsymbol{\psi})}{\partial \psi_u \psi_v}\right], \quad (22)$$

where ψ_u is the uth element of $\boldsymbol{\psi}$, with $u, v \in 1, 2, \cdots, 2D+1$.

The FIM can also be expressed as [43]

$$\frac{1}{T}\boldsymbol{F} = \begin{bmatrix}\Delta_w \\ \Delta_o\end{bmatrix}^H \begin{bmatrix}\Delta_w & \Delta_o\end{bmatrix} = \begin{bmatrix}\Delta_w^H \Delta_w & \Delta_w^H \Delta_o \\ \Delta_o^H \Delta_w & \Delta_o^H \Delta_o\end{bmatrix} \quad (23)$$

where $\Delta_w = (C_{yy}^T \otimes C_{yy})^{-\frac{1}{2}} \left[\frac{\partial r}{\partial w_1}, \cdots, \frac{\partial r}{\partial w_D} \right]$ and $\Delta_o = (C_{yy}^T \otimes C_{yy})^{-\frac{1}{2}} \left[\frac{\partial r}{\partial \sigma_1^2}, \cdots, \frac{\partial r}{\partial \sigma_D^2}, \frac{\partial r}{\partial \sigma_n^2} \right]$ with $r = \text{vec}(C_{yy})$. Then, the CRB of the signal spatial frequencies is obtained as [43]

$$\text{CRB} = \frac{1}{T}(\Delta_\omega^H \Pi_o^\perp \Delta_\omega)^{-1}, \quad (24)$$

where $\Pi_o^\perp = I - \Delta_o(\Delta_o^H \Delta_o)^{-1} \Delta_o^H$.

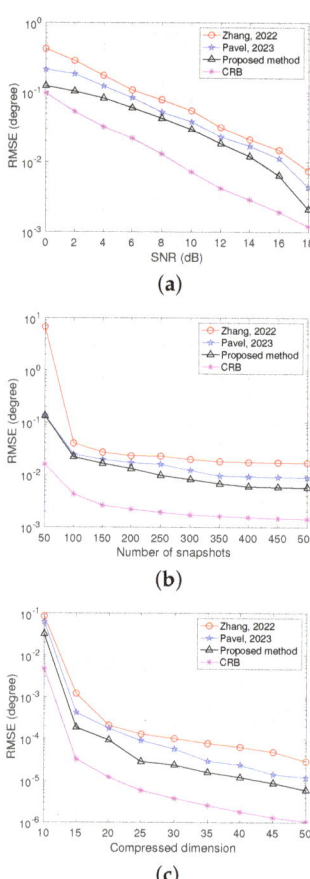

Figure 7. Performance comparison. (**a**) RMSE versus input SNR. (**b**) RMSE versus number of snapshots. (**c**) RMSE versus compressed dimension.

Next, we considered a scenario where nine sources move with an initial position of $-20°$, $-15°$, $-10°$, $-5°$, $0°$, $5°$, $10°$, $15°$, and $20°$ in the positive direction with the same angular rate. They move 1 degree per 20 snapshots. The result of the proposed method is compared with the result of the method described in [34] because both are sequential methods, namely, Φ is sequentially updated. As shown in Figure 8, as the source positions change, the performance of the method described in [34] degrades. This is because this method uses the posterior from the previous time instant as a sufficient statistic of all past observations. Therefore, as each new measurement differs from the previous ones, this method cannot adapt well. In contrast, the proposed method, as depicted in Figure 9, does not have this limitation, resulting in improved DOA estimation performance as the sequential updating continues.

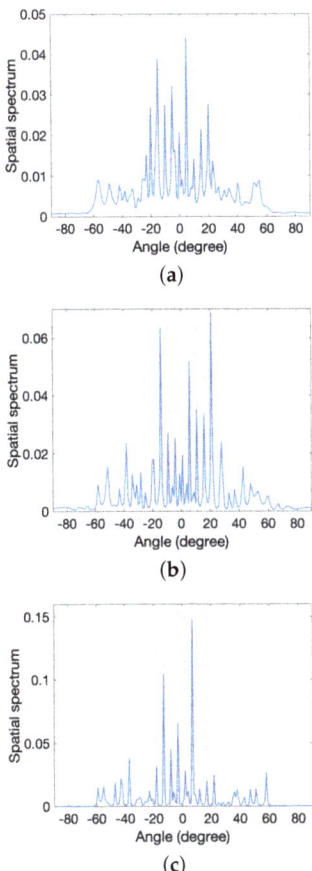

Figure 8. Estimated spectra for moving sources using method in [34]. (**a**) Initial position. (**b**) Next position from (**a**). (**c**) Next position from (**b**).

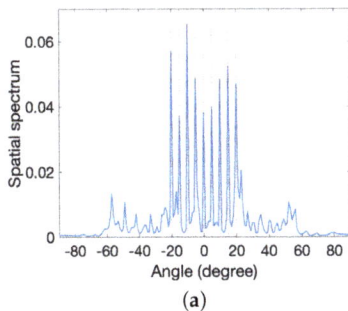

Figure 9. *Cont.*

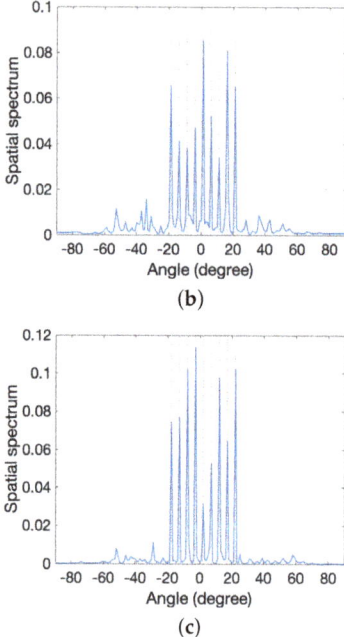

Figure 9. Estimated spectra for moving sources using the proposed method. (**a**) Initial position. (**b**) Next position from (**a**). (**c**) Next position from (**b**).

6. Conclusions

In this paper, we developed an LSTM-based framework to optimize the CMM in a massive MIMO setting. The inherent architecture of an LSTM network is well suited to preserve relevant historical observation, which is useful to design the CMM in a sequential manner. The resulting optimized CMM can then be used to compress high-dimensional received data, which can effectively reduce the number of front-end circuits. Our proposed method exhibits superior DOA estimation performance compared to the existing literature as demonstrated by the simulation results.

Author Contributions: Conceptualization, S.R.P. and Y.D.Z.; methodology, S.R.P.; validation, S.R.P.; writing—original draft preparation, S.R.P.; writing—review and editing, Y.D.Z.; supervision, Y.D.Z. All authors have read and agreed to the published version of the manuscript.

Funding: This research received no external funding.

Data Availability Statement: All data used to support the findings of this study are included within the article.

Conflicts of Interest: The authors declare no conflict of interest.

References

1. De Lamare, R.C. Massive MIMO systems: Signal processing challenges and research trends. *arXiv* **2013**, arXiv:1310.7282.
2. Rusek, F.; Persson, D.; Lau, B.K.; Larsson, E.G.; Marzetta, T.L.; Edfors, O.; Tufvesson, F. Scaling up MIMO: Opportunities and challenges with very large arrays. *IEEE Signal Process. Mag.* **2013**, *30*, 40–60. [CrossRef]
3. Larsson, E.G.; Edfors, O.; Tufvesson, F.; Marzetta, T.L. Massive MIMO for next generation wireless systems. *IEEE Commun. Mag.* **2014**, *52*, 186–195. [CrossRef]
4. Lu, L.; Li, G.Y.; Swindlehurst, A.L.; Ashikhmin, A.; Zhang, R. An overview of massive MIMO: Benefits and challenges. *IEEE J. Sel. Top. Signal Process.* **2014**, *8*, 742–758. [CrossRef]
5. Alkhateeb, A.; El Ayach, O.; Leus, G.; Heath, R.W. Heath, Channel estimation and hybrid precoding for millimeter wave cellular systems. *IEEE J. Sel. Top. Signal Process.* **2014**, *8*, 831–846. [CrossRef]

6. Jiang, F.; Chen, J.; Swindlehurst, A.L.; López-Salcedo, J.A. Massive MIMO for wireless sensing with a coherent multiple access channel. *IEEE Trans. Signal Process.* **2015**, *63*, 3005–3017. [CrossRef]
7. Rappaport, T.S.; Sun, S.; Mayzus, R.; Zhao, H.; Azar, Y.; Wang, K.; Gutierrez, F. Millimeter wave mobile communications for 5G cellular: It will work! *IEEE Access* **2013**, *1*, 335–349. [CrossRef]
8. Wang, C.X.; Haider, F.; Gao, X.; You, X.H.; Yang, Y.; Yuan, D.; Aggoune, H.M.; Hepsaydir, E. Cellular architecture and key technologies for 5G wireless communication networks. *IEEE Commun. Mag.* **2014**, *52*, 122–130. [CrossRef]
9. Molisch, A.F.; Ratnam, S.V.V.; Han, Z.; Li, S.; Nguyen, L.H.; Li, L.; Haneda, K. Hybrid beamforming for massive MIMO: A survey. *IEEE Commun. Mag.* **2017**, *55*, 134–141. [CrossRef]
10. Björnson, E.; Sanguinetti, L.; Wymeersch, H.; Hoydis, J.; Marzetta, T.L. Massive MIMO is a reality—What is next?: Five promising research directions for antenna arrays. *Digital Signal Process.* **2019**, *94*, 3–20. [CrossRef]
11. Fortunati, S.; Sanguinetti, L.; Gini, F.; Greco, M.S.; Himed, B. Massive MIMO radar for target detection. *IEEE Trans. Signal Process.* **2020**, *68*, 859–871. [CrossRef]
12. Lin, T.; Cong, J.; Zhu, Y.; Zhang, J.; Letaief, K.B. Hybrid beamforming for millimeter wave systems using the MMSE criterion. *IEEE Trans. Commun.* **2019**, *67*, 3693–3708. [CrossRef]
13. Zhang, D.; Pan, P.; You, R.; Wang, H. SVD-based low-complexity hybrid precoding for millimeter-wave MIMO systems. *IEEE Commun. Lett.* **2018**, *22*, 2176–2179. [CrossRef]
14. Qi, C.; Ci, W.; Zhang, J.; You, X. Hybrid beamforming for millimeter wave MIMO integrated sensing and communications. *IEEE Commun. Lett.* **2022**, *26*, 1136–1140. [CrossRef]
15. Rossi, M.; Haimovich, A.M.; Eldar, Y.C. Spatial compressive sensing for MIMO radar. *IEEE Trans. Signal Process.* **2013**, *62*, 419–430. [CrossRef]
16. Wen, F.; Gui, G.; Gacanin, H.; Sari, H. Compressive sampling framework for 2D-DOA and polarization estimation in mmWave polarized massive MIMO systems. *IEEE Trans. Wirel. Commun.* **2022**, *22*, 3071–3083. [CrossRef]
17. Pakrooh, P.; Scharf, L.L.; Pezeshki, A.; Chi, Y. Analysis of fisher information and the cramér-rao bound for nonlinear parameter estimation after compressed sensing. In Proceedings of the 2013 IEEE International Conference on Acoustics, Speech and Signal Processing, Vancouver, BC, Canada, 26–31 May 2013; pp. 6630–6634.
18. Gu, Y.; Zhang, Y.D. Compressive sampling optimization for user signal parameter estimation in massive MIMO systems. *Digital Signal Process.* **2019**, *94*, 105–113. [CrossRef]
19. Gu, Y.; Zhang, Y.D.; Goodman, N.A. Optimized compressive sensing-based direction-of-arrival estimation in massive MIMO. In Proceedings of the 2017 IEEE International Conference on Acoustics, Speech and Signal Processing (ICASSP), New Orleans, LA, USA, 5 March 2017; pp. 3181–3185.
20. Guo, M.; Zhang, Y.D.; Chen, T. DOA estimation using compressed sparse array. *IEEE Trans. Signal Process.* **2018**, *66*, 4133–4146. [CrossRef]
21. Zhang, Y.D. Iterative learning for optimized compressive measurements in massive MIMO systems. In Proceedings of the 2022 IEEE Radar Conference (RadarConf22), New York, NY, USA, 21–25 March 2022; pp. 1–5.
22. Nakos, V.; Shi, X.; Woodruff, D.P.; Zhang, H. Improved algorithms for adaptive compressed sensing. *arXiv* **2018**, arXiv:1804.09673.
23. Haupt, J.; Castro, R.M.; Nowak, R. Distilled sensing: Adaptive sampling for sparse detection and estimation. *IEEE Trans. Inform. Theory* **2011**, *57*, 6222–6235. [CrossRef]
24. Sohrabi, F.; Chen, Z.; Yu, W. Deep active learning approach to adaptive beamforming for mmWave initial alignment. *IEEE J. Sel. Areas Commun.* **2021**, *39*, 2347–2360. [CrossRef]
25. Yang, Y.; Zhang, S.; Gao, F.; Xu, C.; Ma, J.; Dobre, O.A. Deep learning based antenna selection for channel extrapolation in FDD massive MIMO. In Proceedings of the 2020 International Conference on Wireless Communications and Signal Processing (WCSP), Nanjing, China, 21–23 October 2020; pp. 182–187.
26. Huang, H.; Peng, Y.; Yang, J.; Xia, W.; Gui, G. Fast beamforming design via deep learning. *IEEE Trans. Vehi. Tech.* **2021**, *69*, 1065–1069. [CrossRef]
27. Zhang, S.S.; Zhang, F.; Gao, J.; Ma, O.; Dobre, A. Deep learning optimized sparse antenna activation for reconfigurable intelligent surface assisted communication. *IEEE Trans. Commun.* **2021**, *69*, 6691–6705. [CrossRef]
28. Jiang, T.; Cheng, H.V.; Yu, W. Learning to reflect and to beamform for intelligent reflecting surface with implicit channel estimation. *IEEE J. Sel. Areas Commun.* **2021**, *39*, 1931–1945. [CrossRef]
29. Wu, L.; Liu, Z.M.; Huang, Z.T. Deep convolution network for direction of arrival estimation with sparse prior. *IEEE Signal Process. Lett.* **2019**, *26*, 1688–1692. [CrossRef]
30. Pavel, S.R.; Chowdhury, M.W.T.; Zhang, Y.D.; Shen, D.; Chen, G. Machine learning-based direction-of-arrival estimation exploiting distributed sparse arrays. In Proceedings of the 2021 55th Asilomar Conference on Signals, Systems, and Computers, Pacific Grove, CA, USA, 31 October–3 November 2021; pp. 241–245.
31. Soltani, M.; Pourahmadi, V.; Mirzaei, A.; Sheikhzadeh, H. Deep learning-based channel estimation. *IEEE Commun. Lett.* **2019**, *23*, 652–655. [CrossRef]
32. Chun, C.-J.; Kang, J.-M.; Kim, I.-M. Deep learning-based channel estimation for massive MIMO systems. *IEEE Wirel. Commun. Lett.* **2019**, *8*, 1228–1231. [CrossRef]
33. He, H.; Wen, C.K.; Jin, S.; Li, G.Y. Deep learning-based channel estimation for beamspace mmWave massive MIMO systems. *IEEE Wirel. Commun. Lett.* **2018**, *7*, 852–855. [CrossRef]

34. Pavel, S.R.; Zhang, Y.D. Deep learning-based compressive sampling optimization in massive MIMO systems. In Proceedings of the ICASSP 2023-2023 IEEE International Conference on Acoustics, Speech and Signal Processing (ICASSP), Rhodes Island, Greece, 4–10 June 2023.
35. Sohrabi, F.; Jiang, T.; Cui, W.; Yu, W. Active sensing for communications by learning. *IEEE J. Sel. Areas Commun.* **2022**, *40*, 1780–1794. [CrossRef]
36. Fernández, S.; Graves, A.; Schmidhuber, J. Sequence labelling in structured domains with hierarchical recurrent neural networks. In Proceedings of the 20th International Joint Conference on Artificial Intelligence, IJCAI, Hyderabad, India, 6–12 January 2007.
37. Schafer, A.M.; Zimmermann, H.G. Recurrent neural networks are universal approximators. In Proceedings of the Artificial Neural Networks—ICANN 2006: 16th International Conference, Athens, Greece, 10–14 September 2006; pp. 632–640.
38. Hochreiter, S.; Schmidhuber, J. Long short-term memory. *Neural Comput.* **1997**, *9*, 1735–1780. [CrossRef]
39. DiPietro, R.; Hager, G.D. Deep learning: RNNs and LSTM. In *Handbook of Medical Image Computing and Computer Assisted Intervention*; Academic Press: Cambridge, MA, USA, 2020; pp. 503–519.
40. Greff, K.; Srivastava, R.K.; Koutník, J.; Steunebrink, B.R.; Schmidhuber, J. Lstm: A search space odyssey. *IEEE Trans. Neural Netw. Learn. Syst.* **2016**, *28*, 2222–2232. [CrossRef]
41. Yu, Y.; Si, X.; Hu, C.; Zhang, J. A review of recurrent neural networks: LSTM cells and network architectures. *Neural Comput.* **2019**, *31*, 1235–1270. [CrossRef]
42. He, T.; Droppo, J. Exploiting LSTM structure in deep neural networks for speech recognition. In Proceedings of the 2016 IEEE International Conference on Acoustics, Speech and Signal Processing (ICASSP), Shanghai, China, 20–25 March 2016; pp. 5445–5449.
43. Liu, C.-L.; Vaidyanathan, P.P. Cramér-Rao bounds for coprime and other sparse arrays, which find more sources than sensors. *Digit. Signal Process.* **2017**, *61*, 43–61. [CrossRef]

Disclaimer/Publisher's Note: The statements, opinions and data contained in all publications are solely those of the individual author(s) and contributor(s) and not of MDPI and/or the editor(s). MDPI and/or the editor(s) disclaim responsibility for any injury to people or property resulting from any ideas, methods, instructions or products referred to in the content.

Article

Recovering the Forcing Function in Systems with One Degree of Freedom Using ANN and Physics Information

Shadab Anwar Shaikh [1,*], Harish Cherukuri [1,*] and Taufiquar Khan [2]

1 Department of Mechanical Engineering and Engineering Science, University of North Carolina at Charlotte, Charlotte, NC 28223-0001, USA
2 Department of Mathematics and Statistics, University of North Carolina at Charlotte, Charlotte, NC 28223-0001, USA
* Correspondence: sshaikh4@uncc.edu (S.A.S.); hcheruku@uncc.edu (H.C.)

Abstract: In engineering design, oftentimes a system's dynamic response is known or can be measured, but the source generating these responses is not known. The mathematical problem where the focus is on inferring the source terms of the governing equations from the set of observations is known as an inverse source problem (ISP). ISPs are traditionally solved by optimization techniques with regularization, but in the past few years, there has been a lot of interest in approaching these problems from a deep-learning viewpoint. In this paper, we propose a deep learning approach—infused with physics information—to recover the forcing function (source term) of systems with one degree of freedom from the response data. We test our architecture first to recover smooth forcing functions, and later functions involving abruptly changing gradient and jump discontinuities in the case of a linear system. Finally, we recover the harmonic, the sum of two harmonics, and the gaussian function, in the case of a non-linear system. The results obtained are promising and demonstrate the efficacy of this approach in recovering the forcing functions from the data.

Keywords: physics informed neural network; dynamic force identification; deep learning; duffing's equation; spring mass damper system; non-linear oscillators

Citation: Shaikh, S.A.; Cherukuri, H.; Khan, T. Recovering the Forcing Function in Systems with One Degree of Freedom Using ANN and Physics Information. *Algorithms* **2023**, *16*, 250. https://doi.org/10.3390/a16050250

Academic Editor: Frank Werner

Received: 10 March 2023
Revised: 3 May 2023
Accepted: 8 May 2023
Published: 12 May 2023

Copyright: © 2023 by the authors. Licensee MDPI, Basel, Switzerland. This article is an open access article distributed under the terms and conditions of the Creative Commons Attribution (CC BY) license (https://creativecommons.org/licenses/by/4.0/).

1. Introduction

Inverse problems are a special class of mathematical problems where the focus is on inferring causal relationships from the set of observations. These problems are often ill-posed and suffer from various numerical issues [1], however, are encountered extensively in different fields of science and engineering. In the past few decades, there has been a plethora of research on solving these problems [2–4].

A subclass of inverse problems, where the interest is in estimating the right-hand side, or "source term", of a governing equation, is known as inverse source problems (ISP). ISPs arise frequently in several domains of physics and engineering, a few noteworthy examples are the following: Optical Molecular Imaging (OMI), where the spatial distribution of bio-luminescent and fluorescent markers in the human tissues is reconstructed from light-intensity measurements [5,6]; Radiative Heat Transfer, where temperature distribution of a medium is reconstructed from radiation intensity measurements and medium properties [6]; Magnetoencephalography (MEG) and Electroencephalography (EEG), where surface electrical and magnetic current measurements on the head are used to determine the source of brain activity [7,8].

In this paper, we study one such ISP known as the dynamic load identification problem. Here, we attempt to recover the 'forcing function' or 'excitation force' of linear and non-linear oscillators from the dynamic response data. This problem can be solved both in the time and frequency domains; however, in this study, we adopt the time domain approach owing to its simplicity and straightforwardness.

In the past few decades, plenty of research has been published discussing various approaches to solving this problem, and it will be difficult to enumerate them all given the scope of this paper; nonetheless, a few notable mentions are as follows. Huang [9] used the conjugate gradient method to estimate the time-dependent forces in a non-linear oscillator. Ma et al. [10] developed a recursive estimator based on the Kalman filter to determine the impulsive load from the measurement data for the single and multi-degree-of-freedom systems. In another interesting work by Azam et al. [11], the authors proposed a dual Kalman filter for estimating the full states of a linear multi-degree of freedom system with unknown input from a limited number of noisy acceleration measurements and a known physical model. Ref. [12] formulated the force identification problem of the duffing oscillator as a Volterra-type integral equation of the first kind and used the regularization technique to stabilize the solution. Feldman [13] proposed a method for predicting forces only from response data without the need for any parametric or governing equation information using the Hilbert transform. Ref. [14] solved the non-linear force identification problem in the frequency domain using ordinary least squares with Tikhonov regularization and its variants. Liu et al. [15] solved the non-linear vibration problem by transforming the non-linear ordinary differential equations into parabolic ordinary differential equations due to their robustness against large noise. Recently, Rice et al. [16] proposed a calibration-based integral formulation for estimating the forcing function in the spring mass damper system from response data. For a detailed review of past and present literature on dynamic load identification techniques, interested readers are advised to refer to [17].

In recent years, there has been a significant interest in applying machine learning and deep learning techniques for load identification. Pravin and Rao [18] proposed a technique for recovering the input forces from acceleration time history using dynamic principal component analysis. Zhou et al. [19] used a deep Recurrent Neural Networks (RNNs) technique with two variants of Long Short Term Memory (LSTM) to recover the impact loads on non-linear structures from response data. They tested their architecture on a damped duffing oscillator subjected to an impact load expressed by normal distribution function and on a composite plate. Another work [20] proposed RNN with different architecture, but this work was mainly focused on recovering the forces on beam structure excited by harmonic, impact, and random forces. In another work by Luca Rosafalco et al. [21], the authors implemented a deep learning based autoencoder for load identification, for structural health monitoring, from multivariate structural vibration data. They employed residual learning and inception modules in their autoencoder network. Ref. [22] proposed an ANN based on Bayesian Probability Framework to estimate the forces from the displacement responses.

In spite of the massive success of deep learning techniques in tackling a variety of problems owing to their ability to explore vast design space and to manage ill-posed problems, deep learning predictions are oftentimes physically inconsistent and generalize poorly [23]. However, this behavior can be alleviated to some extent by embedding various biases; one way of achieving this is by infusing the governing equation in the loss function of a neural network as proposed by [24], known as a "physics-informed neural network" (PINNs). Recently, PINNs have been used to solve inverse source problems; one such account is the paper by He et al. [25]. In this work, the author utilized PINNs to predict the spatially and temporally varying heat source from the simulated temperature data with good accuracy. In this work, we use the PINNs approach for estimating the forcing function of one degree of freedom system.

Recently, two studies [26,27] have been published where the authors utilized machine learning and physics information to solve the vibration problem. The former used the Hilbert transform and a variant of the least-squares method to estimate the non-linear restoring force in a bi-stable structure, and the latter used PINNs to solve forced vibration and plate vibration problems.

Haghighat et al. [27] also used PINNs to solve forced spring mass damper systems similar to ours, but their work was mostly about predicting the displacements for a future time step and natural frequency, whereas our approach is more focused on estimating the excitation forces. We propose PINNs to estimate harmonic or non-harmonic and periodic or aperiodic forcing functions for systems with one degree of freedom subjected to various initial conditions.

Although in this work our attention is on oscillators as a mechanical system, to our understanding, this work also has the potential to be applied to any systems governed by linear or non-linear ordinary differential equations in different domains.

The remainder of the paper is organized as follows: In Section 2, we talk about the mathematical model of duffing's equation followed by Section 3 where we discuss the structure of our neural network and share details about the training process. Later, in the following Section 4, we share our findings and finally conclude this paper with Sections 5 and 6 with discussions and conclusions, respectively.

2. Mathematical Model

Duffing's equation is a nonlinear ordinary differential equation used to model the approximate behavior of various physical systems, such as nano-mechanical resonators [28], ultrasonic cutting systems [29], piezo-ceramics under influence of a magnetic field, and, the flight motor of an insect [30], to name a few. One formulation of Duffing's equation is given by

$$\ddot{x} + \delta \dot{x} + \alpha x + \beta x^3 = f(t). \tag{1}$$

Here, $x(t)$ is the solution to a differential equation. Initial conditions are given by $x(0) = x_0$ and $\dot{x}(0) = \dot{x}_0$, δ is the amount of damping, α is linear stiffness, β is the amount of non-linearity, and $f(t)$ is the forcing function. By rearranging and fixing different values of coefficients, i.e., α, δ, β in Equation (1), the governing equation of various linear and non-linear oscillators can be derived. For a detailed mathematical treatment and understanding of Duffing's equation, interested readers are advised to refer to [31].

In this work, we are going to recover $f(t)$ from the simulated measurement of $x(t)$, its derivative $\dot{x}(t)$, and initial conditions using artificial neural network (ANN) and governing equation information. This is different than solving in a forward manner, where we typically solve the differential equation analytically or numerically, to get the solution $x(t)$ given $f(t)$ and initial conditions.

3. Methodology

In this section, we discuss the structure of the neural network (NN) that was used, followed by details on the loss function, and later, sum up the section by shedding some light on the training algorithm and process that was employed.

3.1. Structure of NN

The structure of NN is shown in Figure 1 and mathematically is represented by

$$\hat{f}, \hat{x}, \dot{\hat{x}} = \Phi^L(t; \mathbf{W}, \mathbf{b}) \tag{2}$$

where the function $\Phi^L : \mathbb{R}^+ \mapsto \mathbb{R}^3$ represents the neural network with L number of layers; $t \in \mathbb{R}^+$ is the input and $\hat{x} \in \mathbb{R}$, $\dot{\hat{x}} \in \mathbb{R}$, $\hat{f} \in \mathbb{R}$ are the outputs; $\mathbf{W} \in \mathbb{R}^{n \times n}$ and $\mathbf{b} \in \mathbb{R}^n$ are the neural network parameters. The architecture was defined in this way since it makes the differentiation of NN output with respect to input more manageable. Differentiation was performed using Automatic Differentiation (AD) with the help of the TensorFlow [32] library functions.

The NN is feed-forward in a sense, such that the first layer is an input to the second, and the second to the next, and so on until the last layer. This can be represented by the composite equation below,

$$\mathbf{x}^j = \sigma^j(\mathbf{W}^j \cdot \mathbf{x}^{j-1} + \mathbf{b}^j), \qquad j \in \{0, \ldots, L\} \tag{3}$$

where j is the layer number, $\sigma^j : \mathbb{R}^n \mapsto \mathbb{R}^n$ is the activation function which adds non-linearity to the NN, and $\mathbf{W}^j$ and $\mathbf{b}^j$ are weights and biases of the specific layer

For example, a 4-layer neural network, i.e., $L = 4$, can be represented by

$$\begin{aligned}
\mathbf{x}^1 &= \sigma^1\left(\mathbf{W}^1 \cdot \mathbf{x}^0 + \mathbf{b}^1\right) \\
\mathbf{x}^2 &= \sigma^2\left(\mathbf{W}^2 \cdot \mathbf{x}^1 + \mathbf{b}^2\right) \\
\mathbf{x}^3 &= \sigma^3\left(\mathbf{W}^3 \cdot \mathbf{x}^2 + \mathbf{b}^3\right) \\
\mathbf{x}^4 &= \mathbf{W}^4 \cdot \mathbf{x}^3 + \mathbf{b}^4
\end{aligned} \tag{4}$$

where $\mathbf{x}^0 = t$ and $\mathbf{x}^4 = [\hat{f}, \hat{x}, \hat{\dot{x}}]$. The output of NN, $\hat{f}$ is constrained by the physical model and $\hat{x}, \hat{\dot{x}}$ are constrained by the displacement and velocity data, respectively. This is discussed in more detail in the Section 3.2.

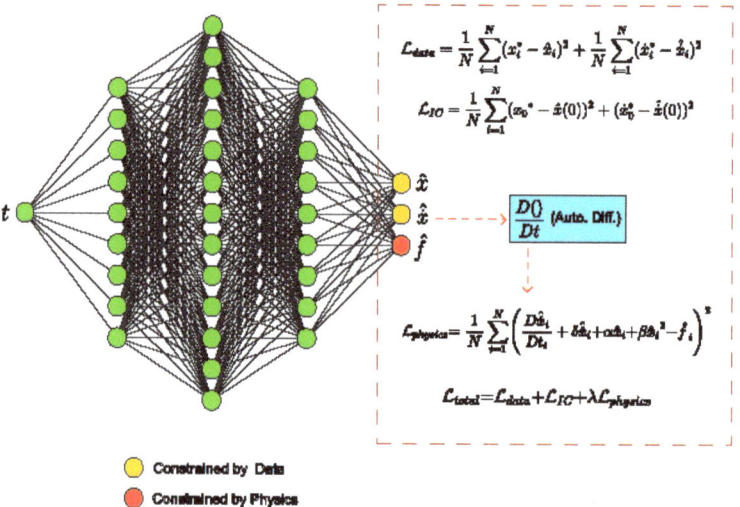

Figure 1. Proposed neural network architecture with input t and output $\hat{x}, \hat{\dot{x}}$ and $\hat{f}$.

The proposed NN architecture was developed using the Keras [33] library with a TensorFlow backend. It consists of $L = 10$ layers with [1,15,30,60,120, 240,120,60,30,15,3] units each. The batch normalization layer is present alternately after every dense layer and, each dense layer is passed through the eLU activation function, which adds the non-linearity to the network.

The optimal hyper-parameters were determined by performing systematic hyper-parameter tuning, which involved exploring different combinations of neural network architectures, initialization methods, activation functions, learning rates, and number of epochs. Initially, a shallow network with a smaller number of trainable parameters and ReLU activation function was used, but this did not yield satisfactory results. Subsequently, other activation functions were experimented with, and it was found that the eLU activation function produced better results. Finally, a deeper architecture with eLU activation function was employed. Similar experiments were conducted to identify other optimal hyper-parameter choices. Additional optimal hyper-parameters choices used in study are discussed in the Section 3.3.

3.2. Loss Function

The workhorse of our approach is the way the neural network loss function is defined. The total loss $\mathcal{L}_{total}$ is composed of the data term $\mathcal{L}_{data}$, $\mathcal{L}_{IC}$ and the physics loss term $\mathcal{L}_{physics}$:

$$\mathcal{L}_{total} = \mathcal{L}_{data} + \mathcal{L}_{IC} + \lambda \mathcal{L}_{physics} \tag{5}$$

such that

$$\mathcal{L}_{data} = \frac{1}{N}\sum_{i=1}^{N}(x_i^* - \hat{x}_i)^2 + \frac{1}{N}\sum_{i=1}^{N}(\dot{x}_i^* - \hat{\dot{x}}_i)^2 \tag{6}$$

and

$$\mathcal{L}_{IC} = (x_0 - \hat{x}(0))^2 + (\dot{x}_0 - \hat{\dot{x}}(0))^2. \tag{7}$$

Here, x_i^* and $\dot{x}_i^*$ are the displacement and velocity from the data, $\hat{x}_i$ and $\hat{\dot{x}}_i$ are displacement and velocity predictions from the neural network, λ represents the regularization term, x_0 and $\dot{x}_0$ are the initial conditions. The task of $\mathcal{L}_{data}$ and $\mathcal{L}_{IC}$ is to constrain the neural network predictions using the data.

The physics loss $\mathcal{L}_{physics}$ term is where the physics information is infused into the neural networks and is given by,

$$\mathcal{L}_{physics} = \frac{1}{N}\sum_{i=1}^{N}\left(\frac{D\hat{\dot{x}}_i}{Dt_i} + \delta\hat{\dot{x}}_i + \alpha\hat{x}_i + \beta\hat{x}_i^3 - \hat{f}_i\right)^2. \tag{8}$$

This equation is obtained by rearranging Equation (1) and replacing velocities and displacements with their equivalent neural network predictions. For calculating the acceleration from velocity prediction, we make use of automatic differentiation, which is represented by $\frac{D}{Dt_i}$ in the above equation. The job of $\mathcal{L}_{physics}$ is to force the $\hat{f}_i$ to take values that obey the governing equation.

3.3. Training

The objective of the proposed NN architecture is to recover the forcing function, $f(t)$, from the displacement and velocity data. The training algorithm is shown below (refer to Algorithm 1). Inputs to the algorithm are t, x^*, $\dot{x}^*$, i.e., time, displacement, and velocity data. The NN takes in t and outputs $\hat{f}$, $\hat{x}$, $\hat{\dot{x}}$, i.e., forcing function, displacement, and velocity predictions, respectively. The weights of the neural network are initialized using He-Normal initialization.

The network was trained on 500 data points in batches of 250 points on NVIDIA GTX 2060 GPU for 60,000 epochs. The training time for all the training instances was around 3 to 3.5 h approximately. The learning rate η was chosen as 0.001 and the regularization term λ was chosen as either 0.1 or 0.01 depending on which provided a better result.

At each epoch, the $\mathcal{L}_{total}$ is calculated from the data and neural network predictions. Later, Adam optimizer [34] takes in $\mathcal{L}_{total}$ and calculates its gradients with respect to NN parameters and propagates them to the network using the back-propagation algorithm. This algorithm uses these gradients to adjust the weights and biases of the network at every epoch. A snapshot of $\mathcal{L}_{total}$, $\mathcal{L}_{data}$ and $\mathcal{L}_{physics}$ progression with respect to epochs for one training instance is shown in the Figure 2. Ideally, for the neural network to learn successfully $\mathcal{L}_{total} \rightarrow 0$, which can be observed in the Figure 2 below.

Algorithm 1 Training Algorithm

Require: $t, x^*, \dot{x}^*$
Ensure: $\mathcal{L}_{total} \to 0$
    $n \leftarrow$ no. of epochs
    $\eta \leftarrow$ learning rate
    $N \leftarrow$ batch size
    $\lambda \leftarrow$ regularization
    while $n > 0$ **do**
        $\hat{f}, \hat{x}, \hat{\dot{x}} \leftarrow \Phi^L(t; \mathbf{W}, \mathbf{b})$
        $\mathcal{L}_{data}, \mathcal{L}_{IC}, \mathcal{L}_{physics}$ ▷ This is calculated using (6)–(8)
        $\mathcal{L}_{total} \leftarrow \mathcal{L}_{data} + \mathcal{L}_{IC} + \lambda \mathcal{L}_{physics}$
        $\mathbf{W}^*, \mathbf{b}^* \leftarrow \text{Adam}(\eta, \mathcal{L}_{total})$
        $\mathbf{W}, \mathbf{b} \leftarrow \mathbf{W}^*, \mathbf{b}^*$
        $n \leftarrow n - 1$
    end while

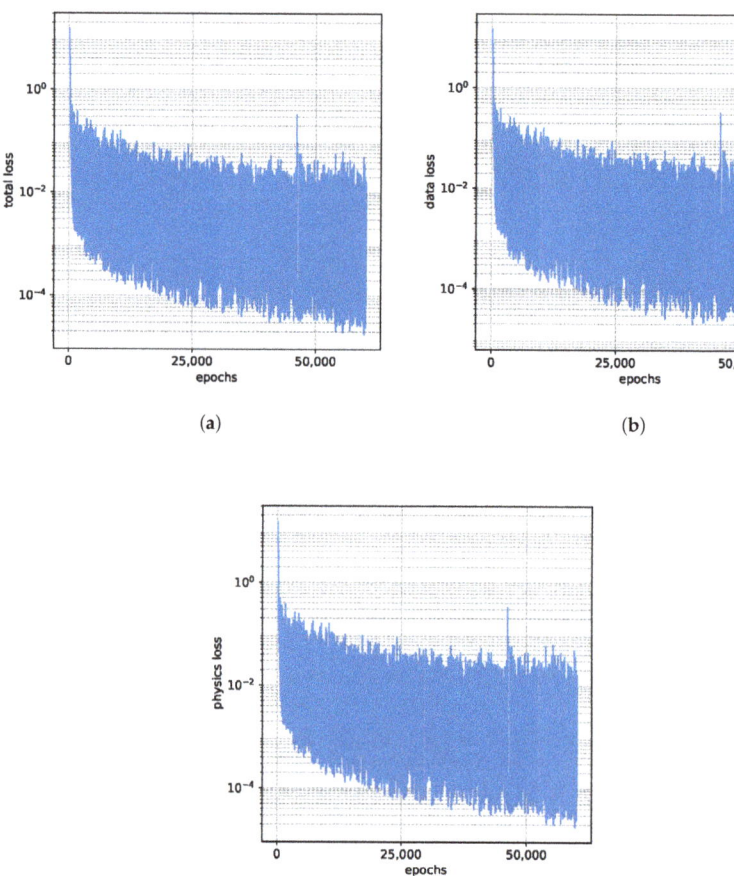

Figure 2. (**a**–**c**) shows the total, data, and physics loss w.r.t the training epochs for one training instance.

4. Results

In this section, we share our findings that were obtained by performing various numerical experiments on our proposed architecture. We start by discussing the results of spring mass damper systems excited by different types of forces and initial conditions and later sum up the section on the results of our experiments with the non-linear oscillator.

The data for training the neural network were generated by simulating Equation (1) using the ode45 routine of MATLAB [35] for different coefficients α, β, δ and initial conditions $x_0, \dot{x}_0$, for all the simulations, $t \in [0, 50 \text{ s}]$. A snapshot of data instance that was generated by simulating ODE is shown in Figure 3.

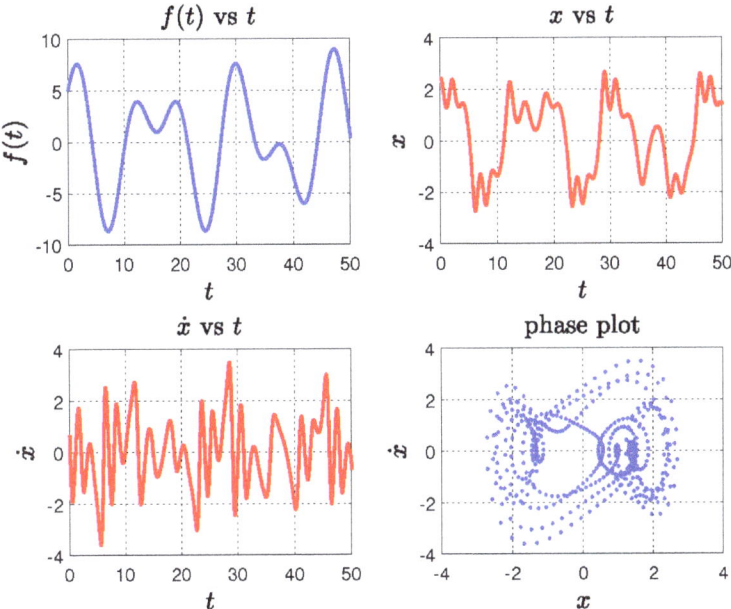

Figure 3. Figure shows the training sample that was obtained by simulating Equation (1) by setting $\alpha = 0.4, \beta = 0.9, \delta = 0.5$ with initial conditions $x_0 = 2.4, \dot{x}_0 = 0.7$ subjected to forcing function given by Equation (14) with $\gamma_1 = 5, \gamma_2 = 4, \omega_1 = 0.4, \omega_2 = 0.7$.

4.1. Linear Case

We convert Equation (1) to a linear ODE by setting $\beta = 0$. Later, by fixing $\alpha = k/m$, $\delta = c/m$ and $f(t) = f(t)/m$ the equation reduces to an equivalent spring mass damper system with mass m, stiffness c and spring constant k. For the remainder of this section, we consider $m = 1, c = 0.2$ and $k = 0.9$ or equivalently $\alpha = 0.9, \delta = 0.2$. Finally, data are generated by solving the linear ODE subjected to sinusoidal, piece-wise, and step-forcing functions.

The neural network was trained on generated data instances and was tested to determine if it can recover the forcing functions from these data. The following sections provide more details of the results that were obtained after training.

4.1.1. Sinusoidal Function

To test whether the neural network can recover a smooth periodic function, we train it on the data generated by subjecting the spring mass damper system to a harmonic excitation given by

$$f(t) = \gamma \cos \omega t \qquad (9)$$

with $x_0 = 4.9, \dot{x}_0 = -2.2, \omega = 0.4$, and $\gamma = 3$. The result obtained is promising and is shown in Figure 4a. It can be observed that the NN prediction and actual function are in excellent agreement.

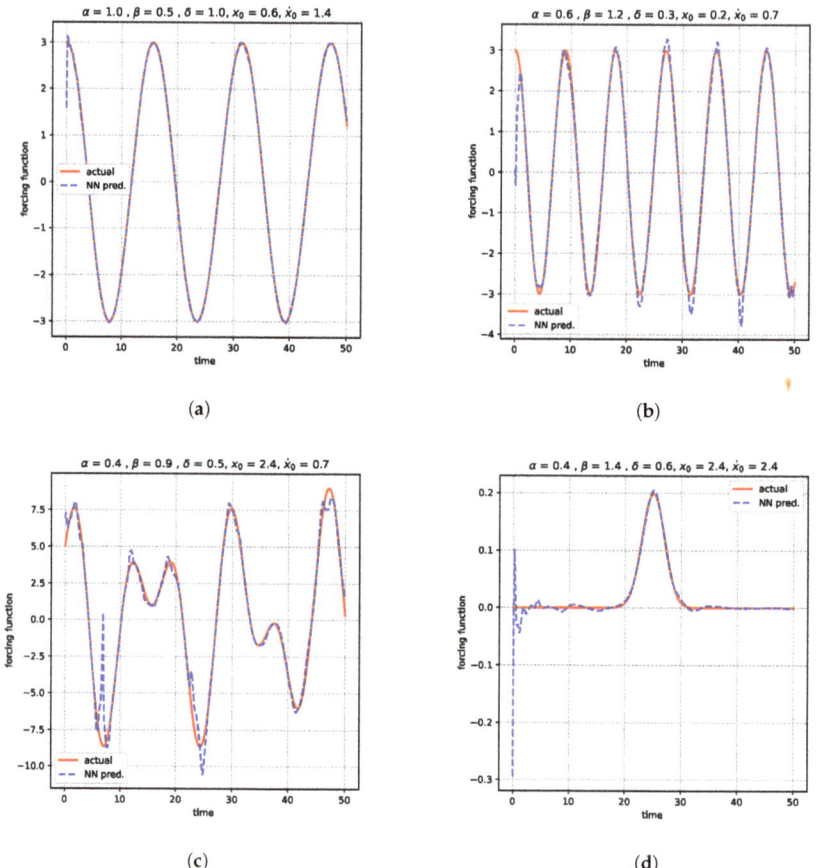

Figure 4. Figure shows the agreement between neural network predictions and actual forcing functions: (**a**) sinusoidal (**b**) sinusoidal with increased non-linearity and frequency (**c**) sum of two sinusoidal (**d**) impulse for duffing's equation.

4.1.2. Piece-Wise Function

Here, we subject the spring mass damper system to piece-wise forcing functions represented by equations,

$$f(t) = \begin{cases} 0 & 0 \leq t < 5 \\ t-5 & 5 \leq t < 10 \\ \dfrac{5}{20}(30-t) & 10 \leq t < 30 \\ 0 & 30 \leq t \leq 50 \end{cases} \tag{10}$$

and,

$$f(t) = \begin{cases} t^2 & 0 \leq t < 10 \\ -2t+120 & 10 \leq t < 30 \\ \dfrac{1}{200}t^3 - \dfrac{1}{2}t^2 + \dfrac{25}{2}t & 30 \leq t \leq 50 \end{cases} \tag{11}$$

the former represents a triangular function, consisting of linearly increasing and decreasing functions at consecutive intervals and the latter is a combination of parabolic, linear, and cubic functions. The functions are characterized by abrupt variations in gradient magnitudes.

Figure 5b,c demonstrate our findings where the network was trained on data instances generated by simulating the spring mass damper system for $x_0 = 4.4, \dot{x}_0 = -4.4$, and $x_0 = 2.2, \dot{x}_0 = -3.8$ initial conditions subjected to forces represented by Equations (10) and (11), respectively.

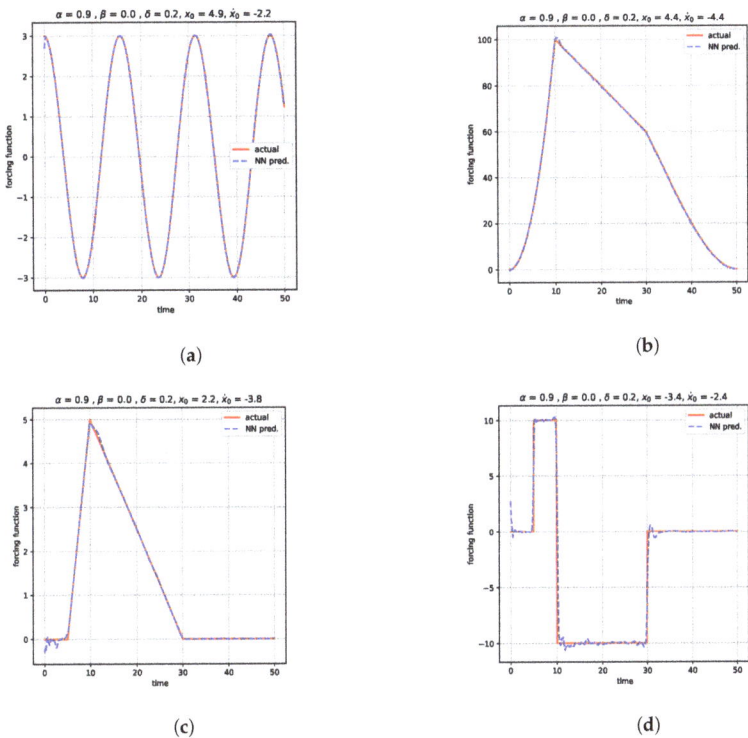

Figure 5. Figure shows the agreement between neural network predictions and actual forcing functions: (**a**) sinusoidal (**b**) combination of parabolic, linear and cubic (**c**) triangular (**d**) step for spring mass damper system.

As observed, the actual forcing function and neural network predictions match very well; however, the network experiences some challenges in predicting the values at the cusp of both functions. For the triangular function, it under-predicts, and for the combination of linear, parabolic, and cubic it over-predicts. In addition, for the interval with a zero value of the function, marking the start of the triangular function, some oscillations are observed in the network predictions.

4.1.3. Step Function

After testing our architecture to recover the piece-wise forcing function in the previous section. In the present section, we attempt to solve a problem that is much more challenging. We try to determine if our architecture can recover functions involving discontinuities.

To answer this question we train the neural network on the data generated by simulating the spring mass damper system with $x_0 = -3.4, \dot{x}_0 = -2.4$ and step function below,

$$f(t) = \begin{cases} 0 & 0 \leq t < 5 \\ 10 & 5 \leq t < 10 \\ -10 & 10 \leq t < 30 \\ 0 & 30 \leq t \leq 50 \end{cases} \quad (12)$$

A step function is marked by constant values on specific intervals followed by sudden jumps in values at the point of transition.

Figure 5d shows our findings. It can be observed NN was able to recover the majority of the function from the data. The constant values of the step function are complemented with oscillatory predictions. These oscillations resemble the Gibbs phenomenon, which is observed when approximating functions with jump discontinuities using the Fourier series.

4.2. Non-Linear Case

After our success with linear ODE in the previous sections, we now evaluate the effectiveness of our proposed architecture on non-linear ODE. We subject Equation (1) to different smooth forcing functions such as sinusoidal, the sum of two sinusoidal, and impulse functions. We share details and findings of our numerical experiments in the following section

4.2.1. Sinusoidal Function

We solve the governing Equation (1) by subjecting it to the sinusoidal forcing function given by,

$$f(t) = \gamma \cos \omega t \quad (13)$$

fixing $\alpha = 1, \delta = 1, \beta = 0.5, \gamma = 3, \omega = 0.4$ and initial conditions $x_0 = 0.6\ \dot{x}_0 = 1.4$ to generate the response data.

Figure 4a demonstrates the performance of our network after training it on the generated data. It can be observed that the neural network was successful in accurately recovering the sinusoidal function from response data without much difficulty; nonetheless, there exists some instability at the starting point.

We now increase the difficulty by setting $\alpha = 0.6, \delta = 0.3, \beta = 1.2, \gamma = 3, \omega = 0.7$ and initial conditions $x_0 = 0.2, \dot{x}_0 = 0.7$. An interesting thing to note here is that the non-linearity $\beta = 1.2$ and frequency $\omega = 0.7$ are now increased versus the previous case.

The finding for this case is shown in Figure 4b. Although seen network predictions are in good agreement with the actual function, for the most part, the neural network over-predicts at the peaks and valleys with the presence of some instabilities at the start of the function.

4.2.2. Sum of Two Sinusoidal Functions

In this section, we attempt to recover the forcing function represented by the sum of two sinusoidal functions represented by the following equation,

$$f(t) = \gamma_1 \cos \omega_1 t + \gamma_2 \cos \omega_2 t \quad (14)$$

The neural network was trained on the data that were generated by fixing the values of $\alpha = 0.4, \beta = 0.9, \delta = 0.5$ and solving the duffing equation subjected to Equation (14) with $\gamma_1 = 5, \gamma_2 = 4, \omega_1 = 0.4, \omega_2 = 0.7$ and $x_0 = 2.4\ \dot{x}_0 = 0.7$ initial conditions. This is somewhat more difficult compared to the previous case involving just one sinusoidal function. The results are shown in Figure 4c, it can be seen that the NN was able to predict the forcing function from response data with acceptable accuracy. Although NN does under-predict and over-predict at certain peaks and valleys of the function, nevertheless, overall the actual function and predictions are almost perfectly aligned.

4.2.3. Impulse Function Idealized by Normal Distribution

Finally, in the present section, we evaluate the efficacy of our network in predicting an impulsive function expressed by a normal distribution given by,

$$f(t) = \frac{e^{-(t-\mu)^2/(2\sigma^2)}}{\sigma\sqrt{2\pi}}. \tag{15}$$

We set $\mu = 25$, and $\sigma = 2$ in Equation (15) and use this to produce the data by simulating Equation (1) with $\alpha = 0.4, \beta = 1.4, \delta = 0.6$ and $x_0 = 1, \dot{x}_0 = -2.2$. This case was used to test if the network can predict an impact excitation force of non-linear oscillators. For the purpose of smoothness, the impact force was expressed by a normal distribution equation. As seen in Figure 4d, the network predictions start with numerical oscillations that later damp out, and, for the most part, the predictions are in good alignment with the actual forcing function that was used for generating the data.

5. Discussion

In Section 4 we shared our findings that demonstrated the effectiveness of our proposed neural network approach for solving the inverse source problem of dynamic load identification by incorporating physics information. The neural network structure and best working hyper-parameter choices were obtained by performing systematic hyper-parameter tuning. The network was later trained on different data instances generated by simulating spring mass damper systems subjected to different types of forcing functions, including smooth, abrupt changes in gradient, and jump discontinuities.

The neural network predictions in all cases were excellent, with slight overshoot and undershoot at the cusp of both piece-wise functions and some small oscillations at the start of the triangular function. However, some numerical oscillations were observed in step function predictions that resemble the Gibbs phenomenon. The findings suggest that the proposed neural network approach was effective in predicting different types of forcing functions.

The study also tested the network to recover the forcing functions of non-linear oscillators from the data. The data were generated by solving duffing equations subjected to various smooth forcing functions. The network was able to predict sinusoidal functions and sinusoidal functions with increased non-linearity and frequency with small amounts of instability and minor overshoot and undershoot at the peak and trough of the periodic function.

Finally, the network was used to predict functions given by the sum of two sinusoidal functions and an impulse, and the network prediction was in close agreement with the actual function. However, some under and over-predictions with small oscillations were observed at the peaks and valleys of the functions in the case of the sum of two sinusoidal functions. In the case of a forcing function involving an impulse, numerical oscillations were observed at the start that dampened out in the later stages of predictions.

Overall, the findings of this study demonstrate that the proposed technique works well in predicting a variety of forcing functions from response data, although, only smooth functions were considered in the case of non-linear oscillators. Additionally, the analysis was based on simulated data without any noise used to train the neural network. Future studies should investigate the effectiveness of this technique using real-world data with noise and compare its performance with other established techniques for dynamic load identification.

6. Conclusions

In this paper, we presented an approach for solving the dynamic load identification problem using neural networks and physics information. We started our analysis by testing the efficacy of our architecture in recovering the forcing functions of the spring mass damper system and finally extending it to non-linear oscillators.

In our analysis of the spring mass damper system, we trained our neural network to recover different types of functions from the data, and it was found that our network was able to seamlessly recover them without much difficulty. Later on, we tried the same for the non-linear ODEs. In the case of non-linear ODEs, we primarily focused on smooth functions, and it was observed that our method was able to recover almost all of the functions, but with minor numerical oscillations at different places.

Though this work was predominantly focused on predicting the source terms of ODEs with mechanical systems in mind, to the best of our understanding, this has the potential to be applied to any system where the interest is in finding the source term from response data.

In the future, this work can be extended by testing whether the architecture can recover discontinuous forcing functions of non-linear ODEs and if similar predictions can be made from data that are corrupted by noise. Also, a similar study can be undertaken for recovering both smooth and discontinuous forcing functions in a multi-degree of freedom system. Another possibility is to test if our neural network architecture can predict the forcing function just from one set of data, i.e., displacement or velocity.

Finally, this work was focused on recovering the forcing function of a specific ODE from its data instances. However, a surrogate model can also be developed that can be trained on huge sets of data and, after training, can predict the forcing function for any instance of a linear or non-linear ODE from its response time histories and initial conditions.

Author Contributions: Methodology, implementation, and writing of manuscript—S.A.S.; supervision, review and editing—H.C. and T.K. All authors have read and agreed to the published version of the manuscript.

Funding: This research received no external funding.

Data Availability Statement: The data that support the findings of this study are available from the corresponding author upon request.

Conflicts of Interest: The authors declare no competing conflict of interest.

References

1. Kabanikhin, S.I. Definitions and examples of inverse and ill-posed problems. *J. Inverse Ill-Posed Probl.* **2008**, *16*, 317–357. Available online: https://www.degruyter.com/document/doi/10.1515/JIIP.2008.019/html (accessed on 9 March 2023). [CrossRef]
2. Sabatier, P.C. Past and future of inverse problems. *J. Math. Phys.* **2000**, *41*, 4082–4124. [CrossRef]
3. Yaman, F.; Yakhno, V.G.; Potthast, R. A Survey on Inverse Problems for Applied Sciences. *Math. Probl. Eng.* **2013**, *2013*, 976837. [CrossRef]
4. Uhlmann, G.; Uhlmann, S.G.F. Inverse problems: Seeing the unseen. *Bull. Math. Sci.* **2014**, *4*, 209–279. [CrossRef]
5. McCormick, N.J. Inverse Radiative Transfer Problems: A Review. *Nucl. Sci. Eng.* **2017**, *112*, 185–198. [CrossRef]
6. Stefanov, P.; Uhlmann, G. An inverse source problem in optical molecular imaging an inverse source problem in optical molecular imaging. *Anal. PDE* **2008**, *1*, 115–116. [CrossRef]
7. Ammari, H.; Bao, G.; Fleming, J.L. An Inverse Source Problem for Maxwell's Equations in Magnetoencephalography. *SIAM J. Appl. Math.* **2006**, *62*, 1369–1382. [CrossRef]
8. Grech, R.; Cassar, T.; Muscat, J.; Camilleri, K.P.; Fabri, S.G.; Zervakis, M.; Xanthopoulos, P.; Sakkalis, V.; Vanrumste, B. Review on solving the inverse problem in EEG source analysis. *J. NeuroEng. Rehabil.* **2008**, *5*, 25. [CrossRef]
9. Huang, C.H. A generalized inverse force vibration problem for simultaneously estimating the time-dependent external forces. *Appl. Math. Model.* **2005**, *29*, 1022–1039. [CrossRef]
10. Ma, C.K.; Tuan, P.C.; Lin, D.C.; Liu, C.S. A study of an inverse method for the estimation of impulsive loads. *Int. J. Syst. Sci.* **1998**, *29*, 663–672. [CrossRef]
11. Azam, S.E.; Chatzi, E.; Papadimitriou, C. A dual Kalman filter approach for state estimation via output-only acceleration measurements. *Mech. Syst. Signal Process.* **2015**, *60*, 866–886. [CrossRef]
12. Jang, T.S.; Baek, H.; Choi, H.S.; Lee, S.G. A new method for measuring nonharmonic periodic excitation forces in nonlinear damped systems. *Mech. Syst. Signal Process.* **2011**, *25*, 2219–2228. [CrossRef]
13. Feldman, M. Mapping nonlinear forces with congruent vibration functions. *Mech. Syst. Signal Process.* **2013**, *37*, 315–337. [CrossRef]

14. Chao, M.; Hongxing, H.; Feng, X. The identification of external forces for a nonlinear vibration system in frequency domain. *Proc. Inst. Mech. Eng. Part C J. Mech. Eng. Sci.* **2014**, *228*, 1531–1539. [CrossRef]
15. Liu, C.S.; Chang, C.W. A real-time Lie-group differential algebraic equations method to solve the inverse nonlinear vibration problems. *Inverse Probl. Sci. Eng.* **2016**, *24*, 1569–1586. [CrossRef]
16. Rice, C.; Frankel, J.I. Estimating the forcing function in a mechanical system by an inverse calibration method. *JVC/J. Vib. Control* **2022**, *28*, 3352–3363. [CrossRef]
17. Liu, R.; Dobriban, E.; Hou, Z.; Qian, K. Dynamic Load Identification for Mechanical Systems: A Review. *Arch. Comput. Methods Eng.* **2022**, *29*, 831–863. [CrossRef]
18. Prawin, J.; Rao, A.R.M. An online input force time history reconstruction algorithm using dynamic principal component analysis. *Mech. Syst. Signal Process.* **2018**, *99*, 516–533. [CrossRef]
19. Zhou, J.M.; Dong, L.; Guan, W.; Yan, J. Impact load identification of nonlinear structures using deep Recurrent Neural Network. *Mech. Syst. Signal Process.* **2019**, *133*, 106292. [CrossRef]
20. Yang, H.; Jiang, J.; Chen, G.; Mohamed, M.S.; Lu, F. A Recurrent Neural Network-Based Method for Dynamic Load Identification of Beam Structures. *Materials* **2021**, *14*, 7846. [CrossRef]
21. Rosafalco, L.; Manzoni, A.; Mariani, S.; Corigliano, A. An autoencoder-based deep learning approach for load identification in structural dynamics. *Sensors* **2021**, *21*, 4207. [CrossRef] [PubMed]
22. Liu, Y.; Wang, L.; Gu, K.; Li, M. Artificial Neural Network (ANN) - Bayesian Probability Framework (BPF) based method of dynamic force reconstruction under multi-source uncertainties. *Knowl.-Based Syst.* **2022**, *237*, 107796. [CrossRef]
23. Karniadakis, G.E.; Kevrekidis, I.G.; Lu, L.; Perdikaris, P.; Wang, S.; Yang, L. Physics-informed machine learning. *Nat. Rev. Phys.* **2021**, *3*, 422–440. [CrossRef]
24. Raissi, M.; Perdikaris, P.; Karniadakis, G.E. Physics-informed neural networks: A deep learning framework for solving forward and inverse problems involving nonlinear partial differential equations. *J. Comput. Phys.* **2019**, *378*, 686–707. [CrossRef]
25. He, Z.; Ni, F.; Wang, W.; Zhang, J. A physics-informed deep learning method for solving direct and inverse heat conduction problems of materials. *Mater. Today Commun.* **2021**, *28*, 102719. [CrossRef]
26. Liu, Q.; Zhao, Z.; Zhang, Y.; Wang, J.; Cao, J. Physics-informed sparse identification of bistable structures. *J. Phys. D Appl. Phys.* **2022**, *56*, 044005. [CrossRef]
27. Haghighat, E.; Bekar, A.C.; Madenci, E.; Juanes, R. Deep learning for solution and inversion of structural mechanics and vibrations. *Model. Comput. Vib. Probl.* **2021**, *1*, 1–17. [CrossRef]
28. Antonio, D.; Zanette, D.H.; López, D. Frequency stabilization in nonlinear micromechanical oscillators. *Nat. Commun.* **2012**, *3*, 806. [CrossRef]
29. Lim, F.; Cartmell, M.; Cardoni, A.; Lucas, M. A preliminary investigation into optimising the response of vibrating systems used for ultrasonic cutting. *J. Sound Vib.* **2004**, *272*, 1047–1069. [CrossRef]
30. Cao, Q.; Xiong, Y.; Wiercigroch, M. A novel model of dipteran flight mechanism. *Int. J. Dyn. Control* **2013**, *1*, 1–11. [CrossRef]
31. Kovacic, I.; Brennan, M.J. *The Duffing Equation: Nonlinear Oscillators and Their Behaviour*; John Wiley & Sons: Hoboken, NJ, USA, 2011.
32. Abadi, M.; Agarwal, A.; Barham, P.; Brevdo, E.; Chen, Z.; Citro, C.; Corrado, G.S.; Davis, A.; Dean, J.; Devin, M.; et al. TensorFlow: Large-Scale Machine Learning on Heterogeneous Systems. 2015. Available online: tensorflow.org (accessed on 8 May 2023).
33. Chollet, F. Keras. 2015. Available online: https://keras.io (accessed on 9 March 2023).
34. Kingma, D.P.; Ba, J.L. Adam: A method for stochastic optimization. *arXiv* **2014**, arXiv:1412.6980.
35. *MATLAB, 9.8.0.1873465 (R2020a) Update 8'*; The MathWorks Inc.: Natick, MA, USA, 2020.

Disclaimer/Publisher's Note: The statements, opinions and data contained in all publications are solely those of the individual author(s) and contributor(s) and not of MDPI and/or the editor(s). MDPI and/or the editor(s) disclaim responsibility for any injury to people or property resulting from any ideas, methods, instructions or products referred to in the content.

 algorithms

Article

Machine-Learning-Based Model for Hurricane Storm Surge Forecasting in the Lower Laguna Madre

Cesar Davila Hernandez [1], Jungseok Ho [2,*], Dongchul Kim [3] and Abdoul Oubeidillah [2]

[1] Department of Civil, Architectural and Environmental Engineering, The University of Texas at Austin, Austin, TX 78705, USA; cesardavilahernandez@utexas.edu
[2] Department of Civil Engineering, The University of Texas Rio Grande Valley, Edinburg, TX 78539, USA; abdoul.oubeidillah@utrgv.edu
[3] Department of Computer Science, The University of Texas Rio Grande Valley, Edinburg, TX 78539, USA; dongchul.kim@utrgv.edu
* Correspondence: jungseok.ho@utrgv.edu

Abstract: During every Atlantic hurricane season, storms represent a constant risk to Texan coastal communities and other communities along the Atlantic coast of the United States. A storm surge refers to the abnormal rise of sea water level due to hurricanes and storms; traditionally, hurricane storm surge predictions are generated using complex numerical models that require high amounts of computing power to be run, which grow proportionally with the extent of the area covered by the model. In this work, a machine-learning-based storm surge forecasting model for the Lower Laguna Madre is implemented. The model considers gridded forecasted weather data on winds and atmospheric pressure over the Gulf of Mexico, as well as previous sea levels obtained from a Laguna Madre ocean circulation numerical model. Using architectures such as Convolutional Neural Networks (CNN) and Long Short-Term Memory (LSTM) combined, the resulting model is capable of identifying upcoming hurricanes and predicting storm surges, as well as normal conditions in several locations along the Lower Laguna Madre. Overall, the model is able to predict storm surge peaks with an average difference of 0.04 m when compared with a numerical model and an average RMSE of 0.08 for normal conditions and 0.09 for storm surge conditions.

Keywords: machine learning; storm surge; hurricane; forecasting; CNN; LSTM

Citation: Davila Hernandez, C.; Ho, J.; Kim, D.; Oubeidillah, A. Machine-Learning-Based Model for Hurricane Storm Surge Forecasting in the Lower Laguna Madre. *Algorithms* **2023**, *16*, 232. https://doi.org/10.3390/a16050232

Academic Editors: Xiang Zhang and Xiaoxiao Li

Received: 10 March 2023
Revised: 26 April 2023
Accepted: 26 April 2023
Published: 28 April 2023

Copyright: © 2023 by the authors. Licensee MDPI, Basel, Switzerland. This article is an open access article distributed under the terms and conditions of the Creative Commons Attribution (CC BY) license (https://creativecommons.org/licenses/by/4.0/).

1. Introduction

The United States mainland has experienced around 280 hurricane strikes since the 1850s. Of these hurricane impacts, nearly a hundred have been classified in the Saffir/Simpson Hurricane Wind Scale (SSHWS) as a category 3 or greater. The monetary damage that such hurricane impacts have can ascend to billions of dollars, as was the case with Hurricane Katrina in 2005 and Ike in 2008. The quantified damages are only a single measure of how destructive a hurricane can be and serve as reminders of the importance of preparation and adequate planning for such events [1,2]. The Laguna Madre, located in South Texas, is one of the six hypersaline lagoons in the world. It is a unique ecological system that provides the perfect environment for the proliferation of numerous species of flora and fauna. This lagoon, and the surrounding region, is impacted by hurricanes that affect the coastal population with flooding and storm surges. Although communities are well aware of the risks that every hurricane season brings, the tools available to prepare and plan are scarce. Storm surge research in this region is paramount to answer the needs of the population. This study seeks to provide a tool that can be used for forecasting storm surge conditions days ahead, without the usage of expensive resources and with automation capabilities. The model proposed here can help first responders and emergency bodies to assemble resources and develop plans ahead of a hurricane impact and subsequential storm surge.

Coastal cities have experienced a boom in growth since the 2000s. The increase has stayed constant at a rate of approximately one percent per year. Leisure has been one of the most cited reasons for growth, and as such, the need for infrastructure in coastal cities has increased proportionately. There have been projects prompted from coastal growth, such as the construction of transportation, water and electrical infrastructure. This has brought many benefits to coastal communities and has allowed and aided their continuous growth, but at the same time, it has also raised a major weakness point. All the infrastructure necessary to sustain and expand communities in coastal areas are just new vulnerabilities. One of the major drivers of hurricane damages in coastal cities are storm surges, due to their proximity to the ocean. Storm surge refers to the abnormal rise in ocean levels beyond the predicted astronomical tides as a result of sustained winds, among other factors [3]. The state of Texas has many coastal cities that could be potentially struck by hurricanes and subsequent storm surges. Major hurricane impacts can bring destruction to vulnerable infrastructure, creating a potential avenue for billions of dollars worth of damages [4]. It is also important to mention that the danger of a hurricane storm surge is not only limited to direct structural damages; it also represents a worrying environmental risk. Many of the coastal cities that could be potentially damaged by hurricanes and storm surges also house ports. These ports expose industrial complexes to catastrophic events. As an example, Hurricane Ike brought USD 30 billion dollars in damages to the cities of Houston and Galveston, where at least 112 deaths occurred. The Houston Ship Channel is one of the busiest seaports in the world and is the host of many petrochemical complexes, which heightens the potential for an environmental disaster [5,6].

Since storm surges have the potential to cause damages worth billions of dollars, as well as cause deaths and possible environmental disasters, it is of the utmost importance to plan accordingly when a major hurricane is approaching a coastal area. It is possible to assess the potential risk that a hurricane poses in terms of storm surge by creating a simulation of the interaction between winds, atmospheric pressure, tides, and waves. To date, the problem of simulating hurricane storm surges has been solved through the usage of computer models capable of capturing these interactions and producing fairly accurate storm surge estimates. Some of the computer models that are available and are currently being used to predict storm surges by agencies such as the Federal Emergency Management Agency (FEMA) or the US Army Corps of Engineers (USACE) are Advanced CIRCulation (ADCIRC), or the Sea, Lake, and Overland Surges from Hurricanes (SLOSH) model [7–9]. There exist other numerical models for different purposes, such as TxBLEND, developed by the Texas Water Development Board (TWDB) used to estimate salinity conditions for Texas estuaries [10]. The estimation of storm surges is not only a matter of accuracy; it is also a problem of time. Emergency preparations are time-sensitive; numerical-based storm surge models such as ADCIRC or SLOSH require a lot of time to be executed, especially if there are not many resources available. Currently, high-performance computer clusters (HPC) are employed to run such models on a large scale and provide enough resources for their computations to be timely. It is important to mention that such models are often coupled with wave models, which add another level of complexity, raising the resource requirements of the models. Some examples of the wave models used in conjunction are the Wave prediction Model (WAM), the Steady-State Spectral Wave Model (STWAVE), and Simulating WAves Nearshore (SWAN) [7,11]. Models such as ADCIRC run their computations based on an unstructured mesh containing bathymetry information of the area to be simulated; this mesh is a discretization of the area that needs sufficient detail near points of interest to better capture the physics involved. It is because of this that there is always a tradeoff between mesh resolution and the time required to complete computations. The ADCIRC code is optimized to scale and parallelize very efficiently, but if, as mentioned, there is a coupled model meant to simulate waves, then the complexity of the model scales vastly, which can hog the computational resources available. It is easy to see how high-fidelity models such as ADCIRC are out of the reach of endeavors without substantial funding, and the long runtime and high costs represent a limiting factor for timely emergency notifications if resources are lacking. The prohibitive costs of a numerical model and the demand for timely storm surge emergency notifications pushed the search for a way to develop an Artificial Intelligence (AI) model for accurately predicting storm surges without the need for large amounts of computational resources. In this study, a machine-learning-based storm surge forecasting model is proposed and created for predicting storm surges at discrete points along the Laguna Madre in Texas. The goal of the study is to create a machine learning model capable of predicting storm surges by using only a fraction of the computational resources that numerical models use.

2. Materials and Methods

To create this study, a literature review was conducted first to gather information on what previous attempts have been made to create machine-learning-based models for storm surge prediction. The literature review shed a light on what types of models were used as well as what predictors are employed.

Literature Review

Machine learning techniques have been employed extensively in the prediction of weather and for the modeling of complex relationships, such as storm surges, precipitation, and floods. Machine learning has proven itself to be a valuable tool in the creation of very accurate, non-resource-intensive models that can capture very complex phenomena. For example, Artificial Neural Networks (ANN) have been utilized for capturing the rainfall–runoff relationship in basins where the declaration of the internal structure of the watershed is not needed [12]. Neural networks have also been used to predict floods with fairly good accuracy [13]. These initially reviewed papers reiterate the possibility of creating a machine learning model for storm surges. Hurricane storm surges are an example of a complex nonlinear relationship where the usage of machine learning methods can prove to be very beneficial. Neural networks are a type of machine learning technique that have already been proven successful for storm surge prediction. In the past, several studies have explored the performance of neural network architectures when it comes to storm surge estimation. Simple ANNs [12,14–21] have already succeeded in recognizing the relationship between weather variables and the subsequent storm surge; however, some problems still remain. For a better visualization, Table 1 contains a sample of 10 reviewed studies.

As it can be seen from Table 1, most of the studies utilized ANN to produce their storm surge predictions. ANNs accept a fixed amount of predictor variables; the most common predictor variables utilized in the studies reviewed are storm parameters. Some of the parameters are the location of the storm, angle of approach, translation speed of the storm, wind speeds, and radius of strong winds. The accuracies obtained by the studies are good; however, there are limitations that could be improved upon.

Table 1. Sample of papers reviewed. Predictors, data types, and metrics used in each paper can be easily referenced in the table.

Paper	Predicted	Model	Predictors	Data Type	Metrics
[16]	Storm surge	ANN	Longitude, latitude at landfall, heading direction, central pressure, moving speed, maximum wind speed, radius of the strong wind speeds	59 Historical storms	CC

Table 1. *Cont.*

Paper	Predicted	Model	Predictors	Data Type	Metrics
[17]	Normalized storm surge	ANN	Pressure, wind velocity, wind direction, estimated astronomical tide	Historical storm descriptive parameters	RMSE and CC
[20]	Storm surge	RBF, GRNN, MLP3, MLP4	Two experiments: (1) daily mean sea level from preceding day, 6 h forecast of wind speed, direction. (2) 4–10 different parameters	Historical storms from 1950–1999	RMSE and CC
[22]	Max still-water inundation, runup, wave height	Stats.	Landfall location, angle at landfall, central pressure, forward speed, radius of maximum winds	1500 synthetic storms	MSE
[15]	Storm surge	ANN	Atmospheric pressure and winds	Historical NCEP-NCAR data	RMSE and CC
[12]	Tide, storm surge	ANN, ANFIS	Wind speed, wind direction, air pressure, simulated water level using hydrodynamic model	Historical data	MAE, RMSE and PE
[19]	Storm tide, coastal inundation	ANN	Landfall location, approach angle, translation speed, wind speed	Computed storm tide, coastal inundation by ADCIRC	CC
[14]	Storm surge	ANN, GPR, SVR	Storm parameters, reference latitude and longitude of storm as well as coastal points	USACE NACCS synthetic data	MSE, RMSE, CC
[21]	Tidal level	SVR, ANN, CNN, LSTM	Previous and current tidal water level	21 years of historical data from tide stations	RMSE, MAPE

The study by [23] developed a multioutput artificial neural network model which was used to predict storm surges in the North Carolinian coast. The authors mention a couple limitations of ANNs; for example, they found out that ANNs often underestimate peak surges. Furthermore, they concluded that the underestimations could be a result of the memoryless approach of ANNs. Naturally, including memory in an ANN-based machine learning model could help improve the results. The usage of memory in neural networks for tidal prediction was explored by [21], where they compared many approaches for predicting ocean water levels at 17 different stations in Taiwan. The model utilized a type of neural network called Long-short Term Memory (LSTM). LSTMs provide a solution to the memoryless problem mentioned by [23] and outperformed other methods. The results of LSTM show their potential for usage in storm surge prediction. It is important to mention that the study in [21] focused only on tidal levels, and no storm surge or weather conditions were considered.

LSTMs are an example of Recurrent Neural Networks (RNNs). These types of neural networks are often used for process control or time series predictions [24]. LSTMs can solve one of the glaring problems that are found in most studies referenced in Table 1, where the usage of ANNs limited the performance of the resulting models due to their lack of 'memory'. Improvement on time series prediction is expected with the usage of LSTMs in comparison with ANNs, and that is why they were chosen for further exploration in this study in comparison with regular ANNs.

Convolutional Neural Networks (CNNs) are another type of neural network architecture that are utilized in this study. CNNs are a very common and well-known neural network architecture. Their structure, often comprised of convolutional, pooling, and fully connected layers, has driven forward the field of computer vision in the past decades. Modern iterations of CNNs were first introduced by [25]. AlexNet [26] brought a scaled-up version of CNNs with around 60 million parameters. Since then, the usage of CNNs has skyrocketed, and their applications in several disciplines have been popularized. In this study, CNNs are used as part of the model to read and interpret weather information obtained in gridded form.

3. Modeling Scenarios and Data Processing

The storm surge forecasting model developed requires two sources of data. The first is a database of ADCIRC numerical model predictions. The second source of data corresponds to forecasted gridded weather data.

3.1. ADCIRC Numerical Model Database

The details of the ADCIRC model utilized to create the database of results for the Laguna Madre can be seen in the following study [27]. To execute ADCIRC and create the dataset necessary for training the machine learning model, it is necessary to develop two files for each simulation. The geometric properties of the model, as well as the nodal parameters, remained constant for all simulations. One of the two files utilized is named Model Parameter and Periodic Boundary Condition file, or 'fort.15' [28]. The 'fort.15' file is used to set the parameters that configure the ADCIRC model for running. The date of the simulation, duration, and tidal constituents are just some relevant parameters that were changed as required, while other parameters remained constant for all simulations, such as the type of input file used.

3.2. Forecasted Gridded Weather Data

The second and perhaps more critical file is 'fort.22', or Meteorological Forcing Data [28]. The machine learning model and the ADCIRC numerical model utilize the same input source: a gridded forecasted weather dataset named the North American Mesoscale Forecast System (NAM) [29]. The NAM dataset provides continuous forecasted gridded atmospheric conditions over the continental United States. The model is distributed by the National Centers for Environmental Information (NCEI) and consists of a 12 km-resolution grid with a forecasting range of up to 84 h. This forecasted gridded dataset is utilized in two forms. First, a set of input files for the ADCIRC numerical model is created; at the same time, the dataset is converted into image files to serve as input for the machine learning storm surge model.

To create both ADCIRC's and the machine learning storm surge model input, the NAM dataset is trimmed to the domain of interest; in this case, the Gulf of Mexico. After the NAM data are trimmed spatially, only the variables that will be used are kept, which includes the U and V components of winds at 10 m elevation and atmospheric pressure. The data is then projected into a regularly spaced grid over the Gulf of Mexico. The resulting grid can be directly used for input in ADCIRC and is also leveraged for the creation of images for their use in the machine learning model. To create the input images, each variable in the data is normalized and its values mapped into the range of an unsigned byte, from 0 to 255, for the creation of PNG stills with three color channels. The resulting composite can be seen below in Figure 1.

Figure 1. Image showing hurricane Hanna (2020) over the Gulf of Mexico as it is approaching the coast of Texas on the morning of July 25th. The image was constructed from retrieved NAM forecasts, where the color channels represent U and V components of winds and atmospheric pressure.

To test the machine learning storm surge forecasting model, a total of five scenarios were prepared from the available data. These five scenarios were selected as representative of the presence and lack of storm surge conditions. Three of the five scenarios are representative of hurricanes that impacted the Laguna Madre directly or caused fluctuations in the ocean levels in the Laguna Madre; the remaining two scenarios provide everyday or normal conditions, meaning no major weather event occurred near the Laguna Madre.

3.2.1. Hurricane Dolly (2008)

Dolly made landfall as a category 1 hurricane on the Saffir–Simpson Hurricane Wind Scale at South Padre Island, Texas, with estimated maximum winds of 86 mph. The storm reached peak intensity at around 1400 UTC on 23 July, 4 h before landfall, centered less than 20 nautical miles east of the Rio Grande River. Part of Hurricane Dolly's track can be seen in Figure 2 below.

3.2.2. Hurricane Alex (2010)

Alex made landfall as a category 2 hurricane on the Saffir–Simpson Hurricane Wind Scale near Soto la Marina, Tamaulipas in northeastern Mexico. At landfall, Alex had an estimated maximum wind speed of 109 mph at around 0200 UTC on 1 July. The path followed by Hurricane Alex as it made landfall can be seen on Figure 2 below.

3.2.3. Hurricane Hanna (2020)

Hanna made landfall as a category 1 hurricane at Padre Island, Texas. The hurricane reached a peak intensity of 92 mph as it was located off the coast of South Texas at 1800 UTC on 25 July. Hanna weakened to a tropical storm by 0600 UTC on 26 July and dissipated at 1800 UTC on 26 July as it neared Monterrey, Mexico. The path Hurricane Hanna took can be seen in Figure 2.

3.2.4. Normal Conditions: June 2008

During this month, precipitation for the southern region of the United States was below normal, with some regions receiving lower than 5% of the average June rainfall. A single tropical storm named Arthur formed on May 30th near the shore of Belize and, after two days, dissipated over the Yucatan Peninsula in Mexico.

3.2.5. Normal Conditions: June 2020

This month was especially dry with a precipitation total for the contiguous U.S. of about 0.21 inches below average. Two tropical storms were recorded in the Atlantic, Amanda and Cristobal. Amanda made landfall in Guatemala and its remnants developed to form Cristobal, which eventually made landfall in Louisiana, just east of Grand Isle.

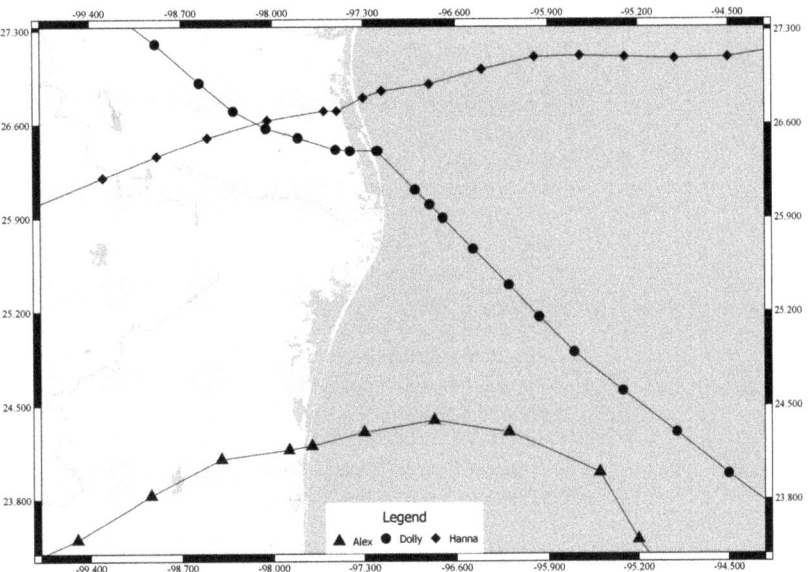

Figure 2. Paths followed by Hurricane Alex, Dolly, and Hanna as they made landfall in Texas. The white line depicts the U.S.–Mexico border.

It is important to note that while data are abundant, a bias was identified, and its impact on the performance is later discussed at the end of the paper. The root of the bias comes from the data available in the area where the study was conducted. Data from NAM provided a total of 13 hurricane seasons for training. Each season translates to six months of data, meaning a total of more than 6 years of continuous data was available. During this period of time, the Lower Laguna Madre saw the impact of around 20 abnormal sea-level conditions due to weather events. On average, the duration of such abnormal events was one week. This translates to 6% of the data being representative of storm surge conditions. This is problematic, since it evidences a bias in the data towards normal conditions; however, this was expected since disastrous impacts of hurricanes are scarce on a local level in the South Texas region.

4. Forecasting Model

There are three forecasting models that were created during this study. The differences between them relies mainly on the machine learning architectures used and their coupling. The two types of architectures used in the models created are CNN, LSTM and CNN+LSTM.

As explained before, CNNs are a type of artificial neural network architecture specialized in the analysis of image data. CNNs are inspired in the biology of the visual cortex of animals. They are great at extracting relevant features out of images and, given that the type of data used for the realization of this study can be interpreted as an image, the usage of CNNs suits the type of problem at hand. The first model created only considers image data as its input and produces a time series of ocean elevations corresponding to a specific time interval in the future. There are a total of 4 CNN-LSTM layers, with pooling operations in between them that accept the time series of images of future weather conditions. Their output is then fed to a series of regular densely connected neural network layers where the final time series output prediction is generated. Training parameters are the same across the CNN and LSTM models: 50 epochs, 6 samples per batch, and a validation split of 25%.

The second model to be evaluated is based on the LSTM neural network architecture. It is composed of 50 LSTM units that connect to a series of regular neural network layers where the output is generated. The training parameters are the same as the CNN model above. The model will not utilize image data for its input; instead, it will use time series data corresponding to past conditions of water surface elevation. Using this information, the model will create a prediction of future conditions.

The third model is a combination of both architectures and can be thought of as the final forecasting model. The two previously described models are simply a set of preliminary attempts to judge the capabilities of the architectures to establish a connection between past ocean surface elevations and weather and future ocean surface elevations. The final surrogate model combines both architectures to take more information into account for the generation of storm surge predictions. The model can be classified as a mixed-input model with two heads. The first head corresponds to the CNN model, using the same architecture discussed in the CNN-only model and accepting the same time series input of images. The second head of the model is the LSTM-only model, with the same architecture and input of time series elevations. Their outputs are then concatenated and fed to a series of densely connected neural network layers that produce the final output. This final model was trained on 100 epochs with a smaller batch size of 3 samples to accommodate the size of the model in the GPU. All three models were trained on the same hardware, an RTX 3060 NVIDIA GPU with 12 GB of VRAM. The training time for the CNN model took around an hour, while the LSTM model only took 5 min to train; however, the CNN+LSTM mixed-input model's total training time was around 7 h. Mixed precision was also leveraged to achieve speed ups.

To train the respective models, two sets of data were utilized. First, a set to train the preliminary models to evaluate their performance based on data from a recording station. Second, a set to train the final surrogate model based on synthetic data generated with the ocean circulation numerical model. Both sets of data have corresponding water surface elevation and forecasted weather conditions data. The first, or preliminary training dataset, contains water surface elevation data coming from the Center for Operational Oceanographic Products and Services (CO-OPS) Port Isabel recording station in Texas, with ID: 8779770. The data obtained from the Port Isabel recording station has the same coverage as the forecasted weather information.

The data obtained from the Port Isabel recording station was leveraged as part of the initial investigation into the feasibility of predicting storm surges with the LSTM and CNN architectures both separately and combined. As part of a pilot, the Port Isabel recordings were used to iterate models by tuning the hyperparameters and their architecture to find the best performance. The best-performing architecture obtained from the Port Isabel pilot models was used in the first iterations of the final model trained on the synthetic water surface elevation data. Subsequent iterations changed the size of the model, integrated mixed precision, and modified training parameters to find the best performance for the final CNN+LSTM model.

The second set of data used to train the final storm surge model comes from the execution of numerical model simulations corresponding to each Atlantic hurricane season from 2008 to 2020. To force the simulations, the forecasted weather information was used. This provides a training dataset for the surrogate model to learn and replicate the performance of the numerical simulations. To evaluate the machine learning model, a set of 10 virtual buoy stations were selected from the numerical model finite element mesh. These virtual stations correspond to points of interest in the Lower Laguna Madre. The set of virtual buoy stations and their location can be seen in Table 2.

Table 2. Table detailing the locations of virtual buoy stations used in the study.

Name	Latitude	Longitude	Numerical Model Mesh ID
South Padre Island (SPI)	26.0854	−97.1562	42195
Laguna–SPI	26.0862	−97.2007	59162
Ship Channel	26.0423	−97.2071	61388
Laguna Heights	26.0854	−97.2518	55382
Laguna Vista	26.1007	−97.2815	52698
Port Isabel	26.062	−97.215	60551
Port Mansfield Inside	26.5588	−97.4201	5684
Port Mansfield Outside	26.564	−97.2593	10629
Arroyo Colorado Inside	26.3616	−97.3266	29783
Arroyo Colorado Outside	26.3814	−97.1979	18356

To better visualize the location of the stations, a map of the Lower Laguna Madre with the virtual stations can be seen below in Figure 3.

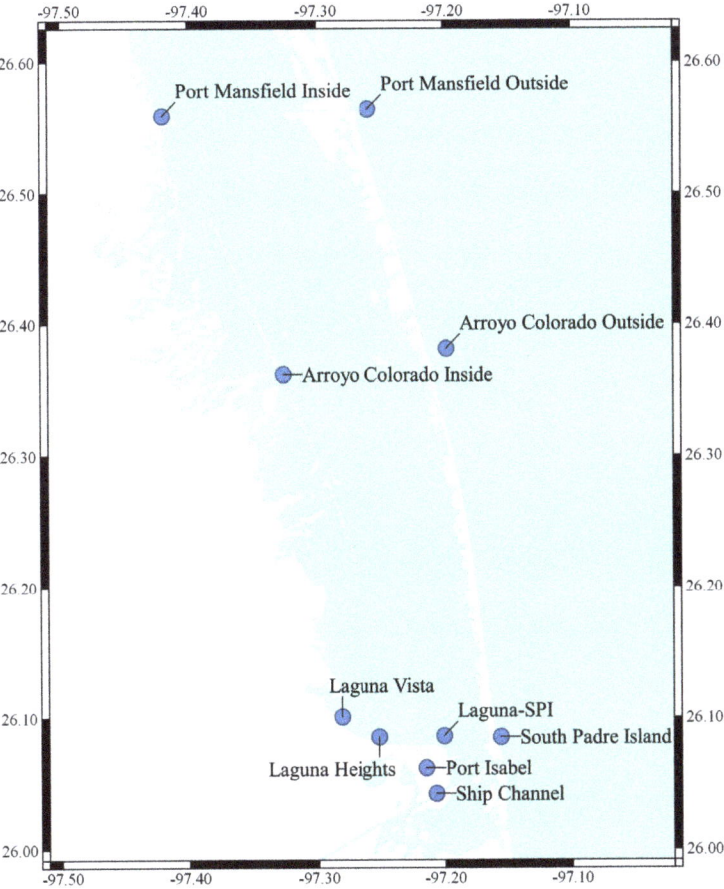

Figure 3. Map for the location of the 10 virtual buoy stations in the study.

5. Results

Two different sets of results are presented. First is the preliminary set of results which corresponds to three different models trained on data recorded by the single Port Isabel station. The first model only utilizes weather information and CNNs to preform storm surge prediction; it is expected that these results are far from accurate since there is no input with relevant information regarding tide harmonics, only weather conditions. The second preliminary model takes into consideration only previous water surface elevations to perform predictions without the influence of weather information using only LSTM. This model was expected to outperform the CNN model in at least normal conditions, since having information about previous tide elevations is sometimes sufficient to predict future conditions. The third preliminary model corresponds to a CNN+LSTM coupled model with mixed input. The third model accepts future weather information in the form of images, as well as past surface elevations as time series data.

The second set of results corresponds to the final machine learning model created for each of the 10 virtual buoy stations with training and validation data generated by the numerical model simulations.

To evaluate the performance of the models, the set of scenarios previously discussed in Section 3 was used.

5.1. Preliminary Modeling Results

These results help to illustrate the influence that the CNN and LSTM architectures have on the final model. The Root Mean Squared Error (RMSE) metric was used to compare their performance.

5.1.1. CNN-Only Model

As previously discussed, the CNN model is expected to be the weakest of the three. This model only takes into consideration weather information, completely ignoring previous water surface elevations. In the case of June 2008, where no major hurricane occurred, the results exhibit a pattern that does not follow water surface elevations, as seen in Figure 4. This period of time was chosen to better illustrate the importance of considering tide harmonics in the model.

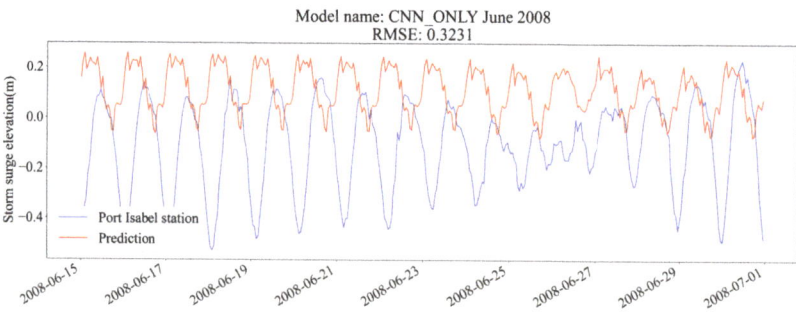

Figure 4. Preliminary CNN-only model prediction for the month of June 2008.

The CNN model does not encounter fluctuations during this month that could hint at a storm surge event. It defaults to an oscillation pattern to maximize its score. The inability of the model to predict the elevation might be due to its lack of knowledge of ocean elevations. It is working, in this case, as a detector of storm surge weather conditions rather than a storm surge predictor. The ability of the model to detect storm surge triggering conditions is reflected in Figure 5.

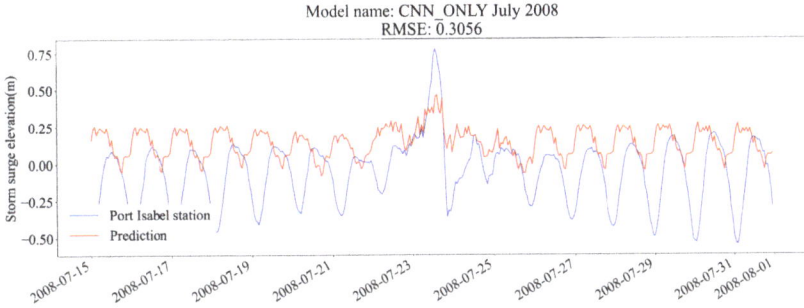

Figure 5. Preliminary CNN-only model prediction for the month of July 2008.

Here, the model defaults to a pattern which is disrupted by the detection of a storm surge triggering weather event. While the estimation is completely inaccurate, the detection of a storm is reflected as a change in the pattern, which hints at the ability of the model to detect storms in image data.

5.1.2. LSTM-Only Model

The LSTM preliminary model only considers past water surface elevations for its prediction and ignores weather information. The month of June 2010 saw the impact of Hurricane Alex in Mexico. The extent of the storm affected the water surface elevation of the Laguna Madre, which can be seen in the peak of the blue line in Figure 6.

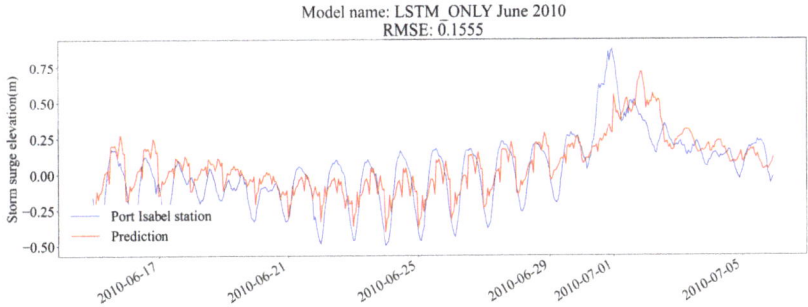

Figure 6. Preliminary LSTM-only model prediction for the month of June 2010.

It can be seen from the prediction that when the storm hits, the model tries to replicate what happened but is delayed in its prediction. This is because the model only considers past elevations to construct its prediction, and since storm surges are produced by weather fluctuations, the model has no information to anticipate the surge. Subsequently, the model tries to continue the surge but cannot estimate it accurately.

Even in storm surge conditions, the LSTM architecture outperforms the CNN model in its overall score but fails to detect the storm as it hits and can only produce a delayed response.

5.1.3. CNN+LSTM Model

This model is expected to perform better than both individual models since it is considering critical information on weather and previous water surface elevations to produce a prediction. The month of June 2008, when there were no storms hitting the Laguna Madre area, can be seen in Figure 7.

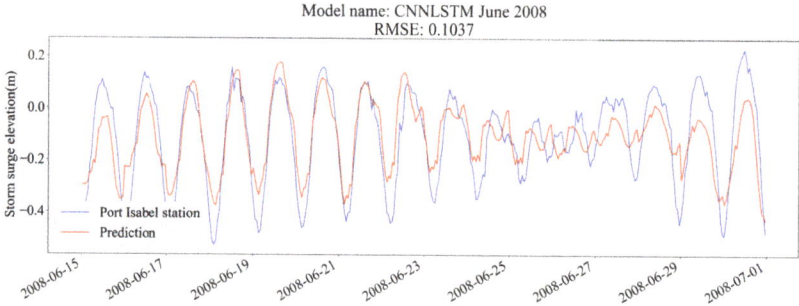

Figure 7. Preliminary CNN+LSTM model prediction for the month of June 2008.

It can be seen from this plot that the model is able to follow the trends closely; however, it still struggles in some places by underestimating both highs and lows. The CNN+LSTM model prediction for the month of June 2010 when the impact of Hurricane Alex was felt in the Laguna Madre is a very good example of the performance of the machine learning model, as shown in Figure 8.

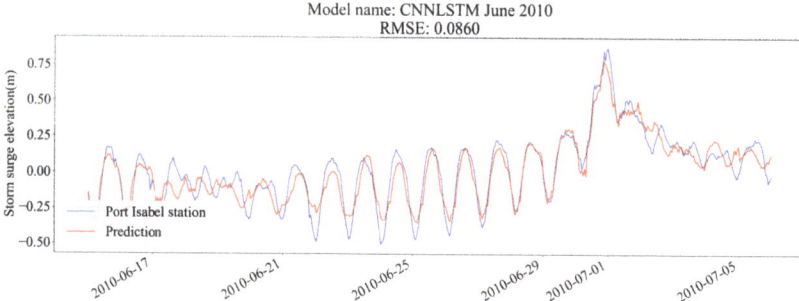

Figure 8. Preliminary CNN+LSTM model prediction for the month of June 2010.

In this case, the model is able to follow the surge correctly but still struggles at some points where normal conditions were expected. However, as it can be seen in the figures, the RMSE was reduced from a maximum of 0.1555 in the LSTM-only model in the month of June 2010 (when Hurricane Alex hit) to 0.0860 during the same period of time in the preliminary model that combines CNN and LSTM.

5.2. Machine Learning Storm Surge Forecasting Model Results

This set of results was produced by the finalized model trained on the full set of virtual buoy stations. For each of the five testing scenarios, a sample of four buoy stations is presented as a scatter plot. The four buoy stations selected represent important socioeconomic areas in the Laguna Madre.

The results are presented as two separated groups: a group that only considers normal conditions and a second group that includes storm surge conditions.

5.2.1. Normal Conditions

The predictions of the final CNN+LSTM model during normal conditions in June 2008 can be seen in Figure 9.

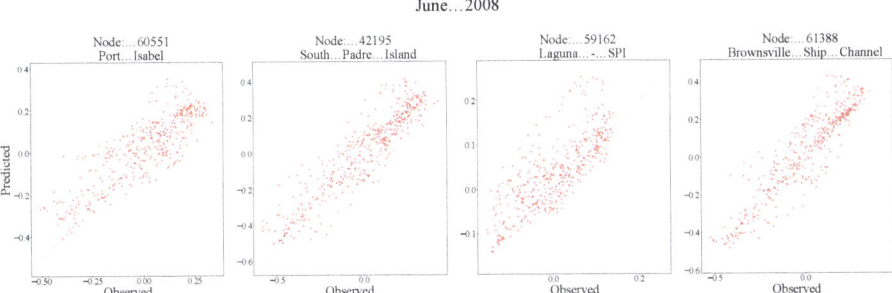

Figure 9. Scatter plot for four nodes in the CNN+LSTM final machine learning model for the month of June 2008.

The RMSEs for the four nodes, Port Isabel, South Padre Island, Laguna-SPI, and Brownsville Ship Channel, during the month of June 2008 are 0.1058, 0.0980, 0.0634, and 0.0990, respectively.

In a similar manner, the RMSE for each virtual buoy station for normal conditions in the month of June 2020 is 0.0730, 0.0832, 0.0541, and 0.0743. The scatter plot can be seen in Figure 10 below.

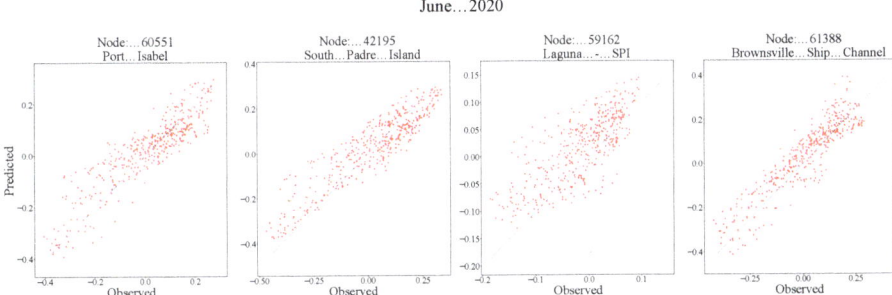

Figure 10. Scatter plot for four nodes in the CNN+LSTM final machine learning model for the month of June 2020.

5.2.2. Storm Surge Conditions

Hurricane Dolly predictions can be seen in Figure 11. The RMSEs for the different stations during Hurricane Dolly are 0.1312, 0.1632, 0.0462, and 0.1430 for nodes 60551, 42195, 59162, and 61388, respectively. There is more spread in these predictions; however, the peak surges observed and predicted do not differ greatly. On average, there is a 0.1183 m difference between the peak observed and the one predicted.

In the case of Hurricane Alex in 2010, the RMSEs for the four stations that can be seen in Figure 12 are 0.065, 0.0822, 0.0549, and 0.075, respectively. The model performed much better during this event than for Hurricane Dolly. The average difference between the observed and predicted peaks is much smaller compared with that of Dolly, being 0.0422 m.

Finally, for Hurricane Hanna in 2020, the RMSE for each of the buoy stations in Figure 13 is 0.1142, 0.1105, 0.0835, and 0.1268, respectively. Interestingly, the peak observed and predicted average difference is -0.0337 m, meaning, the model tended to overestimate storm surge peaks.

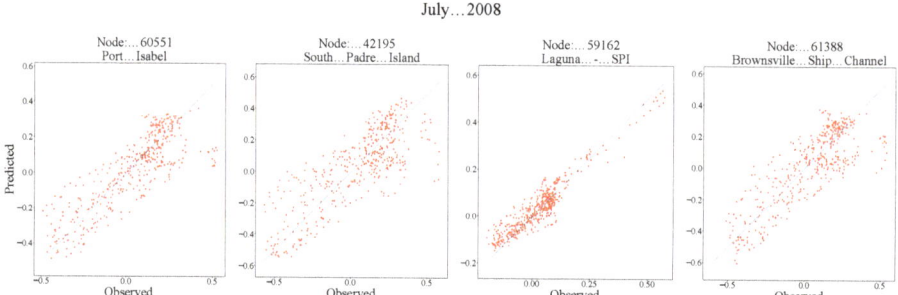

Figure 11. Scatter plot for four nodes in the CNN+LSTM final machine learning model for the month of July 2008.

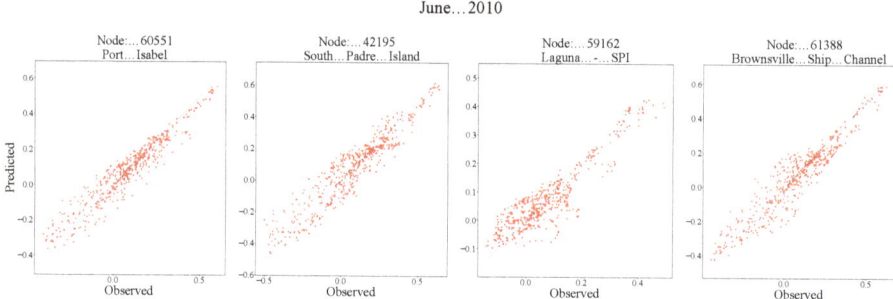

Figure 12. Scatter plot for four nodes in the CNN+LSTM final machine learning model for the month of June 2010.

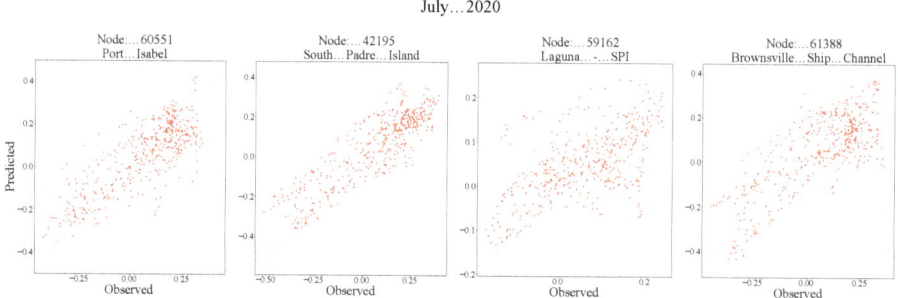

Figure 13. Scatter plot for four nodes in the CNN+LSTM final machine learning model for the month of July 2020.

For most cases, the model was able to produce better estimations for everyday conditions in comparison with storm surge conditions. Limitations in data availability contributed to these results. Data representative of normal conditions constitute nearly 94% of the samples, with the rest corresponding to storm surge conditions. The limitation in data is attributed to the area that the study was conducted in, where, since 2008, around 20 abnormal ocean elevations due to weather were recorded. To improve results without modifying the model, the amount of samples representative of storm surge conditions must be increased. To accomplish this, in the field of image recognition, there are a couple of techniques that allow for the creation of more samples for training. There is no use for these algorithms for the perturbation of existing gridded weather forecasts, since the information contained in the samples is the result of complex atmospheric phenomena, and without a numerical model it is not feasible to perturb the information contained in the samples with traditional image data augmentation algorithms. Nonetheless, the generation of new samples for the improvement of the described machine learning storm surge model is out of the scope of this study. Other possible improvements to the model could come from the input considered which, in essence, is the same type of input used in the numerical model but transformed into a different format. Perhaps the application of feature engineering techniques to the features in the input data could yield better results and a different model architecture that considers a new type of input. Another possible route could be creating an ensemble of models whose output is averaged, which could be achievable without changing the underlying architecture of the model or the input.

6. Conclusions

Throughout the set of experiments that were set up for testing the performance of the model, a very noticeable pattern emerged. The machine learning storm surge forecasting model created in this study was able to constantly provide an accurate estimation of everyday conditions with an average RMSE of 0.0813 among the buoy stations presented. Let us recall that these conditions refer to the absence of any impactful weather event that could change the water surface elevations from the expected astronomical tide harmonics. That is, the model was able to capture the harmonic future oscillations from previous observations while considering normal conditions of winds and pressure. This accomplishment is mainly due to the presence of the LSTM architecture. Ref. [21] demonstrated that LSTM networks are capable of predicting tidal levels effectively with superior performance when compared with other methodologies. Being able to correctly predict tidal levels is imperative to predicting storm surges, since the oscillation of tides have an additive or subtracting effect on the final elevations, as it was noted in Section 5.1. Once this baseline was accomplished during the modeling phase, it was important to build upon it. The next logical step was to attempt to incorporate weather information into the model. The inclusion of the CNN architecture improved everyday conditions and allowed for the estimation of storm surge conditions due to the consideration of input from weather events.

On a more specific note, in the preliminary model results presented in Section 5.1.3, a view of the overall performance of the final storm surge model and the importance of the inclusion of both CNN and LSTM architectures can be seen. The result for normal conditions in the Port Isabel recording station is greatly improved in the CNN+LSTM preliminary model from Figure 7 when compared directly with the CNN model prediction from Figure 4, highlighting the importance of the inclusion of the LSTM architecture, as mentioned. There was a reduction in RMSE from 0.3231 for the CNN-only model to 0.1037 for the CNN+LSTM model. The contribution of the CNN architecture to the final model is also important. Figure 6 shows a delayed response of the predicted storm surge in the presence of a storm event and an RMSE of 0.1555. For storm surge conditions, the inclusion of forecasted weather gridded data as input for the CNN head of the model provides a considerable improvement not only in peak prediction but in its timing, as it is seen in Figure 8. This change further reduced the RMSE to 0.0860 during the same period of predicted time.

In Section 5.2, the prediction of normal conditions and storm surge conditions for the final model shows an important point. Overall, normal condition predictions have a maximum RMSE of 0.1058 and an average RMSE of 0.0813. In the case of storm surge conditions, the maximum RMSE is 0.1632 and the average is 0.0996. From this, we can note that the predictions for storm surge conditions are worse than for normal conditions in the final model. This is important, as it shows a limitation in the storm surge forecasting model presented. However, this limitation in accuracy can be directly attributed to the lack of storm surge data training samples in comparison with normal conditions. The objective of the model presented was to be a storm surge forecasting tool, as such, forecasting-type data were used to train it. These data were obtained from NAM [29] forecasts on winds and atmospheric pressure. This limited the amount of data available, and while there are big collections of parametric data, such as HURDAT2 [30], they were not used in the study because the data are generated after an event and not as a forecast, which could not be directly leveraged in this storm surge forecasting model. Another constraint in data comes from the focus on the Lower Laguna Madre area. A greater model domain will provide better data and plentiful storm events to improve the performance of the model. The logical step is to include a bigger domain and hence more data, which could drive performance further without changing the underlying model architecture. Another approach is data augmentation, which would entail generating synthetic samples of storms.

Overall, the model provided a reliable estimation of storm surge peaks, with the average error between observed and predicted peaks being in the realm of centimeters. The model also tended to underestimate the storm surge peaks, except for the case of Hurricane Dolly, where the model overshot the observed peak by about 0.033 cm on average. Considering the data limitations in this study, a machine learning approach to storm surge prediction using forecasted weather gridded datasets with the inclusion of CNNs is a viable approach. As data continue to be collected and generated, the performance of CNN-based models will continue to improve. This will allow for the possibility of deploying forecasted weather image-based storm surge forecasting solutions that utilize small computational resources during prediction.

Author Contributions: Conceptualization, C.D.H., J.H. and D.K.; methodology, C.D.H.; software, C.D.H.; validation, C.D.H.; investigation, C.D.H.; data curation, C.D.H.; writing—original draft, C.D.H.; writing—review & editing, C.D.H. and J.H.; visualization, C.D.H.; supervision, J.H., D.K. and A.O.; project administration, J.H.; funding acquisition, J.H. All authors have read and agreed to the published version of the manuscript.

Funding: This project was partially funded by the Texas Coastal Management Program, Texas General Land Office Award Number NA18NOS4190153.

Data Availability Statement: The data is not publicly available due to legal reasons.

Conflicts of Interest: The authors declare no conflict of interest.

References

1. Blake, E.S.; Landsea, C.; Gibney, E.J. The deadliest, costliest, and most intense United States tropical cyclones from 1851 to 2010 (and other frequently requested hurricane facts). *NOAA Tech. Memo. NWS NHC* **2011**, *6*. Available online: https://repository.library.noaa.gov/view/noaa/8064 (accessed on 10 March 2023).
2. Morss, R.E.; Hayden, M.H. Storm surge and "certain death": Interviews with Texas coastal residents following Hurricane Ike. *Weather Clim. Soc.* **2010**, *2*, 174–189. [CrossRef]
3. Zachry, B.C.; Booth, W.J.; Rhome, J.R.; Sharon, T.M. A National View of Storm Surge Risk and Inundation. *Weather Clim. Soc.* **2015**, *7*, 109–117. [CrossRef]
4. Cutter, S.L.; Johnson, L.A.; Finch, C.; Berry, M. The US hurricane coasts: Increasingly vulnerable? *Environ. Sci. Policy Sustain. Dev.* **2007**, *49*, 8–21. [CrossRef]
5. Burleson, D.W.; Rifai, H.S.; Proft, J.K.; Dawson, C.N.; Bedient, P.B. Vulnerability of an industrial corridor in Texas to storm surge. *Nat. Hazards* **2015**, *77*, 1183–1203. [CrossRef]
6. Christian, J.; Fang, Z.; Torres, J.; Deitz, R. Modeling the Hydraulic Effectiveness of a Proposed Storm Surge Barrier System for the Houston Ship Channel during Hurricane Events. *Nat. Hazards Rev.* **2015**, *16*, 04014015. [CrossRef]
7. Dietrich, J.C.; Tanaka, S.; Westerink, J.J.; Dawson, C. Performance of the unstructured-mesh, SWAN + ADCIRC model in computing hurricane waves and surge. *J. Sci. Comput.* **2012**, *52*, 468–497. [CrossRef]
8. Jelesnianski, C.; Chen, J.; Shaffer, W.; Gilad, A. SLOSH-A hurricane storm surge forecast model. In Proceedings of the OCEANS IEEE Conference, Washington, DC, USA, 10–12 September 1984; pp. 314–317.
9. Li, J.; Nie B. Storm surge prediction: Present status and future challenges. *Procedia IUTAM* **2017**, *25*, 3–9. [CrossRef]
10. Matsumoto, J. *User's Manual for the Texas Water Development Board's Hydrodynamic and Salinity Model: TxBLEND*; Technical Report Texas Water Development Board: Austin, TX, USA, 1993.
11. Cheung, K.F.; Phadke, A.C.; Wei, Y.; Rojas, R.; Douyere, Y.J.-M.; Martino, C.D.; Houston, S.H.; Liu, P.L.-F.; Lynett, P.J.; Dodd, N.; et al. Modeling of storm-induced coastal flooding for emergency management. *Ocean Eng.* **2003**, *30*, 1353–1386. [CrossRef]
12. Chen, W.B.; Liu, W.C.; Hsu, M.H. Predicting typhoon-induced storm surge tide with a two-dimensional hydrodynamic model and artificial neural network model. *Nat. Hazards Earth Syst. Sci.* **2012**, *12*, 3799–3809. [CrossRef]

13. Mosavi, A.; Ozturk, P.; Chau, K.-W. Flood prediction using machine learning models: Literature review. *Water* **2018**, *10*, 1536. [CrossRef]
14. Al Kajbaf, A.; Bensi, M. Application of surrogate models in estimation of storm surge: A comparative assessment. *Appl. Soft Comput.* **2020**, *91*, 106184. [CrossRef]
15. de Oliveira, M.M.F. Neural network model to predict a storm surge. *J. Appl. Meteorol. Climatol.* **2009**, *48*, 143–155. [CrossRef]
16. Kim, S.W.; Lee, A.; Mun, J. A surrogate modeling for storm surge prediction using an artificial neural network. *J. Coast. Res.* **2018**, *85*, 866–870. [CrossRef]
17. Kim, S.W.; Melby, J.A.; Caraballo, N.C.N.; Ratcliff, J. A time-dependent surrogate model for storm surge prediction based on an artificial neural network using high-fidelity synthetic hurricane modeling. *Nat. Hazards* **2015**, *76*, 565–585. [CrossRef]
18. Lee, T.L. Back-propagation neural network for the prediction of the short-term storm surge in Taichung harbor, Taiwan. *Eng. Appl. Artif. Intell.* **2008**, *21*, 63–72. [CrossRef]
19. Sahoo, B.; Bhaskaran, P.K. Prediction of storm surge and coastal inundation using Artificial Neural Network–A case study for 1999 Odisha Super Cyclone. *Weather Clim. Extrem.* **2019**, *23*, 100196. [CrossRef]
20. Sztobryn, M. Forecast of storm surge by means of artificial neural network. *J. Sea Res.* **2003**, *49*, 317–322. [CrossRef]
21. Yang, C.H.; Wu, C.H.; Hsieh, C.M. Long Short-Term Memory Recurrent Neural Network for Tidal Level Forecasting. *IEEE Access* **2020**, *8*, 159389–159401. [CrossRef]
22. Smith, J.M.; Kennedy, A.B.; Westerink, J.J.; Taflanidis, A.A.; Cheung, K.F. Hawaii hurricane wave and surge modeling and fast forecasting. *Coast. Eng. Proc.* **2012**, *1*, management.8. [CrossRef]
23. Bezuglov, A.; Blanton, B.; Santiago, R. Multi-output artificial neural network for storm surge prediction in north carolina. *arXiv* **2016**, arXiv:1609.07378.
24. Krenker, A.; Bester, J.; Kos, A. Introduction to the artificial neural networks. In *Artificial Neural Networks: Methodological Advances and Biomedical Applications*; InTech: London, UK, 2011; pp. 1–18.
25. LeCun, Y.; Boser, B.; Denker, J.; Henderson, D.; Howard, R.; Hubbard, W.; Jackel, L. Handwritten digit recognition with a back-propagation network. *Adv. Neural Inf. Process. Syst.* **1989**, *2*, 396–404.
26. Krizhevsky, A. Imagenet classification with deep convolutional neural networks. *Adv. Neural Inf. Process. Syst.* **2017**, *60*, 84-90. [CrossRef]
27. Davila, S.E.; Hernandez, C.D.; Flores, M.; Ho, J. South Texas coastal area storm surge model development and improvement. *AIMS Geosci.* **2020**, *6*, 271. [CrossRef]
28. User's Manual-v53-ADCIRC. Available online: https://adcirc.org/home/documentation/users-manual-v53/ (accessed on 21 August 2019).
29. National Centers for Environmental Prediction; National Weather Service; NOAA; U.S. Department of Commerce. *NCEP North American Mesoscale NAM 12 km Analysis*; NCAR: Boulder, CO, USA, 2015.
30. Landsea, C.W. Atlantic hurricane database uncertainty and presentation of a new database format. *Mon. Weather. Rev.* **2013**, *141*, 3576–3592. [CrossRef]

Disclaimer/Publisher's Note: The statements, opinions and data contained in all publications are solely those of the individual author(s) and contributor(s) and not of MDPI and/or the editor(s). MDPI and/or the editor(s) disclaim responsibility for any injury to people or property resulting from any ideas, methods, instructions or products referred to in the content.

Article

Detection of Plausibility and Error Reasons in Finite Element Simulations with Deep Learning Networks

Sebastian Bickel *, Stefan Goetz and Sandro Wartzack

Engineering Design, Friedrich-Alexander-Universität Erlangen-Nürnberg, 91058 Erlangen, Germany; goetz@mfk.fau.de (S.G.); wartzack@mfk.fau.de (S.W.)
* Correspondence: bickel@mfk.fau.de

Abstract: The field of application of data-driven product development is diverse and ranges from requirements through the early phases to the detailed design of the product. The goal is to consistently analyze data to support and improve individual steps in the development process. In the context of this work, the focus is on the design and detailing phase, represented by the virtual testing of products through Finite Element (FE) simulations. However, due to the heterogeneous data of a simulation model, automatic use is a big challenge. A method is therefore presented that utilizes the entire stock of calculated simulations to predict the plausibility of new simulations. Correspondingly, a large amount of data is utilized to support less experienced users of FE software in the application. Thus, obvious errors in the simulation should be detected immediately with this procedure and unnecessary iterations are therefore avoided. Previous solutions were only able to perform a general plausibility classification, whereas the approach presented in this paper is intended to predict specific error sources in FE simulations.

Keywords: deep learning; machine learning; finite element simulation; plausibility checks; convolutional neural networks

1. Introduction

The systematic analysis of data is increasingly established in the product development process and referred to as data-driven product development [1–3]. The range of application is broad, starting at the requirements and continuing through the early phases to the detailed specification of the product. The fundamental principle is the consistent analysis of data to support and improve dedicated (sub-)steps. According to [1], the procedure can be divided into dataset, knowledge base, data-driven method, and the design process step. For each stage, the possibilities are highly dependent on the associated constraints.

In the context of this paper, the focus is on the design and detailing phase, especially on the virtual testing of the products with Finite Element simulations. Due to the heterogeneous data in a simulation model, consisting of input (3D geometry, load cases, surface meshes, etc.), model (mesh, solving methods), and output data (results, reports, etc.), the automatic use of this data is a major challenge [4,5]. An approach for reusing FE simulations was developed by [6], which allows for the retrieval of specific simulations via a database system. As a result, only certain simulations are reused, not the entire pool of calculated simulations. The large amount of data is normally only kept for legal purposes but should be utilized to enable a system to predict the plausibility of new simulations. The aim is to support less experienced users of FE software in their application by directly identifying obvious errors in the simulation and thus avoiding unnecessary iterations. While previous solutions were only able to make general plausibility classifications, the approach presented here targets the prediction of specific error sources. The challenge is to define a suitable transformation method for the simulation data and train a model that is able to predict error sources with high accuracy.

Citation: Bickel, S.; Goetz, S.; Wartzack, S. Detection of Plausibility and Error Reasons in Finite Element Simulations with Deep Learning Networks. *Algorithms* **2023**, *16*, 209. https://doi.org/10.3390/a16040209

Academic Editors: Xiang Zhang and Xiaoxiao Li

Received: 20 February 2023
Revised: 3 April 2023
Accepted: 7 April 2023
Published: 13 April 2023

Copyright: © 2023 by the authors. Licensee MDPI, Basel, Switzerland. This article is an open access article distributed under the terms and conditions of the Creative Commons Attribution (CC BY) license (https://creativecommons.org/licenses/by/4.0/).

1.1. State of the Art

The intention to support users in the application of FE software has been present in the academic landscape for a long time. A very early knowledge-based system was presented by [7] in the late 1980s. With the help of the SACON (Structural Analysis CONsultant) system, the FE calculation of Boeing 747 wings could be improved and access for less experienced engineers was facilitated. Another analysis tool that enhances FE simulation with knowledge-based engineering (KBE) was introduced by [8], with the aim of supporting set up of the FE simulation through knowledge databases. The system was demonstrated with aluminum draw bending components as an example.

In addition to knowledge-based approaches, the use of Machine Learning (ML) techniques in combination with FE simulations has also become popular for facilitating FE simulation tasks. To improve material generation, an approach was presented by [9] that assists the modeling of materials through evolutionary polynomial regression. The approach was integrated into the existing FE simulation process and tested for linear elastic and elastic–plastic material models. The preparation of geometry, a sub-step of preprocessing, can also be optimized by Machine Learning methods. For example, [10] developed a method that detects different ribbon features in components, which enables high-quality meshing of these geometric features. In addition to the recognition, a decomposition into individual areas is also essential for generating a suitable mesh. Another preprocessing upgrade was created from [11], which describes hole detection for mold injection parts. The identified holes are removed from the parts in a subsequent step to facilitate and accelerate the meshing of the different mold components. Furthermore, a contribution dealing with the automatic geometric simplification of components was created by [12]. This approach relies on geometric primitives for segmentation and following morphological investigations of the component. The methods generate a simplified surface model for the simulation from the 3D volume model through dimensional reduction and fitting of the contact surfaces. The authors of [13] provided another contribution to the automation of the preprocessing process by building ontologies via text and data mining, which builds the foundation of the simulation model. In this context, standards or simulation reports serve as the source of the knowledge base and help to automatically set up the simulation. Depending on the analysis requirement, the simulation can be set up accordingly, such as by simplifying bolted connections as beam elements or by modeling them with their threat. Examples of further applications of Machine Learning in the environment of FE simulations are given in [14]. In addition to the listed application fields, other areas such as the efficient optimization of the simulation results and the evaluation of the geometry are also listed.

The presented methods combine assistance to the user with the generation or evaluation of FE simulations. However, these methods [7,8,10,11] only offer solutions for specific problems or use cases. Other approaches [9,12,13] rely on pre-existing knowledge but do not utilize existing simulations from older projects. This gap is filled by the projection method for simulation data developed by [15] and improved in [16].

The objective of this method is to utilize existing simulation data to train a Deep Learning (DL) model that is subsequently capable of classifying new simulations into the classes "plausible" and "non-plausible". The term "plausibility" was defined in the context of FE simulations by [15] as a simulation that does not contain obvious mistakes an experienced simulation engineer would recognize. These errors include incorrect loads such as unit errors for forces (e.g., kN instead of N), meshing of the work piece that is too coarse, or faulty geometry parameters for components. The meaning of plausibility in the simulation context is very well described by the English term "likely valid".

The entire process is shown in Figure 1, starting with the FE simulation and resulting in a classification result. Before a Machine Learning model is trained, a dataset must be created, which consists of the prepared simulations and a corresponding label. Labeling of the simulations should be performed by experienced simulation experts [17]. A parameter study of FE simulations is an effective method for obtaining an adequate number of simulations. After training and examination of the model, it can be employed for the classification of new simulations. For this purpose, new simulations must undergo the same preparation process to be classified as "plausible" and "non-plausible".

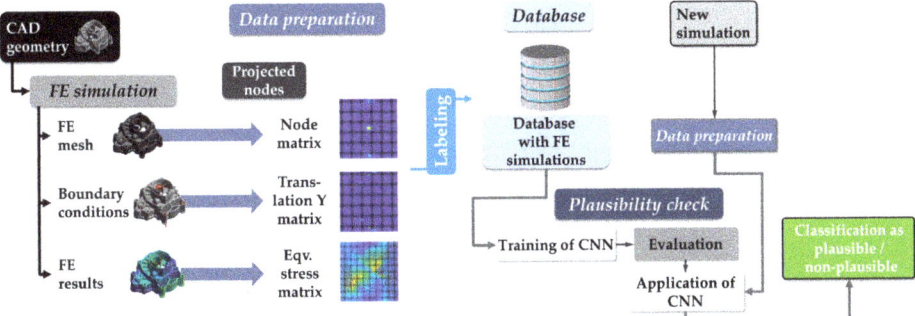

Figure 1. Overview of the Convolutional Neural Network (CNN)-based plausibility check method with example matrices according to [15,16].

In the first step (data preparation), the method uses the projection of points onto a detector sphere to convert the simulation input and results into matrices. In contrast to the unordered simulation data, the matrices are uniformly sized and hence suitable as input for a Neural Network (NN). For conversion of the whole FE simulation into matrices, different point clouds (bearing, loads, mesh, and results) are necessary. The transformation is performed with a projection of nodes onto a detector sphere, which is subdivided into different areas similar to the longitudes and latitudes of a globe. The fields are called pixels and correspond to the respective matrix input. The number of pixels can be chosen independently (for example, 10,000 pixels results in a 100×100 matrix). Detailed calculation of the detector sphere and node projection is explained in more depth in [16] and illustrated in Figure 2 with its main steps.

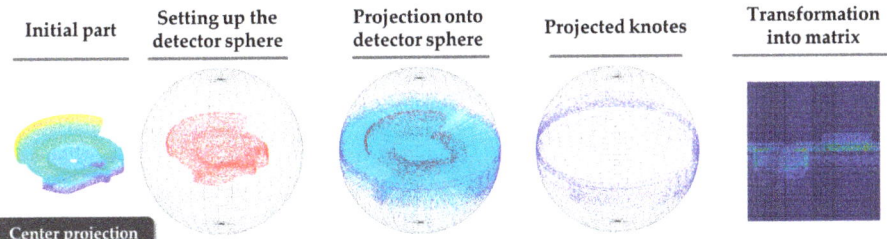

Figure 2. Process steps of the projection method for generating the node matrix according to [15,16].

After projection of the points, the detector sphere is turned into a matrix, similar to transforming a globe into a map. Since the inputs and results of the FE simulation are node-bound, they can be transferred into matrices, allowing the entire simulation to be uniformly transferable. Consequently, different matrices can be created for one simulation, which are arranged channel-wise (comparable to RGB images). The choice of matrices is dependent on the simulation and the objective pursued.

These matrices allow for the training of a Machine Learning model that predicts the two classes "plausible" and "non-plausible". Within this contribution, the aim is to investigate whether a differentiated detection of the cause of the simulation errors is also achievable. For this purpose, it is necessary to examine which classification approach can fulfill the stated goal. Therefore, the methodical background for classification and Deep Learning is presented in the next section.

1.2. Methodical Background

The categorization of Machine Learning algorithms strongly depends on the learning category. According to [18–20], a distinction is typically made between supervised, unsupervised, and reinforcement learning. The classification of objects falls under supervised learning since a labeled dataset must be available. In contrast to regression, where discrete numerical values are determined, classification predicts previously defined categories, as described in [21,22]. In [23,24], the classification task is further divided into the number of labels per input value. If there are only two possible classes, it is called a binary classifier. A multiclass application occurs when there are several possible classes per input, but only one result label. When multiple classes are possible for one input value, this is termed a multilabel classifier. Figure 3 shows the mentioned distinction graphically.

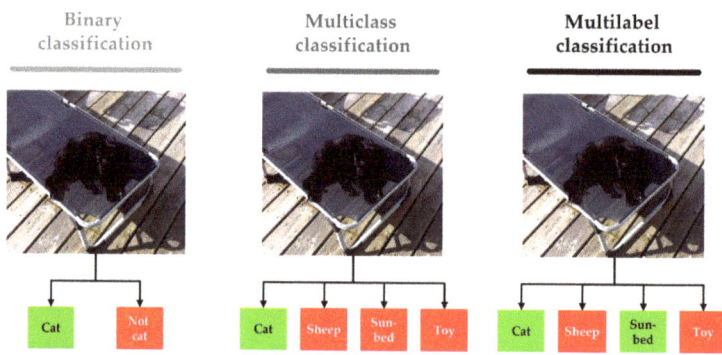

Figure 3. Comparison of different classification approaches according to [23,24] with positive classification results marked in green.

The plausibility detection presented earlier falls under the category of binary classifiers. To classify multiple new error classes, different approaches are feasible. A multilabel classification is performed by converting the classification into a regression task. Each class is converted into numerical values between 0 and 1, resulting in a vector instead of a label for each sample. Subsequently, the vector is determined via the regression algorithm. Afterwards, a threshold value (e.g., 0.5) is used to determine whether the input can be assigned to a class or not. The adaptation of multiclass classification is also an option; however, in this case, the dataset must be supplemented with additional labels. This is necessary to ensure that all label combinations are included in the dataset. With this adjustment of the dataset, multilabel classification is a viable option afterwards. Binary classifiers can also be modified for the task of multilabel classification. In this case, each binary classifier holds one label; thus, multiple models must be trained, which are evaluated afterwards.

A special category in the field of Machine Learning is Deep Learning, which is often linked to the application of Neural Networks [20,25–27]. It differs from classical Machine Learning in the number of layers and feature generation. In a classic ML model, the developer specifies the model features. In contrast, a Deep Learning model creates them in the learning phase. In [20], this process is described as automatically breaking down complicated concepts into more simple ones.

An application of the Deep Learning principle to images is Convolutional Neural Networks (CNNs), which take human vision as a template. The term "convolutional" was first introduced by [28] in 1989 and has been associated with this type of network since then. The structure of a CNN aims to emulate the visual cortex. For this purpose, different neuron, convolutional, and pooling layers are used to filter information from the image data.

One of the most famous CNNs is the LeNet of [29], which was published in 1998 to recognize handwritten letters. As computational power increased and larger datasets became publicly available (e.g., MNIST [29], CIFAR [30], PASCAL VOC [31], or ImageNet [32]), it was possible to put CNNs to practical and beneficial use. As a result of an image detection competition in 2012, AlexNet from [33] attracted particular attention due to its results. In comparison to LeNet-5, AlexNet has more layers and is suitable for higher resolution images. An even deeper network with 16 layers, accordingly named Vgg16, was presented by [34] two years later. All previously mentioned CNN models are serial, which allows the network to pass through all layers in sequence.

According to [35], deeper networks should adapt better to a given task as the parameter space for adjustment increases, though the achieved accuracy tends to saturate and then decrease. Multiple paths through the CNN can solve the described problem, which was implemented through residual blocks in the CNN by [36] and called ResNets. An example of this new component in a network is displayed on the left in Figure 4.

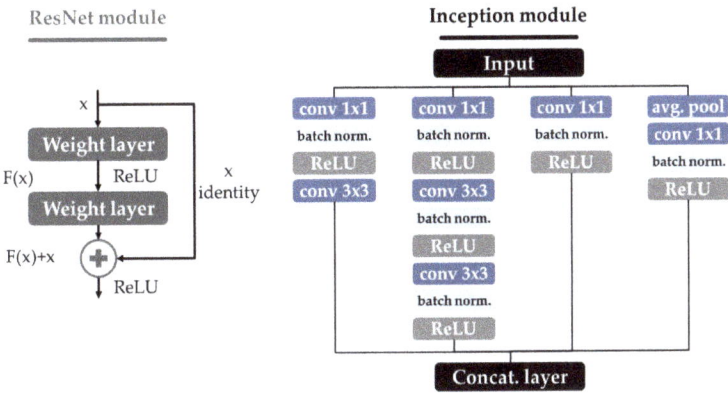

Figure 4. Example of a residual building block and the Inception module according to [36,37].

Since objects in images can occur in different sizes and matching larger kernel sizes increases the complexity of the model and computational requirements, the Inception networks of [37] were developed. The solution is multiple and parallel convolutional operations with fixed sizes, as depicted on the right side in Figure 4. Furthermore, a pooling function is performed, and the results of the concurrent operations are then merged afterwards. This procedure was improved constantly and provided with new updates, hence it is available in the fourth generation [38].

The authors of [39] published another iteration of this idea under the name Densenet. In ResNet models, the merging is always performed after one ResNet module, whereas in Densenet each layer receives the results of all previous layers. An alternative idea to the ever deeper and linked architectures is demonstrated in the creation of MobileNet by [40]. The goal was to design a network that computes fast enough to run on mobile devices. The implementation was achieved through depth-wise separable convolutions, which drastically reduced the number of free parameters. The procedure of depth-wise separable convolution consists of depth-wise and point-wise convolution. After the first version, two more iterations of the idea were published (V2: [41]; V3: [42]).

1.3. Research Gap

After presentation of the current state of the art and the methodological background, two research questions (RQ) for the plausibility check of FE simulations arise.

RQ1: Is there a multilabel classification framework capable of predicting the specific sources of errors for different FE simulations?
RQ2: In combination with the classification model, which CNN architecture is particularly suitable for detecting the causes of errors?

These questions are intended to show whether the detection of specific faults in FE simulations is possible without creating a purely application-specific solution.

2. Methodical Approach

In order to provide conclusive answers to the questions raised, an overview of the planned examinations is presented. Overall, three different influencing factors are relevant to the general investigation: the classification realization, the dataset, and the CNN architecture. All three of these divisions have different influencing parameters that affect the overall result. The objective of the experiment is always the prediction of the plausibility cause, whether it is due to a faulty mesh, wrong load values, or unrealistic geometry parameters. Figure 5 provides an overview, and the following subsections present the different parts in more detail.

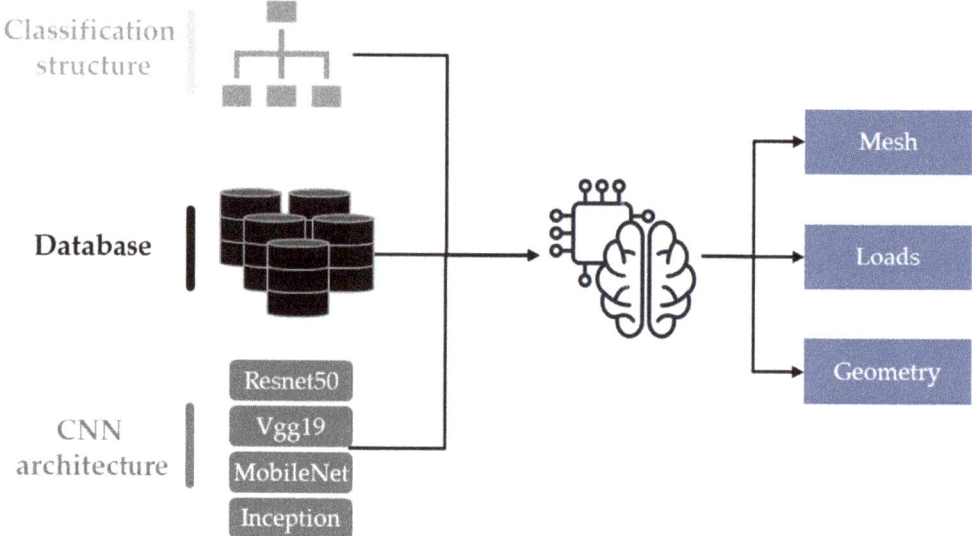

Figure 5. Overview of the relevant experiment parameters.

2.1. Classification Structure

First, the realization of the multilabel classification is explained in greater depth. Two implementation ideas were developed based on the theoretical knowledge from Section 1.2 and are shown schematically in Figure 6. The first concept applies several binary classifiers, each of which predicts one specific class. These consist of a CNN for classification and a dataset extracted from the entire simulation pool. In contrast, the second model uses a conversion of the problem into a regression model. For this purpose, the CNN structure is adapted correspondingly by replacing the softmax and classification layers with sigmoid and cross-entropy loss layers. For this application, the dataset does not require any further processing. The choice of CNN architecture is independent of the selected execution, although the binary classification theoretically offers the advantage of using different CNN models for each classifier.

The third possibility, adaptation of the multiclass classification, was not pursued further since all combinations must be defined as classes, which would correspond to eight (2^3) labels. As a result, very few simulations can be assigned to some classes, such as in a the category in which all three plausibility causes are true. Furthermore, this procedure would become more and more complex to handle when adding further classes, since the number of new necessary classes scales with input classes to the power of two.

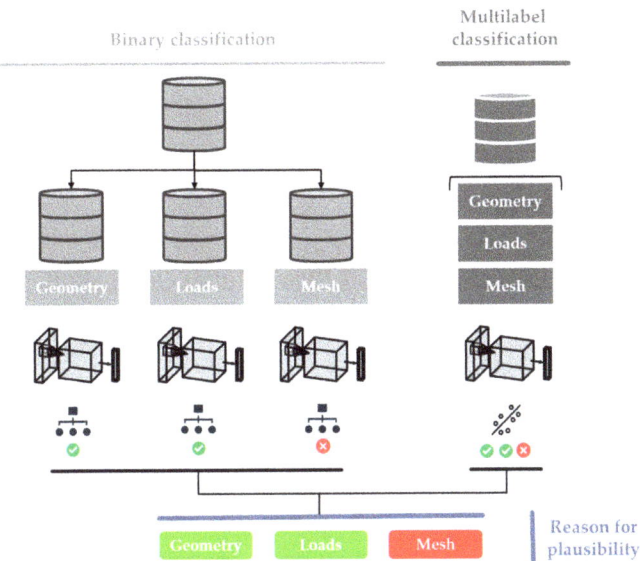

Figure 6. Comparison of multilabel classification approaches.

2.2. Database

In order to test and analyze the new approach, a large dataset with a sufficient number of simulations is necessary. Currently, only structural mechanics simulations with components are considered. The dataset includes already calculated simulations from previous publications [16,43]. The general structure of the entire dataset is organized with the help of the Opitz coding system [44]. The first digit of the code was selected as the distinguishing feature and the aim was to cover the existing categories as broadly as possible. The result with the corresponding simulation parts is listed in Table 1. The variables representing rotatory components stand for the length (L) and the diameter (D), while for the non-rotatory ones the maximum dimensions are sorted in all three directions in space and defined with A as the highest value and C as the lowest value.

Table 1. Categorization of the simulation parts in accordance with the Opitz coding system [44].

	Rotatory			Non-Rotatory			
L/D < 0.5	0.5 < L/D < 3	L/D ≥ 3	A/C > 4	A/B ≤ 3 & A/C ≥ 4	A/B ≤ 3	A/B ≤ 3 & A/C < 4
Vehicle rim		Crankshaft	Inliner frame		Brake lever	Mountain bike rocker

In total, five components from different applications and domains are integrated into the entire dataset, all displayed in Figure 7. All simulations were calculated with parametric CAD models using Ansys Workbench (version 19.2 and 2021 R2). For generation of the results, parameter studies were performed with d-optimal experimental designs (DOE) for the different simulations [45]. After successful calculation of the FE simulation, an APDL script saves the results as a text file, including stresses, deformations, boundary conditions, and the general mesh.

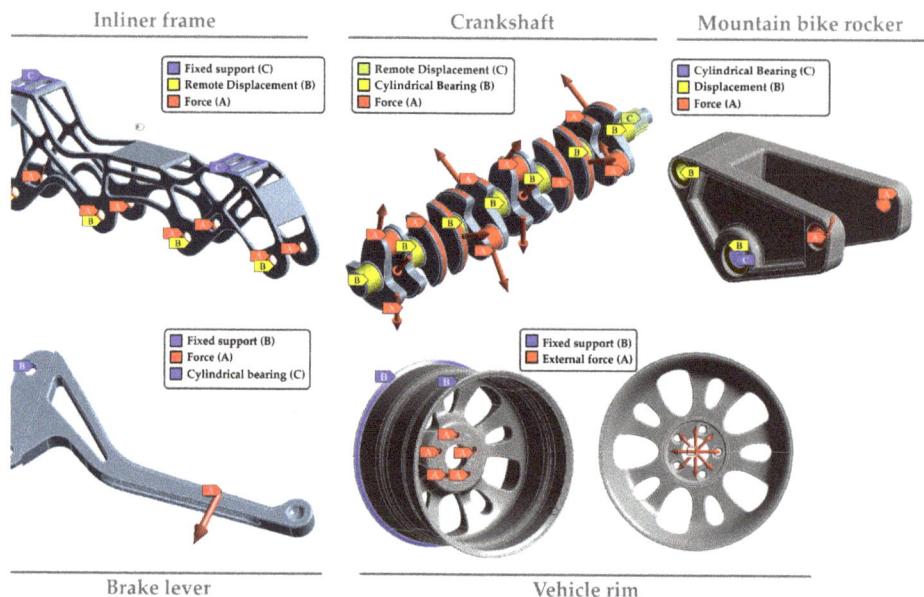

Figure 7. Overview of the different simulation setups.

The simulations were built using real loading conditions (inliner frame or mountain bike rocker) or information from the literature (crankshaft [46,47], brake lever [48], or car rim [49,50]). An overview of the various components and simulation setups is shown in Figure 7, with more detailed information on the simulations listed in [16,43].

For all simulations, the element size of the mesh, the load values, and the geometric variables of the component were used as parameters. These all affect the non-plausibility of FE simulations, and the goal is to detect these certain error sources. Since the focus of previous datasets was not differentiated by plausibility cause, the geometric non-plausibility cases were not taken into account in all parts. To close this gap and to test how the models behave with smaller datasets, supplementary studies focusing on geometric plausibility reasons were created for the vehicle rim and brake lever.

An overview of the calculated simulations and the labeled results is given in Table 2. In total, over 63,000 simulations are in the dataset, corresponding to a storage requirement of almost 13 TB. Most simulations were calculated with the bike rocker and the smallest amount with the crankshaft. In the case of the vehicle rim and brake lever, the second study for the geometrical error cause is added below in brackets as it was calculated with a second DOE plan. The sum of the plausible and different non-plausible classes always exceeds the total number of simulations. This is due to the fact that several reasons for non-plausibility can exist per simulation. The table also shows that the geometrically non-plausible reason is the least represented in the data and accordingly forms an imbalanced dataset, which can thus lead to favoritism toward the majority class from the trained model. Labeling of each parameter study was performed by a combination of automatic (e.g., rule-based for high load values) and manual labeling.

Table 2. General information about the demonstrative study simulation datasets, with the numbers of the additional dataset in brackets.

Dataset	Simulation Numbers	Plausible	Non-Plausible Mesh	Non-Plausible Geometry	Non-Plausible Loads	Storage Space
Vehicle rim	9968	3736	2488	0	4992	676 GB
	(1816)	(80)	(792)	(1520)	(888)	217 GB
Brake lever	9862	5896	2493	0	1987	574 GB
	(1225)	(554)	(315)	(290)	(251)	64 GB
Bike rocker	22,624	12,257	3780	1620	6776	2890 GB
Crankshaft	8640	4800	1440	0	2880	6920 GB
Inliner frame	8952	4344	2172	0	3252	1650 GB
Whole dataset	63,087	31,667	13,480	3430	21,026	12,991 GB

Dataset Preparation

After description and explanation of the available simulation pool, the next step is to demonstrate conversion of the simulation setup and results into matrices. The idea behind the transformation and arrangement of the matrices is to generate the "DNA of the simulation" and represent the simulation setup and results. An example transformation of a simulation is shown in Figure 8 including the input and result variables. With this investigation, the goal was to test a universal approach, which is the reason for including as many loads as possible in the matrix collection. The most common types of loads should be implemented, even if some of them are not part of the simulation pool. Consequently, 26 different matrices are created for one simulation: nodes, fixed translation and rotation in the X-, Y-, and Z-direction, force, external force and pressure in the X-, Y-, and Z-direction, moment around the X-, Y-, and Z-axis, the positive and negative displacements in the X-, Y- and Z-direction, and the equivalent von Mises stress. A resolution of 100 × 100 was chosen to generate the datasets for both classification approaches. The matrices are prepared through a special method of normalization, which is explained in detail in [16]. Through this process, the boundary conditions and result values are normalized differently in order to better represent FE simulations.

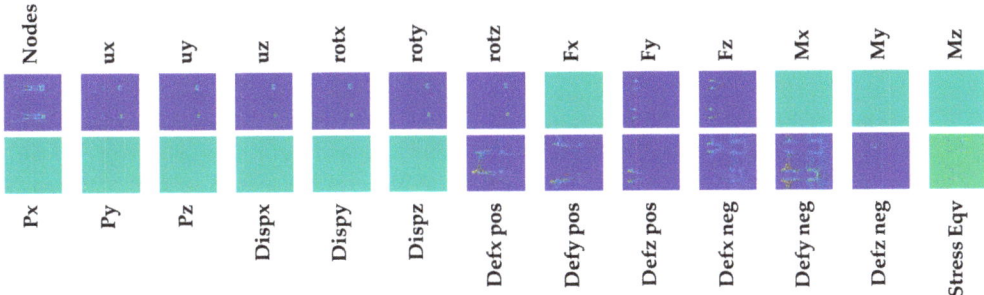

Figure 8. Example of the resulting matrices for one inliner frame simulation.

One additional advantage of projection conversion is the reduced storage space. After execution of the method, the matrices for the entire dataset only need about 10.5 GB compared to the original 13 TB. Of course, size depends on the resolution of the transformation, as the data requirements for higher resolution also increase. For this study, the dataset for each simulation parameter study was split 80/20 into training and testing data. As a result, 10% of the training dataset was selected for validation during training.

2.3. CNN Architecture

After explaining the classification procedure and the dataset, this chapter will focus on applied CNNs. A total of four architectures were investigated: Vgg19, ResNet, Inception-V3, and MobileNet-V2. Figure 9 shows a simplified comparison of the architectures. Due to the size of some architectures, the representation was simplified.

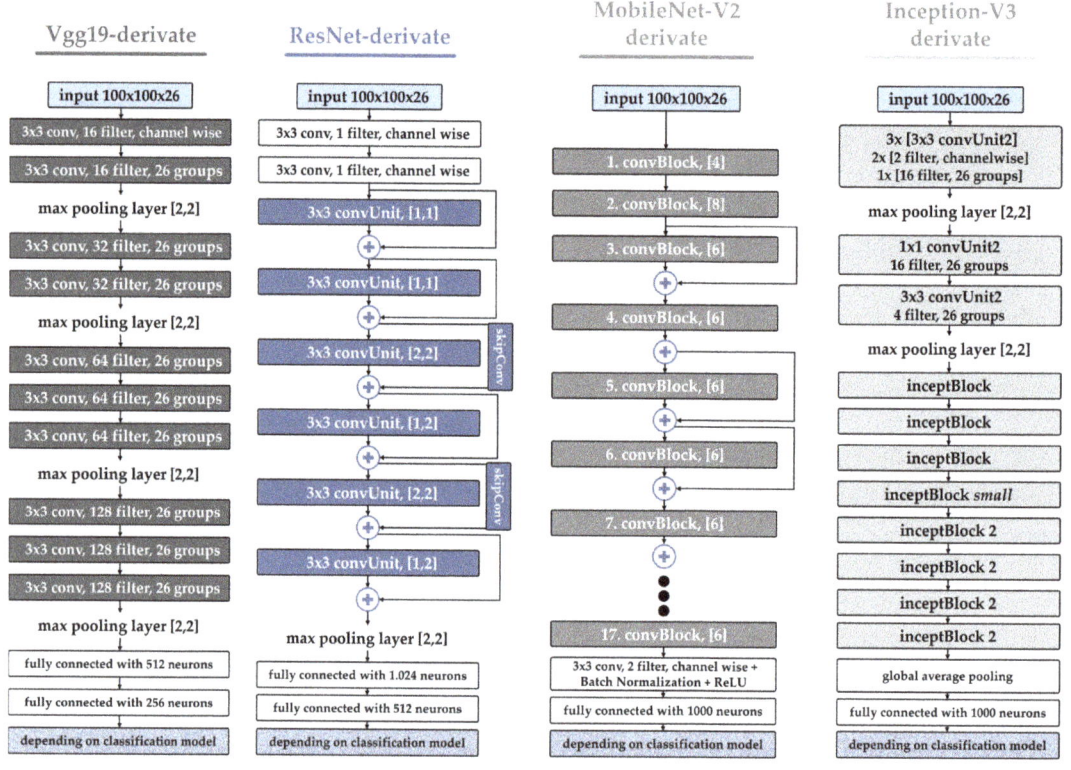

Figure 9. Comparison of different network architectures adapted for channel-wise input of transformed FE simulation matrices.

The Vgg19-derivate uses four groups of sequential convolution layers, each followed by a ReLU (Rectified Linear Unit) layer. Compared to the original Vgg19 architecture, a block of convolutional layers was removed due to the lower resolution of the matrix input. Furthermore, the number of filters per convolutional layer was reduced so a comparable batch size could be applied for all architectures. The variant derived from ResNet is shown in a simplified manner in Figure 9 using *convUnits*, each consisting of a convolution, batch normalization, ReLU activation, convolution, and batch normalization layer. The filter size is 3 × 3 for both convolution layers, and the values in the square brackets describe the number of filters and the stride for the layer. The two *skipConv* blocks contain extra convolution layers and are necessary for the results to have the same format when merging. The third architecture is based on MobileNet-V2 and is illustrated schematically via *convBlock* units in Figure 9. A *convBlock* contains a channel-wise convolution with 6 filters, batch normalization, an ReLU layer, channel-wise convolution with one filter, batch normalization, an ReLU layer, a channel-wise convolution layer with a fixed number of filters (matching the input to the *convBlock*), and a batch normalization layer. A total of

17 blocks are arranged one after the other with partial skip paths, modeled after the original MobileNet-V2. For the adapted Inception-V3 network, the first layers were replaced by *convUnit2* blocks, each composed of a convolution, batch normalization, and ReLU layer, with the convolution parameters listed in the square brackets. The following *inceptBlock* modules are carried over from the original Inception-V3 architecture and contain four threads each with different convolution, batch normalization, ReLU, and pooling layers, as shown in Figure 4. Due to the lower resolution of the input, the last two larger inception blocks were removed from the network.

For all models, the last three layers depend on the classification model. In the case of binary classification, they are a fully connected layer with two neurons and a softmax and classification layer. In contrast, in the multilabel instance, a fully connected layer with three neurons and a sigmoid and cross-entropy loss layer is applied.

The evaluation metric for comparison of the different approaches and models is usually classification accuracy. This metric is derived from the confusion matrix and is calculated for the three datasets: the training dataset, validation dataset, and test dataset. A confusion matrix with the associated variable names is shown in Figure 10, with the variables True Positive (TP), True Negative (TN), False Positive (FP), and False Negative (FN).

		Predicted class		
		positiv	negativ	total
True class	positiv	TP	FN	P
	negativ	FP	TN	N
	total	P'	N'	P+N

Figure 10. Confusion matrix for classification tasks according to [51–53].

For a balanced dataset, classifications accuracy is often applied, which can be calculated according to [52,53]:

$$accuracy = \frac{TP + TN}{TP + TN + FP + FN}$$

However, this metric is not appropriate for the evaluation of imbalanced datasets since it does not consider the uneven distribution of classes. An alternative is the balanced accuracy from [51]:

$$balanced\ accuracy = \frac{1}{2}\left(\frac{TP}{TP + FN} + \frac{TN}{TN + FP}\right)$$

Another metric for imbalanced datasets is the G-Mean (geometric mean) value defined by [54]:

$$G - Mean = \sqrt{\frac{TP}{TP + FN} \cdot \frac{TN}{TN + FP}}$$

Besides the presented metrics, many others have been developed, such as the F-Measure, the Receiver Operator Curve (ROC), the area under the curve (AUC), the Precision Recall (PR) Diagram, and the Index of Balanced Accuracy (IBA), which are explained in detail in [51,54–56].

3. Result Comparison

After explanation of the different classification adaptations and CNN architectures, the following chapter examines them in further depth using the described evaluation metrics. All models were trained on the same computational server, which had two AMD EPYC 7643 processors, 256 GB RAM, and two Nvidia A40 (46 GB) graphics cards installed. The basic set of training parameters is identical for all models, as shown in Table 3. Only the learning rate was adjusted for different models because a uniform rate did not work. Data was divided into training, validation, and test datasets automatically according to the 72%–8%–20% principle and was performed in the same manner for all datasets and models.

Table 3. Training parameters for the CNN models.

Options	Value
Solver Type	adam
Mini Batchsize	128
Max. Epochs	40
Validation Frequency	125
Validation Patience	8
Shuffle	Once
Learning Rate Binary	MobileNet: 0.0001 ResNet: 0.000001 Vgg19: 0.00001 Inception: 0.001
Learning Rate Multilabel	MobileNet: 0.0001 ResNet: 0.000001 Vgg19: 0.00001 Inception: 0.0001

Class distribution for the two variants of training data is shown in Figure 11. The number of non-plausible classes is identical for both cases, with only the plausible instances varying. Since only one cause of error is detected in the binary classifiers, the other two non-plausible cases are still included as plausible. All training datasets consist of 45,444 observations for training. The uneven distribution of classes is particularly evident in the geometry class. Therefore, the metrics balanced accuracy and G-Mean are applied for evaluation to account for the non-uniformity of the distribution.

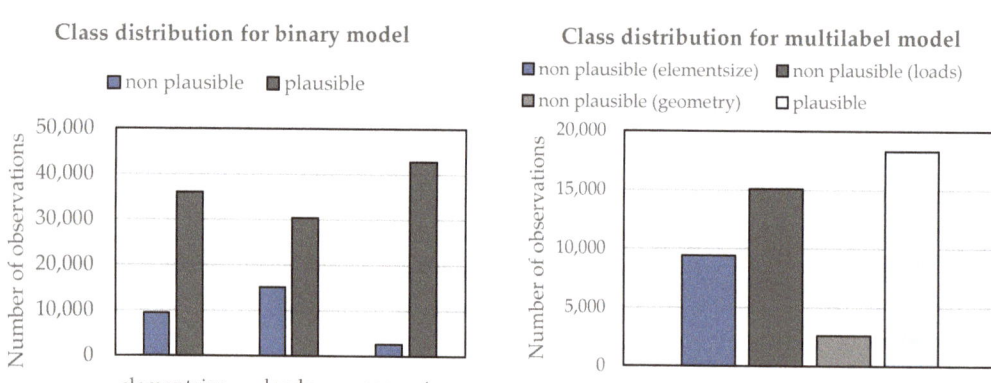

Figure 11. Label distribution for binary and multilabel models.

3.1. Classification Approach

For initial comparison of the classification models, the results of all CNN models were analyzed for all three classes. The derivatives of Vgg19, ResNet, Inception-V3, and MobileNet-V2 serve as the CNN models.

The results are shown in the diagram in Figure 12. The training duration of the CNN models varied between 4 h and 12 h. The plot shows the test results for the error classes in the binary (Bin) and multilabel (MuL) approaches. The boxplot is composed of all four CNN architectures, with all detailed results listed in the Appendix A in Tables A1 and A2.

The scores for all methods are generally very high, with all results above 0.9. Comparison of the G-Mean and balanced accuracy values indicates that scatter is lower for the binary methods over all plausibility causes.

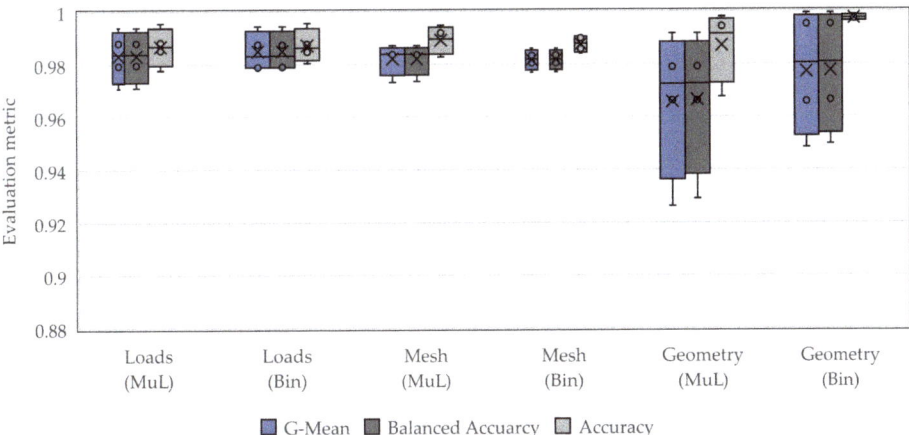

Figure 12. Results for the test dataset with different evaluation metrics for the two classification approaches.

Analysis of the highest classification results also reveals that the binary and multilabel variants achieve nearly identical results for the loads and mesh classes. The absolute differences are very small, in some cases in the third decimal digit. Only in the geometry class is the higher accuracy of the binary classification visible. In evaluation of the geometry cause, it is evident that this class was the most challenging in the classification, recognizable by the high dispersion of both classification variants.

Because of low dispersion and higher accuracy for the geometry class of the binary classifiers, they will be examined in more detail. The aim is to compare the different CNN architectures against each other in order to obtain the best results.

3.2. CNN Architecture

The bar chart in Figure 13 compares the calculated results. In general, the G-Mean values achieved by the respective architectures are very high, and the distribution per class is low in most cases. It is also evident that the geometry class had the most deviations, which is due to the imbalance of the dataset. Furthermore, it is visible that the Inception-V3 derivative best classified the loads and geometry. For the plausibility cause mesh size, ResNet achieved the highest accuracy. The Vgg19 architecture also obtained very high results in the first two classes, though not for the geometric error reason. Here, MobileNet could score very high values, whereas it performed worse in comparison to the other two classes.

Since the Inception network performed the best overall, another study with individual class weights was carried out. For each binary classifier, individual weights were determined depending on the class distribution. Afterwards, the networks were trained again with an adapted learning rate of 0.0005 and the results were compared, which are shown in the confusion matrix in Figure 14. The G-Mean values achieved are as follows: 0.9930 (Loads), 0.9866 (Mesh), and 0.9978 (geometry).

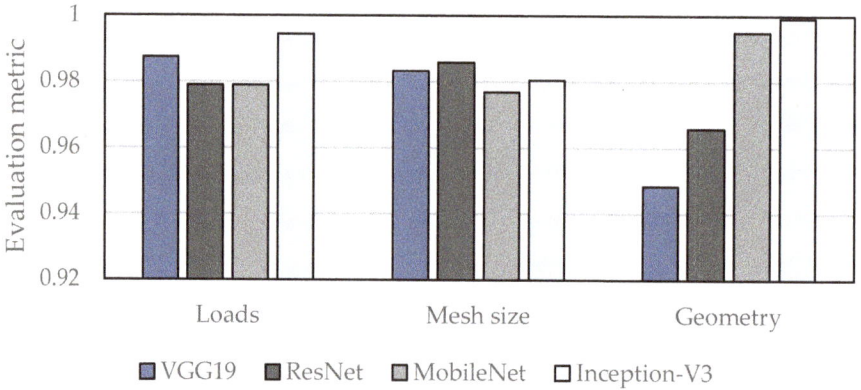

Figure 13. Comparison of different CNN architectures in terms of G-Mean metric for plausibility detection.

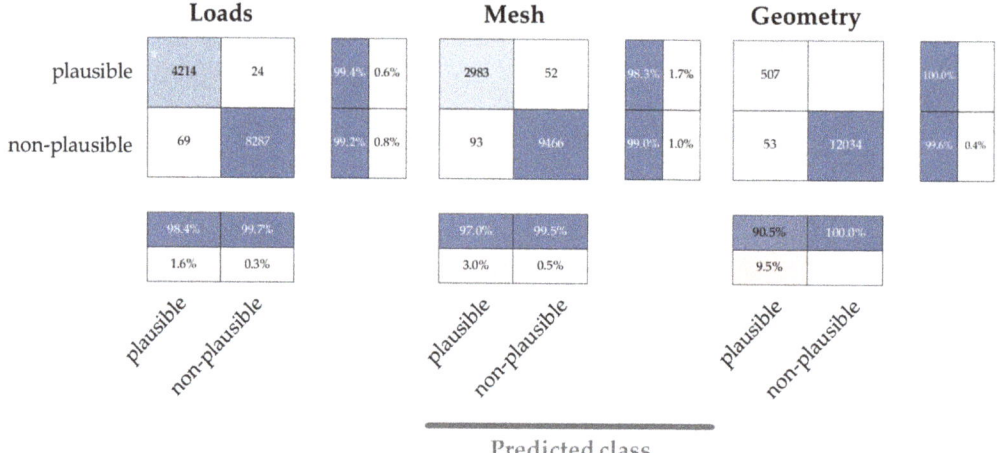

Figure 14. Results of the adapted class weights with the Inception-V3 derivate and binary classification.

The results show that accuracy could again be improved by weighted classes but on a smaller scale, which is inevitable due to the already very high values. Above all, the mesh class was further enhanced, whereas the other two plausibility causes marginally worsened.

4. Discussion

After presentation of the obtained results, it can be concluded that both classification approaches are suitable for the application of specific plausibility cause detection in FE simulations. This answers the first research question as both presented classification approaches provide very good results, and principal detection of the cause of the error is possible with both of them. However, a detailed comparison of the two approaches reveals the different advantages and disadvantages of the procedures.

The advantage of multilabel classification via an adapted regression model is the reduced training time since only one model needs to be trained instead of three in the case of binary classification. Therefore, the model can theoretically be adapted to a new dataset faster. Furthermore, integration of all three labels into the dataset reduces class imbalance compared to a plain binary classifier, as can be seen in Figure 11. Nevertheless, training also showed that there was high sensitivity to the appropriate choice of hyper parameters, which made the training time-consuming in some cases.

In contrast, the advantage of binary classifiers lies in the learning of a specific problem, which thus allows it to predict that problem with higher accuracy at the expense of training time. Additionally, they are much more flexible since the CNN architecture can be chosen specifically for the class. In the case of application as an assistance system for plausibility checking in industry, new data could be brought into the system more easily because only the recognition of an error would cause temporarily interruption.

In addition to the multilabel concept comparison, it is noticeable when comparing the CNN architectures that all networks achieve very good results. However, to answer the second research question, the Inception-V3 adaptation achieves especially high classification results. The other three network types mostly have their strengths in a certain class and are less capable of detecting the other two. The use of specific class weights resulted in a further general improvement, which leads to the conclusion that the combination of binary classifiers with the Inception-V3 network is best suited for the dataset and the application task at hand.

5. Conclusions and Outlook

In summary, this paper tested multilabel classification approaches with different networks to predict the specific plausibility cause. For this purpose, a dataset with over 60,000 simulations was prepared and given as input to different CNNs. The achieved accuracies were reasonably high, which thus allows for the conclusion that a prediction of more accurate error causes in FE simulations is possible.

The next steps could address the analysis of the input vector in more depth. In this paper, the matrices were chosen to ensure that the procedure was generally applicable, although exploring the exact influence of the different matrices on recognition accuracy would be very interesting. In addition, other network architectures and newer Neural Network types (such as Visual Transformer [57]) could be adapted and used for classification. Furthermore, methods from the field of data augmentation could be applied in different ways to reduce the imbalance of the classes. Finally, other causes for non-plausible simulations could be taken into account and the database could be enhanced accordingly.

Author Contributions: Software, conceptualization, methodology, visualization, investigation, resources, data curation, writing—original draft preparation: S.B.; writing—review, conceptualization, and editing: S.G.; project administration, funding acquisition, supervision: S.W. All authors have read and agreed to the published version of the manuscript.

Funding: This research was funded by DFG, grant number WA 2913/47-1.

Institutional Review Board Statement: Not applicable.

Informed Consent Statement: Not applicable.

Data Availability Statement: Not applicable.

Acknowledgments: The authors thank the German Research Foundation for funding this research under grant number WA 2913/47-1. The authors acknowledge financial support by Deutsche Forschungsgemeinschaft and Friedrich-Alexander-Universität Erlangen-Nürnberg within the funding programme "Open Access Publication Funding".

Conflicts of Interest: The authors declare no conflict of interest.

Appendix A

Table A1. All classification results for the binary models and different CNN architectures.

	Dataset Binary			Evaluation Metric
	Loads	Mesh Size	Geometry	
	0.9875	0.9832	0.9484	G-Mean
Vgg19	0.9875	0.9833	0.9497	Balanced Accuracy
	0.9877	0.9906	0.9960	Accuracy
	0.9789	0.9859	0.9658	G-Mean
ResNet	0.9791	0.9859	0.9664	Balanced Accuracy
	0.9848	0.9898	0.9971	Accuracy
	0.9789	0.9768	0.9950	G-Mean
MobileNet-V2	0.9789	0.9770	0.9950	Balanced Accuracy
	0.9805	0.9857	0.9976	Accuracy
	0.9944	0.9804	0.9993	G-Mean
Inception-V3	0.9944	0.9804	0.9993	Balanced Accuracy
	0.9957	0.9840	0.9987	Accuracy

Table A2. All classification results for the multilabel models and different CNN architectures.

	Dataset Multilabel			Evaluation Metric
	Loads	Mesh Size	Geometry	
	0.9709	0.9733	0.9262	G-Mean
Vgg19	0.9711	0.9735	0.9290	Balanced Accuracy
	0.9778	0.9828	0.9942	Accuracy
	0.9795	0.9871	0.9662	G-Mean
ResNet	0.9797	0.9871	0.9662	Balanced Accuracy
	0.9853	0.9919	0.9676	Accuracy
	0.9881	0.9840	0.9788	G-Mean
MobileNet-V2	0.9881	0.9840	0.9790	Balanced Accuracy
	0.9883	0.9871	0.9979	Accuracy
	0.9940	0.9837	0.9916	G-Mean
Inception-V3	0.9940	0.9837	0.9916	Balanced Accuracy
	0.9956	0.9948	0.9886	Accuracy

References

1. Feng, Y.; Zhao, Y.; Zheng, H.; Li, Z.; Tan, J. Data-driven product design toward intelligent manufacturing: A review. *Int. J. Adv. Robot. Syst.* **2020**, *17*, 1729881420911257. [CrossRef]
2. Briard, T.; Jean, C.; Aoussat, A.; Véron, P.; Le Cardinal, J.; Wartzack, S. Data-driven design challenges in the early stages of the product development process. *Proc. Des. Soc.* **2021**, *1*, 851–860. [CrossRef]
3. Quan, H.; Li, S.; Zeng, C.; Wei, H.; Hu, J. Big Data driven Product Design: A Survey. *arXiv* **2021**, arXiv:2109.11424.
4. Iriondo, A.; Oscarsson, J.; Jeusfeld, M.A. Simulation Data Management in a Product Lifecycle Management Context. In *Advances in Manufacturing Technology XXXI*; IOS Press: Amsterdam, The Netherlands, 2017; pp. 476–481.
5. Chari, S. *Addressing Engineering Simulation Data Management (SDM) Challenges: How Engineering Enterprises Can Improve Productivity, Collaboration and Innovation*; Cabot Partners Group, Inc.: Danbury, CT, USA, 2013.
6. Yang, X.; Liang, J.; Liao, Y.; Liu, F.; Feng, X.; Wen, Y. Study of Universal Simulation Data Management System. In Proceedings of the 2009 International Conference on Information Technology and Computer Science, Kiev, Ukraine, 25–26 July 2009; pp. 333–338.
7. Bennet, J.; Creary, L.; Englemore, R.; Melosh, R. *SACON: A Knowledge-Based Consultant for Structural Analysis*; Stanford Heuristic Programming Project; Stanford University—Computer Science Department: Stanford, CA, USA, 1979.
8. Johansson, J. Manufacturability Analysis Using Integrated KBE, CAD and FEM. In *Volume 5: 13th Design for Manufacturability and the Lifecycle Conference; 5th Symposium on International Design and Design Education; 10th International Conference on Advanced Vehicle and Tire Technologies*; ASMEDC: Houston, TX, USA, 2008; pp. 191–200.
9. Javadi, A.A.; Mehrvar, M.; Faramarzi, A.; Ahangar-Asr, A. An artificial intelligence based finite element method. *Comput. Intell. Syst.* **2009**, *1*, 1–120.
10. Lai, J.-Y.; Wang, M.-H.; Song, P.-P.; Hsu, C.-H.; Tsai, Y.-C. Recognition and decomposition of rib features in thin-shell plastic parts for finite element analysis. *Comput. -Aided Des. Appl.* **2018**, *15*, 264–279. [CrossRef]
11. Song, P.-P.; Lai, J.-Y.; Tsai, Y.-C.; Hsu, C.-H. Automatic recognition and suppression of holes on mold bases for finite element applications. *Eng. Comput.* **2019**, *35*, 925–944. [CrossRef]
12. Boussuge, F.; Léon, J.-C.; Hahmann, S.; Fine, L. Idealized models for FEA derived from generative modeling processes based on extrusion primitives. *Eng. Comput.* **2015**, *31*, 513–527. [CrossRef]
13. Kestel, P.; Kügler, P.; Zirngibl, C.; Schleich, B.; Wartzack, S. Ontology-based approach for the provision of simulation knowledge acquired by Data and Text Mining processes. *Adv. Eng. Inform.* **2019**, *39*, 292–305. [CrossRef]
14. Zimmerling, C.; Poppe, C.; Kärger, L. Virtuelle Produktentwicklung mittels Simulationsmethoden und KI. *Lightweight Des.* **2019**, *12*, 12–19. [CrossRef]
15. Spruegel, T.C.; Hallmann, M.; Wartzack, S. A concept for FE plausibility checks in structural mechanics. In Proceedings of the NAFEMS World Congress, San Diego, CA, USA, 21–24 June 2015.
16. Spruegel, T.C.; Bickel, S.; Schleich, B.; Wartzack, S. Approach and application to transfer heterogeneous simulation data from finite element analysis to neural networks. *J. Comput. Des. Eng.* **2021**, *8*, 298–315. [CrossRef]
17. Bickel, S.; Spruegel, T.C.; Schleich, B.; Wartzack, S. How Do Digital Engineering and Included AI Based Assistance Tools Change the Product Development Process and the Involved Engineers. *Proc. Int. Conf. Eng. Des.* **2019**, *1*, 2567–2576. [CrossRef]
18. Bonaccorso, G. *Machine Learning Algorithms*, 1st ed.; Packt Publishing Limited: Birmingham, UK, 2017.
19. Mahesh, B. Machine learning algorithms—A review. *Int. J. Sci. Res.* **2020**, *9*, 381–386.
20. Goodfellow, I.; Courville, A.; Bengio, Y. *Deep Learning*; The MIT Press: Cambridge, MA, USA, 2016.
21. Cleve, J.; Lämmel, U. *Data Mining*, 2nd ed.; De Gruyter Oldenbourg: Berlin, Germany, 2016.
22. Runkler, T.A. *Data Mining: Methoden und Algorithmen Intelligenter Datenanalyse*, 1st ed.; mit 7 Tabellen; Vieweg + Teubner: Wiesbaden, Germany, 2010.
23. Tsoumakas, G.; Katakis, I. Multi-Label Classification. *Int. J. Data Warehous. Min.* **2007**, *3*, 1–13. [CrossRef]
24. Read, J.; Pfahringer, B.; Holmes, G.; Frank, E. Classifier chains for multi-label classification. *Mach. Learn.* **2011**, *85*, 333–359. [CrossRef]
25. Deng, L. Deep Learning: Methods and Applications. *FNT Signal Process.* **2014**, *7*, 197–387. [CrossRef]
26. Janiesch, C.; Zschech, P.; Heinrich, K. Machine learning and deep learning. *Electron Mark.* **2021**, *31*, 685–695. [CrossRef]
27. LeCun, Y.; Bengio, Y.; Hinton, G. Deep learning. *Nature* **2015**, *521*, 436–444. [CrossRef]
28. LeCun, Y.; Boser, B.; Denker, J.S.; Henderson, D.; Howard, R.E.; Hubbard, W.; Jackel, L.D. Backpropagation Applied to Handwritten Zip Code Recognition. *Neural Comput.* **1989**, *1*, 541–551. [CrossRef]
29. LeCun, Y.; Bottou, L.; Bengio, Y.; Haffner, P. Gradient-based learning applied to document recognition. *Proc. IEEE* **1998**, *86*, 2278–2324. [CrossRef]
30. Krizhevsky, A. *Learning Multiple Layers of Features from Tiny Images*; University of Toronto: Toronto, ON, USA, 2009.
31. Everingham, M.; van Gool, L.; Williams, C.K.I.; Winn, J.; Zisserman, A. The Pascal Visual Object Classes (VOC) Challenge. *Int. J. Comput. Vis.* **2010**, *88*, 303–338. [CrossRef]
32. Deng, J.; Dong, W.; Socher, R.; Li, L.-J.; Li, K.; Fei-Fei, L. ImageNet: A large-scale hierarchical image database. In Proceedings of the 2009 IEEE Conference on Computer Vision and Pattern Recognition, Miami, FL, USA, 20–25 June 2009.
33. Krizhevsky, A.; Sutskever, I.; Hinton, G.E. ImageNet classification with deep convolutional neural networks. *Commun. ACM* **2017**, *60*, 84–90. [CrossRef]
34. Simonyan, K.; Zisserman, A. Very Deep Convolutional Networks for Large-Scale Image Recognition. *arXiv* **2014**, arXiv:1409.1556.

35. Srivastava, R.K.; Greff, K.; Schmidhuber, J. Highway Networks. *arXiv* **2015**, arXiv:1505.00387.
36. He, K.; Zhang, X.; Ren, S.; Sun, J. Deep Residual Learning for Image Recognition. In Proceedings of the IEEE Conference on Computer Vision and Pattern Recognition (CVPR), Las Vegas, NV, USA, 27–30 June 2016.
37. Szegedy, C.; Liu, W.; Jia, Y.; Sermanet, P.; Reed, S.; Anguelov, D.; Erhan, D.; Vanhoucke, V.; Rabinovich, A. Going deeper with convolutions. In Proceedings of the 2015 IEEE Conference on Computer Vision and Pattern Recognition (CVPR), Boston, MA, USA, 7–12 June 2015.
38. Szegedy, C.; Ioffe, S.; Vanhoucke, V.; Alemi, A. Inception-v4, Inception-ResNet and the Impact of Residual Connections on Learning. In Proceedings of the AAAI Conference on Artificial Intelligence, San Francisco, CA, USA, 4–9 February 2017; Volume 31.
39. Huang, G.; Liu, Z.; van der Maaten, L.; Weinberger, K.Q. Densely Connected Convolutional Networks. In Proceedings of the IEEE Conference on Computer Vision and Pattern Recognition, Honolulu, HI, USA, 21–26 July 2017.
40. Howard, A.G.; Zhu, M.; Chen, B.; Kalenichenko, D.; Wang, W.; Weyand, T.; Andreetto, M.; Adam, H. MobileNets: Efficient Convolutional Neural Networks for Mobile Vision Applications. *arXiv* **2017**, arXiv:1704.04861.
41. Sandler, M.; Howard, A.; Zhu, M.; Zhmoginov, A.; Chen, L.-C. MobileNetV2: Inverted Residuals and Linear Bottlenecks. In Proceedings of the 2018 IEEE/CVF Conference on Computer Vision and Pattern Recognition, Salt Lake City, UT, USA, 18–22 June 2018.
42. Howard, A.; Sandler, M.; Chen, B.; Wang, W.; Chen, L.-C.; Tan, M.; Chu, G.; Vasudevan, V.; Zhu, Y.; Pang, R.; et al. Searching for MobileNetV3. In Proceedings of the 2019 IEEE/CVF International Conference on Computer Vision (ICCV), Seoul, Korea, 27 October–2 November 2019.
43. Bickel, S.; Schleich, B.; Wartzack, S. Resnet networks for plausibility detection in finite element simulations. In Proceedings of the DS 118: Proceedings of NordDesign 2022, Copenhagen, Denmark, 16–18 August 2022; pp. 1–10.
44. Opitz, H. *A Classification System to Describe Workpieces*; Taylor, A., Translator; Pergamon Press: New York, NY, USA, 1970.
45. Murray-Smith, D.J. *Testing and Validation of Computer Simulation Models: Principles, Methods and Applications*, 1st ed.; Springer International Publishing: Cham, Switzerland, 2015.
46. Van Basshuysen, R. *Handbuch Verbrennungsmotor: Grundlagen, Komponenten, Systeme, Perspektiven*, 7th ed.; mit 1804 Abbildungen und mehr als 1400 Literaturstellen; Springer Vieweg: Wiesbaden, Germany, 2015.
47. Kohler, E. *Verbrennungsmotoren: Motormechanik, Berechnung und Auslegung des Hubkolbenmotors*, 4th ed.; Friedr. Vieweg & Sohn Verlag: Wiesbaden, Germany, 2006.
48. DIN. *Cycles—Safety Requirements for Bicycles—Part 4: Braking Test Methods*; German Institute for Standardization e.V.: Berlin, Germany, 2014.
49. Wang, L.; Chen, Y.; Wang, C.; Wang, Q. Fatigue Life Analysis of Aluminum Wheels by Simulation of Rotary Fatigue Test. *SV-JME* **2011**, *57*, 31–39. [CrossRef]
50. Jape, R.K.; Jadhav, S.G.; Student, M.T. CAD modeling and FEA analysis of wheel rim for weight reduction. *Int. J. Eng. Sci. Comput.* **2016**, *6*, 7404–7411.
51. Brodersen, K.H.; Ong, C.S.; Stephan, K.E.; Buhmann, J.M. The Balanced Accuracy and Its Posterior Distribution. In Proceedings of the 2010 20th International Conference on Pattern Recognition, Washington, DC, USA, 23–26 August 2010.
52. Fawcett, T. An introduction to ROC analysis. *Pattern Recognit. Lett.* **2006**, *27*, 861–874. [CrossRef]
53. Powers, D.M.W. Evaluation: From precision, recall and F-measure to ROC, informedness, markedness and correlation. *arXiv* **2020**, arXiv:2010.16061.
54. Branco, P.; Torgo, L.; Ribeiro, R. A Survey of Predictive Modelling under Imbalanced Distributions. *arXiv* **2015**, arXiv:1505.01658.
55. García, V.; Mollineda, R.A.; Sánchez, J.S. *Index of Balanced Accuracy: A Performance Measure for Skewed Class Distributions*; Springer: Berlin/Heidelberg, Germany, 2009; pp. 441–448.
56. Sun, Y.; Wong, A.K.C.; Kamel, M.S. Classification of imbalanced data: A review. *Int. J. Patt. Recogn. Artif. Intell.* **2009**, *23*, 687–719. [CrossRef]
57. Dosovitskiy, A.; Beyer, L.; Kolesnikov, A.; Weissenborn, D.; Zhai, X.; Unterthiner, T.; Dehghani, M.; Minderer, M.; Heigold, G.; Gelly, S.; et al. An Image is Worth 16x16 Words: Transformers for Image Recognition at Scale. *arXiv* **2020**, arXiv:2010.11929.

Disclaimer/Publisher's Note: The statements, opinions and data contained in all publications are solely those of the individual author(s) and contributor(s) and not of MDPI and/or the editor(s). MDPI and/or the editor(s) disclaim responsibility for any injury to people or property resulting from any ideas, methods, instructions or products referred to in the content.

Article

Unsupervised Cyclic Siamese Networks Automating Cell Imagery Analysis

Dominik Stallmann * and Barbara Hammer *

Faculty of Technology, University of Bielefeld, Universitätsstraße 25, 33615 Bielefeld, Germany
* Correspondence: dstallmann@techfak.uni-bielefeld.de (D.S.); bhammer@techfak.uni-bielefeld.de (B.H.)

Abstract: Novel neural network models that can handle complex tasks with fewer examples than before are being developed for a wide range of applications. In some fields, even the creation of a few labels is a laborious task and impractical, especially for data that require more than a few seconds to generate each label. In the biotechnological domain, cell cultivation experiments are usually done by varying the circumstances of the experiments, seldom in such a way that hand-labeled data of one experiment cannot be used in others. In this field, exact cell counts are required for analysis, and even by modern standards, semi-supervised models typically need hundreds of labels to achieve acceptable accuracy on this task, while classical image processing yields unsatisfactory results. We research whether an unsupervised learning scheme is able to accomplish this task without manual labeling of the given data. We present a VAE-based Siamese architecture that is expanded in a cyclic fashion to allow the use of labeled synthetic data. In particular, we focus on generating pseudo-natural images from synthetic images for which the target variable is known to mimic the existence of labeled natural data. We show that this learning scheme provides reliable estimates for multiple microscopy technologies and for unseen data sets without manual labeling. We provide the source code as well as the data we use. The code package is open source and free to use (MIT licensed).

Keywords: Siamese networks; synthetic data; cyclic learning; unsupervised learning; deep learning; data augmentation; single cell cultivation; bioimage analysis

---

Citation: Stallmann, D.; Hammer, B. Unsupervised Cyclic Siamese Networks Automating Cell Imagery Analysis. *Algorithms* **2023**, *16*, 205. https://doi.org/10.3390/a16040205

Academic Editor: Xiang Zhang and Xiaoxiao Li

Received: 27 February 2023
Revised: 29 March 2023
Accepted: 4 April 2023
Published: 12 April 2023

Copyright: © 2023 by the authors. Licensee MDPI, Basel, Switzerland. This article is an open access article distributed under the terms and conditions of the Creative Commons Attribution (CC BY) license (https://creativecommons.org/licenses/by/4.0/).

1. Introduction

Single cell cultivation is one of the most important steps in single cell analysis [1] and represents an essential means to better understand cell functionality from cellular and subcellular perspectives for diagnosis and therapy, and microfluidic devices constitute fast-rising systems for efficient single cell cultivation. However, the analysis of microfluidic single cell cultivation (MSCC) microscopic images is usually performed manually or supported by technological aiding systems, but requires the work of human experts because of the high spatial and temporal resolution and a variety of visual characteristics that make automation difficult. Flexible image processing pipelines have proven their relevance for certain setups, but are limited to specific scenarios and partially interactive, as the fully automated analysis of non-adhesive cells in the presence of the varying light conditions and various artifacts of microscopic images is challenging [2].

In recent years, the potential of deep convolutional architectures for automated and flexible image analysis has been demonstrated in this area, but training procedures for current deep architectures rely, at least partially, on manually labeled training data [3,4]. A manual procedure is not practical in many applications, creating a demand for effective, fully automated solutions [5]. Therefore, the particular focus of this work is to eradicate the human expert requirement for annotations completely.

Henceforth, we will focus on a relevant generic learning task for MSCC image analysis: the cell count is used as the target variable, which has to be estimated reliably at any point in time of the experiment and is chosen mainly for two reasons: (1) it allows for the extrapolation of other important attributes of the experiment, such as the growth delta over the last few time segments, as well as the overall growth rate, and (2) as a regression task, it is known to be especially difficult to be estimated accurately for unsupervised training methods, i.e., it can be inferred that tasks that are generally considered more simple, such as classification or segmentation, can also be solved with the methodology presented in Section 3.

In the following, we will aim for a solution that does not rely on any manually generated labels. Instead, we will rely on automatically generated artificial labels, i.e., use "fully automated supervision". To prevent misunderstandings, unsupervised deep learning would, in its most exclusive definition, not be able to solve the addressed task, since the lack of labels means that the regression loss cannot be calculated. Therefore, we refer to "unsupervised learning" for this task as the absence of manually curated labels for the experimental data. There needs to be a computable loss on the target variable to achieve actual training, which, in our case, can explicitly and efficiently be defined, based on the available symbolic semantics for auxiliary synthetic data.

Even self-training architectures such as Generative Adversarial Networks (GAN) and Variational Autoencoders (VAE) can only generate losses on predictions and reconstructions of the data, not on the target variable. The Siamese-like architecture described later will therefore not only train on natural data, created by the biotechnological experiments, but also on a collection of synthetic auxiliary data with automatically generated labels and therefore known ground truth. By training this architecture with a special learning scheme, it is not only possible to perform regression learning on the target variable, but also to achieve accuracy that approaches or, in some cases, exceeds the state of the art (see Section 4).

While our own previous work [4] will serve as a basis for the later comparison of results, we would like to clarify the differences between that work and this one in terms of approaches and goals. The novelty of [4] is state of the art accuracy in the domain of semi-supervised cell counting, achieved by transferring a pre-trained model to another type of microscopy data. Due to optimizations in the transfer process, the architecture presented there has also slightly outperformed the previous state of the art. In this work, we instead focus on unsupervised training with the modification of generating pseudo-synthetic images from natural images (and vice versa) in order to use the well-trained regressor that is accustomed to synthetic data representations. The earlier work would not be able to achieve meaningful regression for the fully unlabeled natural data used in this work because the loss of the regressor would not be defined for natural data.

Figure 1 shows examples from the MSCC experiments that we address in the following. It can be seen that lab-on-a-chip technology is used and that the data have a number of visual aspects that make them difficult for classical image processing solutions and non-specialized machine learning models to process. Namely, these are as follows:

- Smudges, in some cases larger than cells. Simple background filtering does not work, as these can move during the experiment.
- Ongoing cell divisions (Figure 1 right), making it unclear in some cases what the actual correct target variable would be, but giving a meaning to comma values as they can represent an ongoing division.
- Varying contrast and light conditions.
- Dying, appearance, and vanishing of cells.
- Overpopulation of the cell chamber or the end of an experiment due to escape of the cells.
- Overlapping and close adherence of cells.
- Continuous changes in the cell membrane and inner organelles, changing the orientation of cells, with variations in shape and perceived size.

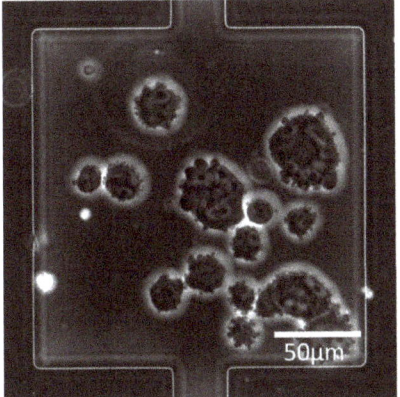 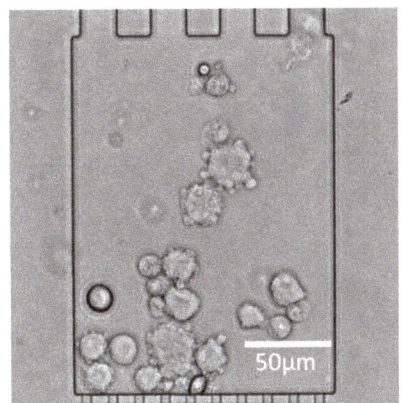

Figure 1. Samples from the data sets of CHO-K1 suspension growth. Bright-field microscopy image on the right, phase-contrast microscopy image on the left. Smudges on the chip can be seen in the form of faint, small circles within the fluid solution. The scale bars do not appear in the working data.

In this article, we propose a novel training scheme for a Siamese deep learning model that can optimally combine information provided by automatically generated synthetic data and real images such that no manual labeling of natural data is required. The contribution and novelty of this work are as follows:

- We achieve high prediction preciseness on the target variable where the state of the art fails to do so.
- We build an effective translation learning pipeline and show, on multiple microscopy data sets, that this pipeline is stable and reliable throughout this domain.
- We gain additional insight into the inner state of the neural network by performing translations twice (cycling), leading to critical parts of the architecture to optimize the network for the domain without overfitting to the specific data, thus contributing to the understanding of deep neural network representations, especially for Siamese networks [6].

In the following sections, we first give an overview of the current state of the art in this research field and take a brief look at previous works in this field of application. In Section 3, we address the underlying machine learning challenge and present our deep Siamese network architecture in detail. Then, the details of the proposed learning procedure are explained and it is analyzed how the unique architecture used affects the learning procedure. Thereafter, Section 4 contains the evaluation for real data sets and ablation studies, as well as the comparison to state of the art alternatives and baselines. Lastly, in Section 5, a discussion followed by a conclusion (see Section 6) completes the contribution.

2. Related Work

In the last few years, convolutional deep neural networks have become the state of the art for image processing that does not require human labor and for the majority of other computer vision tasks [7]. Especially for the task of counting in images, solutions have been worked on for over a decade now (see [8]). Applications in the biomedical domain have become common [9] and cell tracking approaches in images have been an ongoing field of study in recent years [10]. However, the optimization of such methods is often time-consuming and remains prone to errors.

Ulman et al. [11] propose a benchmark suite to compare different imaging technologies and extrapolate the strengths and limitations of different approaches to cell tracking, none of which have been determined as a final solution on this task, even the ones including interactions among bioimage analysis experts [12] or the distributed work of manual labeling [13]. Schmitz et al. [14] show the demand for fleshed out solutions by evaluating the currently used state of the art tools as insufficient for heterogeneity studies of the CHO-K1 mammalian cells that are present in the given data.

In addition, Brent et al. [15] used transfer learning to predict microscope images between different imaging technologies, but without sufficiently accounting for the wide variety of cell images and features. The approach by Falk et al. [16] provides one of the few toolboxes for cell tracking, albeit for adherent rather than suspension cells. It allows for transfer learning based on given models and novel data, whereby data set enrichment technologies limit the number of required samples.

In contrast to adherent cell lines, where already reported single cell cultivation studies [17,18] promise success, we address the more complex scenario of suspension cells with all their visual characteristics listed above, rendering analysis tools of adherent cells deficient. Earlier works have overcome some of the challenges, such as sufficient counting accuracy, by interactive design [19], or detecting overlapping instances in such imagery [20], but they are not yet sufficient for the unsupervised task at hand. Different contrast and light conditions have been addressed by Chen et al. [21]. The adherence of cells and overlaps have been addressed by Xie et al. [22], but additional visual features complicate the process and reduce the applicability of previous solutions.

Siamese networks have been used for a variety of tasks as they can help to facilitate few-shot learning or clustering of the data space by generalizing from unlabeled data. This is done in [23] for genome sequencing and in [24] for text data. These presented architectures are, however, specific to their domains and not applicable to image processing.

There are also Siamese networks that do work in the image processing domain, such as [25], but they focus on change detection as a binary segmentation, suitable for tracking single cells, but not for the regression task at hand. Ref. [26] uses Siamese networks and data augmentation, similar to our approach, but the training is supervised and addresses a four-class classification task. In [27], similar data augmentation and Siamese networks were used and the 20-class classification is closest to the regression task that we address, but the networks used are non-generative CNNs and the data are not used cyclically, rendering it not applicable for our work.

Furthermore, there are no deep learning models that easily and efficiently solve the task, as shown in [3] by comparing the recent state of the art EfficientNet [28] and classical image processing such as Watershed methods [29], and transfer models such as BigTransfer [30] are not reliably able to generate good cell counts by transferring a pretrained model to this domain, as can be seen in our earlier work [4].

Deepak Babu et al. [31] achieved acceptable accuracy for the regression task of crowd counting, a similar task; however, the training was semi-supervised. More generalized few-shot and even zero-shot learning has been done by Schönfeld et al. [32] by using aligned VAEs, achieving high precision, but only on the few-shot tasks, not the zero-shot ones. In our approach, we will fully focus on the idea of the integration of synthetic data, which can itself harvest its semantically meaningful generation, to avoid any additional manual labeling of natural data for training, therefore rendering even these related results insufficient.

Synthetic data have already been used in [33,34], but for natural scene and text recognition, or computer vision tasks more generally, mostly natural domains where powerful deep generative models can build on massive amounts of publicly available data. In contrast, we are interested in synthetic data that are prone to a reality gap due to the limited availability of natural data. In semi-supervised learning, models are often enriched by easily available unlabeled data that describe the underlying input distribution [35]. A view into when unlabeled data can improve the learning rate has been taken by Göpfert et al. [36], suggesting the usage of additional unlabeled data, be it synthetic or natural, as beneficial, confirmed for this case in Section 4. The impact of variability in auxiliary training data on convolutional networks specifically was tested in [37], but for 3D head reconstruction, not intrinsically usable in this domain.

The weight sharing used in our particular learning scheme was used previously to decrease network sizes and improve test and verification performance [38]. In Section 3.3, we show details on the specialized usage of this technique for our architecture.

Lastly, Uniform Manifold Approximation and Projection (UMAP) [39] is used to project the inner state of the network into a two-dimensional representation, allowing us to obtain a glance at the internal state of the latent representation and insight into how the data are processed. In Section 6, such a UMAP is discussed for interpretation.

3. Methodology

3.1. Natural Data

Image data applied in this study were obtained by MSCC of mammalian suspension cells, as introduced before in the literature [40]. The CHO-K1 cells were cultivated in polydimethylsiloxane (PDMS) glass chips. Perfusion of the device constantly provided the cultures with nutrients. An automated inverted microscope performed the live cell imaging, taking images of the relevant positions on-chip every 20 min. The data used in this work are split into two major parts according to the two microscopy technologies, namely bright-field microscopy and phase-contrast microscopy, abbreviated as BF and PC, which were used for the analysis of the architecture. Figure 2 shows example data from both microscopy technologies after the application of the preprocessing described below.

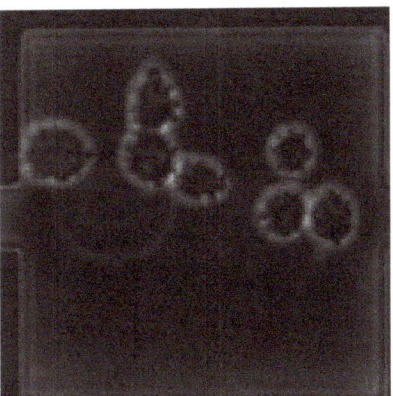
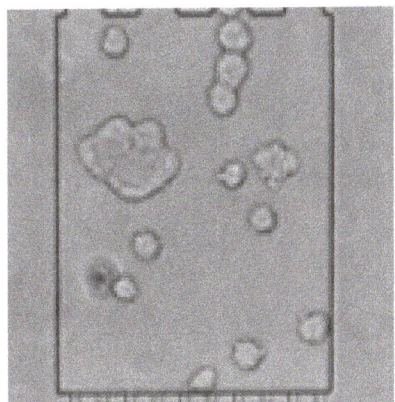

Figure 2. Samples from the natural data sets after application of various data enrichment techniques, described below. Phase-contrast technology on the left, bright-field technology on the right. The image resolution equals the working resolution.

Around 10,000 images were taken over the course of the experiments per microscopy technology; then, images of empty and fully filled cell chambers were removed, since, for these, the experiment had not started yet or the outcome of the experiment was already determined, respectively. In total, 2983 BF images and 3944 PC images remained relevant for the machine learning task. Around 20% of the data were labeled by hand exclusively for testing and will from here on be called Nat-L-Te (natural, labeled test data); the other 80 percent remain unlabeled and are used for training and called Nat-U-Tr (natural, unlabeled training data). The test data were split in half to obtain a verification data set and to prevent accidental specialized training on the test data over the course of the hyperparameter optimization. During the test data selection process, we ensured that full experimental runs as well as randomly picked images from the various experiment series were part of the test and verification data. Table 1 gives an overview over the different types of data sets used in our work.

Table 1. Overview of all data sets used. `Nat-U-Tr` contains natural, unlabeled training data; `Nat-L-Te` natural, labeled test data; `Syn-L-Tr` synthetic, labeled training data, and `Syn-L-Te` contains synthetic, labeled test data. For reasons described in Section 3.2, synthetic data have been generated in a 1:1 ratio to natural data. `Nat-PC` refers to all natural phase-contrast images (i.e., `Nat-L-Te` and `Nat-U-Tr`) and `Nat-BF` refers to all natural bright-field images, respectively. `Syn-PC` and `Syn-BF` denote the groups of training and test data for phase-contrast and bright-field data accordingly, and, lastly, `Nat` and `Syn` denote the full set of natural and synthetic data.

Data Set Name	No. of Phase-Contrast Images	No. of Bright-Field Images
Nat	Nat-PC	Nat-BF
Nat-U-Tr	3.152	2.469
Nat-L-Te	792	514
Syn	Syn-PC	Syn-BF
Syn-L-Tr	3.152	2.469
Syn-L-Te	792	514

We crop and rotate all images to center the cultivation chamber. Further data augmentation beyond this preprocessing is described in Section 3.2. We place our focus on the larger data set called `Nat-PC` from here on. It contains more experimental samples and the biological processes covered are more diverse. In addition, phase-contrast microscopy is more popular, and we will nonetheless show that our method also works reliably on the smaller `Nat-BF` data set, although the variations in cell positions, numbers, and sizes are lower in this data set and therefore the quality of these images is lower in terms of machine learning, similar to what might be the case for entirely different types of cells, such as plant cells.

To make the best use of the poor amount of experimental data, the following enrichment techniques are applied to the data. Flips along both image axes are followed by a random crop up to the edges of the cell chamber, not cropping away cells, except for the entrance tunnel, where precise cell detection is not required. The crop does complicate cell detection, as cells may be in positions where only the chamber rim and the outside of the chamber would be without the crop, but it proved necessary to allow cells to appear anywhere on the images to ensure uniform detection success that is barely affected by the position of the cells within an image. Then, a random rotation of 90° is performed and a randomly generated noise map is multiplied by a small weighting factor and applied to the image to simulate more fluctuation in the cells' visuals, since occasionally there are dead cells in the experimental data that do not change in appearance for multiple images. All augmentations are reapplied to the original data for every epoch of training with seed consistency to ensure reproducibility.

3.2. Synthetic Data

We propose a novel learning scheme in Section 3.3.2 that deals with synthetic data with known ground truth (i.e., the cell count) and a Siamese architecture that can abstract from the fact that the auxiliary data are synthetic. In addition to the common data set enrichment, generating proxy data allows us to create a wide variety of synthetic samples, which are inspired by the natural data, but not limited by their amount or variety.

By enriching the training procedure with synthetic data, we extinguish the need for natural labeled data. Synthetic data are easily obtained in this setting because the architecture does not require that the images are rendered realistically in all respects, such as morphological details. The 128×128 working resolution of the architecture makes the synthetic data generation undemanding, while maintaining sufficient intricacy of visual features such as overlapping (see Figure 3 left). For the specialized training procedure described below, we do not need to synthetically create images that are indistinguishable from natural ones, unlike current data augmentation schemes, such as proposed in the work [41]. This would require a considerate amount of engineering [37], i.e., human expert labor, exactly what we aim to mitigate. We rely merely on modeling simple ellipsoidal shapes to embody cells, ignoring details of the texture and the intricate morphology of real suspension cells. We imposed this limitation on ourselves to suggest that the learning procedure presented below should also work with other types of image data and is neither tailor-made for exactly these microscopy technologies nor requires extensive manual work to generate the most realistic synthetic data possible. In Section 3.3, we show that this approach is adequate for training our architecture described.

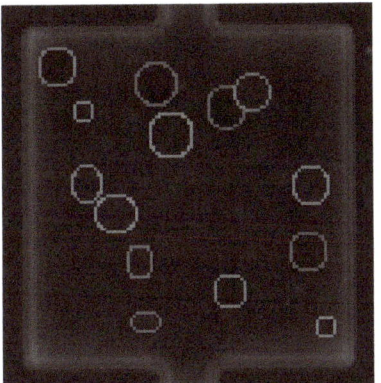 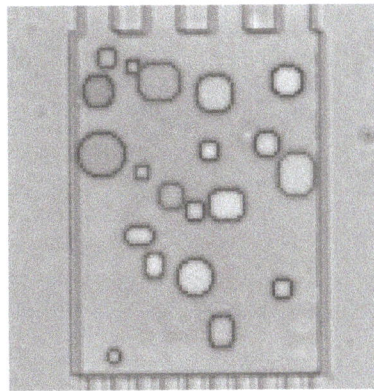

Figure 3. Examples of synthetic data. Syn-PC imagery on the left, Syn-BF imagery on the right. Backgrounds were generated by averaging over natural, nearly empty chamber images (including smudges) and cells are approximated by simple geometric ellipses, but given some of the intricate visual characteristics of natural cells, such as overlapping and differing luminosity, while factors that explicitly only hinder the architecture, such as cells escaping through the chamber funnels and complex visual features such as the inner organelles of cells, have not been recreated.

We ensured that the distribution of cell counts in the auxiliary data was sufficiently close, but not necessarily identical to that of the natural data sets. This allows for an unlimited amount of labeled training data, with only the processing time being the limiting factor for the potential to use enormous amounts of proxy data, not the availability of such. One problem remains, however, which is how to actually improve the regression performance on natural data. Using a large ratio of synthetic data compared to natural data would entail a separation of the two types of data in the inner representation of the network, resulting in high accuracy on the synthetic data, but low accuracy on the natural data (see Section 4). To prevent this separation, two major functionalities are proposed and have been implemented, described in more detail in the following paragraph.

The auxiliary data generator is highly adjustable and produces imagery with a given distribution of cells. As background images, we calculate the mean of the first 20% of data from the experimental series, expecting cell counts to be low and cells to be scattered, so that the background has no visible natural cells in it. The generator takes control of the overlaps, brightness, and blurriness of the cells' inner organelles as well as their membranes, the contrast with the background, a range of possible cell sizes, counts, and crop values, as well as the ellipsoidal deformation range as parameters. All these can be chosen by hand within the code package, or the default values can be used. Combined, these operations can be used to imitate most of the intricate features of the real data, such as ongoing divisions of cells, by requesting a small overlap along with noisy cell boundaries. Smudges, as in Figure 2, are not included because they are a confounding factor and are assumed to only hinder the training process. The cells have been given a roughly circular shape to approximately match the shape of the natural cells. To generate cells, positions are sampled randomly from the valid space, taking the parameter of possible overlaps into account, and are then randomly stretched, deformed, made noisy, and so on according to the chosen parameters; then, brightness fluctuation and Gaussian filters of varying strengths are added to increase the variety of cells in the data. This geometric form can easily be adjusted if natural cells in other data sets have different shape characteristics or when other camera setups produce different ambiences.

This data are generated fully automatically based on simple algorithmic principles and, as a baseline, a ratio between synthetic and natural data of 1:1 is used, since larger amounts increase the training time almost linearly, while the performance improves only with diminishing returns in our experiments. More details on this are given in Section 4. The imagery is produced algorithmically with seed consistency and can therefore be reproduced similarly to the data enrichment on the natural data and can be generated in an arbitrary amount.

3.3. Architecture and Learning Scheme

3.3.1. Architecture

Our aim is to provide reliable cell counting for the microscopic imaging of suspension cells, and since the experimental data are limited in their amount and without annotations, we assemble a novel learning scheme for the `Twin-VAE` architecture previously introduced by us to overcome these limitations.

The architecture circumvents the problem of differences in the appearance of auxiliary and real data by separating the data input for training according to their origin, but requires that the model creates a tightly coupled joint inner representation to avoid high training losses. This is realized by modifying a Variational Autoencoder (VAE), duplicating the outer layers of the encoder and decoder, accounting for the two data sets. Therefore, the weights of the inner layers of both encoder and decoder are shared, as well as the semantic bottleneck in between (see Figure 4). We decided to choose this architecture for the reasons mentioned in Section 2.

The specialized encoders consist of four two-dimensional convolutional layers with kernel sizes of 5 and strides of 2. They are initialized with an orthogonal basis [42]. In between layers, leaky rectified linear units (LReLUs) with a leakiness of 0.2 and a dropout of 0.1 have been added. The channels used for the convolutions in the encoders in order are 32, 64, 128, and 256. The weight-shared encoder contains a single two-dimensional convolutional layer with the same remaining attributes but 512 channels. It is followed by the bottleneck, consisting of three layers of fully connected neurons. The layer sizes are 512, 256, and 512, each with the same dropout as before. The weight-shared decoder therefore also has 512 channels and uses a two-dimensional transposed convolutional operator layer with identical strides and kernel sizes as above, followed by a batch normalization over a four-dimensional input and another LReLU with the same leakiness. The decoders designed for specific data each consist of a total of five layers with kernel sizes 5, 5, 5, 2, 6, and strides of 2, 2, 2, 1, 2, following the convention of a smaller second to last kernel followed by a large last kernel. Then, we include the same LReLUs and a sigmoidal activation function at the end.

The representation in the latent space is not only fed to to the weight-shared decoder, but also to a three-layer fully connected network of neurons as a regressor. The sizes of the layers are 256 and 128 and lastly 1. Linear layers and a dropout of 0.2 are used for the regressor. The rectified Adam (RAdam) [43] optimizer worked best for the training procedure.

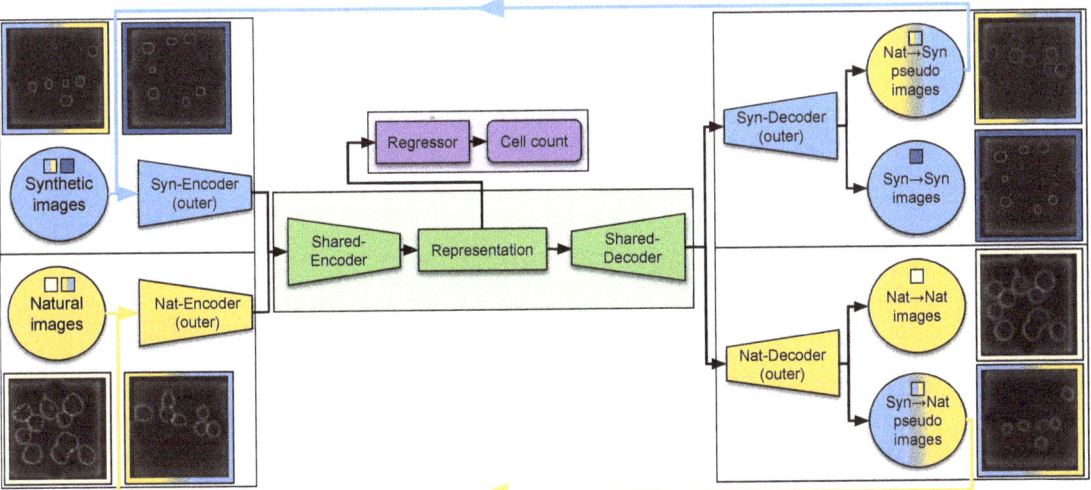

Figure 4. Visualization of the `Siamese-Cycle-VAE` (SC-VAE) architecture. The blue elements represent synthetic data handling, yellow elements depict natural data handling. Green elements are shared by the two VAEs and contain the inner representation of the cell imagery; purple elements result in an estimation for the cell count. The example images that are outlined are samples from the data sets on the left, with their respective results shown on the right. The translated images outlined with color transitioning have been generated from the opposite data type and are of particular interest, as well as the blue and yellow arrows pointing from right to left that indicate the reuse of decoded images. The examples at the very top left and bottom right are of the utmost importance, since they show the conversion of a synthetic image to a natural-looking one, which can then be used as a labeled pseudo-natural image for training of the regressor with natural-looking images.

One of the VAEs works on proxy data, and we will refer to it as `VAE-syn`, while the other one processes natural data (`VAE-nat`). The differing visual features of proxy and real data are accounted for in the separated layers, while the weight-shared encoder and decoder rely on and enforce a similar representation of the determinant image characteristics. In addition to auto-encoding, the architecture works on data with known labels in a supervised manner by the addition of a three-layer fully connected neural network regression model for the actual cell counting, based on the shared representation of the VAEs.

3.3.2. Learning Scheme

For images x of either natural or synthetic type $t \in \{\mathfrak{n}, \mathfrak{s}\}$, the VAEs are able to generate reconstruction losses $\text{Rec}(x, y)$ from reconstructed images y of their decoder. C^t_{Rec} are hand-crafted weighting factors to balance the different reconstruction costs. Choosing these weights to be large results in better reconstruction but worse regression. However, proper reconstruction quality is required to fabricate well-trained encoders, thus demanding the factors to not be too low. The loss for the reconstructions is defined as

$$REC_{loss}(x,t) = C^n_{\text{Rec}} \cdot \text{Rec}(x_n, y_n) + C^s_{\text{Rec}} \cdot \text{Rec}(x_s, y_s) \qquad (1)$$

For synthetic data with cell counts l from 1 to 30, we can also generate a regression loss $\text{Reg}(x_\mathfrak{s}, l)$. However, $\text{Reg}(x_\mathfrak{n}, l)$ cannot be calculated usually, since l is not known for these. In Section 4, our ablation studies show that this is insufficient for effective regression on natural data. The internal representations of the two types of images are naturally being separated in the bottleneck, precisely what VAEs are usually known and used for, resulting in high precision for synthetic data, but nearly arbitrary cell counts for natural data.

The specialized architecture allows an additional learning scheme to generate a loss for pseudo-natural data. This is done by encoding synthetic data in their specialized encoder, but decoding them with the decoder designed for natural data. This translation works both ways and will result in images $x_{s \to n}$ and $x_{n \to s}$.

This new type of data can now be used in the natural pipeline, creating new reconstruction losses $\text{Rec}(x_{s \to n}, y_{s \to n})$, which can be used to train the according encoder and decoder, especially enriching the data available for the natural pipeline immensely.

These images will be called translated or cycled images from here on and they expand the usable image types to $t \in \{n, s, s \to n, n \to s\}$. Examples of translated images and a pipeline of their generation can be seen in Figure 4. Cycled images also generate reconstruction losses, which are defined as

$$\text{REC-}T_{loss}(x,t) = C_{\text{Rec}}^{n \to s} \cdot \text{Rec}(x_{n \to s}, y_{n \to s}) + C_{\text{Rec}}^{s \to n} \cdot \text{Rec}(x_{s \to n}, y_{s \to n}) \qquad (2)$$

These images do not exactly resemble natural images and are distinguishable from them by the human eye, but they are actually close enough in their relevant characteristics to natural images that when designing the learning scheme in the way described below, they are not distinguished as fake natural images by the architecture, a beneficial circumstance that allows the simulation of labeled natural data and shared representations, which becomes more clear when taking a look at the UMAP of the internal representation later in Section 4.3.

This process also leads us to translated natural images, for which the label is known, and therefore allows for the generation of the regression loss $\text{Reg}(x_{s \to n}, l) \neq 0$. This way, we can train the full regression pipeline for natural data, without any labeled natural data at all. Henceforth, we refer to this process as translation learning.

Furthermore, we can translate the same images again, leading to two new types of images yet again $t \in \{x_{s \to n \to s}, x_{n \to s \to n}\}$, which should appear near-identical to the original reconstruction y. We first designed this difference to be a loss as well, but we later omitted this training step for hyperparameter optimization, as it did not improving the accuracy on cell counts significantly while adding another step of the more demanding image backpropagation to the pipeline. However, we still create these bilateral translations for specialized top-performing models (see Table 2) and for reasons mentioned below. Since the cycling of data through the different types is what allows the architecture to perform a regression task on unlabeled natural data, we call it Siamese-Cycle-VAE or SC-VAE for short, and variants with enabled bilateral learning cycles will be called SC-VAE-B from here on.

Table 2. Evaluation of all baselines and SC-VAE on the data sets Nat-PC, Nat-BF, Syn-PC and Syn-BF. For each method and data set, we report the mean absolute (MAE), the mean relative error (MRE), and the accuracy. Ultimately, only performance on natural data (Nat) is important, but we also report the performance on synthetic data (Syn) to provide further context. We use an upward arrow ↑ to indicate that higher is better; a downward arrow ↓ means lower is better. The best results achieved per category are marked in bold, (ss) denotes a semi-supervised method, (u) an unsupervised method.

Method	MAE (Syn) ↓	MRE (Syn) ↓	Acc. (Syn) ↑	MAE (Nat) ↓	MRE (Nat) ↓	Acc. (Nat) ↑
		PC (phase-contrast microscopy)				
EfficientNet (ss)	4.987	79.4%	5.0%	1.67	25.12%	23.4%
BiT (ss)	N/A	N/A	N/A	2.32	29.7%	25.4%
Twin-VAE (ss)	**0.09**	0.68%	68.2%	0.60	5.92%	57.8%
Transfer Twin-VAE (ss)	0.15	0.43%	85.0%	0.66	6.46%	53.7%
Dual Transfer Twin-VAE (ss)	0.12	**0.43%**	**85.0%**	0.58	5.56%	58.7%
Watershed (u)	0.94	18.0%	24.0%	1.66	29.0%	23.1%
C-VAE (u)	0.24	2.65%	54.2%	1.03	19.1%	28.9%
S-VAE (u)	**0.09**	0.53%	76.3%	2.64	41.2%	11.6%
SC-VAE (u)	0.11	0.83%	66.1%	0.49	5.16%	61.7%

Table 2. Cont.

Method	MAE (Syn) ↓	MRE (Syn) ↓	Acc. (Syn) ↑	MAE (Nat) ↓	MRE (Nat) ↓	Acc. (Nat) ↑
SC-VAE-B (u)	0.10	0.81%	67.9%	0.48	5.12%	61.8%
BF (bright-field microscopy)						
EfficientNet (ss)	6.502	67.1%	4.5%	1.13	17.2%	33.9%
BiT (ss)	N/A	N/A	N/A	1.79	22.45%	38.7%
Twin-VAE (ss)	0.48	4.27%	60.1%	0.68	7.6%	53.2%
Transfer Twin-VAE (ss)	0.40	3.87%	66.6%	0.52	5.47%	60.7%
Dual Transfer Twin-VAE (ss)	0.35	3.73%	66.8%	0.51	5.43%	60.8%
Watershed (u)	1.92	39.0%	2.0%	2.39	32.0%	32.0%
C-VAE (u)	0.67	5.72%	50.8%	1.96	21.8%	26.3%
S-VAE (u)	0.33	3.66 %	67.3%	2.09	34.2%	18.6%
SC-VAE (u)	0.41	3.88%	62.5%	0.60	7.1%	56.6%
SC-VAE-B (u)	0.39	3.77%	62.6%	0.56	6.51%	58.7%

As mentioned above, we also generate pseudo-synthetic data $x_{n \to s}$ from natural data (blue arrow in Figure 4). Since, for these pseudo-data, annotations are unknown, they cannot be used to train the regression process, but they can be used for two different purposes. The first is balancing out the encoders and decoders, since, with the learning scheme described above, the synthetic pipeline will go through more training steps than the natural one, although this is the one that should be especially well-trained, as the minimization of regression losses on natural data is the actual goal of this learning scheme. In this way, the natural training pipeline can also be trained on many more cell arrangements than the few that natural images provide, since even with a multitude of data augmentation techniques, the generalization of encoding and decoding can be improved by this step (see Section 4).

Secondly, the decodings of translated synthetic images $y_{n \to s}$ can be used as stability checks of the latent space for the different types of data. Badly decoded pseudo-synthetic images imply a larger than wanted differentiation of natural and synthetic images in the bottleneck. More on this is given in Section 4.1.

Considering the loss functions, let $r(x)$ be the estimated cell count and l remain the label. The mean-squared error (MSE) $||r(x) - l||^2$ and the binary cross-entropy (BCE) $-l \cdot log(r(x)) + (1 - l) \cdot log(1 - r(x))$ yielded similar results as in our previous works, and both resulted in more precise cell counts than common alternatives; therefore, extensive testing has been done with both, but ultimately the MSE was chosen as the default, since it is easier to find appropriate coefficients for the different types of losses due to the diminishing nature of MSE. The weight factors determine the importance of the counting accuracy and change over the course of the training procedure, since deriving accurate cell counts on natural data from synthetic and translated data requires preceding training of the encoders and decoders. The associated $REG_{loss}(x,y)$ term is defined as

$$REG_{loss}(x, l, t) = C_{Reg}^{s,l} \cdot Reg(x_s, l) + C_{Reg}^{s \to n,l} \cdot Reg(x_{s \to n}, l) \qquad (3)$$

When using BCE, the decoder loss factors decays over time with a decaying rate of 3×10^{-5} per epoch. This is necessary because the BCE does not decrease significantly during training, but needs to diminish over time to increase the importance of low regression losses $Reg(x, l)$.

Since it is beneficial for the prevention of overfitting to generate latent vectors that are sufficiently close to a normal distribution, we aim for homogeneous representations of synthetic and natural data in the embedding space of the architecture by applying a regularization cost $\mathcal{D}_{KL}$, which is applied in the form of the Kullback–Leibler divergence (KLD) of the standard VAE [44]. This loss will also ensure that the inner representations of natural, synthetic, and both types of cycled data stay similar, allowing us to use the special training procedure described above. This cost is applied for natural, synthetic, and both types of translated data and is defined as follows:

$$KLD_{loss}(x,t) = C_{\mathcal{D}_{KL}}^{n,n \to s} \cdot \mathcal{D}_{KL}(x_{n,n \to s}) + C_{\mathcal{D}_{KL}}^{s,s \to n} \cdot \mathcal{D}_{KL}(x_{s,s \to n}) \quad (4)$$

All coefficient factors have to be chosen mindfully, balancing the main target of punishing incorrect cell counts on natural data and relaxing the importance of details in visual reconstruction, but not undervaluing the KLD at the same time. Doing so can make the training procedure unstable, while applying very large regularization costs hinders the learning process and slows it down. To minimize the number of hyperparameters that have to be optimized by hand, the weighting factors for the $\mathcal{D}_{KL}$ losses have been grouped and a Bayesian optimization [45] in the form of a Gaussian process regressor [46] was used to quickly find baseline values for the most important hyperparameters, such as the learning rate and the loss weight factors.

We combine these losses to form our overall $SCVAE_{loss}(x,l,t)$, use the coefficients of the different terms to balance the impacts between natural, synthetic, and both types of translated images, and handle input images with missing cell counts by fixing $C_{Reg}^{n,l} = C_{Reg}^{n \to s,l} = 0$:

$$SCVAE_{loss}(x,l,t) = REC_{loss}(x,t) + REC\text{-}T_{loss}(x,t) + REG_{loss}(x,l,t) + KLD_{loss}(x,t) \quad (5)$$

3.3.3. Baselines

For the evaluation in the upcoming section, several baselines have been gathered, to enable a meaningful comparison with the state of the art. The first baseline is a widely practiced classical computer vision pipeline. First, the input images are cropped to only contain the cell chamber, and are then blurred with an averaging kernel-based filter; then, a thresholding filter is applied, followed by a watershed segmentation [29]. The regions of the segmented image are counted and used as a cell estimation. In order to find suitable parameters for this learning scheme, an exhaustive grid search was performed for each data set BF and PC. The code repository contains the best hyperparameters found. We refer to this pipeline as Watershed in the following.

As a second baseline, we fine-tuned a pre-trained state of the art deep convolution neural network, specifically a variant of EfficientNet [28]. We replace the last layer of the pre-trained network with a fully connected layer that outputs a single value, and train it to predict the cell count for a given input image. We apply the same hyperparameter optimization as for our own method, and generate the same data augmentation. Since EfficientNet is a variable architecture that comes in different sizes, referred to as EfficientNet-B0, EfficientNet-B1, and so on, we evaluated EfficientNet-B0 through EfficientNet-B3 and found that the smallest variant EfficientNet-B0 performed best, while larger variants performed progressively worse. We considered to instead use EfficientNetV2 [47], but our preliminary results showed that the same performance degradation applies to its larger variants as well, and since EfficientNet-B0 outperformed the smallest EfficientNetV2-S variant, we retained it and refer to this fine-tuned convolutional neural network as EfficientNet hereafter.

As a third baseline, we compare a state of the art transfer learning model from Kolsenikov et al. called BiT, which produces highly accurate classification results on Cifar-100 and similar data sets in a few-shot learning case of 1 to 10 examples per class. BiT consists of the classical ResNet [48] architecture, but with very long pre-training times on large image sets and a custom hyperrule that determines the training time and learning rate during transfer depending on the size of the new data set. Changes to the hyperrule were tested, but did not cause any significant improvement in accuracy; therefore, the values provided by the authors were used. BiT is given all the natural and synthetic training data per epoch, so it can come up with meaningful cell counts on natural data by abstracting from the labeled synthetic data. We valued the possible cell counts from 1 to 30 as classes, to account for the difference in training methodology.

In addition, we compare our own previous work Twin-VAE (see [3]) and its alterations Transfer Twin-VAE and Dual Transfer Twin-VAE (see [4]). These are based on the same architecture, but perform semi-supervised learning techniques for which the same data are used, albeit with partial annotations on the natural training data of 5–10%. Although this circumstance should allow for higher accuracy on the counting task, the optimized pipeline and cyclic data reuse of the new Siamese-Cycle-VAE is able to keep up with and in some cases even outperform its predecessors, despite not being given any manual labels at all. More on this is given below.

Lastly, ablation studies are done to ensure and show that the specific architectural details and principles of the learning scheme are helpful and optimize the training procedure and therefore the accuracy on the regression task. One study will be called C-VAE from here on. In this alteration of the network, there are no specialized Siamese encoders and decoders, but the cyclic structure is kept. C-VAE should still be able to make meaningful cell predictions, albeit that the abstraction between natural and synthetic data has to happen in the inner layers of the VAE. The cyclic structure and the difference between original and reconstructed images can still help the architecture to enrich the data in a more extensive way than classical data augmentation alone can. The second study is called S-VAE. Here, the Siamese architecture is kept, but we omit the cycling and do not use the reconstructed image data as new input, but merely as reconstruction loss, as in the standard VAE. As there are no labels on the natural data and there is no translated pseudo-natural imagery with labels either, the regressor lacks a loss to meaningfully train for this type of data directly, but could possibly abstract from the differentiation between natural and synthetic data in the latent space and still achieve adequate accuracy on cell counting.

4. Results

As for the hyperparameter choices, the best results were achieved with decoder loss factors $C_{\text{Rec}}^{\text{n}} = 1 \times 10^2$ and $C_{\text{Rec}}^{\text{s}} = 2 \times 10^2$, with the higher loss on synthetic data accounting for the higher image variety of these images, while $C_{\text{Rec}}^{\text{n} \to \text{s}} = C_{\text{Rec}}^{\text{s} \to \text{n}} = 5 \times 10^1$ resulted in the lowest reconstruction losses. While not mandatory to minimize, a degradation in the deconstruction loss of translated images is almost always coupled with lower regression losses. The regressor loss factors for synthetic data $C_{\text{Reg}}^{\text{s}}$ and pseudo-natural data $C_{\text{Reg}}^{\text{s} \to \text{n}}$ are both set to 5 and should inversely account for the ratio between the according types of data. The KLD factor $C_{\mathcal{D}_{\text{KL}}} = 1$ yields the best results for the larger data set Nat-PC, while slightly larger factors work better for Nat-BF, constraining the inner representations of synthetic, natural, and translated images to be coupled tightly. Faster convergence was observed for smaller KLD factors, but the learning scheme tended to separate more between data types, resulting in better reconstructions but poorer regressions. Figure 5 shows the combined losses and indicates convergence.

In addition, a soft weight decay of 2×10^{-5} per epoch, a constant learning rate of 0.75×10^{-5}, and delaying the start of the regressor by 25 epochs are used to achieve the following results. Batch sizes of 128 for both types of microscopy imagery work best and the training runs for up to 20,000 epochs, as there are no significant improvements after this. Ablation studies with more synthetic data relative to natural data have been done as well. In general, the architecture appears to converge faster when measured by epochs, but when taking the increase in training batches per epoch into account and therefore measuring by the number of computations, the training speed is marginally lower in all cases, so we retain the 1:1 ratio.

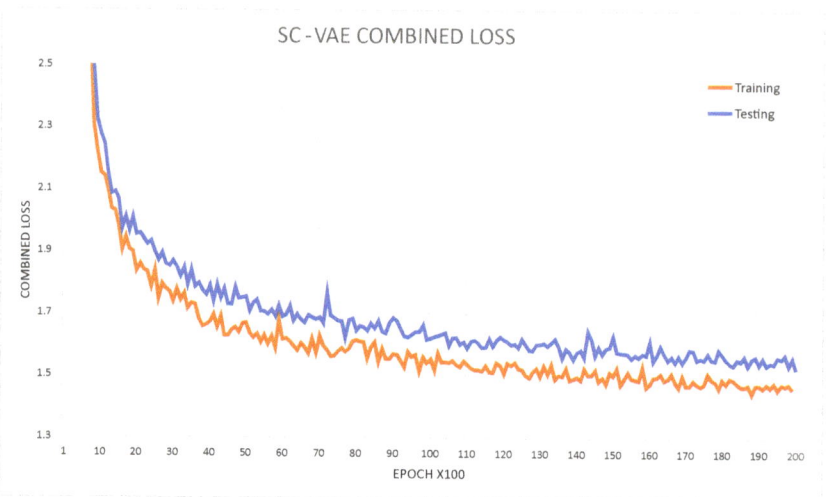

Figure 5. Visualization of the combined losses of SC-VAE top-performing model during training with regularly applied tests, in this case of Nat-PC. It can be seen that after 20,000 epochs, convergence is imminent, but has not fully been reached. Accuracy on cell counts does not improve significantly after this point; only image reconstruction quality does. Since the primary goal is not to diminish the reconstruction and normalization losses to zero, but rather to balance out the different losses, the combined loss can only indirectly be interpreted as a convergence indicator. Nevertheless, larger and faster descents in the combined loss still resemble well-trained models, even if this is insufficient as a sole indicator of such.

4.1. Comparison

We present the results of our method and the comparative baselines in Table 2. The mean relative error (MRE) is a normalized error, taking the ground truth into account, i.e., in high cell count images, small absolute deviations do not increase the error as much as they do for low cell count images. When interpreting experimental results as a biological expert, in most cases, this is the more meaningful indication over the mean absolute error (MAE), which serves as the typical indicator in terms of a regression task. The bilateral alteration SC-VAE-B that uses fully cycled images (back and forth) results in marginal but reliable improvements, assimilating representations in the latent space, and should be considered our top candidate.

Our SC-VAE consistently outperforms the other state of the art methods Watershed, BiT, and EfficientNet by a wide margin. SC-VAE and its alteration SC-VAE-B correctly estimate around 62 % of the cell counts for the Nat-PC data set, and their predictions differ on average by only 0.5 cells from the true cell counts of the images, and they achieve approximately 5.1 % MRE. For the smaller Nat-BF data set, SC-VAE-B accomplishes 0.56 MAE, 6.5 % MRE, and 58.7 % accuracy. While Dual Transfer Twin-VAE achieves slightly better results for these data, they are attained by semi-supervised training, commonly not even compared to unsupervised methods. As such, Siamese-Cycle-VAE holds up against semi-supervised training methods and even exceeds them the case of the larger Nat-PC data set, making it suitable for reliable cell counting with various microscopy techniques.

Moreover, we see that Siamese-Cycle-VAE performs well across the entire range of cell counts in Nat-PC and Nat-BF. By contrast, Watershed and EfficientNet struggle with images that contain few cells, which is the most important range of cell counts for biological tasks, such as estimating the growth rate.

The ablation C-VAE that feeds all data through the same encoder and decoder results in accuracy on synthetic data that is inferior to the other methods, even more so for the important accuracy on natural data. By using the reconstructed images as new input, the learning scheme resembles the optimized scheme of SC-VAE in such a way that visual intricacy on natural data is simplified, but not on the same level as SC-VAE..

S-VAE, on the other hand, worked best on synthetic data, especially so for Nat-BF, but for both types of microscopy data, the MRE and accuracy on the natural data are far from the results from SC-VAE. No translated natural data are generated by S-VAE, which is missing the regression loss for natural data completely. Cell counts on natural data are not random since there is still the shared encoder to unify the two types of data, but since accuracies differ vastly between natural and synthetic data, the S-VAEs encoder fails to do so because of a missing incentive.

4.2. Image Reconstruction and Representation

An analysis of the reconstruction abilities of Siamese-Cycle-VAE is useful to ensure that the shared representation is meaningful, even though our main aim is automatic cell counting, not perfect image reconstruction.

During the training of Siamese-Cycle-VAE, the image inputs are processed by their respective encoder, followed by the general, weight-shared encoder, represented in the bottleneck of the architecture; they are then processed by the shared decoder and finally reconstructed by their specialized decoder accordingly (see Figure 4). The same is true for auxiliary data and both types of translated pseudo-imagery. To ensure that the actual regressive task works as intended for natural images, it must be able to benefit from synthetic data representations in the latent space, so the learned representation must be shared by the four types of data.

This can be verified by encoding natural images with their appropriate encoder, but performing the decoding with the decoder that is designed and trained for auxiliary images, the counterpart to the opposite conversion, which is done in every epoch of training. Minimal changes in the stages of the images that are converted back and forth indicate the close coupling of the representations. The closer the different data types are transformed into the latent space, the greater the potential gain for regression on natural data. Moreover, the conversion makes this fact interpretable on a visual level.

We show examples of perfect translations in Figure 6. For these samples, a natural image is encoded and then decoded as a synthetic image. The number of cells remains unchanged, and the position and size of the cells are also maintained. However, the overall appearance is simplified: Siamese-Cycle-VAE learned to remove noise and to break down the reconstruction to the essentials. Even the very large smudge on the left natural image has not been reconstructed; although it will cause an increased loss in the reconstruction, the weighting of the loss factors makes it more acceptable to forfeit image reconstruction precision in favor of the regression. On the right side, it can be seen that the output does indeed appear more similar to natural data than the synthetic input does, while fine details such as the noisy borders are not recreated.

The ongoing cell division shown in Figure 7 is a prime example to understand how Siamese-Cycle-VAE works. The membrane of the bottom right cell is not fully enclosed and there is no overlap, since a fine bright border of the underlying cell would be seen through the top cell. However, two cell cores can clearly be seen and a human expert would presumably count this situation as two cells, which is exactly what Siamese-Cycle-VAE does. The prediction of 9.65 instead of 10 can be understood as uncertainty and a slightly earlier stage of the division would have arguably led to a slightly smaller prediction, which, when rounded, would be the correct cell count again. The effect of simplified visuals also happens in these non-translated reconstructions; the smudges on the Nat-BF sample are clearly fainter and, in the left image, even the high-contrast dead cell residue on the left is not recreated. This clearly indicates that even when Siamese-Cycle-VAE does not predict the cell count perfectly in an image, the comparison between the original and reconstructed image is useful to understand where an error occurs.

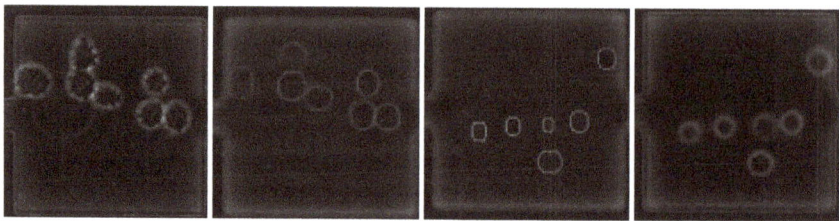

Figure 6. Examples of translations used for cycling. From left to right: natural image, according translated image from natural to synthetic, synthetic image, according translated image from synthetic to natural. Compositions stay the same but the visual style has been transferred. The translated images can now be used in the encoder designed for the type of data that they are imitating and thereby serves a special purpose for each of the two translations: enriching the VAEs process of encoding and decoding with unseen data, which is especially helpful for the natural coders due to the limited availability of natural data ($syn \rightarrow nat$), and allowing the regressor that is well trained to handle synthetic data to count cells in translated natural data ($nat \rightarrow syn$).

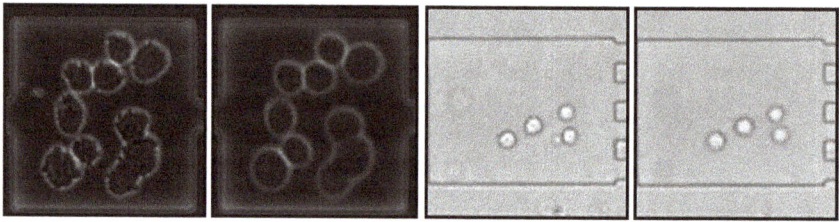

Figure 7. Examples of synthetic-looking reconstructions of a natural images. The reconstructions are to the right of their natural counterparts. The composition of cells stays the same, positions are near identical, cell sizes are preserved, and smudges are not recreated, or, if so, they are very faint, semantically not impacting the regression task too much, since it learns to extract the encoding of large, high-contrast cell boundaries. When rounded to full numbers, the cell counts of 10 on the left and 4 on the right match exactly. Without rounding, on the left side, the predicted cell count is too low by 0.35. This can be interpreted semantically as the ongoing cell division that happens in the bottom right of the image.

4.3. Shared Representation

`Siamese-Cycle-VAE`'s ability to translate back and forth between natural and synthetic images illustrates the semantically shared representation of all four types of data learned by the autoencoder. Below, we visualize this shared representation. Because each image is encoded as a 256-dimensional vector, we need to reduce the dimensionality to do so. Uniform Manifold Approximation and Projection (UMAP) [39] has established itself as the state of the art for nonlinear dimensionality reduction. It computes a topology-preserving embedding that can be used for semantic interpretations of representations. In the resulting embedding (see Figure 8), we see that synthetic and natural data occupy the same space, and we can even observe that both types of translated images also lie on the same projection space.

Therefore, UMAP is unable to separate the latent representations of the different types of data and this allows us to visually understand what is meant by tightly coupled representations. UMAPs are non-parametric; therefore, the axis and scale have no meaning other than the preserving of relations. Since we can observe that, along the main axis, the cell count has been chosen as the most mandatory factor, it is the main determining factor in the latent space, providing perfect conditions for a well-functioning regressor, since images are represented vastly differently, dependent on the number of cells that they include.

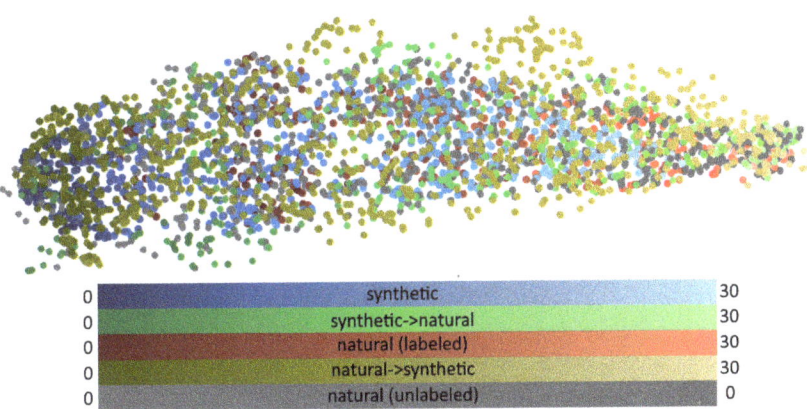

Figure 8. Embedding of the trained representations, determined via UMAP. Illustrated are natural, labeled test samples (red circles); unlabeled test samples (grey); synthetic samples (blue), and both types of translated images, $syn \rightarrow nat$ (green) and $nat \rightarrow syn$ (yellow). Cell counts are separated by brightness, with darker dots indicating low cell counts and brighter dots indicating a high cell count. Since UMAPs are non-parametric, axis and scale have no meaning, but relations are preserved. Since dots become visibly brighter from left to right and this is the main axis along which the dots are separated, UMAP has determined this direction to be the most important and it directly corresponds to cell counts. Simultaneously, natural and auxiliary images do not become separated. If this were the case, it would contradict a truly shared representation between the different types of data.

It can be seen that data that have been translated from synthetic to natural (green) tend to encapsulate the synthetic data (blue); this is more so the case for the natural data that are translated to synthetic (yellow), which encapsulate the original natural data (red and gray). This can be interpreted as semantic coverage, which means that, for every possible natural, unlabeled data point, there are labeled data points nearby, demanding only minor abstractions of the regressor to be able to achieve a meaningful cell prediction.

Another way to ensure meaningful representations and condensed information in the bottleneck of the `Siamese-Cycle-VAE` architecture is to sample images from noise vectors and check two aspects of them: first, they should show deceptive images that could be reconstructions from real data of their type, and, secondly, slight changes to the random vectors should result in similar but not identical images. Both behaviors can be observed in Figure 9; therefore, the latent representation contains information in a semantically meaningful way.

The distribution of the UMAP also suggests that certain areas of the latent space serve to represent a determinable number of cells. We tested this and found that there are indeed areas in the latent space that lead to the reconstruction of low cell counts, and, within the local area, all reconstructions result in low cell counts, while other areas can be found that represent the presence of high cell counts in input images, and this is exactly what is reconstructed by the decoders, when the latent space is sampled in this area.

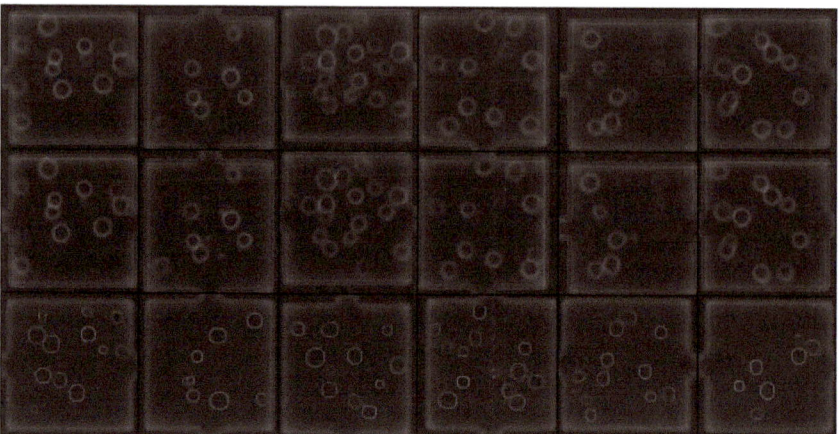

Figure 9. Samples generated from the latent space by inputting noise vectors and deconstructing them with the natural (row 1) and synthetic (row 3) decoder. Appropriate cell imagery can be reconstructed from these; consequently, the latent space meaningfully represents the important information of possible input images for this domain. Adding and subtracting tiny amounts to and from these vectors results in semantically similar images (row 2) with often only one cell more or less, where the cells are slightly larger or smaller and have changed position slightly, while samples from a completely different part of the latent space yield completely different images.

5. Discussion

We now discuss the limitations of this architecture and state possible revisions to overcome them. During analysis, we found that for very small cells in the natural data, only subpar precision is achieved. Since the working resolution of the architecture is 128×128 pixels, these cells are barely visible in the downscaled versions of the images and can therefore not yield low error estimations. In future work, the working resolution could be doubled per axis, which requires new layers in the specialized encoders and decoders, but leaves the rest of the architecture unchanged. Alternatively, local crops of quarters of the images could be used, allowing a quasi-double resolution by answering the question of cell count with the sum of 4 quarters.

Large and high-contrast light reflections can also be problematic for satisfactory regression. When scaling down an image such as the phase-contrast microscopy on the left in Figure 1, the smaller reflections are merely a single bright pixel in the working resolution, too small to impact the cell count. When these reflections are larger, as with the one on the very left, it can lead to quite high reconstruction losses and cause the architecture to replicate these, although they should be filtered out and ignored. To overcome this, a step in the image preprocessing could be added that seeks this effect and dims the affected area. More elegantly, the reconstruction loss could be capped with local maximums, so that the high deviations that derive from this are not fully accounted for in the training of the network. Further, although the proxy image generator is merely auxiliary content for this work, currently, new microscopy imagery makes it obligatory to find appropriate parameters for the generator, accounting for cell sizes, border brightness, etc. A more sophisticated generator could be able to algorithmically generate auxiliary data automatically from given natural data.

Due to the different types of network parts present in the architecture and the resulting loss of Equation (5), it can be difficult to understand the importance of optimization of the different parts of the composite loss. Forcing better reconstructions by setting the according weight factors to high numbers may bring the disadvantage of worse regression, but this is not necessary, because, to some extent, better reconstructions will also help to ensure that the existence of cells is represented in the latent space, which is a major requirement for the regressor to achieve high accuracy.

The amount of hand-crafting meta-parameters could be reduced by the more extensive use of meta-learning systems, such as a modified regressor for the Gaussian process that we used, to enable the creation of a simple tool that users of a complete solution can utilize for cell counting during live cell imaging experiments. Thus far, alternating between automated meta-learning and hand-crafting with multiple parallel runs with different meta-parameter choices has been utilized to find good parameters quickly.

Implementations for the real-time, continuous estimation of cell counts in experiment monitoring would be a practical way to make this architecture and its learning scheme easily usable for biologists. Despite these limitations, with SC-VAE, it is possible to outperform state of the art alternatives, sometimes by a wide margin, and it can compete with its semi-supervised predecessor.

Surprising findings were that the weight factors of the KLD loss in Equation (4) can be quite low and therefore hinder the learning process from ensuring shared representations only very little, only if the parameters of the other losses are chosen well. We are inconclusive regarding what makes them well chosen, but the parameters that we found allow a very high loss factor for regression, especially for translated pseudo-natural images, without the representations becoming separated or the loss or the architecture becoming unstable, a common outcome in other literature when weighing the loss of the main task as too high and devaluing the loss of indirect tasks or those only achievable late in sequential learning schemes.

We will now conclude the contribution and summarize our findings.

6. Conclusions

With our specialized learning scheme, we created a basis for automated cell counting in the domain of microfluidic cell cultivations, and we presented a workflow for the unsupervised image recognition of mammalian suspension cells, obtained by live cell imaging. The auxiliary data generator presented delivers arbitrary amounts of synthetic microscopy imagery and, with only minor adjustments, can also generate images for entirely different types of cells and microscopy technologies. SC-VAE demands only rough similarity between synthetic and natural data, omitting the laborious task of replicating the intricate visual details of the natural data. The presented technique operates independently of the actual cell sizes of the organism being studied, and the adaptation to, e.g., elongated bacterial cells or plant cells can be done easily.

In Section 1, we mentioned that the manual procedure of labeling such imagery by human experts is not feasible and requires automation. We overcome this issue by delivering an end-to-end solution that is usable not only by experts, requires no hand-labeled data at all, and still competes with semi-supervised state of the art solutions that do require manual labels. We also present an innovative means of gaining insights into the latent spaces of these type of Siamese networks by comparing cycled images, i.e., images converted back and forth, to their original counterparts and by translating natural data to pseudo-synthetic data to particularly ensure the stability of the internal representations and a meaningful latent space distribution from which we can sample freely, in such a way that is understandable to the human eye.

The Siamese-Cycle-VAE architecture helps us to understand what requirements exist for the presence, quantity, and quality of natural data in the image processing domain, specifically related to an unsupervised regression task.

Moreover, we show that our specialized learning scheme grants SC-VAE the ability to abstract from the fact that data are synthetic by ensuring that all elements of the architecture that tend to discriminate between different types of data are vastly overruled by elements that do not tend to do so. Only due to the novel learning scheme that we present, it is possible to generate a meaningful loss without any labeled original data.

We encourage future learning methods and architectures in other domains but with similar research questions and obstacles, especially the lack of labeled data, to adapt the general idea of this machine learning scheme and architecture in the future, albeit with different types of difficulties, especially for those cases where the generation of auxiliary data cannot be directly coupled to a target variable or classification, i.e., domains where the full coverage of possible natural data by synthetic data is not trivial.

Author Contributions: Conceptualization, methodology, software, validation, formal analysis, investigation, resources, data curation, writing, and visualization have been performed by D.S. Review, supervision, project administration, and funding acquisition have been performed by B.H. All authors have read and agreed to the published version of the manuscript.

Funding: This research was funded by the Ministerium für Kultur und Wissenschaft NRW, grant number NW21-059A (SAIL).

Data Availability Statement: We have made the data sets available at https://pub.uni-bielefeld.de/record/2960030 (accessed 27 February 2023) and make the source code available at https://github.com/dstallmann/cyclic_siamese_learning (accessed 27 February 2023).

Conflicts of Interest: The authors declare no conflict of interest. The funders had no role in the design of the study, in the collection, analyses, or interpretation of data, in the writing of the manuscript, or in the decision to publish the results.

References

1. Anggraini, D.; Ota, N.; Shen, Y.; Tang, T.; Tanaka, Y.; Hosokawa, Y.; Li, M.; Yalikun, Y. Recent advances in microfluidic devices for single-cell cultivation: methods and applications. *Lab Chip* **2022**, *22*, 1438–1468. [CrossRef] [PubMed]
2. Sachs, C.C. Online high throughput microfluidic single cell analysis for feed-back experimentation. Ph.D. Thesis, Technische Hochschule Aachen, Aachen, Germany, 2018. RWTH-2018-231907. [CrossRef]
3. Stallmann, D.; Göpfert, J.P.; Schmitz, J.; Grünberger, A.; Hammer, B. Towards an Automatic Analysis of CHO-K1 Suspension Growth in Microfluidic Single-cell Cultivation. *Bioinformatics* **2020**, *37*, 3632–3639. [CrossRef] [PubMed]
4. Kenneweg, P.; Stallmann, D.; Hammer, B. Novel transfer learning schemes based on Siamese networks and synthetic data. *Neural Comput. Appl.* **2022**, *35*, 8423–8436. [CrossRef] [PubMed]
5. Theorell, A.; Seiffarth, J.; Grünberger, A.; Nöh, K. When a single lineage is not enough: Uncertainty-Aware Tracking for spatio-temporal live-cell image analysis. *Bioinformatics* **2019**, *35*, 1221–1228. [CrossRef]
6. Jacob, G.; Rt, P.; Katti, H.; Arun, S. Qualitative similarities and differences in visual object representations between brains and deep networks. *Nat. Commun.* **2021**, *12*, 1872. [CrossRef]
7. Ioannidou, A.; Chatzilari, E.; Nikolopoulos, S.; Kompatsiaris, I. Deep Learning Advances in Computer Vision with 3D Data: A Survey. *ACM Comput. Surv.* **2017**, *50*, 3042064. [CrossRef]
8. Lempitsky, V.; Zisserman, A. Learning To Count Objects in Images. In *Proceedings of the Advances in Neural Information Processing Systems 23*; Lafferty, J.D., Williams, C.K.I., Shawe-Taylor, J., Zemel, R.S., Culotta, A., Eds.; Curran Associates, Inc.: Red Hook, NY, USA, 2010; pp. 1324–1332.
9. Razzak, M.I.; Naz, S.; Zaib, A., Deep Learning for Medical Image Processing: Overview, Challenges and the Future. In *Classification in BioApps: Automation of Decision Making*; Springer: Cham, Switzerland, 2018; pp. 323–350. [CrossRef]
10. Moen, E.; Bannon, D.; Kudo, T.; Graf, W.; Covert, M.; Van Valen, D. Deep learning for cellular image analysis. *Nat. Methods* **2019**, *16*, 1233–1246. [CrossRef]
11. Ulman, V.; Maška, M.; Magnusson, K.E.G.; Ronneberger, O.; Haubold, C.; Harder, N.; Matula, P.; Matula, P.; Svoboda, D.; Radojevic, M.; et al. An objective comparison of cell-tracking algorithms. *Nat. Methods* **2017**, *14*, 1141–1152. [CrossRef]
12. Berg, S.; Kutra, D.; Kroeger, T.; Straehle, C.N.; Kausler, B.; Haubold, C.; Schiegg, M.; Ales, J.; Beier, T.; Rudy, M.; et al. ilastik: interactive machine learning for (bio)image analysis. *Nat. Methods* **2019**, *16*, 1226–1232. [CrossRef]
13. Hughes, A.J.; Mornin, J.D.; Biswas, S.K.; Beck, L.E.; Bauer, D.P.; Raj, A.; Bianco, S.; Gartner, Z.J. Quanti.us: a tool for rapid, flexible, crowd-based annotation of images. *Nat. Methods* **2018**, *15*, 587–590. [CrossRef]
14. Schmitz, J.; Noll, T.; Grünberger, A. Heterogeneity Studies of Mammalian Cells for Bioproduction: From Tools to Application. *Trends Biotechnol.* **2019**, *37*, 645–660. [CrossRef] [PubMed]
15. Brent, R.; Boucheron, L. Deep learning to predict microscope images. *Nat. Methods* **2018**, *15*, 868–870. [CrossRef] [PubMed]
16. Falk, T.; Mai, D.; Bensch, R.; Çiçek, Ö.; Abdulkadir, A.; Marrakchi, Y.; Böhm, A.; Deubner, J.; Jäckel, Z.; Seiwald, K.; et al. U-Net: deep learning for cell counting, detection, and morphometry. *Nat. Methods* **2019**, *16*, 67–70. [CrossRef] [PubMed]
17. Di Carlo, D.; Wu, L.Y.; Lee, L.P. Dynamic single cell culture array. *Lab Chip* **2006**, *6*, 1445–1449. [CrossRef]
18. Kolnik, M.; Tsimring, L.S.; Hasty, J. Vacuum-assisted cell loading enables shear-free mammalian microfluidic culture. *Lab Chip* **2012**, *12*, 4732–4737. [CrossRef]

19. Arteta, C.; Lempitsky, V.; Noble, J.A.; Zisserman, A. Interactive Object Counting. In *Computer Vision—ECCV 2014*; Fleet, D., Pajdla, T., Schiele, B., Tuytelaars, T., Eds.; Lecture Notes in Computer Science; Springer: Berlin/Heidelberg, Germany, 2014; Volume 8691, pp. 504–518. [CrossRef]
20. Arteta, C.; Lempitsky, V.; Noble, J.A.; Zisserman, A. Detecting overlapping instances in microscopy images using extremal region trees. *Med Image Anal.* **2016**, *27*, 3–16. [CrossRef]
21. Chen, S.W.; Shivakumar, S.S.; Dcunha, S.; Das, J.; Okon, E.; Qu, C.; Taylor, C.J.; Kumar, V. Counting Apples and Oranges With Deep Learning: A Data-Driven Approach. *IEEE Robot. Autom. Lett.* **2017**, *2*, 781–788. [CrossRef]
22. Xie, W.; Noble, J.A.; Zisserman, A. Microscopy cell counting and detection with fully convolutional regression networks. *Comput. Methods Biomech. Biomed. Eng. Imaging Vis.* **2018**, *6*, 283–292. [CrossRef]
23. Koh, W.; Hoon, S. MapCell: Learning a Comparative Cell Type Distance Metric with Siamese Neural Nets With Applications Toward Cell-Type Identification Across Experimental Datasets. *Front. Cell Dev. Biol.* **2021**, *9*, 767897. [CrossRef]
24. Müller, T.; Pérez-Torró, G.; Franco-Salvador, M. Few-Shot Learning with Siamese Networks and Label Tuning. In Proceedings of the 60th Annual Meeting of the Association for Computational Linguistics (Volume 1: Long Papers), Dublin, Ireland, 22–27 May 2022; pp. 8532–8545. [CrossRef]
25. Yang, L.; Chen, Y.; Song, S.; Li, F.; Huang, G. Deep Siamese Networks Based Change Detection with Remote Sensing Images. *Remote. Sens.* **2021**, *13*, 13173394. [CrossRef]
26. Mehmood, A.; Maqsood, M.; Bashir, M.; Shuyuan, Y. A Deep Siamese Convolution Neural Network for Multi-Class Classification of Alzheimer Disease. *Brain Sci.* **2020**, *10*, 84. [CrossRef] [PubMed]
27. Figueroa-Mata, G.; Mata-Montero, E. Using a Convolutional Siamese Network for Image-Based Plant Species Identification with Small Datasets. *Biomimetics* **2020**, *5*, 10008. [CrossRef] [PubMed]
28. Tan, M.; Le, Q.V. EfficientNet: Rethinking Model Scaling for Convolutional Neural Networks. *arXiv* **2019**, arXiv:1905.11946.
29. Rahman, M.S.; Islam, M.R. Counting objects in an image by marker controlled watershed segmentation and thresholding. In Proceedings of the 3rd IEEE International Advance Computing Conference (IACC), Ghaziabad, India, 22–23 February 2013; pp. 1251–1256. . [CrossRef]
30. Kolesnikov, A.; Beyer, L.; Zhai, X.; Puigcerver, J.; Yung, J.; Gelly, S.; Houlsby, N. Large Scale Learning of General Visual Representations for Transfer. *arXiv* **2019**, arXiv:1912.11370.
31. Sam, D.B.; Sajjan, N.N.; Maurya, H.; Babu, R.V. Almost Unsupervised Learning for Dense Crowd Counting. *Proc. AAAI Conf. Artif. Intell.* **2019**, *33*, 8868–8875. [CrossRef]
32. Schönfeld, E.; Ebrahimi, S.; Sinha, S.; Darrell, T.; Akata, Z. Generalized Zero- and Few-Shot Learning via Aligned Variational Autoencoders. *arXiv* **2019**, arXiv:1812.01784.
33. Jaderberg, M.; Simonyan, K.; Vedaldi, A.; Zisserman, A. Synthetic data and artificial neural networks for natural scene text recognition. In Proceedings of the Workshop on Deep Learning, Advances in Neural Information Processing Systems (NIPS); Palais des Congrès de Montréal, Montréal, QC, Canada, 7 December 2018.
34. Nikolenko, S.I. Synthetic Data for Deep Learning. *arXiv* **2019**, arXiv:1909.11512.
35. van Engelen, J.E.; Hoos, H.H. A survey on semi-supervised learning. *Mach. Learn.* **2020**, *109*, 373–440. [CrossRef]
36. Göpfert, C.; Ben-David, S.; Bousquet, O.; Gelly, S.; Tolstikhin, I.O.; Urner, R. When can unlabeled data improve the learning rate? In Proceedings of the Conference on Learning Theory, COLT 2019, PMLR, Phoenix, AZ, USA, 25–28 June 2019; Beygelzimer, A., Hsu, D., Eds.; Proceedings of Machine Learning Research; Volume 99, pp. 1500–1518.
37. Göpfert, J.P.; Göpfert, C.; Botsch, M.; Hammer, B. Effects of variability in synthetic training data on convolutional neural networks for 3D head reconstruction. In Proceedings of the 2017 IEEE Symposium Series on Computational Intelligence (SSCI), Honolulu, HI, USA, 27 November–1 December 2017; pp. 1–7. [CrossRef]
38. Ullrich, K.; Meeds, E.; Welling, M. Soft Weight-Sharing for Neural Network Compression. *arXiv* **2017**, arXiv:1702.04008.
39. McInnes, L.; Healy, J.; Saul, N.; Grossberger, L. UMAP: Uniform Manifold Approximation and Projection. *J. Open Source Softw.* **2018**, *3*, 861. [CrossRef]
40. Schmitz, J.; Täuber, S.; Westerwalbesloh, C.; von Lieres, E.; Noll, T.; Grünberger, A. Development and application of a cultivation platform for mammalian suspension cell lines with single-cell resolution. *Biotechnol. Bioeng.* **2021**, *118*, 992–1005. [CrossRef] [PubMed]
41. Sandfort, V.; Yan, K.; Pickhardt, P.J.; Summers, R.M. Data augmentation using generative adversarial networks (CycleGAN) to improve generalizability in CT segmentation tasks. *Sci. Rep.* **2019**, *9*, 16884. [CrossRef] [PubMed]
42. Saxe, A.M.; McClelland, J.L.; Ganguli, S. Exact solutions to the nonlinear dynamics of learning in deep linear neural networks. In Proceedings of the International Conference on Learning Representations, ICLR 2013, Scottsdale, AZ, USA, 2–4 May 2013.
43. Liu, L.; Jiang, H.; He, P.; Chen, W.; Liu, X.; Gao, J.; Han, J. On the Variance of the Adaptive Learning Rate and Beyond. *arXiv* **2020**, arXiv:1908.03265.
44. Kingma, D.P.; Welling, M. Auto-Encoding Variational Bayes. *arXiv* **2013**, arXiv:1312.6114.
45. Bergstra, J.; Bardenet, R.; Bengio, Y.; Kégl, B. Algorithms for Hyper-Parameter Optimization. In *Proceedings of the Advances in Neural Information Processing Systems*; Shawe-Taylor, J., Zemel, R., Bartlett, P., Pereira, F., Weinberger, K.Q., Eds.; Curran Associates, Inc.: Red Hook, NY, USA, 2011; Volume 24.
46. Williams, C.K.I.; Rasmussen, C.E. Gaussian Processes for Regression. In *Advances in Neural Information Processing Systems 8*; Touretzky, D.S., Mozer, M.C., Hasselmo, M.E., Eds.; MIT Press: Cambridge, MA, JUSA, 1996; pp. 514–520.

47. Tan, M.; Le, Q.V. EfficientNetV2: Smaller Models and Faster Training. *arXiv* **2021**, arXiv:2104.00298.
48. He, K.; Zhang, X.; Ren, S.; Sun, J. Deep Residual Learning for Image Recognition. *arXiv* **2015**, arXiv:1512.03385.

Disclaimer/Publisher's Note: The statements, opinions and data contained in all publications are solely those of the individual author(s) and contributor(s) and not of MDPI and/or the editor(s). MDPI and/or the editor(s) disclaim responsibility for any injury to people or property resulting from any ideas, methods, instructions or products referred to in the content.

Article

How to Open a Black Box Classifier for Tabular Data

Bradley Walters, Sandra Ortega-Martorell, Ivan Olier * and Paulo J. G. Lisboa

School of Computer Science and Mathematics, Liverpool John Moores University, Liverpool L3 2AF, UK
* Correspondence: i.a.oliercaparroso@ljmu.ac.uk

Abstract: A lack of transparency in machine learning models can limit their application. We show that analysis of variance (ANOVA) methods extract interpretable predictive models from them. This is possible because ANOVA decompositions represent multivariate functions as sums of functions of fewer variables. Retaining the terms in the ANOVA summation involving functions of only one or two variables provides an efficient method to open black box classifiers. The proposed method builds generalised additive models (GAMs) by application of L1 regularised logistic regression to the component terms retained from the ANOVA decomposition of the logit function. The resulting GAMs are derived using two alternative measures, Dirac and Lebesgue. Both measures produce functions that are smooth and consistent. The term partial responses in structured models (PRiSM) describes the family of models that are derived from black box classifiers by application of ANOVA decompositions. We demonstrate their interpretability and performance for the multilayer perceptron, support vector machines and gradient-boosting machines applied to synthetic data and several real-world data sets, namely Pima Diabetes, German Credit Card, and Statlog Shuttle from the UCI repository. The GAMs are shown to be compliant with the basic principles of a formal framework for interpretability.

Keywords: ANOVA; Shapley values; self-explaining neural networks; generalised additive models; interpretability

Citation: Walters, B.; Ortega-Martorell, S.; Olier, I.; Lisboa, P.J.G. How to Open a Black Box Classifier for Tabular Data. *Algorithms* **2023**, *16*, 181. https://doi.org/10.3390/a16040181

Academic Editors: Xiang Zhang and Xiaoxiao Li

Received: 14 February 2023
Revised: 13 March 2023
Accepted: 17 March 2023
Published: 27 March 2023

Copyright: © 2023 by the authors. Licensee MDPI, Basel, Switzerland. This article is an open access article distributed under the terms and conditions of the Creative Commons Attribution (CC BY) license (https://creativecommons.org/licenses/by/4.0/).

1. Introduction

Machine learning models can be inherently interpretable, typically by fitting decision trees [1] or even by representing an existing black box model, such as a neural network, by extracting rules, whether using decompositional methods to explain the activity of individual hidden neurons, or applying pedagogical methods to fit the decision surface with axis-orthogonal hypercubes [2]. Decision trees have been successfully used to build transparent models in high-stakes applications [3].

Alternatively, statistical models, such as logistic regression, have high classification performance for the levels of noise typical for clinical prediction models [4]. Both decision trees and logistic regression have been successful and have global interpretability. However, each has a significant limitation. Rule sets can grow so complex as to become opaque to the user. Generalised linear models, while accurately modelling the nature of chance variation in the data through an appropriate choice of the output distribution function, require a priori choices of attribute factors, often resorting to categorising input variables to better capture non-linearities in the data.

A model that is arguably gold-standard should combine linear additivity with the automatic estimation of the non-linear dependence of the prediction on individual variables or pairs of variables. This can be achieved with generalised additive models (GAMs) [5]. We investigate to what extent it is possible to buck the performance-interpretability trade-off for tabular data by deriving GAMs from existing black box models, or using standard machine learning approaches to seed a GAM, keeping only univariate and bivariate terms.

Opening black boxes with ANOVA in this way is attractive because GAMs quantify Bayesian models in a way that is natural for human thinking. In particular, the representation of the logit as a GAM represents the prediction of the probability of class membership as a combination of independent effects, much in the way that logistic regression does, but allowing for non-linear functions of the input variables. Specifically, for input dimensionality d, the odds ratio of this probability has the form

$$\frac{P(C|x)}{1-P(C|x)} = e^{\varphi_1(x_1)}.e^{\varphi_1(x_2)} \ldots e^{\varphi_d(x_d)}.e^{\varphi_{1,2}(x_1,x_2)} \ldots e^{\varphi_{(d-1),d}(x_{(d-1)},x_d)}.e^{\varphi_0} \quad (1)$$

where the terms $\varphi_i(x_i)$ are univariate functions, hence easily interpreted, $\varphi_{ij}(x_i,x_j)$ are bivariate functions, which can also be easily plotted, and φ_0 is the *null model* for which all of the input variables $\varphi_i(x_i)$ and $\varphi_{i,j}(x_i,x_j)$ are set to 0.

From a Bayesian perspective, each component e^φ models the contribution of an individual variable or pair of variables, which can enhance or suppress the P(C|x) depending on whether the value taken by the argument function φ is positive or negative, acting on the baseline value e^{φ_0}, which, if $\varphi_i(0)$ is always 0, corresponds to the prior odds ratio in the absence of any of the input variables being present.

As the variables are entered into Equation (1), they modulate the prediction of P(C|x), much in the same way as a human observer can start with a prior probability, e.g., for the diagnosis of a clinical state, then modulate that diagnosis as the observations of the symptoms are made; each symptom contributing to increasing or reducing the probability of diagnosing the clinical state according to Equation (1). In the medical domain, many risk models are quantified by exactly this model, usually expressed as a risk score, namely

$$score(x_1,x_2,\ldots,x_d) = \sum_{i=1}^{d} \beta_i \cdot x_i \quad (2)$$

with

$$logit(P(c|x)) = log\left(\frac{P(C|x)}{1-P(C|x)}\right) = \beta_0 + score(x_1,x_2,\ldots,x_d) \quad (3)$$

This corresponds to the GAM defined by Equation (1) with only univariate terms given by

$$\varphi_i(x_i) = \beta_i \cdot x_i \quad (4)$$

1.1. Related Work on Self-Explaining Neural Networks

Interpretable neural network models have a long history starting with generalised additive neural networks (GANNs) [6–8], also called self-Explaining neural networks (SENNs) [9], which consist of a multilayer perceptron with modular structures that are not fully connected but involve sums of sub-networks, each representing functions of a single input variable or pair of variables [6]. However, they lack efficient methods to carry out a model selection to avoid modelling spurious correlations by including too many variables.

Our method relies on the analysis of variance (ANOVA) decompositions [10]. Although ANOVA is well known in mainstream statistics, its potential to derive interpretable models from pre-trained black box machine learning algorithms has not been fully exploited. In his paper introducing gradient boosting machines, Friedman notes that partial dependence functions can help "interpret models produced by any black box prediction method, such as neural networks, support vector machines, etc." [11]. However, this referred to the visualisation of the model's dependence on covariates, which applies locally only at the data median, rather than building a predictor that applies globally and so can be used to make predictions over the complete range of input values with the same additive model.

Other algorithms to derive predictive additive models have been proposed recently. They are neural additive models (NAM), where the univariate functions are each modelled with a separate multilayer perceptron or deep learning neural network [12] and explainable boosting machines (EBM) [13], which includes both univariate and bivariate terms. A recent refinement of these methods is the GAMI-NET [14]. This model estimates main (univariate) effects and pairwise interactions in two separate stages, building bespoke neural networks to model each effect and interaction. None of these models will open an existing black box since they built a SENN structure first rather than applying function decomposition to a given multivariate function, as achieved with ANOVA.

Moreover, all the above models have limitations either in feature selection or in the structure of the model itself. In particular, NAMs favour a model structure that includes univariate functions for all the input variables and lack a clear process for selecting bivariate component functions. In contrast, EBMs incorporate model selection with statistical tests; in fact, ANOVA significance tests applied to partial dependence functions, proposed by [11], which are similar to the marginal functions used in Section 2.1.1 to calculate partial responses from ANOVA decompositions with the Lebesgue measure. This permits the inclusion of bivariate functions in the additive model. However, the EBM component functions are jagged because they are built from hyper box cuts in input space. The GAMI-NET requires explicit sparsity and heredity constraints, along with what is called marginal clarity, which is a penalisation term to enforce orthogonality between the main effects and the pairwise interactions. This is motivated by the functional ANOVA decomposition, implicitly using the marginal distribution, although it is not clear whether this observes the constraint raised in [11] to ensure that correlations among the input variables do not bias the orthogonality calculation. Our approach uses the ANOVA decomposition directly and so keeps the training process much simpler.

All of the above methods are stand-alone algorithms rather than explaining predictions made by pre-trained black boxes. This is also the case for sparse additive models (SAM) [15], where the component univariate and bivariate functions in a GAM are implemented with splines in contrast to our use of neural networks, which are semi-parametric, and hence, less restrictive. Moreover, splines can over-regularise the model and miss important details in the data, as well as being inefficient for estimating bivariate terms due to a proliferation of spline parameters. A further model, sparse additive machines [16], derives GAM structures from SVM models. It is scalable and has a provable convergence rate that is quadratic on the number of iterations, but this is not probabilistic and does not include pairwise terms.

The motivation for considering ANOVA as a method to open black box models is that each measure used in ANOVA is closely related to an intuitive approach for the decomposition of multivariate functions into predictive models with fewer variables. The Dirac measure filters from the multivariate response precisely the terms in the Taylor series, centred at the data median, which are dependent on just one or two variables [17], while the Lebesgue measure marginalises the response surface over one of two variables [18]. The proposed method is computationally efficient and stable for variable selection.

1.2. Contributions to the Literature

The main hypothesis of this paper is that the low-order functions derived by ANOVA from arbitrarily complex machine learning or other probabilistic classifiers contain sufficient information to open the black box models while retaining the classification performance measured by the area under the receiver operating characteristic curve (AUC). The resulting models are interpretable by design [19].

The proposed generic framework to extract GAMs from black boxes is termed partial responses in structured models (PRiSM). An instantiation of the framework has been demonstrated by applying the simplest measure used by ANOVA. This performed well on two medical data sets about intensive care [20] and heart transplants [21]. The focus of the latter is a detailed clinical interpretation of the partial response network (PRN), which is an anchored model, i.e., it combines functions restricted to be zero at the median values of the data. This paper makes a comprehensive approach to the proposed method and contributes novelty in the following respects:

- Comprehensive presentation of the generic framework for deriving PRiSM models from arbitrary black box binary classifiers, reviewing the orthogonality properties of ANOVA for two alternative measures: the Dirac measure, which is similar to partial dependence functions in visualisation algorithms [11] and produces component

functions that are tied to the data median; the Lebesgue measure, which involves estimates of marginal effects and is related to the quantification of effect sizes [7]. The method is tested on nine-dimensional synthetic data to verify that it retrieves the correct generating variables and achieves close to optimal classification performance;
- Derivation of a commonly used indicator of feature attribution, Shapley values [22]. When applied to the logit of model predictions from GAMs and SENNs, it is shown to be identical to the value of the contributions of the partial responses derived from ANOVA;
- Mapping of the properties of the PRiSM models to a formal framework for interpretability, demonstrating compliance with its main requirements [23], known as the three Cs of interpretability. This is complemented by an in-depth analysis of the component functions estimated from three real-world data sets.

The univariate and bivariate component functions representing the additive contributions to the logit of the model prediction are what we call partial responses. Note that while univariate component functions are numerically identical to partial dependence plots, the bivariate functions are not since they are obtained by removing the univariate dependence via the orthogonality properties of ANOVA decompositions. Moreover, the univariate and bivariate component functions are not used here purely for visualisation. Their values are the nomogram of the model, i.e., the ordinate of the figures shown later is in all cases the precise contribution of the variables to the model prediction, which is for every data point merely the summation of the contributions from all of the variables in the logit space.

The derived models retain a direct link between the input variables and the model predictions, meeting the requirements of the three "Cs" outlined earlier, and have comparable classification performance to the original black box models. This is demonstrated by application to four real-world data sets: UCI Diabetes, UCI German Credit Card, and Statlog Shuttle. The first three were used as benchmark data sets, whilst the last one was chosen as it was used in related work [12].

We refer to the overall framework to open pre-trained black boxes by deriving sparse models in the form of GAMs and SENNs as the integration of partial responses into structured models (PRiSM), Figure 1.

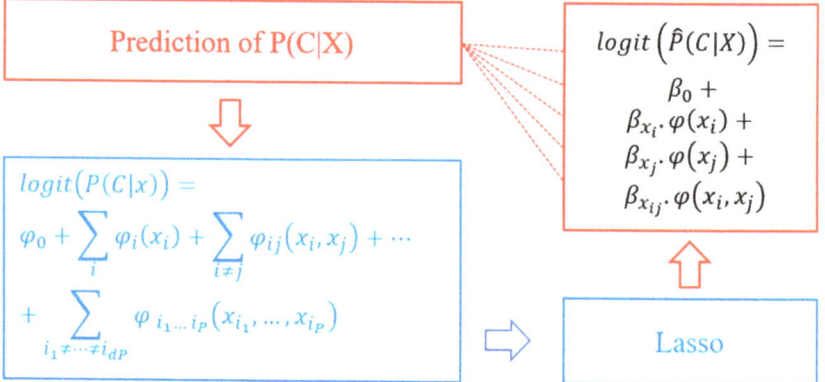

Figure 1. Schematic of the PRiSM framework. Any multidimensional decision function can be represented by a spectrum of additive functions, each with only one or two inputs. The final prediction of the probability of class membership, $\hat{P}(C|X)$, is given by the sum of the univariate and bivariate component functions, scaled by the coefficients β_{x_i}, $\beta_{x_{ij}}$ derived by the least absolute shrinkage and selection operator (LASSO). Since only univariate $\varphi(x_i)$ and bivariate $\varphi(x_i, x_j)$ component functions are in the model, their shapes provide a route towards interpretation by end-users.

2. Materials and Methods
2.1. Methods
2.1.1. ANOVA Decomposition

The first novelty of the paper is to apply an ANOVA decomposition [10] to pre-trained black box probabilistic binary classifiers in order to extract from the $logit(P(C|x))$, which is a multivariate function, component functions of fewer variables.

The ANOVA decomposition is defined as follows

$$logit(P(C|x)) \equiv \log\left(\frac{P(C|x)}{1-P(C|x)}\right)$$
$$= \varphi_0 + \sum_i \varphi_i(x_i) + \sum_{i \neq j} \varphi_{ij}(x_i, x_j) + \ldots + \sum_{i_1 \neq \ldots \neq i_P} \varphi_{i_1 \ldots i_P}(x_{i_1}, \ldots, x_{i_P}) \quad (5)$$

where the general form of the terms in (5) is a recursive function of the nested subsets of the covariate indices $\{i_1, \ldots, i_P\}$ with the property that the term involving all of the covariates $x_i: i = 1 \ldots P$, where P is the dimensionality of the input data is given by

$$\varphi_{i_1 \ldots i_P}(x_{i_1}, \ldots, x_{i_P})$$
$$= logit(P(C|x_{i_1}, \ldots, x_{i_P})) - \sum_{\{i_1 \neq \ldots \neq i_{P-1}\}} \varphi_{i_1 \ldots i_{n-1}}(x_{i_1}, \ldots, x_{i_{P-1}}) - \varphi_0 \quad (6)$$

Note that Decomposition (5) is an identity that exactly reproduces the values of the $logit(P(C|x))$, originally predicted by the black box classifier. We call the component functions $\varphi_{i_1 \ldots i_n}(x_{i_1}, \ldots, x_{i_n})$ partial responses, since they involve only a subset of the input variables.

The general form of the component terms is given by the following equations, which depend only on the chosen measure $\mu(x)$

$$\varphi_0 = \int_{[x]^P} logit(P(C|x)) d\mu(x) \quad (7)$$

$$\varphi_S(x_S) = \int_{[x]^{P-|S|}} logit(P(C|x)) d\mu(x_{-S}) - \sum_{T \subset S} \varphi_T(x_T) \quad (8)$$

where $S \in R^S$ represents a subset of variables with dimensionality $|S| \leq P$. The terms x_S and x_{-S} denote, respectively, the subspace spanned by $S: |S| = n$ in Equation (6) and its complement $-S: |-S| = d - n$.

It follows from (7) and (8) that the terms φ_S are normalised with respect to the chosen measure

$$\int_S \varphi_S(x_S) d\mu(x_j) = 0, \; if \; j \in S \quad (9)$$

and also orthogonal for disjoint variable sets S and T

$$\int_S \varphi_S(x_S) \varphi_T(x_T) d\mu(x) = 0, \; if \; S \neq T. \quad (10)$$

There are two natural choices of measure, each of which will define the functionality of each of the component terms φ_S in response to either one or two arguments:

- Dirac measure

$$d\mu(x) = \delta(x - x_c) dx \quad (11)$$

An arbitrary point x_c that is called anchor point. The partial responses become cuts through the response surface for the $logit(P(C|x)$.

- Lesbesgue measure

$$d\mu(x) = \rho(x) dx \quad (12)$$

where $\rho(x)$ is the density function of the variables in the argument of the integral. This measure calculates the weighted mean of the integrand.

In both cases, the data matrix X is first centred using the overall median of the data and scaled by the marginal standard deviation:

$$X \to (X - median(X)) \Big/ std(X) \tag{13}$$

The absence of a variable now corresponds to fixing it at the median value, since the median point corresponds to a vector of 0 s. Therefore, the logit value then takes the value $logit(P(C|0))$. Similarly, if all of the variables except x_i are set to their median values, then the corresponding values of $logit(P(C|(0,\ldots,x_i,\ldots,0)))$ represent a function of just that one variable. The same principle applies when only two variables are not 0, then three variables, etc.

The partial responses for the Dirac measure are calculated according to

$$\varphi_0 = logit(P(C|0)) \tag{14}$$

$$\varphi_i(x_i) = logit(P(C|(0,\ldots,x_i,\ldots,0))) - \varphi_0 \tag{15}$$

$$\varphi_{ij}(x_i, x_j) = logit(P(C|(0,\ldots,x_i,\ldots,x_j,\ldots,0))) - \varphi_i(x_i) - \varphi_j(x_j) - \varphi_0 \tag{16}$$

In the case of the Lebesgue measure, the integrals in Equations (7) and (8) are calculated empirically using the training data, with sample size N observations

$$\hat{F}_S(x_S) = \frac{1}{N}\sum_{k=1}^{N} logit\left(P(C|x_S, x^k_{-S})\right) \tag{17}$$

where the variables with dimensions x_s take any desired values but those in the complement set with dimension x^k_{-s} are fixed at their actual values in the training set $k = 1\ldots N$ [11]. This corresponds to shifting all onto the coordinate(s) x_s so that in the summation (17), every data point has the same value of this input dimension while retaining the original values for all other coordinates.

The orthogonalised partial responses $\varphi_S(x_s)$ follow by using Equation (8).

$$\hat{\varphi}_0 = \frac{1}{N}\sum_{k=1}^{N} logit\left(P(C|x^k)\right) \tag{18}$$

$$\hat{\varphi}_i(x_i) = \hat{F}_i(x_i) - \hat{\varphi}_0 \tag{19}$$

$$\hat{\varphi}_{ij}(x_i, x_j) = \hat{F}_{ij}(x_i, x_j) - \hat{\varphi}_i(x_i) - \hat{\varphi}_j(x_j) - \hat{\varphi}_0 \tag{20}$$

2.1.2. Model Selection with the LASSO

The resulting terms in the truncated ANOVA decomposition comprising only the univariate and bivariate terms in (5) need to be re-calibrated to maximise the predictive classification performance. In addition, having treated the higher-order terms as noise, the remaining terms need also to be filtered to remove non-informative partial responses.

This is achieved through a second step involving the application of the logistic regression with the LASSO [24], treating $P * (P + 1)/2$ terms in the truncated ANOVA decomposition as the new input variables. The L_1 regularisation is robust for hard model selection by sliding to zero the value of the linear coefficients for the least informative variables, which are now partial responses.

Since the partial responses are generally non-linear functions of one of two variables, they are readily interpretable. This is not new having previously been a widely used approach to visualise non-linear models with partial dependence functions that are functionally equivalent to ANOVA terms with the Dirac measure. What is new is the realisation that when these functions are calculated for the $logit(P(C|x)$ and used for prediction with tabular data, they can achieve comparable AUCs to those of the original black box models from which the partial responses are derived.

2.1.3. Second Training Iteration

If the original black box model is an MLP, it is possible to construct a GANN/SENN to replicate the output of the logistic Lasso by a replication of the weights from the MLP multiplied by the coefficients of the Lasso. This permits an additional step of refining the partial responses themselves by initialising the SENN at the operating point of the GAM.

Given the weights $\{w_{ij}, b_j, v_j, v_0\}$ of the original pre-trained fully connected MLP, Figure 2, with the inputs indexed by i and hidden nodes indexed by j, together with the coefficients $\{\beta_0, \beta_i, \beta_{ij}\}$ fitted by the Lasso, the PRiSM model for the anchored decomposition can be exactly mapped onto an MLP structured in the form of a GANN/SENN, as follows.

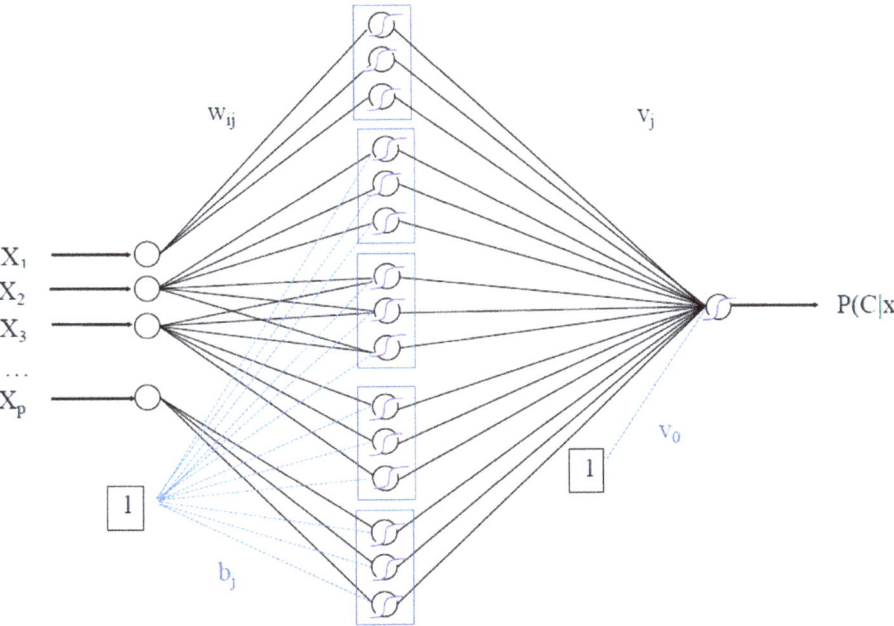

Figure 2. The partial response network (PRN) has the modular structure typical of a self-explaining neural network. In particular, the figure illustrates the connectivity for a univariate function of input variables x_1 and x_p, and a bivariate term involving variables x_2 and x_3. Modelling the interaction term as orthogonal to univariate terms involving the same variables requires three blocks of hidden nodes, as explained in the main text. If there are univariate additive component functions involving either x_2 or x_3 these are added to the structure by inserting additional modules, as shown for x_1 and x_p.

(1) Univariate partial response corresponding to the input x_i

This is shown in Figure 2 for input x_1. Zero inputs for all other inputs will not contribute to the activation of the hidden nodes. The hidden layer weights w_{ij} connected to node x_i remain the same as in the original MLP but the weights and bias to the output node need to be adjusted as follows:

$$v_j \rightarrow \beta_i * v_j \qquad (21)$$

$$v_0 \to \beta_i * (v_0 - logit(P(C|0))) \qquad (22)$$

(2) Bivariate partial response for the input pair $\{x_i, x_j\}$

This is shown in Figure 2 for inputs x_2 and x_3. This time, to replicate the partial response multiplied by the Lasso coefficient, it is necessary to add three elements to the structure, namely, a univariate partial response for each of the inputs involved and a coupled network that both inputs feed into together. We will use the generic input indices k and l to avoid confusion with the hidden node index j. The hidden layer weights once again remain unchanged from the original MLP. The output layer weights and bias for the network structure representing the univariate term associated with input k (and similarly for input l) are adjusted by

$$v_j \to (\beta_k - \beta_{kl}) * v_j \qquad (23)$$

$$v_0 \to (\beta_k - \beta_{kl}) * (v_0 - logit(P(C|0))) \qquad (24)$$

whereas the weights and bias for the coupled network are changed according to

$$v_j \to \beta_{kl} * v_j \qquad (25)$$

$$v_0 \to \beta_{kl} * (v_0 - logit(P(C|0))). \qquad (26)$$

(3) Finally, an amount is added to the total sum of the values calculated for the bias term in the structured neural network. This amount is equal to the intercept of the logistic Lasso, β_0.

Equations (23)–(26) have the property that when an interaction between two variables is identified after the first application of the Lasso, its mapping onto the structured neural network involves also univariate modules, with the consequence that the second back-propagation step can potentially render the bivariate term not statistically significant and replace it with one or more univariate independent effects.

2.1.4. Summary of the Method

The following is the pseudo-code for PRiSM models, taking as a starting point a data set comprising a set of P-dimensional input variables normalised according to (13) and the corresponding black box model predictions.

Algorithm Partial Response Models PRiSM(BB, D):

Input: set D of training examples; predictions $P(C|x)$ from a pre-trained black box model BB.

1. ANOVA decomposition: apply the recursion given by Equation (6) to the $logit(P(C|x))$.

This may use either of the suggested measures, Dirac and Lesbesgue. The former leads to an anchored decomposition referenced to the choice of anchor point; the component functions generated by the latter are summations weighted by the density function of the covariates, $P(x)$.

2. Model selection with the Lasso: input the set of univariate and bivariate partial responses $\varphi_i(x_i)$ and $\varphi_{ij}(x_i, x_j)$ from (6) calculated over the training data set D as new inputs for variable selection with the logistic regression Lasso.

The Lasso will also output a linear coefficient for each partial response, β_i and β_{ij}, as well as an intercept β_0, generally resulting in good calibration.

Output prBB(BB, D): this is the output of the Lasso in Step 2, which has the form of a GAM, shown in Equation (5), truncated to the selected subset of functions $\varphi_i(x_i)$ and $\varphi_{ij}(x_i, x_j)$:

$$logit(prBB(C|x)) \equiv \varphi(0) + \sum_i \beta_i \varphi_i(x_i) + \sum_{i \neq j} \beta_{ij} \varphi_{ij}(x_i, x_j) \qquad (27)$$

Each partial response comprises a non-linear function of its arguments. Consequently, the model prediction equals the sum of all partial responses plus the intercept, weighted by the linear coefficients from Step 2, followed by the application of the sigmoid function, which inverts the $logit(P(C|x))$.

The predictions for anchored decompositions are indexed by the pre-fix *pr* followed by an abbreviation of the black box algorithm, e.g., prSVM and prGBM.

3. Predictions with *PRiSM* models: given a test data point, the $\varphi_i(x_i)$ and $\varphi_{ij}(x_i, x_j)$ are calculated using Equations (14)–(16) or (17)–(20), and the predicted output follows from (27). The input variables are, therefore, directly linked to the predictions through interpretable functions.

Anchored decomposition applied to the MLP:
By denoting the output *prMLP (MLP, D)* by $\overline{MLP\text{-}Lasso}$, it is then possible to continue training as follows:

4. Map the MLP-Lasso into a GANN/SENN: this has the form of a GANN/SENN, meaning that it is not fully connected, as shown in Figure 2. The adjustments to the weights are explained in Equations (21)–(26) and in Section 2.1.3.

Output Partial Response Network [PRN]: having initialised a structured neural network in the previous step, so that it exactly replicates the component functions and output of the MLP-Lasso, back-error propagation is applied to continue the training of this network. The PRN is a probabilistic binary classifier, so training will use the log-likelihood cost function. Note that the component functions no longer conform with the requirements of an ANOVA decomposition as they will have been adjusted without the constraint of orthogonality.

Output PRN-Lasso: Steps 1,2. are then applied to the PRN instead of the original MLP. This generates a new set of partial responses $\varphi_i^*(x_i)$ and $\varphi_{ij}^*(x_i, x_j)$ and corresponding coefficients β_i^* and β_{ij}^* from which the model predictions follow by inserting these coefficients and partial responses into Equation (27).

The second training iteration enables the partial responses to be refined without being adjusted for input variables that were removed from the model by the Lasso in Step 2. Therefore, the PRN–Lasso–BB models will always comprise a subset of the variables in the PRN–BB models, but not necessarily with the same functional form. It is possible that some of the partial responses in the PRN–BB model are no longer selected and even that what may have started as a pure two-way effect can now be split into two independent main effects represented by univariate partial responses.

2.1.5. Exact Calculation of Shapley Values

In common with GAMs generally, the interpretation of a PRiSM model is the model itself, since the components of the logit are additive and the amount contributed by each partial response is clearly quantified.

In addition, the relevance of individual input variables can be calculated using Shapley values [22]. This can be achieved for the overall prediction of the probability of class membership, but also for the logit, which places less emphasis on the non-linearity at the class boundary but takes greater account of the value of the logit across the full range of input values, which is important to ensure the good calibration of the final model.

When the logit has the form shown in Equation (27), the Shapley value ϕ_i corresponding to input variable x_i of dimensionality P can be efficiently computed by summing over all variable subsets that exclude input i, $S \subseteq P\setminus\{i\}$, including $S = \varnothing$, with the usual formula

$$\phi_i(x_i) = \frac{1}{P} \sum_{S \subseteq N\setminus\{i\}} \binom{P-1}{|S|}^{-1} (logit(P(C|S \cup \{i\}) - logit(P(C|S))) \qquad (28)$$

The linear terms in (27) simply add for every combination of input variables excluding i, of which there are $\binom{P-1}{|S|}$; therefore, at each data point the contribution to $\phi_i(x_i)$ is just

$\beta_i(\varphi_i(x_i) - \varphi_i(0))$. In the case of the bivariate terms, the calculation is similar but involves only $\binom{P-2}{|S|}$ combinations giving

$$\frac{1}{P}\sum_{j=1}^{P-1}\left[\frac{\binom{P-2}{j-1}}{\binom{P-1}{j}}\right] = \frac{1}{P}\sum_{j=1}^{P-1}\left[\frac{(P-2)!j!}{(P-1)!(j-1)!}\right] = \frac{1}{P}\sum_{j=1}^{P-1}\left(\frac{j}{P-1}\right) = \frac{1}{2} \quad (29)$$

Therefore, the pairwise terms neatly share their impact among the Shapley values for each of the variables, yielding

$$\phi_i(x_i) = \beta_i(\varphi_i(x_i) - \varphi_i(0)) + \frac{1}{2}\sum_j \beta_{ij}(\varphi_{ij}(x_i, x_j) - \varphi_{ij}(0, x_j)) \quad (30)$$

2.1.6. Experimental Settings

All algorithms were implemented in Matlab [25]. The MLP was trained with automatic relevance determination [26] implemented in Netlab [27], although conjugate gradient descent leads to similar results. The other machine learning algorithms predict scores for a class assignment. In this study, the scores are calibrated for probabilistic classification using the score as the sole input to a logistic regression model, which forms the starting point for PRiSM models by taking the logit in the same way as for the MLP. The SVM was fitted using *fitcSVM* with an RBF kernel and automatic optimisation. The GBM model is implemented with *fitcensemble*, which boosts 100 decision trees using the function *LogitBoost*.

2.2. Data sets used

2.2.1. Synthetic Data

(a) 2D circle. We implemented a sample size of n = 10,000 with unbalanced classes, which is the case for all synthetic data sets in this paper. In this case, the *logit* has two separate univariate components,

$$logit(P(C|(x_1, x_2))) = 10 \times \left[\left(x_1 - \frac{1}{2}\right)^2 + \left(x_2 - \frac{1}{2}\right)^2 - 0.08\right] \quad (31)$$

This data set is similar to that used in [15] but instead of generating clean data by allocating different classes on either side of the boundary, we use noisy data by generating binary targets with a Bernoulli distribution, which is also common for all the synthetic data sets that we report,

$$Y \sim Bin(n, P(C|(x_1, x_2))). \quad (32)$$

The factor of 10 in Equation (31) is to reduce the amount of noise and so ensure a reasonable value for the AUC. The values of (x_1, x_2) are generated using $x_i = 0.5 \times (u_i + w)$, where both u_i and w are uniform distributions in the range [0,1], to demonstrate the prediction accuracy when the two input variables are correlated. There are only two univariate main effects and no interaction term.

(b) XOR function. The purest bivariate interaction is the XOR, represented in the multilinear form appropriate for continuous Boolean algebra [28],

$$P(C|(x_3, x_4)) = x_3 + x_4 - 2x_3x_4, x_i \in]0,1[\quad (33)$$

Each variable will be generated by a uniform distribution in [0,1]. This density function has the property that

$$logit(P(C|(x_3, x_4))) = log\left(\frac{x_3 + x_4 - 2x_3x_4}{1 - x_3 - x_4 + 2x_3x_4}\right) \quad (34)$$

Therefore, $logit\left(P\left(C\middle|\left(x_3, \frac{1}{2}\right)\right)\right) = 0$ making it a pure interaction for the ANOVA decomposition with the *Dirac measure* anchored at (1/2,1/2). Similarly, for the *Lebesgue measure*, it is readily shown that

$$logit(P(C|(x_3, x_4))) = -logit(P(C|(1 - x_3, x_4))) \tag{35}$$

which is similar to the other dimension; therefore, the integrals corresponding to the univariate terms vanish, once again leaving the pure interaction term.

(c) Logical AND function. A combination of univariate and bivariate terms by generating data according to the logical AND function, which in continuous Boolean algebra is represented by the following atomic term:

$$P(C|(x_5, x_6)) = x_5 x_6, x_i \in]0, 1[\tag{36}$$

This time, the ANOVA expansion with the *Dirac measure* anchored at (1/2,1/2) is

$$\begin{aligned} logit(P(C|(x_5, x_6))) \\ = -\log(3) + \sum_i \left[\log\left(\frac{x_i}{2-x_i}\right) + \log(3)\right] \\ + \left[\log\left(\frac{(2-x_5)(2-x_6)}{1-x_5 x_6}\right) - \log(3)\right] \end{aligned} \tag{37}$$

The *Lebesgue measure* yields univariate terms given by

$$\varphi_i^{Lebesgue} = \log\left(x_i / (1 - x_i)\right) + \frac{\log(1 - x_i)}{x_i} + Li_2(1) \tag{38}$$

where $Li_2(1)$ is the polylogarithm function of second order evaluated at 1. The bivariate term is given by the explicit ANOVA decomposition in Equation (5) and does not reduce to a simpler algebraic form.

(d) Three-way interaction. The final synthetic data set comprises a data set that cannot be modelled with univariate and bivariate terms only. The purpose is now to see how well PRiSM models work to model a high-order effect.

$$P(C|(x_7, x_8, x_9)) = x_7 x_8 x_9, x_i \in]0, 1[\tag{39}$$

Note that the complete set of input variables for the synthetic data set is calculated only once. In this way, the same sample of 9-dimensional input data will be used for all classifiers. Only the target classes differ, thus generating four separate binary classification tasks. In each case, two or three variables will carry signal and the others comprise noise. A minimum requirement of all classifiers is to identify the relevant input dimensions and discard the rest. In addition, since we have the data generators, we can calculate the optimal classification performance corresponding to allocating every data point to the correct class, irrespective of the stochastic label generated by the Bernoulli distribution.

2.2.2. Real-World data

A description of the variables included in the starting pool for model selection and any standardisation that was applied to them is provided below.

(a) Diabetes data set:

The Diabetes dataset [29,30] comprises measurements recorded from 768 women, who were at least 21 years old, of Pima Indian heritage, and tested for diabetes using World Health Organization criteria. One of the variables, "Blood Serum" Insulin, has significant amounts of missing data. These rows were removed along with all entries with missing values of "Plasma Glucose Concentration" in a tolerance test, "Diastolic Blood Pressure" (BP), "Triceps Skin Fold Thickness" (TSF) or "Body Mass Index" (BMI), resulting in a reduced data set with n = 532. In line with common practice, a subset was randomly selected for training (n = 314), and the remaining were used for testing (n = 268). The additional variables available are "Age", "Number of Pregnancies", and "Diabetes Pedigree Function" (DPF), a measure of family history of diabetes. A binary target variable indicated diabetes status, with a positive prevalence of 35.7%.

(b) Statlog German Credit Card data set:

We used the numerical version of the Statlog German Credit Card database [31], which contains n = 1000 instances and 24 attributes. The first 700 observations were used for training, with a prevalence of bad credit risks being 29.6%. The remaining 300 observations were used for testing, with a prevalence of bad risks of 31%. The data set was used in the form created for the benchmarking study Statlog, where three categorical variables ("Other Debtors", "Housing", and "Employment") were coded in binary form with multiple columns.

(c) Statlog Shuttle data set:

The Statlog Shuttle database [31,32] from NASA comprises 9 numerical attributes and an outcome label. It is split into 43,500 cases for training and 14,500 for testing. There are 7 outcomes, of which 21% are in the category "Rad Flow". The binary classification task is to separate this category, Class 0, from the others, assigned to Class 1. Given the strong imbalance between classes, the default accuracy for a null model, i.e., predicting the predominant class for all rows, is 79%. The target accuracy is 99–99.9%.

3. Results

The following sections compare the performance and characteristics of different PRiSM models obtained by opening a range of frequently used black box algorithms.

3.1. Synthetic Data

The purpose of the benchmarking on the synthetic data is to ascertain how close each machine learning classifier and the corresponding interpretable PRiSM models get to the optimal classification accuracy, which is obtained using the known class membership probabilities given by the generating formulae for class membership, notwithstanding the presence of noise in the targets.

The classification performance of frequently used machine learning models and their interpretable versions applied to the four synthetic sets are listed in Tables 1–4. The optimal AUC values are in bold, and the values below the confidence interval (CI) are in italics. Two-dimensional plots of the relevant variables from the nine input dimensions are plotted in Figures 3–5, showing the actual training data with Bernoulli noise and the ideal class allocations used to find the best achievable AUC. The generated data set was split into three parts for training, model parameter optimisation with out-of-sample data, and performance estimation in generalisation. It is interesting to see how much the optimal AUC varies between three slices from the same noisy data. This illustrates the importance of calculating confidence intervals. The model with marginally the best point estimate of the AUC for the optimisation data may not have the highest AUC estimated on the independent sample.

Table 1. Classification performance for the 2D circle measured by the AUC [CI]. The input variables x_1 and x_2 are ideally selected solely for their univariate responses.

AUC [CI]	No. Input Variables	Training (n = 6000)	Optimisation (n = 2000)	Performance Estimation (n = 2000)
Optimal classifier	2	0.676 [0.662,0.689]	0.657 [0.634,0.681]	0.666 [0.643,0.690]
MLP	9	0.676 [0.663,0.690]	0.659 [0.635,0.682]	0.660 [0.636,0.684]
SVM	9	0.695 [0.682,0.708]	0.646 [0.622,0.670]	0.648 [0.624,0.672]
GBM	9	*0.697 [0.684,0.710]*	*0.649 [0.625,0.673]*	*0.641 [0.617,0.665]*

Table 1. Cont.

AUC [CI]	No. Input Variables	Training (n = 6000)	Optimisation (n = 2000)	Performance Estimation (n = 2000)
PRiSM models	*Components*		*Dirac measure*	
Lasso	2	0.675 [0.661,0.688]	0.658 [0.634,0.682]	0.661 [0.637,0.685]
PRN	2	0.676 [0.662,0.689]	0.659 [0.636,0.683]	0.664 [0.640,0.687]
PRN–Lasso	2	0.676 [0.662,0.689]	0.659 [0.636,0.683]	0.664 [0.640,0.688]
prSVM	2	0.676 [0.662,0.689]	0.658 [0.634,0.681]	0.664 [0.640,0.688]
prGBM	5	0.681 [0.667,0.694]	0.655 [0.631,0.679]	0.655 [0.632,0.679]
PRiSM models	*Components*		*Lebesgue measure*	
Lasso	2	0.675 [0.662,0.689]	0.659 [0.636,0.683]	0.661 [0.637,0.685]
PRN	2	0.676 [0.662,0.689]	0.659 [0.636,0.683]	0.664 [0.640,0.687]
PRN–Lasso	2	0.676 [0.662,0.689]	0.660 [0.636,0.683]	0.664 [0.640,0.687]
prSVM	3	0.675 [0.662,0.689]	0.657 [0.634,0.681]	0.665 [0.641,0.689]
prGBM	2	0.673 [0.659,0.686]	0.656 [0.632,0.679]	0.654 [0.630,0.678]

Table 2. Classification performance for the XOR function measured by the AUC [CI]. The input variables x_3 and x_4 are ideally selected solely for their bivariate response.

AUC [CI]	No. Input Variables	Training (n = 6000)	Optimisation (n = 2000)	Performance Estimation (n = 2000)
Optimal classifier	1	0.689 [0.675,0.702]	0.663 [0.639,0.687]	0.671 [0.648,0.695]
MLP	9	0.692 [0.678,0.705]	0.665 [0.641,0.688]	0.669 [0.646,0.693]
SVM	9	0.708 [0.695,0.721]	0.652 [0.628,0.676]	0.660 [0.637,0.684]
GBM	9	0.713 [0.700,0.726]	0.586 [0.561,0.610]	0.609 [0.584,0.633]
PRiSM models	*Components*		*Dirac measure*	
Lasso	1	0.688 [0.675,0.701]	0.663 [0.639,0.686]	0.672 [0.648,0.695]
PRN	1	0.690 [0.677,0.703]	0.664 [0.640,0.687]	0.670 [0.646,0.694]
PRN–Lasso	1	0.688 [0.675,0.702]	0.663 [0.639,0.686]	0.672 [0.648,0.695]
prSVM	14	0.691 [0.678,0.705]	0.663 [0.640,0.687]	0.671 [0.648,0.695]
prGBM	1	0.687 [0.674,0.700]	0.656 [0.633,0.680]	0.661 [0.638,0.685]
PRiSM models	*Components*		*Lebesgue measure*	
Lasso	1	0.689 [0.676,0.702]	0.664 [0.640,0.688]	0.670 [0.647,0.694]
PRN	1	0.690 [0.677,0.703]	0.664 [0.640,0.687]	0.670 [0.646,0.693]
PRN–Lasso	1	0.690 [0.676,0.703]	0.664 [0.641,0.688]	0.670 [0.647,0.694]
prSVM	7	0.690 [0.677,0.703]	0.633 [0.640,0.687]	0.672 [0.648,0.695]
prGBM	1	0.688 [0.675,0.702]	0.656 [0.632,0.680]	0.659 [0.635,0.682]

Table 3. Classification performance for the logical AND function measured by the AUC [CI]. The input variables x_5 and x_6 are ideally selected with two univariate responses and a bivariate response.

AUC [CI]	No. Input Variables	Training (n = 6000)	Optimisation (n = 2000)	Performance Estimation (n = 2000)
Optimal classifier	3	0.816 [0.802,0.830]	0.836 [0.813,0.860]	0.817 [0.793,0.841]
MLP	9	0.816 [0.803,0.830]	0.833 [0.809,0.857]	0.815 [0.791,0.839]
SVM	*9*	*0.803 [0.790,0.817]*	*0.797 [0.772,0.821]*	*0.786 [0.762, 0.809]*
GBM	9	0.822 [0.810,0.834]	0.826 [0.805,0.847]	0.808 [0.787,0.830]
PRiSM models	*Components*		*Dirac measure*	
Lasso	3	0.815 [0.801,0.828]	0.833 [0.809,0.857]	0.813 [0.789,0.837]
PRN	3	0.816 [0.802,0.829]	0.835 [0.811,0.858]	0.814 [0.790,0.838]
PRN–Lasso	3	0.816 [0.802,0.830]	0.835 [0.811,0.859]	0.814 [0.791,0.838]
prSVM	6	0.800 [0.787,0.813]	0.813 [0.790,0.835]	0.797 [0.774, 0.820]
prGBM	6	0.820 [0.807,0.832]	0.828 [0.807,0.848]	0.807 [0.786,0.829]

Table 3. Cont.

AUC [CI]	No. Input Variables	Training (n = 6000)	Optimisation (n = 2000)	Performance Estimation (n = 2000)
PRiSM models	*Components*		*Lebesgue measure*	
Lasso	3	0.815 [0.801,0.828]	0.832 [0.808,0.856]	0.813 [0.789,0.837]
PRN	3	0.816 [0.802,0.829]	0.835 [0.811,0.858]	0.814 [0.790,0.838]
PRN–Lasso	3	0.816 [0.802,0.830]	0.835 [0.811,0.858]	0.815 [0.791,0.839]
prSVM	4	0.799 [0.786,0.812]	0.812 [0.790,0.834]	0.796 [0.773,0.819]
prGBM	8	0.817 [0.805,0.829]	0.828 [0.808,0.849]	0.810 [0.789,0.831]

Table 4. Classification performance for the three-way interaction measured by the AUC [CI]. Three input variables are involved, x_7, x_8, and x_9.

AUC [CI]	No. Input Variables	Training (n = 6000)	Optimisation (n = 2000)	Performance Estimation (n = 2000)
Optimal classifier	3	**0.840 [0.822,0.859]**	**0.817 [0.783,0.851]**	**0.836 [0.805,0.868]**
MLP	9	0.840 [0.822,0.859]	0.809 [0.775,0.843]	0.832 [0.801,0.864]
SVM	*9*	*0.797 [0.779,0.815]*	*0.764 [0.729,0.798]*	*0.786 [0.755,0.817]*
GBM	9	0.831 [0.816,0.847]	0.796 [0.767,0.826]	0.813 [0.786,0.840]
PRiSM models	*Components*		*Dirac measure*	
Lasso	3	0.837 [0.818,0.855]	0.811 [0.777,0.845]	0.821 [0.797,0.861]
PRN	3	0.837 [0.819,0.856]	0.812 [0.778,0.846]	0.830 [0.799,0.862]
PRN–Lasso	3	0.837 [0.819,0.856]	0.812 [0.778,0.846]	0.830 [0.799,0.862]
prSVM	6	0.813 [0.796,0.829]	0.777 [0.744,0.810]	0.807 [0.778,0.836]
prGBM	3	0.832 [0.817,0.847]	0.797 [0.768,0.826]	0.813 [0.786,0.841]
PRiSM models	*Components*		*Lebesgue measure*	
Lasso	3	0.834 [0.816,0.853]	0.808 [0.774,0.842]	0.828 [0.796,0.860]
PRN	3	0.837 [0.819,0.856]	0.812 [0.778,0.846]	0.831 [0.799,0.862]
PRN–Lasso	3	0.837 [0.819,0.856]	0.812 [0.778,0.846]	0.831 [0.799,0.862]
prSVM	6	0.808 [0.792,0.824]	0.776 [0.745,0.808]	0.805 [0.777,0.833]
prGBM	4	0.825 [0.809,0.841]	0.798 [0.768,0.828]	0.810 [0.781,0.839]

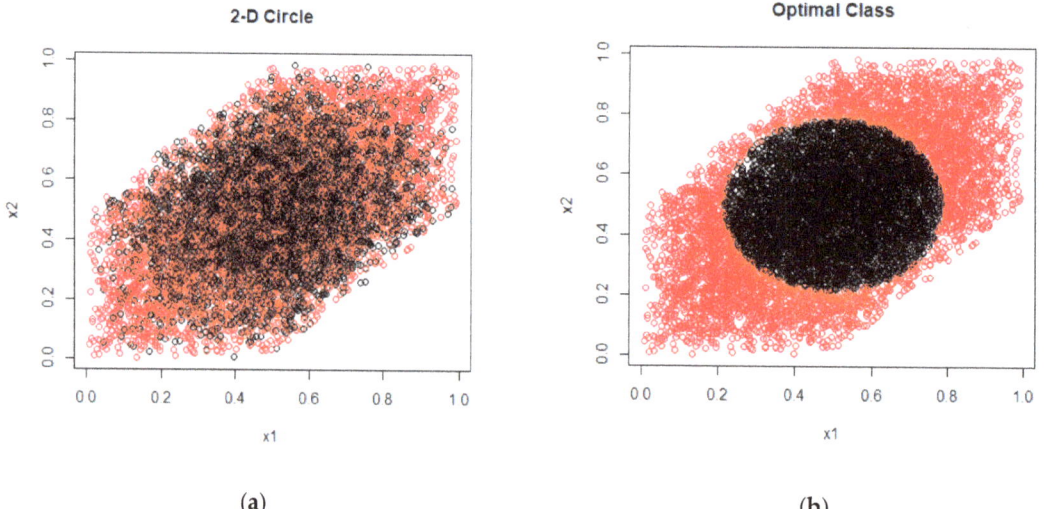

Figure 3. Class allocation for the 2-circle synthetic data set as a function of x_1 and x_2 showing: (**a**) The stochastic class labels; and (**b**) The correct classes that are used to find the optimal AUC.

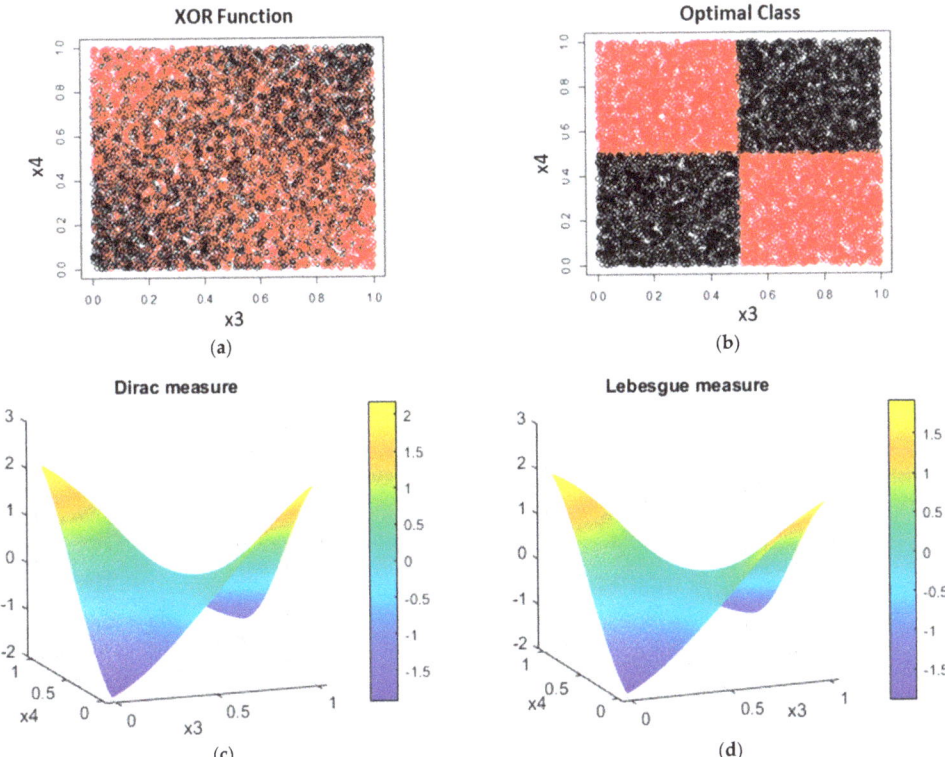

Figure 4. Class allocation for the XOR data set as a function of x_3 and x_4 showing: (**a**) The stochastic class labels; (**b**) The correct classes used to find the optimal AUC; (**c**) The two-way interaction term identified by the Dirac measure; and (**d**) The interaction estimated with the Lebesgue measure, which is almost identical to the curve in (**c**). Both surfaces are the only terms in the GAM, and closely correspond to the logit of the ideal XOR prediction surface. The main difference to theory is that the values at the four corners that saturate at finite values, whereas in theory, they extend to infinity in both vertical directions. This, however, has little impact on the crucial region for classification, which is the class boundary.

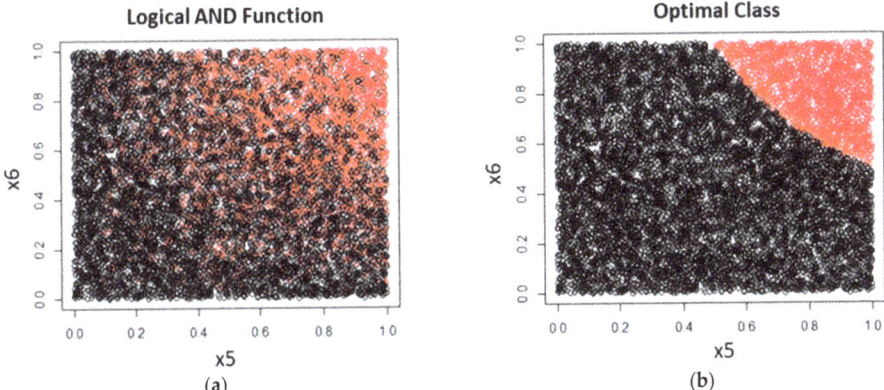

Figure 5. Class allocation for the synthetic data set representing the logical AND a function of x_5 and x_6 showing: (**a**) The stochastic class labels; and (**b**) The correct classes to find the optimal AUC.

The MLP-derived PRiSM models identified the correct ANOVA components for all data sets, with both the Dirac and Lebesgue measures. The three-way interaction term is a product of three inputs, not a pure interaction term. Therefore, its decision boundary can be approximated even in the absence of a third-order term, with three univariate partial responses sufficient to get close to the optimal prediction accuracy. Note that the predicted response in Figure 4c,d for the XOR task is very close to the bilinear surface corresponding to the theoretically correct response given by multilinear algebra (Tsukimoto, 2000).

Some machine learning models can be prolific in model selection with the ANOVA decomposition, followed by the Lasso, for either measure. The models always include the relevant variables but may also suffer from overfitting. However, it is remarkable how the interpretable models frequently achieve AUC values within 1% of the optimal value.

The models that filtered out the correct number of components to model each data set all have consistent interpretations. The partial responses correspond to the data generators in the vicinity of the class boundary, although the responses tend to level off away from the boundary, where the precise value of the logit is less important since the class membership probabilities are close to zero or one.

3.2. Real-World Data

The benchmarking results for the interpretable models against the original black box classifiers are summarised in Table 5. Values below the CI of the AUC are in italics.

Table 5. Classification performance for the real-valued data sets. The label 'D' indicates the number of input variables for the black boxes and component functions for the PRiSM models.

AUC [CI]	D	Diabetes	D	Credit Card	D	Shuttle
MLP	7	0.902 [0.850,0.954]	24	0.815 [0.758,0.872]	6	0.999 [0.998,1.000]
SVM	7	0.817 [0.749,0.884]	24	0.793 [0.733,0.852]	6	0.999 [0.999,1.000]
GBM	7	0.816 [0.748,0.884]	24	0.784 [0.724,0.845]	6	1.000 [0.999,1.000]
PRiSM models				*Dirac measure*		
MLP–Lasso	5	0.902 [0.851,0.954]	12	0.818 [0.762,0.875]	3	0.999 [0.999,1.000] *
PRN	5	0.903 [0.851,0.954]	12	0.809 [0.752,0.867]	3	0.999 [0.998,1.000] *
PRN–Lasso	5	0.903 [0.851,0.955]	12	0.815 [0.758,0.872]	2	0.998 [0.997,0.999] *
prSVM	5	0.884 [0.829,0.940]	13	0.798 [0.739,0.857]	3	0.998 [0.997,0.999] *
prGBM	8	0.847 [0.784,0.910]	10	0.763 [0.700,0.825]	2	0.998 [0.997,0.999]
PRiSM models				*Lebesgue measure*		
MLP–Lasso	4	0.889 [0.835,0.944]	12	0.819 [0.763,0.876]	3	0.999 [0.998,1.000] *
PRN	4	0.903 [0.852,0.955]	12	0.817 [0.760,0.874]	3	0.999 [0.998,1.000] *
PRN–Lasso	4	0.905 [0.853,0.956]	11	0.819 [0.762,0.875]	2	0.999 [0.998,1.000] *
prSVM	6	0.896 [0.842,0.949]	12	0.803 [0.745,0.861]	3	0.998 [0.997,0.999] *
prGBM	7	0.881 [0.824,0.937]	9	0.791 [0.732,0.851]	2	0.997 [0.995,0.998]

* Indicates a two-stage model selection process, explained in the text.

All methods use the same data sets, and the AUCs are quoted for test data only. Measuring statistical significance with the McNemar test shows that the performance difference between any pair of models is not significant at the 5% level.

While the accuracy of all models is comparable, the PRiSM models use fewer variables and are intuitive to interpret. It is also apparent that the two different measures lead to very similar classification performances. The coefficients of the Lasso used for re-calibration are close to unity for all models.

The number of component functions in Table 5 shows the effect of variable selection by the Lasso. The Diabetes data set generates only univariate responses. However, the Credit Card and Shuttle data sets require two-way interactions, as well as univariate effects. Note that the Credit Card data set generates 300 partial responses to choose from.

The GAMs, seeded by the SVM and GBM, are calibrated by the LASSO, resulting in the prSVM and prGBM. The univariate and bivariate structure of these models can be used to define a PRN model, which is a SENN with MLP components, initialised either with random weights or with univariate and bivariate modules trained to replicate each of the selected partial responses. This will replicate the PRN and, following orthogonalization, the PRN–Lasso.

The sparsity of the models and their potential for interpretation are illustrated by the partial responses of two models, the MLP–Lasso and the PRN, shown in Figures 6–11. These functions are derived from the training data and are always used for prediction on out-of-sample data. The corresponding component functions for the other PRiSM models have similar values, although, if derived from random forests, e.g., in the case of the prGBM, they are stepwise constant rather than smooth. This is shown in [20] for a different data set.

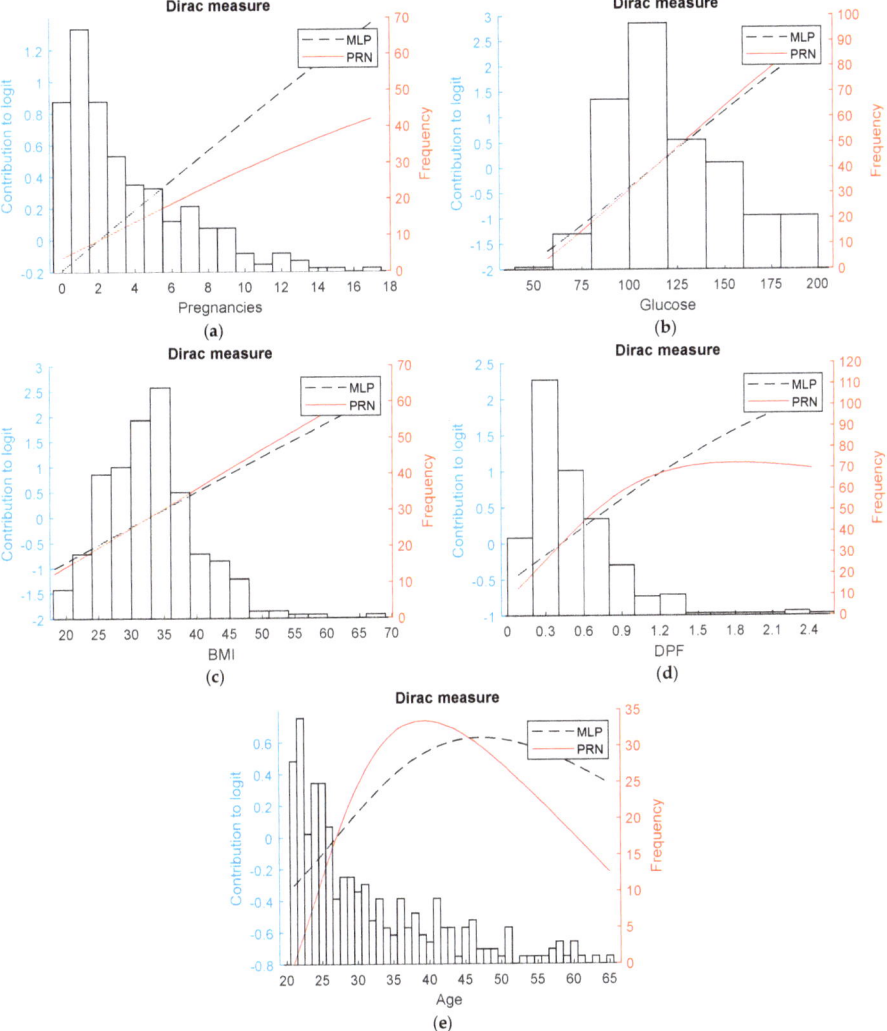

Figure 6. Contributions to the logit from partial responses to the logit (left axis) for the Diabetes data set, obtained with the Dirac measure, overlapped with the histogram of the training data (right axis). The final partial responses derived at the second application gradient descent (solid lines) are shown alongside the partial responses from the original MLP (dashed lines). Five covariates are represented, namely (**a**) Pregnancies, (**b**) Glucose, (**c**) BMI, (**d**) DPF and (**e**) Age.

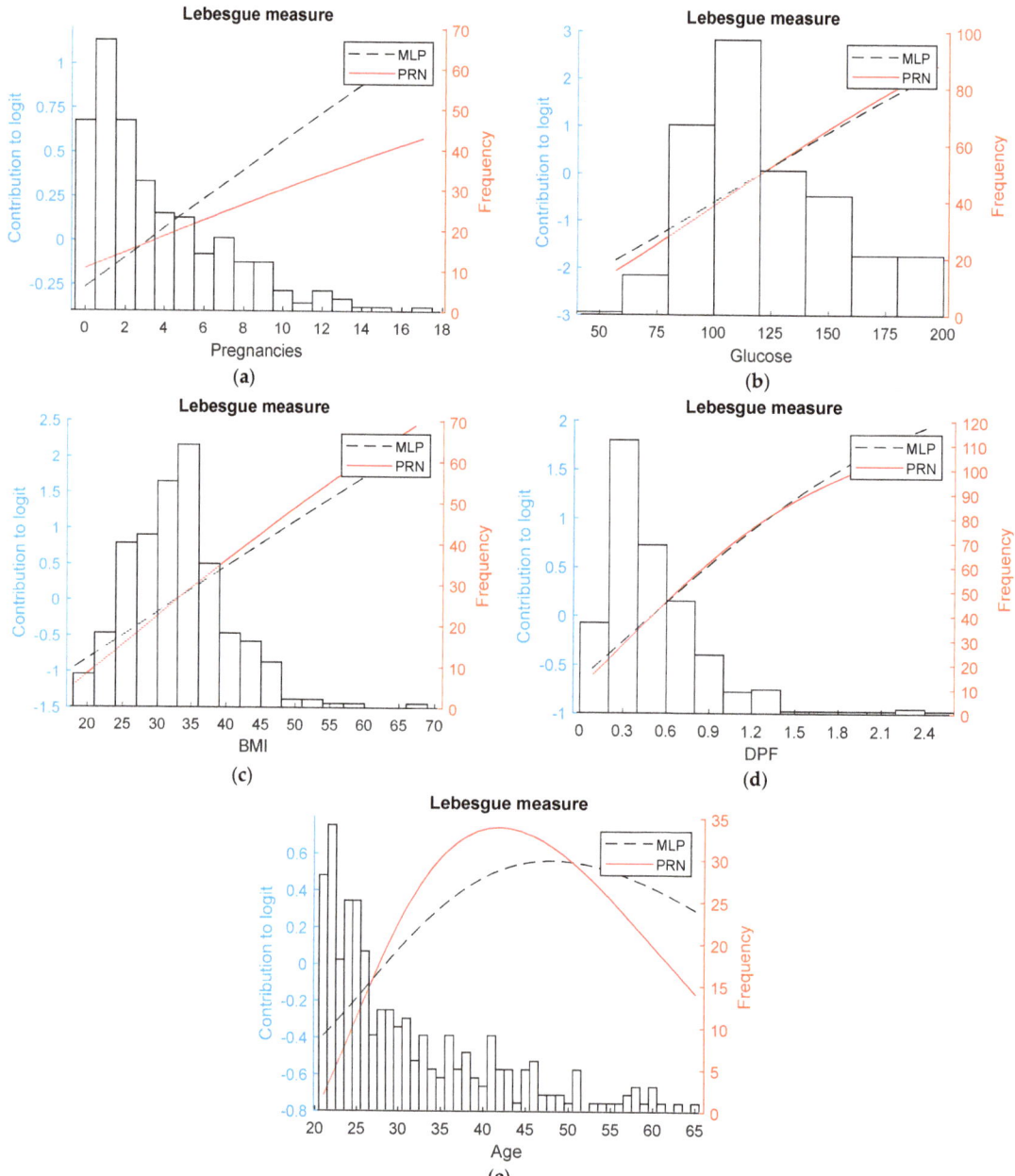

Figure 7. As for Figure 6, with the Lebesgue measure, the component functions of the GAM are very similar for both measures. They have a similar structure and range of contributions to the logit. Despite being fitted with a generic non-linear model, the MLP, several of the partial responses are linear. Variable "DPF" shows a saturation effect, as might be expected, while the log odds of "Age" as an independent effect peak around the age of 40. Note that data sparseness for higher values will result in greater uncertainty in the estimation of the partial response. The same size covariates are represented (**a**–**e**) as in Figure 6.

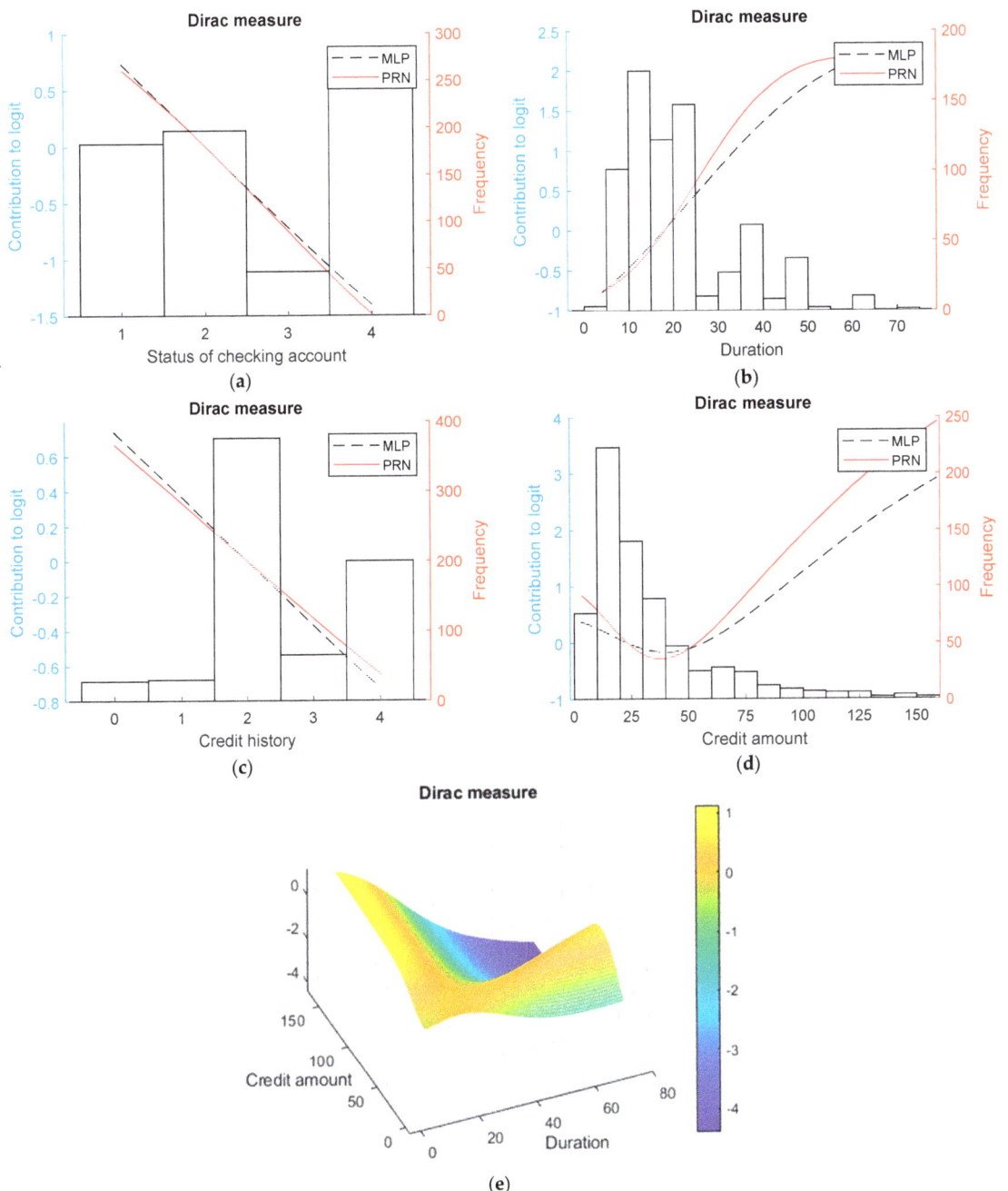

Figure 8. Partial responses for the German Credit Card data set, using the same notation as the previous figures. Four univariate responses and a bivariate response are shown namely for the covariates (**a**) Status of checking account, (**b**) Duration of loan, (**c**) Credit history and (**d**) Credit amount, together with (**e**) the pairwise interaction between Credit amount and Duration of loan.

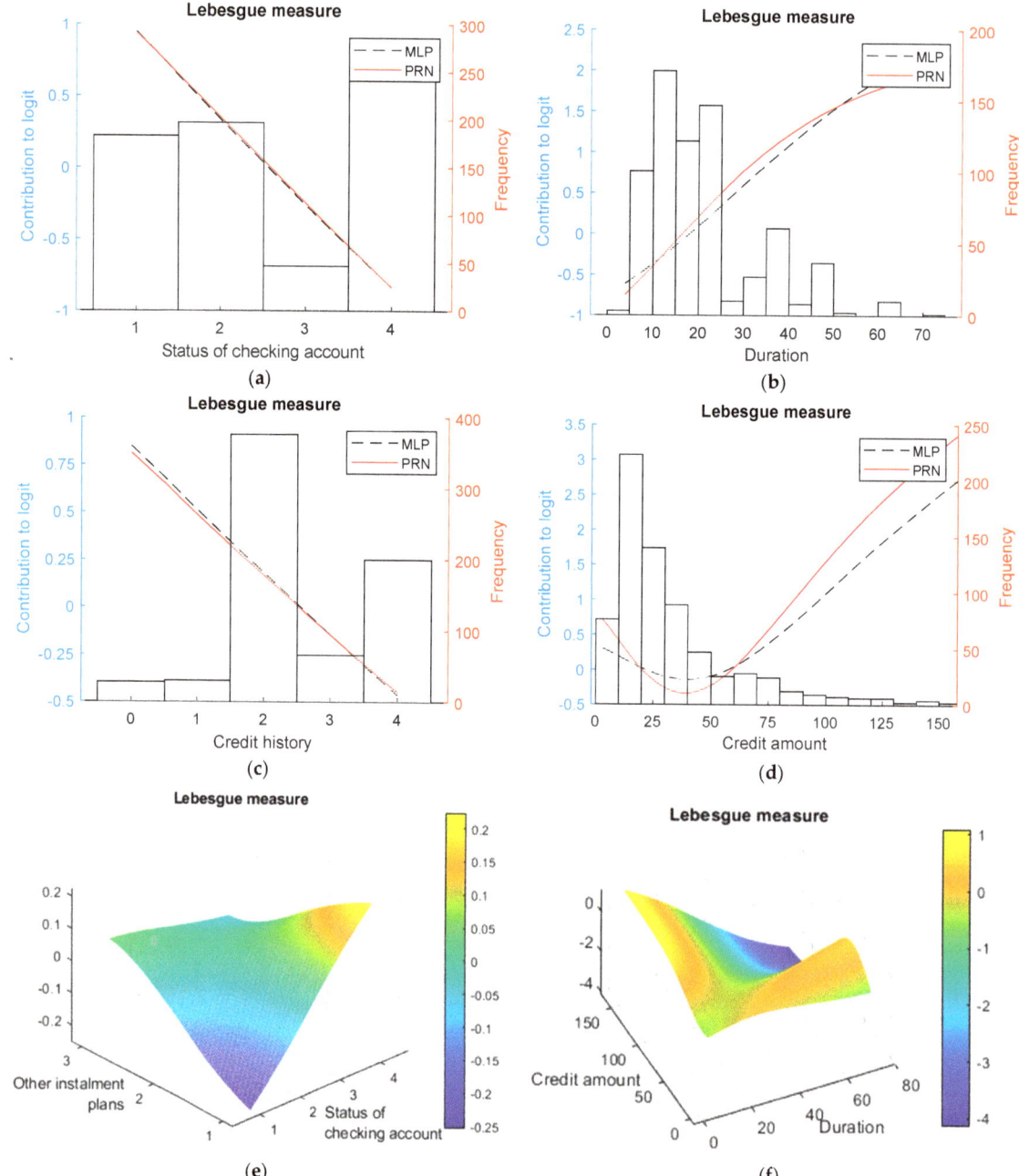

Figure 9. As for Figure 8, with the Lebesgue measure for the same covariates in (**a**–**d**), but with two pairwise interactions involving the variables listed in (**e**,**f**). Despite the different nature of the two measures, they offer entirely consistent interpretations, with the only difference being the selection by the Lasso model of a second bivariate interaction term, albeit with a range in contribution to the logit that is five times smaller than for the interaction term involving "Credit amount" and "Duration".

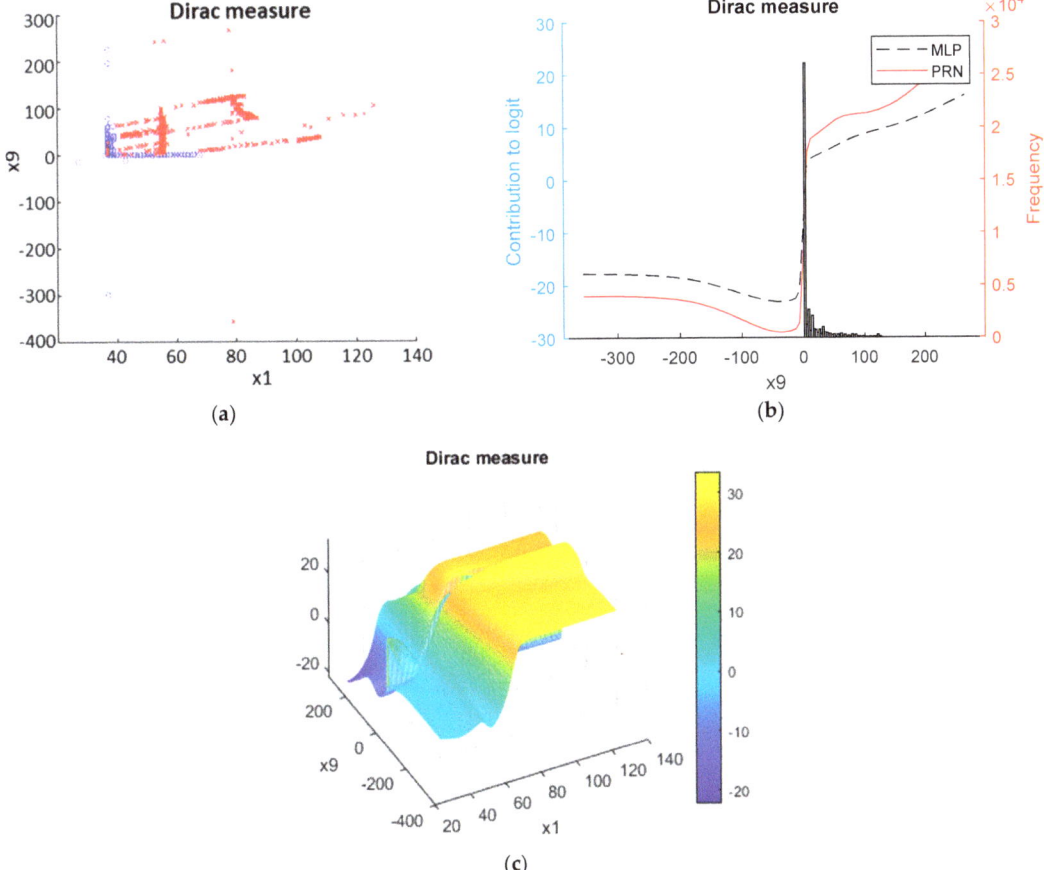

Figure 10. Nomogram of the PRN–Lasso model obtained for the Statlog Shuttle data set using the Dirac measure with a training/test split of n = 43,500 and 14,500, respectively: (**a**) Shows the raw data for the two variables selected, which corresponds well with two partial responses in the final model, namely: (**b**) shows the main effect involving x_9; and (**c**) plots the two-way interaction between the two variables in the model, x_1 and x_9.

Among the seven covariates in the Diabetes data set, five occurred together as univariate responses in all of the random initialisations for the MLP–Lasso, PRN–Lasso, and the two measures. They are "Pregnancies", "Glucose", "BMI", "DPF", and "Age". An interaction term involving "Glucose" and "DPF" was present in three random initialisations. The set of models obtained is, therefore, remarkably stable. The partial responses for the recurrent univariate effects are shown in Figures 6 and 7.

The German Credit Card data set is more challenging. Out of 24 variables, six were present in all initialisations for both measures: "Duration", "Credit history", "Savings accounts", "Period of employment", and the two variables labelled x_{16} and x_{17}. In the case of the Lebesgue measure, three more variables recurred in all 10 initialisations, namely "Status of checking account", "Other instalment plans", and "Worker status". In addition, the variable "Credit amount" featured as a univariate or a bivariate term in eight initialisations. These ten variables were selected to obtain the models for which a selection of component functions is shown in Figures 8 and 9.

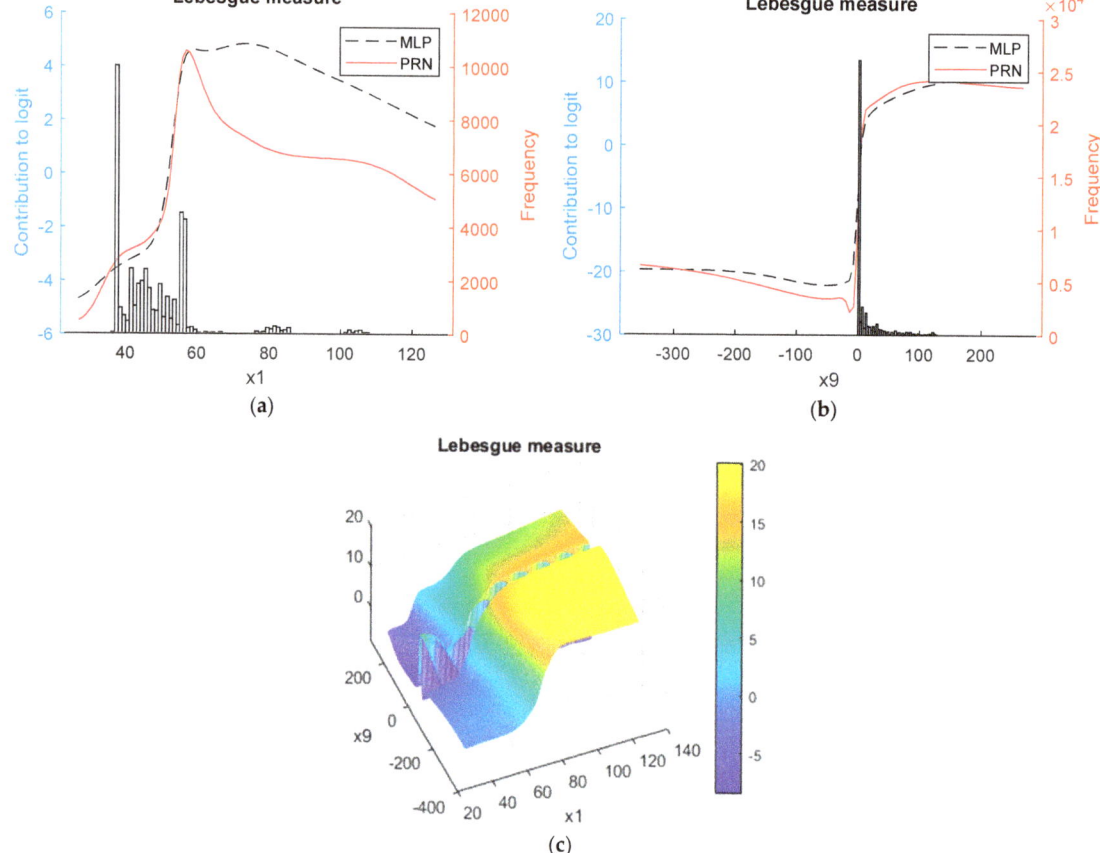

Figure 11. As for Figure 7, with the Lebesgue measure, the same two variables were used as with the Dirac measure, and similar AUC performance was achieved albeit involving an additional univariate term. Shown are the two main effects involving covariates x_1 in (**a**) and x_9 in (**b**) together with the pairwise interaction between them in (**c**).

Four univariate functions for multi-valued input variables are consistently monotonically decreasing and very close to linear, suggesting that these indicators are well calibrated as independent effects on credit risk, quantifying reductions in risk with rising input values. "Duration" shows saturation in its contribution to risk for large values, and "Credit amount" has a non-linear response with a minimum value. The bivariate responses suggest that to optimise the overall calibration of the model, adjustments are required in addition to the main effects. This includes a risk reduction when the "Credit amount" and "Duration" are both high, and a slight enhancement when either is small compared with the median value.

After mapping the structure derived with the Dirac measure from the prSVM onto the PRN–Lasso, good discrimination was achieved with an AUC of 0.812 [0.755,0.869] with just ten univariate effects. They comprised the six variables identified also by the PRN, together with the variables 'Personal status', 'Property', and 'Other instalment plans'.

For both the Diabetes and Credit Card data, the other benchmarked algorithms, SVM and GBM, generally select more components than the MLP and have worse generalisation performance, as evident from Table 5. If the partial response models derived from each machine learning algorithm are mapped onto a SENN and further trained, then their performance becomes similar for all of the models and they select consistent input variables, although some models will include additional ones.

The scalability and power of the method can be illustrated using the Statlog Shuttle data set. This data set is challenging because all of the variables have non-normal distributions, often with very peaked histograms, hence very small entropy. Two of the variables, x_5 and x_9, have a Pearson correlation of -0.875.

When applying MLP, the weight decay parameters estimated for variables x_2, x_4, and x_6 are noticeably larger than the others, indicating that these variables are less informative. They were, therefore, removed from the data. In the case of the Dirac measure, univariate component functions for x_1 and x_9 were selected by the PRN–Lasso with an AUC of 0.996 [0.994,0.998]. Selecting just these two variables as the inputs resulted in the performance listed in Table 5, involving a univariate effect for x_9 together with the interaction between x_1 and x_9. The Lebesgue measure behaved similarly but for the same Lasso selection procedure, and included also a univariate effect for x_1 albeit without an appreciable performance improvement.

The prSVM model selection process also followed a two-stage process, ending with the same two variables, x_1 and x_9, for both measures, each time involved in two univariate effects and a bivariate term. Interestingly, the prGBM model converged straight away on the two-component solution involving a univariate effect for x_9 and an interaction between x_1 and x_9 with the Dirac measure; with the Lebesgue measure, it converged on two univariate effects.

4. Discussion

A potential advantage of the PRN model over other PRiSM models in their current formulation is that the PRN allows for a second step of training, where the univariate and bivariate responses are re-estimated without the constraints of the ANOVA framework. The PRN–Lasso then applies the ANOVA framework to the refined univariate and bivariate models obtained by the PRN, followed by re-calibration, using logistic regression with L_1 regularisation.

We now turn to three key questions for explainable machine learning methods: the accuracy of the resulting models, their stability in model selection and their interpretability. In particular, accuracy and stability are critical requirements for any interpretable model.

4.1. Predictive Accuracy

The ability to model data depends primarily on the capacity of the machine learning algorithm to fit the data structure given the observational noise. Each of the methods shown is capable of fitting the benchmark data although some of the point estimates of the AUC are close to the confidence limit boundaries of the best performing methods. Therefore, the different methods have different efficiencies for modelling specific data sets. However, all of the models have comparable performance, which is uniformly high and with no evidence of an interpretability vs. performance trade-off.

4.2. Stability

The discussion of the empirical results shows that model selection is stable for multiple random initialisations of the MLP algorithm. This suggests that the PRiSM framework resolves two major limitations of the MLP: different predictions for multiple initialisations and lack of interpretation. It turns out that re-shaping the MLP to become a SENN also stabilises the predictions for different initialisations.

Stability is also good between models, with consistency between the input variables selected by all of the methods. This is perhaps most striking for the Shuttle data, where all of the methods picked the two key variables and identified an important interaction between them from a highly non-linear but remarkably noise-free set of measurements.

4.3. Interpretability

This can be referred to a formal framework involving the three Cs of interpretability [23]:

- Completeness—the proposed models have global coverage in the sense that they provide a direct and causal explanation of the model output from the input data, over the complete range of input data. The validity of the model output is evidenced by the AUC and calibration measures;
- Compactness—the explanations are as succinct, ensured by the application of logistic regression modelling with the Lasso. The component functions, both univariate and bivariate, are shown in the results to be stable, as are the derived GAMs;
- Correctness—the explanation generates trust in the sense that:
    - They are sufficiently correct to ensure good calibration for all data sets. This means that deviations from the theoretical curves for the synthetic data occur in regions where the model is close to saturated, i.e., making predictions close to 0 or 1;
    - The label coherence of the instances covered by the explanation is assured by the shape of the component functions so that the neighbouring instances have similar explanations.

The partial responses for the real-world data sets are plausible. In the case of the medical and credit card classifiers, some variables show remarkably linear dependence over their full range, while others are monotonic but their values saturate, showing a levelling-up beyond a certain point. In some cases, there is a turning point, and, interestingly, this was seen consistently for the two measures, e.g., for the added risk associated with credit amount, shown in Figures 8d and 9d. There is also a clear impact from data sparsity, which causes variability in the component functions in the less densely sampled regions of the data.

A more thorough appraisal of the plausibility of a PRiSM model using the Dirac measure applied to heart transplants is discussed in [21].

Finally, we note that PRiSM models are counterfactual because their predictions are directly connected to the input values. In the case of the PRN, the logit of the probabilistic prediction is simply the sum of the univariate and bivariate responses, whereas for the MLP–Lasso, PRN–Lasso, and the remaining PRiSM models seeded by other machine learning algorithms, the prediction is the sum of the response functions re-scaled by the linear coefficients of the Lasso.

5. Conclusions

We propose ANOVA decompositions of multivariate logit functions into sums of functions of fewer variables as a computationally efficient way to open probabilistic black box binary classifiers. Empirical results on the synthetic and real-world data show that the resulting interpretable models do not suffer from the interpretability vs. performance trade-off when applied to tabular data. Moreover, two alternative measures, Dirac and Lebesgue, lead to consistent interpretations for any given data set. The proposed method is accurate, stable, and scalable. Benchmarking it against a range of machine learning algorithms confirms this.

This paper formalizes the complete framework for the derivation of GAMs from black box classifiers, links the formalism to a commonly used attribution measure, Shapley values, and demonstrates its compliance with a user-led interpretability framework [23]. The paper extends previous results from related work focusing on clinical interpretations of a particular realization of the framework with anchored decomposition [20,21]. An unexpected finding of this study is that although the two measures are distinct, in that the Dirac measure represents a cut through a response surface at a particular point in the data and so is dependent on the choice of anchor point, while the Lebesgue measure integrates the surface over the range of the data and so is closer to the evaluation of size effects, both measures lead to similar interpretable models. This result is encouraging and suggests that the PRiSM framework may be a viable method to derive globally interpretable models from arbitrary binary classifiers.

The resulting partial responses form a nomogram, which is a broadly used method of communicating complex models to users without the need for a detailed mathematical formulation [33]. We show that the components in the nomogram of a GAM agree exactly with the Shapley values, which are increasingly used for the explanation of machine learning in some high-stakes applications [34].

The component functions derived with the two measures, while close, are not identical. Further work is required to explore with end-users the preference for either measure and by which model they are seeded. In addition, confidence intervals for the univariate and bivariate terms need to be quantified. There are also clear parallels with regression models and a possible extension of the binary classifier to survival modelling within the framework of partial logistic cost functions [35]. Note that the method applies to any classifier that predicts the probability of class membership since it does not use the internal structure of the classifier but only the overall response function.

Author Contributions: P.J.G.L. conceptualised the method and led the study. P.J.G.L., S.O.-M. and I.O. implemented the code and ran the experiments. B.W. contributed to the discussions, implementation, and experiments. All authors evaluated the results. P.J.G.L., S.O.-M. and I.O. drafted the early versions of the manuscript. All authors contributed to the writing, reviewing, and editing, and approved the final manuscript. All authors have read and agreed to the published version of the manuscript.

Funding: This was partially funded by Liverpool John Moores University via a PhD scholarship.

Data Availability Statement: The real-world data analysed in the current study are available in Kaggle, the UCI Machine Learning repository, and PhysioNet, as follows: Diabetes (Pima Indians diabetes database): https://www.kaggle.com/datasets/uciml/pima-indians-diabetes-database (access on 11 October 2021) German Credit Card (Statlog German credit card data set): https://archive.ics.uci.edu/ml/datasets/statlog+(german+credit+data) (access on 11 October 2021). Statlog Shuttle data set: https://archive.ics.uci.edu/ml/datasets/Statlog+(Shuttle) (access on 11 October 2021). Medical Information Mart for Intensive Care (MIMIC-III): https://physionet.org/content/mimiciii/1.4/ (access on 11 October 2021).

Conflicts of Interest: The authors declare no conflict of interest.

References

1. Angelino, E.; Larus-Stone, N.; Alabi, D.; Seltzer, M.; Rudin, C. Learning Certifiably Optimal Rule Lists for Categorical Data. *J. Mach. Learn. Res.* **2018**, *18*, 1–78.
2. Rögnvaldsson, T.; Etchells, T.A.; You, L.; Garwicz, D.; Jarman, I.; Lisboa, P.J.G. How to Find Simple and Accurate Rules for Viral Protease Cleavage Specificities. *BMC Bioinform.* **2009**, *10*, 149. [CrossRef]
3. Poon, A.I.F.; Sung, J.J.Y. Opening the Black Box of AI-Medicine. *J. Gastroenterol. Hepatol.* **2021**, *36*, 581–584. [CrossRef]
4. Christodoulou, E.; Ma, J.; Collins, G.S.; Steyerberg, E.W.; Verbakel, J.Y.; van Calster, B. A Systematic Review Shows No Performance Benefit of Machine Learning over Logistic Regression for Clinical Prediction Models. *J. Clin. Epidemiol.* **2019**, *110*, 12–22. [CrossRef] [PubMed]
5. Guidotti, R.; Monreale, A.; Ruggieri, S.; Turini, F.; Giannotti, F.; Pedreschi, D. A Survey of Methods for Explaining Black Box Models. *ACM Comput. Surv.* **2018**, *51*, 93. [CrossRef]
6. Sarle, W.S. Neural Networks and Statistical Models. In Proceedings of the Nineteenth Annual SAS Users Group International Conference, Dallas, TX, USA, 10–13 April 1994; pp. 1538–1550.
7. Brás-Geraldes, C.; Papoila, A.; Xufre, P. Odds Ratio Function Estimation Using a Generalized Additive Neural Network. *Neural Comput. Appl.* **2019**, *32*, 3459–3474. [CrossRef]
8. Lee, C.K.; Samad, M.; Hofer, I.; Cannesson, M.; Baldi, P. Development and Validation of an Interpretable Neural Network for Prediction of Postoperative In-Hospital Mortality. *NPJ Digit. Med.* **2021**, *4*, 8. [CrossRef]
9. Alvarez-Melis, D.; Jaakkola, T.S. Towards Robust Interpretability with Self-Explaining Neural Networks. In Proceedings of the 32nd Conference on Neural Information Processing Systems (NeurIPS 2018), Montréal, QC, Canada, 2–8 December 2018.
10. Hooker, G. Generalized Functional ANOVA Diagnostics for High-Dimensional Functions of Dependent Variables. *J. Comput. Graph. Stat.* **2007**, *16*, 709–732. [CrossRef]
11. Friedman, J.H. Greedy Function Approximation: A Gradient Boosting Machine. *Ann. Stat.* **2001**, *29*, 1189–1232. [CrossRef]
12. Agarwal, R.; Melnick, L.; Frosst, N.; Zhang, X.; Lengerich, B.; Caruana, R.; Hinton, G.E. Neural Additive Models: Interpretable Machine Learning with Neural Nets. *Adv. Neural Inf. Process. Syst.* **2020**, *6*, 4699–4711. [CrossRef]

13. Nori, H.; Jenkins, S.; Koch, P.; Caruana, R. InterpretML: A Unified Framework for Machine Learning Interpretability. *arXiv* **2019**, arXiv:1909.09223 2019.
14. Yang, Z.; Zhang, A.; Sudjianto, A. GAMI-Net: An Explainable Neural Network Based on Generalized Additive Models with Structured Interactions. *Pattern Recognit.* **2021**, *120*, 108192. [CrossRef]
15. Ravikumar, P.; Lafferty, J.; Liu, H.; Wasserman, L. Sparse Additive Models. *J. R. Stat. Soc. Ser. B* **2009**, *71*, 1009–1030. [CrossRef]
16. Chen, H.; Wang, X.; Deng, C.; Huang, H. Group Sparse Additive Machine. *Adv. Neural Inf. Process. Syst.* **2017**, *30*, 97–207.
17. van Belle, V.; Lisboa, P. White Box Radial Basis Function Classifiers with Component Selection for Clinical Prediction Models. *Artif. Intell. Med.* **2014**, *60*, 53–64. [CrossRef]
18. Saltelli, A.; Annoni, P.; Azzini, I.; Campolongo, F.; Ratto, M.; Tarantola, S. Variance Based Sensitivity Analysis of Model Output. Design and Estimator for the Total Sensitivity Index. *Comput. Phys. Commun.* **2010**, *181*, 259–270. [CrossRef]
19. Rudin, C. Stop Explaining Black Box Machine Learning Models for High Stakes Decisions and Use Interpretable Models Instead. *Nat. Mach. Intell.* **2019**, *1*, 206–215. [CrossRef]
20. Walters, B.; Ortega-Martorell, S.; Olier, I.; Lisboa, P.J.G. Towards Interpretable Machine Learning for Clinical Decision Support. In Proceedings of the International Joint Conference on Neural Networks, Padua, Italy, 18–23 July 2022. [CrossRef]
21. Lisboa, P.J.G.; Jayabalan, M.; Ortega-Martorell, S.; Olier, I.; Medved, D.; Nilsson, J. Enhanced Survival Prediction Using Explainable Artificial Intelligence in Heart Transplantation. *Sci. Rep.* **2022**, *12*, 19525. [CrossRef]
22. Lundberg, S.; Lee, S.-I. A Unified Approach to Interpreting Model Predictions. *Adv. Neural Inf. Process. Syst.* **2017**, *30*, 4765–4774.
23. Carvalho, D.V.; Pereira, E.M.; Cardoso, J.S. Machine Learning Interpretability: A Survey on Methods and Metrics. *Electronics* **2019**, *8*, 832. [CrossRef]
24. Tibshirani, R. Regression Shrinkage and Selection Via the Lasso. *J. R. Stat. Soc. Ser. B* **1996**, *58*, 267–288. [CrossRef]
25. The MathWorks Inc. *MATLAB*; The MathWorks Inc.: Natick, MA, USA, 1994.
26. MacKay, D.J.C. The Evidence Framework Applied to Classification Networks. *Neural Comput.* **1992**, *4*, 720–736. [CrossRef]
27. Nabney, I. *NETLAB: Algorithms for Pattern Recognitions*; Springer: Berlin/Heidelberg, Germany, 2002.
28. Tsukimoto, H. Extracting Rules from Trained Neural Networks. *IEEE Trans. Neural Netw.* **2000**, *11*, 377–389. [CrossRef] [PubMed]
29. Ripley, B.D. *Pattern Recognition and Neural Networks*; Cambridge University Press: Cambridge, UK, 1996.
30. Smith, J.W.; Everhart, J.E.; Dickson, W.C.; Knowler, W.C.; Johannes, R.S. Using the ADAP Learning Algorithm to Forecast the Onset of Diabetes Mellitus. In Proceedings of the Annual Symposium on Computer Application in Medical Care, Washington, DC, USA, 6–9 November 1988; p. 261.
31. Newman, D.J.; Hettich, S.; Blake, C.L.; Merz, C.J. UCI Repository of Machine Learning Databases. Available online: http://www.ics.uci.edu/~mlearn/MLRepository.html (accessed on 1 January 2022).
32. Abe, N.; Zadrozny, B.; Langford, J. Outlier Detection by Active Learning. In Proceedings of the ACM SIGKDD International Conference on Knowledge Discovery and Data Mining, Philadelphia, PA, USA, 20–23 August 2006; pp. 504–509. [CrossRef]
33. Balachandran, V.P.; Gonen, M.; Smith, J.J.; DeMatteo, R.P. Nomograms in Oncology: More than Meets the Eye. *Lancet Oncol.* **2015**, *16*, e173–e180. [CrossRef] [PubMed]
34. Roder, J.; Maguire, L.; Georgantas, R.; Roder, H. Explaining Multivariate Molecular Diagnostic Tests via Shapley Values. *BMC Med. Inform. Decis. Mak.* **2021**, *21*, 1–18. [CrossRef]
35. Biganzoli, E.; Boracchi, P.; Mariani, L.; Marubini, E. Feed Forward Neural Networks for the Analysis of Censored Survival Data: A Partial Logistic Regression Approach. *Stat. Med.* **1998**, *17*, 1169–1186. [CrossRef]

Disclaimer/Publisher's Note: The statements, opinions and data contained in all publications are solely those of the individual author(s) and contributor(s) and not of MDPI and/or the editor(s). MDPI and/or the editor(s) disclaim responsibility for any injury to people or property resulting from any ideas, methods, instructions or products referred to in the content.

Article

Framework for Evaluating Potential Causes of Health Risk Factors Using Average Treatment Effect and Uplift Modelling

Daniela Galatro [1], Rosario Trigo-Ferre [2], Allana Nakashook-Zettler [1], Vincenzo Costanzo-Alvarez [3,*], Melanie Jeffrey [4], Maria Jacome [5], Jason Bazylak [3] and Cristina H. Amon [1,3]

1. Department of Chemical Engineering and Applied Chemistry, University of Toronto, Toronto, ON M5S 3E5, Canada
2. Faculty of Applied Science and Engineering, University of Toronto, Toronto, ON M5S 3E5, Canada
3. Department of Mechanical and Industrial Engineering, University of Toronto, Toronto, ON M5S 3G8, Canada
4. Centre for Indigenous Studies, University of Toronto, Toronto, ON M5S 2J7, Canada
5. Faculty of Applied Sciences and Technology, Humber Institute of Technology and Advanced Learning, Toronto, ON M9W 5L7, Canada
* Correspondence: v.costanzo@utoronto.ca

Abstract: Acute myeloid leukemia (AML) is a type of blood cancer that affects both adults and children. Benzene exposure has been reported to increase the risk of developing AML in children. The assessment of the potential relationship between environmental benzene exposure and childhood has been documented in the literature using odds ratios and/or risk ratios, with data fitted to unconditional logistic regression. A common feature of the studies involving relationships between environmental risk factors and health outcomes is the lack of proper analysis to evidence causation. Although statistical causal analysis is commonly used to determine causation by evaluating a distribution's parameters, it is challenging to infer causation in complex systems from single correlation coefficients. Machine learning (ML) approaches, based on causal pattern recognition, can provide an accurate alternative to model counterfactual scenarios. In this work, we propose a framework using average treatment effect (ATE) and Uplift modeling to evidence causation when relating exposure to benzene indoors and outdoors to childhood AML, effectively predicting causation when exposed indoors to this contaminant. An analysis of the assumptions, cross-validation, sample size, and interaction between predictors are also provided, guiding future works looking at the universalization of this approach in predicting health outcomes.

Keywords: acute myeloid leukemia; risk factors; average treatment effect; uplift modelling; machine learning; benzene

1. Introduction

Acute myeloid leukemia (AML) is a cancer of the myeloid line of blood cells; AML starts in the blood stem cells and is characterized by its rapid growth [1]. While AML is the most common type of leukemia in adults, it also affects children; and about 500 children are diagnosed with AML in the U.S. annually [2]. Childhood AML is most prevalent during the first two years of life and adolescence. Epidemiological and genetic studies have confirmed that most infant leukemias develop in utero [3,4].

Chemical exposure to significant benzene concentrations is reported as a possible cause of AML in occupationally exposed workers [5]. Benzene exposure has also been reported to increase the risk of developing AML in children. Most existing reports are retrospective case-control studies [6], which are inherently limited since benzene exposure is typically measured indirectly (biased) as parents of sick versus healthy children may differentially recall them [5].

Moreover, some positive findings may be due to confounding factors instead, as other biases are added when specific segments of the population are under-represented in the study or control cohorts [6]. It has also been noted that exposure to various solvents and hydrocarbons increases the chance of developing childhood AML [7,8]. Both groups of chemicals fall into a vast range of toxicological profiles, benzene being the one of greatest concern.

In the following subsections, we briefly review the traditional approaches to establishing the relationship between Benzene Exposure and AML and current trends in estimating causation for health outcomes using Machine Learning outcomes.

1.1. Traditional Approaches to Establishing the Relationship between Benzene Exposure and AML

The Bradford Hill criteria [9,10] have been extensively used to evaluate causation when human epidemiologic relationships are found between exposure to a contaminant such as benzene and the disease outcome, such as AML or other hematopoietic and pulmonary diseases [10]. Despite its extensive use, this method is still debated among epidemiologists, as they question, among many arguments, its scope of application and the possibility of ruling out causality in some specific scenarios.

The assessment of the potential relationship between environmental benzene exposure and childhood AML includes studying exposures prior to conception, during pregnancy, or while breastfeeding [5]. Parental exposure to benzene, for instance, has been studied as a potential risk factor for infant AML, with conflicting results among researchers. Kaatsch et al. [11] and Shu et al. [12] did not find any association between parental exposure and childhood AML. On the other hand, Buckley et al. [13] and Magnani et al. [14] reported elevated rates of childhood AML associated with benzene, solvents, and paternal petroleum occupational exposure (prenatal).

Households' exposures to benzene have also been investigated, showing no increases in childhood AML related to home use of solvents [15,16]. Nevertheless, cigarette smoke, the main non-occupational source of benzene, is associated with an increased risk of developing this disease, even at low-level exposure to benzene, through parental smoking during pregnancy [17,18].

Other exposure surrogates for benzene as an air pollutant are traffic density and proximity to chemical plants, refineries, and gas stations. While several air pollutants are typically present in different concentrations, their risks are ranked by odds ratios. Norlinder and Jarkvolm [19] observed an increase in childhood AML related to car density with an incidence greater than 20 cars/km^2, possibly attributable to benzene in the gasoline. Reynolds [20] reported correlations between traffic density between benzene and butadiene air concentrations. The corresponding odds ratios for children reveal a relationship with the incidence rate of childhood AML. Similarly, Crosignani et al. [21] also reported an association between elevated rates of childhood AML to traffic density, attributable to high benzene exposure. Steffan et al. [22] reported an increased risk of this disease in proximity to gas stations, while Harrison et al. [23] found no association. These opposing results have also been reported when analyzing the risks of nearby petrochemical plants [5].

The discrepancies found in the literature may be due to the method of estimating exposures, potential confound from correlated pollutants, and the intrinsically anisotropic nature of the control volumes defined for the studies. For instance, air measurements in outdoor volumes, show considerable variability in space and time, compared to values reported for indoor control volumes. Benzene has undoubtedly been classified as a human carcinogen causing AML in adults when exposed to relatively high concentrations at work. Nevertheless, it is not clear if low concentrations of this compound in outdoor air cause childhood AML, although some studies reveal some association [24].

Previous studies involving benzene exposure and childhood AML statistically reported their results as odds ratio (OR) and/or risk ratio (RR). OR stands for the ratio of an event's odds in one group (for example, the exposed group) to its odds in the other group (for example, the nonexposed group); the risk ratio (RR) stands for the ratio of the risk of an event in one group to the risk of an event in the other group. An OR or RR greater than 1.0 indicates an increase in odds or risk among the exposed group compared to the unexposed one. Conditional and unconditional logistic regressions are typically used to fit the data of these studies, hence estimating the ORs, and RRs [25–27]. Matching is used in case-control studies to adjust for confounding data, ensuring that regression is possible when there is not enough overlap in confounding variables between cases and a set of controls. Age, sex, and race are typical confounders suggested by descriptive epidemiology [28]. Since the distribution of these variables may differ between cases and controls, matching is commonly used to select cases and controls with similar distributions of similar variables. Unmatched case-control studies, on the other hand, are typically analyzed using unconditional logistic regression (ULR) due to their robust estimates and effectiveness if there are few confounders to adjust for [23,27]. ULR involves producing exposure-disease strata for each level of the confounder and then producing an average effect across the data. This method is also effective when there are no problems with sparse data, no loss of validity, and a potential increase in precision [29].

ULR makes the events log-odds a linear mixture of one or more independent factors, predicting the likelihood that an event will occur [30]. Similar to other regressions, this method shows where there is a relationship between these variables. Nevertheless, this relationship cannot always imply causation; in other words, regression does not determine causation. In statistics, the causal analysis goes one step further than the standard statistical analysis in assessing the parameters of a distribution, aiming to infer probabilities under changing conditions and understanding the actual effect of a specific phenomenon happening in a system.

1.2. Current Trends in Estimating Causation for Health Outcomes Using Machine Learning Methods

Causal analysis can be sometimes inaccurate, as in complex systems, it is difficult to make causal arguments based on single correlation coefficients. To overcome this challenge, recent machine learning (ML) approaches have been developed, based on causal pattern recognition, providing robustness in accurately modeling counterfactual scenarios [31].

ML methods have been applied to health sciences for causal inference [32]. For counterfactual prediction, ML has been used to address causal questions using methods such as Random Forest [33] and Bayesian additive regression trees (BART) [34]. Some common research goals that can be tackled with these techniques are [30] (i) the evaluation of potential causes of health outcomes, (ii) the assessment of treatment options, and (iii) the assessment of bias in the statistical analysis. Some ML predictors proved to be assertive when causally inferring the influence of a health outcome while being controlled by confounders. One study, for instance, showed that the targeted maximum likelihood estimation (TMLE) technique outperformed traditional models when analyzing the effect of fruit density on the nutrition of pregnant women on birth outcomes [35]. Despite being a promising alternative to causal analysis, it is still in the foreseeable future when we will be able to identify high-level causal variables from low-level data using these techniques, as causal modeling approaches such as meta-learning and meta-modeling will be able to find causal relationships accurately. Moreover, the potential case of being exposed to complex mixtures of chemical contaminants causing adverse health outcomes can have additive or synergistic effects, posing a challenge where the strength of the ML approach could be used in combination with existing human data to infer causality [36].

Uplift modeling has been used by several companies to estimate the effect of an action on some customer outcomes [37]. Estimating customer uplift is a causal inference since it requires determining the difference between two outcomes that are mutually exclusive for an individual (counterfactual nature); this is carried out using randomized experiments for the treatment group and the control group. At the same time, the Uplift estimation is also a machine learning problem because different models must be trained to finally select the one that yields the most reliable prediction, requiring a sensible cross-validation process [38]. The combination of these features taken from both approaches, causal inference, and machine learning, make Uplift modeling a suitable alternative in determining causation. To our knowledge, Uplift modeling has not been applied to health sciences. Uplift modeling might become unstable when predicting causation, as with any other ML technique, as the sample size decreases. Moreover, its convergence might be affected since it can depend on variables not typically used in response models.

In this work, we propose a novel framework, for evaluating potential causes of health outcomes using the average treatment effect (ATE) to compare the effects in our computational experiments and Uplift modeling, as a machine learning technique employed for cross-validation of the ATEs. This simple approach effectively estimates the causation of health outcomes using two levels of confirmation, integrating causal inference and machine learning features. Our case study includes the causation of benzene exposure (as an air pollutant) to childhood AML, analyzing the counterfactual nature of the OR-based relationships found indoors and outdoors. The case study selected for our framework was presented by Heck et al. [25] and includes childhood AML data collected from California birth records over 17 years. Health outcomes based solely on relationships between variables can be challenged when the outcome is not proven to result from the occurrence of the other event (s). This paper aims to describe the development and use of this framework and discuss its significance as a reliable causation framework that can potentially be effectively used to prevent, monitor, and treat diseases.

2. Methods

The methodological workflow (Figure 1) can be applied as a framework for any study involving the causation of a pollutant exposure to the risk of developing a disease through machine learning techniques and the analysis of the counterfactual nature of the OR-based relationships.

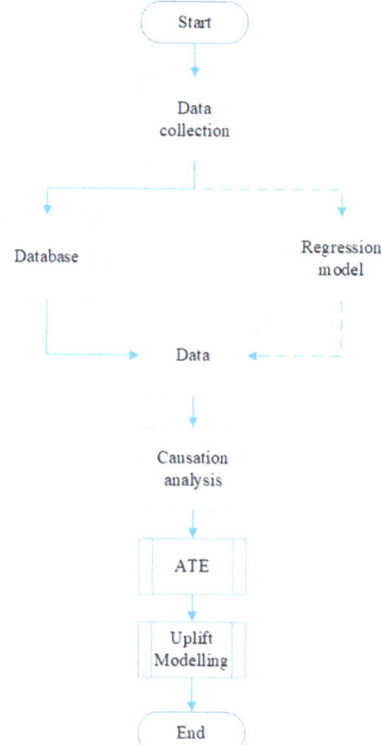

Figure 1. Framework for causation analysis of a pollutant exposure to the risk of developing a disease using machine learning techniques.

The proposed ATE-Uplift framework is depicted in Figure 1, where the data is collected either from an existing database or by obtaining simulated data from a regression model. Typically, health outcome studies in the literature comprise strata of data that are fitted using logistic regressions, as discussed in Section 2.1. Once collected, our causation analysis includes two stages: (i) estimating the ATEs and (ii) cross-validating the previous estimation using the Uplift modeling. The two levels strategy based on cross-validation integrating causal inference and machine learning is crucial to support the reliability of our framework since the consequences of determining causation can have several implications in the prevention, monitoring, and treatment of diseases. Ultimately, our framework provides two integrated causation indicators, the ATE values, and Qini coefficients. The results from these stages allow researchers to conclude the causation of pollutant exposure to the risk of developing a disease.

2.1. Case Study

The data for the case study selected in this work was presented by Heck et al. [25]. In their work, they ascertained 46 cases of AML from the California Cancer Registry records of children with ages less than six years and 19,209 controls from California birth records between 1990 and 2007 and within 6 km of air monitoring stations. Risks of developing AML were reported as ORs, including the ones associated with exposure to benzene, butadiene, toluene, and other air pollutants, concluding that there is an increased risk for AML when exposed to these air pollutants. A 1-M-matched case-control study was performed using unconditional logistic regression (ULR), adjusted for the year of birth as a matching variable, with 1:M = 1:20, to compare several characteristics of cases and controls, primarily demographics (socioeconomic status, race, birthplace, and parity). Then, ULR was employed to estimate the risk of AML from each interquartile range increase in air toxic exposure for the different pollutants separately. The data might require evaluating the correlations between pollutants. Heck et al. [25] recommended performing a factor analysis with varimax rotation to group highly correlated pollutants based on eigenvalues greater than 1. We have selected the OR related to exposure to benzene, which reveals a relationship between this exposure and the risk of developing childhood AML.

2.2. Data Generation and Preparation for Uplift

This section summarizes the process used to generate data from the 1-M matched control case study fitted with URL [23], as the original numerical and categorical data of the study was unavailable, and its consequent preparation for ATE-Uplift, including factual and counterfactuals. The data generation involves drawing samples from the existing ULR model by Heck et al. [23].

Let y be the case-control study, where $y = 1$ for a case and $y = 0$ for the control. Let $x_m = \{x_{m1}, x_{m2}\}$ a vector of matching variables, x_e and exposure associated with the case-control status, and x_0 a vector of unmatched dummy variables corresponding to the strata of the matched variables. The ULR model, assuming no interaction between the predictors, is given by,

$$logit(\pi) = \beta_0 + \beta_e x_e + \beta_m^T x_m + \beta_0^T x_0 \qquad (1)$$

where π is the probability of developing the disease, and β's are the regression coefficients. T denotes transpose.

The input data for the ATE model must be generated as a table of factual and counterfactual cases. 'Factuals' are persons in the factual universe (where a 'zero' value is assigned to benzene, or benzene = 0), and 'counterfactuals' are persons in a counterfactual universe (where 'one' value is assigned to benzene, or benzene = 1). The table is generated from the expected propensity of AML conditional on the inputs, which are predicted and converted into a binary variable, as shown in Table 1.

Table 1. Factuals and counterfactuals input for the ATE model.

Person	Socioeconomic Status				Race		Birthplace	Parity	Benzene	BINaml
1	0	0	0	0	0	0	0	0	0	0
2	0	0	0	0	0	0	0	1	0	0
3	0	0	0	0	0	0	1	0	0	0
...	...	...	...	...	...	...	...	...	...	...
61	0	0	0	0	0	0	0	0	1	0
62	0	0	0	0	0	0	0	1	1	0
63	0	0	0	0	0	0	1	0	1	0

In Table 1, person 1 and person 61 are identically theoretical persons, except for having different binary exposures to benzene and potentially different binary AML outcomes. Similarly, and with the same proviso, person 2 and person 62 are identical, person 3 and person 63 are identical, and so on.

We used simulated data from the ULR of the case study; the simulation assumes no interaction between the benzene exposure and the rest of the predictors (socioeconomic status, race, birthplace, and parity); hence, Simpson's paradox is ruled out. This paradox emerges when groups of data show one trend, but this is reversed when the groups are combined. Our factual and counterfactuals table, in particular, the BINaml column (the presence or absence of AML), is generated by the projection of the target variable of Equation (1) or its substitute, Equation (2), that is $logit(\pi(x))$ of AML and its associated binary AML variable.

$$logit(\pi(x)) = \beta_0 + \beta_e x_e + \beta_m^T x_m \quad (2)$$

This projection requires Equation (1) to be completely specified, including the intercepts, which was omitted by Heck et al. [25] as is usual in matched case-controlled studies. Therefore, we substitute Equation (1) with Equation (2) to estimate the intercept, where β_0 is a single number rather than a vector, yet β_e, β_m^T are the same β_e, β_m^T [25]. We estimate β_0 using Equation (2) following Haneuse's et al. [38] optimization approach by using an estimated overall prevalence of AML for the years 1990–2007 and the simulated benzene exposure data. As input to this projection, we use two levels of benzene exposure: the minimum and maximum values of the benzene distribution. Having projected the binary AML variable, we inserted it into the BINaml column of the factual and counterfactuals table, along with the corresponding benzene exposures and other predictor values. Finally, we generated the factual and counterfactuals table by converting the benzene exposures from numerical to categorical (i.e., from a maximum value to 1 and from a minimum value to 0). We carry out this last conversion following the approach by Lebel [39] and the California of Environmental Health Hazzard Assessment's reference exposure level for benzene as 0.940 ppm (0.903 ppb) [40].

2.3. Distribution of Benzene Exposure

Heck et al. [23] provide a description of the distribution of outdoor benzene exposure, reproduced in Table 2.

Table 2. Outdoor benzene distribution [23].

Agent	Mean/Standard Deviation	Inter-Quartile Range (IQR)	Minimum	Percentile				Maximum
				10th	25th	75th	90th	
Benzene, ppbv *	1.268/0.830	1.197	0.151	0.410	0.591	1.788	2.574	4.600

* ppbv is parts per billion by volume.

For our benzene exposure data simulation, we use a normal distribution centered at 1.268 with a standard deviation of 0.830, a truncated minimum of 0.151, and a truncated maximum of 4.600. Heck et al. [25] calculate the risk of AML associated with one interquartile range increase in benzene exposure; we normalize the benzene distribution parameters (mean, standard deviation, minimum, and maximum) by the IQR = 1.197 as well.

As for the observed prevalence of pediatric AML in California, we use an incidence of 46/19,255 (observed ratio of cases over controls) [25], reflecting their 1:20 matching.

In addition to the outdoor distribution, we also provide a causation analysis using an indoor benzene exposure distribution from locations near garages (Table 3) [41].

Table 3. Indoor benzene distribution [38].

| Agent | Mean/Standard Deviation | Inter-Quartile Range (IQR) * | Minimum | Percentile | | | | Maximum |
				10th	25th	75th	90th	
Benzene, ppbv	5.650/2.825	1.197	0.700	-	-	-	-	12.000

* Assumed the same as the outdoor distribution.

We normalized the parameters by the IQR of the outdoor benzene exposure to be able to compare the results using two different distributions.

2.4. Causation between Exposure to Benzene and Risk of Developing AML

We estimated the causal effects of the benzene exposure to AML using the average treatment effect and typical validation indicators obtained from Uplift modeling.

The average treatment effect (ATE) is a special case of an average partial effect for a binary explanatory variable. It is used to compare the effects in our randomized computational experiments. The ATE measures the difference in mean outcomes between units assigned to the study and units assigned to the control and is given by,

$$ATE = \frac{1}{N}\Sigma_i \left(y_{1(i)} - y_{0(i)} \right) \quad (3)$$

where the treatment effect for individual i is given by $y_{1(i)} - y_{0(i)} = \beta(i)$; the summation occurs over all N individuals in the population.

The value of the potential outcome $y(i)$ must not be affected by how the treatment and exposure are assigned among all other individuals, according to the stable unit treatment value assumption that is required for the estimation of the ATE. Extrapolation based on strata must be assumed, or monotonicity instead, which denotes the absence of definers in the population. Therefore, if the experiment experiences non-compliance, the ATE can no longer be recovered. Instead, a local ATE can be obtained as the average treatment effect for a particular subpopulation, limiting its extrapolation. Generalization for the causal inference can be, hence, affected. The extrapolation based on ignobility or monotonicity, are difficult assumptions to verify; once the data is available, the foundations of the design of the experiment might reveal signals of homogeneity across groups that can verify them or not, for which further data analysis is required. A stronger argument for Uplift modeling can be made, as they provide a solution for isolating effects. Thus, Uplift models the difference between conditional response probabilities in both the treatment and control groups, clearly identifying groups of individuals on which an action or intervention will have the most 'positive effect'. A binary outcome is assumed for Uplift modeling, aligned to the odds ratio, as per the nature of the problem described in this work.

There are various Uplift modeling approaches. The response probabilities that differ between the study and control groups are used by the Two-Model approach to model the uplift. This leads to a methodology based on two models as these probabilities are calculated separately for each group. In Lo's approach (Figure 2), the independent variables change in logistic regression. The model is based (and learned) on one model; however, the predicted probabilities are calculated for both groups. For the calculation of the predicted probabilities, there is a dummy treatment variable in the test dataset, which is set to 0 for the control group and 1 for the treatment group [42].

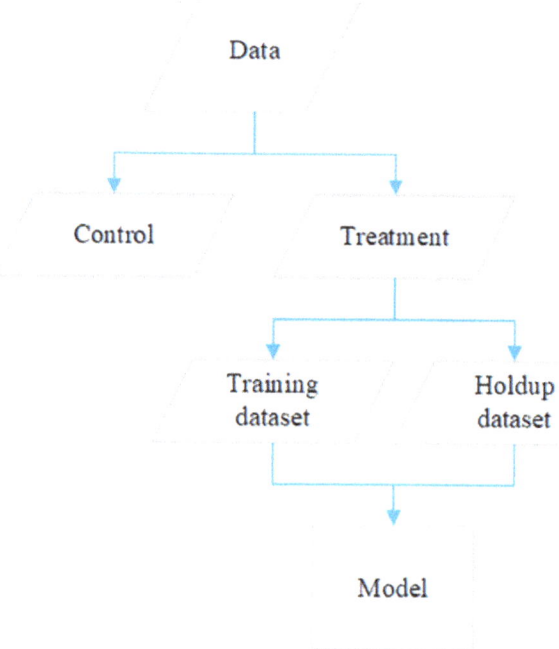

Figure 2. Uplift Two-model Approach.

The Uplift model validation is performed by selecting an appropriate cost function measuring the difference between the actual and predicted values of the response variable. In economics, the Gini coefficient is used to measure the model's goodness-of-fit. It is typically plotted to show the Lorenz curve where the predicted scores of the targeted observations are sorted in decreasing order. The extension of this curve and the Gini coefficient for Uplift modeling is called the Qini curve [43]. Figure 3 shows a typical Qini curve for an application in Econometrics.

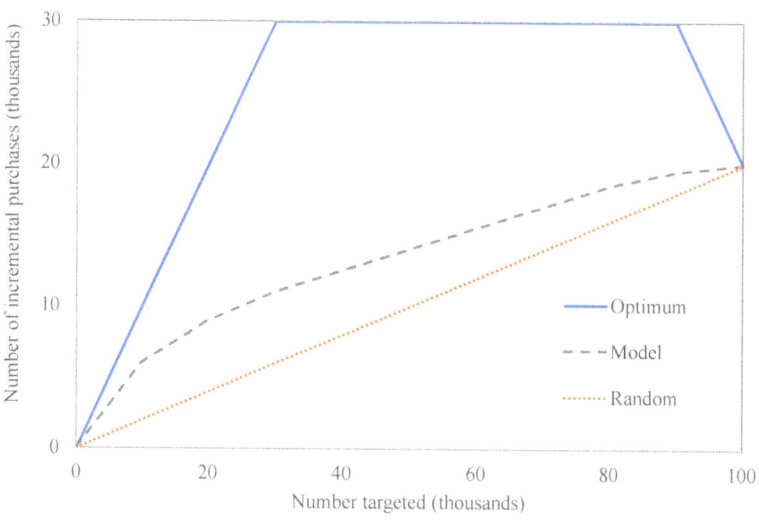

Figure 3. Typical Qini curve for Uplift model evaluation, used in Econometrics.

The y-axis shows the cumulative incremental gains, and the x-axis the proportion of the population targeted. There is an Uplift curve and a random curve based on the calculation of every segment. The Qini coefficient is the difference between the area under these curves. A positive Qini-coefficient represents a good performance of the model, while a value approximating zero represents a poorer performance.

2.5. Causation Codes

The Uplift data generation code (datagen.rmd) uses the βs provided by Heck et al. [23] and benzene distributions indoors and outdoors to find the corrected intercept $β\_0$ via optimization. This code, developed with the software R, is a modification of the program presented by Haneuse et al. [38]. The main results obtained include the ATE and the data table prepared as input for Uplift modeling.

We also developed an R code (*uplift.R*) for the Uplift modeling, using the library *tools4uplift*. The data is split into train and validation data for further fitting using the baseline model two-model estimator through the embedded function *DualUplift*. The results are interpreted from the QiniArea from the function *PerformanceUplift*.

Both codes datagen.r and uplift.rmd are available in Available online: https://github.com/CHE408UofT/AML_Uplift (accessed on 18 March 2023) [44].

2.6. Results Interpretation

ATE values equal to zero reveal no causation, while values different than zero reveal causation between exposure to benzene and the risk of developing childhood AML. We look at two different scenarios, as we included indoor and outdoor benzene distributions, looking at finding causation indoors and/or outdoors; therefore, we reported ATE values for both scenarios.

Regarding the Uplift modeling, the goodness-of-fit of the model is evaluated using the *QiniArea* function in R, which computes the area under the Qini curve. A positive value attests to a good performance of the model, while a value near 0 shows a worse performance.

3. Results

This section presents the results of using our ATE-Uplift framework to estimate the causation of benzene exposure (as an air pollutant) to childhood AML, through the analysis of the counterfactual nature of the OR-based relationships found indoors and outdoors.

3.1. Indoor Benzene Distribution

The results of generating a set of factual/counterfactuals tables for indoor benzene distribution to estimate their ATEs, show an average ATE of 0.203. This positive value reveals the causation between indoor exposure to benzene and the risk of developing AML in early childhood.

When analyzing the Uplift modeling results, we look at a variant of the Qini curve, representing the incremental uplift as a function of the proportion of the population target. Incremental Uplift measures whether an event would not have occurred without a specific interaction; hence positive Qinis attest to the goodness-of-fit of the Uplift model. Figure 4 shows a typical Qini curve for the indoor benzene distribution scenario.

The data is first partitioned into subsets that keep the same distribution of treated versus non-treated and responders versus non-responders values. The training was achieved using the formula *DualUplift* which fits the data using the two-model estimator or approach (logistic regression model), with splits of the data in 70% for the training and 30% for the validation. The first element of the *DualUplift* class is the baseline model fitted for nontreated individuals, and the second is the baseline model fitted for treated individuals. Using the two-model estimator, a baseline model is fitted for comparison purposes. Using the validation set, the function *predict* infers the uplift. Finally, to evaluate the quality of the baseline model, we plot the Qini curve, as shown in Figure 4. The Qini coefficients are single indexes of the Uplift model. The x-axis represents the fraction of targeted individuals and the y-axis represents the incremental number of positive responses relative to the total number of targeted individuals. The straight line between the origin and (100, y-max) in Figure 4 represents a benchmark to compare the model's performance to a strategy that randomly targets subjects, as we explained before. In our case, the Qini coefficient is positive (with a value of 0.14) and outperforms random targeting. The uplift percentages are detailed in Figure 5. This reinforces the goodness-of-fit of the Uplift modeling approach, as the observed uplifts are ordered from highest to lowest.

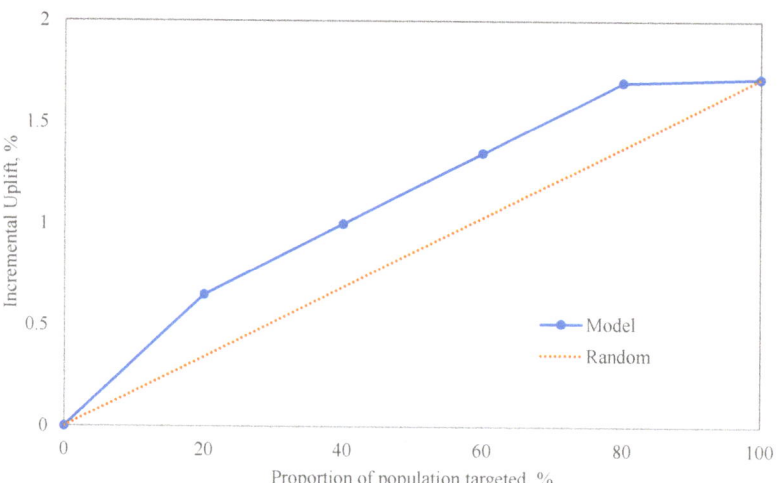

Figure 4. Qini curve for Uplift modeling for the validation data—indoor benzene distribution.

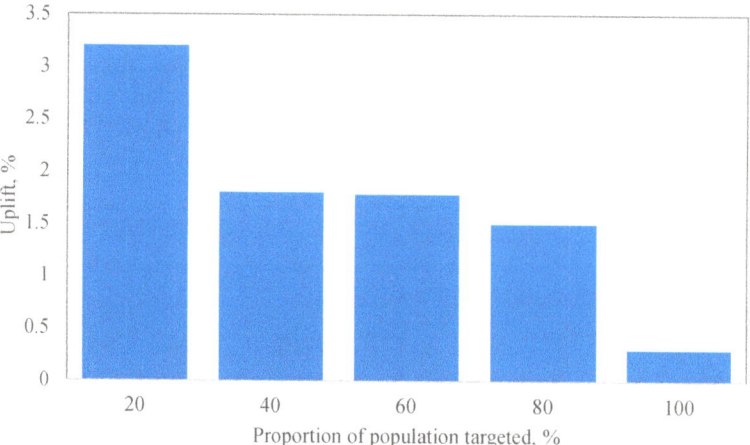

Figure 5. Uplift versus proportion of population targeted.

Our combined ATE/Uplift modeling framework allows us to conclude that there is a causation of benzene exposure (as an air pollutant) to AML in early childhood, analyzing the counterfactual nature of the OR-based relationship found indoors for the simulated data from Heck et al. [25] and the benzene exposure distribution considered [25].

3.2. Outdoor Benzene Distribution

The results of generating a set of factual/counterfactuals tables for outdoor benzene distribution to estimate their ATEs show an average value of zero, which indicates no causation between outdoor exposure to benzene and the risk of developing AML in early childhood. The incremental uplift, in this case, is also zero at any proportion of the targeted population.

4. Discussion

The ATE-Uplift framework effectively predicts causation in health outcomes when fitted using ULR. Uplift modeling acts as a cross-validation technique of the ATE estimation, integrating its causal inference and machine learning features. Moreover, Uplift modeling ensures the goodness-of-fit of the regression. Thus, categorical factual/counterfactuals tables generated from the original data are input to obtain ATEs, with positive values revealing causation. Then, Uplift modeling is employed, where positive Qini coefficients confirm causation.

For the data considered by Heck et al. [25], their corresponding ULR fitting and distribution of benzene exposure [38], our framework was useful in revealing the causation between indoor exposure to benzene and the risk of developing childhood AML. In contrast, no causation was revealed when considering outdoor exposure. Nevertheless, it was observed that, for this scenario, low ATE values (<0.05) near zero are somehow related to inconsistent Uplift modeling results, as the corresponding Qini coefficients also show low values (<0.03), different than zero. In these instances, we recommend, using a third cross-validation method when reporting low ATE values.

While our preference is to have the original data to perform exploratory data analysis (EDA), evaluate the interaction between predictors, and consequently preselect -and later compare- applicable ML methods for estimating causation, in this work, we cautiously tested ATE-Uplift for generated data, with one predictor, benzene, as ATE and Uplift modeling are complementary methods for binary outcomes, working with factual and counterfactuals to consequently estimating causality. ML methods, although promising, must be carefully supported by a detailed EDA and a sample size evaluation. We noticed, for instance, that inconsistent Uplift modeling results are obtained when decreasing the sample size, an effect that must be minimized as per most ML predictors. Our future work will add to our framework an EDA that will allow us to observe trends among and within data groups, potentially fit and compare different surrogate models to establish the 'best' relationship between variables, and ultimately, perform a meta-analysis and comparison between causation-based ML methods. Some techniques to be explored in future works include meta-analysis and machine learning tools such as meta-learning causal structures and causal Bayesian networks.

It is important to note that the reliability of the results obtained through the application of our ATE-Uplift framework depends largely on the completeness of the data used and how well-defined the assumptions are. Thus, once the numerical and categorical data is available, it is recommended to perform data analysis to verify or not the main assumptions regarding the absence of definers in the population required by the ATE model and, therefore, frame the limitations of the model extrapolation.

Finally, we have assumed that there is no interaction between the benzene exposure and the rest of the predictors. Such interaction will be considered in future works adapting our framework once the data is available. ORs might be readjusted, and correlations between pollutants might be revisited for more accurate correlations representing the interaction within the strata predictors and benzene exposure.

Our research's scientific and practical novelty lies simply and effectively in estimating the causation of health outcomes using two levels of confirmation or cross-validation. We use ATE values and Uplift modeling, integrating causal inference and machine learning features. Causation is, per se, the main goal when evaluating health outcomes since confirmed relationships between variables might not indicate that the outcome is indeed the result of the occurrence of the other event(s). A reliable causation approach may lead to effective disease prevention, monitoring, and treatment.

5. Conclusions

In this work, we have presented the ATE-Uplift framework to predict causation in health outcomes. Uplift modeling and estimating ATE values effectively integrate causal inference and machine learning capabilities. We tested our framework to estimate the causation between benzene exposure and AML, verified when considering indoor exposure to this air pollutant. Causation is confirmed with two indicators, an ATE value different than zero and positive Qini coefficients. Further considerations to validate and universalize the use of this approach include an exhaustive exploratory data analysis (EDA) to observe trends that might allow confirming the assumptions for its applicability and analyzing the interaction between predictors, as its comparison with emerging ML methods being evaluated for causation.

Author Contributions: Conceptualization and visualization: D.G., R.T.-F., V.C.-A. and C.H.A. Data collection and methodology: D.G., R.T.-F. and A.N.-Z. Software: D.G. and R.T.-F. Formal analysis: D.G., R.T.-F. and V.C.-A. Validation: A.N.-Z., M.J. (Melanie Jeffrey), M.J. (Maria Jacome), J.B. and C.H.A. Computing resources: D.G., R.T.-F. and C.H.A. Writing—original draft: D.G. and R.T.-F. Preparation: D.G., R.T.-F. and A.N.-Z. Writing—review and editing: D.G., R.T.-F., V.C.-A., M.J. (Melanie Jeffrey), M.J. (Maria Jacome), J.B. and C.H.A. Supervision: D.G., R.T.-F., V.C.-A. and C.H.A.; funding acquisition: C.H.A. All authors have read and agreed to the published version of the manuscript.

Funding: This research was funded by a Healthy Cities Implementation Science Team Grants (LOI) 202110LT5 from the Canadian Institutes of Health Research.

Data Availability Statement: Not applicable.

Acknowledgments: We are grateful to Julia E. Heck from the UCLA Fielding School of Public Health, Department of Epidemiology, for the information and support provided throughout this research.

Conflicts of Interest: The authors declare that they have no known competing financial interests or personal relationships that could have appeared to influence the work reported in this paper.

References

1. What Is Acute Myeloid Leukemia (AML)? What Is AML? Available online: https://www.cancer.org/cancer/acute-myeloid-leukemia/about/what-is-aml.html (accessed on 8 February 2023).
2. Administrator Just Diagnosed, Just Diagnosed with Acute Myeloid Leukemia (AML). Available online: https://childrensoncologygroup.org/just-diagnosed-with-acute-myeloid-leukemia-aml- (accessed on 8 February 2023).
3. Ross, J.A.; Potter, J.D.; Robison, L.L. Infant leukemia, topoisomerase II inhibitors, and the MLL gene. *JNCI J. Natl. Cancer Inst.* **1994**, *86*, 1678–1680. [CrossRef]
4. Ross, J.A.; Davies, S.M.; Potter, J.D.; Robison, L.L. Epidemiology of childhood leukemia, with a focus on infants. *Epidemiol. Rev.* **1994**, *16*, 243–272. [CrossRef] [PubMed]
5. Pyatt, D.; Hays, S. A review of the potential association between childhood leukemia and benzene. *Chem.-Biol. Interact.* **2010**, *184*, 151–164. [CrossRef]
6. Belson, M.; Kingsley, B.; Holmes, A. Risk factors for acute leukemia in children: A review. *Environ. Health Perspect.* **2007**, *115*, 138–145. [CrossRef] [PubMed]
7. Rinsky, R.A. Benzene and leukemia: An epidemiologic risk assessment. *Environ. Health Perspect.* **1989**, *82*, 189–191. [CrossRef]
8. Costantini, A.S.; Dsc, A.B.; Vineis, P.; Kriebel, D.; Tumino, R.; Ramazzotti, V.; Rodella, S.; Stagnaro, E.; Crosignani, P.; Amadori, D.; et al. Risk of leukemia and multiple myeloma associated with exposure to benzene and other organic solvents: Evidence from the Italian Multicenter Case-control study. *Am. J. Ind. Med.* **2008**, *51*, 803–811. [CrossRef] [PubMed]
9. Hill, S.A.B. The environment and disease: Association or causation? *J. R. Soc. Med.* **2015**, *108*, 32–37. [CrossRef]
10. Cox, L.A. Modernizing the Bradford Hill criteria for assessing causal relationships in observational data. *Crit. Rev. Toxicol.* **2018**, *48*, 682–712. [CrossRef]
11. Kaatsch, P.; Kaletsch, U.; Meinert, R.; Miesner, A.; Hoisl, M.; Schüz, J.; Michaelis, J. Erman case control study on childhood leukaemia—Basic considerations, methodology and summary of the results. *Klin. Pädiatrie* **1998**, *210*, 185–191. [CrossRef]
12. Shu, X.O.; Gao, Y.T.; Tu, J.T.; Zheng, W.; Brinton, L.A.; Linet, M.S.; Fraumeni, J.F. A population-based case-control study of childhood leukemia in Shanghai. *Cancer* **1988**, *62*, 635–644. [CrossRef]
13. Buckley, J.D.; Chard, R.L.; Baehner, R.L.; Nesbit, M.E.; Lampkin, B.C.; Woods, W.G.; Denman Hammond, G. Improvement in outcome for children with acute nonlymphocytic leukemia. A report from the Childrens Cancer Study Group. *Cancer* **1989**, *63*, 1457–1465. [CrossRef]

14. Magnani, C.; Pastore, G.; Luzzatto, L.; Terracini, B. Parental occupation and other environmental factors in the etiology of leukemias and Non-Hodgkin'S lymphomas in childhood: A case-control study. *Tumori J.* **1990**, *76*, 413–419. [CrossRef] [PubMed]
15. Freedman, D.M.; Stewart, P.; Kleinerman, R.A.; Wacholder, S.; Hatch, E.E.; Tarone, R.E.; Robison, L.L.; Linet, M.S. Household solvent exposures and childhood acute lymphoblastic leukemia. *Am. J. Public Health* **2001**, *91*, 564–567. [CrossRef]
16. Alderton, L.E.; Spector, L.G.; Blair, C.K.; Roesler, M.; Olshan, A.F.; Robison, L.L.; Ross, J.A. Child and maternal household chemical exposure and the risk of acute leukemia in children with Down's syndrome: A Report from the Children's Oncology Group. *Am. J. Epidemiol.* **2006**, *164*, 212–221. [CrossRef]
17. Chang, J.S. Parental smoking and childhood leukemia. *Methods Mol. Biol.* **2009**, *472*, 103–137. [CrossRef] [PubMed]
18. Lichtman, M.A. Cigarette smoking, cytogenetic abnormalities, and acute myelogenous leukemia. *Leukemia* **2007**, *21*, 1137–1140. [CrossRef] [PubMed]
19. Nordlinder, R.; Jarvholm, B. Environmental exposure to gasoline and leukemia in children and young adults-an ecology study. *Int. Arch. Occup. Environ. Health* **1997**, *70*, 57–60. [CrossRef] [PubMed]
20. Reynolds, P.; Von Behren, J.; Gunier, R.B.; Goldberg, D.E.; Hertz, A. Residential exposure to traffic in California and childhood cancer. *Epidemiology* **2004**, *15*, 6–12. [CrossRef]
21. Crosignani, P.; Tittarelli, A.; Borgini, A.; Codazzi, T.; Rovelli, A.; Porro, E.; Contiero, P.; Bianchi, N.; Tagliabue, G.; Fissi, R.; et al. Childhood leukemia and road traffic: A population-based case-control study. *Int. J. Cancer* **2003**, *108*, 596–599. [CrossRef]
22. Steffen, C.; Auclerc, M.F.; Auvrignon, A.; Baruchel, A.; Kebaili, K.; Lambilliotte, A.; Leverger, G.; Sommelet, D.; Vilmer, E.; Hémon, D.; et al. Acute childhood leukaemia and environmental exposure to potential sources of benzene and other hydrocarbons; a case-control study. *Occup. Environ. Med.* **2004**, *61*, 773–778. [CrossRef]
23. Harrison, R.M.; Leung, P.L.; Somervaille, L.; Smith, R.; Gilman, E. Analysis of incidence of childhood cancer in the West Midlands of the United Kingdom in relation to proximity to main roads and petrol stations. *Occup. Environ. Med.* **1999**, *56*, 774–780. [CrossRef]
24. Raaschou-Nielsen, O.; Hvidtfeldt, U.A.; Roswall, N.; Hertel, O.; Poulsen, A.H.; Sørensen, M. Ambient benzene at the residence and risk for subtypes of childhood leukemia, lymphoma and CNS tumor. *Int. J. Cancer* **2018**, *143*, 1367–1373. [CrossRef]
25. Heck, J.E.; Park, A.S.; Qiu, J.; Cockburn, M.; Ritz, B. Risk of leukemia in relation to exposure to Ambient Air Toxics in pregnancy and early childhood. *Int. J. Hyg. Environ. Health* **2013**, *217*, 662–668. [CrossRef]
26. Wan, F. Conditional or unconditional logistic regression for frequency matched case-control design? *Stat. Med.* **2022**, *41*, 1023–1041. [CrossRef]
27. Kuo, C.-L.; Duan, Y.; Grady, J. Unconditional or conditional logistic regression model for age-matched case–control data? *Front. Public Health* **2018**, *6*, 57. [CrossRef]
28. De Graaf, M.A.; Jager, K.J.; Zoccali, C.; Dekker, F.W. Matching, an appealing method to avoid confounding? *Nephron Clin. Pract.* **2011**, *118*, c315–c318. [CrossRef] [PubMed]
29. Pearce, N. Analysis of matched case-control studies. *BMJ* **2016**, *352*, i969. [CrossRef]
30. Stoltzfus, J.C. Logistic Regression: A brief primer. *Acad. Emerg. Med.* **2011**, *18*, 1099–1104. [CrossRef]
31. Gonfalonieri, A. Introduction to Causality in Machine Learning. Medium. 9 July 2020. Available online: https://towardsdatascience.com/introduction-to-causality-in-machine-learning-4cee9467f06f (accessed on 8 February 2023).
32. Sanchez, P.; Voisey, J.P.; Xia, T.; Watson, H.I.; O'Neil, A.Q.; Tsaftaris, S.A. Causal machine learning for healthcare and Precision Medicine. *R. Soc. Open Sci.* **2022**, *9*, 220638. [CrossRef] [PubMed]
33. Venkatasubramaniam, A.; Mateen, B.A.; Shields, B.M.; Hattersley, A.T.; Jones, A.G.; Vollmer, S.J.; Dennis, J.M. Comparison of causal forest and regression-based approaches to evaluate treatment effect heterogeneity: An application for type 2 diabetes precision medicine. *medRxiv* **2022**. [CrossRef]
34. Chipman, H.A.; George, E.I.; McCulloch, R.E. Bart: Bayesian additive regression trees. *Ann. Appl. Stat.* **2010**, *4*, 266–298. [CrossRef]
35. Côté, M.; Lamarche, B. Artificial intelligence in nutrition research: Perspectives on current and future applications. *Appl. Physiol. Nutr. Metab.* **2022**, *47*, 1–8. [CrossRef] [PubMed]
36. Fedak, K.M.; Bernal, A.; Capshaw, Z.A.; Gross, S. Applying the Bradford Hill criteria in the 21st Century: How data integration has changed causal inference in molecular epidemiology. *Emerg. Themes Epidemiol.* **2015**, *12*, 14. [CrossRef] [PubMed]
37. Gailmard, S. Causal Inference: Inferring causation from Correlation. In *Statistical Modeling and Inference for Social Science*; Cambridge University Press: Cambridge, UK, 2018; pp. 335–357. [CrossRef]
38. Haneuse, S.; Saegusa, T.; Lumley, T. osDesign: An r package for the analysis, evaluation, and design of two-phase and case-control studies. *J. Stat. Softw.* **2011**, *43*, 1–29. [CrossRef] [PubMed]
39. Lebel, E.D.; Michanowicz, D.R.; Bilsback, K.R.; Hill, L.A.L.; Goldman, J.S.W.; Domen, J.K.; Jaeger, J.M.; Ruiz, A.; Shonkoff, S.B.C. Composition, emissions, and air quality impacts of hazardous air pollutants in unburned natural gas from residential stoves in California. *Environ. Sci. Technol.* **2022**, *56*, 15828–15838. [CrossRef] [PubMed]
40. Centers for Disease Control and Prevention. United States and Puerto Rico Cancer Statistics, 1999–2019 Incidence Request. Available online: https://wonder.cdc.gov/cancer-v2019.HTML (accessed on 8 February 2023).
41. Mann, H.S.; Crump, D.; Brown, V. Personal exposure to benzene and the influence of attached and integral garages. *J. R. Soc. Promot. Health* **2001**, *121*, 38–46. [CrossRef] [PubMed]

42. Uplift Modelling—Github Pages. Available online: https://humboldt-wi.github.io/blog/research/theses/uplift_modeling_blogpost/ (accessed on 9 February 2023).
43. Quality Measures for Uplift Models—Stochastic Solutions. Available online: https://www.stochasticsolutions.com/pdf/kdd2011late.pdf (accessed on 9 February 2023).
44. CHE408UofT—Overview. Available online: https://github.com/CHE408UofT (accessed on 14 March 2023).

Disclaimer/Publisher's Note: The statements, opinions and data contained in all publications are solely those of the individual author(s) and contributor(s) and not of MDPI and/or the editor(s). MDPI and/or the editor(s) disclaim responsibility for any injury to people or property resulting from any ideas, methods, instructions or products referred to in the content.

Article

Nearest Neighbours Graph Variational AutoEncoder

Lorenzo Arsini [1,2], **Barbara Caccia** [3], **Andrea Ciardiello** [2,*], **Stefano Giagu** [1,2,*] **and Carlo Mancini Terracciano** [1,2]

[1] Department of Physics, Sapienza University of Rome, 00185 Rome, Italy
[2] INFN Section of Rome, 00185 Rome, Italy
[3] Istituto Superiore di Sanità, 00161 Rome, Italy
* Correspondence: andrea.ciardiello@gmail.com (A.C.); stefano.giagu@uniroma1.it (S.G.)

Abstract: Graphs are versatile structures for the representation of many real-world data. Deep Learning on graphs is currently able to solve a wide range of problems with excellent results. However, both the generation of graphs and the handling of large graphs still remain open challenges. This work aims to introduce techniques for generating large graphs and test the approach on a complex problem such as the calculation of dose distribution in oncological radiotherapy applications. To this end, we introduced a pooling technique (ReNN-Pool) capable of sampling nodes that are spatially uniform without computational requirements in both model training and inference. By construction, the ReNN-Pool also allows the definition of a symmetric un-pooling operation to recover the original dimensionality of the graphs. We also present a Variational AutoEncoder (VAE) for generating graphs, based on the defined pooling and un-pooling operations, which employs convolutional graph layers in both encoding and decoding phases. The performance of the model was tested on both the realistic use case of a cylindrical graph dataset for a radiotherapy application and the standard benchmark dataset sprite. Compared to other graph pooling techniques, ReNN-Pool proved to improve both performance and computational requirements.

Keywords: graph neural network; variational autoencoder; pooling; nearest neighbours

1. Introduction

Deep Generative Modeling involves training a deep neural network to approximate the high-dimensional probability distribution of the training data, enabling the generation of new examples from that distribution. There are various approaches to deep generative modeling, such as Generative Adversarial Networks (GANs) [1], Variational AutoEncoders (VAEs) [2], and Normalizing Flow models [3]. A comprehensive review of deep generative modeling can be found in [4].

In some cases, the architecture includes both an encoding and a decoding scheme, as is the case with models such as VAEs. The encoding process is typically used to obtain compact representations of the data distribution, often achieved through pooling operations that reduce the dimensionality of the data. The creation of a "bottleneck" by embedding the input samples in lower and lower dimensional spaces enables the extraction of essential features of the data. The decoding scheme, on the other hand, often employs reverse techniques used in the encoding, such as un-pooling operations, to restore the original dimensionality of the data.

In recent years, there has been a growing interest in utilizing Deep Learning in the field of Medical Physics. Specifically, in Radiotherapy (RT), Deep Generative modeling presents a valuable opportunity to streamline the calculation of deposited dose distributions by radiation in a given medium. These data, which are currently computed using more resource-intensive methods, can be utilized to optimize and validate RT treatment plans. Little effort has been made so far in this area, except for in the works of [5,6]. Models for this application should possess two key properties. Firstly, a high resolution in dose prediction is crucial and requires the ability to process large data efficiently. Secondly,

Citation: Arsini, L.; Caccia, B.; Ciardiello, A.; Giagu, S.; Mancini Terracciano, C. Nearest Neighbours Graph Variational AutoEncoder. *Algorithms* **2023**, *16*, 143. https://doi.org/10.3390/a16030143

Academic Editors: Xiang Zhang and Xiaoxiao Li

Received: 20 December 2022
Revised: 7 February 2023
Accepted: 7 February 2023
Published: 6 March 2023

Copyright: © 2023 by the authors. Licensee MDPI, Basel, Switzerland. This article is an open access article distributed under the terms and conditions of the Creative Commons Attribution (CC BY) license (https://creativecommons.org/licenses/by/4.0/).

models should be lightweight to enable their use in resource-constrained medical devices and for online training. In the future, real-time imaging may enable real-time treatment planning optimization, making it imperative to use fast Deep Learning models during both training and inference.

Deep Learning applications can find a role in specialised hardware for both resource efficient deployment and fast inference tasks. These models are referred to as Lightweight models and they are designed to be small and efficient, making them well-suited for use on resource-constrained devices. Notable applications are embedded software in Internet of Things (IoT) devices [7], wearable medical devices [8], and real-time applications such as online video analysis, e.g., online crowd control [9]. A similar need is also present for models developed for fast inference on accelerated hardware, for which a keypoint example is the trigger analysis in high energy physics experiments [10]. These models are typically smaller and less complex than traditional deep learning models, which allow them to run on devices with limited computational power and memory. Moreover, designing them often involves trade-offs between computational resources and performance.

Deep Generative Modeling is commonly based on Convolutional Neural Networks (CNNs) for many applications, as they are one of the most powerful tools for processing grid-like data in Deep Learning frameworks. However, a significant amount of real-world data is better described by more flexible data structures, such as graphs.

A graph is defined by a pair $\mathcal{G} = (V, E)$. $V = \{v_i\}_{i=1}^{N}$ is a set of N vertices, or nodes, while $E = \{e_{ij}\}_{i,j=1}^{N}$ is the set of edges, which carry the relational information between nodes. The edge set E can be organised into the adjacency matrix A, an NxN binary matrix, whose elements A_{ij} are equal to 1 if a link between i-th and j-th node exists and is equal to 0 otherwise.

To address learning tasks on graphs, there has been an increasing interest in Graph Neural Networks (GNNs). These architectures typically use Graph Convolutional layers (GCNs), which allow for the processing of data on graphs, generalizing the concept of convolutions in CNNs. There are currently several types of GCNs available, ranging from the simplest models [11,12], to those based on graph spectral properties [13], and those that include attention mechanisms [14]. Although it is currently possible to achieve excellent results in solving various problems of classification, regression, or link prediction on graphs, graph generation remains an open challenge [15].

Unlike images, graphs often have complex geometric structures that are difficult to reproduce, particularly in an encoder–decoder framework. Despite various approaches existing, there is currently no standard method for addressing this class of problems. Standard classes of models for graph generation are Graph AutoEncoders (GAEs) and Variational Graph AutoEncoders (VGAEs) [16], which apply the concepts of AutoEncoders and Variational AutoEncoders (VAEs) to graphs. However, these architectures can only reconstruct or generate the adjacency matrix of the graphs, not the features of their nodes. Additionally, while these models can learn meaningful embeddings of node features, the graph structure and number of nodes remain fixed during the encoding process, resulting in no compression of input data through pooling operations and no bottleneck.

Different strategies have been developed for pooling operations on graphs. Early works used the eigen-decomposition for graph coarsening operations based on the graph topological structure, but these methods are often computationally expensive. An alternative algorithm is the Graclus algorithm [17], used in [13] and later adopted in other works on GNNs. Approaches like this aim to define a clustering scheme on graphs, on top of which it is possible to apply a standard max or mean pooling. Other approaches, such as SortPooling [18], select nodes to pool based on their importance in the network. There is also a stream of literature that bases pooling operations on spectral theory [19,20]. Finally, state-of-the-art approaches rely on learnable operators that, such as message-passing layers, can adapt to a specific task to compute the optimal pooling, such as DiffPool [21], Top-K pooling [22], and ASAPooling [23]. These pooling methods have been demonstrated to perform well when integrated into GNN models for graph classification, but all have limitations. For example, DiffPool learns a dense matrix to assign nodes to clusters, thus it is not scalable to large graphs. Top-k pooling samples the top-k aligned nodes with a learnable vector, not considering the graph connectivity. In this way, after the pooling, a good connectivity between the surviving nodes is not guaranteed. ASAPooling uses a self-attention mechanism for cluster formation and a top-k scoring algorithm for cluster selection, also taking into account graph connectivity. While overcoming some limitations of previous methods, this pooling requires more computations, which can lead to high computing needs for large graphs.

In contrast to pooling procedures, there is currently a lack of solutions for un-pooling operations for graphs that can be considered the inverse of pooling. The only works that attempt to define such operations are described in [22,24]. Other decoding schemes for graph generation are designed in different ways, most of which are task-specific. For example, in many algorithms for protein or drug structure generation, decoding is conducted by adding nodes and edges sequentially [25,26]. On the other hand, there are also works on "one-shot" graph generation, with decoding architectures that can output the node and edge features in a single step [27,28]. However, in various works that use this approach, the decoding of nodes and edges are considered separately and do not take into account the structure of the graphs. For example, in [29], a 1D-CNN is used to decode node features and a 2D-CNN is used for edge features.

In summary, we found that the current literature lacks:

- A pooling operation for graph data that takes into account graph connectivity and, at the same time, is lightweight and scalable to a large graph;
- A graph generative model based on an encoder–decoder architecture;
- A decoding solution that is based on the message passing algorithm.

In this study, we propose a model for graph generation based on Variational AutoEncoders. We focus on the case of graph data with a fixed, regular, and known geometric structure. To this end, we have developed:

- Simple, symmetrical, and geometry-based pooling and unpooling operations on graphs, which allow for the creation of bottlenecks in neural network architectures and that are scalable to large graphs;
- A Variational AutoEncoder for regular graph data, where both the encoding and decoding modules use graph convolutional layers to fully exploit the graph structure during the learning process.

The remainder of the study is organized as follows. In Section 2, we describe our proposed deep learning architecture and the datasets used. First, in Section 2.1, we introduce our Nearest Neighbors Graph VAE, describing how the developed pooling and unpooling techniques work and how they are integrated into the generative model. Then, in Section 2.2, we describe the benchmark sprite dataset and present our own set of cylindrical-shaped graph data for a Medical Physics application. In Section 3, we present the results of applying our Graph VAE to the described datasets. We also conduct an ablation study to compare the performance of our model using different pooling and unpooling techniques. The paper concludes with a final discussion in Section 4.

2. Materials and Methods

2.1. Nearest Neighbour Graph VAE

In this section, we introduce our Nearest Neighbour Graph VAE model, which uses graph convolutions in both the encoding and decoding operations. To create a bottleneck in the architecture, we propose new symmetrical graph pooling and un-pooling techniques, which we refer to as Recursive Nearest Neighbour Pooling and Un-Pooling (ReNN-Pool and Un-Pool). Such operations enable the construction of a VAE decoder based on graph convolutions.

2.1.1. ReNN-Pool and Un-Pool

In CNNs, pooling operations are widely used to decrease the dimensionality of feature maps while increasing the receptive fields of neurons when processing grid-like data. This is easily possible on images, where a standard pooling layer typically involves a downsampling operation such as the max or mean function applied to groups of nearby pixels. Conversely, applying this idea to graph structures is generally a challenging task.

However, there are cases where, although data does not have a grid-like shape and can be better processed with GNNs, the graph structures are fixed and have a regular and known geometry. For example, some datasets may contain examples whose data are arranged in a cylindrical or spherical structure. For these cases, we developed a simple pooling operation (ReNN-Pool) that can sub-sample graph nodes in a regular way.

The ReNN-Pool consists in a masking operation and a subsequent update of the adjacency matrix of the graph. First of all, nodes are sorted on the basis of their position in the graph. For example, if samples have a cylindrical structure, nodes can be hierarchically ordered on the basis of their positions along the z, θ and r axes. Then, the masking operation is carried out. Masking consists in dropping, i.e., removing, certain nodes from the graph. The process is performed in a recursive manner on the sorted node list. It begins with the first node, which is preserved, while all its nearest neighbours are dropped and removed from the node list. The process then continues with the next node and repeats, until all nodes in the list have been processed.

After the masking, we rewire links between the "survived" nodes, connecting the ones that were 2nd order neighbours before the masking. This is conducted substituting the adjacency matrix A with A^2. If we call M the vector that contains all the indices of the "survived" nodes, $X = \{x_i\}_{i=1}^N$ and A, respectively, and the nodes' feature matrix and the adjacency matrix before the pooling, the application of ReNN-Pool gives in output:

$$X' = \{x'_i\}_{i=1}^N, \text{ where } x'_i = \begin{cases} x_i, & \text{if } i \in M \\ 0, & \text{otherwise} \end{cases} \qquad A' = \begin{cases} A^2_{ij}, & \text{if } i,j \in M \\ 0, & \text{otherwise} \end{cases}$$

The process is illustrated in Figure 1.

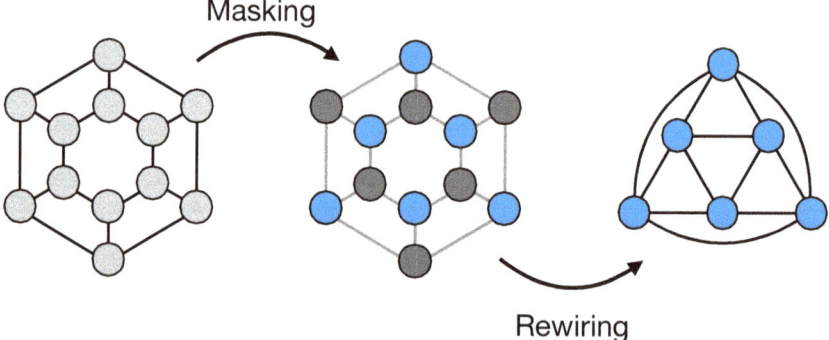

Figure 1. Pooling. The ReNN-Pool operation consists of two steps: masking and rewiring. In the first step, recursively on the whole graph, a node is selected and all its nearest neighbours are dropped. In the second step, nodes are linked to the ones that were their 2nd order neighbours.

In the case of regular geometrical graph structures, by construction, pooled and not-pooled nodes are evenly spread across the graph; thus, the choice of the starting node does not affect the performances of the model in which the ReNN-Pool is used. For irregular graph structures, the performance can depend on the choice of the first node. However, in principle this can become an hyperparameter to optimize using a validation set. Such a possibility will be explored in future works.

On regular graphs, the masking operation allows one to define evenly spread clusters of nodes. In fact, the surviving nodes can be thought as centroids of the clusters made up by their nearest neighbours. These clusters can be used to perform a mean or max pooling on graphs in addition to the simple masking. A comparison of these methods is presented in Section 3.

Due to the fact that the creation of masks and the adjacency matrices' augmentation in our pooling only depends on the graph structure of data, it is possible to compute and store them before the training. This has two main advantages. First, the pooling operation has no influence on the computational needs both in the training and the inference phase. Thus, it can be used inside lightweight models for resource-constrained devices and it is scalable for graphs of any size. Second, such masks and adjacencies can also be used to define an un-pooling operation that is symmetrical to the pooling one. Such a possibility is particularly relevant for the construction of generative encoder–decoder models, but also crucial for symmetrical architectures such as U-nets [30], where skip connections connect graphs with the same geometrical structure. Starting from a lower dimensional (pooled) representation of the graph with a feature matrix X and adjacency A^2, the Un-Pool layer embeds back the nodes in their original position in the higher dimensional representation of the graph, that has an adjacency matrix A. All other restored nodes are initialized to 0. A similar idea for the un-pooling was already explored [22]. An illustration of the un-pooling operation is shown in Figure 2.

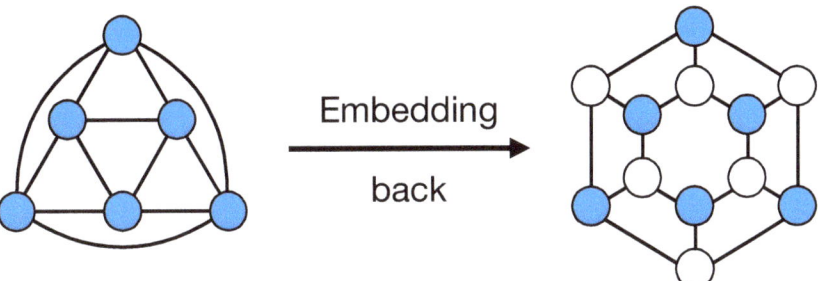

Figure 2. Un-Pooling. The Un-Pool operation consists in embedding the nodes of a pooled graph in their initial position in the bigger original graph structure. All other restored nodes are initialized to 0.

2.1.2. ReNN Graph VAE Architecture

A Variational AutoEncoder is a generative model with an encoder–decoder structure. First the encoder learns to represent high dimensional input data as a distribution in a low dimensional space, called "latent space". The decoder is then trained to recover the original data, sampling a point from such distribution. We refer the reader to the Appendix B and the original paper [2] for a detailed description of the model.

In our architecture, the encoding consists of three subsequent repetitions of two operations: a graph convolution and a ReNN-Pool operation. For the graph convolution, we chose to use the GraphConv layer [11]. With this convolution, the new features of nodes are just linear combinations between their old features and the mean of the features of their neighbourhood, followed by a ReLu activation:

$$x'_i = ReLu\left(W_1 x_i + W_2 \frac{1}{|N(i)|} \sum_{j \in N(i)} x_j\right). \tag{1}$$

Eventually, to increase the expressive power of the network, one can also include edge features e_{ij} in the computation, considering instead:

$$x'_i = ReLu\left(W_1 x_i + W_2 \frac{1}{|N(i)|} \sum_{j \in N(i)} e_{ij} x_j\right). \tag{2}$$

In particular, we consider edge features e_{ij} to be learned parameters of the Neural Network.

The number of output channels of the GraphConv in the three subsequent repetitions is set to 16, 32, and 64.

After the three graph encoding steps, the node features are put together and flattened. Then, the dimensionality of data is further reduced through a linear layer.

The encoded data is processed as in a standard VAE architecture with Gaussian prior to that.

Data points are mapped to Gaussian distributions in the latent space and, using the reparameterisation trick, a variable Z is sampled from those distributions.

The decoding uses the same graph representations employed for the encoding, but in reverse order. After an initial decoding linear layer, we repeat for three times the series of an un-pooling layer and a graph convolution. For the convolutions, we employ again the GraphConv layers with the output channels' number set to 32, 16 and 1. In this way, the original dimensionality of the data is recovered. The activation function of the last convolutional layer is a sigmoid. The model is trained minimizing the standard β-VAE loss function, defined in Appendix B, with binary cross entropy as the reconstruction term.

The concatenation of a graph convolution and a pooling operation can be thought of as an "encoding block", while the union of an un-pooling operation and a convolution can be thought of as a "decoding block". Various architectures can be built using different numbers of blocks. In Figure 3, for example, our VAE architecture is illustrated, but with only two blocks in the encoder and decoder.

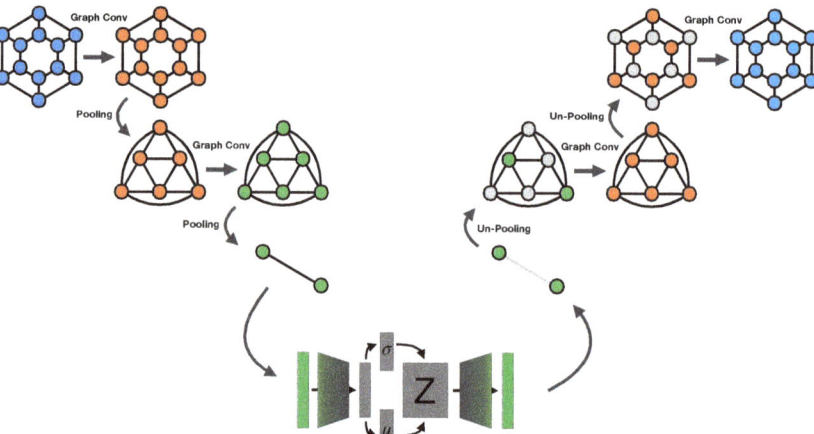

Figure 3. Full scheme. Schematic representation of our Re-NN Graph VAE with two encoding blocks and two decoding blocks. Each block is made up of a graph convolution and a pooling (un-pooling) operation. In the lower part of the picture, the VAE sampling and the encoding (decoding) linear layers are represented.

2.2. Datasets

2.2.1. Energy Deposition Datasets

The architecture presented in this work was developed for a specific application in Medical Physics, which is the generation of the distribution of the dose absorbed by a medium interacting with a given particle beam, conditioned to beam parameters and medium density. Specifically, the approach was developed for a frontier application in radiation oncology therapy, which makes use of high-energy electron beams (Flash Therapy [31]).

The datasets for this task are built simulating an electron beam interacting with a material using Geant4 [32], a toolkit in C++ for Monte Carlo simulations in particle physics.

The two datasets differ on the material in which electrons deposit their energy. In the first case, this material is a cubic volume filled with water. We will refer to this dataset as "Water Dataset". In the second case, to increase the complexity of the task, we inserted a slab of variable density in the water volume. This slab is orthogonal to the electrons' beam and has a fixed position and thickness. The density of the slab is uniformly sampled at each run of the simulation between 0 and 5 g/cm^3 (for reference, water density is 1 g/cm^3). We will refer to this dataset as "Water + Slab Dataset". In both cases, the particles' energies are sampled uniformly between 50 and 100 MeV, which is the typical range of energies for the FLASH radiotherapy with high-energy electrons.

Energy deposition data are collected in a cylindrical scorer, aligned with the electron beam, and divided in $28 \times 28 \times 28$ voxels along z, θ and r axes. The cylindrical shape is particularly useful in our application because it allows for higher precision near the beamline.

Each example in the dataset is therefore a set of 28^3 voxels arranged in a cylindrical shape. Voxels have only one feature, and correspond to the amount of energy deposited in them by the simulated particle beam. Each example of the Water Dataset is labelled by the initial energy of the electron beam, while in the other dataset examples are labelled by both the particles' initial energy and the slab's density. An illustration of a typical example from these datasets is shown in Figure 4. Besides the representation of the original data in the left panel, we also show how the ReNN-Pool operates on nodes. As it is possible to see, the nodes' pooling is conducted in a spatial and uniform way.

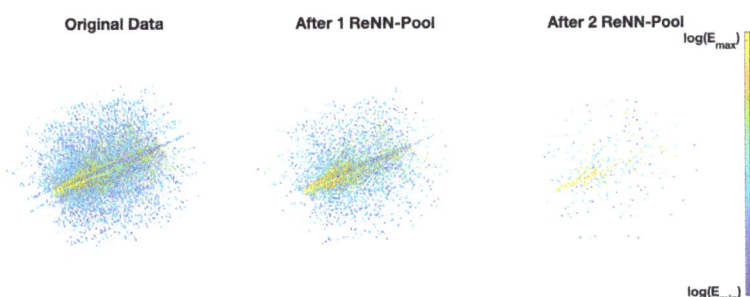

Figure 4. Dataset and ReNN-Pool. From the left, the panels show the representation of a typical example from the energy deposition datasets and two pooled representations of the same example. The nodes in light grey have null features, while all others show an energy distribution within the considered range.

Datasets, respectively, consist of 4662 and 6239 examples and are divided in train, validation and test sets on the basis of particle energy and slab density. In particular, in the Water Dataset, the test set is made up of examples with a particle's energy ranging between 70 and 80 MeV. In the Water + Slab Dataset test set, the examples have the same range of initial energies and slab density values, ranging between 2 and 3 g/cm^3. In both cases, the rest of the dataset is used for validation and trains with a ratio of 1/10.

Test sets have been chosen in this way in order to test the network ability to interpolate between samples and generalise to unseen configurations.

For both datasets, we imposed a graph structure on the data. Each voxels was associated with a node and nodes were linked within each other with a nearest neighbours connectivity. In this way, the nodes in the center and on the outer surface of the cylinder have five neighbours, while all others have six neighbours.

2.2.2. Sprite Dataset

The sprite dataset is a benchmark dataset for the latent space feature disentaglement in VAEs and consist of a set of 2D images representing pixelized video game "sprites". The aim of testing our Graph VAE on such a dataset is to show that our model can also work as a standard Variational AutoEncoder on tasks that are different from the one for which it was developed. Although a CNN would reasonably be the best choice for this dataset, images can also be thought of as graphs with a regular structure; therefore, they should also be processed effectively by our model.

We used part of the dataset employed in [33], available online (https://github.com/YingzhenLi/Sprites, accessed on 17 November 2022). Such a dataset consists of 9000 examples for training and 2664 for testing. Each example is a sequence of 8 frames of a sprite performing an action. We decided to keep the first frame for each example, so we ended up with 9000 images, divided into a training and validation set with a 1/8 ratio, and 2664 images for testing. Each image is 64×64 pixels and represents a standing sprite whose attributes are organized in 4 categories (skin color, tops, pants and hairstyle) with 6 variations each, and 3 orientations (left, center and right).

To process such a dataset with our architecture, we had to impose a graph structure on the data. Therefore, we associated a node to each pixel and connected nodes with a grid-like connectivity. In this way, internal nodes have 4 edges, border nodes have 3 edges and corner nodes have 2 edges.

3. Results

3.1. Results on Energy Deposition Datasets

We trained our VAE with the two energy deposition datasets described in the previous section. Here, we present the results that regard the reconstruction of the energy deposition distribution from the test set. The DL model was trained for 200 epochs and the best set of learnable parameters was chosen as the one that minimizes the validation loss. We set the latent space dimensionality to 1, for the Water Volume dataset, and to 2 for the other dataset. For the weight update, we used the Adam optimiser with an initial learning rate of 0.003 and an exponential scheduler with $\lambda = 0.9$. The hyperparameter β of the VAE, defined in Appendix B, was set to 1.

To evaluate the performance of our model, we considered both local node-per-node and global reconstruction metrics. As a node-per-node reconstruction metric, we use the δ-index, developed by [5]. This metric is inspired by the standard γ-index [34], used for the clinical validation of treatment plans, and is currently used in the field to evaluate DL models for energy deposition data generation. The reconstruction error on each node is defined as:

$$\delta = \frac{X_{reco} - X_{GT}}{max(X_{GT})} \qquad (3)$$

where X_{reco} is the node feature predicted by the VAE, while X_{GT} is the ground truth node feature in the corresponding example. Then, as a reconstruction performance measure, we consider the 3% passing rate, which is the percentage of nodes with a δ index smaller than 3%. In the water volume case, our Network reaches 99.4% of nodes with a 3% passing rate, while the water volume + Slab case reaches 98.4%, as reported in Table 1.

Table 1. Results on energy deposition reconstruction. We report mean relative errors on energy profiles and total energy along with the mean 3% δ-index passing rate. Uncertainties are computed as standard deviations. Values are computed on test sets.

Dataset	z Profile Error	r Profile Error	Total Energy Error	$\delta < 3\%$
Water	5.8 ± 3.4%	2.6 ± 1.6%	2.2 ± 1.6%	99.3 ± 0.1%
Water + Slab	6.9 ± 3.4%	3.0 ± 1.2%	2.2 ± 1.6%	98.6 ± 0.3%

As global evaluation metrics, we consider the error on relevant physical quantities that the generative model should reconstruct well. To this end, we compute the relative error on three quantities:

- **Total energy**: computed by summing the features of all nodes.
- **z profile**: computed by integrating, i.e., by summing, the features of all nodes along the r and θ axes.
- **r profile**: computed by integrating, i.e., by summing, the features of all nodes along the z and θ axes.

In Figure 5, we show the energy profiles along the z and r axes. The upper Figure 5a regards the Water Dataset, while the lower Figure 5b refers to the Water + Slab one. In each panel, the blue line correspond to the ground truth, i.e., Monte Carlo simulated data, while the orange line refers to the reconstructed data from our Network. In both cases, the Network reconstructs the profiles well. The mean relative errors on profiles and total energy deposition are reported in Table 1, along with their standard deviation on the test set.

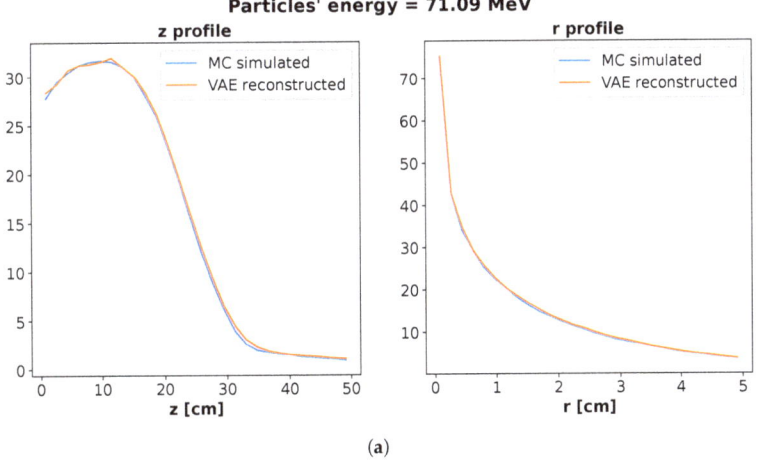

Figure 5. Cont.

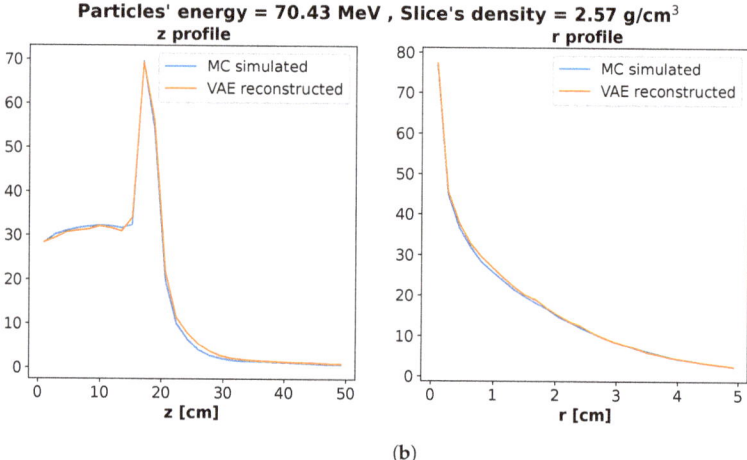

(b)

Figure 5. Energy profiles reconstruction. Distribution of energy deposition along z and r axes from the test sets of the Water dataset (**a**) and the Water + Slab dataset (**b**). The blue lines correspond to the Monte Carlo simulated data, while the orange lines refer to the reconstructed data from our Network.

While the errors on the r profile, total energy and overall reconstruction are quite low and around 1–3%, the errors on the z profile are around 6%. To understand such a result, we included in the analysis the variance in the Monte Carlo simulations. We fixed the particle energy and slab density to be the ones in the example in Figure 5b, and we ran 100 Monte Carlo simulations computing the mean and standard deviation of the energy deposition profile along the z axis. We also generated 100 energy deposition distributions for feeding our VAE the test set example relative to the chosen particles' energy and slab density, as well as computed the mean and standard deviation for the z profile.

In Figure 6, we show the comparison of the standard deviation over the mean of the energy profile along the z axis between Monte Carlo simulations (left) and VAE reconstruction (right). The red dashed lines represent the slab with different (in this case higher) density, where most of the energy is released. Note that most of the errors in the reconstruction is relative to regions where there are fluctuations in the energy deposition, and so in our training set generated by Monte Carlo simulations, they are not negligible.

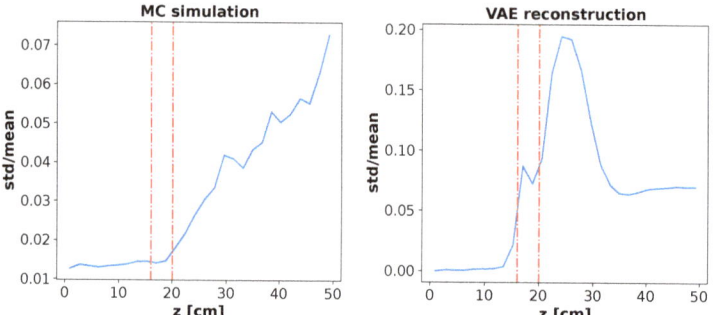

Figure 6. Standard deviations in MC and VAE. Comparison of standard deviation over mean of the energy profile along the z axis between Monte Carlo simulations and VAE reconstruction in the Water + Slab setting. Values are estimated for 100 MC runs with fixed parameters and 100 VAE execution with the same example as input. Results demonstrate how VAE's largest errors are in regions where energy deposition fluctuation, and so Monte Carlo's ones, are not negligible.

3.2. Results on Sprite Dataset

For this task, to increase the expressive power of the architecture, we used both variants of the GraphConv layers. In particular, in the first layer of the encoder (and in a symmetrical way in the last layer of the decoder), we used the GraphConv without edge weights described in Equation (1). In the other layers, we used the GraphConv with edge weights (Equation (2)). Such weights are learned using Linear layers. A full description of the model is given in Appendix A.

We trained our Graph VAE for 50 epochs with a batch size of 50 and set the latent space to have 5 dimensions.

For the weight update, we used the Adam optimiser with an initial learning rate of 0.005 and an exponential scheduler with $\lambda = 0.95$. In this case, The hyperparameter β of the VAE, defined in Appendix B, was set to 2.

As shown in Figure 7, our model can also work like a standard CNN VAE for image generation. In the upper panel, we show a comparison between the input images and the reconstructed ones. In the lower panel, we show how the VAE can learn a disentangled representation of features and can also interpolate through samples. In particular, we show how when fixing all dimensions of the latent space but one, it is possible to generate samples with a continuously changing hair style. A direct comparison with a standard 2D CNN VAE is presented in Appendix C.

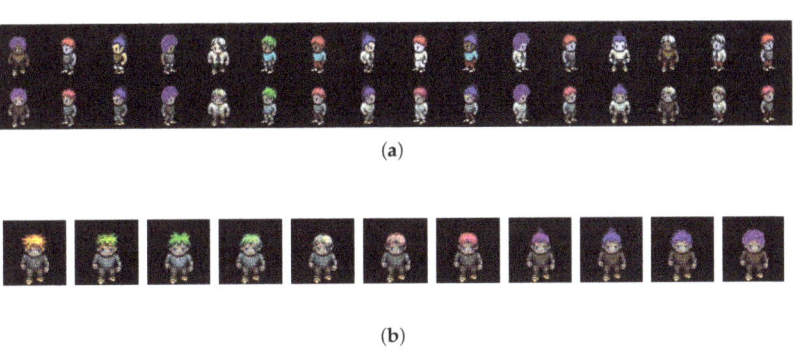

Figure 7. Results on sprite dataset. (**a**) Comparison between input sprite images (first row) and reconstructed ones (second row). (**b**) Images generated fixing all the latent variables' dimensions but one, which is varied. Generated sprites have fixed attributes but a continuously varying hair style.

3.3. Ablation Study on Pooling

We performed an ablation study to asses the impact of the pooling technique on the model's performance. The model was evaluated on the Water + Slab dataset using the reconstruction metrics discussed in Section 3.1. Five pooling techniques were considered:

- ReNN-Pool: the one proposed in this work with only the simple node masking;
- ReNN Mean Pool: mean pooling on clusters defined by the masking operation of ReNN-Pool;
- ReNN Max Pool: max pooling on clusters defined by the masking operation of ReNN-Pool;
- Random Pool: dropping random nodes in the graph;
- Top-k Pool: defined in [22], dropping nodes on the base of features' alignment with a learnable vector.

For the Random Pool and Top-k Pool, we fixed the ratios of the pooled nodes to be the same as the one of the ReNN-Pool. Such ratios are sequentially: 50%, 87% and 84%. After the node dropping, the adjacency matrix is updated from A to A^2, connecting second order neighbours, as conducted in this work and recommended in [22], where the Top-k pooling was introduced. The un-pooling operations employ the same node masks and adjacency matrices of the pooling operations; thus, they are always symmetrical to them. The results of the ablation study are presented in Table 2, where it is demonstrated how the architectures with the ReNN-Pool and Un-Pool operations outperform the other models. The results relative to the addition of mean and max operations are very likely related to the kind of data processed, which are smooth energy distributions in a cylinder. With such data, it is reasonable that the ReNN Mean Pool performs similarly to the simple ReNN-Pool and that adding the max operation leads to worse results.

Table 2. Results of ablation study on pooling. Comparison of the results on the test set of the Water + Slab dataset using different pooling and un-pooling techniques. Mean relative errors on energy profiles and total energy along with the mean 3% δ-index passing rate on test sets are reported.

Pooling	z Profile Error	r Profile Error	Total Energy Error	$\delta < 3\%$
ReNN-Pool	6.9 ± 3.4%	3.0 ± 1.2%	2.2 ± 1.6%	98.6 ± 0.3%
ReNN Mean Pool	6.4 ± 3.0%	2.8 ± 1.1%	2.0 ± 1.4%	98.6 ± 0.3%
ReNN Max Pool	22.6 ± 9.9%	5.0 ± 1.8%	3.2 ± 2.3%	97.5 ± 0.7%
Random Pool	172.6 ± 21.7%	52.2 ± 3.7%	2.0 ± 1.5%	92.4 ± 0.4%
Top-k Pool	51.7 ± 3.4%	75.1 ± 9.1%	4.0 ± 2.6%	79.9 ± 1.3%

A plausible explanation of the better performances of ReNN-Pool-based techniques with respect to the Random and Top-k Pool relates to the connectivity of the graphs. ReNN-Pool is specifically designed for data to always be represented by a single connected graph. Indeed, after each pooling operation, the receptive field of the remaining nodes is enlarged but there is no loss of information due to the disconnected clusters of nodes. Conversely, with random pooling or Top-k pooling there is no guarantee that this will happen. Actually, in most cases, after such pooling operations, the graph structure breaks up in different unconnected clusters. That is particularly true when the graph exhibits only local connectivity.

4. Discussion

In this work, we presented our Nearest Neighbour Graph VAE, a Variational AutoEncoder that can generate graph data with a regular geometry. Such a model fully takes advantage of the Graph convolutional layers in both encoding and decoding phases. For the encoding, we introduced a pooling technique (ReNN-Pool), based on the graph connectivity that allows us to sub-sample graph nodes in a spatially uniform way and to alter the graph adjacency matrix consequently. The decoding is carried out using a symmetrical un-pooling operation to retrieve the original graphs. We demonstrated how our model can reconstruct well the cylindrical-shaped graph data of energy deposition distributions of a particle beam in a medium.

We also evaluated the performance of the model on the sprite benchmark dataset, after transforming the image data into graphs. Although it can not be directly compared with more sophisticated and task specific algorithms for image synthesis, our model has the ability to generate good quality images, create disentangled representations of features, and interpolate through samples as well as a standard CNN VAE. Finally, we performed an ablation study on pooling. The results show how, on our task on large regular graphs, using the ReNN-Pool is more efficient and leads to better performances versus using a state-of-the-art technique, such as Top-k Pool.

Finally, we believe that ReNN-Pool represents a simple, lightweight and efficient solution to pool regular graphs. It requires no computation during either the training or inference of models because node masks and adjacency matrices can be computed and stored early on. Thus, it is directly scalable to graphs of any size, contrarily to state-of-the-art pooling techniques. Moreover, the definition of a symmetrical un-pooling technique enables the construction of graph decoding modules, which can take advantage of graph convolutional layers. The current limitation of our pooling is that it has been only tested on regular graphs. However, a test on irregular graphs is among our future research directions. Although ReNN-Pool is not directly usable on all types of graphs, such as fully or highly connected ones, we believe that it could also be an efficient solution for irregular graphs with small to medium-sized node neighbourhoods. We also plan to test our method on graph U-Net architectures, where the symmetry between encoding and decoding is needed.

Author Contributions: Conceptualization, L.A., B.C., A.C., S.G. and C.M.T.; methodology, L.A., B.C., A.C., S.G. and C.M.T.; software, L.A.; validation, L.A. and A.C.; formal analysis, L.A.; investigation, L.A. and A.C.; resources, B.C., S.G. and C.M.T.; data curation, L.A. and C.M.T.; writing—original draft preparation, L.A.; writing—review and editing, L.A., A.C. and S.G.; visualization, L.A.; supervision, S.G. and C.M.T. All authors have read and agreed to the published version of the manuscript.

Funding: This research received no external funding.

Data Availability Statement: The Sprite dataset is publicly available in https://lpc.opengameart.org/, (accessed on 17 November 2022); the Energy deposition datasets and the code used for this study are available on request by contacting the authors.

Conflicts of Interest: The authors declare no conflict of interest. The funders had no role in the design of the study; in the collection, analyses, or interpretation of data; in the writing of the manuscript; or in the decision to publish the results.

Abbreviations and Symbols

The following abbreviations and symbols are used in this manuscript:

DL	Deep Learning
CNN	Convolutional Neural Network
GAN	Generative Adversarial Networks
VAE	Variational AutoEncoder
RT	Radiotherapy
GNN	Graph Neural Networks
GCN	Graph Convolutional layers
GAE	Graph AutoEncoders
VGAE	Variational Graph AutoEncoders
ReNN-Pool	Recursive Nearest Neighbour Pooling
ELBO	Evidence Lower Bound
(z, θ, r)	Cylindrical coordinate system
$X = \{x_i\}_{i=1}^N$	Node feature vector
$A = \{A_{i,j}\}_{i,j=1}^N$	Adjacency matrix
M	ReNN-Pool masking vector
N	Number of nodes in the graph
$N(i)$	Number of neighbours of node i
e_{ij}	Weight of the edge between node i and j
W_k	Generic weight of the Neural network
Z	Latent space variable
δ	δ-index

Appendix A. Full Model Description

In the following Tables, we report a detailed list of the layers that compose the models we used to run the experiments described in Section 3. Next to the name of each layer, we report the number of parameters in it and the number of nodes and edges in the graphs after the layer execution. In particular, in Table A1, we describe the model used on the Water + Slab dataset. For the Water dataset, we used the same architecture except for the last two linear layers of the encoder and the first one of the decoder, whose output (input) number of channels was set to 1, instead of 2, in accordance with the latent space dimensionality.

In Table A2, the version of the Re-NN Graph VAE used for the Sprite dataset is described. The linear layers between the pooling (un-pooling) operations and the graph convolutions are responsible for learning the edge features which enter in the computation of the GraphConv marked with e_{ij}.

Table A1. ReNN Graph VAE used for the Water + Slab dataset. For the Water dataset, the same architecture was used but the parameter marked with an asterisk was changed to 1, in accordance with the latent space dimensionality.

	Layers	Parameters	N Nodes	N Edges
Graph Encoder	GraphConv (1, 16, 'mean')	48	21,952	128,576
	ReNN-Pool	-	10,976	188,216
	GraphConv (16, 32, 'mean')	1056	10,976	188,216
	ReNN-Pool	-	1470	21,952
	GraphConv (32, 64, 'mean')	4160	1470	21,952
	ReNN-Pool	-	236	6206
	Linear (64 × 236, 64)	966,720	-	-
	Linear (64, 2*)	130	-	-
	Linear (64, 2*)	130	-	-
Graph Decoder	Linear (2*, 64)	192	-	-
	Linear (64, 64 × 236)	981,760	-	-
	ReNN-Unpool	-	1470	21,952
	GraphConv (64, 32, 'mean')	4128	1470	21,952
	ReNN-Unpool	-	10,976	188,216
	GraphConv (32, 16, 'mean')	1040	10,976	188,216
	ReNN-Unpool	-	21,952	128,576
	GraphConv (16, 1, 'mean')	33	21,952	128,576

Table A2. ReNN Graph VAE for sprite dataset.

	Layers	Parameters	N Nodes	N Edges
Graph Encoder	GraphConv (3, 16, 'mean')	112	4096	16,128
	ReNN-Pool	-	2048	15,874
	Linear (1, 15,874)	31,748	-	-
	GraphConv (16, 32, 'mean', e_{ij})	1056	2048	15,874
	ReNN-Pool	-	528	3906
	Linear (1, 3906)	7812	-	-
	GraphConv (32, 64, 'mean', e_{ij})	4160	528	3906
	ReNN-Pool	-	136	930
	Linear (64 × 136, 64)	557,120	-	-
	Linear (64, 5)	325	-	-
	Linear (64, 5)	325	-	-
Graph Decoder	Linear (5, 64)	384	-	-
	Linear (64, 64 × 136)	565,760	-	-
	ReNN-Unpool	-	528	3906
	Linear (1, 3906)	7812	-	-
	GraphConv (64, 32, 'mean', e_{ij})	4128	528	3906
	ReNN-Unpool	-	2048	15,874
	Linear (1, 15,874)	31,748	-	-
	GraphConv (32, 16, 'mean', e_{ij})	1040	2048	15,874
	ReNN-Unpool	-	4096	16,128
	GraphConv (16, 3, 'mean')	99	4096	16,128

Appendix B. Variational AutoEncoder

A Variational AutoEncoder is a generative Deep Learning model first proposed by Kingma and Welling [2]. It is a special AutoEncoder based on the variational Bayes inference, whose goal is to learn the distribution of the training data and to be able to sample new datapoints from it. The underlying hypothesis is that datapoints $\{x\}$ are the results of a generative process controlled by a variable z that lives in a low dimensional space, called latent space, and their distribution is thus:

$$p(x) = \int p(x|z)p(z)dz,$$

where the prior $p(z)$ is often considered Gaussian. The model is made up of two networks: the encoder and the decoder. The encoder $q_\psi(z|x)$ maps the input data to a distribution in the latent space. Thanks to the reparemeterisation trick, a point from such a distribution is sampled in a fully differentiable way and processed by the decoder $p_\psi(x|z)$ to retrieve the original data. The model is trained maximising the evidenced lower bound (ELBO) of the data likelihood:

$$\{\psi,\phi\} = argmax_{\psi,\phi}\left[\mathbb{E}_{x\sim q_\psi(\cdot|x)}\left[logp_\phi(x|z) - D_{KL}(q_\psi(z|x)|p(z))\right]\right]$$

After training, new datapoints x can be generated sampling z in the latent space and passing it to the decoder. Starting from a standard VAE, it is also possible to slightly modify the loss function by adding a scalar hyperparameter $\beta > 1$:

$$\{\psi,\phi\} = argmax_{\psi,\phi}\left[\mathbb{E}_{x\sim q_\psi(\cdot|x)}\left[logp_\phi(x|z) - \beta D_{KL}(q_\psi(z|x)|p(z))\right]\right].$$

The model with such a modification is known as β-VAE [35] and is recognised to promote a better disentangling of features' embedding in the latent space.

Appendix C. ReNN Graph VAE vs. CNN VAE

We performed a quantitative comparison between our ReNN Graph VAE and a standard 2D CNN VAE on the Sprite benchmark dataset. The CNN comprise 2D convolutional layers and mean pooling in the encoder and 2D transpose convolutions and upsampling in the decoder. A full description of the model is given in Table A3. The model was trained for 50 epochs with a batch size of 50, setting the latent space to have 5 dimensions. For the weight update, we used the Adam optimiser with an initial learning rate of 0.005 and an exponential scheduler with λ = 0.95. In order to obtain a disentangled representation for the hair style in the latent space, we had to set the β parameter to 4.

To quantitatively evaluate the performance of our model on this dataset, we considered the Structure Similarity Index Measure (SSIM). It is a perception-based measure that considers image degradation as the perceived change in structural information. While pixel-per-pixel reconstruction metrics, such as as MSE or the previously used δ-index, estimate absolute errors, the structural information considers the strong inter-dependencies between spatially close pixels that carry important information about the image as a whole. Both CNN VAE and ReNN Graph VAE reached an average SSIM on the test set of 0.90.

In Figure A1, we also report a comparison between some ground truth, ReNN Graph VAE reconstructed sprites and CNN VAE reconstructed sprites from the test set. Both VAEs work well, but it is possible to spot some differences. CNN VAE reconstructed images are slightly blurrier that the originals, while the ReNN Graph VAE has slightly less bright colours.

Figure A1. *Ground truth vs. reconstructed sprites*. Comparison between sprites from the test set with their reconstructed counterpart by ReNN Graph VAE and a standard CNN VAE.

Table A3. Two-dimensional CNN VAE for sprite dataset.

	Layers	Parameters
Graph Encoder	Conv2d (3, 16, kernel_size = (3, 3, 3))	448
	AvgPool2d (kernel_size = 2, stride = 2)	-
	Conv2d (16, 32, kernel_size = (3, 3, 3))	4640
	AvgPool2d (kernel_size = 2, stride = 1)	-
	Conv2d (32, 64, kernel_size = (3, 3, 3))	18,496
	AvgPool2d (kernel_size = 2, stride = 2)	-
	Linear (64 × 169, 64)	692,288
	Linear (64, 5)	325
Graph Decoder	Linear (64, 5)	325
	Linear (5, 64)	384
	Linear (64, 64 × 169)	703,040
	Upsample (size = (26, 26), mode = 'bilinear')	-
	ConvTranspose2d (64, 32, kernel_size = (3, 3, 3))	18,464
	Upsample (size = (29, 29), mode = 'bilinear')	-
	ConvTranspose2d (32, 16, kernel_size = (3, 3, 3))	4624
	Upsample (size = (62, 62), mode = 'bilinear')	-
	ConvTranspose2d (16, 3, kernel_size = (3, 3, 3))	435

References

1. Goodfellow, I.J.; Pouget-Abadie, J.; Mirza, M.; Xu, B.; Warde-Farley, D.; Ozair, S.; Courville, A.; Bengio, Y. Generative Adversarial Networks. *arXiv* **2014**, arXiv:1406.2661.
2. Kingma, D.P.; Welling, M. Auto-Encoding Variational Bayes. *arXiv* **2014**, arXiv:1312.6114.
3. Rezende, D.; Mohamed, S. Variational Inference with Normalizing Flows. In Proceedings of the Machine Learning Research (PMLR), Proceedings of the 32nd International Conference on Machine Learning, Lille, France, 6–11 July 2015; Volume 37, pp. 1530–1538.
4. Bond-Taylor, S.; Leach, A.; Long, Y.; Willcocks, C.G. Deep Generative Modelling: A Comparative Review of VAEs, GANs, Normalizing Flows, Energy-Based and Autoregressive Models. *IEEE Trans. Pattern Anal. Mach. Intell.* **2022**, *44*, 7327–7347.
5. Mentzel, F.; Kröninger, K.; Lerch, M.; Nackenhorst, O.; Paino, J.; Rosenfeld, A.; Saraswati, A.; Tsoi, A.C.; Weingarten, J.; Hagenbuchner, M.; et al. Fast and accurate dose predictions for novel radiotherapy treatments in heterogeneous phantoms using conditional 3D-UNet generative adversarial networks. *Med. Phys.* **2022**, *49*, 3389–3404. [CrossRef]
6. Zhang, X.; Hu, Z.; Zhang, G.; Zhuang, Y.; Wang, Y.; Peng, H. Dose calculation in proton therapy using a discovery cross-domain generative adversarial network (DiscoGAN). *Med. Phys.* **2021**, *48*, 2646–2660. [CrossRef] [PubMed]
7. Mendonça, R.V.; Silva, J.C.; Rosa, R.L.; Saadi, M.; Rodriguez, D.Z.; Farouk, A. A lightweight intelligent intrusion detection system for industrial internet of things using deep learning algorithms. *Expert Syst.* **2022**, *39*, e12917. [CrossRef]
8. Beniczky, S.; Karoly, P.; Nurse, E.; Ryvlin, P.; Cook, M. Machine learning and wearable devices of the future. *Epilepsia* **2021**, *62*, S116–S124. [CrossRef]
9. Khan, N.; Ullah, A.; Haq, I.U.; Menon, V.G.; Baik, S.W. SD-Net: Understanding overcrowded scenes in real-time via an efficient dilated convolutional neural network. *J. Real-Time Image Process.* **2021**, *18*, 1729–1743. [CrossRef]
10. Francescato, S.; Giagu, S.; Riti, F.; Russo, G.; Sabetta, L.; Tortonesi, F. Model compression and simplification pipelines for fast deep neural network inference in FPGAs in HEP. *Eur. Phys. J. C* **2021**, *81*, 969. [CrossRef]
11. Morris, C.; Ritzert, M.; Fey, M.; Hamilton, W.L.; Lenssen, J.E.; Rattan, G.; Grohe, M. Weisfeiler and Leman Go Neural: Higher-order Graph Neural Networks. *arXiv* **2021**, arXiv:1810.02244.
12. Kipf, T.N.; Welling, M. Semi-Supervised Classification with Graph Convolutional Networks. *arXiv* **2017**, arXiv:1609.02907.
13. Defferrard, M.; Bresson, X.; Vandergheynst, P. Convolutional Neural Networks on Graphs with Fast Localized Spectral Filtering. *arXiv* **2017**, arXiv:1606.09375.
14. Veličković, P.; Cucurull, G.; Casanova, A.; Romero, A.; Liò, P.; Bengio, Y. Graph Attention Networks. *arXiv* **2018**, arXiv:1710.10903.
15. Zhu, Y.; Du, Y.; Wang, Y.; Xu, Y.; Zhang, J.; Liu, Q.; Wu, S. A Survey on Deep Graph Generation: Methods and Applications. *arXiv* **2022**, arXiv:2203.06714.
16. Kipf, T.N.; Welling, M. Variational Graph Auto-Encoders. *arXiv* **2016**, arXiv:1611.07308.
17. Dhillon, I.S.; Guan, Y.; Kulis, B. Weighted Graph Cuts without Eigenvectors A Multilevel Approach. *IEEE Trans. Pattern Anal. Mach. Intell.* **2007**, *29*, 1944–1957. [CrossRef]
18. Zhang, M.; Cui, Z.; Neumann, M.; Chen, Y. An End-to-End Deep Learning Architecture for Graph Classification. In Proceedings of the AAAI Conference on Artificial Intelligence, New Orleans, LA, USA, 2–7 February 2018; Volume 32. [CrossRef]
19. Bianchi, F.M.; Grattarola, D.; Livi, L.; Alippi, C. Hierarchical Representation Learning in Graph Neural Networks with Node Decimation Pooling. *IEEE Trans. Neural Netw. Learn. Syst.* **2022**, *33*, 2195–2207.

20. Bravo-Hermsdorff, G.; Gunderson, L.M. A Unifying Framework for Spectrum-Preserving Graph Sparsification and Coarsening. *arXiv* **2020**, arXiv:1902.09702.
21. Ying, R.; You, J.; Morris, C.; Ren, X.; Hamilton, W.L.; Leskovec, J. Hierarchical Graph Representation Learning with Differentiable Pooling. *arXiv* **2019**, arXiv:1806.08804.
22. Gao, H.; Ji, S. Graph U-Nets. *arXiv* **2019**, arXiv:1905.05178.
23. Ranjan, E.; Sanyal, S.; Talukdar, P. Asap: Adaptive structure aware pooling for learning hierarchical graph representations. In Proceedings of the AAAI Conference on Artificial Intelligence, New York, NY, USA, 7–12 February 2020; Volume 34, pp. 5470–5477.
24. Guo, Y.; Zou, D.; Lerman, G. An Unpooling Layer for Graph Generation. *arXiv* **2022**, arXiv:2206.01874.
25. Liu, Q.; Allamanis, M.; Brockschmidt, M.; Gaunt, A.L. Constrained Graph Variational Autoencoders for Molecule Design. *arXiv* **2019**, arXiv:1805.09076.
26. Bresson, X.; Laurent, T. A Two-Step Graph Convolutional Decoder for Molecule Generation. *arXiv* **2019**, arXiv:1906.03412.
27. Guo, X.; Zhao, L.; Qin, Z.; Wu, L.; Shehu, A.; Ye, Y. Interpretable Deep Graph Generation with Node-Edge Co-Disentanglement. In Proceedings of the 26th ACM SIGKDD International Conference on Knowledge Discovery & Data Mining, Virtual, 6–10 July 2020; pp. 1697–1707. [CrossRef]
28. Assouel, R.; Ahmed, M.; Segler, M.H.; Saffari, A.; Bengio, Y. DEFactor: Differentiable Edge Factorization-based Probabilistic Graph Generation. *arXiv* **2018**, arXiv:1811.09766.
29. Du, Y.; Guo, X.; Cao, H.; Ye, Y.; Zhao, L. Disentangled Spatiotemporal Graph Generative Models. In Proceedings of the AAAI Conference on Artificial Intelligence, Virtual, 22 February–1 March 2022; Volume 36, pp. 6541–6549. [CrossRef]
30. Shelhamer, E.; Long, J.; Darrell, T. Fully Convolutional Networks for Semantic Segmentation. *IEEE Trans. Pattern Anal. Mach. Intell.* **2017**, *39*, 640–651. [CrossRef]
31. Lin, B.; Gao, F.; Yang, Y.; Wu, D.; Zhang, Y.; Feng, G.; Dai, T.; Du, X. FLASH Radiotherapy: History and Future. *Front. Oncol.* **2021**, *11*. [CrossRef]
32. Agostinelli, S.; Allison, J.; Amako, K.; Apostolakis, J.; Araujo, H.; Arce, P.; Asai, M.; Axen, D.; Banerjee, S.; Barrand, G.; et al. Geant4—A simulation toolkit. *Nucl. Instruments Methods Phys. Res. Sect. A Accel. Spectrometers Detect. Assoc. Equip.* **2003**, *506*, 250–303. [CrossRef]
33. Li, Y.; Mandt, S. Disentangled Sequential Autoencoder. *arXiv* **2018**, arXiv:1803.02991.
34. Low, D.A.; Harms, W.B.; Mutic, S.; Purdy, J.A. A technique for the quantitative evaluation of dose distributions. *Med. Phys.* **1998**, *25*, 656–661. [CrossRef]
35. Higgins, I.; Matthey, L.; Pal, A.; Burgess, C.; Glorot, X.; Botvinick, M.; Mohamed, S.; Lerchner, A. beta-VAE: Learning Basic Visual Concepts with a Constrained Variational Framework. In Proceedings of the International Conference on Learning Representations, Toulon, France, 24–26 April 2017.

Disclaimer/Publisher's Note: The statements, opinions and data contained in all publications are solely those of the individual author(s) and contributor(s) and not of MDPI and/or the editor(s). MDPI and/or the editor(s) disclaim responsibility for any injury to people or property resulting from any ideas, methods, instructions or products referred to in the content.

Article

Acoustic Echo Cancellation with the Normalized Sign-Error Least Mean Squares Algorithm and Deep Residual Echo Suppression

Eran Shachar *, Israel Cohen * and Baruch Berdugo *

Andrew and Erna Viterbi Faculty of Electrical & Computer Engineering, Technion–Israel Institute of Technology, Technion City, Haifa 3200003, Israel
* Correspondence: eranshachar@campus.technion.ac.il (E.S.); icohen@ee.technion.ac.il (I.C.); bbaruch@technion.ac.il (B.B.)

Abstract: This paper presents an echo suppression system that combines a linear acoustic echo canceller (AEC) with a deep complex convolutional recurrent network (DCCRN) for residual echo suppression. The filter taps of the AEC are adjusted in subbands by using the normalized sign-error least mean squares (NSLMS) algorithm. The NSLMS is compared with the commonly-used normalized least mean squares (NLMS), and the combination of each with the proposed deep residual echo suppression model is studied. The utilization of a pre-trained deep-learning speech denoising model as an alternative to a residual echo suppressor (RES) is also studied. The results showed that the performance of the NSLMS is superior to that of the NLMS in all settings. With the NSLMS output, the proposed RES achieved better performance than the larger pre-trained speech denoiser model. More notably, the denoiser performed considerably better on the NSLMS output than on the NLMS output, and the performance gap was greater than the respective gap when employing the RES, indicating that the residual echo in the NSLMS output was more akin to noise than speech. Therefore, when little data is available to train an RES, a pre-trained speech denoiser is a viable alternative when employing the NSLMS for the preceding linear AEC.

Keywords: residual echo suppression; acoustic echo cancellation; deep-learning; speech enhancement

1. Introduction

Acoustic echo cancellation is a long-standing problem in real-life telecommunication scenarios where a near-end speaker communicates with a far-end speaker. A loudspeaker plays the far-end signal, and a microphone captures the echo of the loudspeaker signal, and the near-end signal and background noise [1].

Traditional acoustic echo cancellers (AECs) employ linear adaptive filters [2]. Linear AECs commonly use the least mean squares (LMS) algorithm [3,4] and its normalized version, the normalized LMS (NLMS) [5,6]. The improvement introduced by the normalization is that the step size can be set independently of the reference signal's power [7]. Variants of the LMS and NLMS algorithms are the sign-error LMS (SLMS), and normalized SLMS (NSLMS) algorithms [8]. In contrast to the NLMS, the NSLMS adjusts the weight for each filter tap, based on the polarity (sign) of the error signal. Several studies have shown the advantages of the NSLMS over the NLMS. For example, Freire and Douglas [9] used the NSLMS adaptive filter to cancel geomagnetic background noise in magnetic anomaly detection systems and demonstrated its superiority over the NLMS. Pathak et al. [10] utilized the NSLMS adaptive filter to perform speech enhancement in noisy magnetic resonance imaging (MRI) environments. According to their experiments, the NSLMS achieved faster convergence than the NLMS, and residual noise produced by the NSLMS had characteristics of white noise. In contrast, residual noise produced by the NLMS was more structured.

The linear AECs lack the ability to cancel the nonlinear components of the echo. Therefore, further suppression of the residual echo is required, and a residual echo suppressor (RES) is typically employed. While traditional residual echo suppression relies on filter-based techniques [11,12], recent advances in deep learning have shifted the focus toward neural network-based approaches [13–16]. Under challenging real-life conditions, for example, low signal-to-echo ratios (SERs) and changing acoustic echo paths, the performance of the linear AEC preceding the RES model has a significant impact on the overall performance. Hence, it may be beneficial to investigate the AECs in conjunction with deep-learning models for residual echo suppression.

The output of a linear AEC is expected to contain a distorted weaker version of the echo signal, while keeping the near-end signal almost distortionless. Therefore, denoising the estimated near-end signal with a designated speech denoiser might suppress the residual echo, while eliminating other noises. Research on deep-learning-based speech enhancement algorithms has seen significant progress over the last few years, with many models exhibiting excellent performances [17–19]. For a speech denoiser to achieve good performance as an RES, the AEC must produce residual echo that closely resembles noise, rather than human speech.

In this paper, two aspects of residual echo suppression were investigated: the impact of the preceding linear AEC on the performance of the residual echo suppression deep-learning model and the utilization of a pre-trained speech denoiser as an alternative to an RES. In addition, an echo suppression system, that employs NSLMS to perform linear acoustic echo cancellation and a deep complex convolutional recurrent network (DCCRN) [18] to achieve residual echo suppression, is proposed. The performances of the NSLMS and the commonly-used NLMS algorithms were compared, and the utilization of a speech denoiser to the output of the linear AEC to suppress the residual echo and additional noises was evaluated. The results showed that the performances of systems using NSLMS were superior to those using NLMS in all settings. This suggested that NSLMS was better suited for acoustic echo cancellation and residual echo suppression tasks, emphasizing the importance of choosing the right linear AEC. Additionally, the performance of the pre-trained denoiser in combination with each linear AECs was investigated to determine which of the outputs contained residual echo that resembled noise more closely than speech. The results indicated that, contrary to the NLMS, the outputs of the NSLMS were more akin to noise than speech. Therefore, the preceding linear AEC choice had an even more significant impact when employing a pre-trained speech denoiser model for the residual echo suppression task. With the NSLMS, a speech denoiser might be a suitable alternative when insufficient data is available to train an RES model. Finally, the advantages and efficacy of the proposed RES model over a larger pre-trained denoiser model are shown. To summarize the contributions of the presented study, the main findings are highlighted below:

- The performance of the NSLMS is superior to that of the common NLMS, both as a standalone linear AEC and combined with a deep-learning residual echo suppressor. More generally, the reported findings indicated that the linear AEC significantly impacted the performance of the following residual echo suppressor and should be carefully chosen.
- When combined with a pre-trained speech denoiser, the NSLMS brings a more significant performance improvement than when combined with a residual echo suppressor. This indicated that the outputs of the NSLMS were less structured and more akin to noise than the NLMS outputs. Therefore, with the NSLMS, employing a pre-trained speech denoiser might be a viable alternative to training a residual echo suppressor.
- The DCCRN architecture, initially proposed for speech enhancement, is offered to perform residual echo suppression. While requiring only a minor modification to adapt to the residual echo suppression task, the proposed residual echo suppressor outperformed the larger, pre-trained speech denoiser.

The presented study focused on challenging real-life scenarios, such as echo–path changes, low signal-to-echo ratios (SERs), and real-time considerations.

Following is the outline of the manuscript. In Section 2, formulation of the residual echo suppression problem is provided, the relevant signals are denoted, the different systems and their components are described, and details regarding the datasets and experimental procedures are provided. In Section 3, the experimental results are provided. The results are discussed and interpreted in this section as well. The manuscript is concluded in Section 4.

2. Materials and Methods

This section is organized as follows. First, the different signals of concern are denoted and explained. A high-level overview of the residual echo suppression setting is also provided. Next, the different systems and system components are described in detail. Lastly, the training and evaluation data are described, and experimental, and implementation details are provided.

2.1. Problem Formulation

First, the different signals presented in the manuscript are denoted. The far-end reference signal is denoted by $x(n)$. The echoic loudspeaker signal is denoted by $s(n)$, and the near-end signal is denoted by $d(n)$. The value $v(n)$ denotes the background noise. The microphone signal is given by:

$$m(n) = s(n) + d(n) + v(n). \qquad (1)$$

The linear AEC receives as inputs, $x(n)$ and $m(n)$, and outputs two signals: $a(n)$, the estimate of the echo signal $s(n)$, and the estimate of the noisy near-end signal, i.e. the error signal $e(n) = m(n) - a(n)$. The filter tap weights vector of length N is denoted by $\mathbf{c}(n) = [c_1(n), ..., c_N(n)]^T$, where $(\cdot)^T$ represents the transposed vector. Similarly, the far-end signal's vector at time n and length N is denoted by $\mathbf{x}_N(n) = [x(n), x(n-1), ..., x(n-N+1)]^T$.

The error signal $e(n)$ contains noise and residual echo components. The goal was to enhance $e(n)$ by further suppressing the residual echo and possibly removing noise. This is done either by a speech denoising model, in which case it receives $e(n)$ as a single input to be denoised, or by an RES model, in which case it also receives as inputs $x(n)$, $m(n)$, and $a(n)$. The RES/denoiser block predicts $\tilde{d}(n)$. The problem's setup and the related signals are depicted in Figure 1. When referring to the short-time Fourier transform (STFT) [20] domain transformations of the above signals, f denotes the frequency index, and k denotes the time index of the transformed signals. For example, $E(f,k)$ is the STFT of $e(n)$.

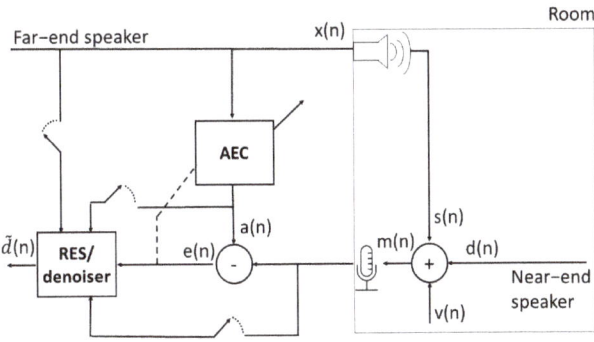

Figure 1. Residual echo suppression setup.

2.2. System Components

A residual echo suppression system comprises a linear AEC and an RES model. Two linear AECs were compared: NSLMS and NLMS. For residual echo suppression, two alternatives were considered: the proposed RES model and a pre-trained speech-denoising model.

2.2.1. Linear Acoustic Echo Cancellers

For linear acoustic echo cancellation, an AEC with the NSLMS algorithm was employed. The algorithm operates in the subband domain by transforming the signals with uniform single-sideband filter banks [21]. The filters' tap weights update equation for each subband is given by:

$$\mathbf{c}(n+1) = \mathbf{c}(n) + \frac{\mathbf{x}_N(n)\text{sgn}(e(n))\alpha(n)}{||\mathbf{x}_N(n)||^2} \quad (2)$$

where $\alpha(n)$ is the step size, and $\text{sgn}(\cdot)$ is the signum function. The performance of NSLMS was compared to that of NLMS, for which the tap weights update equation is given by:

$$\mathbf{c}(n+1) = \mathbf{c}(n) + \frac{\mathbf{x}_N(n)e(n)\alpha(n)}{||\mathbf{x}_N(n)||^2}. \quad (3)$$

2.2.2. Residual Echo Suppression Model

The DCCRN [18] architecture, which employs a complex convolutional encoder–decoder structure and a complex long short-term memory (LSTM), was adopted for residual echo suppression. The model was initially developed for speech enhancement in the time–frequency (T–F) domain. It estimates a complex ratio mask (CRM) applied to the STFT of the input signal. For residual echo suppression, the model was adapted to have 4 input channels instead of one, and its inputs were all available signals: $e(n)$, $a(n)$, $x(n)$, and $m(n)$. The estimated CRM was applied to the STFT of the error signal, $E(f,k)$. Figure 2 depicts the model's architecture.

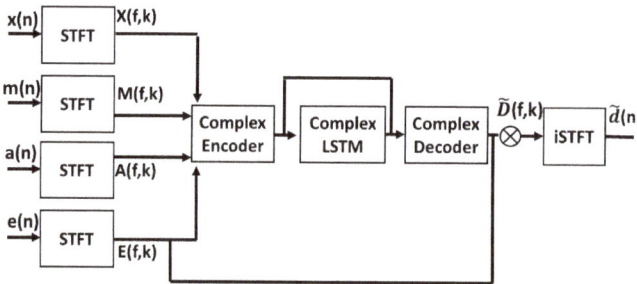

Figure 2. Residual echo suppression model architecture.

The encoder and decoder branches of the model were symmetrical, where the outputs of each encoder block were used as the inputs of the next encoder block and as additional inputs to the decoder block of the same level. These connections between the different encoder and decoder blocks are termed skip connections. Skip connections have two advantages: they provide an alternative path for the gradient during back-propagation, which is beneficial for model convergence, and they allow re-use of features from the encoder in the decoder. Each encoder/decoder block comprised a complex 2-D convolution layer, a complex batch-normalization layer, and a real parametric rectified linear unit (PReLU) activation function [22], as depicted in Figure 3.

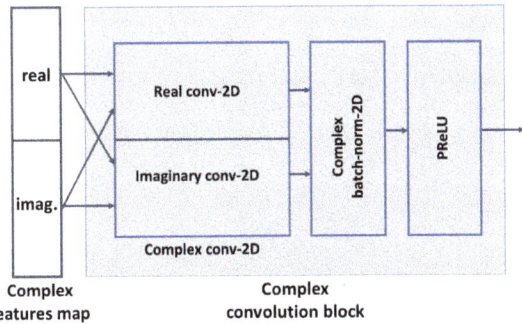

Figure 3. Structure of a complex convolution block. The input features map, consisting of real and imaginary parts, was fed to a complex 2-D convolution layer, the outputs of which were fed to a complex 2-D batch normalization layer. A PReLU activation function provided the block's output.

A complex 2-D convolution layer comprised two real 2-D convolution layers, each operating on the real and imaginary parts of its input. The output of a complex 2-D convolution layer, denoted by O_c, is formulated as:

$$O_c = (X_r * W_r - X_i * W_i) + j(X_r * W_i + X_i * W_r), \tag{4}$$

where X_r and X_i are the real and imaginary parts of the input, respectively, W_r and W_i are the real and imaginary convolution kernels, respectively, and $*$ is the convolution operation. Like the complex 2-D convolution layer, the complex LSTM layer comprised two real LSTM layers, denoted by LSTM_r and LSTM_i. The output of the complex LSTM, denoted by F_c, is formulated as:

$$F_c = (\text{LSTM}_r(X_r) - \text{LSTM}_i(X_i)) + j(\text{LSTM}_i(X_r) + \text{LSTM}_r(X_i)). \tag{5}$$

Further details regarding the original model's architecture and the structure of the different layers can be found in [18].

Since a clean near-end signal is unavailable when training with real, recorded data, the noisy near-end signal $d(n) + v(n)$ was the training target. The training objective was the waveform ℓ_1 loss, combined with the multi-resolution STFT magnitude loss adopted from [17]. For an estimated signal $\tilde{y}$ and its ground-truth y, the loss is defined as:

$$\text{Loss} = \frac{1}{T}[||y - \tilde{y}||_1 + \sum_{i=1}^{M} L_{\text{mag}}^{(i)}(y, \tilde{y})] \tag{6}$$

$$L_{\text{mag}}^{(i)}(y, \tilde{y}) = \frac{1}{T}||\log|\text{STFT}(y)| - \log|\text{STFT}(\tilde{y})|||_1 \tag{7}$$

where T denotes the total time steps number, $||\cdot||_1$ is the ℓ_1 norm, M is the number of STFT resolutions, and i is the resolution index.

2.2.3. Speech Denoising Model

As an alternative to the RES model, an off-the-shelf, pre-trained speech-denoising deep-learning model [17], which accepts a single input $e(n)$ and outputs $\tilde{d}(n)$, was utilized. A speech-denoising model might be considered an alternative to an RES in cases where the residual echo resembles noise more closely than speech. In these cases, the residual echo might be suppressed while preserving the near-end speech. The utilized speech-denoising model was based on the DEMUCS architecture [23]. The model operated in the time domain, and similarly to DCCRN, it employed a convolutional encoder–decoder structure and an LSTM between the encoder and the decoder. A single encoder block consisted of two 1-D convolution layers. The activation function of the first convolution layer was the rectified linear unit (ReLU) [24] and the activation function of the second convolution layer was the gated linear unit (GLU) [25]. The output of the encoder block was passed to the next encoder block (or to the LSTM when it was the final encoder block) and to its matching decoder block via a skip connection. A decoder block received both the output of the matching encoder block and the output of the previous decoder block (or the output of the LSTM when it was the first decoder block). The inputs were summed element-wise. The structure of the decoder block mirrored that of the encoder block, except after the first convolution layer, a 1-D transpose convolution layer was employed to upsample the signal. The structure of the encoder and decoder blocks is depicted in Figure 4. The general structure of the speech-denoising model is depicted in Figure 5. Further details regarding the model's architecture can be found in [17].

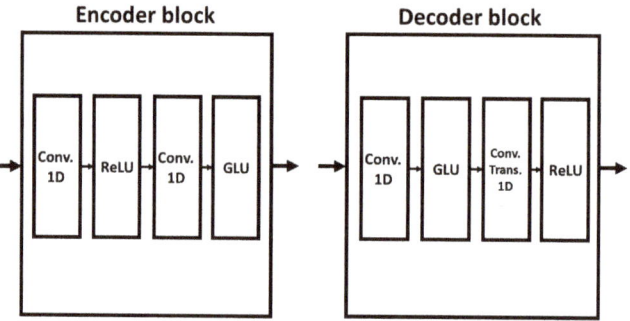

Figure 4. Structure of the speech-denoising model's encoder and decoder blocks. Conv. stands for convolution, and Trans. stands for transpose.

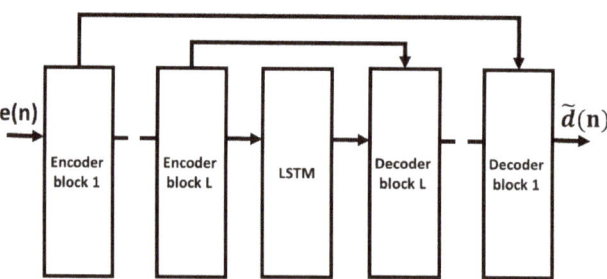

Figure 5. High-level structure of the speech denoising model.

As mentioned in Section 1, the speech enhancement field is well-studied, with an abundance of excellent works and a variety of readily-available, pre-trained models trained on large and diverse datasets. With careful fine-tuning, the features learned by such pre-trained models might be effectively utilized for the residual echo suppression task. This might be especially effective when there is only a small amount of data to train a residual echo suppression model. Therefore, a pre-trained model, provided by the authors [17], was employed. The model was pre-trained on the Valentini dataset [26] and the INTERSPEECH 2020 deep noise suppression (DNS) challenge dataset [27]. The model was subsequently fine-tuned with the same training data used for training the RES models, once with the NSLMS outputs and once with the NLMS outputs. The loss function that was minimized is given in (6).

2.3. Datasets

Two datasets were employed for training the different models: the ICASSP 2021 AEC challenge synthetic dataset [28] and an independently recorded dataset. Unlike the synthetic data, the independent recordings were taken in real-life conditions with low SERs. Various scenarios were considered, including echo–path changes, variations in near-end source positions and distances from the microphone, and varying room sizes. A total of 11 hours of speech data were taken from the LibriSpeech [29] corpus and the TIMIT [30] corpus. Spider MT503^{TM} or Quattro MT301^{TM} speakerphones (Shure Inc., Niles, IL, USA) were utilized to simulate low-SER scenarios. The loudspeaker and microphone were positioned 5 cm from each other in these devices. Echo path changes were simulated by moving a Logitech type Z120^{TM} loudspeaker (Logitech International S.A., Lausanne, Switzerland), playing the echo signal. The loudspeaker's distance from the microphone was either 1, 1.5, or 2 m. The near-end speech was simulated using mouth simulator type 4227-A^{TM} of Bruel&Kjaer (Bruel&Kjaer, Naerum, Denmark). The distance of the mouth simulator from the microphone also varied between recordings and was either 1, 1.5, or 2 m from the microphone. Double-talk utterances always contained two different speakers, so the average overlap between the two was 90%. Rooms of different sizes were used for the recordings (sizes varied between $3 \times 3 \times 2.5$ m^3 and $5 \times 5 \times 4$ m^3). Reverberation time (RT$_{60}$) varied between 0.3 and 0.6 seconds. The training data SER was distributed on $[-24, 18]$ decibels, and the test data SER was distributed on $[-18, 5]$ decibels. Test data speakers were unique and not used in the training set. Further details regarding the data creation can be found in [14].

The ICASSP 2021 AEC challenge synthetic dataset was used to augment the training data. About 27.7 h of data were generated, with different scenarios, including double-talk, far-end or near-end single-talk, with/without near-end noise, and likewise for far-end. In addition, several nonlinear distortions were applied, with different SERs and signal-to-noise ratios. Further details regarding the dataset can be found in [28].

2.4. Implementation Details

All signals were sampled with a sampling rate of 16 kHz. Initially, the input signals were transformed to the subband domain by uniform 32-band single-sideband filter banks [21]. Each subband consisted of 150 taps. These were the equivalent of filters in the time domain with 2400 taps and of length 150 ms.

For the RES model, the transformation of the input signals to the T-F domain was achieved by a 512-point STFT, resulting in 257 frequency bins. The STFT window length was 25 ms, and the hop length was 6.25 ms. The number of convolution kernels for the different encoder layers was $[16, 32, 64, 128, 256, 256]$. The LSTM had two layers with a 128 hidden size. The model comprised 2.07 M parameters. The Adam optimizer [31] was employed for model optimization. Training started with a learning rate of 5×10^{-4}. The learning rate was decreased by a factor of 2 if the validation loss did not improve after 3 consecutive epochs. The mini-batch size was 16, and the training continued for a maximum number of 100 epochs.

The number of encoder and decoder blocks for the speech-denoising model was 5. The number of the first encoder block's output channels was 64, and each encoder block doubled the number of channels. Subsequently, each decoder block halved the number of channels, where the output of the last decoder block consisted of 1 channel. The convolution kernel size was 8, and its stride was 4. The LSTM consisted of two layers, and its hidden size matched the number of channels of the last encoder block (and the number of channels of the first decoder block). The input to the model was normalized by its standard deviation. The model was pre-trained using the Valentini dataset [26] and the INTERSPEECH 2020 DNS challenge dataset [27]. The model comprised 18.87 M parameters. For a fair comparison with the RES model, the causal version of the denoiser was employed. For both linear AECs, the model was fine-tuned using the same data used to train the RES model. Training continued for 20 epochs with a learning rate of 3×10^{-4} using the Adam optimizer [31]. Further details regarding the model architecture can be found in [17].

3. Results

This section presents performance measures and experimental results.

3.1. Performance Measures

Performance was evaluated in two scenarios: far-end single-talk and utterances containing near-end speech, either double-talk or near-end single-talk. When only the far-end speaker spoke, the goal was to reduce the output signal's energy as much as possible. Optimally, the enhanced signal was silent during these periods. We utilized the echo return loss enhancement (ERLE) measure to evaluate performance during far-end-only periods. The ERLE in decibels is defined as:

$$\text{ERLE} = 10\log_{10}\frac{||m||^2}{||\tilde{d}||^2}. \tag{8}$$

During double-talk periods, the goal was to maintain near-end speech quality while suppressing the residual echo. Since the performance measures used during these periods focused on speech quality rather than echo reduction, these measures were also used during near-end single-talk periods. Two different measures were employed to evaluate performance during these periods. Perceptual evaluation of speech quality (PESQ) [32] aimed to approximate a subjective assessment of an enhanced speech signal. PESQ was intrusive, i.e., the enhanced signal was compared to the clean, ground-truth signal. PESQ score was in the range $[-0.5, 4, 5]$. PESQ is known to only sometimes correlate well with subjective human ratings. Therefore, deep noise-suppression meant opinion score (DNSMOS) [33] was also used to evaluate performance during these periods. DNSMOS is traditionally used to assess noise suppressors, although it can be employed to estimate speech quality in any setting. DNSMOS is non-intrusive, i.e., it does not require a clean near-end signal to evaluate speech quality. DNSMOS is a neural network trained with hundreds of hours of ground-truth subjective human speech quality ratings. The model predicted a score in the $[1, 5]$ range.

Further measures used in the next section included the SER, measured in double-talk scenarios and defined in decibels as:

$$\text{SER} = 10\log_{10}\frac{||d||^2}{||s||^2}, \tag{9}$$

and the echo-to-noise ratio (ENR), measured in far-end-only scenarios and defined in decibels as:

$$\text{ENR} = 10\log_{10}\frac{||s||^2}{||v||^2}. \tag{10}$$

3.2. Experimental Results

Table 1 shows the different methods' performances on the test set: the linear AECs (NLMS and NSLMS), the denoiser [17] operating on the outputs of each of the linear AECs (NLMS + Denoiser and NSLMS + Denoiser), and the RES model combined with each of the linear AECs (NLMS + RES and NSLMS + RES). First, the performances of the NLMS and NSLMS acoustic echo cancellers were compared. As the table shows, NSLMS had significantly better echo cancellation performance than NLMS, as indicated by the 4.57 dB gap in ERLE. NSLMS also outperformed NLMS in preserving near-end speech quality, as shown by DNSMOS and PESQ, both in near-end single-talk and double-talk periods. PESQ and DNSMOS results for the double-talk-only scenario (DT) were differentiated from the respective results when including the near-end-only scenario (DT + NE). Notably, the performance gap during DT was more significant than during DT + NE: the DNSMOS difference between NSLMS and NLMS was 0.05 for DT + NE and 0.09 for DT, and the PESQ score difference was 0.33 for DT + NE and 0.56 for DT. These results indicated that a proper choice of a linear AEC was even more crucial when considering the challenging double-talk scenario, and NSLMS was notably superior to NLMS in this scenario. Overall, the performance of the NSLMS as a linear AEC was superior to that of the NLMS in all scenarios.

Table 1. Performance comparison of the different systems. FE stands for far-end-only scenarios, NE stands for near-end-only scenarios, and DT stands for double-talk scenarios. Results in bold represent the best result in the column and row group (where row groups are separated with bold lines.)

	FE	DT		DT + NE	
	ERLE	DNSMOS	PESQ	DNSMOS	PESQ
NLMS	16.60	2.62	2.42	2.81	3.33
NSLMS	**21.17**	**2.71**	**2.98**	**2.86**	**3.66**
NLMS + Denoiser	32.63	2.44	2.32	2.72	3.23
NSLMS + Denoiser	**39.44**	**2.65**	**3.13**	**2.84**	**3.63**
NLMS + RES	38.55	2.46	2.53	2.76	3.34
NSLMS + RES	**40.34**	**2.64**	**3.11**	**2.84**	**3.70**

Next, the performance of the proposed RES was considered, both with the NLMS and the NSLMS. It can be seen from the table that the NSLMS + RES system's performance was superior to the NLMS + RES system's performance in all scenarios. When comparing the performance of the NLMS + RES and NSLMS + RES systems to the respective linear AECs (NLMS and NSLMS), different trends in DNSMOS and PESQ scores were observed. For both systems, DNSMOS deteriorated, and PESQ improved. This emphasized the differences between the two measures and the importance of examining several measures when evaluating the performance of residual echo suppression systems. While NLMS + RES DNSMOS deteriorated by 0.05 for DT + NE and 0.16 for DT, NSLMS+RES DNSMOS deteriorated by 0.02 for DT + NE and by 0.07 for DT. In other words, the NSLMS RES system saw a smaller degradation in DNSMOS than the NLMS RES system, further showing the advantage of employing NSLMS over NLMS. Furthermore, the NLMS+RES PESQ increased by 0.01 for DT + NE and by 0.11 for DT, while the NSLMS+RES PESQ increased by 0.04 for DT + NE and by 0.13 for DT. In other words, the improvement in PESQ was greater for the NSLMS system than for the NLMS system. A different trend could be seen in the far-end-only performance. For the NLMS, ERLE increased by 21.95 dB compared to the linear AEC, and for the NSLMS system, ERLE increased by 19.17 dB. These results indicated that, when combined with the deep-learning RES, the NLMS achieved a greater performance gain than the NSLMS. Overall, it could be seen that the NLMS was more efficient than the NSLMS when combined with the deep-learning RES model during far-end-only periods, but NSLMS was more efficient than the NLMS in near-end-only and double-talk scenarios. While it might be worthwhile to investigate these different trends, the overall performance of the NSLMS + RES system was superior to the performance of the NLMS + RES system, indicating that NSLMS was a better choice for a linear AEC than the NLMS when combined with a deep-learning RES model.

When comparing the performances of the NLMS + Denoiser and the NSLMS + Denoiser systems, it could be seen again that the system using NSLMS as a linear AEC was superior to the system using NLMS in all settings. NSLMS + Denoiser ERLE was 6.81 dB greater than the NLMS + Denoiser ERLE. Similarly to the RES systems, DNSMOS deteriorated for both denoisers compared to the linear AECs, both during DT + NE and during DT. NLMS + Denoiser DNSMOS deteriorated by 0.09 during DT + NE and by

0.18 during DT, while NSLMS+Denoiser DNSMOS deteriorated by 0.02 during DT + NE and by 0.06 during DT. Contrary to the RES system, the NLMS + Denoiser PESQ decreased both for DT + NE and DT, while the NSLMS+Denoiser PESQ increased. Notably, the PESQ score of the denoiser with the NSLMS linear AEC was 0.81 greater than the PESQ score of the denoiser using the NLMS linear AEC during double-talk periods. Furthermore, the Denoiser + NSLMS DNSMOS was 0.21 greater than the Denoiser + NLMS DNSMOS during double-talk periods. These significant gaps in performance during double-talk periods, and the notable ERLE gap during far-end-only periods, further asserted the claim that the NSLMS produced a residual echo that was more akin to noise than speech when compared to the NLMS. In light of all the above observations, it was clear that when employing a pre-trained speech denoising model to the task of residual echo suppression, the preceding linear AEC significantly impacted the denoiser's performance, and NSLMS was preferable over NLMS to a large degree.

Next, the performances of the NSLMS + Denoiser and NSLMS + RES systems were compared. The RES system achieved better far-end single-talk performance, as indicated by the 0.9 dB gap in ERLE. The DNSMOS of both systems was on-par, with a minor difference during DT periods. The RES system's PESQ was 0.07 greater during DT + NE and 0.02 lower during DT. Overall, it could be concluded that the performance of the RES system was superior to the denoiser system's performance during far-end single-talk periods, and the performances were on-par during near-end single-talk and double-talk periods, which indicated that the overall performance of the RES system was superior to the performance of the denoiser system. These results asserted the efficacy of the proposed RES model, which consisted of 10 times fewer model parameters than the denoiser model, which was also pre-trained on a large corpus with diverse speakers and noises. Nevertheless, the performance gap was not significant, which suggested that in cases where a large dataset for training a residual echo suppressor is not available, fine-tuning an off-the-shelf speech denoiser might be a reasonable alternative to a residual echo suppressor.

To complete the comparison between the different systems, the different measures' gaps between the NLMS and the NSLMS systems for the denoiser and the RES models were compared. During far-end single-talk periods, the gap between the NSLMS + RES and NLMS + RES ERLE was 1.79 dB, while the gap between the respective denoiser systems was 6.81 dB. In other words, the denoiser brought a more significant performance improvement between the NLMS and NSLMS systems, compared to the gap in the residual echo suppression setting. During DT + NE periods, the DNSMOS gap between the NLMS + RES and the NSLMS + RES systems was 0.08, and the respective gap in the denoiser setting was 0.12. During DT, the DNSMOS gap in the residual echo suppression setting was 0.18, and the DNSMOS gap in the denoiser setting was 0.21. Again, the denoiser brought a greater DNSMOS improvement between the NLMS and NSLMS compared to the improvement between the respective systems in the RES settings. For PESQ, the same trend could be observed: during DT + NE, the PESQ gap was 0.36 in the residual echo suppression setting and 0.40 in the denoiser setting, and during DT, the gap in the residual echo suppression setting was 0.58 and 0.81 in the denoiser setting. Overall, it could be seen that in all scenarios, the gap between the NLMS and NSLMS performances in the denoiser setting was greater than the respective gap in the residual echo suppression settings. In other words, the denoiser benefited more from choosing NSLMS over NLMS than the proposed RES, which further asserted that the outputs produced by the NSLMS were more akin to noise than the outputs produced by the NLMS. Therefore, although NSLMS was preferable over NLMS in all settings when employing a pre-trained speech denoiser to the task of residual echo suppression, using NSLMS as a linear AEC resulted in significantly superior performance compared to using NLMS, showing that the proper choice of a linear AEC was even more critical in this setting.

Finally, the performances of the NSLMS and NLMS as linear AECs, as well as combined with the proposed RES model, were compared for different SERs and ENRs. Figure 6 shows the PESQ scores for different values of SER in the double-talk scenario. NSLMS achieved superior PESQ over NLMS in all SERs, both as a standalone linear AEC and combined with the RES model. Furthermore, in all SERs, the RES model did not improve PESQ when employing the NLMS linear AEC. On the other hand, in the more challenging scenarios of lower SERs, the RES model improved in PESQ when employing the NSLMS linear AEC. Figure 7 shows the ERLE for different values of ENR during far-end single-talk periods. Again, NSLMS achieved superior performance over NLMS in all ENRs, both as a standalone linear AEC and combined with the RES model. In the challenging low ENR scenarios, the performance gap between the NLMS + RES and NSLMS + RES systems was greater than the respective gap in higher ENRs, further showing the advantage of using NSLMS over using NLMS in challenging scenarios. Overall, the graphs show the superiority of NSLMS over NLMS, both as standalone linear AECs and combined with the proposed RES model, in various conditions and settings. Furthermore, the graphs show that the advantage of using NSLMS over NLMS was even more significant in challenging scenarios and conditions.

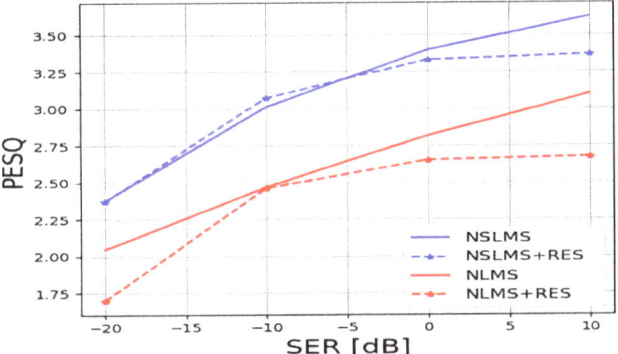

Figure 6. PESQ in double-talk-only scenarios for different SERs.

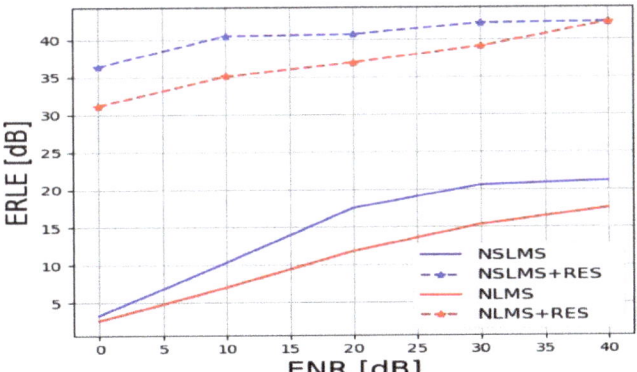

Figure 7. ERLE in far-end-only scenarios for different ENRs.

4. Conclusions

In this study, an echo suppression system, based on the NSLMS linear AEC and the DCCRN speech enhancement model, was presented. Experiments in challenging real-life conditions with low SER were conducted. The performances of the proposed system and a pre-trained speech-denoising model operating on the AEC output that was fine-tuned with the same training data were compared. The proposed system's ERLE was 0.9 dB greater than the denoiser's ERLE, indicating better far-end single-talk performance. The near-end single-talk and double-talk performances of the systems were on-par. These results showed that, although the speech denoising model was pre-trained on a large corpus with diverse speakers and conditions and was 10 times larger concerning the number of parameters, the proposed RES model was favorable. A comparison of the performances of all the systems using NSLMS–AEC and NLMS–AEC was also made. The NSLMS was favorable over NLMS in all settings and scenarios. Notably, NSLMS's ERLE was 4.57 db greater than NLMS's ERLE as a stand-alone linear AEC. When combined with the proposed RES, NSLMS's DNSMOS was 0.18 greater than the NLMS, and its PESQ score was 0.58 greater, both in the challenging double-talk scenario. Overall, the results showed that, although the NLMS algorithm is commonly employed for linear acoustic echo cancellation, the NSLMS may be a better choice, which raises a more general question regarding the importance of choosing a proper linear AEC and its effect on the performance of the deep-learning residual echo suppressor. When analyzing the performance of the pre-trained speech denoiser, both with the NLMS and the NSLMS, a notable ERLE gap of 6.81 dB was observed. This gap was considerably larger than the respective 1.79 dB gap in the RES setting. Furthermore, there was a 0.81 gap in double-talk PESQ scores, which was also considerably larger than the respective 0.58 gap in the RES setting. When including near-end single-talk periods, the differences between the different measures' gaps were less notable. These observations supported the claim that the NSLMS produced a residual echo that was less structured than the output produced by the NLMS. Therefore, when the complexity of the model is not an important consideration, fine-tuning a readily available denoiser could be a reasonable alternative to creating a new RES model. However, the choice of linear AEC becomes more critical, and NSLMS is preferable to NLMS.

Author Contributions: Conceptualization, E.S., I.C. and B.B.; methodology, E.S., I.C. and B.B.; software, E.S. and B.B.; validation, E.S.; formal analysis, E.S.; investigation, E.S., I.C. and B.B.; resources, I.C. and B.B.; data curation, E.S. and B.B.; writing—original draft preparation, E.S.; writing—review and editing, I.C. and B.B.; visualization, E.S.; supervision, I.C. and B.B.; project administration, I.C.; funding acquisition, I.C. All authors have read and agreed to the published version of the manuscript.

Funding: This research received no external funding.

Data Availability Statement: The data presented in this study are available on request from the corresponding author.

Conflicts of Interest: The authors declare no conflict of interest.

Abbreviations

The following abbreviations were used in this manuscript:

AEC	Acoustic echo canceller
CRM	Complex ratio mask
DCCRN	Deep complex convolution network
DNS	Deep noise suppression
DNSMOS	Deep noise suppression mean opinion score
ENR	Echo-to-noise ratio
GLU	Gated linear unit
LSTM	Long short-term memory
MRI	Magnetic resonance imaging
NLMS	Normalized least mean squares
NSLMS	Normalized sign-error least mean squares
PESQ	Perceptual evaluation of speech quality
PReLU	Parametric rectified linear unit
ReLU	Rectified linear unit
RES	Residual echo suppressor
SER	Signal-to-echo ratio
SLMS	Sign-error least mean squares
STFT	Short-time Fourier transform
T-F	Time-frequency

References

1. Sondhi, M.; Morgan, D.; Hall, J. Stereophonic Acoustic Echo Cancellation-an Overview of the Fundamental Problem. *IEEE Signal Process. Lett.* **1995**, *2*, 148–151. [CrossRef] [PubMed]
2. Benesty, J.; Gänsler, T.; Morgan, D.R.; Sondhi, M.M.; Gay, S.L. *Advances in Network and Acoustic Echo Cancellation*; Springer: Berlin/Heidelberg, Germany, 2001.
3. Macchi, O. *Adaptive Processing: The Least Mean Squares Approach*; John Wiley and Sons, Inc.: Hoboken, NJ, USA, 1995.
4. Rusu, A.G.; Ciochină, S.; Paleologu, C.; Benesty, J. An Optimized Differential Step-Size LMS Algorithm. *Algorithms* **2019**, *12*, 147. [CrossRef]
5. Bershad, N. Analysis of the Normalized LMS Algorithm with Gaussian Inputs. *IEEE Trans. Acoust. Speech Signal Process.* **1986**, *34*, 793–806. [CrossRef]
6. Rusu, A.G.; Paleologu, C.; Benesty, J.; Ciochină, S. A Variable Step Size Normalized Least-Mean-Square Algorithm Based on Data Reuse. *Algorithms* **2022**, *15*, 111. [CrossRef]
7. Koike, S. Analysis of Adaptive Filters Using Normalized Signed Regressor LMS Algorithm. *IEEE Trans. Signal Process.* **1999**, *47*, 2710–2723. [CrossRef]
8. Farhang-Boroujeny, B. *Adaptive Filters: Theory and Applications*; John Wiley and Sons, Inc.: Hoboken, NJ, USA, 1998.
9. Freire, N.; Douglas, S. Adaptive Cancellation of Geomagnetic Background Noise Using a Sign-Error Normalized LMS algorithm. In Proceedings of the IEEE International Conference on Acoustics, Speech, and Signal Processing (ICASSP), Minneapolis, MN, USA, 27–30 April 1993; Volume 3, pp. 523–526.
10. Pathak, N.; Panahi, I.; Devineni, P.; Briggs, R. Real Time Speech Enhancement for the Noisy MRI Environment. In Proceedings of the Annual International Conference of the IEEE Engineering in Medicine and Biology Society, Minneapolis, MN, USA, 3–6 September 2009; pp. 6950–6953.
11. Guerin, A.; Faucon, G.; Le Bouquin-Jeannes, R. Nonlinear Acoustic Echo Cancellation Based on Volterra Filters. *IEEE Trans. Speech Audio Process.* **2003**, *11*, 672–683. [CrossRef]
12. Malik, S.; Enzner, G. State-Space Frequency-Domain Adaptive Filtering for Nonlinear Acoustic Echo Cancellation. *IEEE Trans. Audio Speech Lang. Process.* **2012**, *20*, 2065–2079. [CrossRef]
13. Wang, Z.; Na, Y.; Liu, Z.; Tian, B.; Fu, Q. Weighted Recursive Least Square Filter and Neural Network Based Residual Echo Suppression for the AEC-Challenge. In Proceedings of the International Conference on Acoustics, Speech, and Signal Processing (ICASSP), virtual, 6–11 June 2021; pp. 141–145.
14. Ivry, A.; Cohen, I.; Berdugo, B. Deep Residual Echo Suppression with A Tunable Tradeoff Between Signal Distortion and Echo Suppression. In Proceedings of the IEEE International Conference on Acoustics, Speech, and Signal Processing (ICASSP), virtual, 6–11 June 2021; pp. 126–130.
15. Franzen, J.; Fingscheidt, T. Deep Residual Echo Suppression and Noise Reduction: A Multi-Input FCRN Approach in a Hybrid Speech Enhancement System. In Proceedings of the IEEE International Conference on Acoustics, Speech, and Signal Processing (ICASSP), Singapore, 22–27 May 2022; pp. 666–670.
16. Ma, L.; Huang, H.; Zhao, P.; Su, T. Acoustic Echo Cancellation by Combining Adaptive Digital Filter and Recurrent Neural Network. *arXiv* **2020**, arXiv:2005.09237.
17. Defossez, A.; Synnaeve, G.; Adi, Y. Real Time Speech Enhancement in the Waveform Domain. *arXiv* **2020**, arXiv:2006.12847.
18. Hu, Y.; Liu, Y.; Lv, S.; Xing, M.; Zhang, S.; Fu, J.; Wu, J.; Zhang, B.; Xie, L. DCCRN: Deep Complex Convolution Recurrent Network for Phase-Aware Speech Enhancement. *arXiv* **2020**, arXiv:2008.00264.
19. Koizumi, Y.; Yatabe, K.; Delcroix, M.; Masuyama, Y.; Takeuchi, D. Speech Enhancement Using Self-Adaptation and Multi-Head Self-Attention. In Proceedings of the IEEE International Conference on Acoustics, Speech, and Signal Processing (ICASSP), Barcelona, Spain, 4–8 May 2020; pp. 181–185.
20. Ortiz-Echeverri, C.J.; Rodríguez-Reséndiz, J.; Garduño-Aparicio, M. An approach to STFT and CWT learning through music hands-on labs. *Comput. Appl. Eng. Educ.* **2018**, *26*, 2026–2035. [CrossRef]
21. Crochiere, R.E.; Rabiner, L.R. Section 7.6. In *Multirate Digital Signal Processing*; Prentice Hall PTR: Hoboken, NJ, USA, 1983.
22. He, K.; Zhang, X.; Ren, S.; Sun, J. Delving Deep into Rectifiers: Surpassing Human-Level Performance on ImageNet Classification. *arXiv* **2015**, arXiv:1502.01852.
23. Défossez, A.; Usunier, N.; Bottou, L.; Bach, F. Music Source Separation in the Waveform Domain. *arXiv* **2019**, arXiv:1911.13254.
24. Xu, B.; Wang, N.; Chen, T.; Li, M. Empirical Evaluation of Rectified Activations in Convolutional Network. *arXiv* **2015**, arXiv:1505.00853.
25. Dauphin, Y.N.; Fan, A.; Auli, M.; Grangier, D. Language Modeling with Gated Convolutional Networks. *arXiv* **2016**, arXiv:1612.08083.
26. Valentini-Botinhao, C. *Noisy Speech Database for Training Speech Enhancement Algorithms and TTS Models*; Centre for Speech Technology Research (CSTR), School of Informatics, University of Edinburgh: Edinburgh, UK, 2017.
27. Reddy, C.K.A.; Beyrami, E.; Dube, H.; Gopal, V.; Cheng, R.; Cutler, R.; Matusevych, S.; Aichner, R.; Aazami, A.; Braun, S.; et al. The INTERSPEECH 2020 Deep Noise Suppression Challenge: Datasets, Subjective Speech Quality and Testing Framework. *arXiv* **2020**, arXiv:2001.08662.
28. Sridhar, K.; Cutler, R.; Saabas, A.; Parnamaa, T.; Loide, M.; Gamper, H.; Braun, S.; Aichner, R.; Srinivasan, S. ICASSP 2021 Acoustic Echo Cancellation Challenge: Datasets, Testing Framework, and Results. In Proceedings of the IEEE International Conference on Acoustics, Speech, and Signal Processing (ICASSP), virtual, 6–11 June 2021; pp. 151–155.

29. Panayotov, V.; Chen, G.; Povey, D.; Khudanpur, S. Librispeech: An ASR Corpus Based on Public Domain Audio Books. In Proceedings of the IEEE International Conference on Acoustics, Speech, and Signal Processing (ICASSP), Toronto, ON, Canada, 6–11 June 2015; pp. 5206–5210.
30. Garofolo, J.S.; Lamel, L.F.; Fisher, W.M.; Fiscus, J.G.; Pallett, D.S.; Dahlgren, N.L. *DARPA TIMIT Acoustic Phonetic Continuous Speech Corpus CDROM. NIST Speech Disc 1-1.1.*; Technical Report LDC93S1; National Institute of Standards Technolology: Gaithersburg, MD, USA, 1993.
31. Kingma, D.P.; Ba, J. Adam: A Method for Stochastic Optimization. *arXiv* **2017**, arXiv:1412.6980.
32. Rix, A.; Beerends, J.; Hollier, M.; Hekstra, A. Perceptual Evaluation of Speech Quality (PESQ)-A New Method for Speech Quality Assessment of Telephone Networks and Codecs. In Proceedings of the IEEE International Conference on Acoustics, Speech, and Signal Processing (ICASSP), Salt Lake City, UT, USA, 7–11 May 2001; Volume 2, pp. 749–752.
33. Reddy, C.K.A.; Gopal, V.; Cutler, R. DNSMOS: A Non-Intrusive Perceptual Objective Speech Quality Metric to Evaluate Noise Suppressors. In Proceedings of the IEEE International Conference on Acoustics, Speech, and Signal Processing (ICASSP), virtual, 6–11 June 2021; pp. 6493–6497.

Disclaimer/Publisher's Note: The statements, opinions and data contained in all publications are solely those of the individual author(s) and contributor(s) and not of MDPI and/or the editor(s). MDPI and/or the editor(s) disclaim responsibility for any injury to people or property resulting from any ideas, methods, instructions or products referred to in the content.

Article

Fourier Neural Operator Network for Fast Photoacoustic Wave Simulations

Steven Guan [†], Ko-Tsung Hsu [†] and Parag V. Chitnis *

Bioengineering Department, George Mason University, Fairfax, VA 22030, USA
* Correspondence: pchitnis@gmu.edu
† These authors contributed equally to this work.

Abstract: Simulation tools for photoacoustic wave propagation have played a key role in advancing photoacoustic imaging by providing quantitative and qualitative insights into parameters affecting image quality. Classical methods for numerically solving the photoacoustic wave equation rely on a fine discretization of space and can become computationally expensive for large computational grids. In this work, we applied Fourier Neural Operator (FNO) networks as a fast data-driven deep learning method for solving the 2D photoacoustic wave equation in a homogeneous medium. Comparisons between the FNO network and pseudo-spectral time domain approach were made for the forward and adjoint simulations. Results demonstrate that the FNO network generated comparable simulations with small errors and was orders of magnitude faster than the pseudo-spectral time domain methods (~26× faster on a 64 × 64 computational grid and ~15× faster on a 128 × 128 computational grid). Moreover, the FNO network was generalizable to the unseen out-of-domain test set with a root-mean-square error of 9.5×10^{-3} in Shepp–Logan, 1.5×10^{-2} in synthetic vasculature, 1.1×10^{-2} in tumor and 1.9×10^{-2} in Mason-M phantoms on a 64 × 64 computational grid and a root mean squared of $6.9 \pm 5.5 \times 10^{-3}$ in the AWA2 dataset on a 128 × 128 computational grid.

Keywords: photoacoustic imaging; image processing; computer vision; simulation; reconstruction; deep learning

Citation: Guan, S.; Hsu, K.-T.; Chitnis, P.V. Fourier Neural Operator Network for Fast Photoacoustic Wave Simulations. *Algorithms* **2023**, *16*, 124. https://doi.org/10.3390/a16020124

Academic Editors: Xiang Zhang and Xiaoxiao Li

Received: 19 January 2023
Revised: 14 February 2023
Accepted: 16 February 2023
Published: 19 February 2023

Copyright: © 2023 by the authors. Licensee MDPI, Basel, Switzerland. This article is an open access article distributed under the terms and conditions of the Creative Commons Attribution (CC BY) license (https://creativecommons.org/licenses/by/4.0/).

1. Introduction

Photoacoustic imaging is a non-invasive hybrid imaging modality that combines the advantages of optical (e.g., high contrast and molecular specificity) and ultrasound (e.g., high penetration depth) imaging [1]. It has been applied for many preclinical and clinical imaging applications, such as small-animal whole-body imaging, breast and prostate cancer imaging and image-guided surgery [2–6]. Specifically, in breast cancer detection, tumors have been successfully revealed by single-breath-hold photoacoustic computed tomography (SBH-PACT) without the need of ionizing radiation and exogenous contrast agents based on the higher blood vessel density characteristics associated with tumors [7]. Multispectral photoacoustic imaging can be used for functional imaging, such as measuring blood oxygen saturation and metabolism in biological tissues [8]. In addition to applying multispectral photoacoustic imaging to differentiate oxyhemoglobin from deoxyhemoglobin in breast cancer, ultrasound and photoacoustic tomography (US-OT) can reveal differences in lipids and collagen in breast fibroglandular tissue, providing more clinically meaningful insights for diagnosis [9]. Photoacoustic imaging provides both structural and functional information that can potentially reveal novel insights into biological processes and disease pathologies [10].

In photoacoustic tomography (PAT), a tissue medium is illuminated using a short-pulsed laser. Optically absorbing molecules within the medium are excited and undergo thermoelastic expansion, resulting in the generation of photoacoustic waves that are subsequently measured using an array of acoustic sensors [1]. An image representing the initial pressure distribution can be reconstructed from the measured time-dependent signals using analytical solutions, numerical methods and model-based iterative methods [11–15]. A detailed understanding of parameters describing the imaging medium (e.g., optical, thermal and acoustic properties of the tissue) and the imaging system (e.g., arrangement and characteristics of the laser source and acoustic sensors) is needed to reconstruct a high-quality PAT image.

PAT simulation is a highly useful tool that provides quantitative and qualitative insights into these parameters affecting image quality [16]. It is commonly used prior to experimentation and imaging to optimize the system configuration. It also plays an integral role in PAT image reconstruction and provides numerical phantom data for the development of advanced algorithms, such as iterative methods and deep learning methods [17–22]. Simulating PAT image acquisition comprises two components: optical illumination and photoacoustic propagation. For this work, we are primarily focused on the photoacoustic propagation component. The equation for photoacoustic wave propagation can be solved numerically using classical methods, such as the time domain finite element method [23,24]. These methods generally solve the equation via approximation on a mesh and can be computationally expensive, such as for large three-dimensional (3D) simulations.

Recently, deep learning has been explored as an alternative method for solving partial differential equations (PDE) [25,26]. It has the potential to greatly impact scientific disciplines and research by providing fast PDE solvers that approximate or enhance conventional ones. Applications requiring repeated evaluations of a PDE can greatly benefit from the reduced computation times offered by deep learning. Here, we provide a brief overview of three deep learning methods for solving PDEs—finite dimensional operators, neural finite element models and Fourier Neural Operators (FNO).

Finite dimensional operators use a deep convolutional neural network (CNN) to solve the PDE on a finite Euclidean Space [27,28]. This approach is mesh-dependent, meaning the CNN needs to be retrained for solving the PDE at different spatial resolutions and discretization. Neural finite element models are mesh-independent and closely resemble traditional finite element methods [25,29]. It replaces the set of local basis functions in the finite element models with a fully connected neural network. It requires prior knowledge of the underlying PDE and is designed to solve for one specific instance of the PDE. The neural network needs to be retrained for new instances where the underlying PDE is parameterized with a different set of functional coefficients. FNO is a mesh-free approach that approximates the mapping between two infinite dimensional spaces from a finite collection of input–output paired observations [30,31]. The neural operator is learned directly in the Fourier and image space using a CNN. The same learned operator can be used without retraining to solve PDEs with different discretization and parameterization. Fourier Neural Operators have been demonstrated to achieve state-of-the-art results for a variety of PDEs (e.g., Burgers' equation, Darcy Flow and Navier–Stokes) and outperform other existing deep learning methods [31].

To the best of our knowledge, this is the first paper to apply deep learning for solving the photoacoustic wave equation for simulating PAT. FNOs were chosen for this task given their flexibility in discretization and superior performance compared to other deep learning methods. Prior work with FNOs demonstrated solutions to the Navier–Stokes and Burgers' equations, which have relatively smooth spatio-temporal solutions [31]. Unlike these works, photoacoustic signals have high broadband frequencies and contain sharp transitions. Specifically, this paper highlights the following innovative contributions:

- Adapting the FNO neural network and applying it as a fast PDE solver for simulating the forward and adjoint 2D photoacoustic operator.
- Simulations from the FNO network and the widely used k-Wave toolbox for time domain acoustic wave propagation [16] were compared in terms of accuracy and computation times.

- Further experiments were also conducted to evaluate the generalizability of the FNO network beyond the training data and the impact of key hyperparameters on network performance and complexity.

The remainder of the article is organized as follows. The forward problem and the inverse problem of PAT are described in Section 2. Acoustic wave simulation techniques for the PAT based on conventional methods and FNO networks are presented in Section 2. The data generation and training process of the FNO network and its detailed implementation are also given in Section 2. Simulation results of the FNO network on the different test set with different spatial grid sizes and hyperparameter optimizations are provided in Section 3. Furthermore, the simulation results of zero-shot super-resolution with the FNO network are also given in Section 3. The conclusion and discussion are presented in Sections 4 and 5, respectively.

2. Materials and Methods

2.1. Photoacoustic Signal Generation and Imaging

The photoacoustic signal is generated by irradiating the medium with a nanosecond laser pulse (Figure 1). Chromophores within the image medium are excited by the laser and undergo thermoelastic expansion to generate acoustic pressure waves. Assuming negligible thermal diffusion and volume expansion during illumination, the initial photoacoustic pressure x can be defined as

$$x(r) = \Gamma(r)A(r), \tag{1}$$

where $A(r)$ is the spatial absorption function, and $\Gamma(r)$ is the Grüneisen coefficient describing the conversion efficiency from heat to pressure [32]. The photoacoustic pressure wave $p(r,t)$ at position r and time t can be modeled as an initial value problem, where c is the speed of sound [33].

$$\left(\partial_{tt} - c_0^2 \Delta\right)p(r,t) = 0, \quad p(r,t=0) = x, \quad \partial_t p(r,t=0) = 0 \tag{2}$$

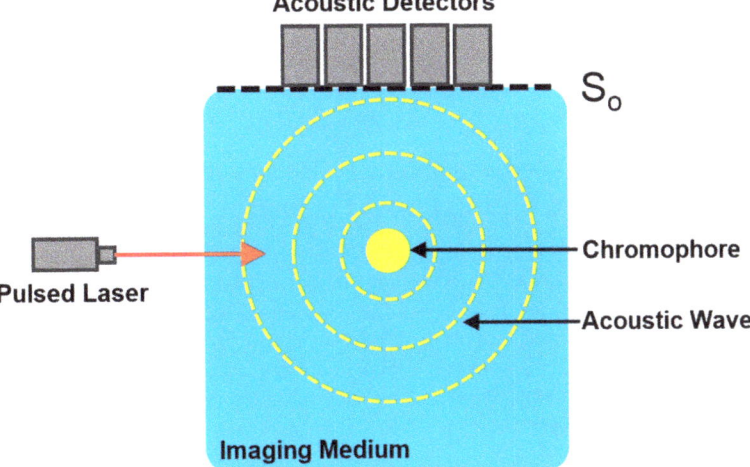

Figure 1. Diagram illustrating the process of photoacoustic signal generation and detection. Chromophores absorb the incident pulsed laser light and undergo thermoelastic expansion to generate acoustic waves. Acoustic detectors along the measurement boundary So are used to measure the acoustic waves.

In photoacoustic imaging, sensors located along a measurement surface S_o, surrounding the medium, are used to measure a time series signal. The linear operator $\mathcal{M}$ acts on $p(r,t)$ restricted to the boundary of the computational domain Ω over a finite time T

and provides a linear mapping to the measured time-dependent signal y. The forward photoacoustic operator W maps the initial acoustic pressure to the measured signal.

$$y = \mathcal{M}_{p|\partial\Omega \times (0,T)} = Wx \qquad (3)$$

The measured sensor data are then used to form an image representing the initial acoustic pressure distribution. Photoacoustic image reconstruction is a well-studied inverse problem that can be solved using analytical solutions, numerical methods and model-based iterative methods [11–13,15,34]. The adjoint photoacoustic operator W^* maps the measured signal to the initial acoustic pressure.

$$x = W^*y \qquad (4)$$

Time reversal is a robust reconstruction method that works well for homogenous and heterogeneous mediums and also for any arbitrary detection geometry [15,34]. The acoustic waves that are generated are measured along the measurement surface S_o. After a long period of time T, the acoustic field within the medium becomes zero, which is guaranteed by Huygens' principle in homogeneous mediums [35]. A PAT image is formed by running a numerical model of the forward problem and transmitting the measured sensor data in a time-reversed order into the medium, where the detectors along S_o are time-varying pressure sources. Thus, time reversal is modeled as a time-varying boundary value problem, and the resulting acoustic field at $t = 0$ is the initial acoustic pressure distribution to be recovered.

2.2. Conventional Solvers for the Wave Equation

Numerical approaches, such as the finite difference and finite element methods, are commonly used to solve PDEs by discretizing the space into a grid [36]. However, these methods are often slow for time domain modeling broadband or high-frequency waves due to the need for a fine grid with small time steps [16]. Computational efficiency can be improved using pseudo-spectral and k-space methods. The pseudo-spectral method fits a Fourier series to the data and reduces the number of grid points per wavelength required for an accurate solution [37]. The k-space method incorporates a priori information regarding the governing wave equation into the solution [38]. This allows for larger time steps and improves numerical stability in the case of acoustically heterogeneous media. The k-Wave toolbox, a widely used MATLAB tool for photoacoustic simulations, uses the pseudo-spectral k-space approach for solving time domain photoacoustic wave simulations [39].

Conventional numerical approaches are typically used to solve a single instance of PDEs and require the PDEs' explicit form. Because these approaches solve the PDE via approximation on a mesh, there is a trade-off between accuracy and computation time. In comparison, the FNO network is a data-driven and black-box approach that learns a solution for a family of PDEs from the training data and does not require the PDEs' explicit form. It is also resolution- and mesh-invariant, meaning that the trained network can be used for solving PDEs at varying levels of resolution and discretization. However, the FNO network is dependent on the quality of the data and is slow to train. Although modifications to the functional form of the PDE can be easily accounted for in conventional approaches to solve a single instance, the FNO network would need to be retrained with a new training dataset.

2.3. Fourier Neural Operator Networks

The FNO network [31] was adapted for solving the 2D photoacoustic wave equation. In the original implementation, the input a to the FNO was the first several time steps of the solution acquired using a conventional solver. Using insights from the physics of photoacoustic imaging, we determined that only the initial pressure distribution (time = 0) was needed as the input a to the FNO for solving the wave equation because the generated acoustic pulses propagate in an omni-directional manner. This removed the need for conventional solvers, and the full spatio-temporal solution could be obtained using only the FNO. To avoid instabilities and keep our solution bounded, we replaced previously used element-wise Gaussian normalizers with a peak-normalization scheme, where the initial source distribution map was normalized by its maximum value. We empirically found that the Gaussian normalizer was not appropriate for simulating wave propagation because the distribution of pressures over time at any given element in the computational grid was not normally distributed.

The network begins by projecting the input a (initial pressure distribution) onto a higher dimensional latent representation using the fully connected layer FC_1 with a single shallow layer (Figure 2). The dimensionality of this latent representation is defined by the hyperparameter termed channels. Four Fourier layers are then used to iteratively update the projected features. In each Fourier layer, the features initially undergo a Fourier transform, which plays a key role in enabling the network to efficiently learn mesh- and resolution-invariant features for solving the PDE. Features learned in the Fourier space are global by nature and represent patterns spanning the whole computational grid. In contrast, features learned in a standard CNN are local by nature and represent patterns spanning over a local region (e.g., edges and shapes).

Pseudo-code for the FNO
```
def FNO(x):
    x = fc 0(x)

    for i in range( 3):
        x1 = SpectralConv 3d(x)
        x2 = conv 3d(x)
        x = x1 + x2
        x = gelu (x)

    x1 = SpectralConv 3d( x)
    x2 = conv 3d(x)
    x = x1 + x2

    x = fc 1(x)
    x = gelu (x)
    x = fc 2(x)

    return x
```

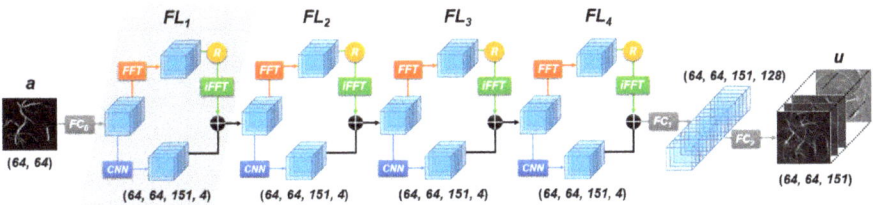

Figure 2. Neural network architecture for the FNO network. The input a (initial pressure distribution a) is mapped to a higher dimensional space using a fully connected layer (FC_0). The transformed feature is passed through four Fourier Layers (FLs). Finally, a fully connected layer (FC_2) is used to obtain the final output u (solution to the wave equation u) with the desired dimensions. The input goes through two paths in each Fourier layer. In the top path, the input undergoes a Fourier Transform FFT, linear transform R and inverse Fourier Transform iFFT. In the bottom path, the input undergoes a linear transform. Outputs from each path are summed together and undergo GeLU activation. The dimension of the feature representation for each operation is given in the parentheses.

After the Fourier transform, the resulting Fourier modes can be truncated to optimize computational efficiency. This is useful as a regularization technique and for PDEs with smooth solutions that can be accurately represented with fewer Fourier modes, as previously demonstrated for the 2D Navier–Stokes equation [31]. Following the Fourier layers, the updated features are projected in FC_2 to a higher dimensional representation with 128 channels in the hidden layer and finally to the desired dimensions in the final shallow layer to obtain the output u (solution to the wave equation). Through a combination of Fourier, linear and non-linear transformations, the FNO network can approximate highly complex and non-linear operators in PDEs.

Channels and modes are the two main hyperparameters for the FNO network. Channels represent the dimensionality of the latent representation in the FNO network, and modes define the number of Fourier modes retained in each Fourier layer. Increasing the channel parameter generally increases the representational power of the model to learn more complex operators but can lead to issues of overfitting. There is no upper limit to the number of channels that can be used. Choosing the number of Fourier modes to retain largely depends on the smoothness of the PDE's solution. The maximum number of modes is defined by the size of the computational grid.

PDE solvers using Fourier methods assume a periodic boundary condition. Although the FNO network heavily uses the Fourier transform, it is not limited by this assumption and can be applied to solve PDEs with non-periodic boundary conditions, such as Burgers' equation and the Navier–Stokes equation [31]. This is important because the photoacoustic wave equation also has non-periodic boundary conditions.

The photoacoustic wave equation can be solved using either a 2D or 3D FNO architectural implementation. In the 2D architecture, the FNO network performs 2D convolutions in space and finds a solution for some fixed interval length Δt. The solution is then recurrently propagated in time and used to solve for the next interval length. In the 3D architecture, the FNO network performs 3D convolutions in space-time and can directly output the full time series solution with any time discretization. Both implementations were demonstrated to have similar performance. In this work, the 3D FNO network was used because it was found to be more expressive and easier to train [31].

2.4. Data Generation

The MATLAB toolbox k-Wave was used for photoacoustic wave simulation and to generate data for training and testing the FNO network [16]. The simulation medium was defined as a 64 × 64 computational grid, non-absorbing and homogenous with a speed of sound of 1480 m/s and density of 1000 kg/m^3. Forward simulations were performed with a time step of 20 ns for T = 151 steps. The initial photoacoustic pressure was initialized using anatomically realistic breast vasculature phantoms that were numerically generated [40]. The training dataset (n = 500) and testing dataset (n = 100) comprised images representing the initial photoacoustic pressure (the input to the FNO network) and the corresponding simulation of the photoacoustic wave propagation (output of the FNO network). Simulations for the Shepp–Logan, synthetic vasculature, tumor and Mason-M phantoms were also generated to evaluate the generalizability of the FNO network [16,41].

A second dataset was generated based on images from the Animals with Attributes 2 (AWA2) dataset originally developed for zero-shot image classification [42]. The AWA2 dataset has over 32,000 images categorized into 50 animal classes. This highly diverse dataset with many varied animals and backgrounds provides a more challenging task to train and evaluate the FNO. Forward simulations were performed with a similar medium as described previously, except with a 128 × 128 computational grid for T = 302 steps. With the same medium, the adjoint simulations were also performed using a 128-sensor linear array at the top of the computational grid. Images from 10 animal classes were used to create a training dataset (n = 1500). Images from 5 different animal classes were used to create a testing dataset (n = 500). The forward and adjoint simulations had their own respective datasets.

2.5. Model Training and Evaluation

The FNO network was implemented in PyTorch v1.7.1, a popular open-source deep learning library for Python [43]. The Adam optimizer with a mean squared error loss function was used to train the FNO network for 2000 epochs over approximately two days on an NVIDIA Tesla K80 GPU. The trained model was used to solve the wave equation for all time steps in a single forward pass.

The simulations from k-Wave served as the ground truth and were used to evaluate the quality of the FNO simulations. The root-mean-square error (RMSE) was used to quantitatively measure FNO simulation quality. Prior to calculating the RMSE, the k-Wave and FNO simulations were normalized to have values between 0 and 1 based on the peak value in the entire time series data. Normalization was applied to the entire time series and not to each individual time step. The RMSE was calculated at each time step and for the whole simulation.

For further validation, an in silico experiment of PAT imaging with a 64-sensor linear array was conducted. In general, any sensor array geometry could be used because the photoacoustic simulation and data sampling were independent events. A linear geometry was chosen because it is a widely available sensor array that is often used in experimental and clinical settings. Sensor data for the image reconstruction experiment were generated from the k-Wave and FNO network simulations by sampling the photoacoustic pressures at the top of the computational grid. The sampled time series sensor data were then used to reconstruct an image with the time reversal method [16].

The execution times to run the k-Wave and FNO simulations were measured on the same machine with an NVIDIA GeForce GTX 1080 Ti GPU and an Intel i7-12700K CPU. Simulations were repeated for 200 iterations, and the mean execution time was recorded. Torchinfo v1.6.5 was used to estimate the model size and GPU memory requirements.

3. Results

3.1. Breast Vasculature Simulation

An FNO network with the hyperparameters of 5 channels and 64 Fourier modes was trained using the breast vasculature dataset. The trained FNO network was used to predict and simulate photoacoustic wave propagation for $n = 100$ initial photoacoustic sources in the breast vasculature testing dataset. The photoacoustic wave simulations produced by the FNO network and k-Wave were remarkably similar and essentially identical to the naked eye (Figure 3). The FNO simulations successfully maintained the sharp edges and fine image details of the acoustic waves as they propagated throughout the medium. This demonstrated that the FNO network can model the broadband and high-frequency waves required for photoacoustic simulations.

Errors in the FNO network were quantitatively measured using the RMSE. The distribution of normalized photoacoustic pressures decreased as the simulation continued forward because energy dissipated within the medium as the acoustic waves propagated and exited the medium (Figure 4). For the testing dataset, the RMSE was several orders of magnitude smaller than the distribution of photoacoustic pressures in the simulations. This indicated that the errors in the FNO network simulations were small compared to the actual acoustic pressures, and the FNO network simulations were highly accurate approximations of the k-Wave simulations for photoacoustic wave propagation. Here, the RMSE was orders of magnitude smaller than the photoacoustic pressure distribution in the simulations, which can be attributed to the inherent model properties of globally learning frequency domain features and using the entire Fourier mode without any truncation. Therefore, the broadband frequency components originally distributed in the photoacoustic time series data can be described by sufficient frequency components.

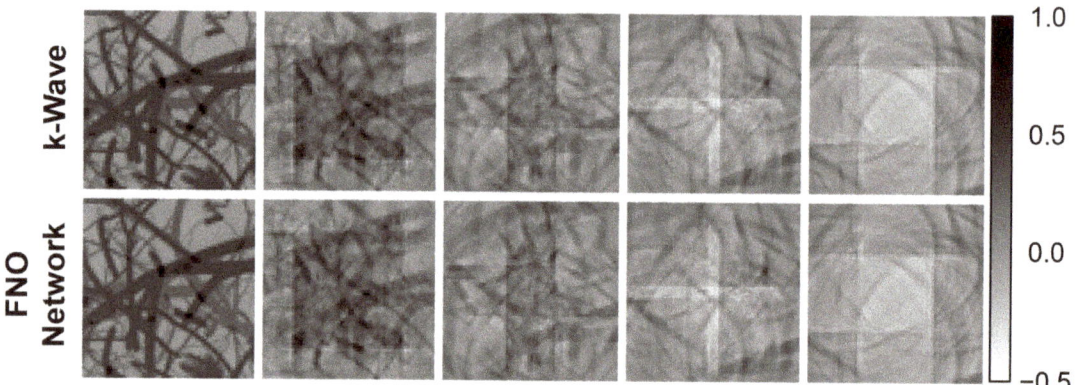

Figure 3. Visual comparison of the ground truth (**Top** Row) using k-Wave and the FNO network (**Bottom** Row) simulated photoacoustic wave propagation for an example vasculature image in a homogeneous medium at t = [1, 20, 40, 60, 80] time steps. The RMSE over all time steps was 3.8×10^{-3} for this example.

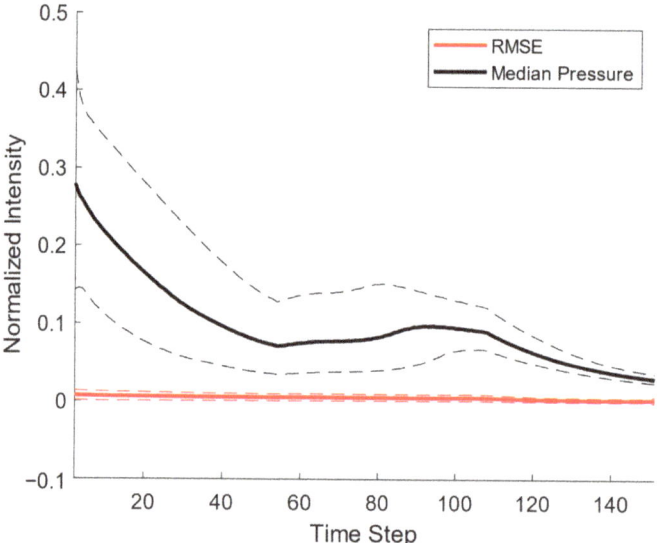

Figure 4. RMSE and standard deviation bands between the k-Wave and FNO simulations on the breast vasculature test dataset. Distribution of pressures (25th, 50th and 75th percentiles) are provided as a frame of reference.

A key advantage of data-driven PDE solvers over traditional ones is the vast reduction in computation time. In general, the time required to solve the photoacoustic wave equation largely depends on the discretization of the computational grid. For a computational grid of 64×64, k-Wave on average required 1.63 s to complete the simulation on a GPU. The FNO network on average required 0.061 s to complete it on the same GPU. This was approximately a $26\times$ reduction in computation time.

3.2. Image Reconstruction

The reconstructed PAT images from the FNO network and k-Wave simulations were almost visually identical (Figure 5). Vasculature structures and artifacts arising from the limited-view nature of the linear array can be seen in both the k-Wave and FNO network images. The reconstructed images were quantitatively compared using the RMSE and the structural similarity index metric (SSIM), a metric ranging from 0 to 1 that measures the similarity between two images based on factors relevant to human visual perception (e.g., structure, contrast and luminance) [44]. For the testing dataset ($n = 100$), the similarity between the FNO network and k-Wave images were measured with the RMSE ($7.1 \pm 1.5 \times 10^{-3}$), SSIM ($0.98 \pm 0.01$) and maximum error pixelwise (0.05 ± 0.01). These small errors and high similarity scores demonstrated that the time series sensor data produced using the FNO network and k-Wave simulations were highly similar.

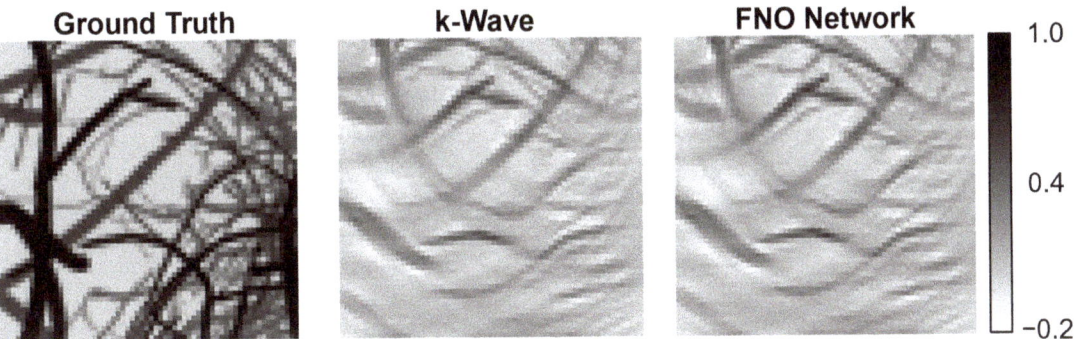

Figure 5. FNO and k-Wave were used to simulate wave propagation for the ground truth image. Sensor data were sampled from the resulting simulations and reconstructed into PAT images. The k-Wave and FNO images are almost identical. RMSE (0.011), SSIM (0.97) and max error (0.06).

3.3. Generalizability of Trained FNO Network

The FNO network was trained on photoacoustic simulations of breast vasculature. To evaluate its generalizability, the trained FNO network was used to simulate photoacoustic wave propagation with initial photoacoustic sources for the Shepp–Logan, synthetic vasculature, breast tumor and Mason-M logo phantoms. These phantoms contain many features not observed in the training dataset. For example, the breast vasculature phantoms typically occupy a majority of the space in the computational grid and have a mixture of large and small vessels, whereas the other phantoms occupy a fraction of the space and have small vessels or non-vasculature structures.

The FNO network and k-Wave simulations for each phantom tested were highly similar, but small visual differences could be observed (Figure 6). For example, the Mason-M logo has a mostly uniform grayscale background in the k-Wave simulation at t = 1, but a small gradient or shading could be seen in the FNO network simulation (average RMSEs across all time steps in the FNO network simulations: Shepp–Logan (9.5×10^{-3}), synthetic vasculature (1.5×10^{-2}), tumor (1.1×10^{-2}) and Mason-M (1.9×10^{-2}) phantoms). The Mason-M FNO simulation likely had the highest RMSE because it was a non-biological phantom unlike the other phantoms and the training dataset.

These results were promising and provided evidence that the trained FNO network is generalizable to other initial photoacoustic sources not in the training data. However, the FNO network did overfit the training data, as shown by the larger RMSE of the additional phantoms. Having a more diverse and larger training dataset can further improve the generalizability of the FNO network.

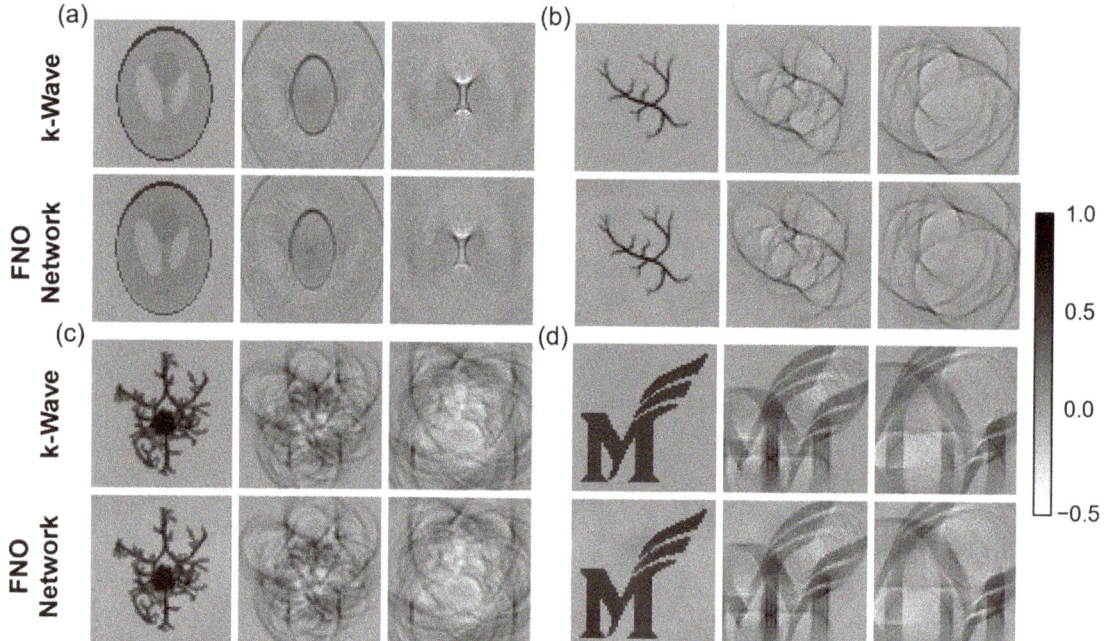

Figure 6. Comparison between FNO Network and k-Wave simulations for initial pressure sources using the (**a**) Shepp–Logan, (**b**) synthetic vasculature, (**c**) tumor and (**d**) Mason-M phantoms at t = [1, 10, 20] time steps.

3.4. Hyperparameter Optimization

A study was conducted to investigate the impact of hyperparameter selection on the FNO network's accuracy. All FNO networks were trained on the breast vasculature dataset for 200 epochs, which was sufficient for all networks to converge to a minimum loss. The number of Fourier modes had the largest impact on the FNO network because it directly affected the truncation error in the Fourier layers. FNO networks with fewer modes typically produced simulations with a blurred appearance (Figure 7). This was due to the loss of high-frequency information necessary for accurately simulating the sharp transitions of the acoustic wavefront. For a computational grid of 64 × 64, the FNO network with a maximum number of 64 modes produced the highest quality photoacoustic simulations.

Increasing the number of channels improved the FNO network's accuracy with diminishing returns (Table 1). Results show that there was little benefit in having an FNO network with more than five channels. Parameterizing the FNO network with a higher number of modes or channels results in a more complex model that requires more GPU memory. Interestingly, the time for a trained network to complete a simulation remained approximately the same. There was a small increase in computation time for the larger FNO networks with 64 modes and a higher number of channels.

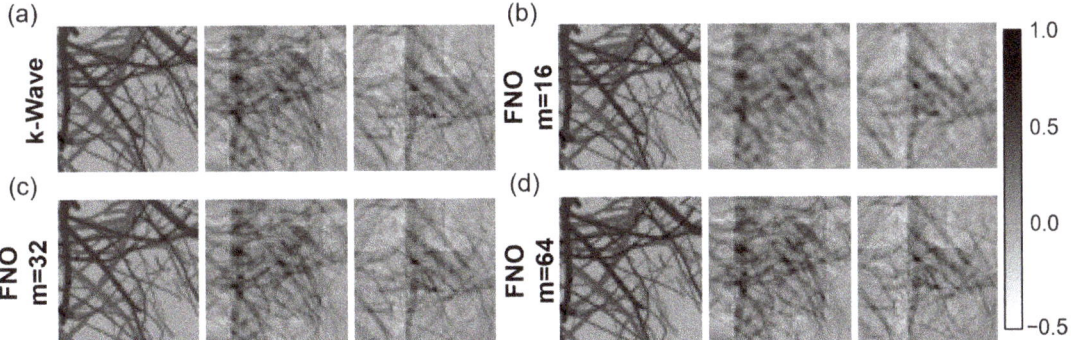

Figure 7. Comparison of FNO simulations at t = 1, 5, 10, 15 and 20 time steps. (**a**) k-Wave simulation. (**b**) The FNO network were parametrized with channels = 5 and modes = 16. (**c**) The FNO network were parametrized with channels = 5 and modes = 32. (**d**) The FNO network were parametrized with channels = 5 and modes = 64.

Table 1. Comparison of FNO network hyperparameters.

Grid Size	M	C	RMSE	Std. Dev.	Time (s)	GPU Mem. (GB)
64 × 64 × 151	16	5	2.4×10^{-2}	2.7×10^{-2}	0.016	0.85
64 × 64 × 151	32	5	8.5×10^{-3}	7.9×10^{-3}	0.021	0.94
64 × 64 × 151	64	5	4.7×10^{-3}	4.6×10^{-3}	0.061	1.68
64 × 64 × 151	64	2	1.3×10^{-2}	1.2×10^{-2}	0.048	0.84
64 × 64 × 151	64	3	8.5×10^{-3}	8.2×10^{-3}	0.051	1.05
64 × 64 × 151	64	4	5.4×10^{-3}	5.4×10^{-3}	0.055	1.33
64 × 64 × 151	64	5	4.7×10^{-3}	4.6×10^{-3}	0.061	1.68
64 × 64 × 151	64	6	5.1×10^{-3}	4.9×10^{-3}	0.066	2.09
64 × 64 × 151	64	7	4.4×10^{-3}	4.3×10^{-3}	0.074	2.57
64 × 64 × 151	64	8	5.1×10^{-3}	6.2×10^{-3}	0.082	3.12
128 × 128 × 302	64	5	6.9×10^{-3}	5.5×10^{-3}	0.110	6.45

Comparison between FNO networks with varying grid sizes, Fourier modes (M) and channels (C).

3.5. AWA2 Simulations

FNO networks with 5 channels and 64 Fourier modes were trained using the AWA2 datasets to perform the forward and adjoint simulations on a 128 × 128 computational grid. The simulations by the FNO network and k-Wave were visually almost identical (Figure 8). The RMSE in the forward simulation was consistently several orders of magnitude smaller than the normalized pressure across all time steps (Figure 9). The RMSE in the adjoint simulation increased over time but remained smaller than the normalized pressure (Figure 10). An increasing error was expected because the adjoint simulations began with a zero computational grid, and the pressure waves entered the grid from the top over time. The RMSE over the entire testing dataset ($n = 500$) was similarly small for the forward ($6.9 \pm 5.5 \times 10^{-3}$) and adjoint ($5.2 \pm 5.5 \times 10^{-3}$) simulations.

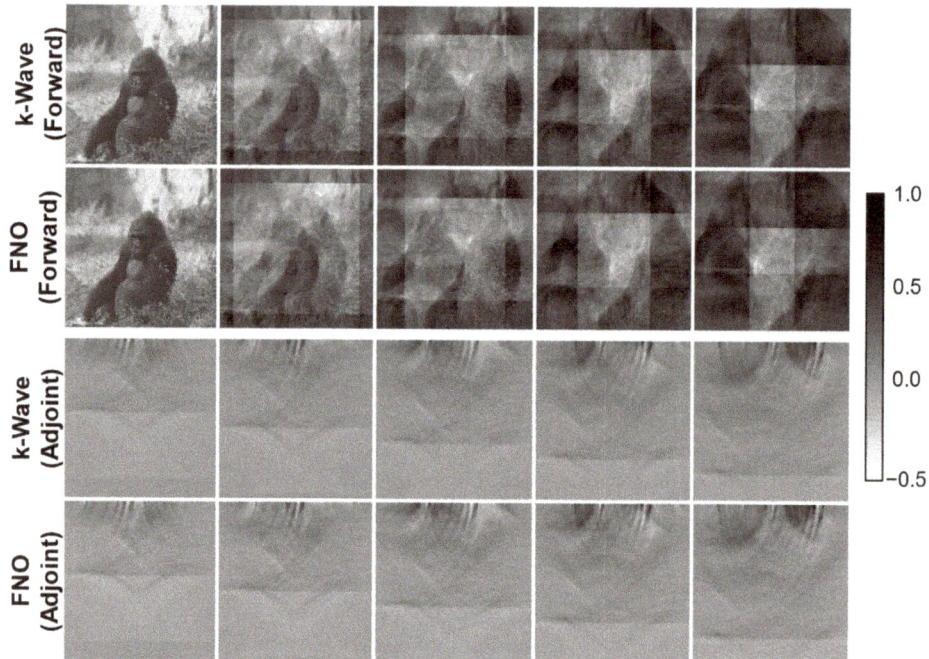

Figure 8. Simulations shown are for a 128 × 128 computation grid. (**Top**) Comparison between FNO and k-Wave forward simulations at t = [1, 40, 80, 120, 160] time steps. (**Bottom**) Comparison between FNO and k-Wave adjoint simulation t = [200, 220, 240, 260, 280] time steps. The input to both adjoint simulations was sensor data sampled with a linear array from the k-Wave forward simulation.

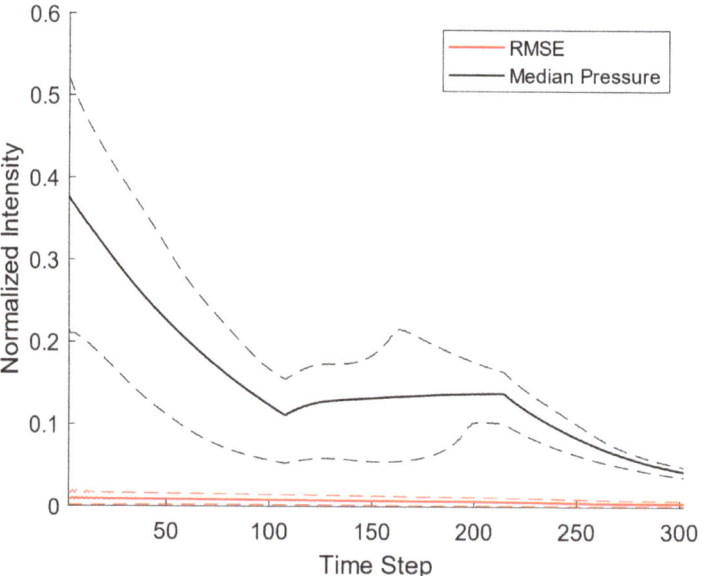

Figure 9. RMSE and standard deviation bands between the k-Wave and FNO forward simulations on the AWA2 test dataset. Distribution of pressures (25th, 50th and 75th percentiles) are provided as a frame of reference.

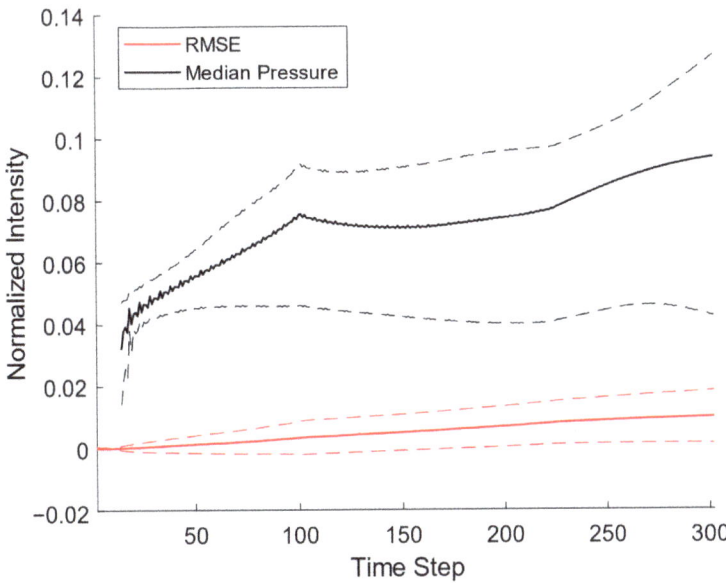

Figure 10. RMSE and standard deviation bands between the k-Wave and FNO adjoint simulations for the AWA2 test dataset. Distribution of pressures (25th, 50th and 75th percentiles) is provided as a frame of reference.

3.6. Zero-shot Super Resolution

The FNO was trained on simulations with a $128 \times 128 \times 302$ computational grid and was then used for zero-shot super resolution to simulate wave propagation on larger-sized grids. This was completed on an animal image from the testing dataset and a vasculature image to evaluate generalizability. The FNO simulations for both images strongly resembled their respective higher-resolution simulations using k-Wave (Figure 11). Errors could be seen in the background. The FNO simulations also had a more blurred appearance, as seen in the zoomed regions. This was likely due to the truncation of Fourier modes leading to the loss of high-frequency information that is useful for retaining sharper details in an image. Truncation errors became more prevalent for larger grid sizes using the FNO's super resolution feature (Table 2).

For a computational grid of $128 \times 128 \times 302$, k-Wave required on average 1.66 s to complete a simulation on a GPU. The FNO network on average required 0.11 s on the same GPU. This was approximately a $15\times$ reduction in computation time.

Table 2. FNO super resolution RMSE.

Grid Size	Animal	Vasculature
$128 \times 128 \times 302$	9.8×10^{-3}	2.7×10^{-3}
$152 \times 152 \times 302$	5.2×10^{-2}	3.4×10^{-2}
$176 \times 176 \times 302$	7.1×10^{-2}	4.5×10^{-2}
$200 \times 200 \times 302$	8.6×10^{-2}	5.5×10^{-2}
$224 \times 224 \times 302$	1.0×10^{-1}	6.3×10^{-2}

RMSE errors between k-Wave simulations and FNO zero-shot super resolution simulations for varying computational grid sizes.

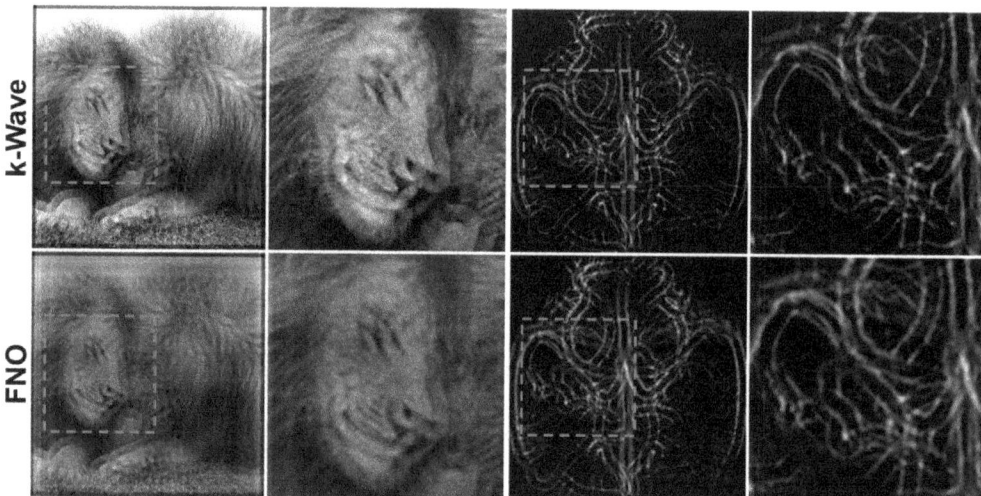

Figure 11. Zero-shot super resolution using an FNO trained on a 128 × 128 × 302 computational grid to perform simulations on a 224 × 224 × 302 grid. Images from the FNO and k-Wave simulations at t = 5 and zoomed regions are shown. (**Left**) Animal image of a lion from the testing dataset. (**Right**) Vasculature image to evaluate FNO generalizability.

4. Discussion

A key motivation for an FNO network is that a trained network can quickly produce accurate solutions for both forward and adjoint simulations. For a comparable simulation, the FNO network was ~26× faster on a 64 × 64 grid and ~15× faster on a 128 × 128 grid than k-Wave. This reduction in computation time with minimal loss in accuracy is ideal for applications requiring repeated evaluations of the photoacoustic operator. For example, advanced image reconstruction techniques, such as iterative methods, yield state-of-the-art results but are computationally expensive due to the repeated evaluation of the forward and adjoint operators. Therefore, the FNO network can greatly accelerate these methods by replacing traditional solvers for those operators.

The FNO network is parameterized by the number of Fourier modes and channels. Increasing either parameter typically improves model performance but at the cost of increased memory and computation requirements. PDEs with generally smoother solutions require fewer modes to achieve a satisfactory solution. However, the photoacoustic operator contains broadband frequency information, which means that a higher number of modes is needed for an accurate solution. The optimal number of Fourier modes retained is related to the spatial resolution of the initial photoacoustic source and not necessarily the size of the computational grid, meaning that not all simulations with a computational grid of 64 × 64 require the maximum 64 Fourier modes for the FNO network to produce an accurate solution. Hyperparameter optimization is especially important for simulations with large computational grids where limited GPU memory can become a problem.

Optimizing the FNO for larger computational grids can be partially addressed via hyperparameter selection. There are other approaches that can be employed to further reduce GPU memory limitations. In this work, a 3D CNN architecture was used, but there are other CNN architectures, such as the recurrent 2D network, that are more memory-efficient [31]. Instead of solving for the full temporal solution in a single step, the FNO can be used iteratively to solve the wave equation for n time steps in each forward pass over the full time interval. Conventional solvers typically require sufficiently small time steps for solution stability, but the FNO is likely not limited by this requirement. Thus, it is possible that the FNO can use larger time steps and obtain an accurate solution for downstream image reconstruction and processing tasks.

In this work, we chose to simulate the full spatio-temporal wave field to decouple the tasks of simulation from sampling. This allowed the same trained FNO to be used for any sensor configuration. The FNO could be configured and trained to directly output the sampled sensor data. This would reduce memory requirements but would also need to be retrained for each sensor geometry and configuration.

A practical limitation in data-driven PDE solvers, such as the FNO network, is the need for high-quality training data. Traditional solvers are often used to create arbitrarily large datasets to train the network. Depending on the size of the computational grid, this can be computationally formidable, such as the case of 3D photoacoustic simulations. To create a large dataset in these scenarios, a high-performance computing environment would be needed to generate the training data in a reasonable timeframe. Transfer learning could also be employed to partially address this challenge after training the initial FNO model. Rather than training from scratch, a pre-trained model can be fine-tuned with smaller datasets for specific tasks or simulation environments. This would make the model more accessible for other downstream users.

Zero-shot super resolution is a unique feature to the FNO and has been previously demonstrated to work well for the Navier–Stokes equation. Given the difficulty of zero-shot tasks, it is highly encouraging that the FNO could generate larger-sized simulations resembling the k-Wave simulations. However, the truncation of Fourier modes led to blurring and errors for larger computation grids. For example, the computational grid of 224×224 produced 224 Fourier modes, but only 64 were retained. The information loss in that scenario was greater than that in the case of 128×128 computational grid.

5. Conclusions

Solving the 2D photoacoustic wave equation with traditional methods typically requires a fine discretization of the computational grid and can be time-consuming to complete. Deep learning methods directly learn from data to solve PDEs and can be orders of magnitude faster with minimal losses in accuracy. In this work, we applied the FNO network as a fast data-driven PDE solver for the 2D photoacoustic wave equation in a homogeneous medium. The photoacoustic simulations generated by a traditional solver with the k-Wave toolbox and the FNO network for the breast vasculature testing dataset were remarkably similar, both visually and quantitatively. The RMSE between the k-Wave and FNO simulations was several orders of magnitude smaller than the pressure intensities.

Model generalizability is a highly desirable property for an FNO network. If the trained FNO network is to be a reliable alternative to traditional PDE solvers, then it needs to be capable of solving the photoacoustic operator for any arbitrary initial pressure source within an acceptable degree of error. Having a generalizable network minimizes the need to retrain the network for instances not observed in the training dataset. The generalizability of the trained FNO network was evaluated using phantoms not in the training data. Shepp–Logan, synthetic vasculature, tumor and Mason-M phantoms were used for 64×64 simulations, and the vasculature phantom was used for the 128×128 simulation. In general, the FNO network and k-Wave simulations were visually similar. The RMSE was relatively small for these phantoms but was larger than those in the testing dataset. This indicated that the FNO was overfitting the training data. These results provide evidence for the FNO network being generalizable and can be used for simulations with any arbitrary initial pressure source. Moreover, the FNO network was learning the photoacoustic operator and not memorizing specific solutions related to the training data.

In this work, the FNO network was trained for solving the 2D acoustic wave equation in a homogeneous medium. Simulations with homogeneous media are widely used in many applications because the spatial distribution of heterogeneities is often unknown. Nevertheless, an FNO network can be used for simulations with heterogeneous media by providing the spatial distribution of medium properties as additional inputs to the FNO network. During the training process, the FNO network can leverage these inputs and learn from training examples generated with varying heterogeneous media to perform simulations with heterogeneous media. The operator for a heterogeneous medium is more complex than that of the homogeneous case. Thus, a larger and more diverse dataset is likely needed to adequately train the FNO network.

The significance of our work is that it provides a comprehensive study on solving the 2D photoacoustic wave equation with an FNO, demonstrating its application potential in downstream reconstruction and image-processing tasks. The FNO performs orders of magnitude faster than traditional solvers and can generalize to unseen out-of-domain datasets. However, for simulations in a larger computational grid, a higher Fourier mode is necessarily required to learn the broadband frequency residing in the whole time series data. Consequently, it increases GPU memory and can be an intractable problem while simulating in a larger domain, which usually requires the output of more time steps. Furthermore, the current framework is limited to simulating the 2D photoacoustic wave equation. Simulating the 3D photoacoustic source to output entire 4D time series data is impossible to handle with modern GPUs. In addition, zero-shot super resolution using an FNO tends to output blurry images due to the insufficient number of Fourier modes used to train the network to support broadband frequency components in a larger computational grid. In the future, research addressing these issues will benefit the use of FNOs in more complex settings.

Author Contributions: Conceptualization, S.G.; methodology, S.G.; validation, S.G. and K.-T.H.; writing—original draft preparation, S.G.; writing—review and editing, S.G., K.-T.H. and P.V.C.; visualization, S.G.; supervision, P.V.C. All authors have read and agreed to the published version of the manuscript.

Funding: This research received no external funding.

Institutional Review Board Statement: Not applicable.

Informed Consent Statement: Not applicable.

Data Availability Statement: Animals with attributes 2 (AWA2) dataset is available at https://cvml.ista.ac.at/AwA2/. Software for generating breast phantom dataset is available at https://breastphantom.readthedocs.io/en/latest/.

Acknowledgments: This project was supported by resources provided by the Office of Research Computing at George Mason University URL: https://orc.gmu.edu (accessed on 1 January 2022). The authors would like to acknowledge Matthias Eyassu from the George Mason Biomedical Imaging Laboratory for providing the breast vasculature phantoms, and we acknowledge the source code for Fourier Neural Operators available at https://github.com/zongyi-li/fourier_neural_operator.

Conflicts of Interest: The authors declare no conflict of interest.

References

1. Xia, J.; Yao, J.; Wang, L.V. Photoacoustic tomography: Principles and advances. *Electromagn. Waves Camb. Mass* **2014**, *147*, 1–22. [CrossRef] [PubMed]
2. Xia, J.; Wang, L.V. Small-animal whole-body photoacoustic tomography: A review. *IEEE Trans. Biomed. Eng.* **2014**, *61*, 1380–1389. [CrossRef] [PubMed]
3. Nyayapathi, N.; Xia, J. Photoacoustic imaging of breast cancer: A mini review of system design and image features. *J. Biomed. Opt.* **2019**, *24*, 121911. [CrossRef]
4. Bungart, B.L.; Lan, L.; Wang, P.; Li, R.; Koch, M.O.; Cheng, L.; Masterson, T.A.; Dundar, M.; Cheng, J.-X. Photoacoustic tomography of intact human prostates and vascular texture analysis identify prostate cancer biopsy targets. *Photoacoustics* **2018**, *11*, 46–55. [CrossRef] [PubMed]
5. Moore, C.; Jokerst, J.V. Strategies for Image-Guided Therapy, Surgery, and Drug Delivery Using Photoacoustic Imaging. *Theranostics* **2019**, *9*, 1550–1571. [CrossRef]
6. Rao, A.P.; Bokde, N.; Sinha, S. Photoacoustic Imaging for Management of Breast Cancer: A Literature Review and Future Perspectives. *Appl. Sci.* **2020**, *10*, 767. [CrossRef]
7. Lin, L.; Hu, P.; Shi, J.; Appleton, C.M.; Maslov, K.; Li, L.; Zhang, R.; Wang, L.V. Single-breath-hold photoacoustic computed tomography of the breast. *Nat. Commun.* **2018**, *9*, 2352. [CrossRef]
8. Li, M.; Tang, Y.; Yao, J. Photoacoustic tomography of blood oxygenation: A mini review. *Photoacoustics* **2018**, *10*, 65–73. [CrossRef]

9. Goh, Y.; Balasundaram, G.; Tan, H.M.; Putti, T.C.; Tang, S.W.; Ng, C.W.Q.; Buhari, S.A.; Fang, E.; Moothanchery, M.; Bi, R.; et al. Biochemical "decoding" of breast ultrasound images with optoacoustic tomography fusion: First-in-human display of lipid and collagen signals on breast ultrasound. *Photoacoustics* **2022**, *27*, 100377. [CrossRef]
10. Wang, L.V. Prospects of photoacoustic tomography. *Med. Phys.* **2008**, *35*, 5758–5767. [CrossRef]
11. Li, S.; Montcel, B.; Liu, W.; Vray, D. Analytical model of optical fluence inside multiple cylindrical inhomogeneities embedded in an otherwise homogeneous turbid medium for quantitative photoacoustic imaging. *Opt. Express* **2014**, *22*, 20500–20514. [CrossRef]
12. Xu, M.; Wang, L.V. Universal back-projection algorithm for photoacoustic computed tomography. *Phys. Rev. E* **2005**, *71*, 016706. [CrossRef]
13. Hristova, Y.; Kuchment, P.; Nguyen, L. Reconstruction and time reversal in thermoacoustic tomography in acoustically homogeneous and inhomogeneous media. *Inverse Probl.* **2008**, *24*, 055006. [CrossRef]
14. Huang, C.; Wang, K.; Schoonover, R.W.; Wang, L.V.; Anastasio, M.A. Joint Reconstruction of Absorbed Optical Energy Density and Sound Speed Distributions in Photoacoustic Computed Tomography: A Numerical Investigation. *IEEE Trans. Comput. Imaging* **2016**, *2*, 136–149. [CrossRef]
15. Cox, B.T.; Treeby, B.E. Artifact Trapping During Time Reversal Photoacoustic Imaging for Acoustically Heterogeneous Media. *IEEE Trans. Med. Imaging* **2010**, *29*, 387–396. [CrossRef] [PubMed]
16. Treeby, B.E.; Cox, B.T. k-Wave: MATLAB toolbox for the simulation and reconstruction of photoacoustic wave fields. *J. Biomed. Opt.* **2010**, *15*, 021314. [CrossRef] [PubMed]
17. Xu, M.; Xu, Y.; Wang, L.V. Time-domain reconstruction algorithms and numerical simulations for thermoacoustic tomography in various geometries. *IEEE Trans. Biomed. Eng.* **2003**, *50*, 1086–1099. [CrossRef] [PubMed]
18. Paltauf, G.; Viator, J.A.; Prahl, S.A.; Jacques, S.L. Iterative reconstruction algorithm for optoacoustic imaging. *J. Acoust. Soc. Am.* **2002**, *112*, 1536–1544. [CrossRef]
19. Guan, S.; Khan, A.; Sikdar, S.; Chitnis, P. Fully Dense UNet for 2D Sparse Photoacoustic Tomography Artifact Removal. *IEEE J. Biomed. Health Inform.* **2019**, *24*, 568–576. [CrossRef] [PubMed]
20. Guan, S.; Khan, A.A.; Sikdar, S.; Chitnis, P.V. Limited-View and Sparse Photoacoustic Tomography for Neuroimaging with Deep Learning. *Sci. Rep.* **2020**, *10*, 8510. [CrossRef]
21. Antholzer, S.; Haltmeier, M.; Schwab, J. Deep learning for photoacoustic tomography from sparse data. *Inverse Probl. Sci. Eng.* **2019**, *27*, 987–1005. [CrossRef]
22. Hauptmann, A.; Lucka, F.; Betcke, M.M.; Huynh, N.; Adler, J.; Cox, B.T.; Beard, P.C.; Ourselin, S.; Arridge, S.R. Model-Based Learning for Accelerated, Limited-View 3-D Photoacoustic Tomography. *IEEE Trans. Med. Imaging* **2018**, *37*, 1382–1393. [CrossRef]
23. Baumann, B.; Wolff, M.; Kost, B.; Groninga, H. Finite element calculation of photoacoustic signals. *Appl. Opt.* **2007**, *46*, 1120–1125. [CrossRef] [PubMed]
24. Xia, W.; Piras, D.; van Hespen, J.C.G.; van Veldhoven, S.; Prins, C.; van Leeuwen, T.G.; Steenbergen, W.; Manohar, S. An optimized ultrasound detector for photoacoustic breast tomography. *Med. Phys.* **2013**, *40*, 032901. [CrossRef]
25. Raissi, M.; Perdikaris, P.; Karniadakis, G.E. Physics-informed neural networks: A deep learning framework for solving forward and inverse problems involving nonlinear partial differential equations. *J. Comput. Phys.* **2019**, *378*, 686–707. [CrossRef]
26. Greenfeld, D.; Galun, M.; Basri, R.; Yavneh, I.; Kimmel, R. Learning to Optimize Multigrid PDE Solvers, in International Conference on Machine Learning, May 2019, pp. 2415–2423. Available online: http://proceedings.mlr.press/v97/greenfeld19a.html (accessed on 22 May 2021).
27. Khoo, Y.; Lu, J.; Ying, L. Solving parametric PDE problems with artificial neural networks. *Eur. J. Appl. Math.* **2021**, *32*, 421–435. [CrossRef]
28. Adler, J.; Öktem, O. Solving ill-posed inverse problems using iterative deep neural networks. *Inverse Probl.* **2017**, *33*, 124007. [CrossRef]
29. E, W.; Yu, B. The Deep Ritz Method: A Deep Learning-Based Numerical Algorithm for Solving Variational Problems, ArXiv171000211 Cs Stat, September 2017. Available online: http://arxiv.org/abs/1710.00211 (accessed on 22 May 2021).
30. Lu, L.; Jin, P.; Karniadakis, G.E. DeepONet: Learning Nonlinear Operators for Identifying Differential Equations Based on the Universal Approximation Theorem of Operators, ArXiv191003193 Cs Stat, April 2020. Available online: http://arxiv.org/abs/1910.03193 (accessed on 22 May 2021).
31. Li, Z.; Kovachki, N.; Azizzadenesheli, K.; Liu, B.; Bhattacharya, K.; Stuart, A.; Anandkumar, A. Fourier Neural Operator for Parametric Partial Differential Equations, ArXiv201008895 Cs Math, October 2020. Available online: http://arxiv.org/abs/2010.08895 (accessed on 29 December 2020).
32. Beard, P. Biomedical photoacoustic imaging. *Interface Focus* **2011**, *1*, 602–631. [CrossRef] [PubMed]
33. Xu, M.; Wang, L.V. Universal back-projection algorithm for photoacoustic computed tomography. *Int. Soc. Opt. Photonics* **2005**, *5697*, 251–255. [CrossRef]
34. Treeby, B.E.; Zhang, E.Z.; Cox, B.T. Photoacoustic tomography in absorbing acoustic media using time reversal. *Inverse Probl.* **2010**, *26*, 115003. [CrossRef]
35. Piaggio, H.T.H. The Mathematical Theory of Huygens' Principle. *Nature* **1940**, *145*, 531–532. [CrossRef]
36. Tadmor, E. A review of numerical methods for nonlinear partial differential equations. *Bull. Am. Math. Soc.* **2012**, *49*, 507–554. [CrossRef]

37. Treeby, B.E.; Pan, J. A practical examination of the errors arising in the direct collocation boundary element method for acoustic scattering. *Eng. Anal. Bound. Elem.* **2009**, *33*, 1302–1315. [CrossRef]
38. Mast, T.D.; Souriau, L.P.; Liu, D.-L.D.; Tabei, M.; Nachman, A.I.; Waag, R.C. A k-space method for large-scale models of wave propagation in tissue. *IEEE Trans. Ultrason. Ferroelectr. Freq. Control* **2001**, *48*, 341–354. [CrossRef] [PubMed]
39. Treeby, B.E.; Jaros, J.; Rendell, A.P.; Cox, B.T. Modeling nonlinear ultrasound propagation in heterogeneous media with power law absorption using a k-space pseudospectral method. *J. Acoust. Soc. Am.* **2012**, *131*, 4324–4336. [CrossRef] [PubMed]
40. Badano, A.; Graff, C.G.; Badal, A.; Sharma, D.; Zeng, R.; Samuelson, F.W.; Glick, S.J.; Myers, K.J. Evaluation of Digital Breast Tomosynthesis as Replacement of Full-Field Digital Mammography Using an In Silico Imaging Trial. *JAMA Netw. Open* **2018**, *1*, e185474. [CrossRef] [PubMed]
41. Arridge, S.; Beard, P.; Betcke, M.; Cox, B.; Huynh, N.; Lucka, F.; Ogunlade, O.; Zhang, E. Accelerated high-resolution photoacoustic tomography via compressed sensing. *Phys. Med. Biol.* **2016**, *61*, 8908. [CrossRef]
42. Xian, Y.; Lampert, C.H.; Schiele, B.; Akata, Z. Zero-Shot Learning—A Comprehensive Evaluation of the Good, the Bad and the Ugly. *IEEE Trans. Pattern Anal. Mach. Intell.* **2019**, *41*, 2251–2265. [CrossRef]
43. Paszke, A.; Gross, S.; Massa, F.; Lerer, A.; Bradbury, J.; Chanan, G.; Killeen, T.; Lin, Z.; Gimelshein, N.; Antiga, L.; et al. PyTorch: An Imperative Style, High-Performance Deep Learning Library. *arXiv* **2019**, arXiv:1912.01703.
44. Wang, Z.; Bovik, A.C.; Sheikh, H.R.; Simoncelli, E.P. Image quality assessment: From error visibility to structural similarity. *IEEE Trans. Image Process.* **2004**, *13*, 600–612. [CrossRef]

Disclaimer/Publisher's Note: The statements, opinions and data contained in all publications are solely those of the individual author(s) and contributor(s) and not of MDPI and/or the editor(s). MDPI and/or the editor(s) disclaim responsibility for any injury to people or property resulting from any ideas, methods, instructions or products referred to in the content.

Article

Development and Implementation of an ANN Based Flow Law for Numerical Simulations of Thermo-Mechanical Processes at High Temperatures in FEM Software

Olivier Pantalé

Laboratoire Génie de Production, Institut National Polytechnique/Ecole Nationale d'Ingénieurs de Tarbes, Université de Toulouse, 47 Av d'Azereix, F-65016 Tarbes, France; olivier.pantale@enit.fr; Tel.: +33-562442933

Abstract: Numerical methods based on finite element (FE) have proven their efficiency for many years in the thermomechanical simulation of forming processes. Nevertheless, the application of these methods to new materials requires the identification and implementation of constitutive and flow laws within FE codes, which sometimes pose problems, particularly because of the strongly non-linear character of the behavior of these materials. Computational techniques based on machine learning and artificial neural networks are becoming more and more important in the development of these models and help the FE codes to integrate more complex behavior. In this paper, we present the development, implementation and use of an artificial neural network (ANN) based flow law for a GrC15 alloy under high temperature thermomechanical solicitations. The flow law modeling by ANN shows a significant superiority in terms of model prediction quality compared to classical approaches based on widely used Johnson–Cook or Arrhenius models. Once the ANN parameters have been identified on the base of experiments, the implementation of this flow law in a finite element code shows promising results in terms of solution quality and respect of the material behavior.

Keywords: ANN flow law; constitutive behavior; radial return algorithm; numerical implementation; VUHARD; GrC15; Abaqus Explicit

1. Introduction

Numerical methods for simulating the behavior of structures subjected to high thermomechanical loads, as in the case of the high-temperature forming of metallic materials, are generally based on the use of commercial finite element (FE) codes, such as Abaqus, or laboratory codes, such as DynELA [1]. These FE codes are based on two types of equations: conservation equations and constitutive equations. If the first equations are well established on the basis of physics and mechanics, it is not the same for the second type of equations: the constitutive equations. Thus, in a general way, the conservation equations concern the fundamental principles of physics, such as the mass conservation law, the momentum law (fundamental equation) and the energy law (declined as the first and second principles of thermodynamics). By themselves, these laws are not sufficient to describe the behavior of a material or a structure subjected to thermomechanical solicitations because the nature of the material's behavior translated through the behavior laws is not included in the system previously proposed. Therefore, for each type of material, it is necessary to define behavior laws whose formulation is based on observation in order to describe the behavior of this material under external forces. The quality and the accuracy of the results of any numerical simulation depend on the choice of these behavior laws and on the ability of the user to identify the coefficients of these behavior laws for a given material by performing experiments under conditions close to those encountered during the real stress of the structure in service that one wishes to design [2]. Depending on the nature of the solicitations, these tests are based on quasi-static or dynamic tensile or compression tests, tests on thermomechanical simulators such as Gleeble [3] or impact tests using gas launchers or Hopkinson bars [4].

In the thermomechanical simulation of forming processes, these behavior laws define the dependence [5] of the flow stress of the material σ^y as a function of the three input variables, which are the plastic strain ε^p, the strain rate $\dot{\varepsilon}$ and the temperature T of the material, so that the general form of the flow law can be written with the following expression:

$$\sigma^y = f(\varepsilon^p, \dot{\varepsilon}, T) \qquad (1)$$

These laws, due to the nature of materials and the phenomena involved [6,7] (work hardening, movement of dislocations, structural hardening, phase transformations, etc.) are highly non-linear, and their validity is restricted to a certain range of strains ε, strain rates $\dot{\varepsilon}$ and temperatures T. From the observations made, we can define two main classes of behavior laws: the flow laws based on physics and the empirical flow laws. From the mechanics of continuous media and experimental tests and depending on the materials used, several flow models have been developed in the past, including the Johnson–Cook flow law [8,9], the Zerilli–Armstrong flow law [10] and their respective derived forms [11–19], the Hansel–Spittle [20,21] or the Arrhenius [22–24] flow laws, to name only a few of the most widely used in the metal-forming processes at high temperature. As an example, and because it is widely used in numerical simulation of metal forming processes, the equation that describes the Johnson–Cook flow law [8] is given as follows:

$$\sigma^y = \left(A + B\varepsilon^{p^n}\right)\left[1 + C\ln\left(\frac{\dot{\varepsilon}}{\dot{\varepsilon}_0}\right)\right]\left[1 - \left(\frac{T - T_0}{T_m - T_0}\right)^m\right], \qquad (2)$$

where A is the initial elastic limit of the material, B is the strain hardening coefficient, n is the strain hardening exponent, and C and m are the material constants that describe the strain rate hardening coefficient and the thermal softening coefficient, respectively. The Johnson–Cook model is the most widely used because it is simple to identify and use and has few parameters to determine [25,26].

Once the choice has been made concerning the type of flow law to be used for a material, it is then necessary, from a set of experimental tests carried out in the laboratory under conditions close to those of the structure in service, to identify the parameters of these flow laws by machine learning methods based on approaches of minimization of the calculated experiment. Therefore, the use of the Johnson–Cook flow law defined by Equation (2) requires the identification of 5 material parameters.

The main problem that researchers are confronted with after the phase of realization of the experimental tests concerns the choice of the flow law to use according to the observations made on these test results. This choice of flow law is also restricted by the FE code used and the availability of such flow laws. Thus, a user of the Abaqus FE code will turn more particularly to a Johnson–Cook [8] flow law, where it is natively implemented in this software. The choice of another form of flow law, Zerilli–Armstrong, or Arrhenius, for example, obliges the user to program himself the computation of the flow stress σ^y of the material through a VUMAT subroutine in FORTRAN 77 as proposed by Gao et al. [27], Ming et al. [28] for a Johnson–Cook flow law, or Liang et al. [24] for an Arrhenius type flow law with the following expression:

$$\sigma^y = \frac{1}{\alpha(\varepsilon)}\ln\left\{\left(\frac{Z(\varepsilon)}{A(\varepsilon)}\right)^{1/n(\varepsilon)} + \sqrt{1 + \left(\frac{Z(\varepsilon)}{A(\varepsilon)}\right)^{2/n(\varepsilon)}}\right\} \qquad (3)$$

with

$$Z(\varepsilon) = \dot{\varepsilon}\exp\left(\frac{Q(\varepsilon)}{RT}\right), \qquad (4)$$

where Z is the Zenner–Hollomon parameter [29], $Q(\varepsilon)$ is the apparent activation energy (J mol^{-1}), R is the universal gas constant (8.314 J mol^{-1}K^{-1}). $Q(\varepsilon)$, $A(\varepsilon)$, $\alpha(\varepsilon)$ and $n(\varepsilon)$ are expressed as a function of the strain ε through polynomial functions of degree m (varying from 1 to 9), which leads to the identification of up to 36 material parameters.

Implementing the flow law as a VUMAT FORTRAN subroutine requires the computation of the derivatives $\partial \sigma^y / \partial \varepsilon^p$, $\partial \sigma^y / \partial \dot{\varepsilon}$ and $\partial \sigma^y / \partial T$ of the flow stress σ^y, which can quickly become relatively complex as the complexity of the flow law increases, i.e., the relative complexity of the Arrhenius flow law defined by Equations (3) and (4), regarding the relative simplicity of the Johnson–Cook model defined by Equation (2), one can refer to the work proposed by Liang et al. [24] for details concerning this implementation using the safe version of the Newton–Raphson method proposed by Ming et al. [28]. The choice of the flow law to use for a problem is therefore doubly guided by the behavior of the material on the one hand, but a more important aspect is the list of flow laws implemented natively in the FE code we plan to use for the numerical simulation. At this time, there is not yet a flow law generic enough to cover a wide range of material behavior that is simple to implement and use.

As we have seen in the previous paragraph, the choice of the flow law to use is guided mainly by the list of flow laws available in the finite element code used, and very often, this choice is made at the expense of the quality of the model. For example, Zhou et al. [14], proposed the identification of the flow law of a GCr15 alloy for a continuous casting bloom with heavy reduction application as introduced by Ji et al. [30], who performed compression tests on this material. In their study, Ji et al. [30] performed compression tests on GCr15 cylinders in a temperature range of 750 °C to 1300 °C in 50 °C steps, strain rates of 0.001 s^{-1}, 0.01 s^{-1} and 0.1 s^{-1} and strains up-to 0.7. The results of these compression tests, plotted in Figure 1, show a decrease in flow stress σ^y with respect to an increase in the temperature T and a increase of σ^y with respect to an increase in the strain rate $\dot{\varepsilon}$, as in most metallic materials.

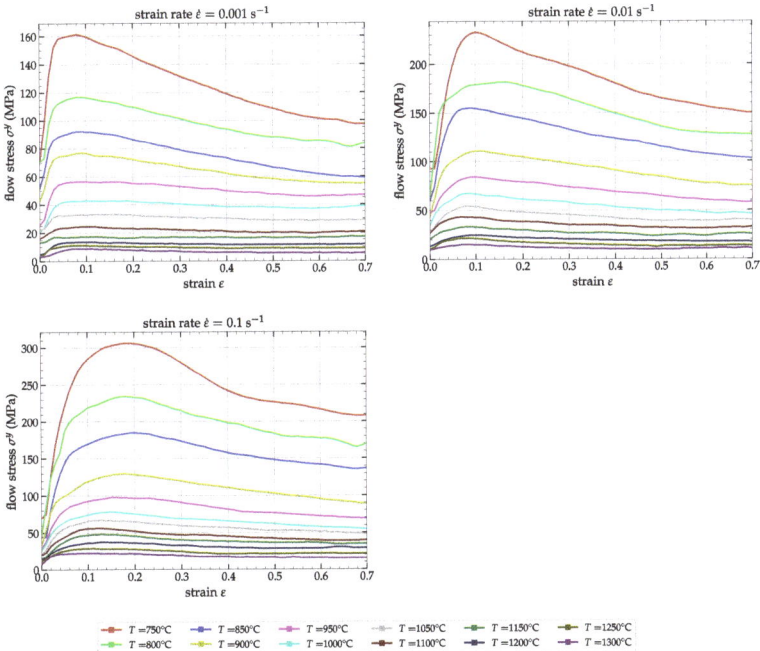

Figure 1. Original data extracted from the publication of Ji et al. [30].

The evolution of the flow stress as a function of the plastic deformation shows the presence of a dynamic recrystallization (DRX) phenomenon within the material. This phenomenon is an additional non-linearity of this type of material compared to other materials, mainly because of high temperatures and low strain rates, which should be considered when describing the material behavior. As stated in the publication of Zhou et al. [14], depending on the flow model used—Johnson–Cook, modified Zerilli–Armstrong, Arrhenius or new modified Johnson–Cook—the fidelity of considering the real behavior varies widely with the complexity of the flow model, which includes between 5 parameters for the Johnson–Cook model and 16 parameters for the Arrhenius model. Thus, and for the input data provided by Ji et al. [30], the two most common models, Johnson–Cook and Zerilli–Armstrong do not correctly describe the material behavior. Only the modified Johnson–Cook and Arrhenius models can describe correctly the behavior of the material during the compression process. Unfortunately, and this is not part of their study, if these last two models are satisfactory from a theoretical point of view, from a practical point of view for the user of a FE code such as Abaqus, it will be necessary to carry out a numerical implementation in a FORTRAN 77 VUMAT subroutine of the modified Johnson–Cook flow law or the Arrhenius law as carried out by a few authors [24,27,28] to use these laws for numerical simulation. This requires a certain expertise in the development and implementation of flow laws, which is not available to all users of the Abaqus FE code.

From this observation, and from the necessity to select a flow law for a type of material, then to identify the parameters of this flow law according to experimental tests, and finally to implement this flow law as a user subroutine in FORTRAN in the Abaqus FE code, we recently proposed in Pantalé et al. [31] an alternative approach based on the ability of artificial neural networks (ANNs) to behave as universal approximators as reported by Minsky et al. [32] and Hornik et al. [33]. In fact, artificial neural networks can solve problems that are difficult to conceptualize using traditional computational methods. Unlike a classical approach based on a regression method, an ANN does not need to know the mathematical form of the model it seeks to reproduce; hence, we do not need anymore to postulate the mathematical form of the constitutive equation to use it in a FE simulation using this kind of approach. Using a neural network instead of an analytical constitutive law can lead to a bias related to the validity of the answers according to the domain of use and the learning domain. Thus, if ANNs are efficient for the interpolation of results inside the learning domain, their behavior outside of it is not controlled. Therefore, if the input values are far from those provided during the training, the outputs can be far from the physical reality of the process. It is, of course, the same for analytical laws when modeling non-linear behavior, but if the choice of the model is made properly, based on physical considerations, they will provide results closer to reality than the ANN model. Therefore, care should be taken when using ANN-based flow laws, and the validity of the model input data should always be verified.

Implementing ANNs for plasticity in thermomechanics has been studied, and a review of the literature can be found, for example, in the work of Gorji et al. [34] concerning the use of recurrent neural networks, in that of Jamli et al. [35] concerning their application in finite element analysis of metal forming processes, or in that of Jiao et al. [36] concerning the applicability to meta-materials and their characterization. A distinction must be made between ANN-based flow models (the focus of this study) and ANN-based constitutive models. Both approaches have been studied by many researchers during the last thirty years. Ghaboussi [37] proposed an ANN-based constitutive model for concrete under monotonic biaxial loading and cyclic uniaxial loading. They extended their work by introducing adaptive and auto-progressive networks in [38,39], where the architecture of the network evolves during the learning phase to better learn the complex stress–strain behavior of the materials using a global load-deflection response, where the evaluation of the flow stress of the material computed by the ANN is combined with a radial return algorithm. Lin et al. [40] proposed an ANN to predict the flow stress of 42CrMo4 steel in hot compression tests on a Gleeble thermomechanical device and showed a very good correlation between the experimental results and the model predictions. Ashtiani et al. [41] compared the predictive capabilities of an ANN versus an analytical model for Johnson–Cook, Arrhenius, and strain-compensated Arrhenius laws and concluded that the neural network had better efficiency and accuracy in predicting the hot behavior of the Al–Cu–Mg–Pb alloy.

The underlying idea proposed in our approach is to implement a flow law described by a trained ANN as a FORTRAN 77 subroutine in the Abaqus FE code. This ANN was previously trained from the data extracted from mechanical tests of the material and can directly define the value of the flow stress σ^y as a function of the plastic strain ε^p, the strain rate $\dot{\varepsilon}$ and the temperature T. After a training phase based on the use of the Python library TensorFlow [42,43], the weights and biases of the trained neural network are transcoded into a subroutine in FORTRAN 77, which is compiled and linked with the libraries of the Abaqus FE code to include the behavior of the material by allowing the computation of the flow stress σ^y as a function of ε^p, $\dot{\varepsilon}$ and T, and of its three derivatives $\partial \sigma^y / \partial \varepsilon^p$, $\partial \sigma^y / \partial \dot{\varepsilon}$ and $\partial \sigma^y / \partial T$.

The structure of this paper is as follows: Section 2 addresses the presentation of a neural-network-based flow law and its training from the data proposed by Ji et al. [30] and reported in Figure 1. The comparison of several neural network architectures regarding accuracy and implementation complexity will be presented and compared. In Section 3, we will present the transposition of this neural network into a FORTRAN 77 subroutine for the Abaqus FE code. Validation is based on the numerical simulation Abaqus Explicit FE code of a compression test in the same configuration as the one proposed by Ji et al. [30] using four different ANN flow laws. In this Section, we will present the problems of overfitting the neural network and its visible consequences on the results concerning numerical simulations. Finally, a conclusion and perspective section will conclude this paper.

2. Training of the ANN Flow Law

In this section, we briefly recall, as an introduction, some basic principles of artificial neural networks that apply to this work. The global architecture chosen to model the behavior of a material is based on a multi-layer feed-forward ANN, which, as proposed by Hornik et al. [33], can be used as a universal approximator. The architecture retained for this study concerns a neural network with two hidden layers containing a variable number of neurons on these two layers, 3 input nodes corresponding to the plastic strain ε^p, the strain rate $\dot{\varepsilon}$ and the temperature T, respectively, and a single output node for the flow stress σ^y of the material. Figure 2 shows a graphical representation of the global architecture of this neural network.

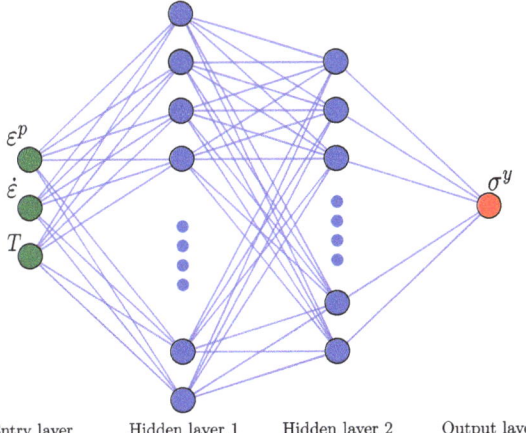

Figure 2. Global structure of the ANN flow law with two hidden layers, 3 input neurons (ε^p, $\dot{\varepsilon}$, T) and one output neuron σ^y.

The choice of the number of neurons in the two hidden layers is free, but must be reasonable. Indeed, the more neurons the network contains, the more it will reproduce faithfully the training data, but the less it will generalize to new data (the classical problem of the over-learning of neural networks). Moreover, the more neurons it contains, the more complex its mathematical structure will be, and the more computation time it will require for propagating the data inside of it within the routine included in the FE code. It is therefore necessary to respect a balance between the capacity of the network to minimize errors during the learning phase, its complexity and the computing CPU time once it is transcribed into the FE code.

2.1. Neural Network Governing Equations

According to Figure 2, the proposed neural network has 3 inputs (referred as the input vector $\vec{x}$) corresponding to the plastic strain ε^p, the strain rate $\dot{\varepsilon}$ and the temperature T, respectively. These inputs are first normalized within the range $[0, 1]$ to avoid an ill-conditioning of the system as presented by many other authors in the literature [40,44] since these three variables represent different physical data with very different amplitudes (0.7 for the plastic strain, 100 s^{-1} for the strain rate and 550 °C for the temperature in the case of the training data reported in Figure 1). Therefore, the three components of the input vector $\vec{x}$ are coming from the plastic strain ε^p, the strain rate $\dot{\varepsilon}$ and the temperature T using the following expressions:

$$\vec{x} = \begin{cases} x_1 = \frac{\varepsilon^p - [\varepsilon^p]_{min}}{[\varepsilon^p]_{max} - [\varepsilon^p]_{min}} \\ x_2 = \frac{\ln(\dot{\varepsilon}/\dot{\varepsilon}_0) - [\ln(\dot{\varepsilon}/\dot{\varepsilon}_0)]_{min}}{[\ln(\dot{\varepsilon}/\dot{\varepsilon}_0)]_{max} - [\ln(\dot{\varepsilon}/\dot{\varepsilon}_0)]_{min}} \\ x_3 = \frac{T - [T]_{min}}{[T]_{max} - [T]_{min}} \end{cases}, \quad (5)$$

where $[\ ]_{min}$ and $[\ ]_{max}$ are the boundaries of the range of the corresponding field. Concerning the strain rate $\dot{\varepsilon}$, and considering that its amplitude in a real case can reach 10^5 s^{-1}, as proposed in Pantalé et al. [31], we chose initially to substitute $\ln(\dot{\varepsilon}/\dot{\varepsilon}_0)$, with $\dot{\varepsilon}_0$ equal to the lowest strain rate test, for the value of $\dot{\varepsilon}$. After normalization, these three input variables are introduced into the neural network and are propagated within it by the feed-forward propagation mechanism.

Conforming to the structure of the ANN reported in Figure 2 any hidden layer k, containing n neurons, takes a weighted sum of the outputs $\vec{\hat{y}}^{(k-1)}$ of the immediately previous layer $(k-1)$, containing m neurons, given by the following equation:

$$y_i^{(k)} = \sum_{j=1}^{m} w_{ij}^{(k)} \hat{y}_j^{(k-1)} + b_i^{(k)}, \quad (6)$$

where $y_i^{(k)}$ is the entry of the ith neuron of layer k, $\hat{y}_j^{(k-1)}$ is the output of the jth neuron of layer $(k-1)$, $w_{ij}^{(k)}$ is the associated weight parameter between the ith neuron of layer k and the jth neuron of layer $(k-1)$ and $b_i^{(k)}$ is the associated bias of the ith neuron of layer k. Those weights w_{ij} and bias b_i, for each layer, are the training parameters of the ANN that we have to adjust during the training process. For the proposed model, we selected the sigmoid activation function so that each neuron in the hidden layer k provides an output value $\hat{y}$ from the input value y of the same neuron defined by Equation (6) according to the following equation:

$$\hat{y} = \frac{1}{1 + e^{-y}} \quad (7)$$

According to Equations (6) and (7), the output of each of the two hidden layers ($\vec{y}_1$ for the first hidden layer and $\vec{y}_2$ for the second hidden layer) are given by the following two equations:

$$\vec{y}_1 = \left[1 + \exp\left(-\mathbf{w}_1 \cdot \vec{x} - \vec{b}_1\right)\right]^{-1} \tag{8}$$

$$\vec{y}_2 = \left[1 + \exp\left(-\mathbf{w}_2 \cdot \vec{y}_1 - \vec{b}_2\right)\right]^{-1} \tag{9}$$

Then we compute the output s of the ANN from the output vector of the second hidden layer $\vec{y}_2$ using the following equation:

$$s = \vec{w}^T \cdot \vec{y}_2 + b \tag{10}$$

Finally, since no activation function is used for the output neuron of the ANN as is usually done in regression ANN, the flow stress σ^y can be obtained from the output s using the following equation:

$$\sigma^y = ([\sigma]_{max} - [\sigma]_{min})s + [\sigma]_{min} \tag{11}$$

2.2. Computation of the Derivatives of the Neural Network

As introduced in Section 1, implementing a flow law in a FE code requires both the computation of the flow stress σ^y as a function of the input data, performed using the previous Equations (5)–(11), but also the evaluation of the three derivatives of σ^y with respect to the input data to use a Newton–Raphson algorithm within the stress integration scheme, as proposed by many authors [24,28,45,46] based on the radial return algorithm in the Abaqus FE code. It is, therefore, necessary to perform a numerical evaluation of these three derivatives based on the ANN to obtain these quantities. It seems obvious that it is not possible to train a neural network to evaluate these values of derivatives insofar as the training data are not physically collectible data during the experimental tests. It is, therefore, necessary to predict these derivatives from the neural network architecture itself. One straightforward, but not recommended, solution to this problem is to compute numerically the derivative of σ^y with respect to ε^p, $\dot{\varepsilon}$ and T using the following relation:

$$\frac{\partial \sigma(x)}{\partial x} = \frac{\sigma(x + \delta x) - \sigma(x)}{\delta x}, \tag{12}$$

where δx is a small increase ($\delta x = 10^{-6}$ for example) applied to one of the 3 variables ε^p, $\dot{\varepsilon}$ and T. As reported in [31], we need to compute a result from the ANN 4 times to compute the flow stress and approximate the three derivatives, which is quite time consuming. The solution for this study consists, insofar as the architecture of the neural network is known through Equations (6)–(10), in analytically deriving the output s of the network with respect to the input $\vec{x}$, then integrating the data normalization operations defined by Equations (5) and (11). Given Equations (5)–(11), we can then establish in the case of a neural network containing two hidden layers and a sigmoid activation function on the two hidden layers that the derivative of σ^y with respect to the input data ε^p, $\dot{\varepsilon}$ and T is given by the following procedure.

- First, we compute the internal terms of the ANN to compute the derivative of the ANN with respect to the input vector $\vec{x}$:

$$\begin{cases} \vec{z}_1 = \exp\left(-\mathbf{w}_1 \cdot \vec{x} - \vec{b}_1\right) \\ \vec{z}_2 = \exp\left(\mathbf{w}_2 \cdot \frac{1}{1+\vec{z}_1} + \vec{b}_2\right) \\ \vec{z}_3 = \vec{w} \circ \frac{\vec{z}_2}{(1+\vec{z}_2)^2} \\ \vec{z}_4 = \frac{\vec{z}_1}{(1+\vec{z}_1)^2} \end{cases}, \tag{13}$$

- where ∘ is the element-wise product, known as the Hadamard product, which is a binary operation that takes two matrices A and B of the same dimensions and produces another matrix C of the same dimension as the operands, where each element $C_i = A_i B_i$.
- Then, from the two terms $\vec{z}_3$ and $\vec{z}_4$, we can therefore compute the three derivatives of the output s with respect to the input vector $\vec{x}$ with the following equation, where $\vec{s}'$ is a vector of 3 components containing the 3 derivatives $\partial s/\partial \varepsilon^p$, $\partial s/\partial \dot{\varepsilon}$ and $\partial s/\partial T$:

$$\vec{s}' = \mathbf{w}_1^T \cdot \left[\left(\mathbf{w}_2^T \cdot \vec{z}_3\right) \circ \vec{z}_4\right] \tag{14}$$

- Finally, from Equation (14) and conforming to the normalization of the inputs introduced earlier, one can obtain the 3 derivatives of the yield stress σ^y with respect to the three inputs ε^p, $\dot{\varepsilon}$ and T using the following final equation:

$$\begin{cases} \partial \sigma/\partial \varepsilon^p = s'_1 \frac{[\sigma]_{max} - [\sigma]_{min}}{[\varepsilon^p]_{max} - [\varepsilon^p]_{min}} \\ \partial \sigma/\partial \dot{\varepsilon} = \frac{s'_2}{\dot{\varepsilon}} \frac{[\sigma]_{max} - [\sigma]_{min}}{[\dot{\varepsilon}]_{max} - [\dot{\varepsilon}]_{min}} \\ \partial \sigma/\partial T = s'_3 \frac{[\sigma]_{max} - [\sigma]_{min}}{[T]_{max} - [T]_{min}} \end{cases} \tag{15}$$

Equations (13)–(15) define the derivatives of the yield stress σ^y with respect to ε^p, $\dot{\varepsilon}$ and T, as computed by the ANN, and, as shown in [31], these derivatives can be used for the numerical implementation of the ANN constitutive law in a FE code.

2.3. Training of the Neural Networks

In neural network learning, it is necessary to define the objective function to be minimized and the evaluation of the model error. In this study, the error evaluation is based on the mean square error (E_{MS}) and the root mean square error (E_{RMS}) given by the following equation:

$$E_{RMS}(\text{MPa}) = \sqrt{E_{MS}} = \sqrt{\frac{1}{N}\sum_{i=1}^{N}\left(\sigma_i^e - \sigma_i^y\right)^2}, \tag{16}$$

where N is the total number of numerical training data used, σ_i^y is the ith value predicted by the neural network, and σ_i^e is the corresponding experimental value coming from the experimental tests. The accuracy and predictive ability of the models is assessed by the mean absolute relative error (E_{MAR}) defined by Equation (17):

$$E_{MAR}(\%) = \frac{1}{N}\sum_{i=1}^{N}\left|\frac{\sigma_i^y - \sigma_i^e}{\sigma_i^e}\right| \times 100 \tag{17}$$

The numerical implementation of the learning phase of the neural network was done in Python language, using the TensorFlow library [42,43]. The minimization procedure of the objective function is based on the use of the adaptive moment estimation (ADAM) solver proposed by Kingma et al. [47].

The training data used in this section are taken from the publication of Ji et al. [30]. Thus, data for which compression tests were performed for the 3 strain rates $\dot{\varepsilon} = 0.001$ s^{-1}, $\dot{\varepsilon} = 0.01$ s^{-1} and $\dot{\varepsilon} = 0.1$ s^{-1}, and the 12 temperature values between 750 °C and 1300 °C in 50 °C steps are used. For each pair of data ($\dot{\varepsilon}$, T), we have a record of 71 values of flow stress σ^e corresponding to values of deformation between 0 and 0.7, regularly spaced of 0.01. We use a database of 2556 quadruplets of values (ε^p, $\dot{\varepsilon}$, T, σ^e) for the training of the ANNs.

The set of these data is used as training data for the neural network. Several neural network architectures have been studied in this work; they differ from each other by the number of neurons present in the two hidden layers. Among them, we selected 4 different architectures named 3-7-4-1, 3-9-4-1, 3-9-7-1 and 3-15-7-1 for which the name 3-n-m-1 translates an ANN with 2 hidden layers, having n neurons on the first layer and m neurons on the second layer.

All models have been trained for the same number of iterations (50,000 iterations), and around 50 min of training on a Dell XPS-13 7390 laptop running Ubuntu 22.04 LTS 64 bits with 16 GB of RAM and an Intel 4-core i7-10510U processor allow obtaining the converged parameters of the ANN models. Figure 3 shows the evolution of the training error defined by the $\log_{10}$ of the mean square error ($\log_{10}[E_{MS}]$) during the training phase.

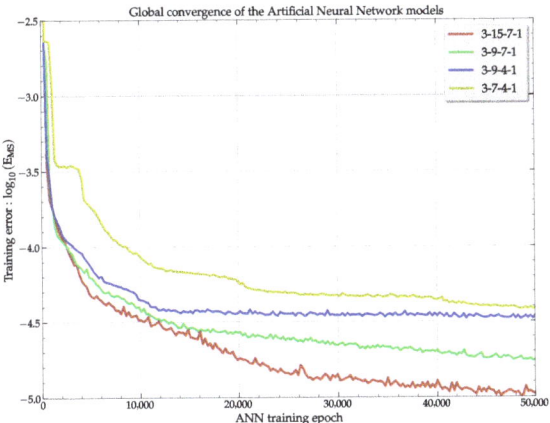

Figure 3. Convergence of the ANN models during the training phase.

As we can see on this figure, after 50,000 iterations, we can consider that we have reached a stationary state of the model learning and that it is useless to continue the learning phase. As expected, the more neurons the model contains, the more it can follow the non-linear evolution of the material's behavior and therefore the more the mean square error (E_{MS}) during the learning phase decreases. Table 1 shows the main results of the training of these neural networks.

Table 1. Results concerning the training of the four ANN flow laws.

ANN	n_v	t (min)	E_{MS} $\times 10^{-5}$	E_{MAR} (%)	E_{RMS} (MPa)
3-7-4-1	65	48	3.91	1.88	3.05
3-9-4-1	81	48	3.29	1.70	2.75
3-9-7-1	114	49	1.83	1.25	2.44
3-15-7-1	180	50	1.01	0.97	2.30

It can be noted that the number of internal variables n_v of the networks varies from 65 to 180 for the most complex and the most powerful one, but that this complexity has no real influence on the learning time t which oscillates around a value of 50 min, regardless of the architecture chosen. Concerning the internal accuracy E_{MS} of the network, it varies in proportions in accordance with the graphical representation of Figure 3. From the plot in Figure 3 and the results reported in Table 1, the user would normally be tempted to select the most complex model, namely 3-15-7-1, as it gives the smallest deviation between predicted and experimental values of flow stress σ^y. This will be analyzed in the next section concerning the numerical simulation of the compression of a cylinder on the Abaqus Explicit software using the ANN flow law.

Since, as reported in Figure 3, the 3-7-4-1 model seems to have converged after the training phase, we are going to compare it with the 'accurate' model, the 3-15-7-1 model. From a more physical point of view, Figures 4 and 5 show the correlation between the data predicted by the neural network and the experimental data for the 3-7-4-1 and 3-15-7-1 networks, respectively.

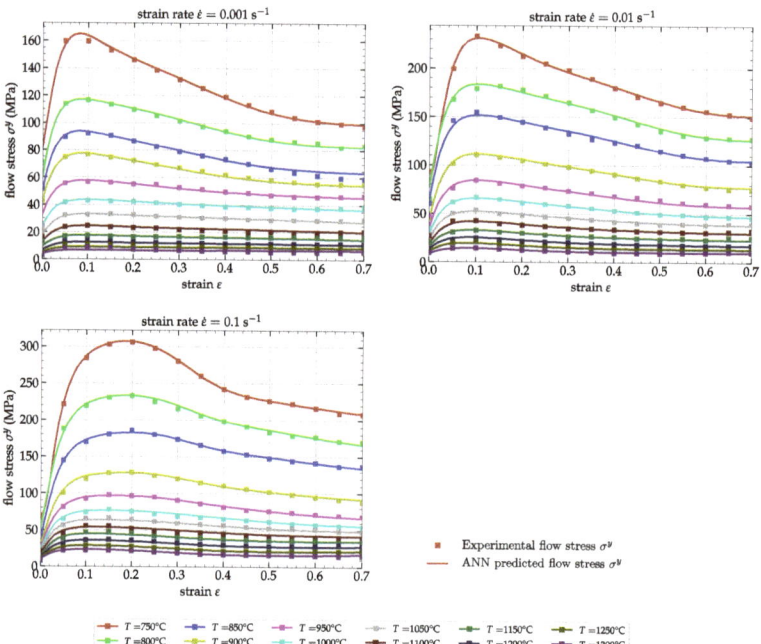

Figure 4. Comparison of the flow stress σ^y predicted by the 3-7-4-1 ANN (continuous line) and the experimental data for the GCr15 (square markers).

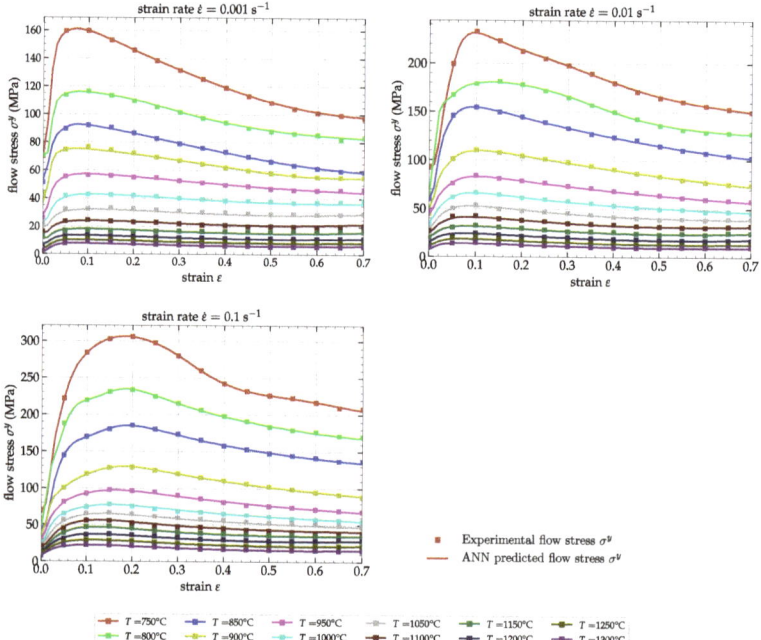

Figure 5. Comparison of the flow stress σ^y predicted by the 3-15-7-1 ANN (continuous line) and the experimental data for the GCr15 (square markers).

Analysis of Figures 4 and 5 shows a very good correlation between the ANN results and the experimental results, which is reflected by the very low values of the E_{MAR} and E_{RMS} coefficients reported in Table 1. As reported by Phaniraj [48], the correlation coefficient (R) is generally not a good measure in our case of study because it only shows the correlation of the model with respect to the data and not its accuracy, which is a determining factor in the qualification of a model. Therefore, this type of coefficient is not used in this work for comparing the different models.

Concerning the performance of the ANN flow laws, the correlation results for both reported models, are much better than the ones obtained by Zhou et al. [14] during his work on the same material with four different analytical flow laws, especially since he had to split the data into two groups according to the temperature value (one on the range $T = 750$–$850\ °C$ and one on the range $T = 850$–$1300\ °C$) and to identify two sets of parameters for each flow law to reduce the error of his identified analytical models. This of course raises the question of the usability of those analytical laws where the temperature of the material changes from one group to the other during a thermomechanical transformation.

In our approach and by using an ANN flow law, the identified law is not only valid over the whole temperature range, but it displays a E_{MAR} value 5 times lower than the best flow law proposed by Zhou et al. [14]: the Arrhenius law with an $E_{MAR} = 3.74\%$ over the range $T = 750$–$850\ °C$ and $E_{MAR} = 5.76\%$ over the range $T = 850$–$1300\ °C$, while the $E_{MAR} = 0.97\%$ for the 3-15-7-1 and $E_{MAR} = 1.88\%$ for the 3-7-4-1 ANN flow laws proposed here.

The disadvantage of developing a flow law model based on neural networks is the number of internal variables in the network (180 in the case of the 3-15-7-1 network), which makes it difficult to translate the network into printable results. Using a Johnson–Cook-type flow law, for example, allows the reader to quickly get an idea of the law, where the analytical formulation of the law is known to the users, and the behavior of a material is based on the knowledge of only 5 internal parameters to be identified, which makes it easy to publish in a table. Concerning an Arrhenius law, this task becomes a little more complex, as one can have from 24 to 36 coefficients. However, in our case, the publication of the 65 coefficients of the 3-7-4-1 model or the 180 coefficients of the 3-15-7-1 model makes this task delicate. As an illustration, we provide in the Appendix A all the coefficients of the 3-7-4-1 model identified during this study.

Once the identification phase is complete, it is now necessary to transpose this ANN model into a subroutine in FORTRAN or C++ that can be used by a FE code, such as Abaqus (for the FORTRAN 77 version) or DynELA (for the C++ version not presented in this paper). This is the main topic of the next section.

3. ANN Flow Law Implementation in FE Software

Once the neural network is trained as presented in Section 2.3, it can be used in a finite element code for the numerical simulation of a structure subjected to thermomechanical loading. This requires the extraction of the internal variables of the neural network and their transfer as a subroutine in FORTRAN 77 based on equations proposed in Sections 2.1 and 2.2.

3.1. Implementation of the ANN Flow Law

If we refer to the general flowchart of a finite element code as shown in Figure 6, integrating the flow law described by the ANN concerns the computation of the stress tensor σ_1 at the end of an increment, in the yellow rectangle on the figure.

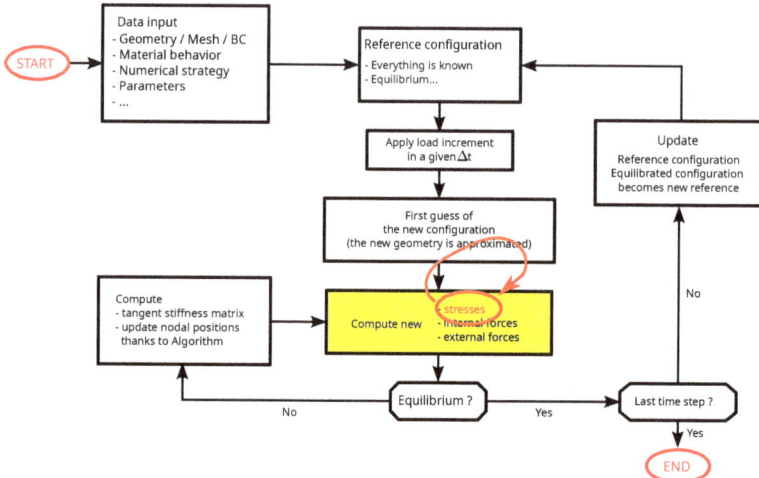

Figure 6. General flowchart of a FE code, focus on the stresses computation using an iterative solving procedure.

Within the framework of a FE formulation in large deformations such as the one used in thermomechanical modeling of processes, this computation of the stress tensor σ_1 is to be carried out on all the integration points of each element of the studied structure. Since the numerical model can include thousands of elements, themselves comprising between 1 and 8 integration points depending on the elements used, this stress computation must be as fast as possible in order not to increase the CPU time too much, but precise enough so that the results are under the physics of the process. This is even more important if we want to integrate this flow law in an explicit FE code, such as Abaqus/Explicit, for which one second of physical simulation corresponds to several million iterations of these stress computations. Thus, the complexity of the ANN, i.e., the number of computational steps that must be performed to compute the flow stress as a function of the input variables, is a major parameter in the choice of the neural network. As an example, for the model presented in Section 2.3, 180 internal variables, 15 neurons on the first hidden layer and 7 neurons on the second hidden layer were listed. Given the equations described in Sections 2.1 and 2.2, it will be necessary to compute 22 exponentials, to make matrix–vector products of size 15×3 and 15×7 plus many other numerical operations to compute the flow stress σ^y and the 3 derivatives of it with respect to ε^p, $\dot{\varepsilon}$ and T.

Implementing the ANN flow law identified above is realized here in a VUHARD subroutine, similarly as proposed by van Rensburg et al. [49], used by the Abaqus Explicit FE code in order to allow a user to program the computation of the flow stress σ^y and its 3 derivatives as a function of the model input data. This subroutine is used when calculating the stress tensor σ_1 at the end of an increment from the stress tensor at the beginning of the increment σ_0, the deformations, the material parameters and the history of the deformation at each finite element integration points, according to the stress integration algorithm based on the radial return method as described in Simo et al. [46] for the general aspects, Ming et al. [28] for Abaqus Explicit FE code, or Pantalé et al. [1] for the DynELA FE code. Thus, without going into too much detail about the stress integration scheme used in finite element codes (the curious reader can refer to [1,24,28,45] for details about this method), Figure 7 shows the location of the VUHARD subroutine used to compute the flow stress σ^y and its derivative $\partial \sigma^y / \partial \Gamma$ used in the writing of the two quantities $\gamma(\Gamma)$ and $\gamma'(\Gamma)$ used in the Newton–Raphson solving procedure from the following relation:

$$\frac{d\sigma^y}{d\Gamma} = \sqrt{\frac{2}{3}} \left(\frac{\partial \sigma^y}{\partial \varepsilon^p} + \frac{1}{\Delta t} \frac{\partial \sigma^y}{\partial \dot{\varepsilon}^p} + \frac{\eta \sigma^y}{\rho C_p} \frac{\partial \sigma^y}{\partial T} \right), \tag{18}$$

where Γ is the consistency parameter used in the radial return algorithm as defined by Simo et al. [46], Δt is the time increment, η is the Taylor–Quinney coefficient defining the amount of plastic work converted into heat energy, C_p is the specific heat coefficient, ρ is the density of the material and $\partial \sigma^y / \partial \varepsilon^p$, $\partial \sigma^y / \partial \dot{\varepsilon}$ and $\partial \sigma^y / \partial T$ are the three derivatives defined in Equation (15).

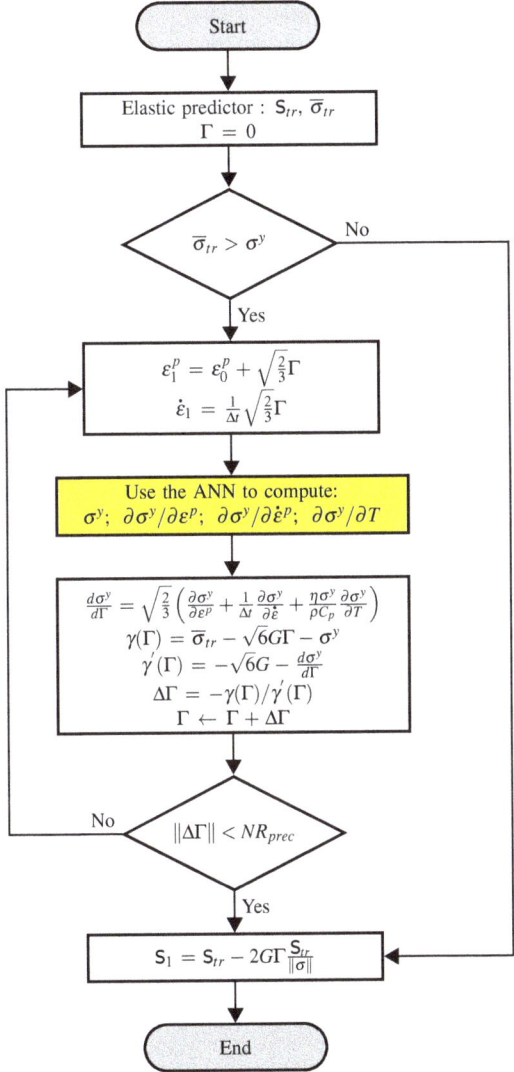

Figure 7. General flowchart of the radial return algorithm to compute the final stress tensor σ_1.

3.2. Numerical Simulations and Benchmarks Tests

To validate the proposed approach and to compare the different neural network architectures proposed in Section 2.3, we propose here to simulate on the Abaqus Explicit FE code the high-temperature compression of a cylinder on a Gleeble-type thermomechanical device. We consider a cylinder in compression with an initial diameter $d_0 = 8$ mm and an initial height $h_0 = 12$ mm made of GCr15 material, for which the final height after compression is $h = 6$ mm, which is a reduction of 50% of its total height. The compression of the sample is done in 10 s so that the strain rate $\dot{\varepsilon}$ is in the corresponding range of the characterization of the material behavior defined by Ji et al. [30]. Concerning the flow laws, the 4 models presented in Section 2.3 will be used and compared between them. Unfortunately, it is not possible here to compare these results with the experimental results, even if the initial shape of the specimen is the same, as these are not available in the references of the work of Zhou et al. [14] or Ji et al. [30].

The mesh of the sample is made with 850 axis-symmetric quadrilateral finite elements with 4 nodes and reduced integration (named CAX4R in the Abaqus software) with 50 elements in the vertical direction and 17 elements in the radial direction, respectively. The cylinder is between two rigid surfaces, and the Coulomb friction law with a friction coefficient at the contact surfaces was set to $\mu = 0.15$. The simulation time being fixed at 10 s in order to reduce the simulation time, considering that an explicit integration scheme is used, a global mass scaling is used for all simulations. The VUHARD subroutine is compiled using the GNU gfortran 11.3.0 and linked to the main Abaqus Explicit executable. All benchmarks tests were solved using Abaqus Explicit 2022 on a Dell XPS 13 laptop running Ubuntu 20.04 64 bits with 16 GiB of RAM and one 4 core i7-10510U Intel Processor. All computations were performed using the double precision option of Abaqus, with parallel threads execution on two cores.

Figure 8 shows the plastic strain field ε^p contourplot within the structure at the end of the simulation for both the 3-7-4-1 (left side) and the 3-15-7-1 (right side) flow laws, while Figure 9 shows the temperature field T contourplot for the same models.

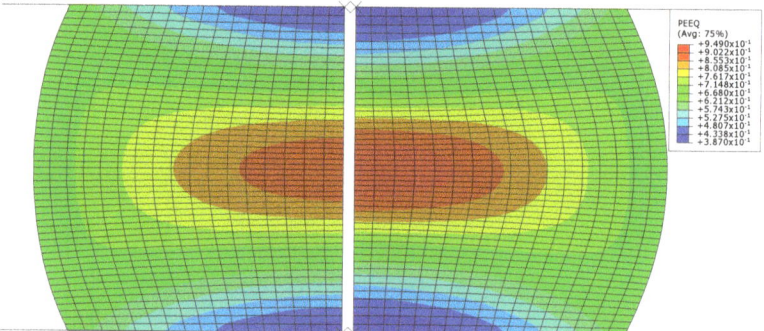

Figure 8. Equivalent plastic strain ε^p contourplot for the compression of a cylinder using the 3-7-4-1 (**left side**) and the 3-15-7-1 (**right side**) ANN flow laws.

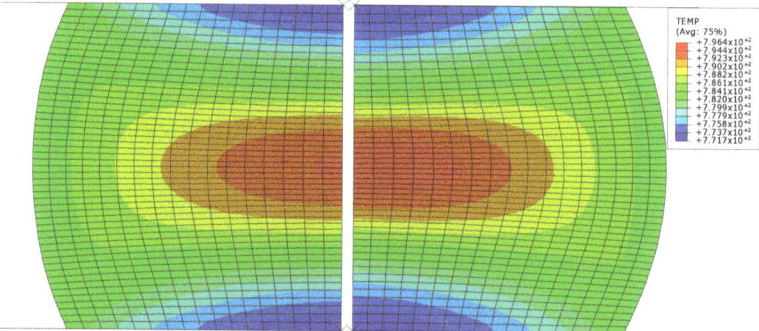

Figure 9. Temperature T contourplot for the compression of a cylinder using the 3-7-4-1 (**left side**) and the 3-15-7-1 (**right side**) ANN flow laws.

Both sides of the figures look more or less the same with some visible differences from the left to the right concerning the shape of the isovalues zones and the maximum value, but in fact, the two models with the lowest and the highest number of neurons give coherent results concerning for the plastic strain ε^p and temperature T contourplots. The maximum plastic strains are concentrated in the center of the specimen with a maximum value of $\varepsilon^p = 0.89$ for the 3-7-4-1 model and $\varepsilon^p = 0.95$ for the 3-15-7-1 model, which is slightly beyond the limit set by the training data, which varies from 0 to 0.7. As shown by Pantalé et al. [31], the flow laws defined by neural networks are able to correctly extrapolate the flow stresses σ^y when the plastic deformations are higher than at least 150% of the maximum plastic strain used during training. Concerning the temperature T, the maximum value is around $T = 795\,°C$ and $T = 799\,°C$, which is very close and in accordance to the experiments used for the learning phase.

Figure 10 shows the evolution of the maximum radius r of the cylinder (measured at the middle of the sample height) as a function of the vertical displacement of the top of the cylinder.

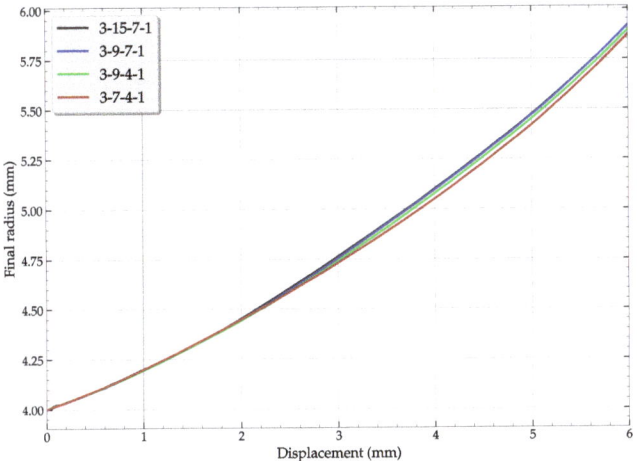

Figure 10. Evolution of the external radius r of the specimen during the compression process using the four ANN flow laws (only the 3-15-7-1 model differs).

This figure shows a slight difference of the four models during the numerical simulation. In the rest of this section, the four models will be referred to as M_{1234}. The final value therefore differs from $r = 5.870$ mm for M_1 to $r = 5.917$ mm for M_{34}.

Table 2 gathers the results allowing the comparison of the four identified flow laws.

Table 2. Compression of a cylinder using the four ANN flow laws, results for the center element of the structure.

Model	ANN	N_{inc}	t (s)	r (mm)	ε^p	T (°C)	σ (MPa)
M_1	3-7-4-1	1,367,147	886	5.870	0.891	794.74	161.95
M_2	3-9-4-1	1,405,471	941	5.895	0.927	798.29	178.78
M_3	3-9-7-1	1,408,680	1023	5.917	0.965	798.76	164.25
M_4	3-15-7-1	1,418,586	1263	5.917	0.950	796.56	165.80

It appears from the study of this table that the modification of the number of neurons in the hidden layers has an influence on the computation time t, which increases with the complexity of the network structure as expected and varies within the range from 886 s to 1263 s approximately since this information is hard to capture from a commercial software that does not contain accurate CPU time reports as the Abaqus software. It is obvious from this table that all models do not give exactly the same results. The computing time increases from M_1 to M_4, proof that the increase in complexity of the ANN has an influence on the global computation time t.

The results, both from the point of view of the dimensional characteristics of the sample (maximum radius r), or the internal fields, such as the temperatures T and the plastic strains ε^p and equivalent stresses σ in the center of the sample, are more or less the same for all M_{1234} flow models.

To have a better analysis of the difference between models M_{1234}, Figure 11 shows the evolution of the equivalent von Mises stress σ for the element in the center of the cylinder during the compression.

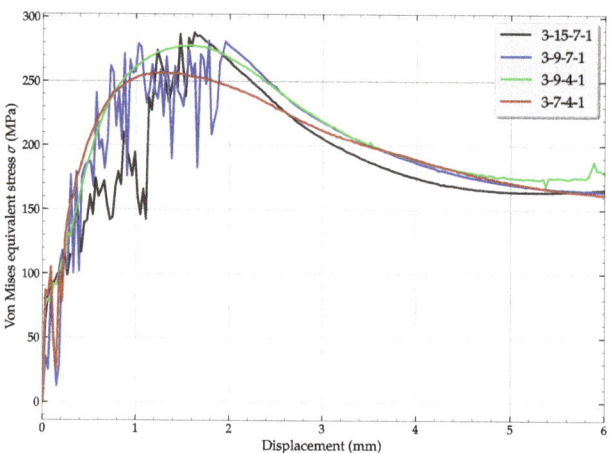

Figure 11. Evolution of the equivalent von Mises stress σ of the specimen during the compression process using the four ANN flow laws.

As shown in this figure, the M_{1234} models give equivalent results with more or less the same value of the equivalent stress σ at the end of the cylinder compression as shown in Table 2. The appearance of the curve for the M_3 and M_4 models is very oscillating in the first 1/3 of the graph. This is probably related to the fact that the M_{34} models are over-fitted and cannot serve as a universal approximator for the flow stress.

To verify this assumption, Figure 12 shows a plot of the predicted flow stress σ^y using the 3-15-7-1 ANN model as a function of the plastic strain ε^p and the plastic strain rate $\dot{\varepsilon}$ for a fixed temperature $T = 750\ °C$.

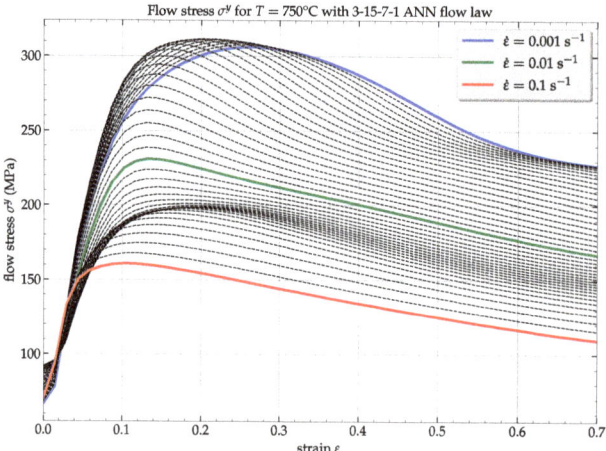

Figure 12. Predicted flow stress σ^y as a function of $(\varepsilon^p, \dot{\varepsilon})$ for a fixed temperature $T = 750\ °C$ using the 3-15-7-1 model.

This figure shows that when $\dot{\varepsilon}$ varies between 0.001 s^{-1} and 0.01 s^{-1}, and for a value of $\varepsilon^p < 0.3$, the representative curves of σ^y 'cross' demonstrate the poor interpolation of the flow stresses σ^y when the strain rate varies (there is a zone in black dashed lines above the blue line). Thus, for a strain rate between 0.001 s^{-1} and 0.01 s^{-1}, and for a plastic strain less than 0.3, the flow stress σ^y is greater than the value of σ^y calculated for the same plastic strain and $\dot{\varepsilon} = 0.001$ s^{-1}, which is physically not admissible for the behavior of GCr15 material. This causes the oscillations visible in Figure 11. For comparison, Figure 13 shows a similar study to Figure 12 for the 3-7-4-1 model.

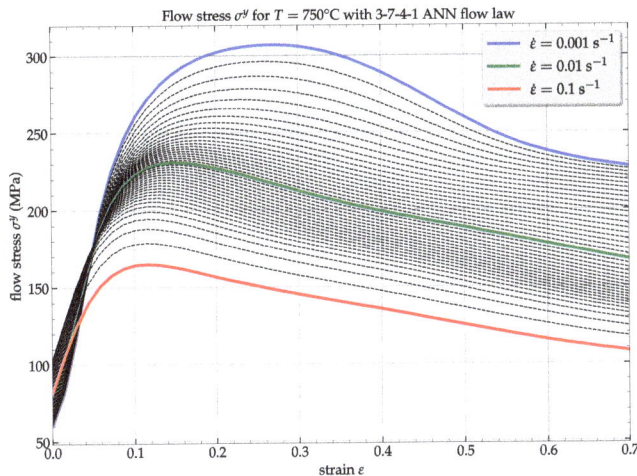

Figure 13. Predicted flow stress σ^y as a function of $(\varepsilon^p, \dot{\varepsilon})$ for a fixed temperature $T = 750$ °C using the 3-7-4-1 model.

This time, there is no visible area where the representative curves 'cross', except perhaps for low values of the strain, where it is hard to distinguish the curves.

This problem occurs for the 3-15-7-1 ANN because we do not have enough training points regarding the strain rate $\dot{\varepsilon}$ (only 3 strain rates are used) regarding the number of internal variable of the ANN, and this leads to erroneous calculations of the flow stress σ^y when the strain rate values differ from those used during training (0.001 s^{-1}, 0.01 s^{-1} and 0.1 s^{-1}). Even though the M_4 model has the lowest values of E_{MAR} and E_{RMS} during the training phase, it is not usable for numerical simulation of the GCr15 flow law in FE simulations. The same type of conclusions can be drawn for the M_3 model.

We can conclude here that only the two first models M_{12} can be used for numerical simulation of the compression of a cylinder, but we must avoid the models M_{34}, as it seems to be over-fitted, and the behavior of the GCr15 alloy is badly represented, even if the curves reported in Figure 5 show that the prediction of model M_4 is excellent.

4. Conclusions and Future Work

In this paper, a flow law based on an artificial neural network capable of predicting the flow stress of a material as a function of input data, such as the plastic strain ε^p, the strain rate $\dot{\varepsilon}$ and the temperature T, for a metallic material subjected to high thermomechanical loading is presented.

From the equations that govern the writing of the neural network, the expressions of the derivatives of the flow stress of the model as a function of the plastic strain ε^p, the strain rate $\dot{\varepsilon}$ and the temperature T were established. These expressions allow the transfer of the neural network behavior into a VUHARD subroutine written in FORTRAN 77 language to allow the use of this network for the computation of the material flow stresses within the Abaqus FE code.

In a first step, data from the works of Ji et al. [30] and Zhou et al. [14], allowed to train several architectures of the proposed model and to compare the results of these ANN models regarding the fidelity of reproduction of the experimental behavior. The comparison of the results obtained allowed to validate the approach and to show the superiority of the ANN model compared to the analytical models based on Johnson–Cook or Arrhenius flow laws, both in terms of the fidelity of the model and quality of the results. In a second step, after transferring the training data to the VUHARD subroutines for the Abaqus FE code, we showed the consistency and quality of the numerical results obtained during the numerical simulation of the compression of a GCr15 alloy cylinder. In the same section, we also discussed the problems of over-fitting the ANN when the number of neurons is too large compared to the training data ranges. It is therefore important to always adjust the structure and size of the neural network to the experimental data that we wish to approximate to avoid this over-fitting phenomenon.

This work thus allowed to highlight the significant contributions of flow laws based on neural networks in numerical simulation by finite elements on a commercial FE code, such as the Abaqus software. The quality of the results obtained allows us to go further in the use of the simulation results and in particular to consider that the results of these finite element simulations can predict the phase transformations and the dynamic recrystallization within the material during the thermomechanical transformation at high temperature.

Funding: This research received no external funding.

Data Availability Statement: Source files of the numerical simulations are available from the author.

Conflicts of Interest: The author declare no conflict of interest.

Abbreviations

The following abbreviations are used in this manuscript:

ANN	Artificial Neural Network
DRX	Dynamic Recrystallization
CPU	Central Processing Unit
FE	Finite Element
VUMAT	User subroutine to compute the stress tensor for Abaqus/Explicit
VUHARD	User subroutine to compute the flow stress for Abaqus/Explicit

Appendix A. ANN Flow Law Coefficients

In order to complete this paper, we report here after the computing process and the 65 coefficients of the artificial neural network ANN-3-7-4-1 model used in Section 2.3. The weight matrix for the first hidden layer w_1 is a 7×3 matrix:

$$w_1 = \begin{bmatrix} -0.4234 & 0.6361 & -3.3756 \\ 0.9035 & -2.0141 & -85.3653 \\ 6.3799 & -1.9357 & -0.3671 \\ -26.7227 & 0.9218 & -2.5756 \\ -0.7105 & 0.7599 & 11.5957 \\ -0.4727 & -18.4137 & 11.6583 \\ 3.4733 & 6.0173 & -2.2098 \end{bmatrix}$$

The biases of the first hidden layer $\vec{b_1}$ is a 7-component vector:

$$\vec{b}_1 = \begin{bmatrix} 1.1200 \\ 0.8351 \\ -2.9032 \\ -1.1547 \\ -4.7023 \\ -3.9429 \\ -7.2849 \end{bmatrix}$$

The weight matrix for the second hidden layer w_2 is a 4×7 matrix:

$$w_2^T = \begin{bmatrix} 1.0488 & -2.2694 & 4.7134 & -8.6149 \\ 1.2225 & 1.7295 & 0.6877 & 8.2364 \\ -0.9681 & -16.4026 & -1.9820 & -0.2577 \\ -2.2942 & -7.3726 & -14.0394 & 16.5637 \\ -11.3020 & -2.9066 & -1.9601 & 0.3557 \\ -35.7421 & -3.0537 & -1.8083 & 0.1603 \\ 0.9444 & 3.5816 & 0.4988 & -0.6497 \end{bmatrix}$$

The biases of the second hidden layer $\vec{b_2}$ are a 4-component vector:

$$\vec{b}_2 = \begin{bmatrix} -1.0302 \\ -1.6695 \\ -1.6705 \\ 1.7122 \end{bmatrix}$$

The weight vector for the output layer $\vec{w}$ is a 4-component vector:

$$\vec{w} = \begin{bmatrix} 0.6684 \\ 3.0013 \\ 0.1998 \\ -0.1879 \end{bmatrix}$$

The bias of the output layer b is a scalar:

$$b = 0.1631$$

The boundaries of the range of the corresponding field are as follows:
- $\varepsilon^p \in [0.0, 0.7]$
- $\dot{\varepsilon} \in [0.001 \text{ s}^{-1}, 0.1 \text{ s}^{-1}]$
- $T \in [750\ °C, 1300\ °C]$
- $\sigma \in [3.052\ \text{MPa}, 306.096\ \text{MPa}]$.

The reference strain rate is $\dot{\varepsilon}_0 = 0.001\ \text{s}^{-1}$.

References

1. Pantalé, O.; Caperaa, S.; Rakotomalala, R. Development of an object-oriented finite element program: Application to metal-forming and impact simulations. *J. Comput. Appl. Math.* **2004**, *168*, 341–351. [CrossRef]
2. Dey, S.; Borvik, T.; Hopperstad, O.S.; Langseth, M. On the influence of constitutive relation in projectile impact of steel plates. *Int. J. Impact Eng.* **2007**, *34*, 464–486. [CrossRef]
3. Lin, Y.C.; Chen, M.S.; Zhang, J. Modeling of flow stress of 42CrMo steel under hot compression. *Mater. Sci. Eng. A* **2009**, *499*, 88–92. [CrossRef]
4. Kolsky, H. An Investigation of the Mechanical Properties of Materials at very High Rates of Loading. *Proc. Phys. Society. Sect. B* **1949**, *62*, 676–700. [CrossRef]
5. Lee, W.S.; Liu, C.Y. The effects of temperature and strain rate on the dynamic flow behaviour of different steels. *Mater. Sci. Eng. A* **2006**, *426*, 101–113. [CrossRef]

6. Lennon, A.M.; Ramesh, K.T. The influence of crystal structure on the dynamic behavior of materials at high temperatures. *Int. J. Plast.* **2004**, *20*, 269–290. [CrossRef]
7. Zhang, J.; Chen, B.; Baoxiang, Z. Effect of initial microstructure on the hot compression deformation behavior of a 2219 aluminum alloy. *Mater. Des.* **2012**, *34*, 15–21. [CrossRef]
8. Johnson, G.R.; Cook, W.H. A Constitutive Model and Data for Metals Subjected to Large Strains, High Strain Rates, and High Temperatures. In Proceedings of the 7th International Symposium on Ballistics, The Hague, The Netherlands, 19–21 April 1983; pp. 541–547.
9. Johnson, G.R.; Holmquist, T.J. Evaluation of cylinder-impact test data for constitutive model constants. *J. Appl. Phys.* **1988**, *64*, 3901–3910. [CrossRef]
10. Zerilli, F.J.; Armstrong, R.W. Dislocation-mechanics-based constitutive relations for material dynamics calculations. *J. Appl. Phys.* **1987**, *61*, 1816–1825. [CrossRef]
11. Lin, Y.; Chen, X.M. A critical review of experimental results and constitutive descriptions for metals and alloys in hot working. *Mater. Des.* **2011**, *32*, 1733–1759. [CrossRef]
12. Li, H.Y.; Wang, X.F.; Duan, J.Y.; Liu, J.J. A modified Johnson Cook model for elevated temperature flow behavior of T24 steel. *Mater. Sci. Eng. A* **2013**, *577*, 138–146. [CrossRef]
13. Zhang, D.N.; Shangguan, Q.Q.; Xie, C.J.; Liu, F. A modified Johnson–Cook model of dynamic tensile behaviors for 7075-T6 aluminum alloy. *J. Alloy. Compd.* **2015**, *619*, 186–194. [CrossRef]
14. Zhou, Q.; Ji, C.; Zhu, M.y. Research on Several Constitutive Models to Predict the Flow Behaviour of GCr15 Continuous Casting Bloom with Heavy Reduction. *Mater. Res. Express* **2020**, *6*, 1265f2. [CrossRef]
15. Jia, Z.; Guan, B.; Zang, Y.; Wang, Y.; Lei, M. Modified Johnson-Cook model of aluminum alloy 6016-T6 sheets at low dynamic strain rates. *Mater. Sci. Eng. A* **2021**, *820*, 141565. [CrossRef]
16. Rule, W.K.; Jones, S.E. A revised form for the Johnson-Cook Strengh Model. *Int. J. Impact Eng.* **1998**, *21*, 609–624. [CrossRef]
17. Lin, Y.; Chen, X.M.; Liu, G. A modified Johnson–Cook model for tensile behaviors of typical high-strength alloy steel. *Mater. Sci. Eng. A* **2010**, *527*, 6980–6986. [CrossRef]
18. Lennon, A.M.; Ramesh, K.T. On the performance of modified Zerilli-Armstrong constitutive model in simulating the metal-cutting process. *J. Manuf. Process.* **2017**, *28*, 253–265. [CrossRef]
19. Cheng, C.; Mahnken, R. A modified Zerilli–Armstrong model as the asymmetric visco-plastic part of a multi-mechanism model for cutting simulations. *Arch. Appl. Mech.* **2021**, *91*, 3869–3888. [CrossRef]
20. Hensel, A.; Spittel, T. *Kraft- und Arbeitsbedarf Bildsamer Formgebungsverfahren*; Deutscher Verlag für Grundstoffindustrie: Leipzig, Duchland, 1978.
21. Chadha, K.; Shahriari, D.; Jahazi, M. An Approach to Develop Hansel–Spittel Constitutive Equation during Ingot Breakdown Operation of Low Alloy Steels. In *Frontiers in Materials Processing, Applications, Research and Technology*; Springer: Hyderabad, India, 2018; pp. 239–246. [CrossRef]
22. Jonas, J.; Sellars, C.; Tegart, W.M. Strength and structure under hot-working conditions. *Metall. Rev.* **1969**, *14*, 1–24. [CrossRef]
23. He, A.; Xie, G.; Zhang, H.; Wang, X. A comparative study on Johnson–Cook, modified Johnson–Cook and Arrhenius–type constitutive models to predict the high temperature flow stress in 20CrMo alloy steel. *Mater. Des. (1980–2015)* **2013**, *52*, 677–685. [CrossRef]
24. Liang, P.; Kong, N.; Zhang, J.; Li, H. A Modified Arrhenius-Type Constitutive Model and its Implementation by Means of the Safe Version of Newton–Raphson Method. *Steel Res. Int.* **2022**, *94*, 2200443. [CrossRef]
25. Nemat-Nasser, S.; Guo, W.G. Thermomechanical response of DH-36 structural steel over a wide range of strain rates and temperatures. *Mech. Mater.* **2003**, *35*, 1023–1047. [CrossRef]
26. Khan, A.S.; Sung Suh, Y.; Kazmi, R. Quasi-static and dynamic loading responses and constitutive modeling of titanium alloys. *Int. J. Plast.* **2004**, *20*, 2233–2248. [CrossRef]
27. Gao, C.Y. FE Realization of a Thermo-Visco-Plastic Constitutive Model Using VUMAT in ABAQUS/Explicit Program. In *Computational Mechanics*; Springer: Berlin/Heidelberg, Germany, 2007; p. 301.
28. Ming, L.; Pantalé, O. An Efficient and Robust VUMAT Implementation of Elastoplastic Constitutive Laws in Abaqus/Explicit Finite Element Code. *Mech. Ind.* **2018**, *19*, 308. [CrossRef]
29. Zener, C.; Hollomon, J.H. Effect of Strain Rate Upon Plastic Flow of Steel. *J. Appl. Phys.* **1944**, *15*, 22–32. [CrossRef]
30. Ji, C.; Wang, Z.; Wu, C.; Zhu, M. Constitutive Modeling of the Flow Stress of GCr15 Continuous Casting Bloom in the Heavy Reduction Process. *Metall. Mater. Trans. B* **2018**, *49*, 767–782. [CrossRef]
31. Pantalé, O.; Tize Mha, P.; Tongne, A. Efficient implementation of non-linear flow law using neural network into the Abaqus Explicit FEM code. *Finite Elem. Anal. Des.* **2022**, *198*, 103647. [CrossRef]
32. Minsky, M.L.; Papert, S. *Perceptrons: An Introduction to Computational Geometry*; MIT Press: Cambridge, UK, 1969.
33. Hornik, K.; Stinchcombe, M.; White, H. Multilayer Feedforward Networks Are Universal Approximators. *Neural Netw.* **1989**, *2*, 359–366. [CrossRef]
34. Gorji, M.B.; Mozaffar, M.; Heidenreich, J.N.; Cao, J.; Mohr, D. On the Potential of Recurrent Neural Networks for Modeling Path Dependent Plasticity. *J. Mech. Phys. Solids* **2020**, *143*, 103972. [CrossRef]
35. Jamli, M.; Farid, N. The Sustainability of Neural Network Applications within Finite Element Analysis in Sheet Metal Forming: A Review. *Measurement* **2019**, *138*, 446–460. [CrossRef]

36. Jiao, P.; Alavi, A.H. Artificial Intelligence-Enabled Smart Mechanical Metamaterials: Advent and Future Trends. *Int. Mater. Rev.* **2020**, *66*, 365–393. [CrossRef]
37. Ghaboussi, J.; Garrett, J.H.; Wu, X. Knowledge-Based Modeling of Material Behavior with Neural Networks. *J. Eng. Mech.* **1991**, *117*, 132–153. [CrossRef]
38. Ghaboussi, J.; Pecknold, D.A.; Zhang, M.; Haj-Ali, R.M. Autoprogressive Training of Neural Network Constitutive Models. *Int. J. Numer. Methods Eng.* **1998**, *42*, 105–126. [CrossRef]
39. Ghaboussi, J.; Sidarta, D. New Nested Adaptive Neural Networks (NANN) for Constitutive Modeling. *Comput. Geotech.* **1998**, *22*, 29–52. [CrossRef]
40. Lin, Y.; Zhang, J.; Zhong, J. Application of Neural Networks to Predict the Elevated Temperature Flow Behavior of a Low Alloy Steel. *Comput. Mater. Sci.* **2008**, *43*, 752–758. [CrossRef]
41. Ashtiani, H.R.; Shahsavari, P. A Comparative Study on the Phenomenological and Artificial Neural Network Models to Predict Hot Deformation Behavior of AlCuMgPb Alloy. *J. Alloy. Compd.* **2016**, *687*, 263–273. [CrossRef]
42. Abadi, M.; Barham, P.; Chen, J.; Chen, Z.; Davis, A.; Dean, J.; Devin, M.; Ghemawat, S.; Irving, G.; Isard, M.; et al. TensorFlow: A System for Large-Scale Machine Learning. In Proceedings of the 12th USENIX Conference on Operating Systems Design and Implementation, OSDI'16, Savannah, GA, USA, 2–4 November 2016; USENIX Association: Berkeley, CA, USA, 2016; pp. 265–283.
43. Mattmann, C. *Machine Learning with Tensorflow*; O'REILLY MEDIA: Shelter Island, NY, USA, 2020.
44. Lu, Z.; Pan, Q.; Liu, X.; Qin, Y.; He, Y.; Cao, S. Artificial Neural Network Prediction to the Hot Compressive Deformation Behavior of Al–Cu–Mg–Ag Heat-Resistant Aluminum Alloy. *Mech. Res. Commun.* **2011**, *38*, 192–197. [CrossRef]
45. Ponthot, J.P. Unified Stress Update Algorithms for the Numerical Simulation of Large Deformation Elasto-Plastic and Elasto-Viscoplastic Processes. *Int. J. Plast.* **2002**, *18*, 91–126. [CrossRef]
46. Simo, J.C.; Hughes, T.J.R. *Computational Inelasticity*; Interdisciplinary Applied Mathematics, Springer: New York, NY, USA, 1998.
47. Kingma, D.P.; Lei, J. Adam: A method for stochastic optimization. *arXiv Preprint* **2014**, arXiv:1412.6980
48. Phaniraj, M.P.; Lahiri, A.K. The applicability of neural network model to predict flow stress for carbon steels. *J. Mater. Process. Technol.* **2003**, *141*, 219–227. [CrossRef]
49. Jansen van Rensburg, G.; Kok, S. Tutorial on State Variable Based Plasticity: An Abaqus UHARD Subroutine. In Proceedings of the Eighth South African Conference on Computational and Applied Mechanics—SACAM2012, Johannesburg, South Africa, 3–5 September 2012.

Disclaimer/Publisher's Note: The statements, opinions and data contained in all publications are solely those of the individual author(s) and contributor(s) and not of MDPI and/or the editor(s). MDPI and/or the editor(s) disclaim responsibility for any injury to people or property resulting from any ideas, methods, instructions or products referred to in the content.

Article

Investigating Novice Developers' Code Commenting Trends Using Machine Learning Techniques

Tahira Niazi [1], Teerath Das [2], Ghufran Ahmed [3], Syed Muhammad Waqas [4], Sumra Khan [1], Suleman Khan [5,*], Ahmed Abdelaziz Abdelatif [6] and Shaukat Wasi [1]

[1] Department of Computer Science, Mohammad Ali Jinnah University, Karachi 75400, Pakistan
[2] Faculty of Information Technology, University of Jyväskylä, 40014 Jyväskylä, Finland
[3] School of Computing, National University of Computer Emerging Sciences, Karachi 75400, Pakistan
[4] Department of Computer Science, Bahria University, Karachi 75260, Pakistan
[5] School of Psychology and Computer Science, University of Central Lancashire, Preston PR1 2HE, UK
[6] Khawarizmi International College, Al Bahya, Abu Dhabi 25669, United Arab Emirates
* Correspondence: skhan92@uclan.ac.uk

Abstract: Code comments are considered an efficient way to document the functionality of a particular block of code. Code commenting is a common practice among developers to explain the purpose of the code in order to improve code comprehension and readability. Researchers investigated the effect of code comments on software development tasks and demonstrated the use of comments in several ways, including maintenance, reusability, bug detection, etc. Given the importance of code comments, it becomes vital for novice developers to brush up on their code commenting skills. In this study, we initially investigated what types of comments novice students document in their source code and further categorized those comments using a machine learning approach. The work involves the initial manual classification of code comments and then building a machine learning model to classify student code comments automatically. The findings of our study revealed that novice developers/students' comments are mainly related to *Literal* (26.66%) and *Insufficient* (26.66%). Further, we proposed and extended the taxonomy of such source code comments by adding a few more categories, i.e., *License* (5.18%), *Profile* (4.80%), *Irrelevant* (4.80%), *Commented Code* (4.44%), *Autogenerated* (1.48%), and *Improper* (1.10%). Moreover, we assessed our approach with three different machine-learning classifiers. Our implementation of machine learning models found that *Decision Tree* resulted in the overall highest accuracy, i.e., 85%. This study helps in predicting the type of code comments for a novice developer using a machine learning approach that can be implemented to generate automated feedback for students, thus saving teachers time for manual one-on-one feedback, which is a time-consuming activity.

Keywords: source code comments; classification; machine learning techniques

1. Introduction

Code comments are considered an integral and indispensable activity across various tasks in the software development life cycle (SDLC). Indeed, it is necessary for the developers and peer reviewers to understand what the code is intended to perform and how it works. In recent times, with the increase in software complexity and the number of developers working on a single project, it has become necessary to write code comments to make any sense of what is happening within the software. With growing team sizes, it is important for all the developers in the team to have a better understanding of the code. This can be achieved by adhering to good programming conventions to better understand the codebase by all the developers within a team. Many code conventions are followed to make the code readable across the development teams, e.g., naming conventions, source code comments, etc. Code conventions are a set of formats, rules, and guidelines followed while writing code. The code is written in a specific format to make the program easy to read and understand. There are many research studies that discuss the impact of adopting coding standards on their particular projects [1]. Many studies reveal that coding conventions significantly and positively impact the readability of code [2]. These programming conventions help developers produce more readable code that is better understood by others. At the same time, it also helps to produce adaptable code, which is easy to fix when it comes to bug fixing. Basic code conventions are generalized across all programming languages. However, the way code comments are written varies according to the programming language's syntax. Figure 1 illustrates different types of comments in Java program such as block, single-line and multi-line comments.

As discussed above, source code commenting is one of the programming practices widely followed by developers to explain their code to others, who intend to gain an understanding for either improving the code or bug fixing. For a particular project, the same development team is not always the one to work on that project continuously. Therefore, it is not guaranteed that the next developer will be as experienced as the development team that worked on it before. No matter how well the code is written or refactored, it still requires that the documentation be included in the source code, and therefore, code commenting is one of the good practices for documenting the code.

Code comments are part of the source code that developers produce in natural language to describe the purpose and implementation details of the programming code. The purpose of source code comments is not just limited to the code's explanation; developers also include comments to highlight any pending bug fixes, technical debt, or references to other code snippets. They play a pivotal role in many software engineering tasks, such as software maintainability, code modification, and code reuse. Multiple researches suggest that commenting on a source code enhances its readability [3,4], leads to bug detection [5,6], and improves testing [7].

```
1  public class STSubscriptExpression extends STExpression {
2
3      private static CSpellingService fInstance;
4
5      /**
6       * Returns the created expression, or null in case of error.
7       * @deprecated Replaced by {@link #getExpression()}
8       */
9      @Deprecated
10     public STExpression getSubscriptExpression(){
11         if (fInstance == null) {
12             fInstance = new Expression(ConsoleEditors.getPreferenceStore());
13         }
14         return fInstance;
15     }
16
17     /**
18      * Handle terminated sub-launch
19      * @param launch a terminable launch object.
20      * @author Jesse MC Wilson
21      */
22     private void STLaunchTerminated(ILaunch launch) {
23         // See com.vaadin.data.query.QueryDelegate#getPrimaryKeyColumns
24         if (this == launch)
25             return;
26         // Remove sub launch, keeping the processes of the terminated launch to
27         // show the association and to keep the console content accessible
28         if (subLaunches.remove(launch) != null) {
29             // terminate ourselves if this is the last sub launch
30             if (subLaunches.size() == 0) {
31                 // TODO: Check the possibility to exclude it
32                 //monitor.exlude();
33                 monitor.subTask("Terminated"); //$NON-NLS-1$
34                 fTerminated = true;
35                 fireTerminate();
36                 // %%%
37             }
38         }
39     }
40 }
```

Figure 1. Example of code comments in Java program file. Reprinted/adapted with permission from [8] Copyright 2019, by Luca Pascarella, Magiel Bruntink, Alberto Bacchelli.

This research study has provided the key contributions to taxonomy introduced in [9,10] by analyzing student code comments. Further, we implemented machine learning models to achieve the automated classification of students'/developers' source code comments.

The main contributions of our study are:

- An extension to the *taxonomy* of the source code comments introduced in [9,10];
- Automated *classification* of students'/developers' source code comments using machine learning techniques.

The remainder of this paper is structured as follows: The related research work is highlighted in Section 2 to find the significant gap. Section 3 describes the methodology exploited to conduct the research, and the experiment is explained in Section 4. The results and analysis of the research are reported in Section 5. Finally, Section 6 represents the conclusions and provides potential future research directions.

2. Related Work

Research on code comments has been an active area of research in the past decades. Many researchers have investigated code comments regarding their relation to code concerning various factors. These studies help us understand the effectiveness of code comments and their influence on different aspects of software design and implementation. The related literature is divided into six categories connected to our study: (i) code comments for code maintainability, (ii) code comments for bug detection, (iii) comments generation and code summarizing, (iv) code comments as a means of documentation, (v) code comments quality aspect and categorization, and (vi) analysis of student code comments.

2.1. Code Comments for Code Maintainability

Many researchers have studied the source code comments and revealed interesting findings that encourage programmers to follow this useful code convention. The benefits of good commenting extend beyond the primary benefit of providing information to the reader. Comments are an important element of code quality. They help document how the code is supposed to work. This increases programmer understanding, making the code more maintainable. Tenny et al. [3,4] suggested that commenting on a source code enhances its readability, as discussed in that leads to bug detection, discussed by Rubio-Gonz et al. and Subramanian et al. [5,6] and improved testing, discussed by Goffi et al. [7]. Hartzman et al. [11] studied the roles of comments in the maintenance of large software systems depicting the need for source code comments for maintainability. Jiang et al. [12] suggested that outdated comments that no longer align with the associated method entities result in confusion for the developers and hinder the process of future code-changing. As evident from the results, writing quality source code comments in a program is regarded as a good practice, as studied by de Souza et al. [13]. Oman et al. and Garcia et al. [14,15] introduced a quality metric called the code/comment ratio to quantify the quality of the overall code. Further tools are developed to assess the quality of the source code comments. For example, Khami [16] designed a tool called JavaDocMiner to check the quality of JavaDoc comments. It is based on natural language processing and evaluates the comment content concerning "language" and its relevance with the associated code. Steidl et al. [17] suggested that for analyzing the quality of code comments, a machine learning model was used, and assessment was carried out on various comment categories, including "header comments, member comments, in-line comments, section comments, code comments, and task comments." Similarly, as an extension to the previous work, Sun et al. [18] gave useful recommendations by performing a comprehensive assessment of the comments in jdk8.0 and jEdit.

2.2. Code Comments for Bug Detection

Many researchers have exploited code comments to gain useful insights for software quality assurance perspectives. The developers often overlook inconsistencies between code and comments as the codebase grows. Tan et al. [19] suggest that bugs can be automatically detected between inconsistent code and comments. The experimental results present evidence that their tool, iComment, can extract 1832 rules from comments with 90.8–100% accuracy and detect 60 comment-code inconsistencies, 33 new bugs, and 27 bad comments in the latest versions of the four programs. Nineteen of these issues (twelve bugs and seven bad comments) were confirmed by the corresponding developers, while the other issues are currently under investigation by the developers. Ratol et al. [20] studied the process of refactoring a source code. Code comments can be used to facilitate the change introduced by the refactoring. Code comments were used to help in the refactoring activities, thus enhancing the code's maintainability. Few studies have been conducted to analyze GitHub commits; for example, Das et al. [21] analyzed GitHub commits to investigate the performance issues in Android application.

2.3. Comments Generation and Code Summarizing

Various studies have been conducted in the context of experimenting with comment generation and code summarizing to produce comments from the existing code. The techniques employed by machine translation were suggested by Allamanis et al. and Hu et al. [22,23], and information retrieval was suggested by Haiduc et al. and Huang et al. [24–26] to generate comments. The study by Lawrie et al. [27] employed an information retrieval approach using the cosine similarity for assessing the program's quality with the hypothesis that "if the code is high quality, then the comments give a good description of the code". Marcus et al. [28] introduced an innovative information retrieval approach to distinguish traceability links between source code and comments. Chen et al. [29] worked on automatically identifying the scope of the code comments in Java programs by employing machine learning techniques. However, they propose that natural language processing techniques can also be applied to evaluate the similarities between code comments and the corresponding code entities.

2.4. Code Comments as a Means of Documentation

In the literature, researchers also investigated the contents of comments in their work to further assess the need for writing informative and meaningful code comments. Hata et al. [30] investigated the role of links in code comments, their prevalence, purpose, and targets. Their investigation reveals diversity in the usage of links in comments, and links decay over time and evolve after they have been referenced in the source code comments. Similarly, Alghamdi et al. [31] studied comments concerning the presence of primitive data types through advanced lexical methods and demonstrated that developers document the primitive data types in the code comments to give additional information regarding purpose and usage.

2.5. Code Comments Quality Aspect and Categorization

As apparent from the above sections, code commenting practice varies among developers, and different code comments serve different purposes and meanings. Eventually, this leads to an interesting research area of comment classification. Some of the earliest studies by Haouari et al. and Steidl et al. [17,32] that worked on comment classification presented valuable results. Additionally, Zhai et al. [33] introduced a taxonomy by considering the code entities and the code perspectives of the comments. They also experimented with the propagation of comments from one code entity to another. However, classifying comments was not their primary purpose. Moreover, Pascarella et al. [8] introduced a more fine-grained taxonomy of code comments by studying comments from six open-source Java projects and mobile applications. It resulted in two-layered taxonomy having 6 top layers and 16 sub-layer categories. A statistically representative 1925 comments from files were selected and then manually classified by the two authors using the COMMEAN application. The authors used the supervised machine learning technique, probabilistic (Naïve Bayes Multinomial), and the Decision Tree algorithm (Random Forest or J48).

2.6. Analysis of Student Code Comments

Mohammadi-Aragh et al. [9] also assessed the commenting habits of students and categorized them into different types. Beck et al. [10] collected student source code comments and labeled them as "sufficient" or "insufficient" according to their codebook from their previous research work and then implemented supervised machine learning techniques. Their results suggest that introducing the lemmatization technique improved the performance of the Random Forest classifier. However, it lowered the performance on Multinomial Naïve Bayes on average. Additionally, Random Forest exceeded Naïve Bayes classifier in both testing rounds based on the results. Vieira et al. [34] worked on promoting in-code comments to self-explain the code written by students. Beck et al. [35] studied the structure and proportion of student comments and code.

Furthermore, various studies have been conducted to build the taxonomy of source code comments. For example, Table 1 contains the various aspects along with their names and descriptions. It presents the aspects that were considered in various types of research work on source code comments carried out in this particular domain. Table 2 is an overview of the research studies that cover specific aspects of Table 1.

Table 1. Aspects considered in research.

Aspect Category	Aspect Name	Description
A1	Analysis of student code commenting habit	Whether the dataset was taken of the professional developers or students
A2	Taxonomy based on code cognition	Types of comment categories based on comments insights from the author re-flection
A3	Taxonomy based on program aspect	Types of comment categories based on program structure and related code entities
A4	Classification using machine learning method	Any classification techniques that are applied to carry out the research

Table 2. Analysis of existing research (A = Addressed, NA = Not Addressed).

Research Work	A1	A2	A3	A4
J. Zhai et al. [33]	NA	NA	A	A
L. Pascarella and A. Bacchelli, [8]	NA	NA	A	A
P. Beck et al. [10]	A	A	NA	A
L. Pascarella [36]	NA	NA	A	A
R. E. Garcia [34]	NA	NA	NA	NA
M. J. Mohammadi-Aragh et al. [9]	A	A	NA	NA
H. Hata, C. Treude et al. [30]	NA	NA	A	NA
M. Alghamdi et al. [31]	NA	NA	A	NA
P. J. Beck [35]	A	NA	NA	A

The research study discussed herein mainly differs from the existing research work in all the above aspects. In particular, previous studies were mostly based on codebases produced by professional developers, whereas the current study investigates the code commenting habits of novice developers. The work by Mohammadi-Aragh et al. [9] is also related to students' commenting habits, but the experiment was carried out for the Python language; however, this research work has taken Java as the programming language. To illustrate this point, consider the fact that programming languages differ in their structure, as the former is a dynamically typed language and the latter is a statically typed language, therefore, having a consequent impact on the programming concepts. Moreover, the research work mentioned above used supervised machine learning methods to train a binary classifier. In contrast, our model is capable of classifying data into different categories, i.e., a multi-class classification model. Another aspect is a difference in the granularity of the classification with respect to comment categorization.

3. Methodology

The study aims to analyze the activities performed in the Java source code with the purpose of manually investigating and classifying the source code activities using machine learning techniques. The study was conducted from the viewpoint of novice developers and researchers. The context of the study is based on the projects of novice students/developers that were developed at Mohammad Ali Jinnah University.

3.1. Research Questions

The main objectives that drive the motivation behind this study are: is it possible to analyze the code activities by novice developers and further classify the source code comments that would help novice student developers to write meaningful code comments? The intent is to make their code more readable. We formulated two research questions (RQs) to investigate this study further.

RQ-1. *Which kind of code activities are performed by novice students/developers in the source code?*

Rationale: The primary rationale behind this research question is to analyze the key activities developers mention in their source code comments. This research question provides an idea to novice developers regarding the essential aspects that should be considered for development. The features exploited in this **RQ-1** are *comment_content* and *code*, as shown in Table 3. As already described, the main idea is to see the novice developers' activities by analyzing comment code and its corresponding source code and building a meaningful set of categories. The outcome of this research question will be a taxonomy of categories mentioned in the source code.

Table 3. Description of the features extracted for the dataset preparation.

No.	Feature Name	Description
1	comment_content	This feature contains the comment text written by the student
2	code	This feature contains the relevant code about which the comment was written.
3	begin_line	The line number of the file at which the comment begins.
4	end_line	The end line of the comment.
5	code_start_line	The start line for the relevant code section.
6	type	The type of the comment, i.e., single-line or multi-line.
7	category	This is the class that was labeled to the dataset using the taxonomy.

RQ-2. *Is it possible to classify novice students'/developers' source code comments using machine learning techniques?*

Rationale: This research question is dedicated to automatically classifying the novice students'/developers' source code comment categories obtained in **RQ-1** using machine learning techniques. Furthermore, the objective of this research question is to apply different machine-learning approaches to source code comments and eventually find the best machine-learning approach for classifying code comments. This will help novice developers to categorize the new comments in the correct categories.

It is important to note here that the work examines student code comments with a finer categorization of their comments, as discussed at the end of Section 2.6. The objective of this research question is also to lay out the methodology of machine learning techniques based on multi-label classification, which will provide an outcome of how effective this approach is at predicting code comments for novice developers.

The proposed method in Listing 1 represents the high-level pseudo-code algorithm, which describes the overall methodology. The methodology of our study consists of two parts: (i) Preparation of taxonomy of code comments using source code comments (M1), and (ii) classification of source code comments categories using machine learning techniques (M2). M1 aims to address **RQ-1**, whereas M2 is dedicated to **RQ-2**, described in the research question section. For the **RQ-2** methodology, we used three machine learning techniques to classify the source code's comments: (i) Support Vector Machine, (ii) Random Forest, and (iii) Decision Tree.

Listing 1. Pseudo code of classification of code comments.

```
Input: Comments extracted from the source code
Parameter: Hyperparamter tuning
Output: Label comments
Steps of M1: Preparation of dataset of source code comments
building taxonomy of source code comments

1. Pre-processing the raw java source code.
2. Building the parser to parse the raw source code and extract code comments in JSON object format
3. The JSON object is converted into CSV
4. Building Taxonomy and Dataset Annotation

Steps of M2: Classification of source code comments categories using machine learning techniques

5. Extract the dependent feature.
6. Add the dependent feature to the original dataset.
7. Split the dataset into training and testing
8. Hyperparameter Tuning
```

3.2. Context Selection

The context of this study is 70 web development projects written in Java language by novice students/developers at the Department of Computer Science, Mohammad Ali Jinnah University. We built the dataset of source code comments from the Java code projects, and these comments are extracted by the *parser*, which is built in JavaScript. There are two approaches used in Java programming to comment in the source code, i.e., (i) single-line comment and (ii) multi-line comment.

Single-line comments start with //.
Example System.out.println("Hello World");//This is the example comment
Multi-line comments start with /* and end with */.
Example:///* The code will print the character of words to the screen, then use it in line 4*/

Figure 2 represents the flow chart of the classification of code comments that describes the overall flow of our algorithm. The raw Java code is initially pre-processed, and then we parse it to create a JSON object, which is then converted to CSV. In CSV, we obtain our dataset, which consists of 5000 total comments, and then annotate it using our designed taxonomy, represented in Table 4. We then extract the dependent features, and add those features to our dataset. The dataset was then split into training and testing to apply the machine learning algorithm and tune their hyper-parameters to improve the results even further.

Table 4. Taxonomy and annotation with new categories.

SNO	Category	Frequency	Description
1	Literal	1333 (26.66%)	A comment that just restates the source code and does not provide any additional insight into the program's logic.
2	Insufficient	1333 (26.66%)	Code comments might be classified as "insufficient," either if they do not provide enough information for understanding the code or if, even if they are verbose, they add no value.
3	Conceptual	1111 (22.22%)	Conceptual comments explain source code functionality without simply restating the source code. Conceptual comments are not mere translations of source code in English but explain its functionality in greater detail to a code reviewer or another outside developer.

Table 4. Cont.

SNO	Category	Frequency	Description
4	License	259 (5.18%)	The code comments that contain information on the terms of use and the licensing of the source code.
5	Profile	240 (4.80%)	These code comments provide references to the authors and their ownership of the work, as well as source credentials in the form of an "@author" tag.
6	Irrelevant	240 (4.80%)	The type of code comments for which it is not easy to comprehend their meaning and they do not clearly describe the associated code and are not related.
7	Commented code	222 (4.44%)	This category includes all comments that contain source code commented out by developers.
8	Organizational	92 (1.84%)	Organizational comments are used to communicate the structure of code. They typically take the form of a short comment that explains a module or block of code, separating one functional unit from another. This demonstrates that the programmer is attempting to present code in a way that helps other coders easily understand it.
9	Autogenerated	74 (1.48%)	This category includes Auto-generated code. These are typically the metadata left behind by an IDE and contain only the skeleton with a placeholder provided by the IDE.
10	Improper	55 (1.10%)	This category includes comments that are not properly implemented, e.g., a comment should have an associated code directly below the comment body without any empty lines in between.
11	Empty	41 (0.82%)	This category includes the comments that do not contain anything, for example //

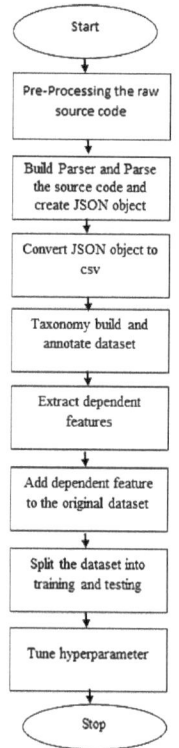

Figure 2. Flow chart of classification of code comments.

3.3. Data Extraction

As already discussed, we split the methodology for **RQ-1** and **RQ-2** as M1 and M2, respectively. The data extraction process of the research questions is described in M1 and M2.

3.3.1. M1: Preparation of Dataset of Source Code Comments and Building Taxonomy of Source Code Comments

As shown in Figure 3 and Listing 1, the steps from 1 to 4 of the figure and algorithm cover the data extraction of *RQ-1*. It defines the overall procedure of dataset preparation which is sub-divided into four parts, (i) pre-processing of java source code, (ii) building the parser, (iii) the JSON object is converted into CSV, and (iv) building taxonomy and dataset annotation, which are described as follows:

- **Pre-processing of java source code:** The dataset required to carry out this research was prepared by pre-processing the raw source code. This raw source code is obtained from the lab assignments of sophomore-year students in the computer science discipline. We only considered the java source code files for our study. Initially, we prepared a dedicated script to obtain all the projects that are: (i) complete projects and (ii) programs built in java language. This results in a total of 70 projects.
- **Build the parser and Parse the raw source code to create JSON object:** A parser was developed in JavaScript language to parse the java source code files and extract the code-comment pairs. The parser goes through a directory, traverses all sub-directories within that directory, and searches all files with a .java file extension. It reads the files one by one, extracts the code-comments pairs from those files, and creates a JSON object. That extended JSON object is later converted to CSV file format so that this can be used for machine learning experiments.
- **The JSON object converted into CSV:** Data pre-processing is the first and most crucial phase in the research analysis. Data pre-processing is applied to the CSV file that is obtained by the parser. Intensive pre-processing would be required to convert the raw code into a usable dataset.
- **Building Taxonomy and Dataset Annotation:** The generated dataset was carefully analyzed, the annotation for the dataset was performed from the existing taxonomy [9,10], and new categories in the taxonomy were also introduced. Table 4 below contains all the information about the taxonomy, which consists of the comment type name and its description (the types in bold text are newly introduced types in the taxonomy).

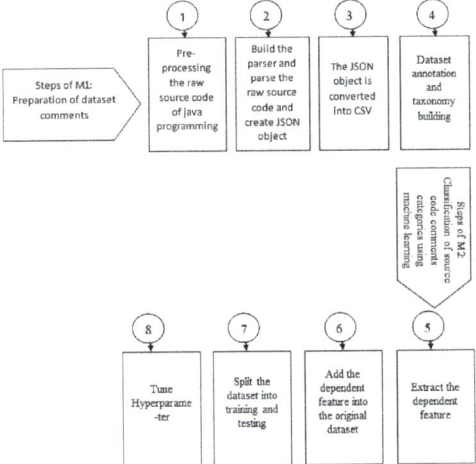

Figure 3. Overall methodology.

Figure 3 depicts the overall methodology, which consists of two steps (M1 and M2), each represented by an arrow symbol and each sub-step by a number. The first step, which we called M1, was the preparation of the dataset represented by 1–4. In substep 1, the raw source code is pre-processed. In the second sub-step, the parser is built through which the raw source code is parsed to create a JSON object containing the source code comments. In the third sub-step, the JSON object is converted into CSV. In the fourth sub-step, a taxonomy is built, and the annotation is performed on a CSV file. The second step, M2, involves the classification of source code using various machine learning algorithms; the second part is represented as 5–8. In the fifth sub-step, feature extraction is performed, and in the sixth sub-step, we divided the dataset into training and testing. Then, in the seventh sub-step, a machine learning classification model was implemented, and in the last sub-step, three evaluation measures were used to evaluate the performance of the algorithm.

3.3.2. M2: Classification of Source Code Comments Categories Using Machine Learning Techniques

The methodology (M2) covers points from 5 to 8 in the algorithm and aims to answer *RQ-2*. M2 consists of 4 steps, i.e., (i) extract the dependent features from data, (ii) add the extracted features to the original dataset, (iii) split the dataset into training and testing, and (iv) tune the hyper-parameter for the machine learning model. We further explain these steps in detail in the next Experiment section.

4. Experiment

Several experiments are performed to assess the effectiveness of the suggested method. A machine equipped with an Intel Xeon E5-2630 v4 CPU, 64G RAM, Windows 10 with 64-bit OS, and the Jupyter notebook was used to conduct the tests. We exploited precision, recall, and accuracy as the performance metrics to report the results.

4.1. Characteristics of Datasets

In order to run machine learning experiments, it is important to have datasets available for these experiments. Often, the data required for an experiment are not readily available in the desired format. Therefore, it must be created from scratch. Similarly, this was the case in our experiment, and we had to prepare our datasets. A total of 5000 samples were acquired in the dataset preparation process. The information contained in Table 3 describes each feature/attribute present in our dataset.

4.2. Performing Feature Extraction

The feature engineering step was carried out on the data, and some new features were created from the existing data. This step is also called feature extraction. These new features were extracted to improve the machine learning results and enrich the feature set. Table 5 describes the new features that resulted after the feature engineering step.

Table 5. New features introduced in the dataset during feature engineering process.

No.	Feature Name	Description
1	comment_length	The number of characters present in the comment content.
2	is_license	Indicates whether the comment falls in the License category with a value of 1 or 0 (1: yes, 0: no)
3	comment_token_length	The number of tokens present in the comment content.
4	is_profile	Indicates whether the comment falls in the Profile category with a value of 1 or 0 (1: yes, 0: no)

4.3. Training and Testing the Model

After feature extraction, the dataset is split into the training and test set. The training set is used to train the classifier with the help of hyperparameter tuning, and later the model was evaluated according to accuracy and other parameters by using the test set for predictions.

Code comments written by students are often too general or premature and lack the precision of those written by more experienced developers. From the code perspective, the apparent characteristics of the code comments can be extracted as the features, e.g., what is the text that creates a comment, from where does the comment start, etc. The features listed in Table 3 were extracted based on these apparent characteristics of comments to prepare the initial dataset for this experiment. The initial dataset was examined, and a feature engineering process was performed to derive more meaningful features that can enhance the overall prediction of the machine learning model. The impact of features from Table 5 is demonstrated in the Result and Discussion section.

4.4. Hyperparameter Tuning

Hyperparameters are the adjustable parameters of a machine learning model architecture, and these cannot be assigned randomly, but rather optimizing and selecting the ideal parameters is needed to improve the machine learning model's performance. Therefore, this process is called hyperparameter tuning. We performed the hyperparameter tuning of the machine learning model in our experiments to enhance their overall performance. K-fold cross-validation of 5 folds was applied to tune the machine learning model and gain the values for the hyperparameters.

Among the three classifiers, Decision Tree was the most accurate classifier for predicting the comment categories, and then Random Forest also gave relatively better results. However, Support Vector Machine only performed well on the textual data; therefore, we performed hyperparameter tuning on the Random Forest to further improve its results. As discussed above, the 5-fold cross-validation method was used to obtain the values for the hyperparameters. We employed *GridSearchCV* from the *Scikit-learn* library; it is a method that exhaustively considers all parameter combinations (as shown in Listing 2), providing a means for finding the best parameter settings.

Listing 2. Parameter combinations for the hyperparmater tuning of Random Forest classifier.

```
1    param_grid_rf = {
2      'n_estimator': [200, 300, 400, 500, 600, 700, 800, 1000],
3      max_features': [' auto '],
4      'max_depth': [20, 22, 24, 26, 28, 30],
5      'random_state': [ x for x in range (6,100,2)]
6    }
```

4.5. Evaluation and Performance Metrics

Every experiment evaluation requires some performance measure to validate the results. We used four performance measures in our study, i.e., *accuracy, precision, recall,* and *F1-Scores*. The main reasons for selecting these measures are their widespread acceptance in machine learning. These performance measures are obtained from the classification report of the machine learning model.

Model accuracy measures how accurately a classification model predicts classifications. A model's accuracy is defined by the number of correct classifications divided by the number of total predictions.

$$Accuracy = \frac{Total\ Number\ of\ Correct\ reponses\ for\ a\ class}{Total\ Number\ of\ responses\ for\ a\ class}$$

The precision measure is also known as *positive predictive value (PPV)*, which indicates the proportion of positive instances among all the positive class predictions. This prediction measure is defined for each class output individually. The outcome is different for each parameter.

$$Precision_{(class)} = \frac{Total\ Number\ of\ Correct\ predictions\ for\ a\ class}{Total\ Number\ of\ resulting\ predictions\ for\ a\ class}$$

The *recall* tells how many of all the positive samples were correctly identified as such by the classifier. It is also known as *true positive rate (TPR)* or sensitivity. Recall measure is also defined for each class output individually.

$$Recall_{(class)} = \frac{Total\ Number\ of\ Correct\ predictions\ for\ a\ class}{Total\ Number\ of\ Actual\ predictions\ for\ a\ class}$$

By calculating the harmonic mean of a classifier's precision and recall, the *F1-score* integrates both into a single metric.

$$F1-Score_{(class)} = \frac{2 \times Precision \times Recall}{Precision + Recall}$$

5. Results and Discussion

5.1. RQ-1 Which Kind of Code Activities Are Performed by Novice Students/Developers in the Source Code?

In order to answer this research question, we manually analyzed each comment's content and assigned them a suitable category. The category should be a representation of the whole source code comment. Master's students performed this activity for all the source code comments. The student's supervisor and co-supervisor cross-checked the labels to verify this activity. The outcome of this labeling activity was a taxonomy of categories representing different aspects of the source code.

According to our results, the source code comments are mainly distributed in the categories such as *Literal, Insufficient, Conceptual, License, Profile, Irrelevant, Commented code, Autogenerated, Improper,* and *Empty*. The distribution of the dataset according to the "category" is reported in Table 4 and Figure 4. We observed that the more frequent source code comment categories in our dataset are "*Insufficient*" and "*Literal*" (1333, 26.66% each). This may be due to students' inability to write better comments as the large proportion of comments falls in the "*Insufficient*" and "*Literal*" categories. The *Literal* category just restates the source code and does not provide any additional insight into the program logic. Whereas in the *Insufficient* category, comments either do not provide enough information for understanding or are verbose, i.e., adding no value. Moreover, large numbers of *conceptual* comments (1111, 22.22%) are present in our dataset, followed by *License* (259, 5.18%). This makes sense because, generally, students write some *conceptual* comments to explain the functionality of source code in detail without simply restating the code. *License* comments are more focused on the terms of use and the licensing of the source code. It usually appears at the top of the source code.

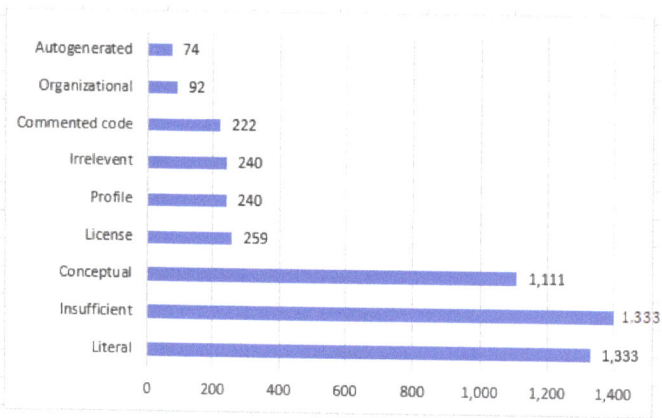

Figure 4. Distribution of code-comments data by the type column feature.

Empty (41, 0.82%) category source code comments are rare in our dataset. We presume that developers very rarely write "//" or does not write any comment on the source code.

Furthermore, as discussed, Table 4 depicts the complete taxonomy that is obtained after pre-processing, carefully analyzing, and annotation of the source code comments. The *bold* category type, frequency, and description are indicated as our *contribution* as new categories to the existing taxonomy. The new categories of the taxonomy that emerged from our dataset are:

- **License (259, 5.18%):** License is the code comments that contain information on the terms of use and the licensing of the source code. It usually appears at the top of the source code.
- **Profile (240, 4.80%):** This comment contains the information of authors and the ownership of the work; it usually begins with the "@author" tag.
- **Irrelevant (240, 4.80%):** It is not easy to comprehend the meaning of the comment. This type of comment does not describe the associated code.
- **Commented code (222, 4.44%):** This category contains all the comments that contain source code which were commented out by the developer.
- **Auto-generated (74, 1.48%):** This category contains metadata left behind by an IDE and contains only the skeleton with a placeholder provided by the IDE.
- **Improper (55, 1.10%):** This category includes comments that are not properly implemented, e.g., a comment should have an associated code directly below the comment body without any empty lines in between.

From the above results, these obtained categories can be used as a checklist for novice developers to check what types of comments developers focus on during software development. It is interesting to note that novice developers frequently mention the *Literal* type of comments in their source code. This is reasonable because the comments of novice developers are more specific to what they are implementing in their source code. Moreover, the comments type *Empty* has been used significantly less by novice developers, which means developers tend to comment on what activities are performed in source code.

Distribution of Data According to Type of Comments

We further analyzed that there are two types of comments present in our dataset: (i) single-line comments and (ii) multi-line comments. The data distribution according to the "type" column is shown in Table 6, along with its graphical representation in Figure 5. It is evident from the figure that students are more comfortable writing single-line comments than writing more detailed comments in the form of multi-line. We attribute this to the fact that students are still in the learning phase and lack attention to the code documentation aspect.

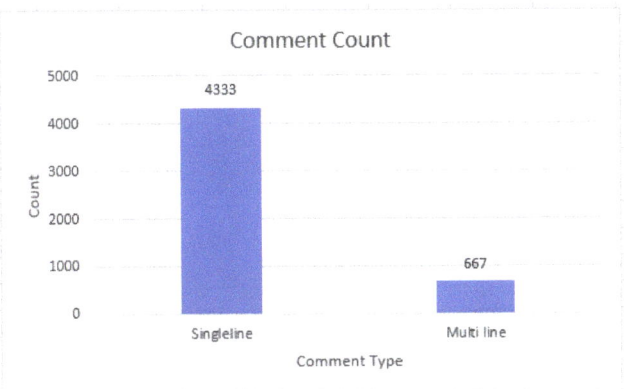

Figure 5. Distribution of code-comments data by the type column feature.

Table 6. Distribution of data by "type" column.

Type	Total
Single-line	4333
Multi-line	667

After the dataset and taxonomy preparation, the experiments were carried out in Python using the Jupyter notebook. Mainly, three machine learning algorithms were implemented to conduct the experiment: *Support Vector Machine, Random Forest, and Decision Trees*. Table 7 reports the results of three models for their accuracy measure with a comparison of the after and before feature extraction steps. The results show that all three classifiers' performance was enhanced after implementing feature extraction.

Table 7. Accuracy measure of proposed machine learning algorithm.

Method	Before Feature Extraction	After Feature Extraction
Random Forest	0.68 (68%)	0.84 (84%)
Decision Tree	0.72 (72%)	0.85 (85%)
Support Vector Machine	0.31 (31%)	0.59 (59%)

5.2. RQ-2 Is It Possible to Classify Student Source Code Comments Using Machine Learning Techniques?

In order to answer this research question, we applied three machine learning algorithms to our labeled dataset obtained in **RQ-1**. The algorithms considered in our study to classify the source code comments are: (i) *Support Vector Machine (SVM)*, (ii) *Decision Tree*, and (iii) *Random Forest*. After the machine learning models were implemented, the results were recorded. We analyzed the results with three performance parameters, i.e., *accuracy, precision, and recall*.

Table 7 and Figure 6 represent the comparison of the *accuracy* measure for all three classifiers. The feature extraction helped in improving the overall performance of all three classifiers. As apparent from the results, the *Decision Tree* algorithm outperformed the rest of the two models with an overall accuracy of 0.85 (85%). The performance of the *Support Vector Machine* was poor. We presume that this is the one main reason it was not used previously for such a problem, i.e., classification of source code comments.

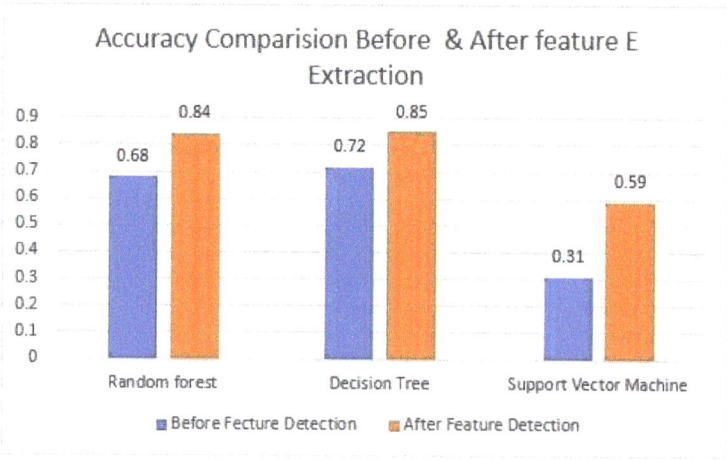

Figure 6. Classifiers accuracy before and after feature extraction.

Figure 6 shows a graphical representation of the accuracy before feature extraction and after feature extraction.

One interesting aspect to note from Table 8 and Figure 7 is that the *Support Vector Machine* classifier produced good results when only the text feature (i.e., comment content) was selected as the only predictor for the machine learning model. However, when both quantitative data (numerical information such as token comment size, length, etc.) and textual data (e.g., comment text) were used as predictors, both *Random Forest* and *Decision Tree* achieved good performance.

Table 8. Accuracy of all three classifiers on text data.

Method	Accuracy on Text Feature
Random Forest	0.83 (83%)
Decision Tree	0.86 (86%)
Support Vector Machine	0.83 (83%)

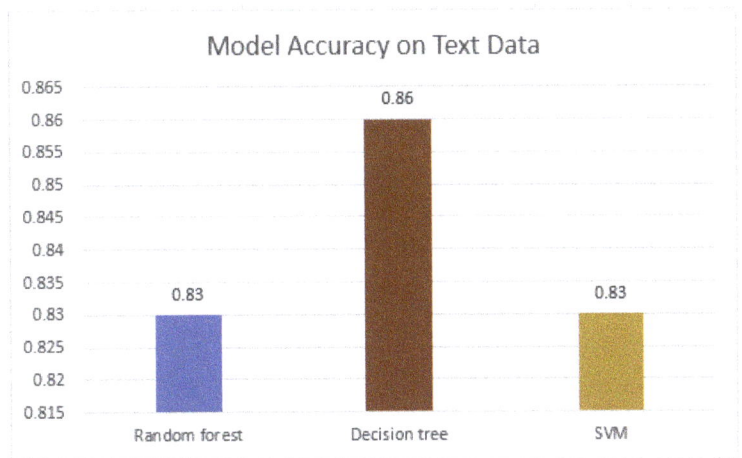

Figure 7. Accuracy of all three classifiers on text data only.

P. Beck et al. [10] evaluated and analyzed the code comments with a single label as either sufficient or insufficient using a binary classifier. In their research study, they only considered the text feature of the comments. They demonstrated that after the reduction in the vocabulary size due to lemmatization, the Multinomial Naive Bayes classifier's accuracy was reduced by 5%, but Random Forest Classifier's accuracy was improved by 6%. The results of their study reveal that they achieved an overall precision rate of 82% using Multinomial Naïve Bayes. By using a Random Forest classifier and lemmatization, they were able to achieve a classification precision of 90%. In another study, L. Pascarella [36] compared the performance of two machine learning models to automatically classify code comments in five open-source mobile applications. Their aim was to assess code comments produced by professional developers. Specifically, they used two well-known classes of supervised machine learning algorithms based on probabilistic classifiers and Decision Tree algorithms: Naive Bayes Multinomial and Random Forest. According to their results, Random Forest outperformed the Naive Bayes Multinomial classifier in automatically classifying the code comments. In our research study, we employed three different machine learning classifiers to compare their performance results. All three models produced better results on text data; however, when the other quantitative features were taken into account, both Random Forest and Decision Tree produced good results than the Support Vector Machine, with Decision Tree having the highest accuracy, i.e., 85%. It is interesting to note that previous studies, as discussed above, also revealed the effectiveness of the Random Forest classifier for classifying source code comments.

Table 9 and Figure 8 represent the *precision, recall* and *F1-Score* of *Random Forest* and *Decision Tree* on all the source code comments categories of our dataset. The overall accuracy achieved in the case of *Random Forest* is 0.84 (84%), whereas the overall accuracy in the case of *Decision Tree* is 0.85 (85%), which means we obtain the best result on the Decision Tree.

Table 9. The Precision, Recall anf F1-Score for Random Forest and Decision Tree.

	Random Forest			Decision Trees		
	Precision	Recall	F1-score	Precision	Recall	F1-score
Autogenerated	1	0.5	0.67	1	0.5	0.67
Commented code	1	0.75	0.86	1	1	1
Conceptual	0.75	0.9	0.82	0.75	0.9	0.82
Improper	0	0	0	0	0	0
Insufficient	0.86	0.95	0.9	0.9	0.95	0.92
Irrelevant	1	0.67	0.8	0.67	0.67	0.67
License	1	1	1	1	1	1
Literal	0.78	0.74	0.76	0.82	0.74	0.78
Organizational	1	1	1	1	1	1
Profile	1	0.67	0.67	1	0.67	0.8
	Overall Accuracy 0.84			Overall Accuracy 0.85		

Figure 8. The precision and recall for Random Forest and Decision Tree.

6. Conclusions

In this study, initially, we manually classified the source code comments and then presented a machine-learning approach to classify source code comments written by novice developers/students enrolled at Mohammad Ali Jinnah University. This work is inspired by many aspects, such as student metacognition, focusing on internal student processes while writing code; teacher–student feedback activity, introducing automated feedback and reducing teacher dependency; and studying the machine learning approach to code-comment analysis. The results of our study depicted that novice developers/students' comments are mainly related to *Literal* (26.66%) and *Insufficient* (26.66%). Further, we proposed and extended a taxonomy of such source code comments by adding a few more categories, i.e., *License* (5.18%), *Profile* (4.80%), *Irrelevant* (4.80%), *Commented Code* (4.44%),

Autogenerated (1.48%), and *Improper* (1.10%). Moreover, after applying different machine learning algorithms, we found that the *Decision Tree* has the overall highest accuracy, i.e., 85%, and performed better than other studied techniques. Classification of source code comments is important from the perspective of how students utilize this important code convention in providing the documentation for their programming code. This study helps not only in predicting the type of code comments using the machine learning approach but also can serve as a basis for designing a utility that can be implemented to generate automated feedback for students, thus, saving teachers' time for manual one-on-one feedback, which is a time-consuming activity. The objectives of this study included building a source code parser, designing a taxonomy for the categorization of source code comments, and implementing the different machine learning models and their results and evaluations. The datasets for this research study were not available. Therefore, they were extracted from the raw source code of student programming tasks. The machine learning models performed classification with a reasonably good accuracy of 85%, achieved by *Decision Tree*, and hence, outperformed the other two algorithms.

7. Future Work

This study provides a foundation for future directions in this area of research. As previously discussed, the research in this software engineering domain is ongoing and offers much potential for further study. This also opens more ways for pursuing research in this field of study. In the future, other machine learning models can be analyzed by their performance. Furthermore, the NLP approach to classifying source code comments can be carried out and compared with the machine learning approach as a comparison. Moreover, in the future, the idea related to predicting the contribution of each feature to the classification model using Random Forest variables with SHAP can be implemented as an extension to the current work with anticipation of further enhancing the effectiveness and accuracy of our research objective. We also aim to incorporate the code context and CodeBert in our intended extension of this research effort.

Author Contributions: Conceptualization, T.N. and S.W.; Methodology, T.N., T.D. and S.M.W.; Software, T.N. and S.K. (Sumra Khan); Validation, T.D.; Investigation, T.D., S.K. (Sumra Khan) and S.W.; Resources, G.A.; Data curation, G.A. and S.W.; Writing—original draft, S.M.W.; Writing—review & editing, S.K. (Suleman Khan) and A.A.A.; Supervision, G.A. and S.W. All authors have read and agreed to the published version of the manuscript.

Funding: This research received no external funding.

Data Availability Statement: Not applicable.

Conflicts of Interest: The authors declare no conflict of interest.

References

1. Smit, M.; Gergel, B.; Hoover, H.J.; Stroulia, E. Maintainability and source code conventions: An analysis of open source projects. *Univ. Alta. Dep. Comput. Sci. Tech. Rep. TR11* **2011**, 6.
2. dos Santos, R.M.; Gerosa, M.A. Impacts of coding practices on readability. In Proceedings of the 26th Conference on Program Comprehension, Gothenburg, Sweden, 27–28 May 2018; pp. 277–285.
3. Tenny, T. Program readability: Procedures versus comments. *IEEE Trans. Softw. Eng.* **1988**, *14*, 1271. [CrossRef]
4. Tenny, T. Procedures and comments vs. the banker's algorithm. *Acm Sigcse Bull.* **1985**, *17*, 44–53. [CrossRef]
5. Rubio-González, C.; Liblit, B. Expect the unexpected: Error code mismatches between documentation and the real world. In Proceedings of the 9th ACM SIGPLAN-SIGSOFT Workshop on Program Analysis for Software Tools and Engineering, Toronto, ON, Canada, 5–6 June 2010; pp. 73–80.
6. Subramanian, S.; Inozemtseva, L.; Holmes, R. Live API documentation. In Proceedings of the 36th International Conference on Software Engineering, Hyderabad, India, 31 May–7 June 2014; pp. 643–652.
7. Goffi, A.; Gorla, A.; Ernst, M.D.; Pezzè, M. Automatic generation of oracles for exceptional behaviors. In Proceedings of the 25th International Symposium on Software Testing and Analysis, Saarbrücken, Germany, 18–20 July 2016; pp. 213–224.
8. Pascarella, L.; Bacchelli, A. Classifying code comments in Java open-source software systems. In Proceedings of the 2017 IEEE/ACM 14th International Conference on Mining Software Repositories (MSR), Buenos Aires, Argentina, 20–28 May 2017; pp. 227–237.

9. Mohammadi-Aragh, M.J.; Beck, P.J.; Barton, A.K.; Reese, D.; Jones, B.A.; Jankun-Kelly, M. Coding the coders: A qualitative investigation of students' commenting patterns. In Proceedings of the 2018 ASEE Annual Conference Exposition, Salt Lake City, UT, USA, 23–27 July 2018.
10. Beck, P.; Mohammadi-Aragh, M.J.; Archibald, C. An Initial Exploration of Machine Learning Techniques to Classify Source Code Comments in Real-time. In Proceedings of the 2019 ASEE Annual Conference & Exposition, Tampa, FL, USA, 15 June–19 October 2019.
11. Hartzman, C.S.; Austin, C.F. Maintenance productivity: Observations based on an experience in a large system environment. In Proceedings of the 1993 Conference of the Centre for Advanced Studies on Collaborative Research: Software Engineering, Toronto, ON, Canada, 22–25 November 1993; Volume 1, pp. 138–170.
12. Jiang, Z.M.; Hassan, A.E. Examining the evolution of code comments in PostgreSQL. In Proceedings of the 2006 International Workshop on Mining Software Repositories, Shanghai, China, 22–23 May 2006; pp. 179–180.
13. de Souza, S.C.B.; Anquetil, N.; de Oliveira, K.M. A study of the documentation essential to software maintenance. In Proceedings of the 23rd Annual International Conference on Design of Communication: Documenting & Designing for Pervasive Information, Coventry, UK, 21–23 September 2005; pp. 68–75.
14. Oman, P.; Hagemeister, J. Metrics for assessing a software system's maintainability. In Proceedings of the Conference on Software Maintenance 1992, IEEE Computer Society, Orlando, FL, USA, 9–12 November 1992; pp. 337–338.
15. Garcia, M.J.B.; Granja-Alvarez, J.C. Maintainability as a key factor in maintenance productivity: A case study. In Proceedings of the Icsm, Monterey, CA, USA, 4–8 November 1996; p. 87.
16. Khamis, N.; Witte, R.; Rilling, J. Automatic quality assessment of source code comments: The JavadocMiner. In Proceedings of the International Conference on Application of Natural Language to Information Systems, Cardiff, UK, 23–25 June 2010; Springer: Berlin/Heidelberg, Germany, 2010; pp. 68–79.
17. Steidl, D.; Hummel, B.; Juergens, E. Quality analysis of source code comments. In Proceedings of the 2013 21st International Conference on Program Comprehension (icpc), San Francisco, CA, USA, 20–21 May 2013; pp. 83–92.
18. Sun, X.; Geng, Q.; Lo, D.; Duan, Y.; Liu, X.; Li, B. Code comment quality analysis and improvement recommendation: An automated approach. *Int. J. Softw. Eng. Knowl. Eng.* **2016**, *26*, 981–1000. [CrossRef]
19. Tan, L.; Yuan, D.; Krishna, G.; Zhou, Y. comment: Bugs or bad comments? In Proceedings of the ACM Symposium on Operating Systems Principles: Proceedings of Twenty-First ACM SIGOPS Symposium on Operating Systems Principles, New York, NY, USA, 3–6 November 2007; Volume 14, pp. 145–158.
20. Ratol, I.K.; Robillard, M.P. Detecting fragile comments. In Proceedings of the 2017 32nd IEEE/ACM International Conference on Automated Software Engineering (ASE), Urbana-Champaign, IL, USA, 30 October–3 November 2017; pp. 112–122.
21. Das, T.; Penta, M.D.; Malavolta, I. A Quantitative and Qualitative Investigation of Performance-Related Commits in Android Apps. In Proceedings of the 2016 IEEE International Conference on Software Maintenance and Evolution, ICSME 2016, IEEE Computer Society, Raleigh, NC, USA, 2–7 October 2016; pp. 443–447. [CrossRef]
22. Allamanis, M.; Peng, H.; Sutton, C. A convolutional attention network for extreme summarization of source code. In Proceedings of the International Conference on Machine Learning, New York City, NY, USA, 19–24 June 2016; pp. 2091–2100.
23. Hu, X.; Li, G.; Xia, X.; Lo, D.; Jin, Z. Deep code comment generation. In Proceedings of the 2018 IEEE/ACM 26th International Conference on Program Comprehension (ICPC), Gothenburg, Sweden, 27 May–3 June 2018; pp. 200–20010.
24. Haiduc, S.; Aponte, J.; Marcus, A. Supporting program comprehension with source code summarization. In Proceedings of the 2010 ACM/IEEE 32nd International Conference on Software Engineering, Cape Town, South Africa, 1–8 May 2010; Volume 2, pp. 223–226.
25. Haiduc, S.; Aponte, J.; Moreno, L.; Marcus, A. On the use of automated text summarization techniques for summarizing source code. In Proceedings of the 2010 17th Working Conference on Reverse Engineering, Washington, DC, USA, 13–16 October 2010; pp. 35–44.
26. Huang, Y.; Zheng, Q.; Chen, X.; Xiong, Y.; Liu, Z.; Luo, X. Mining version control system for automatically generating commit comment. In Proceedings of the 2017 ACM/IEEE International Symposium on Empirical Software Engineering and Measurement (ESEM), Toronto, ON, Canada, 9–10 November 2017; pp. 414–423.
27. Lawrie, D.J.; Feild, H.; Binkley, D. Leveraged quality assessment using information retrieval techniques. In Proceedings of the 14th IEEE International Conference on Program Comprehension (ICPC'06), Athens, Greece, 14–16 June 2006; pp. 149–158.
28. Marcus, A.; Maletic, J.I. Recovering documentation-to-source-code traceability links using latent semantic indexing. In Proceedings of the 25th International Conference on Software Engineering, Portland, OR, USA, 3–10 May 2003; pp. 125–135.
29. Chen, H.; Huang, Y.; Liu, Z.; Chen, X.; Zhou, F.; Luo, X. Automatically detecting the scopes of source code comments. *J. Syst. Softw.* **2019**, *153*, 45–63. [CrossRef]
30. Hata, H.; Treude, C.; Kula, R.G.; Ishio, T. 9.6 million links in source code comments: Purpose, evolution, and decay. In Proceedings of the 2019 IEEE/ACM 41st International Conference on Software Engineering (ICSE), Montreal, QC, Canada, 27 May 2019; pp. 1211–1221.
31. Alghamdi, M.; Hayashi, S.; Kobayashi, T.; Treude, C. Characterising the Knowledge about Primitive Variables in Java Code Comments. In Proceedings of the 2021 IEEE/ACM 18th International Conference on Mining Software Repositories (MSR), Madrid, Spain, 17–19 May 2021; pp. 460–470.

32. Haouari, D.; Sahraoui, H.; Langlais, P. How good is your comment? A study of comments in java programs. In Proceedings of the 2011 International Symposium on Empirical Software Engineering and Measurement, Banff, AB, Canada, 22–23 September 2011; pp. 137–146.
33. Zhai, J.; Xu, X.; Shi, Y.; Tao, G.; Pan, M.; Ma, S.; Xu, L.; Zhang, W.; Tan, L.; Zhang, X. CPC: Automatically classifying and propagating natural language comments via program analysis. In Proceedings of the ACM/IEEE 42nd International Conference on Software Engineering, Seoul, Republic of Korea, 27 June–19 July 2020; pp. 1359–1371.
34. Vieira, C.; Magana, A.J.; Falk, M.L.; Garcia, R.E. Writing in-code comments to self-explain in computational science and engineering education. *ACM Trans. Comput. Educ. (TOCE)* **2017**, *17*, 1–21. [CrossRef]
35. Beck, P.J.; Mohammadi-Aragh, M.J.; Archibald, C.; Jones, B.A.; Barton, A. Real-time metacognition feedback for introductory programming using machine learning. In Proceedings of the 2018 IEEE Frontiers in Education Conference (FIE), Lincoln, NE, USA, 13–16 October 2018; pp. 1–5.
36. Pascarella, L. Classifying code comments in Java mobile applications. In Proceedings of the 2018 IEEE/ACM 5th International Conference on Mobile Software Engineering and Systems (MOBILESoft), Gothenburg, Sweden, 27 May–3 June 2018.

Disclaimer/Publisher's Note: The statements, opinions and data contained in all publications are solely those of the individual author(s) and contributor(s) and not of MDPI and/or the editor(s). MDPI and/or the editor(s) disclaim responsibility for any injury to people or property resulting from any ideas, methods, instructions or products referred to in the content.

Article

Fourier Neural Operator for Fluid Flow in Small-Shape 2D Simulated Porous Media Dataset

Abouzar Choubineh [1,2,*], Jie Chen [2,*], David A. Wood [3], Frans Coenen [1] and Fei Ma [2]

1. Department of Computer Science, University of Liverpool, Liverpool L69 7ZX, UK
2. Department of Applied Mathematics, Xi'an Jiaotong-Liverpool University, Suzhou 215123, China
3. DWA Energy Limited, Lincoln LN5 9JP, UK
* Correspondence: a.choubineh@liverpool.ac.uk or a.choubineh20@student.xjtlu.edu.cn (A.C.); jie.chen01@xjtlu.edu.cn (J.C.)

Abstract: Machine Learning (ML) and/or Deep Learning (DL) methods can be used to predict fluid flow in porous media, as a suitable replacement for classical numerical approaches. Such data-driven approaches attempt to learn mappings between finite-dimensional Euclidean spaces. A novel neural framework, named Fourier Neural Operator (FNO), has been recently developed to act on infinite-dimensional spaces. A high proportion of the research available on the FNO has focused on problems with large-shape data. Furthermore, most published studies apply the FNO method to existing datasets. This paper applies and evaluates FNO to predict pressure distribution over a small, specified shape-data problem using 1700 Finite Element Method (FEM) generated samples, from heterogeneous permeability fields as the input. Considering FEM-calculated outputs as the true values, the configured FNO model provides superior prediction performance to that of a Convolutional Neural Network (CNN) in terms of statistical error assessment based on the coefficient of determination (R^2) and Mean Squared Error (MSE). Sensitivity analysis considering a range of FNO configurations reveals that the most accurate model is obtained using $modes = 15$ and $width = 100$. Graphically, the FNO model precisely follows the observed trend in each porous medium evaluated. There is potential to further improve the FNO's performance by including physics constraints in its network configuration.

Keywords: subsurface fluid flow; Fourier neural operator; small-shape data; finite element method; convolutional neural network; sensitivity analysis

1. Introduction

A wide range of phenomena/processes in science and engineering are described via measurable/estimable quantities that rely on independent variables. As an example, in subsurface fluid flow, pressure and temperature are typically measured based on the time and location variables. Given the available fundamental laws, it is feasible to determine the relationships among the rates of change of these physical quantities. The mathematical correlations typically used to do this are Ordinary and/or Partial Differential Equations (ODEs/PDEs). In ODEs, the derivatives of the dependent variable(s) are taken with respect to only one independent variable. On the other hand, partial derivatives are required in PDEs when there are two or more independent variables involved.

Theories, methods, and tools available in scientific computing (also called computational science) make it possible to solve mathematical models of physical phenomena described in terms of ODEs and/or PDEs [1]. The theories and methods are together called numerical analysis/numerical mathematics, and tools refer to computer systems on which codes are run. The more complex the mathematical models, the more advanced the computational hardware requirements are to solve them. There are various numerical methods available that can provide approximate solutions to such problems. These include the finite difference method [2], Finite Element Method (FEM) [3], finite volume method [4], spectral method [5], and meshless method [6]. Such methods are usually time-consuming to apply.

One way to mitigate the problem of the high computational cost in numerical calculations required to determine complex systems is to apply Machine Learning (ML) and/or Deep Learning (DL) techniques. Machine learning methods such as Neural Network (NN), adaptive-neuro-fuzzy-inference system, support-vector machine, and decision tree are widely employed to find and predict relevant patterns within datasets. Machine learning is now used to great advantage in various fields [7–10]. Deep learning methods represent more complex extensions of existing ML methods, particularly neural networks, and have demonstrated improved performance, particularly when applied to large datasets [11–15]. There are various DL algorithms, including Convolutional Neural Network (CNN), deep auto-encoder, deep-belief network, recurrent neural network, and generative adversarial network. There are some differences between ML and DL. For instance, manual feature engineering tends to be performed with ML algorithms, sometimes requiring domain knowledge about a given problem. To make the point clear, consider 'filling missing values'. A dataset can include missing values due to the difficulty of collecting complete data. Missing values can be manually filled in based on expert knowledge, which is sometimes a tedious process. However, with DL algorithms this is more often not required, being performed automatically.

Classical neural networks concentrate on learning mappings between finite-dimensional spaces. This makes such networks, when configured, confined to a particular discretization (i.e., they are mesh-dependent). Mesh-independent networks have been developed to reduce such constraints. In this regard, the Fourier Neural Operator (FNO) has recently been proposed to learn a continuous function via parameterizing the model in its function space [16]. This makes it possible for FNO to be trained on one mesh and subsequently evaluated on another. Unlike standard feed-forward networks that use activation functions (e.g., sigmoid, tanh, relu), training an FNO model using the Fourier transform to find optimum weights and biases is performed by employing sines and cosines as activation functions [17–19].

The Fourier neural operator has demonstrated its capabilities in solving parametric PDEs. Different models were developed to solve the Navier–Stokes equation for a viscous, incompressible fluid in vorticity form on the unit torus [16]. The viscosity was set to 0.001, 0.0001, and 0.00001. The resolution was 64×64 for both training and testing. Based on the results, the FNO-3D had the best performance in the case of available sufficient data. When the amount of data was not sufficient, the FNO-2D achieved the lowest error.

An improved FNO-based DL model, U-FNO, was developed to solve a CO_2-water multiphase flow problem over a wide range of rock–fluid properties, such as permeability, anisotropy, and flow rate [20]. The predictions generated for gas saturation and pressure buildup confirmed the superiority of the U-FNO model compared to FNO and CNN models applied to the same dataset. Additionally, U-FNO requires few training data to match the prediction accuracy of CNN.

As a substitute for physics-based solvers, an FNO framework was employed to learn/map certain mechanical responses of 2D composites [21]. The FNO models, trained with few data, were able to predict high-resolution stress/strain tensor fields for geometrically complex microstructures. Additionally, the models exhibited zero-shot generalization with high precision on random geometries previously unseen by the trained FNO model. Moreover, the trained FNO models were able to predict high-resolution stress/strain fields when presented with low-resolution inputs.

An FNO model has also been applied to a Large Eddy Simulation (LES) of a 3D turbulence system [22]. Filtered direct numerical simulation flow-field of isotropic turbulence recorded at different times comprised the training data. In the a posteriori test of LES, The FNO model outperformed dynamic Smagorinsky and dynamic mixed models to predict the velocity spectrum, probability density functions of vorticity and velocity increments, and the instantaneous flow structures.

In addition to solving parametric PDEs, FNO has been successfully applied to solve other problems. For example, FNO was used to classify images contained in the CIFAR-10 image database comprised of 60,000 distinct samples [23]. The input samples were color images of ten different classes. A total of 83% of the total dataset was used to train the FNO, and the remaining images were used to test the trained model. According to the different evaluation criteria, the FNO performed slightly better than ResNet20. However, the FNO model was computationally more costly.

As described, some research has been conducted applying FNO models to various existing datasets. However, much of that research addresses problems involving big-shape data (e.g., 421 × 421 and 256 × 256). Thus, there is a critical lack of analysis regarding the performance of FNO models on small-shape data. Consequently, the major contribution of this paper is to apply and evaluate an FNO model to predict pressure distribution in small-shape data (30 × 30). Specifically, the study answers the following questions:

1. Can FNO models perform accurately on small-shape data problems in terms of the prediction error metrics?
2. How do mode and width affect the performance of FNO models?
3. Does downsampling have a positive or negative effect on FNO model performance when applied to small-shape data?
4. Can FNO models satisfy the pattern applicable to porous media problems?
5. How does the performance of FNO models compare to that of CNN?

A 30 × 30 uniform mesh problem from the domain of petroleum engineering is evaluated as a relevant topic with a suitable dataset to address the research questions identified. Continued constraints on the ability of the available energy supply to meet global energy demand make it important to improve our understanding of subsurface oil and gas reservoirs to improve production and resource recovery. The problem evaluated is designed to do that.

Comparing the FNO model performance with that of a CNN model applied to the same dataset is justified because CNNs are proven in their applications to 2D arrays and the mathematical basis underpinning convolutional-filter functionality is well established. Convolutional neural networks are also able to learn the spatial hierarchy of dataset characteristics on an unsupervised basis leading to good prediction performance based on relatively sparse feature selections.

The remaining sections of this article are arranged as follows. Section 2 describes the problem configuration and the dataset evaluated; Section 3 explains the configurations of the FNO and CNN models applied to the dataset and how their performances are optimized; Section 4 presents and compares the results generated by those two models; Section 5 discusses the limitations of the research; and Section 6 draws conclusions and makes recommendation for required future research.

2. Problem Setup with Governing Equations

The flow of fluids through porous media can be effectively described in terms of: (i) the Darcy (or momentum) law, (ii) mass conservation, (iii) energy drive, and (iv) case-specific rock–fluid correlations including compressibility and saturation equations, where more than one fluid is involved (e.g., gas, oil and/or water) [24]. Energy conservation can in many cases be disregarded if isothermal conditions are considered. However, for reservoir systems in which temperature changes over time, such as for surface water injected into subsurface reservoirs, energy conservation cannot be disregarded. For a single, incompressible fluid phase with constant viscosity in a 2D linear and isothermal system, Darcy's law, assuming steady-state flow and ignoring gravitational effects, can be expressed as [24]:

$$k^{-1}\mu u + \nabla p = 0 \tag{1}$$

where k = permeability, μ = fluid viscosity, u = Darcy velocity, and ∇p = gradient pressure $\left(\frac{\partial p}{\partial x}, \frac{\partial p}{\partial y}\right)$.

The formulation for the mass conservation law (also known as the continuity equation) is [24]:

$$\nabla . u = f \qquad (2)$$

here, $\nabla . u$ = divergence velocity ($\frac{\partial u_x}{\partial x} + \frac{\partial u_y}{\partial y}$), and f = source term.

By combining Equations (1) and (2) and assigning values to the viscosity and source term of one and zero, respectively, and assuming the permeability to be a diagonal tensor in the isotropic medium, the below is obtained [24]:

$$\nabla . (-k \nabla p) = 0 \qquad (3)$$

In a homogeneous porous medium, k is constant, so the formulation becomes [24]:

$$k(\nabla . \nabla p) = k \Delta p = k(\frac{\partial^2 p}{\partial x^2} + \frac{\partial^2 p}{\partial y^2}) = 0 \qquad (4)$$

where Δp = Laplace pressure.

A heterogeneous porous medium indicates that it is not homogeneous, and thus formation-related properties can have multiple scales. For example, in petroleum reservoirs, there may be numerous fractures (connected or disconnected) with different lengths, whose width is much smaller than the domain size. For a heterogeneous medium, Equation (3) changes to [24]:

$$\frac{\partial (k \frac{\partial p}{\partial x})}{\partial x} + \frac{\partial (k \frac{\partial p}{\partial y})}{\partial y} = 0 \qquad (5)$$

To solve PDEs, Boundary Conditions (BCs) and Initial Conditions (ICs) need to be specified as additional constraints on the system. The main types of BCs applied are those defined by: (i) Dirichlet (the first kind), (ii) Neumann (the second kind), and (iii) Robin or Dankwerts (the mixed or third kind). In the first type, values are assigned to the certain dependent variable(s) (e.g., pressure) while the derivatives of the certain dependent variable(s) are known in Neumann's condition. Robin's BC is a weighted combination of the first two BCs. An IC refers to a value (or a correlation) of a parameter at time $t = 0$.

For the system analyzed here, the computational domain was defined as $\Omega = [0,1] \times [0,1]$, representing a square 2D domain. Dirichlet's condition was applied on two sides: $p = 100$ (left-side boundary) and $p = 0$ (right-side boundary). Neumann's condition was applied to the other two sides: $\partial p = 0$ (top and bottom sides).

The grid selected to define each square system consisted of a 30×30 uniform mesh with the option to incorporate (or not) horizontal and/or vertical fractures. The permeability is defined as the ability of a rock to permit fluids to pass through it. The permeability in fractures is generally much higher than that of the matrix. In this research, the permeability of the matrix (K_m) and fracture (K_f) were assigned fixed values of 1 and 1000 millidarcy (md), respectively. The number of fractures (N_f) available in a porous medium was set to 5, and fractures are allowed to intersect with each other. The length of individual fractures was randomly distributed. A total of 1400 sample grids were generated in MatLab software to constitute the training dataset, and a further 300 sample grids were generated to constitute the testing dataset. The testing data, therefore, made up 17.65% of the generated grids and the training data 82.35%. Permeability fields were randomly assigned to each generated grid using the Karhunen–Loeve expansion [25], and duplicate fields were not allowed to exist in the training and/or testing datasets. Only two of the generated grids were removed during pre-processing to avoid intruding bias to specific permeability fields. Although the grid shape of each sample is small, the number of elements it covers in 1698 samples is large (1698 $\times$ 30 $\times$ 30), which makes the dataset too large to be handled by ML/DL methods.

3. Methodology

3.1. FNO Architecture

While conducting research on heat propagation, Joseph Fourier introduced the idea of a harmonic series, later called the Fourier series, which can represent any periodic function as an infinite sum of sine and cosine waves [26]. Assuming $f(x)$ defined over the interval $(-T, T)$ and outside this space $f(x + 2T) = f(x)$, the Fourier series of this periodic function is written as follows [26]:

$$f(x) = \frac{a_0}{2} + \sum_{n=1}^{\infty} [a_n \cos(\frac{n\pi x}{T}) + b_n \sin(\frac{n\pi x}{T})] \tag{6}$$

in which a_n and b_n are the Fourier series coefficients expressed in the form of integral and also a_0 is the first term of a_n when $n = 0$.

Subsequently, the Fourier transform was developed to extend the Fourier series to non-periodic functions [27]. The Fourier transform involves the decomposition of functions into frequency components. Supposing that $f(x)$ is the original function, 'i' is the imaginary number ($\sqrt{-1}$), and 's' is the angular frequency, then the mathematical definition of a continuous FT is defined as [27]:

$$F(s) = \int_{-\infty}^{\infty} f(x) e^{-2\pi i s x} dx \tag{7}$$

It is appropriate to consider the inverse of the continuous FT as [27]:

$$f(x) = \int_{-\infty}^{\infty} F(s) e^{2\pi i s x} ds \tag{8}$$

The Fourier neural operator is an operator for a neural network that performs convolutions applying the Fourier transform. This causes the higher modes to be removed from the Fourier space, leaving only the lower modes. In the following, a linear transform is applied along with an inverse Fourier transform. This makes the training process independent of the number of cells in a specific mesh.

At any location (x, y) within a mesh, the FNO algorithm first raises the input $I(x, y)$ to a higher-dimension channel space $Z_0(x, y)$, where $Z_0(x, y) = P(I(x, y))$ (Figure 1). It does this by locally applying the transform $P: \mathbb{R} \to \mathbb{R}^{d_z}$, with a parametric procedure using either a Fully Connected (FC) neural network or a simple linear layer. Z_0 is defined on the similar mesh to I and the values of Z_0 can be displaced as an image with d_z channels. Then, four successive Fourier layers are applied to Z_0. Subsequently, another transform is applied locally $Q: \mathbb{R}^{d_z} \to \mathbb{R}$. This final transform projects $Z_4(x, y)$ to the output by $O(x, y) = Q(Z_4(x, y))$. Meantime, Z_4 is the output of the fourth (final) Fourier layer and Q is parameterized by a fully connected neural network.

$Z(x, y)$ passes through two routes in the Fourier layers. In the top path, a Fourier transform F, a linear transform R on the lower Fourier modes, and an inverse Fourier transform F^{-1} are applied. $Z(x, y)$ undergoes only a local linear transform W in the bottom path. Outputs of each path are added together and then subjected to an activation function σ (here ReLu).

To establish an optimum FNO architecture, PyTorch [28] was employed with Python version 3.9.12. The models developed for the dataset applied *batch size* = 5, *epochs* = 500, *step size* = 100, *gamma* = 0.9, and *downsampling rate* = 1 in this research. Additionally, 'Adam' [29] was used as the optimizer with a learning rate of 0.001 and a weight decay of 0.0001. Adam uses a distinct learning rate for each scalar parameter and adapts these rates during the whole training process considering the historical values of the partial derivatives of each parameter. This gradient-based algorithm combines the ability of (i) AdaGrad to handle sparse gradients and (ii) RMSProp to function in online and non-stationary settings. The input and output shapes defined were 30 × 30 × 1 and 30 × 30, respectively. Moreover, fast Fourier transform [30] was used as a fast algorithm to compute discrete Fourier transforms and their inverses.

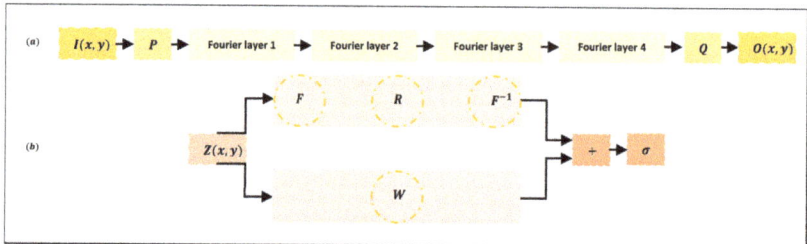

Figure 1. (**a**) Architecture of the neural operator and (**b**) Architecture of a Fourier layer.

3.2. CNN Architecture

In preparing a CNN simulation involving a unit square, a 30×30 uniform mesh was selected. On the other hand, the input/output values were defined as a 900×1 1D tensor (vector). The input shape was then changed to $30 \times 30 \times 1$ for processing through 2D convolutional filters. Regarding to the output in CNN, there were two options: keeping the initial shape or reshaping to a 2D tensor. While reshaping to 30×30, the accuracy achieved by the CNN model became substantially impaired. On the other hand, many fewer errors were generated by CNN models that retained the initial 900×1 shape. Therefore, the CNN model was developed and its computational layers processed with the 900×1 shape and only reshaped to the 30×30 output size for final visualization purposes (Figure 2).

An optimum CNN architecture was developed with five convolutional layers and two FC layers (Figure 2). The kernel numbers in the convolutional layers (referred to as CONV1 to CONV5) were 5, 45, 85, 125, and 165, respectively. Padding was set to 'same' only in CONV5 to prevent the size from changing. A 3×3 kernel size and 1×1 stride were applied to all convolutional layers, providing those layers with sizes 28×28, 26×26, 24×24, 22×22, and 22×22, respectively. A batch normalization layer (referred to as BN1 to BN5) followed CONV1 to CONV5, without changing size. Normalization of the input layer makes the CNN converge more quickly to outputs that collectively average nearly zero with a standard deviation of nearly one. The layers FC1 and FC2 contain 1500 neurons. The ReLu activation function was applied to CONV1 to CONV5, whereas the sigmoid activation function was applied to FC1 and FC2, with a linear transformation applied to generate the output layer.

The CNN model was coded using the Keras/TensorFlow packages [31] executed in virtual environments in Python version 3.9.12. It was specifically configured with the Mean Squared Error (MSE) as the loss (objective) function and 'Adam' [29] with the default values as the optimizer. The CNN was trained to apply a batch size of 16 samples and run with 500 epochs.

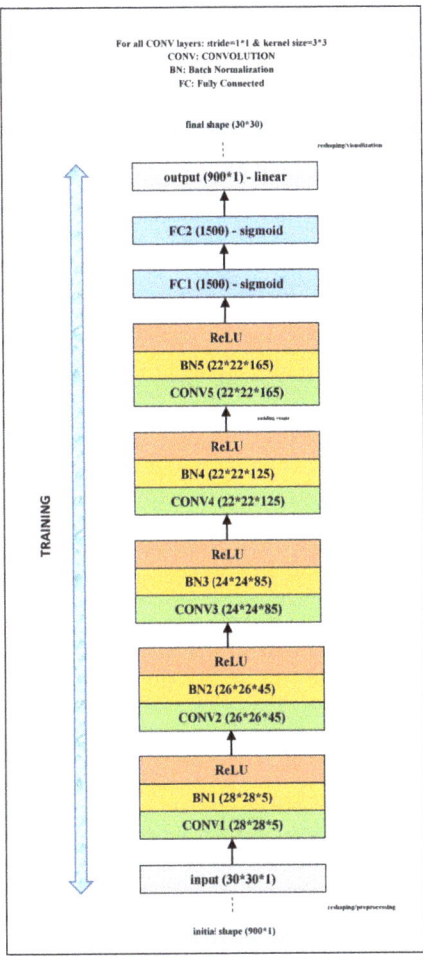

Figure 2. The structure of the CNN model used in this study.

4. Results

There are two main hyperparameters in FNO: the number of channels and modes. The former defines the width of the FNO network, referring to the number of features learned in each layer. The latter defines the number of lower Fourier modes retained when truncating the Fourier series. The size of the grid space controls the maximum allowable number of modes. In this research, five values were evaluated for the width: 20, 60, 100, 140, and 180, and four cases were evaluated for the mode: 5, 10, 15, and 20.

Figure 3a reveals that the FNO models generated very similar errors, based on MSE, when calculated based on initial pressure values (actual non-normalized values) for the training data when the number of modes is 10, 15, or 20. However, the errors increased slightly for models configured with $modes = 5$. The coefficient of determination (R^2) values for the training data varied from 0.9945 to 0.9971, according to Figure 3b. As a general result, all models were able to predict pressure with acceptable error levels for the training subset.

Figure 3c,d display the FNO results for the testing subset. The model with modes of 5 generated the poorest prediction performance, i.e., highest MSE and lowest R^2. As width increased (with modes held at 5), MSE decreased from 109.9231 to 86.3347 and R^2 increased from 0.7661 to 0.8163. When the number of modes was increased to 10, the FNO performance improved. Additionally, an increase in width had a positive effect on accuracy when modes were held at 10. The model with $modes = 15$ performed better than models with modes of 5 or 10, as it generated MSE and R^2 displaying ranges of 42.1611–65.5664 and 0.8605–0.9103, respectively. In general, the prediction performance of the FNO model with modes of 20 overlapped with that of modes of 15. Considering all twenty cases, the model with $modes = 15$ and $width = 100$ generated the best performance with an MSE of 1.4087 and R^2 of 0.997 for the training subset, and an MSE of 42.1611 and R^2 of 0.9103 for the testing subset. In addition to the graphical comparisons (Figure 3), the MSE and R^2 values achieved by all FNO cases evaluated are listed in Table 1.

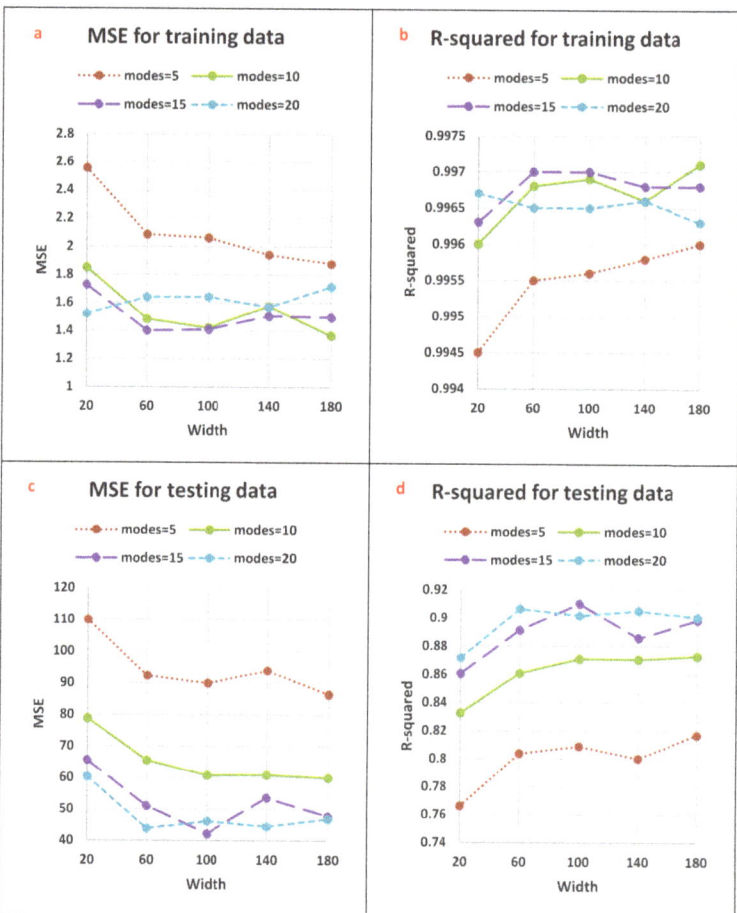

Figure 3. Prediction error graphical analysis of the developed FNO models: (**a**) MSE for training data, (**b**) R^2 for training data, (**c**) MSE for testing data, and (**d**) R^2 for testing data.

Table 1. Performance of the developed FNO models with different modes and widths based on MSE and R^2.

Mode	Width	MSE (Training)	R^2 (Training)	MSE (Testing)	R^2 (Testing)
5	20	2.5543	0.9945	109.9231	0.7661
5	60	2.0832	0.9955	92.2014	0.8038
5	100	2.0605	0.9956	89.8219	0.8089
5	140	1.943	0.9958	93.8539	0.8003
5	180	1.878	0.996	86.3347	0.8163
10	20	1.8483	0.996	78.7648	0.8324
10	60	1.4814	0.9968	65.4587	0.8607
10	100	1.4196	0.9969	60.6803	0.8709
10	140	1.5745	0.9966	60.8775	0.8705
10	180	1.3643	0.9971	59.8904	0.8726
15	20	1.7253	0.9963	65.5664	0.8605
15	60	1.4007	0.997	51.0625	0.8914
15	**100**	**1.4087**	**0.997**	**42.1611**	**0.9103**
15	140	1.505	0.9968	53.6779	0.8858
15	180	1.4966	0.9968	47.783	0.8983
20	20	1.5206	0.9967	60.3367	0.8716
20	60	1.6387	0.9965	43.8621	0.9067
20	100	1.6409	0.9965	46.167	0.9018
20	140	1.5687	0.9966	44.5223	0.9053
20	180	1.7145	0.9963	46.8985	0.9002

To assess whether downsampling has a positive or negative impact on the FNO model performance with respect to small-shape data (in the dataset modeled: 30 × 30), a downsampling rate was set to 2. By applying that rate, the data shape was reduced to 15 × 15, which led to poor prediction results. For example, with $modes = 10$ and $width = 100$, the FNO model achieved pressure predictions with MSE of 27.3128 and R^2 of 0.9411 for the training subset, and with MSE of 410.7709 and R^2 of 0.1259 for the testing subset. As to be expected, further downsampling of the initial case caused prediction accuracy to deteriorate further. A likely explanation for this outcome is that the size of the grid space controls the maximum allowable number of modes. This means that by downsampling, the allowable number of FNO modes also decreases. Meantime, because CNN acts on discretized vectors, downsampling with CNN is not reasonable.

In order to improve visualization of the pressure changes occurring over the defined shapes, three examples are illustrated for selected training (Figure 4) and testing (Figure 5) subsets. The plots in the left-side columns display the permeability fields, for representative sample grids. The plots in the left-central columns display the pressure distribution derived by FEM (considered to be true distribution). The plots in the right-central columns display the predicted pressure distributions of the best-performing FNO model developed. The plots in the right-side columns display the pressure difference between the FEM and FNO outputs $[p_{(FNO)} - p_{(FEM)}]$. Generally, there was a very close match between the true pressure distributions and those predicted by the FNO model, especially for the training dataset.

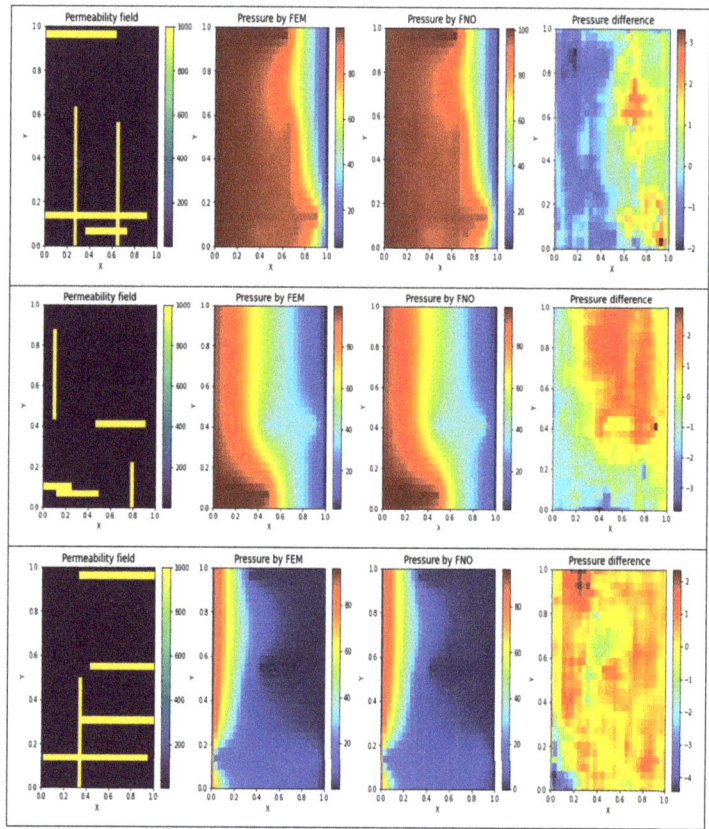

Figure 4. A comparison between the actual pressure distributions and those obtained by FNO for three representative training subset samples. The pressure difference is based on a point-by-point absolute error. Outputs are displayed as rectangles rather than squares due to a scaling issue.

The prediction performance of the CNN model is similar to that of the FNO model in terms of R^2 with regard to the training subset (Table 2). Indeed, the MSE generated by the CNN model (0.3074) is slightly less than that generated by the FNO model (1.4087). Nonetheless, the FNO model clearly provided superior results in terms of R^2 and MSE when the trained models were applied to the testing data subset. The results (Table 2) suggest that whereas the trained FNO model is well-fitted to the dataset, the trained CNN model is somewhat over-fitted to the same dataset.

Table 2. A comparison between the performance of the best-performing FNO model and the CNN model in terms of MSE and R^2.

Model	MSE (Training)	R^2 (Training)	MSE (Testing)	R^2 (Testing)
FNO ($mode = 15$ and $width = 100$)	1.4087	0.997	42.1611	0.9103
CNN	0.3074	0.9993	86.1818	0.8166

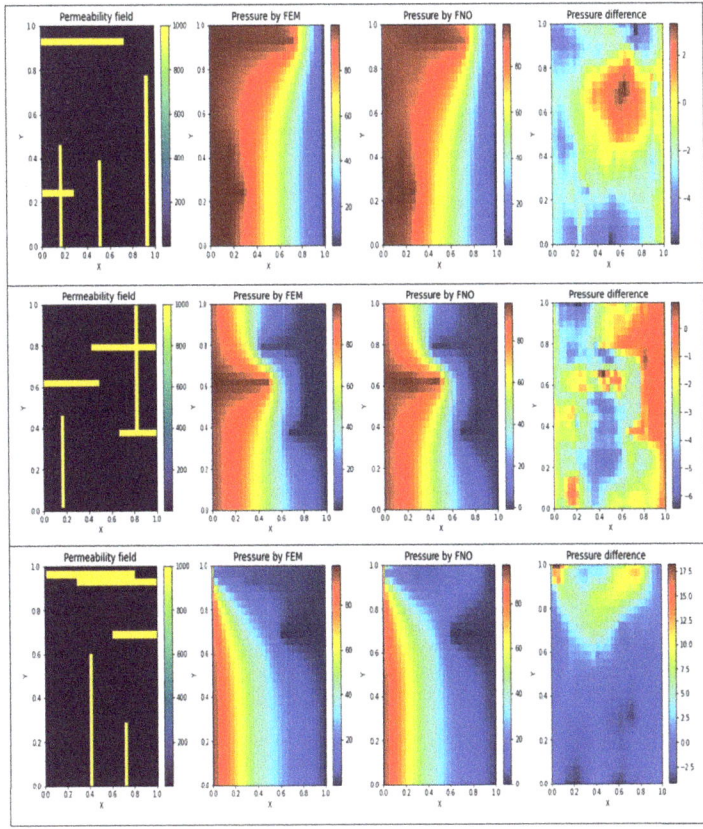

Figure 5. A comparison between the actual pressure distributions and those obtained by FNO for three representative testing subset samples. The pressure difference is based on a point-by-point absolute error. Outputs are displayed as rectangles rather than squares due to a scaling issue.

5. Discussion

The FNO model is underpinned by a rigorous mathematical methodology, as described. Furthermore, the statistical/graphical pressure prediction results associated with the small-size grids simplistically simulating fluid flow in a subsurface reservoir indicate promising prediction accuracy, which outperforms that of a CNN model. However, there is a drawback associated with the FNO model applied to these small-size grids. As with other data-driven ML/DL methods, FNO relies on the number of data samples it is provided with, and it may require a large number of small-size grids to adequately train it to fully learn the full range of possible variations in complex subsurface systems. For this reason, FNO was applied to a relatively simple example dataset, i.e., based on relatively limited assumptions of $K_m = 1$ md, $K_f = 1000$ md, and $N_f = 5$. As opposed to data-driven neural networks such as FNO, which rely exclusively on the provided data points, Physics-Informed Neural Networks (PINNs) use the PDE itself as a data source. In PINNs, the PDEs are explicitly encoded into the NN via automatic differentiation algorithms. The weighted summation of the MSE of the PDE residuals, BCs, ICs, and possibly known solution points could then be minimized as a loss function based on the NN parameters. Therefore, it could be beneficial to combine PINN and FNO to find out how the performance changes compared to a stand-alone FNO. In this sense, the model uses available data and/or physics constraints to learn the solution operator, conquering the limitations of purely data-driven and physics-based techniques.

6. Conclusions

Classical NNs attempt to learn mappings between finite-dimensional Euclidean spaces, making them confined to a particular discretization. On the other hand, the FNO, as a mesh-independent algorithm, tries to learn function-to-function mappings. This makes it possible for FNO to be trained on one mesh and subsequently assessed on another. This study further extended the capabilities of FNO by applying it to a new simulated dataset made up of small-shape samples. The generated dataset simulates single-phase fluid flow in a porous reservoir assessed by 1700 2D grid samples, each constructed as a unit square with a 30 × 30 uniform mesh. The models of FNO and CNN are trained to predict the pressure distribution of each grid sample based on its permeability field. The statistical-graphical results confirm the good ability of the FNO to predict the pressure distribution based on the permeability field. The FNO model provided better prediction performance than the CNN model when applied to the testing dataset. Analysis of the results leads to three recommendations for future research. These are: (i) training the FNO models for fluid flow in porous media with more data covering a wider range of matrix and fracture permeabilities and a variable number of fractures in each small-shape grid sample, (ii) applying FNO to solve other types of small-shape data problems, and (iii) designing and testing novel more complex FNO architectures.

Author Contributions: Conceptualization, A.C. and J.C.; methodology, A.C.; formal analysis, A.C., J.C. and D.A.W.; data curation, A.C. and J.C.; writing original draft, A.C.; writing—review and editing by A.C., D.A.W. and F.C.; visualization, A.C.; supervision, J.C., F.C. and F.M. All authors have read and agreed to the published version of the manuscript.

Funding: This work is partially supported by the Key Program Special Fund in XJTLU (KSF-E-50), XJTLU Postgraduate Research Scholarship (PGRS1912009), and XJTLU Research Development Funding (RDF-19-01-15).

Institutional Review Board Statement: Not applicable.

Informed Consent Statement: Not applicable.

Data Availability Statement: The datasets generated and supporting the findings of this article are obtainable from the corresponding author(s) upon reasonable request.

Acknowledgments: We would like to thank Zongyi Li for clarifying some points related to FNO.

Conflicts of Interest: The authors declare no conflict of interest.

Abbreviations

The following abbreviations are used in this manuscript:

a_0	first term of a_n
a_n	Fourier series coefficient
BC	Boundary Condition
BN	Batch Normalization
b_n	Fourier series coefficient
CNN	Convolutional Neural Network
CONV	convolutional layers
DL	Deep Learning
Δp	Laplace pressure
f	source term
F	Fourier transform
F^{-1}	inverse Fourier transform
FC	Fully Connected
FEM	Finite Element Method

FNO	Fourier Neural Operator
i	imaginary number ($\sqrt{-1}$)
IC	Initial Condition
$I(x,y)$	input layer
K_f	permeability of the fracture
K_m	permeability of the matrix
LES	Large Eddy Simulation
ML	Machine Learning
N_f	number of fractures
MSE	Mean Squared Error
μ	fluid viscosity
NN	Neural Network
∇p	gradient pressure ($\frac{\partial p}{\partial x}, \frac{\partial p}{\partial y}$)
$\nabla \cdot u$	divergence velocity ($\frac{\partial u_x}{\partial x} + \frac{\partial u_y}{\partial y}$)
ODE	Ordinary Differential Equation
$O(x,y)$	output layer
PDE	Partial Differential Equation
PINN	Physics-Informed Neural Network
R	linear transform
R^2	coefficient of determination
s	angular frequency
k	permeability
u	Darcy velocity
W	local linear transform
$Z_0(x,y)$	higher-dimension channel space
Z_4	output of the fourth (final) Fourier layer

References

1. Golub, G.H.; Ortega, J.M. *Scientific Computing and Differential Equations: An Introduction to Numerical Methods*; Academic Press: Cambridge, MA, USA, 1992.
2. Tao, Z.; Cui, Z.; Yu, J.; Khayatnezhad, M. Finite difference modelings of groundwater flow for constructing artificial recharge structures. *Iran. J. Sci. Technol. Trans. Civ. Eng.* **2022**, *46*, 1503–1514. [CrossRef]
3. Fathollahi, R.; Hesaraki, S.; Bostani, A.; Shahriyari, E.; Shafiee, H.; Pasha, P.; Chari, F.N.; Ganji, D.D. Applying numerical and computational methods to investigate the changes in the fluid parameters of the fluid passing over fins of different shapes with the finite element method. *Int. J. Thermofluids* **2022**, *15*, 100187. [CrossRef]
4. Afzal, A.; Saleel, C.A.; Prashantha, K.; Bhattacharyya, S.; Sadhikh, M. Parallel finite volume method-based fluid flow computations using OpenMP and CUDA applying different schemes. *J. Therm. Anal. Calorim.* **2021**, *145*, 1891–1909. [CrossRef]
5. Han, C.; Wang, Y.L.; Li, Z.Y. Numerical Solutions of Space Fractional Variable-Coefficient Kdv–Modified Kdv Equation by Fourier Spectral Method. *Fractals* **2021**, *29*, 2150246. [CrossRef]
6. Bhardwaj, A.; Kumar, A. A meshless method for time fractional nonlinear mixed diffusion and diffusion-wave equation. *Appl. Numer. Math.* **2021**, *160*, 146–165. [CrossRef]
7. Keybondorian, E.; Soltani Soulgani, B.; Bemani, A. Application of ANFIS-GA algorithm for forecasting oil flocculated asphaltene weight percentage in different operation conditions. *Pet. Sci. Technol.* **2018**, *36*, 862–868. [CrossRef]
8. Mohammadi, M.; Safari, M.; Ghasemi, M.; Daryasafar, A.; Sedighi, M. Asphaltene adsorption using green nanocomposites: Experimental study and adaptive neuro-fuzzy interference system modeling. *J. Pet. Sci. Eng.* **2019**, *177*, 1103–1113. [CrossRef]
9. Mai, H.; Le, T.C.; Chen, D.; Winkler, D.A.; Caruso, R.A. Machine learning for electrocatalyst and photocatalyst design and discovery. *Chem. Rev.* **2022**, *122*, 13478–13515. [CrossRef] [PubMed]
10. Kazemi, P.; Ghisi, A.; Mariani, S. Classification of the Structural Behavior of Tall Buildings with a Diagrid Structure: A Machine Learning-Based Approach. *Algorithms* **2022**, *15*, 349. [CrossRef]
11. Chen, W.; Wang, S.; Zhang, X.; Yao, L.; Yue, L.; Qian, B.; Li, X. EEG-based motion intention recognition via multi-task RNNs. In Proceedings of the 2018 SIAM International Conference on Data Mining, SIAM, San Diego, CA, USA, 3–5 May 2018; pp. 279–287.
12. Choubineh, A.; Chen, J.; Coenen, F.; Ma, F. An innovative application of deep learning in multiscale modeling of subsurface fluid flow: Reconstructing the basis functions of the mixed GMsFEM. *J. Pet. Sci. Eng.* **2022**, *216*, 110751. [CrossRef]
13. Choubineh, A.; Chen, J.; Coenen, F.; Ma, F. A quantitative insight into the role of skip connections in deep neural networks of low complexity: A case study directed at fluid flow modeling. *J. Comput. Inf. Sci. Eng.* **2022**, *23*, 014502. [CrossRef]
14. Pawar, P.; Ainapure, B.; Rashid, M.; Ahmad, N.; Alotaibi, A.; Alshamrani, S.S. Deep Learning Approach for the Detection of Noise Type in Ancient Images. *Sustainability* **2022**, *14*, 11786. [CrossRef]

15. Mijalkovic, J.; Spognardi, A. Reducing the False Negative Rate in Deep Learning Based Network Intrusion Detection Systems. *Algorithms* **2022**, *15*, 258. [CrossRef]
16. Li, Z.; Kovachki, N.; Azizzadenesheli, K.; Liu, B.; Bhattacharya, K.; Stuart, A.; Anandkumar, A. Fourier neural operator for parametric partial differential equations. *arXiv* **2020**, arXiv:2010.08895.
17. Gallant, A.R.; White, H. There exists a neural network that does not make avoidable mistakes. In Proceedings of the ICNN, San Diego, CA, USA, 24–27 July 1988; pp. 657–664.
18. Silvescu, A. Fourier neural networks. In Proceedings of the IJCNN'99, International Joint Conference on Neural Networks, Proceedings (Cat. No. 99CH36339), Washington, DC, USA, 10–16 July 1999; Volume 1, pp. 488–491.
19. Liu, S. Fourier neural network for machine learning. In Proceedings of the 2013 International Conference on Machine Learning and Cybernetics, Tianjin, China, 14–17 July 2013; Volume 1, pp. 285–290.
20. Wen, G.; Li, Z.; Azizzadenesheli, K.; Anandkumar, A.; Benson, S.M. U-FNO—An enhanced Fourier neural operator-based deep-learning model for multiphase flow. *Adv. Water Resour.* **2022**, *163*, 104180. [CrossRef]
21. Rashid, M.M.; Pittie, T.; Chakraborty, S.; Krishnan, N.A. Learning the stress-strain fields in digital composites using fourier neural operator. *iScience* **2022**, 105452. [CrossRef] [PubMed]
22. Li, Z.; Peng, W.; Yuan, Z.; Wang, J. Fourier neural operator approach to large eddy simulation of three-dimensional turbulence. *Theor. Appl. Mech. Lett.* **2022**, 100389. [CrossRef]
23. Johnny, W.; Brigido, H.; Ladeira, M.; Souza, J.C.F. Fourier Neural Operator for Image Classification. In Proceedings of the 2022 17th Iberian Conference on Information Systems and Technologies (CISTI), Madrid, Spain, 22–25 June 2022; pp. 1–6.
24. Chen, Z. *Reservoir Simulation: Mathematical Techniques in Oil Recovery*; SIAM: Philadelphia, PA, USA, 2007.
25. Fukunaga, K.; Koontz, W.L. Application of the Karhunen-Loeve expansion to feature selection and ordering. *IEEE Trans. Comput.* **1970**, *100*, 311–318. [CrossRef]
26. Lasser, R. *Introduction to Fourier Series*; CRC Press: Boca Raton, FL, USA, 1996; Volume 199.
27. Strichartz, R.S. *A Guide to Distribution Theory and Fourier Transforms*; World Scientific Publishing Company: Hackensack, NJ, USA, 2003.
28. Subramanian, V. *Deep Learning with PyTorch: A Practical Approach to Building Neural Network Models Using PyTorch*; Packt Publishing Ltd.: Birmingham, UK, 2018.
29. Reddi, S.J.; Kale, S.; Kumar, S. On the convergence of adam and beyond. *arXiv* **2019**, arXiv:1904.09237.
30. Nussbaumer, H.J. The fast Fourier transform. In *Fast Fourier Transform and Convolution Algorithms*; Springer: Berlin/Heidelberg, Germany, 1981; pp. 80–111.
31. Joseph, F.J.J.; Nonsiri, S.; Monsakul, A. Keras and TensorFlow: A hands-on experience. In *Advanced Deep Learning for Engineers and Scientists*; Springer: Cham, Switzerland, 2021; pp. 85–111.

Disclaimer/Publisher's Note: The statements, opinions and data contained in all publications are solely those of the individual author(s) and contributor(s) and not of MDPI and/or the editor(s). MDPI and/or the editor(s) disclaim responsibility for any injury to people or property resulting from any ideas, methods, instructions or products referred to in the content.

Article

Predicting Dissolution Kinetics of Tricalcium Silicate Using Deep Learning and Analytical Models

Taihao Han [1], Sai Akshay Ponduru [1], Arianit Reka [1,2], Jie Huang [3], Gaurav Sant [4] and Aditya Kumar [1,*]

[1] Department of Materials Science and Engineering, Missouri University of Science and Technology, Rolla, MO 65409, USA
[2] Faculty of Natural Sciences and Mathematics, University of Tetova, 1220 Tetovo, North Macedonia
[3] Department of Electrical and Computer Engineering, Missouri University of Science and Technology, Rolla, MO 65409, USA
[4] Civil and Environmental Engineering, University of California, Los Angeles, CA 90095, USA
* Correspondence: kumarad@mst.edu; Tel.: +1-573-341-6994; Fax: +1-573-341-6934

Abstract: The dissolution kinetics of Portland cement is a critical factor in controlling the hydration reaction and improving the performance of concrete. Tricalcium silicate (C_3S), the primary phase in Portland cement, is known to have complex dissolution mechanisms that involve multiple reactions and changes to particle surfaces. As a result, current analytical models are unable to accurately predict the dissolution kinetics of C_3S in various solvents when it is undersaturated with respect to the solvent. This paper employs the deep forest (DF) model to predict the dissolution rate of C_3S in the undersaturated solvent. The DF model takes into account several variables, including the measurement method (i.e., *reactor connected to inductive coupled plasma spectrometer* and *flow chamber with vertical scanning interferometry*), temperature, and physicochemical properties of solvents. Next, the DF model evaluates the influence of each variable on the dissolution rate of C_3S, and this information is used to develop a closed-form analytical model that can predict the dissolution rate of C_3S. The coefficients and constant of the analytical model are optimized in two scenarios: *generic* and *alkaline* solvents. The results show that both the DF and analytical models are able to produce reliable predictions of the dissolution rate of C_3S when it is undersaturated and far from equilibrium.

Keywords: tricalcium silicate; analytical model; ion activity; dissolution kinetics; deep forest

Citation: Han, T.; Ponduru, S.A.; Reka, A.; Huang, J.; Sant, G.; Kumar, A. Predicting Dissolution Kinetics of Tricalcium Silicate Using Deep Learning and Analytical Models. *Algorithms* 2023, 16, 7. https://doi.org/10.3390/a16010007

Academic Editors: Xiang Zhang and Xiaoxiao Li

Received: 14 November 2022
Revised: 19 December 2022
Accepted: 21 December 2022
Published: 22 December 2022

Copyright: © 2022 by the authors. Licensee MDPI, Basel, Switzerland. This article is an open access article distributed under the terms and conditions of the Creative Commons Attribution (CC BY) license (https://creativecommons.org/licenses/by/4.0/).

1. Introduction

Portland cement (PC) is the fundamental material for modern infrastructure, but its production contributes significantly to global CO_2 emissions, accounting for about 9% of total emissions [1–3]. To improve the sustainability and performance of PC, it is important to understand the hydration reaction of its primary component, tricalcium silicate (C_3S). C_3S is the most abundant component in PC, making up more than 50% of its composition [4–6]. When C_3S reacts with water, it undergoes a series of chemical reactions that result in the dissolution of calcium and silicate ions, followed by the formation of calcium silicate hydrate and portlandite [4]. While the phase transformations that occur at later stages of the hydration are well documented [4,7], the dissolution kinetics of C_3S at early stages remains a controversial subject. However, it is important to understand the dissolution kinetics of C_3S when it is undersaturated with respect to solvent. The undersaturation of C_3S solution presents the initial and induction periods of cement hydration [4,6]. The dissolution mechanisms of C_3S are different when the solution is in undersaturation and saturation (i.e., hydration products form) [6,8]. By studying the dissolution behaviors of C_3S, we can gain a better understanding of the factors that affect the hydration kinetics of cement. This knowledge can be used to develop novel cement formulations and improve cement performance.

Despite many studies that have sought to uncover the mechanisms (e.g., protective phase [9–11] and double layer theory [12]) behind the dissolution of C_3S and minerals in recent decades, a definitive rate-controlling mechanism remains elusive due to the complex interaction of physicochemical parameters between solids and aqueous solvents. The most widely accepted theory to explain the dissolution kinetics of C_3S and minerals is the inverse crystal nucleation theory [6,13,14]. This theory posits that, similar to the process of crystal growth, the dissolution of C_3S and minerals is primarily determined by the density of pre-existing steps on the surface of minerals [14]. These steps are formed by dislocation defects and the nucleation of two-dimensional vacancy islands at impurities or homogenous sites. The growth of vacancy islands on a surface is determined by the Gibbs–Thomson effect, a thermodynamic principle that dictates their critical size [15,16]. If a vacancy exceeds this critical size, it will continue to grow. At the critical size, the free energy change reaches a maximum, creating an energy barrier that must be overcome for vacancy growth to continue. The energy barriers that must be overcome by the vacancy islands have a proportional relationship with the interfacial energy, but an inverse relationship with the degree of undersaturation [15,16]. While the solution is near the equilibrium, the density of steps of the solid is dominated by dislocation defects, as the energy barriers are too high for vacancy islands to overcome.

Except for surface defects, other experimental parameters—for example, solvent chemistry [8,17], surface geometry [18–23], and mineral composition [24–26]—also substantially influence the dissolution kinetics of C_3S and minerals. By incorporating these parameters into analytical models, it is possible to reveal underlying structures between dissolution kinetics and physicochemical properties of minerals and solvents. The following review focuses on existing analytical models (shown in Table 1) that have been used to predict the dissolution kinetics of C_3S and minerals. Some of these models have been successful in accurately predicting the dissolution kinetics of minerals. The symbols used in these models are defined as follows: ΔG_r is the Gibbs free energy of the overall reaction; T is the temperature; R is the gas constant; A is the effective surface area of material; a_i is the ion activity of species i; E_a is the activation energy; n, n_i, k, and k_i are constants; and $g(I)$ is the function of ionic strength.

The analytical model developed by Burch et al. [27] is based on the transition state theory and the Burton–Cabrera–Frank theory. It shows that the dissolution rate of a mineral depends exponentially on the Gibbs free energy of the overall dissolution and the temperature. However, this model cannot accurately predict the dissolution kinetics of a solid–solvent system that is near the equilibrium. This is because the model does not account for the transition from step retreat to dislocation-controlled dissolution. The model developed by Lasaga et al. [28] accounts for various factors such as surface area, temperature, ionic strength, H^+ concentration in the solvent, and the change in Gibbs free energy related to dissolution. This model is widely used in the cement community to predict the dissolution kinetics of C_3S [6]. In addition to modeling from a thermodynamic perspective, several studies [29–33] have explained the dissolution kinetics of minerals using the ion leaching theory. Strachan's model [29] accounts for both H^+ and OH^- in the leaching process, as these ions leach species from mineral surfaces with different activation energies. Other studies [32–36] have found that cations (excluding H^+) in solvents can also contribute to mineral surface leaching. Oelkers et al. [32] have emphasized the role of the ion activity ratio of H^+ to cations in mineral dissolution kinetics. This model divides the process into two scenarios: if the ion activity ratio is small, a large number of cations remain on the material surface, which dominates the leaching and dissolution processes; if the ratio is large, the dissolution rate is independent of cations. This model has been used to predict the dissolution kinetics of various minerals [33].

Table 1. Summary of current dissolution kinetics models for C_3S and minerals.

$Rate = k_1 \left[1 - \exp\left(-n\left(\frac{\Delta G_r}{RT}\right)^{n_1}\right)\right] + k_2\left[1 - \exp\left(-\frac{\Delta G_r}{RT}\right)\right]^{n_2}$	Burch et al. [27]
$Rate = k_0 \cdot A_{min} \cdot \exp\left(-\frac{E_a}{RT}\right) \cdot a_{H+}^{nH+} \cdot \prod_i a_i^{ni} \cdot g(I) \cdot f(\Delta G_r)$	Lasaga et al. [28]
$Rate = k\left[a_{H+}^{n_{OH-}} + a_{OH-}^{n_{OH-}}\right]$	Strachan [29]
$Rate = k \prod_{i=1, i \neq k}^{i} \frac{k_i\left(\frac{a_{H+}^{Vi}}{a_{Mi}^{Vi}}\right)^n}{1+k_i\left(\frac{a_{H+}^{Vi}}{a_{Mi}^{Vi}}\right)^n}$	Oelkers et al. [32]

Although previous studies have proposed various models for predicting dissolution kinetics of minerals based on disparate theories, none of these models can predict the dissolution kinetics of C_3S in a high-fidelity manner with a coefficient of determination (R^2) above 0.90. This is because there are several knowledge gaps in the state-of-the-art analytical models. First, it is not possible to account for all the influential variables (e.g., ions in the solvent; physicochemical properties of C_3S particles; temperature; etc.) in a single analytical model. Moreover, it is difficult to incorporate a variable into analytical models without a clear understanding of its role in the dissolution process. Next, coefficients are not generic, thus requiring additional calibration while applying the model to a new C_3S-solvent systems. Lastly, some parameters (e.g., ion activity; Gibbs free energy; activation energy; etc.) are obtained from additional quantitative and qualitative analyses of experimental results, which makes the model difficult to use and increases the likelihood of human error.

Measuring the dissolution rate of C_3S is a challenge because the solubility of calcium silicate hydrate is much lower than that of C_3S, which means calcium silicate hydrate will precipitate before C_3S completely dissolves, unless a very small amount of C_3S is used. As a result, only a few studies have attempted to measure the C_3S dissolution rate. Those studies have applied two different methods to measure the dissolution rate of C_3S: *reactor connected to inductive coupled plasma (ICP) spectrometer* [37,38]; and *flow chamber with vertical scanning interferometry (VSI)* [39]. In the first method, C_3S particles dissolve into the solvent in a reactor, and the ICP spectrometer measures ion concentrations of the solution for the first couple of minutes to determine the dissolution rate. The change in C_3S surface area can be ignored because of the short measurement duration. In the second method, the solvent is flushed over the surface of the C_3S bulk for a period of time, and the VSI is used to measure the leaching depth and determine the dissolution rate. Because these two methods are based on different experimental principles and use different parameters, a single analytical model cannot be used to predict the dissolution rate from both methods.

Machine learning (ML), a data-driven framework, has been employed in many studies [40–50] to predict properties for multi-component systems (e.g., cement, glass, and biomaterials) in a high-fidelity manner. ML models acquire knowledge of underlying input-output correlations (all possible correlations can be included) from a training dataset, and subsequently utilize such knowledge to produce predictions for new mixture designs, without requiring an understanding of the mechanisms behind the materials. Elçiçek et al. [49] have successfully employed an artificial neural network to discover the underlying structure between the dissolution kinetics of colemanite, a type of boron mineral, in complex dissolution environments. A decision-tree-based ensemble model has demonstrated remarkable performance, in terms of $R^2 \approx 0.98$, on predictions of dissolution rate for bioactive glasses in various pH environments [40]. ML models incorporating topological constraints of glasses have been employed to predict and extrapolate dissolution kinetics of silicate glasses without violating fundamental material laws [43]. Although extensive studies have applied ML methods to predictions of material dissolution kinetics, there is currently no literature that shows that an ML model is a valid approach to predict the dissolution rate of C_3S when it is undersaturated with respect to the solvent.

In this study, a deep forest (DF) model is trained using a heterogenous database of C_3S dissolution rate measured by the *reactor connected to ICP spectrometer* and *flow chamber with VSI* methods. The rigorously trained model produces high-fidelity, a priori predictions of the C_3S dissolution rate. It is notable that ML models can predict the hydration kinetics of PC at any given age, which has been shown in our previous studies [51–53]. This study only focuses on the dissolution kinetics at the initial period (i.e., undersaturated solution) because the hydration products precipitate and cause the solution to reach saturation after a short time of the dissolution of C_3S. Then, the influence of each input variable on the dissolution rate is evaluated, and this knowledge is used to develop a simple, closed-form analytical model based on fundamental thermodynamic and kinetic frameworks, such as ion activity, ion strength, and ion activity product (IAP). The analytical model reveals fundamental correlations behind the C_3S dissolution process, which are the critical information that cannot be provided by ML models due to their "black-box" nature. Furthermore, the analytical model can be used by all end users, regardless of their background or of their access to ML models. Overall, this study is the first to develop an ML model to predict with high fidelity the dissolution kinetics of C_3S dissolved in various solvents when it is undersaturated and far from equilibrium.

2. Database Collection

The C_3S dissolution database used in this study consists of 292 data records, which were consolidated from Nicoleau et al. [37,38] and Juilland and Gallucci [39]. However, these data records are not compatible with our database due to differences in experimental parameters. For example, Bellmann et al. [54] measured the dissolution rate of C_3S at the induction period and later ages; Damidot et al. [55] and Barret et al. [56] used the filter dissolution technique; and Robin et al. [57] used the face-specific dissolution method to measure the dissolution rate of C_3S. The database used in this study contains 11 input parameters: temperature (°C); specific surface area (SSA) of C_3S (m^2/g); flow rate (mL/min/mm^2) initial concentration of Na, Cl, Ca, Si, Cs, K, and SO_4 (mM); and initial pH (unitless). The output is the dissolution rate of C_3S (umol/m^2/s). There are 92 data-records from Nicoleau et al. [37,38] measured by the *reactor connected to ICP spectrometer* method. Since the flow rate is not applicable in this method, it was set as 0. Several solvents with different ions were utilized in the *reactor connected to ICP spectrometer* method. There were 200 data records from Juilland and Gallucci [39] measured with the *flow chamber with VSI* method. Moreover, since the SSA of C_3S is not applicable in this method, it was set as 0. The solvents only contained calcium ions at different concentration levels. Four statistical parameters associated with inputs and output of the C_3S dissolution database are summarized in Table 2.

Table 2. Four statistical parameters pertaining to the 12 parameters (11 inputs and 1 output in bold) of the C_3S dissolution database. The database consists of 292 unique data records.

Attribute	Unit	Min.	Max.	Mean	Std. Dev.
Temperature	°C	10	60	21.07	5.437
SSA of C_3S	m^2/g	0	0.400	0.112	0.171
Flow Rate	mL/min/mm^2	0	1273	79.22	201.8
Initial Na Concentration	mM	0	1000	29.19	101.5
Initial Cl Concentration	mM	0	1000	18.74	113.6
Initial Ca Concentration	mM	0	20	5.824	6.561
Initial Si Concentration	mM	0	0.876	0.006	0.062
Initial Cs Concentration	mM	0	1000	5.513	65.45
Initial K Concentration	mM	0	1000	5.513	65.45
Initial SO4 Concentration	mM	0	200	8.904	34.95
Initial pH	Unitless	6.516	13.09	10.69	2.316
C_3S Dissolution rate	**umol/m^2/s**	**0.3800**	**154.6**	**27.92**	**32.61**

The ML model was trained by 219 randomly selected data records from the original database. The remaining 73 data records were used to validate the performance of the model. The prediction performance was evaluated by five statistical parameters: mean absolute error (MAE); coefficient of determination (R^2); mean absolute percentage error ($MAPE$); Pearson correlation coefficient (R); and root mean square error ($RMSE$).

3. Deep Forest Model

In this study, a DF model was utilized to predict C_3S dissolution kinetics based on the physicochemical properties of C_3S and solvents. The DF model was developed based on the modified classification-and-regression tree (CART) model with a combination of bagging and random selection techniques [58,59]. The DF model grows a large number of independent trees through a recursive binary split at each node [58]. To be specific, the root node receives information from a bootstrap extracted from the training dataset, and then splits to create two child nodes. This process is repeated until the homogeneity of the child nodes cannot be improved. The tree can grow as deep as it can because none of the usual pruning or smoothing algorithms are applied. This allows the DF model to maintain diversity among trees. The DF model usually contains hundreds of independent trees. Usually, a large-size forest is required to produce reliable predictions while the database contains thousands of data-records. When a testing dataset is applied to a trained DF model, trees produce independent outputs, and subsequently a bagging algorithm averages them to derive the final output. A unique feature (i.e., two-stage randomization) allows the DF model to reduce the variance and bias errors in predictions. The first randomization is that the bootstrap randomly selects data records from the parent database. Second, at each split, several randomly selected variables, instead of all variables, are used to determine the optimal split. The randomization features ensure the decorrelation between trees. Furthermore, due to the growth of a large number of trees, errors from generalization and the likelihood of overfitting are minimized. Owing to those unique features, the DF model can effectively learn input–output correlations from complex databases. Overall, the architecture of the DF can be summarized in the following steps:

N bootstrap samples are randomly selected from the training dataset. N is equal to the number of trees. In this study, N was 200. Each bootstrap can contain ~66% [60–62] of the data records of the training dataset. The remaining data records are "out-of-bag" (OOB) data [58].

- Each bootstrap iteration in the DF model grows a single tree. At each split, a subset of input variables is randomly selected and used to determine the optimal split scenario. The number of leaves, or the subset size, was set to five in this study. The cost function (i.e., MAE) is used to evaluate all split scenarios, and the scenario with the minimum cost is selected. Unlike other models, the DF model allows trees to grow to their maximum size without pruning or smoothing.
- Next, the DF model produces predictions for OOB data. The DF model aggregates and averages these predictions to produce an overall OOB prediction and OOB error rate. This OOB error rate can be used to evaluate the importance of each variable in influencing the model's output.
- Lastly, at the testing stage, the DF model averages outcomes from trees to produce predictions for a new data domain.

4. Predictions from Deep Forest Model

To optimize the DF model's performance on new data records, it is crucial to meet the following criteria. First, the model requires sufficient and diverse data records to learn adequate input–output correlations (e.g., pH–dissolution rate). Second, outliers should be included in the database to ensure that the DF model comprehensively learns input–output correlations [63,64]. Herein, the outliers indicated that one or more data-records—although measured and reported properly—did not fit into the trends exhibited by the majority of the data records in the neighborhood because of some underlying (chemical, or kinetic, or thermodynamic) mechanism. Third, it is important to avoid both underfitting and overfitting to datasets. Underfitting occurs when the model is unable to learn the underlying correlations in the data, often due to a small training dataset that does not contain enough information for the model to learn from. On the other hand, overfitting occurs when the model learns local trends instead of global ones from highly similar data, resulting in poor performance on the testing dataset. To address this issue, the hyperparameters of the DF model were the 10-fold cross-validation (CV) [41,65] and grid-search methods [48,52]. These methods can help to prevent underfitting and overfitting by evaluating the model's performance on multiple splits of the training data and using a range of different hyperparameter settings, respectively. Predictions of C_3S dissolution rate (from training and testing datasets), as produced by the DF model, are demonstrated in Figure 1. The five statistical parameters listed in Table 3 provide further evidence of the model's performance and accuracy. Overall, by meeting the aforementioned criteria, the DF model can be trained to make highly accurate predictions on new data records.

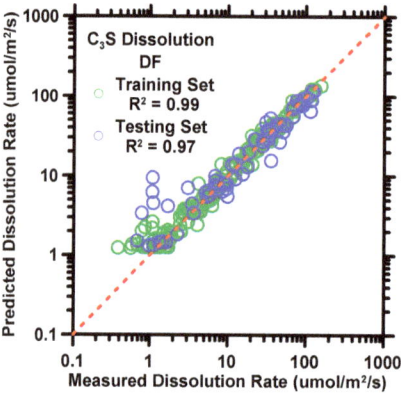

Figure 1. DF model's predictions of C_3S dissolution rate against experimental measurements of training and testing datasets. Coefficient of determination (R^2) is shown in the legend, providing a measure of the prediction performance. The dashed line represents the ideal prediction.

Table 3. R, R^2, MAE, $MAPE$, and $RMSE$ evaluating prediction accuracy of the DF model against the testing dataset.

Model Name	R	R^2	MAE	MAPE	RMSE
DF	Unitless	Unitless	μmol/m²/s	%	μmol/m²/s
	0.9672	0.9354	5.297	47.33	9.373

The predicted results from the DF model for the dissolution rate of C_3S, as shown in Figure 1 and Table 3, demonstrate the model's accuracy and reliability. The R^2 and $RMSE$ values for the dissolution rate predictions were 0.94 and 9.4 μmol/m²/s, respectively, indicating a strong correlation between the predicted and measured values. In Figure 1, the predictions show a larger deviation at low dissolution rates than at high dissolution rates, but this is largely due to the use of a logarithmic scale on the y-axis. The prediction errors, as measured by the mean absolute error (MAE), were 2.01 μmol/m²/s for low dissolution rates (below 20 μmol/m²/s) and 8.67 μmol/m²/s for high dissolution rates, indicating that the DF model is able to produce reliable predictions of the dissolution rate of C_3S, regardless of the experimental method. This is a significant improvement over analytical models, which typically have a prediction accuracy of only 0.78 in terms of R^2 for silicate compounds [66]. The capability of the DF model to yield reliable predictions of C_3S dissolution rate is largely due to its inherent architecture [59,60,62]. First, by growing a large number (more than 100) of independent trees without smoothing or pruning, the model is able to significantly reduce the variance error in its output. Next, bias error is minimized by adopting the randomization at bootstrap and feature selections [59], which ensures that the output of one tree does not interfere with that of others. Lastly, the utilization of the 10-fold cross-validation method [65] and grid-search method [48,67] autonomously optimized the hyper-parameters so as to establish optimal input–output correlations as well as account for outliers.

The DF model can estimate the influence (in terms of importance) of input variables on the dissolution rate of C_3S. The results of this analysis are shown in Figure 2, which is organized in descending order based on the magnitude of variables' influence. This rank is also utilized as a guide for feature selection in the development of the analytical model in Section 5.

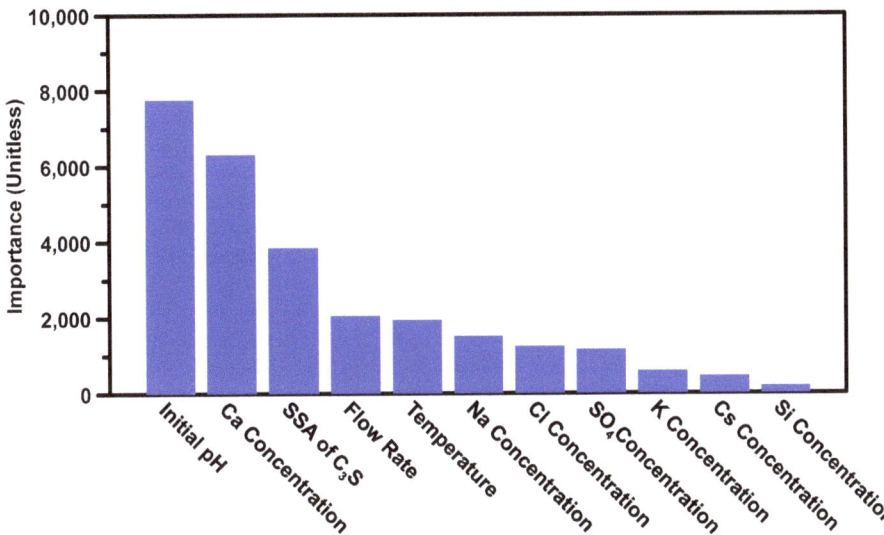

Figure 2. The influence (importance) of input variables based on their contributions towards the C_3S dissolution rate. The permutation of the rank is shown in a descending manner, where variables on the left side have more influence.

As can be seen in Figure 2, the initial pH, Ca concentration, SSA of C_3S, and flow rate—ranked from high to low—exhibited the strongest influences on the dissolution rate of C_3S. This is expected because the Ca and OH ions (in terms of pH value) are known to be the main factors that affect the dissolution reaction according to *IAP* (described in Section 5) of C_3S dissolution, where a high concentration of these ions significantly reduces the dissolution rate. The SSA of C_3S is the third important variable because an increase in the interface between C_3S particles and solvent leads to a monotonical increase of the dissolution rate [20]. Similarly, the flow rate in the *flow chamber with VSI* method plays a significant role, as it determines the speed at which ions are leached from the surface of the C_3S particles, with higher flow rates leading to an increase in the leaching speed. Temperature is also an important variable, as previous research [27] has shown that the dissolution rate of minerals increases exponentially with an increase in temperature. Other ions in the solvent contribute less significantly to the dissolution rate. This is not a surprise, because no literature has found direct correlations between C_3S dissolution rate and those ions. Interestingly, the Si ion, one of the major ions that affect the dissolution rate of C_3S, was ranked much lower in terms of importance. This is likely because there are only three solvents in the database that contain Si ions, and the dissolution rates for these systems show little variation. As a result, the Si ions are less important than they would be in a larger and more diverse dataset. It should be noted that the importance of input variables can vary depending on the dataset used. Some variables may be found to be more important in one dataset, while being less significant in another. In this study, only a few variables were found to have a strong influence on the dissolution rate of C_3S. However, in a different dataset, different variables may exhibit a greater importance.

5. Analytical Model Development

The abovementioned results demonstrate that the DF model can produce predictions of the dissolution rate of C_3S in a high-fidelity manner. However, the use of machine learning (ML) techniques can have some limitations, such as the "black-box" issue, where the underlying input–output correlations learned by the model are difficult to interpret. Additionally, ML models may not be accessible to end users who do not have a programming background. To address these issues, this section introduces an original, closed-form analytical model that has been distilled from the DF model. This model can be used to predict the dissolution rate of C_3S and provide a better understanding of the input–output correlations involved.

The development of a reliable analytical model involves a wise selection of input variables. The inclusion of influential variables is vital to enhance the performance of the analytical model. Simultaneously, the exclusion of inconsequential variables reduces the complexity of the model. The new analytical model is developed based on Lasaga's model [28], and some new input variables are added to it. We selected Lasaga's model as the baseline model because it is the most used model to predict C_3S dissolution kinetics. This model accounts for the SSA of C_3S, solvent pH, temperature, and ions in solvents. The feature importance, shown in Figure 2, also confirms that those parameters dominated the dissolution rate of the C_3S. It is worth pointing out that only data from Nicoleau et al. [37,38] was employed to develop the analytical model. This is because the SSA of C_3S is not applicable in Juilland and Gallucci [39].

In the baseline model, the Gibbs free energy of the overall reaction is one of the major influential variables. To properly quantify this variable, it is important to understand the dissolution mechanism of C_3S. The dissolution process of C_3S can be considered as an inverse nucleation process [13], which is controlled by two major factors: interfacial properties and the driving force. The interfacial properties include chemical composition, chemical bond, surface defects, and impurities in crystals. Generally, the dissolution process can be divided into three steps: (1) horizontal movement at the atomic scale to form a 2D vacancy; (2) etch pit formation at dislocation; and (3) step retreat at pre-existing roughness [6,19]. The driving force of the C_3S dissolution reaction is defined as the energy to overcome the activation energy barriers for the first two steps of the dissolution process. The equation to calculate the driving force is shown in Equation (1) [6,68]:

$$\sigma = \frac{\Delta \mu}{kT} = \frac{\Delta G^*}{RT} = \ln\left(\frac{IAP}{K_{SP}}\right) \tag{1}$$

Here, σ is the undersaturation coefficient; $\Delta \mu$ is the difference in chemical potential; k is the Boltzmann constant; T is the temperature; ΔG^* is the free energy difference between the undersaturated solution and the solution in equilibrium; R is the gas constant; IAP is the ion activity product to reactant species; and K_{SP} is the mineral solubility products. The dissolution reaction of C_3S is expressed in Equation (2) [8], and the IAP is defined in Equation (3). a_i is the ion activity of species i. The chemical equilibrium constant (K_{SP}) for C_3S dissolution has been estimated as $10^{-17.65}$ [8,69].

$$(CaO)_3 SiO_2 + 3H_2O \rightarrow 3Ca^{2+} + H_2SiO_4^{2-} + 4OH^- \tag{2}$$

$$IAP = a_{Ca^{2+}}^3 \cdot a_{OH^-}^4 \cdot a_{H_2SO_4^{2-}} \tag{3}$$

Equation (3) suggests that the value of IAP is solely determined by calcium and hydroxide ion activity. Thus, a high calcium ion activity leads to an equilibrium for the

C_3S dissolution, resulting in a slower dissolution rate compared to a solvent without calcium ions [6,70]. Similarly, a basic solvent significantly decreases the dissolution rate of C_3S by containing a large amount of hydroxide ions. In this study, only $H_2SiO_4^{2-}$ was considered in the *IAP* calculation because H_4SiO_4 and $H_3SiO_4^-$ can deprotonate to form $H_2SiO_4^{2-}$ [71,72]. To clearly observe the influence of *IAP* on dissolution rate, Figure 3 shows the correlation between the degree of undersaturation (IAP/K_{sp}) and the dissolution rate of C_3S. The general trend of the correlation and order of magnitude of changes in the dissolution rate observed herein are in good agreement with previous studies [6,28]. It is not surprising that the dissolution rate of C_3S decreases as the degree of undersaturation increases, as a high degree of undersaturation indicates that the solution is approaching an equilibrium, which reduces the driving force for dissolution.

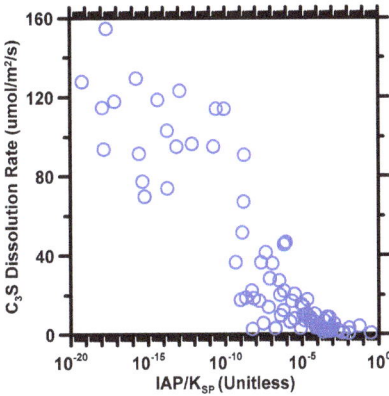

Figure 3. The correlation between the degree of undersaturation (IAP/K_{sp}) and the dissolution rate of C_3S. The x-axis shows in a logarithmic scale due to the small magnitude of the degree of undersaturation.

As previously discussed in the introduction, Strachan [29] has demonstrated that H^+ and OH^- leach mineral surfaces in different activation energies. Since Lasaga's model only accounts for the H^+, the new model includes the ion activities of both H^+ and OH^- in order to interpret the leaching process. Moreover, especially for C_3S dissolution, OH^- is one of the main products of the dissolution reaction, as shown in Equation (2).

Previous studies [32–36] have also shown that the concentration of major cations (excluding H^+) in the solvent can influence the dissolution rate, and this is supported by the data shown in Figure 2, which highlights the importance of Ca concentration in the analytical model. However, previous studies have not explored the relationship between the activity of Ca^{2+} and the dissolution rate of C_3S. Using data from Nicoleau et al. [37,38], we show this relationship in Figure 4, which plots the natural logarithm of the dissolution rate of C_3S against the initial activity of Ca^{2+}. The correlation is observed as linear (shown as the red line). This means the relationship between C_3S dissolution rate and Ca^{2+} activity is exponential. Some outliers can be seen in the Figure, which may be due to the influence of other parameters, such as temperature and the specific surface area of C_3S, on the dissolution rate. If all other parameters are kept constant, a more ideal linear relationship should be observed. After embodying OH^- and Ca^{2+}, the new analytical model, with seven input variables, is formed as Equation (4). Here, C_i is the coefficient for each attribute; T is Temperature (°C); A is the specific surface area of C_3S (m^2/g); $a_{i,j}$ is ion activity of i species at initial/final state (unitless); I is ion strength of initial state (mM); *IAP* is ion activity product of final state (unitless); K_{sp} is C_3S solubility product ($\approx 10^{-17.65}$ [8,69]).

$$rate = e^{C_0} * e^{\frac{C_1}{T}} * A^{C_2} * e^{C_3 a_{Ca,initial}} * a_{OH,initial}^{C_4} * a_{H,initial}^{C_5} * I^{C_6} * \left(\frac{IAP}{K_{sp}}\right)^{C_7} \quad (4)$$

$$\ln(rate) = C_0 + \frac{C_1}{T} + C_2 \ln(A) + C_3 a_{Ca,inital} + C_4 \ln(a_{OH,inital}) + C_5 \ln(a_{H,inital})$$
$$+ C_6 \ln(I) + C_7 \ln\left(\frac{IAP}{K_{sp}}\right) \qquad (5)$$

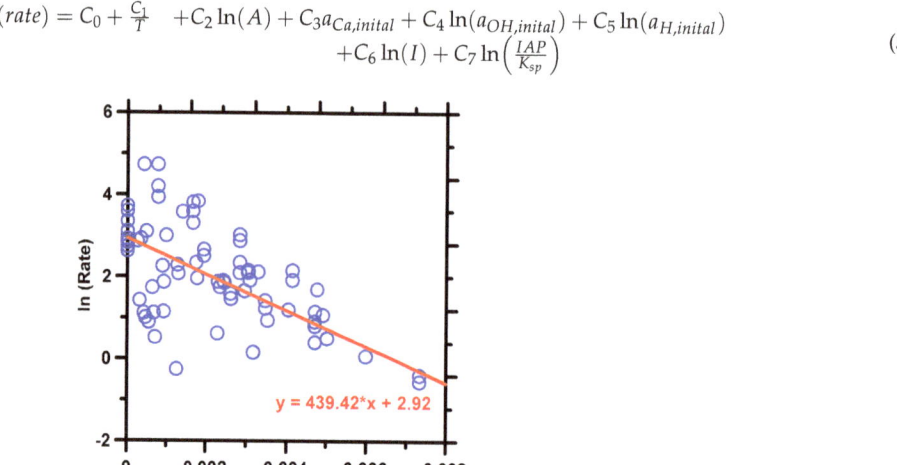

Figure 4. The dissolution rate of C_3S, expressed in terms of natural logarithm, against the ion activity of Ca^{2+} in solvents. The red line indicates the linear correlation.

Phreeqc version 3, a geochemical modeling package, was used to simulate chemical reactions and ion transportations in natural and polluted water for laboratory and industrial purposes. The program is based on the equilibrium chemistry of aqueous solutions interacting with other components, including mineral, gas, solid solution, and sorption surface. The model can produce the concentration of an element, molarity of a compound, activity of aqueous species, pH, and phase transformation to achieve equilibrium based on reversible and irreversible chemical reactions [73–75]. In this study, the geochemical Phreeqc code was employed to calculate ion activity and ion strength of ions in solutions. Thermodynamic data were obtained from the specific ion interaction theory database to account for the non-ideality of aqueous solutions and used to calculate the speciation and saturation index [73,76]. Temperature and concentration of the species are given as initial conditions with pH as charge balance to calculate the pH, ion strength and ion activity of Na^+, Cl^-, OH^-, Ca^{2+}, $H_2SiO_4^{2-}$, Cs^+, K^+, and SO_4^{2-}.

There are seven coefficients and one constant (i.e., C_i) that ought to be optimized. Two scenarios are considered to optimize the coefficients: (1) C_3S dissolves in *generic* solvent (pH ≈ 7–13) with a pH range of approximately 7–13, where both H^+ and OH^- can leach the surface of C_3S; and (2) C_3S dissolves in *alkaline* solvent (pH ≈ 11–13) with a pH range of approximately 11–13, where OH^- is the primary leaching ion. An independent optimization for the alkaline scenario was performed in order to improve the prediction accuracy. The optimal values of coefficients were derived from a nonlinear, gradient-descent scheme [40,42,52,77–79] and Nelder–Mead multi-dimensional simplex algorithm [80,81].

Table 4 shows the optimal coefficients of the analytical model for the *generic* solvent scenario. Predicted results of the C_3S dissolution rate as produced by the analytical model based on the coefficient in Table 4 are demonstrated in Figure 5a. Five statistical parameters pertaining to the predicted results are listed in Table 5. As demonstrated in Figure 5a and Table 5, the accuracy for predictions made by *generic* solvent scenario was moderate in terms of $R^2 \approx 0.69$ and $RMSE \approx 32.9$ µ mol/m²/s. This is expected, because the analytical model cannot account for all influential factors (e.g., other ions in solvents and some processing parameters) compared to the DF model. Furthermore, a large deviation of H^+ concentration in neutral and alkaline solvents increases the difficulty of optimizing the simple-structure analytical model.

Table 4. Seven coefficients and one constant (for seven input variables corresponding to the physicochemical properties of C_3S and solvents) optimized for the analytical model of the *generic* solvent scenario.

C_0	59.7404	C_1	−17.0531	C_2	−0.3166
C_3	−231.8133	C_4	1.7087	C_5	1.7798
C_6	0.0256	C_7	−0.0646		

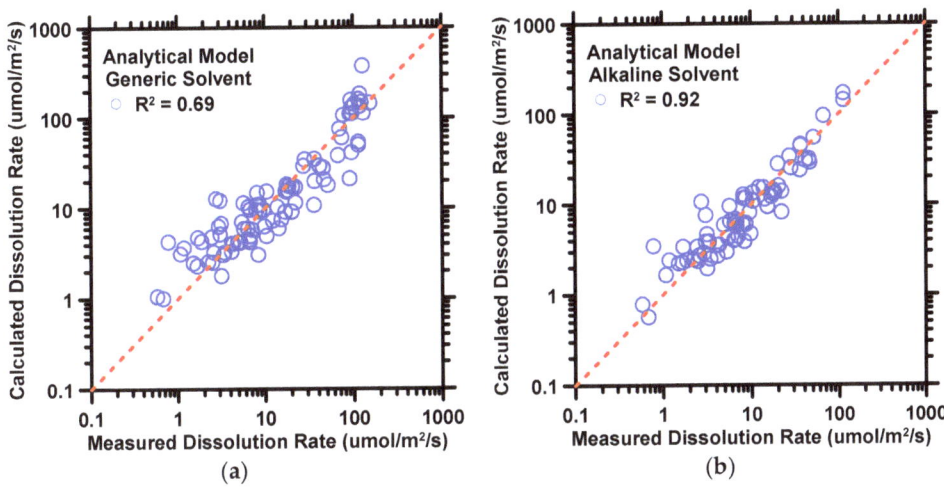

Figure 5. The analytical model's predictions of C_3S dissolution rate against experimental measurements for (**a**) *generic* solvent and (**b**) *alkaline* solvent. Coefficient of determination (R^2) is shown in the legend, providing a measure of the prediction performance. The dashed line represents the ideal prediction.

Table 5. R, R^2, *MAE*, *MAPE*, and *RMSE* evaluating the prediction performance of the analytical model for *generic* and *alkaline* solvent scenarios against experimental measurements.

	Model Name	R	R^2	MAE	MAPE	RMSE
		Unitless	Unitless	µmol/m²/s	%	µmol/m²/s
Generic Solvent	Analytical model	0.8277	0.6851	13.76	55.05	32.90
Alkaline Solvent	Analytical model	0.9566	0.9151	4.921	39.77	9.545

Table 6 shows the optimal coefficients of the analytical model for *alkaline* solvent scenario. Predicted results of the C_3S dissolution rate, as produced by the analytical model based on the coefficient in Table 6, are demonstrated in Figure 5b. Five statistical parameters pertaining to the results are listed in Table 5. As shown in Figure 5b and Table 6, predictions for the dissolution rate of C_3S were high-fidelity, with R^2 of 0.92 and *RMSE* of 9.545 µmol/m²/s, respectively. The predictions of the *alkaline* solvent scenario are superior, in terms of R^2, to those from *generic* solvent scenario. The high-quality prediction is expected because the *alkaline* solvent scenario minimizes the effect from H^+; in other words, the input–output correlations become simpler due to the reduction of the influence of H^+. Therefore, the trend for the simple system can be captured by the analytical model exactly.

Table 6. Seven coefficients and one constant (for seven input variables corresponding to the physicochemical properties of C_3S and solvents) optimized for the analytical model of the *alkaline* solvent scenario.

C_0	−1160.8543	C_1	−1476.3562	C_2	−0.6632
C_3	−256.4132	C_4	−37.9113	C_5	−37.9089
C_6	−0.3445	C_7	−0.0978		

6. Conclusions

In this study, the DF and analytical models were demonstrated to predict the dissolution rate of C_3S. The DF model was used to predict the dissolution rate of C_3S in relation to temperature, ion concentration in solvent, and pH, which can be directly obtained from experimental measurements. To the best of the authors' knowledge, this is the first study to employ ML to predict the dissolution rate of C_3S when it is undersaturated with respect to a wide range of solvents. Another novel point of this study is the leveraging of the DF model for evaluating the influence of input variables and using such knowledge to develop an analytical model.

The database was collected from two distinct experimental setups: *reactor connected to ICP spectrometer* and *flow chamber with VSI*. The DF model was rigorously trained by 75% of the parent database that consisted of 292 data records. Subsequently, the model was tested against the remaining 25% of the data records to evaluate prediction performance. The results demonstrated that the DF model was able to yield reliable predictions, with an R^2 value of approximately 0.97, of C_3S dissolution rate in the undersaturated solution. The DF model allows researchers to acquire the dissolution rate of C_3S by simply knowing the ion concentration and temperature of solvents without the cumbersome dissolution experiments. The DF model was also employed to evaluate the influence of input variables on the dissolution rate of C_3S. It was found that the pH value of solvents and the concentration of Ca^{2+} exerted significant influences on the dissolution process, while the concentration of silicate ions had little influence.

The analytical model (only using data from the *reactor connected to ICP spectrometer* method) was classified into two scenarios: *generic* solvent and *alkaline* solvent. The coefficients of the *generic* solvent and *alkaline* solvent scenarios were optimized by 92 data records and 75 data records, respectively. The physiochemical properties—which were used as inputs for both scenarios—comprised SSA of C_3S, temperature, ion activity of Ca^{2+}, OH^-, and H^+, ionic strength of solvent, and degree of undersaturation. The results showed that the analytical model was able to produce reliable predictions of *generic* solvent with $R \approx 0.83$ and *alkaline* solvent with $R \approx 0.96$ when all coefficients were rigorously optimized. Unlike ML, the analytical model can quantitively interpret aqueous chemistry-dissolution correlations.

Overall, the DF model is an apposite platform that can be used in the future to study the dissolution kinetics of cementitious materials. A large volume and diverse database can further enhance prediction accuracy. By incorporating a wide range of data, the model can better capture the complex dissolution behavior of cementitious materials. This can improve the reliability of the model's predictions, allowing it to be used more effectively in the design of cementitious materials. Overall, the DF model has the potential to be a valuable tool for studying the dissolution kinetics of cementitious materials.

Author Contributions: Conceptualization, development, training, and validation of machine learning and analytical models, and preparation of original manuscript, T.H.; development of analytical model and preparation of original manuscript, S.A.P.; manuscript review and editing, A.R.; supervision, manuscript review and editing; and funding acquisition, J.H.; supervision, manuscript review and editing, and funding acquisition, G.S.; conceptualization, manuscript review and editing, and funding acquisition, A.K. All authors have read and agreed to the published version of the manuscript.

Funding: This study was financially supported by the Leonard Wood Institute (LWI: W911NF-07-2-0062); the National Science Foundation (NSF-CMMI: 1661609; NSF-CMMI: 1932690; NSF-DMR: 2034856); and the Federal Highway Administration (Award no: 693JJ31950021); the Ministry of Education and Science of North Macedonia.

Data Availability Statement: The data used in this study are available on request.

Acknowledgments: The authors thank Missouri S&T for providing facilities to accomplish the experimental and computational work of this research.

Conflicts of Interest: The authors declare that they have no known competing financial interests or personal relationships that could have appeared to influence the work reported in this paper.

References

1. Gartner, E.; Hirao, H. A Review of Alternative Approaches to the Reduction of CO_2 Emissions Associated with the Manufacture of the Binder Phase in Concrete. *Cem. Concr. Res.* **2015**, *78 Pt A*, 126–142. [CrossRef]
2. Schneider, M. Process Technology for Efficient and Sustainable Cement Production. *Cem. Concr. Res.* **2015**, *78 Pt A*, 14–23. [CrossRef]
3. Ludwig, H.-M.; Zhang, W. Research Review of Cement Clinker Chemistry. *Cem. Concr. Res.* **2015**, *78 Pt A*, 24–37. [CrossRef]
4. Bullard, J.W.; Jennings, H.M.; Livingston, R.A.; Nonat, A.; Scherer, G.W.; Schweitzer, J.S.; Scrivener, K.L.; Thomas, J.J. Mechanisms of Cement Hydration. *Cem. Concr. Res.* **2011**, *41*, 1208–1223. [CrossRef]
5. Juilland, P.; Kumar, A.; Gallucci, E.; Flatt, R.J.; Scrivener, K.L. Effect of Mixing on the Early Hydration of Alite and OPC Systems. *Cem. Concr. Res.* **2012**, *42*, 1175–1188. [CrossRef]
6. Juilland, P.; Gallucci, E.; Flatt, R.; Scrivener, K. Dissolution Theory Applied to the Induction Period in Alite Hydration. *Cem. Concr. Res.* **2010**, *40*, 831–844. [CrossRef]
7. Taylor, H.F.W. *Cement Chemistry*; Thomas Telford: London, UK, 1997.
8. Oey, T.; Kumar, A.; Falzone, G.; Huang, J.; Kennison, S.; Bauchy, M.; Neithalath, N.; Bullard, J.W.; Sant, G. The Influence of Water Activity on the Hydration Rate of Tricalcium Silicate. *J. Am. Ceram. Soc.* **2016**, *99*, 2481–2492. [CrossRef]
9. Gartner, E.M.; Jennings, H.M. Thermodynamics of Calcium Silicate Hydrates and Their Solutions. *J. Am. Ceram. Soc.* **1987**, *70*, 743–749. [CrossRef]
10. Gartner, E.; Gaidis, J.M. Hydration Mechanisms. In *Materials Science of Concrete*; Skalny, J.P., Ed.; The American Ceramic Society: Westerville, OH, USA, 1989.
11. Brown, P.W.; Franz, E.; Frohnsdorff, G.; Taylor, H.F.W. Analyses of the Aqueous Phase during Early C_3S Hydration. *Cem. Concr. Res.* **1984**, *14*, 257–262. [CrossRef]
12. Tadros, M.E.; Skalny, J.; Kalyoncu, R.S. Early Hydration of Tricalcium Silicate. *J. Am. Ceram. Soc.* **1976**, *59*, 344–347. [CrossRef]
13. Cabrera, N.; Levine, M.M. XLV. On the Dislocation Theory of Evaporation of Crystals. *Philos. Mag.* **1956**, *1*, 450–458. [CrossRef]
14. Dove, P.M.; Han, N.; De Yoreo, J.J. Mechanisms of Classical Crystal Growth Theory Explain Quartz and Silicate Dissolution Behavior. *Proc. Natl. Acad. Sci. USA* **2005**, *102*, 15357–15362. [CrossRef] [PubMed]
15. Jackson, C.L.; McKenna, G.B. The Melting Behavior of Organic Materials Confined in Porous Solids. *J. Chem. Phys.* **1990**, *93*, 9002–9011. [CrossRef]
16. Perez, M. Gibbs–Thomson Effects in Phase Transformations. *Scr. Mater.* **2005**, *52*, 709–712. [CrossRef]
17. Cailleteau, C.; Angeli, F.; Devreux, F.; Gin, S.; Jestin, J.; Jollivet, P.; Spalla, O. Insight into Silicate-Glass Corrosion Mechanisms. *Nat. Mater.* **2008**, *7*, 978–983. [CrossRef]
18. Anbeek, C. Surface Roughness of Minerals and Implications for Dissolution Studies. *Geochim. Cosmochim. Acta* **1992**, *56*, 1461–1469. [CrossRef]
19. Brantley, S.L. Kinetics of Mineral Dissolution. In *Kinetics of Water-Rock Interaction*; Springer: Berlin, Germany, 2008; pp. 151–210. [CrossRef]
20. Nicoleau, L.; Nonat, A. A New View on the Kinetics of Tricalcium Silicate Hydration. *Cem. Concr. Res.* **2016**, *86*, 1–11. [CrossRef]
21. Marchon, D.; Juilland, P.; Gallucci, E.; Frunz, L.; Flatt, R.J. Molecular and Submolecular Scale Effects of Comb-Copolymers on Tri-Calcium Silicate Reactivity: Toward Molecular Design. *J. Am. Ceram. Soc.* **2017**, *100*, 817–841. [CrossRef]
22. Fierens, P.; Kabuema, Y.; Tirlocq, J. Influence de La Temperature de Recuit Sur La Cinetique de l'hydratation Du Silicate Tricalcique. *Cem. Concr. Res.* **1982**, *12*, 455–462. [CrossRef]
23. Fischer, C.; Luttge, A. Pulsating Dissolution of Crystalline Matter. *Proc. Natl. Acad. Sci. USA* **2018**, *115*, 897–902. [CrossRef]
24. Casey, W.; Westrich, H. Control of Dissolution Rates of Orthosilicate Minerals by Divalent Metal–Oxygen Bonds. *Nature* **1992**, *355*, 157–159. [CrossRef]
25. Ohlin, C.A.; Villa, E.M.; Rustad, J.R.; Casey, W.H. Dissolution of Insulating Oxide Materials at the Molecular Scale. *Nat. Mater.* **2010**, *9*, 11–19. [CrossRef] [PubMed]
26. Zhang, L.; Lüttge, A. Aluminosilicate Dissolution Kinetics: A General Stochastic Model. *J. Phys. Chem. B* **2008**, *112*, 1736–1742. [CrossRef] [PubMed]

27. Burch, T.E.; Nagy, K.L.; Lasaga, A.C. Free Energy Dependence of Albite Dissolution Kinetics at 80 °C and PH 8.8. *Chem. Geol.* **1993**, *105*, 137–162. [CrossRef]
28. Lasaga, A.C. *Kinetic Theory in the Earth Sciences*; Princeton University Press: Princeton, NJ, USA, 1998.
29. Strachan, D. Glass Dissolution Asa Function of PH and Its Implications for Understanding Mechanisms and Future Experiments. *Geochim. Cosmochim. Acta* **2017**, *219*, 111–123. [CrossRef]
30. Ganor, J.; Lasaga, A.C. Simple Mechanistic Models for Inhibition of a Dissolution Reaction. *Geochim. Cosmochim. Acta* **1998**, *62*, 1295–1306. [CrossRef]
31. Lasaga, A.C. Chapter 2. Fundamental Approaches in Describing Mineral Dissolution and Precipitation Rates. In *Chemical Weathering Rates of Silicate Minerals*; White, A.F., Brantley, S.L., Eds.; De Gruyter: Berlin, Germany, 1995; pp. 23–86.
32. Oelkers, E.H.; Schott, J.; Devidal, J.-L. The Effect of Aluminum, PH, and Chemical Affinity on the Rates of Aluminosilicate Dissolution Reactions. *Geochim. Cosmochim. Acta* **1994**, *58*, 2011–2024. [CrossRef]
33. Oelkers, E.H. General Kinetic Description of Multioxide Silicate Mineral and Glass Dissolution. *Geochim. Cosmochim. Acta* **2001**, *65*, 3703–3719. [CrossRef]
34. Oelkers, E.H.; Schott, J. An Experimental Study of Enstatite Dissolution Rates as a Function of PH, Temperature, and Aqueous Mg and Si Concentration, and the Mechanism of Pyroxene/Pyroxenoid Dissolution. *Geochim. Cosmochim. Acta* **2001**, *65*, 1219–1231. [CrossRef]
35. Hellmann, R. The Albite-Water System: Part II. The Time-Evolution of the Stoichiometry of Dissolution as a Function of pH at 100, 200, and 300 °C. *Geochim. Cosmochim. Acta* **1995**, *59*, 1669–1697. [CrossRef]
36. Brantley, S.L.; Stillings, L. Feldspar Dissolution at 25 °C and Low pH. *Am. J. Sci.* **1996**, *296*, 101–127. [CrossRef]
37. Nicoleau, L.; Nonat, A.; Perrey, D. The Di- and Tricalcium Silicate Dissolutions. *Cem. Concr. Res.* **2013**, *47*, 14–30. [CrossRef]
38. Nicoleau, L.; Schreiner, E.; Nonat, A. Ion-Specific Effects Influencing the Dissolution of Tricalcium Silicate. *Cem. Concr. Res.* **2014**, *59*, 118–138. [CrossRef]
39. Juilland, P.; Gallucci, E. Morpho-Topological Investigation of the Mechanisms and Kinetic Regimes of Alite Dissolution. *Cem. Concr. Res.* **2015**, *76*, 180–191. [CrossRef]
40. Han, T.; Stone-Weiss, N.; Huang, J.; Goel, A.; Kumar, A. Machine Learning as a Tool to Design Glasses with Controlled Dissolution for Application in Healthcare Industry. *Acta Biomater.* **2020**, *107*, 286–298. [CrossRef]
41. Cook, R.; Lapeyre, J.; Ma, H.; Kumar, A. Prediction of Compressive Strength of Concrete: A Critical Comparison of Performance of a Hybrid Machine Learning Model with Standalone Models. *ASCE J. Mater. Civ. Eng.* **2019**, *31*, 04019255. [CrossRef]
42. Han, T.; Siddique, A.; Khayat, K.; Huang, J.; Kumar, A. An Ensemble Machine Learning Approach for Prediction and Optimization of Modulus of Elasticity of Recycled Aggregate Concrete. *Constr. Build. Mater.* **2020**, *244*, 118271. [CrossRef]
43. Liu, H.; Zhang, T.; Anoop Krishnan, N.M.; Smedskjaer, M.M.; Ryan, J.V.; Gin, S.; Bauchy, M. Predicting the Dissolution Kinetics of Silicate Glasses by Topology-Informed Machine Learning. *npj Mater. Degrad.* **2019**, *3*, 32. [CrossRef]
44. Chou, J.-S.; Tsai, C.-F. Concrete Compressive Strength Analysis Using a Combined Classification and Regression Technique. *Autom. Constr.* **2012**, *24*, 52–60. [CrossRef]
45. Omran, B.A.; Chen, Q.; Jin, R. Comparison of Data Mining Techniques for Predicting Compressive Strength of Environmentally Friendly Concrete. *J. Comput. Civ. Eng.* **2016**, *30*, 04016029. [CrossRef]
46. Duan, Z.H.; Kou, S.C.; Poon, C.S. Using Artificial Neural Networks for Predicting the Elastic Modulus of Recycled Aggregate Concrete. *Constr. Build. Mater.* **2013**, *44*, 524–532. [CrossRef]
47. Bangaru, S.S.; Wang, C.; Hassan, M.; Jeon, H.W.; Ayiluri, T. Estimation of the Degree of Hydration of Concrete through Automated Machine Learning Based Microstructure Analysis—A Study on Effect of Image Magnification. *Adv. Eng. Inform.* **2019**, *42*, 100975. [CrossRef]
48. Gomaa, E.; Han, T.; ElGawady, M.; Huang, J.; Kumar, A. Machine Learning to Predict Properties of Fresh and Hardened Alkali-Activated Concrete. *Cem. Concr. Compos.* **2021**, *115*, 103863. [CrossRef]
49. Elçiçek, H.; Akdoğan, E.; Karagöz, S. The Use of Artificial Neural Network for Prediction of Dissolution Kinetics. *Sci. World J.* **2014**, *2014*, e194874. [CrossRef]
50. Xu, X.; Han, T.; Huang, J.; Kruger, A.A.; Kumar, A.; Goel, A. Machine Learning Enabled Models to Predict Sulfur Solubility in Nuclear Waste Glasses. *ACS Appl. Mater. Interfaces* **2021**, *13*, 53375–53387. [CrossRef]
51. Cook, R.; Han, T.; Childers, A.; Ryckman, C.; Khayat, K.; Ma, H.; Huang, J.; Kumar, A. Machine Learning for High-Fidelity Prediction of Cement Hydration Kinetics in Blended Systems. *Mater. Des.* **2021**, *208*, 109920. [CrossRef]
52. Lapeyre, J.; Han, T.; Wiles, B.; Ma, H.; Huang, J.; Sant, G.; Kumar, A. Machine Learning Enables Prompt Prediction of Hydration Kinetics of Multicomponent Cementitious Systems. *Sci. Rep.* **2021**, *11*, 3922. [CrossRef]
53. Han, T.; Ponduru, S.A.; Cook, R.; Huang, J.; Sant, G.; Kumar, A. A Deep Learning Approach to Design and Discover Sustainable Cementitious Binders: Strategies to Learn from Small Databases and Develop Closed-Form Analytical Models. *Front. Mater.* **2022**, *8*, 796476. [CrossRef]
54. Bellmann, F.; Sowoidnich, T.; Ludwig, H.-M.; Damidot, D. Dissolution Rates During the Early Hydration of Tricalcium Silicate. *Cem. Concr. Res.* **2015**, *72*, 108–116. [CrossRef]
55. Damidot, D.; Bellmann, F.; Sovoidnich, T.; Möser, B. Measurement and Simulation of the Dissolution Rate at Room Temperature in Conditions Close to a Cement Paste: From Gypsum to Tricalcium Silicate. *J. Sustain. Cem.-Based Mater.* **2012**, *1*, 94–110. [CrossRef]

56. Barret, P.; Ménétrier, D. Filter Dissolution of C$_3$S as a Function of the Lime Concentration in a Limited Amount of Lime Water. *Cem. Concr. Res.* **1980**, *10*, 521–534. [CrossRef]
57. Robin, V.; Wild, B.; Daval, D.; Pollet-Villard, M.; Nonat, A.; Nicoleau, L. Experimental Study and Numerical Simulation of the Dissolution Anisotropy of Tricalcium Silicate. *Chem. Geol.* **2018**, *497*, 64–73. [CrossRef]
58. Breiman, L. Bagging Predictors. *Mach. Learn.* **1996**, *24*, 123–140. [CrossRef]
59. Breiman, L. Random Forests. *Mach. Learn.* **2001**, *45*, 5–32. [CrossRef]
60. Chen, X.; Ishwaran, H. Random Forests for Genomic Data Analysis. *Genomics* **2012**, *99*, 323–329. [CrossRef]
61. Ibrahim, I.A.; Khatib, T. A Novel Hybrid Model for Hourly Global Solar Radiation Prediction Using Random Forests Technique and Firefly Algorithm. *Energy Convers. Manag.* **2017**, *138*, 413–425. [CrossRef]
62. Svetnik, V.; Liaw, A.; Tong, C.; Culberson, J.C.; Sheridan, R.P.; Feuston, B.P. Random Forest: A Classification and Regression Tool for Compound Classification and QSAR Modeling. *J. Chem. Inf. Comput. Sci.* **2003**, *43*, 1947–1958. [CrossRef]
63. Carlini, N.; Erlingsson, Ú.; Papernot, N. Distribution Density, Tails, and Outliers in Machine Learning: Metrics and Applications. *arXiv* **2019**. [CrossRef]
64. Chakravarty, S.; Demirhan, H.; Baser, F. Fuzzy Regression Functions with a Noise Cluster and the Impact of Outliers on Mainstream Machine Learning Methods in the Regression Setting. *Appl. Soft Comput.* **2020**, *96*, 106535. [CrossRef]
65. Schaffer, C. Selecting a Classification Method by Cross-Validation. *Mach. Learn.* **1993**, *13*, 135–143. [CrossRef]
66. Crundwell, F.K. On the Mechanism of the Dissolution of Quartz and Silica in Aqueous Solutions. *ACS Omega* **2017**, *2*, 1116. [CrossRef] [PubMed]
67. Bergstra, J.; Bengio, Y. Random Search for Hyper-Parameter Optimization. *J. Mach. Learn. Res.* **2012**, *13*, 281–305.
68. Dove, P.M.; Han, N. Kinetics of Mineral Dissolution and Growth as Reciprocal Microscopic Surface Processes across Chemical Driving Force. *AIP Conf. Proc.* **2007**, *916*, 215. [CrossRef]
69. Flatt, R.J.; Scherer, G.W.; Bullard, J.W. Why Alite Stops Hydrating below 80% Relative Humidity. *Cem. Concr. Res.* **2011**, *41*, 987–992. [CrossRef]
70. Kumar, A.; Bishnoi, S.; Scrivener, K.L. Modelling Early Age Hydration Kinetics of Alite. *Cem. Concr. Res.* **2012**, *42*, 903–918. [CrossRef]
71. Zhang, Z.; Han, F.; Yan, P. Modelling the Dissolution and Precipitation Process of the Early Hydration of C$_3$S. *Cem. Concr. Res.* **2020**, *136*, 106174. [CrossRef]
72. Bullard, J.W.; Scherer, G.W.; Thomas, J.J. Time Dependent Driving Forces and the Kinetics of Tricalcium Silicate Hydration. *Cem. Concr. Res.* **2015**, *74*, 26–34. [CrossRef]
73. USGS—Description of Input and Examples for PHREEQC Version 3—A Computer Program for Speciation, Batch-Reaction, One-Dimensional Transport, and Inverse Geochemical Calculations. Available online: https://pubs.usgs.gov/tm/06/a43/pdf/tm6-A43.pdf (accessed on 13 November 2022).
74. Bothe, J.V.; Brown, P.W. PhreeqC Modeling of Friedel's Salt Equilibria at 23 ± 1 °C. *Cem. Concr. Res.* **2004**, *34*, 1057–1063. [CrossRef]
75. Halim, C.E.; Short, S.A.; Scott, J.A.; Amal, R.; Low, G. Modelling the Leaching of Pb, Cd, As, and Cr from Cementitious Waste Using PHREEQC. *J. Hazard. Mater.* **2005**, *125*, 45–61. [CrossRef]
76. Benavente, D.; Brimblecombe, P.; Grossi, C.M. Thermodynamic Calculations for the Salt Crystallisation Damage in Porous Built Heritage Using PHREEQC. *Environ. Earth Sci.* **2015**, *74*, 2297–2313. [CrossRef]
77. Friedman, J.H. Stochastic Gradient Boosting. *Comput. Stat. Data Anal.* **2002**, *38*, 367–378. [CrossRef]
78. Lapeyre, J.; Kumar, A. Influence of Pozzolanic Additives on Hydration Mechanisms of Tricalcium Silicate. *J. Am. Ceram. Soc.* **2018**, *101*, 3557–3574. [CrossRef]
79. Meng, W.; Lunkad, P.; Kumar, A.; Khayat, K. Influence of Silica Fume and Polycarboxylate Ether Dispersant on Hydration Mechanisms of Cement. *J. Phys. Chem. C* **2016**, *120*, 26814–26823. [CrossRef]
80. Nelder, J.A.; Mead, R. A Simplex Method for Function Minimization. *Comput. J.* **1965**, *7*, 308–313. [CrossRef]
81. McKinnon, K.I.M. Convergence of the Nelder–Mead Simplex Method to a Nonstationary Point. *SIAM J. Optim.* **1998**, *9*, 148–158. [CrossRef]

Disclaimer/Publisher's Note: The statements, opinions and data contained in all publications are solely those of the individual author(s) and contributor(s) and not of MDPI and/or the editor(s). MDPI and/or the editor(s) disclaim responsibility for any injury to people or property resulting from any ideas, methods, instructions or products referred to in the content.

Article

RoSummary: Control Tokens for Romanian News Summarization

Mihai Alexandru Niculescu [1], Stefan Ruseti [1] and Mihai Dascalu [2],*

[1] Computer Science & Engineering Department, University Politehnica of Bucharest, 313 Splaiul Independentei, 060042 Bucharest, Romania
[2] Research Technology, 19D Soseaua Virtutii, 060782 Bucharest, Romania
* Correspondence: mihai.dascalu@upb.ro

Abstract: Significant progress has been achieved in text generation due to recent developments in neural architectures; nevertheless, this task remains challenging, especially for low-resource languages. This study is centered on developing a model for abstractive summarization in Romanian. A corresponding dataset for summarization is introduced, followed by multiple models based on the Romanian GPT-2, on top of which control tokens were considered to specify characteristics for the generated text, namely: counts of sentences and words, token ratio, and n-gram overlap. These are special tokens defined in the prompt received by the model to indicate traits for the text to be generated. The initial model without any control tokens was assessed using BERTScore (F_1 = 73.43%) and ROUGE (ROUGE-L accuracy = 34.67%). Control tokens improved the overall BERTScore to 75.42% using <LexOverlap>, while the model was influenced more by the second token specified in the prompt when performing various combinations of tokens. Six raters performed human evaluations of 45 generated summaries with different models and decoding methods. The generated texts were all grammatically correct and consistent in most cases, while the evaluations were promising in terms of main idea coverage, details, and cohesion. Paraphrasing still requires improvements as the models mostly repeat information from the reference text. In addition, we showcase an exploratory analysis of the generated summaries using one or two specific control tokens.

Keywords: RoGPT2; control tokens; summarization; text generation; human evaluation

1. Introduction

A remarkable development in Natural Language Processing (NLP) towards creating models that understand human languages has been observed in recent years. Text generation is one of the main challenges in the field of NLP, and this task has seen an important development after the introduction of Transformers [1]. The Transformer uses an encoder–decoder architecture, self-attention, and positional encodings to facilitate parallel training. The GPT-2 model developed by OpenAI [2] was the first model with remarkable text generation capabilities. GPT-2 was trained for predicting the next token in a sequence and could easily be adjusted for specific tasks. The follow-up improving the GPT-3 model [3] is more than 10-times larger in terms of the parameters and deduces the task only from the provided prompt. There have been several open-source variations of the model, such as GPT-Neo [4] and GPT-J [5]. Other architectures consider a unified framework to cover text-to-text formats and convert text-based language problems, such as the Text-To-Text Transfer Transformer (T5) [6]. This model can perform zero-shot learning and deduce the task from the context of the prompt received as the input, even if it was not presented in the training stage.

For the Romanian language, there are not many specific resources (i.e., pre-trained models and datasets), although there has been significant progress in recent years. The most notable models for Romanian consider the BERT architecture (e.g., RoBERT [7], BERT-base-ro [8], Distil-BERT [9]) and the GPT-2 architecture (e.g., RoGPT2 [10]) and were developed in the last 2 years. Romanian has only one available benchmark, namely LiRo [11]. However, the models are small compared to their English counterparts, and there are no available datasets for common NLP tasks. Overall, Romanian remains a low-resource language with low international usage (https://www.worlddata.info/languages/romanian.php; last accessed on 20 October 2022), despite recent efforts in terms of datasets and models; as such, we argue for the necessity of our efforts to develop tools tailored to this language.

Text summarization is a task of particular importance in NLP centered on extracting critical information from the text using two approaches. First, extractive summarization involves removing the most-important phrases or sentences that include the main ideas of a text. Second, abstractive summarization considers the generation of a new summary starting from the text. One of the most popular datasets in English used for this task is *CNN/Daily Mail* [12], having a total number of 280,000 examples; the dataset was afterward extended to other languages, including French, German, Spanish, Russian, and Turkish, thus generating the large-scale multilingual corpus *MLSUM* [13]. Another dataset used in studies for abstractive summarization is Extreme Summarization (*X-Sum*) [14] to generate a short, one-sentence summary for each news article; X-Sum was derived from BBC news and consists of 220,000 examples. Another dataset is *Webis-TLDR-17 Corpus* [15] with approximately three million examples constructed with the support of the Reddit community. Extractive summarization in Romanian has been previously tackled by Cioaca et al. [16] and Dutulescu et al. [17] with small evaluation datasets. We now introduce the first dataset for Romanian abstractive summarization (https://huggingface.co/datasets/readerbench/ro-text-summarization; last accessed on 20 October 2022).

A wide variety of architectures has been employed for text summarization, including general Transformer-based models [6,18–20] and specific models such as BRIO [21], ProphetNet [22], or PEGASUS [23]. We aim to provide a baseline abstractive summarizer for Romanian built on top of RoGPT2 [10] and to control the characteristics of the generated text. This is an additional step to better imitate human capabilities by considering one or more specifications that improve the summary. As such, we assessed the extent to which text generation is influenced by using control tokens specified in the prompt received by the model to induce specific characteristics of a text. The idea of specifying control tokens directly in the prompt was exploited first in MUSS [24] and CONTROL PREFIXES [25]. The GPT-2 model was also used in combination with BERT [26]; however, to our knowledge, the generation task was not tackled until now in combination with control tokens to manipulate the characteristics of the generated summary.

Following the introduction of various models for text summarization, evaluating the quality of a generated text is a critical challenge, which can be even more difficult than the text generation task itself. Text evaluation is generally performed using synthetic metrics developed for machine translation, such as Bilingual Evaluation Understudy (BLEU) [27], Recall Oriented Understudy for Gisting Evaluation (ROUGE) [28], or Metric for Evaluation for Translation with Explicit Ordering (METEOR) [29]; however, these metrics are limited as they focus on the lexical overlap. Newer metrics based on Transformers, such as BERTScore [30], BARTScore [31], or Bilingual Evaluation Understudy with Representations from Transformers (BLEURT) [32], are much more accurate compared to the classical metrics. Still, they require more resources (i.e., pre-trained models and higher computing power) and have longer processing times. Besides comparing automated similarity metrics, Celikyilmaz et al. [33] argued that a human evaluation is the gold standard for evaluating a Natural Language Generation (NLG) task; nevertheless, it is the most expensive and cumbersome to accomplish.

Thus, our research objective is threefold: create a dataset for summarization in Romanian, train a model that generates coherent texts, and introduce control tokens to manipulate the output easily. Following this objective, our main contributions are the following:

- Publish a clean version of the dataset for Romanian text summarization (https://huggingface.co/datasets/readerbench/AlephNews; last accessed 20 October 2022).

- Develop and publicly release a baseline model built on top of RoGPT-2 available on HuggingFace (https://huggingface.co/readerbench/RoSummary-large; last accessed on 20 October 2022), with the corresponding code released on GitHub (https://github.com/readerbench/RoSummary; last accessed on 20 October 2022).
- Study the use of control tokens for the text characteristics in the case of our summarization task.

2. Method

This section presents the dataset created for the summarization task, the model architecture, the training method with the control tokens, as well as the methods employed to evaluate the generated text.

2.1. Corpus

The dataset for the summarization task was constructed by crawling all articles from the AlephNews website (https://alephnews.ro/; last accessed on 20 October 2022) until July 2022. The site presents a section with the news summary as bullet points with sentences representing the main ideas for most articles. This peculiarity of the site enabled the automatic creation of a reasonably qualitative dataset for abstractive summarization. The news articles that did not have a summary or were too short were eliminated by imposing a minimum limit set of 20 characters. This resulted in 42,862 collected news articles. The news and summary texts were cleaned using several heuristics: these were the repair of diacritics, the elimination of special characters, the elimination of emoticons, and fixing punctuation (if it has more points, if it has no punctuation mark, a period is added at the end of the sentence), eliminating words such as "UPDATE", "REPORT", "AUDIO", etc. The dataset was split into 3 partitions (i.e., train, dev, and test) with proportions of 90%–5%–5%. Articles with a maximum of 715 tokens based on the RoGPT2 tokenizer were selected for the test partition; out of 724 tokens, 9 were reserved for the control tokens. After analyzing the dataset and based on the limitations regarding the sequence length of a context, the maximum size was set to 724 tokens. In the case of entries from the training and dev partitions having the combined length of the article and the summary greater than 724, the article content was divided into a maximum of 3 distinct fragments, which had the last sentences removed; this was applied to approximately 10% of the entries to increase the number of examples and to keep the beginning of the news, which contains key information to be considered. We chose not to apply this augmentation technique for the entries in the test partition, as this would have altered the content of the original texts and would have generated multiple artificial test entries; moreover, we limited the text to the first 715 tokens so that control tokens could also be added when running various configurations. The total number of examples for each partition was: 47,525 for training, 132 for validation, and 2143 for testing.

2.2. RoGPT2 Model for Summarization

The model was trained to predict the next token using the previous sequence, similar to the RoGPT2 [10] training for the Romanian language. The model architecture consists of several decoder layers of architecture Transformers [1], as presented in Figure 1. There are 3 versions of the model, each with a different number of decoder layers: 12 layers were used for the base version, 24 layers for the medium version, and 36 layers for the large version.

Control tokens were used to indicate the task and the characteristics of the generated text, which are presented in the following subsections. This assumes that the model maximizes the probability of a subword depending on the context and the previously generated subwords:

$$P(w_{1...m}) = \prod_{i=1}^{m} P(w_m|w_1, w_2, w_3, ..., w_{m-1}) \qquad (1)$$

Cross-entropy was the loss function for the supervised learning task:

$$L_{CE} = -\sum_{i=1}^{n} t_i log(p_i) \qquad (2)$$

where t_i is the label and p_i is the probability of the ith class, or more specifically, a class is considered the *id* of a token.

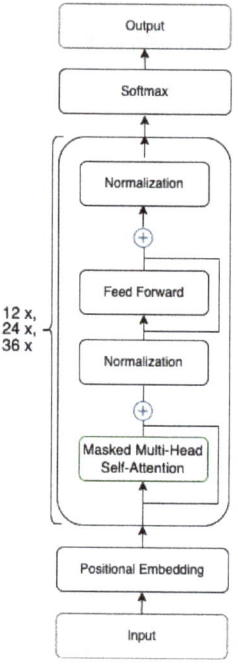

Figure 1. RoGPT2 architecture.

Due to a large number of parameters, the model was trained on TPU v3-8. The batch size was limited to fit into memory 724 tokens per entry. The Adam optimizer [34], the ReduceLROnPlateau (https://keras.io/api/callbacks/reduce_lr_on_plateau/; last accessed on 20 October 2022) and EarlyStopping (https://keras.io/api/callbacks/early_stopping/; last accessed on 20 October 2022) callbacks were used.

Three decoder methods for text generation were considered to choose the next token depending on the tokens generated up to that point and the probability distribution over the vocabulary.

Greedy search: This strategy is based on choosing a local optimum, in this case the token with the highest probability, which converges to a local maximum. First, the probability distribution is generated, and then, the next token is selected by choosing the highest probability. The procedure continues until the desired length is achieved or the token indicating the end is found. An advantage of this method is that it is efficient and intuitive, but it does not guarantee finding a global optimum for the generated sequence; this can lead to the non-exploration of some branches with a higher probability.

Beam search: Beam search [35] partially solves the maximum global problem by keeping the best beam width sequences with a higher total probability. Multiple contents are generated for each step, and the sequence with the highest probability is chosen at each step. The advantage of this method is that it obtains better results for relatively small beam widths, but it requires more memory for a larger beam width or longer sequences, whereas the text does not vary much, being quite monotone. Beam search also does not guarantee finding the global optimum. Beam search works quite well when it can approximate the generated text's length, but has issues when the corresponding length varies greatly. Holtzman et al. [36] argued that people do not choose the phrase with the highest probability as the element of unpredictability is important.

Top-p (nucleus) sampling: This method involves choosing the smallest subset of words with a probability equal to p. Based on the new probability distribution, a new token is chosen. The advantage of this method is that it achieves results quite close to human ones and does not require many resources. The disadvantage is that p is fixed and not dynamic.

2.3. Control Tokens

Starting from previous studies presented in the Introduction and related to the specifics of the summarization task, we chose to specify a set of 4 control tokens representative of various characteristics of the text, namely:

- **NoSentences** indicates the number of sentences that the summary should have;
- **NoWords** indicates the number of words to be generated within the summary;
- **RatioTokens** reflects how many times the sequence of tokens of the summary must be longer than the input;
- **LexOverlap** is the ratio of the number of 4-grams from the summary that also appears in the reference text; stop words and punctuation marks were omitted.

The first 3 control tokens are purely quantitative and reflect different use-case scenarios: a summary containing at most a specific number of sentences, a summary having an imposed number of words, or a compression ratio to be used globally. The last control token ensures a lower or higher degree of lexical overlap between the two texts.

The prompt for the summarization task was the following:

$$Text : \{article\} \; Summary : \{summary\} < |endoftext| > \quad (3)$$

The model learns that, after the control token **"Summary:"**, it must generate the summary of the text preceding that token. Control tokens are specified before the token that indicates the input (i.e., marked by the **Text** token), while the token specific to the task is placed after the end. The prompt used for an item from the dataset used for training is the following:

$$FeatureToken : \{value\} \; Text : \{article\} \; Summary : \{summary\} < |endoftext| > \quad (4)$$

where FeatureToken is <NoSentences>, <NoWords>, <RatioTokens>, or <LexOverlap>.

Following the initial experimentation, we noticed that the model learns best when subsequent entries have the same input text, but with different values for the control tokens and a different text to be generated; this refers to the extraction of fragments from the original summary and their use as the output. This variation is reflected in the text to be generated and was used for the <NoSentences>, <NoWords>, and <RatioToken> control tokens. The generation of multiple variations was applied if the summary text had more than 3 sentences; thus, incremental examples were generated by adding sentences and calculating the value for the control token each time. An example for a summary comprising 4 sentences s_1, s_2, s_3, s_4 and <NoWords> would consider two entries in the training dataset: the first item would consist of the first 3 sentences and the corresponding <NoWords> for this first shorter summary and a second item where the s_4 sentence would be added and <NoWords> is set at the global count of words from the summary.

Besides training the summarization model with each control token individually, we also considered combinations of 2 control tokens, namely: <NoWords>-<NoSentences>, <RatioTokens>-<NoSentences>, and <LexOverlap>-<NoWords>. The combination <NoWords>-<NoSentences> was chosen because it reflects the most straightforward manner to manually enforce the length of the summary by an end user (i.e., specify an approximate number of words and the number of sentences that the generated summary should have). <RatioTokens> presents the same idea as <NoWords>, only that it is much more difficult to learn by the model as it represents the ratio between the length of the news and that of the summary. The combination of <LexOverlap>-<NoWords> is interesting because it forces the model to generate a text with an approximate number of words. Still, the generated text must not match the one received by the model. <NoWords> indicates how many words the summary should have, while <LexOverlap> restricts the percentage of combinations of words that are present in the news and generated text by the model; a small value for <LexOverlap> indicates that the model must reformulate an idea from the news, whereas a large value makes the model extract the most important phrases within a word limit.

2.4. Evaluation Metrics

Our evaluations considered both automated and human evaluations of the generated summaries. We wanted the evaluation of the model to be a sustainable one; for this, the three evaluation metric methods used were: Recall Oriented Understudy for Gisting Evaluation (ROUGE) [28] as a classic metric, which is used in the majority of research in the field of abstract summarization, BERTScore [30], a metric that uses a pre-trained model to understand the generated text and the reference to provide a better comparison, and human evaluation. To evaluate the characteristics of the control token, the following metrics were used: Mean Absolute Error (MAE) and Mean-Squared Error (MSE) for <NoSentences> and <NoWords>, and the Pearson and Spearman coefficients were used for <RatioTokens> and <LexOverlap>.

2.4.1. BERTScore

Metrics based on Transformers [1], such as BERTScore [30], have been introduced to better capture the similarity between texts. BERTScore shows how good and realistic a text generated by a model is at the semantic level (i.e., the metric considers the meaning of the text by computing the cosine similarity between token embeddings from the generated sentences versus the tokens in the given sentences as a reference). The token embeddings are the numerical representations of subwords obtained using the BERT [37] tokenizer. The precision, recall, and F_1 scores are computed based on the scalar product between the embeddings in the two texts. Precision refers to the generated text and is calculated as the average value for the largest scalar product between the embeddings of the generated sentence and those of the reference sentence; in contrast, recall is centered on the reference text and is computed in an equivalent manner while considering the embedding of the reference versus the generated sentence embeddings. The original paper showed good correlations to human evaluations. Even if BERTScore is more accurate when compared to classical machine translation metrics, which account for the overlap between words using n-grams or synonyms (e.g., BLEU, ROUGE), the metric requires a language model for the targeted language. We used the implementation offered by HuggingFace (https://huggingface.co/spaces/evaluate-metric/bertscore; last accessed on 20 October 2022), which considers mBERT [37] for the Romanian language. The performance metrics are computed as follows:

$$P_{BERT} = \frac{1}{|\hat{x}|} \sum_{\hat{x}_j \in \hat{x}} max_{x_i \in x}(x_i^T \hat{x}_j) \qquad (5)$$

$$R_{BERT} = \frac{1}{|x|} \sum_{x_i \in x} max_{\hat{x}_j \in \hat{x}}(x_i^T \hat{x}_j) \qquad (6)$$

$$F_{BERT} = 2 * \frac{P_{BERT} * R_{BERT}}{P_{BERT} + R_{BERT}} \qquad (7)$$

where:
- x is the embedding for the text given as a reference;
- $\hat{x}$ is the embeddings for the text generated by the model.

2.4.2. Human Evaluation

Human evaluation is considered the gold standard in measuring the quality of generated text [33], but it is costly and difficult to achieve. For human evaluation, the most-used method is the one by which a form is created, and the respondents are asked to evaluate the generated text. In our case, correspondents were asked to assess the generated text from the point of view of five metrics: main idea (i.e., the main idea of the article is present within the summary), details (i.e., the key information is found in the generated text for irrelevant ideas), cohesion (i.e., phrases and ideas have a logic), wording/paraphrasing (i.e., the text is not the same as that of the news and the model-made changes), and language beyond the source text (i.e., there is a varied range of lexical and syntactic structures). The scores ranged from 1 to 4, the best being 4. The summary scoring rubric is based on the studies of Taylor [38] and Westley, Culatta, Lawrence, and Hall-Kenyon [39]. The raters were asked to evaluate 5 examples chosen randomly from the texts generated using the 3 decoding methods, and for 3 variants of the model; in total, 45 questions were included in the form. The Intraclass Correlation Coefficient (ICC3) [40] was calculated for each configuration and model-version-decoding method to measure the consistency of the evaluations. The form was sent to people collaborating with our research laboratory to obtain the relevant results, primarily due to the complexity of the 5 metrics used.

2.5. Experimental Setup

The Adam [34] optimizer started from a learning rate equal to 1×10^{-4} and was reduced to 4×10^{-6} using the callback ReduceLROnPlateau, for patience equal to 2 and a factor of $1/e$. The patience parameter was set to 1 for combinations of control tokens due to the task's complexity and the dataset's size; the training was more aggressive, modifying the learning rate if there were no improvements after an epoch. The training was stopped if no improvements were noticed after 3 epochs for baseline summarization or 4 epochs for the control token. A context size equal to 724 was considered, and the batch size varied for each model version: 128 for the base, 24 for the medium, and 16 for the large models. Three decoding methods were used for text generation: greedy, beam-search, and top-p sampling. The experiments were performed on TPU v3.8 for training, while the NVIDIA Tesla A100 and NVIDIA Tesla P100 were used for text generation and evaluation. The model received prompts that contained the summary token and those that specified the characteristics of the text to be generated.

3. Results

This section presents the results obtained by the models for the summarization task and the experiments for control tokens. In most experiments, the same configuration was used for text generation. After training, the following generation strategies were used: greedy, beam search with a width equal to four, and top p sampling (with top k = 25 and $p = 0.94$). In addition, we introduced an exploratory analysis to highlight the benefits of using control tokens when generating summaries with various specificities.

3.1. News Summary

This experiment aimed to generate summaries for news articles without any particular characteristics. The model knows that it must generate text after the control token <Summary>. The evaluation of the model was performed using the metrics: ROUGE [28] score (the F1-score average was calculated for ROUGE-1, ROUGE-2, ROUGE-L) and BERTScore [30]. The results are available in Table 1. The medium version using beam search achieved the best scores (74.34% for BERTScore F_1 and 34.67% for ROUGE-L F_1), surpassing the large version with beam search by 0.1% for BERTScore.

Table 1. Results for the evaluation of news summaries (bold marks the best results).

Model	Decode Method	BERT Score			ROUGE		
		Precision (%)	Recall (%)	F$_1$ (%)	ROUGE-1 (%)	ROUGE-2 (%)	ROUGE-L (%)
Base	Greedy	73.35	73.99	73.58	33.60	18.62	33.33
	Beam Search	73.54	74.68	74.04	34.80	19.91	34.16
	Top-p Sampling	72.96	72.99	72.92	30.58	14.52	29.51
Medium	Greedy	73.78	74.01	73.80	34.22	19.22	33.94
	Beam Search	73.90	**74.93**	**74.34**	**35.46**	**20.61**	**34.67**
	Top-p Sampling	73.15	72.85	72.94	30.42	14.00	29.21
Large	Greedy	73.76	74.24	73.91	34.14	18.95	33.55
	Beam Search	**73.94**	74.70	74.24	34.92	19.95	33.84
	Top-p Sampling	73.11	73.01	72.99	30.51	14.18	29.31

3.2. Human Evaluations

The next experiment was to evaluate the model trained on the AlephNews dataset to generate summaries on the DigiNews test dataset introduced by Niculescu et al. [10]. As the DigiNews dataset does not have a summary for a news story, a human evaluation was performed to assess the quality of the generated text. The form was completed by six raters, and the scores from Table 2 consider the average for the five evaluated texts from each combination.

Table 2. Results for human evaluation (bold marks the best results).

Model	Decode Method	Main Idea	Details	Cohesion	Paraphrasing	Language	ICC3(1)	ICC3(k)
Base	Greedy	3.10	2.93	3.10	2.46	3.26	0.88	0.98
	Beam Search	2.73	2.86	2.86	2.03	3.40	0.93	0.99
	Top-p Sampling	2.70	2.50	2.53	1.90	3.00	0.92	0.98
Medium	Greedy	2.76	2.36	2.46	2.06	2.73	0.88	0.98
	Beam Search	3.43	**3.36**	3.30	2.00	3.56	**0.98**	**1.00**
	Top-p Sampling	2.56	2.30	3.16	2.63	3.33	0.92	0.98
Large	Greedy	**3.73**	3.06	**3.53**	2.30	**3.73**	0.92	0.99
	Beam Search	2.23	2.06	2.33	1.56	2.93	0.95	0.99
	Top-p Sampling	2.50	2.33	3.26	**2.70**	3.26	0.85	0.97

3.3. Control Tokens

For the following experiments, control tokens were used individually or in combination to indicate the characteristics of the generated text, in addition to the one indicating the task. For the more complex scenarios, we wanted to observe if the model learns a combination of several control tokens that were not reproduced in the training stage and if the order of tokes from the prompt matters. BERTScore [30] was used holistically as a means to compare different combinations; the Mean Absolute Error (MAE) and Mean-Squared Error (MSE) were considered for <NoSentences> and <NoWords>, whereas the Pearson and Spearman coefficients were used for <RatioTokens> and <LexOverlap>. Table 3 shows the best BERTScores obtained for each control token separately; the beam search and top-p sampling decoding methods were selected because they obtained the most revealing results. Detailed results for each control token are presented in Tables A1–A4. The best score was 75.42% with the <LexOverlap> control token.

Subsequently, we explored the extent to which the model succeeded in learning combinations of control tokens, having only examples for each one in the training stage. The following combinations of control tokens were chosen in line with the argumentation from the Method Section: <RatioTokens>-<NoSentences>, <NoWords>-<NoSentences>, <NoWords>-<LexOverlap>. We decided to focus only on the condensed results that consider BERTScore for the medium and large versions using beam search and the top-p sample as the decoding methods (see Table 4). Tables A5–A10 present the full results of the previous combinations. The best score was achieved by the combination of <NoWords>-<LexOverlap> using the medium version with beam search (F1 = 74.95%).

Table 3. BERTScore [30] for control tokens taken individually (bold marks the best results).

Control Token	Model	Decode Method	BERTScore		
			Precision (%)	Recall (%)	F_1 (%)
NoSentences	Base	Beam Search	73.69	73.53	73.54
		Top-p Sampling	72.52	72.24	72.32
	Medium	Beam Search	73.49	74.42	73.89
		Top-p Sampling	72.72	73.04	72.83
	Large	Beam Search	73.90	74.78	74.27
		Top-p Sampling	73.34	72.99	73.11
NoWords	Base	Beam Search	74.17	73.67	73.88
		Top-p Sampling	72.84	72.56	72.67
	Medium	Beam Search	74.71	74.45	74.55
		Top-p Sampling	73.43	73.07	73.23
	Large	Beam Search	74.90	74.67	74.75
		Top-p Sampling	73.53	73.27	73.37
RatioTokens	Base	Beam Search	74.81	72.48	73.55
		Top-p Sampling	73.22	71.59	72.32
	Medium	Beam Search	75.45	73.41	74.34
		Top-p Sampling	74.11	72.49	73.22
	Large	Beam Search	74.35	74.66	74.48
		Top-p Sampling	73.22	73.37	73.26
LexOverlap	Base	Beam Search	75.62	74.32	74.89
		Top-p Sampling	73.48	73.17	73.27
	Medium	Beam Search	75.90	**74.94**	75.36
		Top-p Sampling	73.95	73.88	73.87
	Large	Beam Search	74.37	73.83	74.05
		Top-p Sampling	**76.30**	74.66	**75.42**

Table 4. BERTScore [30] for complex control tokens (bold marks the best results).

Control Token	Model	Decode Method	BERTScore		
			Precision (%)	Recall (%)	F_1 (%)
RatioTokens-NoSentences	Medium	Beam Search	74.47	74.34	74.36
		Top-p Sampling	73.48	73.00	73.20
	Large	Beam Search	74.81	74.54	74.63
		Top-p Sampling	73.77	73.18	73.43
NoSentences-RatioTokens	Medium	Beam Search	72.67	75.28	73.91
		Top-p Sampling	71.76	73.96	72.81
	Large	Beam Search	73.25	75.51	74.33
		Top-p Sampling	72.48	73.99	73.19
NoWords-NoSentences	Medium	Beam Search	73.98	74.71	74.30
		Top-p Sampling	72.94	73.21	73.04
	Large	Beam Search	74.43	74.71	74.52
		Top-p Sampling	73.66	73.47	73.52
NoSentences-NoWords	Medium	Beam Search	73.91	75.33	74.58
		Top-p Sampling	72.61	73.74	73.15
	Large	Beam Search	73.46	75.34	74.35
		Top-p Sampling	72.73	74.11	73.38
LexOverlap-NoWords	Medium	Beam Search	**75.05**	74.84	**74.90**
		Top-p Sampling	73.49	73.52	73.46
	Large	Beam Search	74.89	74.60	74.69
		Top-p Sampling	73.71	73.69	73.66
NoWords-LexOverlap		Top-p Sampling	73.64	73.76	73.66
	Large	Beam Search	74.81	74.59	74.65
		Top-p Sampling	73.53	73.56	73.50

3.4. Exploratory Analysis of Generated Summaries Using Control Token

Besides assessing the performance of various configurations, our aim was also to explore the extent to which control tokens change the generated texts. As such, we generated summaries for the same news by varying the values for the control token(s), while assessing the impact on the quality of the generated summary and its resemblance to the original text. Given the previous best results, medium and large RoGPT models with beam search configurations were chosen for this experiment. We experimented with an individual control token (i.e., <NoSenentences>) that is easily explainable, as well as with a more complex scenario that forces a compression/expansion of the generated text (i.e., a combination used of <NoSentences>-<NoWords>). The range for <NoSenentences> was 2–5; there were extremely few training samples with only 1 sentence within the summary, and our model is incapable of generating such over-condensed summaries. The <NoWords> control token considered five values −50%, −25%, 0%, +25%, +50%, which signified a compression of −50% words from the reference summary, all the way to an expansion with +50% additional words. A sample of 100 news articles from the test partition was chosen, and BERTScore F_1 was calculated for each value of the control token(s); the corresponding results are presented in Figures 2 and 3. An example of text generation when only the <NoSentence> was varied is presented in Appendix C.1, whereas Appendix C.2 showcases the example for <NoSentence>-<NoWords>.

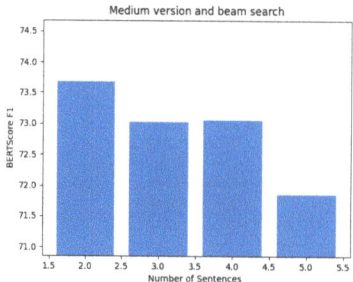 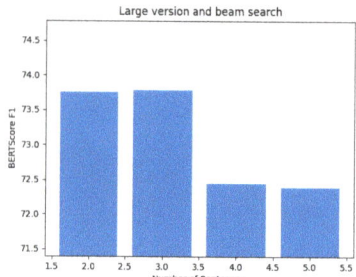

Figure 2. BERTScore for NoSentences.

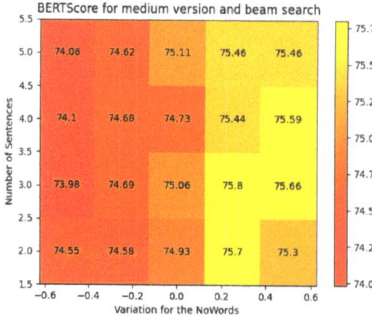 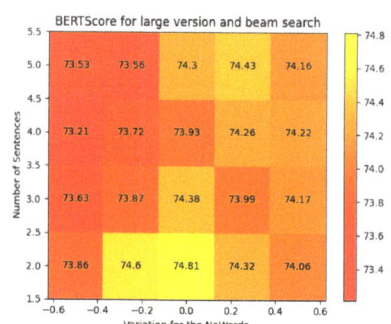

Figure 3. BERTScore for NoSentences-NoWords.

4. Discussion

The baseline model managed to achieve good results (see Table 1) for the summarization task, and the best results for ROUGE-L (34.67%) and BERTScore (74.34%) were obtained by the medium version with the beam search decoding method. It is worth noting that the best results were obtained with the beam search decoding method regardless of the considered model. Poorer results obtained by the large version are arguable, given the relatively small size of the dataset.

Results from the human evaluations (see Table 2) were also consistent, based on the obtained ICC3 score. The best score for the main idea was obtained by the large model with greedy decoding (3.73/4), followed by the medium version with beam search with a score of 3.43/4, thus arguing that the models managed to identify the main idea from the news. In terms of the provided details, the best score (3.36/4) was achieved by the medium model with beam search decoding (see Appendix A.1 for an example). The model managed to have coherent sentences with an elevated language; this was also shown in the paper that introduced RoGPT2 [10]. The large model obtained the highest overall score in terms of cohesion with greedy decoding (3.27/4), followed by the medium model with beam search with a score of 3.13/4; this lower score is justifiable since the contents of some randomly sampled news articles were challenging to summarize (see Appendix A.2 for a horoscope example). Paraphrasing was the main problem of the texts generated by the model since the models mostly repeated information from the reference text. Nevertheless, the results obtained by the model are impressive, considering that the human-evaluated news articles originated from a dataset on which the model was not trained.

The summaries using control tokens obtained better scores than the baseline summarization task (see Table 3). The small differences indicate that a winning configuration cannot be determined with certainty as the largest difference was up to 2%; however, we observed that beam search consistently obtained the best results. Despite being the most complex token, the largest improvement in BERTScore F_1 with 1.08% was obtained with the <LexOverlap> control token. The worst results for controlling text characteristics were obtained by <NoSentences>, whereas <RatioTokens> obtained a lower BERTScore than <NoWords> because it is a token more difficult to understand by the model.

Lower performance for combinations of tokens was expected because the dataset is relatively small and the task difficulty was higher. Then, comparing the performance of the models on each control token individually, we noticed that a higher performance was obtained for the second token specified in the prompt; this suggests that the model was influenced more by the second token from the prompt. The combination <NoWords>-<LexOverlap> obtained the best overall results, highlighting the benefits of complementarity between control tokens. Overall, the best decoding method was beam search.

When considering the exploratory analysis, the best results when varying the number of sentences were obtained for values of 2 and 3; this was expected as most summaries had 3 sentences. The example from Appendix C.1 highlights that the model seems to only extract sentences from the original text without paraphrasing. With <NoSentences> set at three, the model copied a central sentence and reiterated it based on a repetition present in the source text (i.e., the news article contained "Roxana Ispas este fondatoarea brandului Ronna Swimwear." and "Roxana Ispas, fondatoare Ronna Swimwear", which confused the model). Furthermore, there was a problem when setting the control token to 5 as the model failed to generate five sentences; nevertheless, it generated considerably longer sentences than the previous use case with only four sentences.

The best results for the experiment with the <NoSentences>-<NoWords> combination were obtained when the number of sentences was equal to 2 or 3 and the number of words was equal to +25% or +50% more words than the original summary. The best BERTScore was obtained for the medium version with <NoSentence> = 3 and <NoWords> = +25%, followed by a similar scenario with <NoSentences> = 2 and the same value for <NoWords>. As exemplified in Appendix C.2, the model takes into account the number of words that must be generated, i.e., there is a proportional relationship between the length of the summary and the value of the control token. Furthermore, a higher compression rate given by a smaller number of words forced the model to generate one less sentence than specified.

5. Conclusions

This paper introduced a novel dataset, a baseline model, and control tokens for manipulating text characteristics when summarizing texts in Romanian; all previous resources have been publicly released. Our model obtained overall good results (F1-scores above

0.73 in most configurations), indicating that the models learn even from limited samples. The generated texts were grammatically correct and primarily consistent, as highlighted by the human evaluation. Using control tokens led to the improvement of BERTScore [30]. The best results were obtained when using beam search as a decoding strategy, while medium and large models shared similar performances; however, the medium models are more suitable given the size of the dataset. Higher scores were obtained when only one control token was used. In contrast, the model emphasized the second token specified in the prompt when generating the text in complex scenarios.

In terms of future work, we aim to increase the quality and size of our dataset with examples originating from other news websites targeting specific fields in contrast to AlephNews, which is a generalist news site. This will ensure a higher diversity of text characteristics and introduce the possibility of new control tokens specific to the new categories. Moreover, we plan to register the summarization task in the LiRo benchmark [11] to ensure the development of robust natural-language-understanding systems for Romanian.

Author Contributions: Conceptualization, M.D. and S.R.; methodology, M.D., S.R. and M.A.N.; software, M.A.N. and S.R.; validation, M.A.N., S.R. and M.D.; formal analysis, S.R.; investigation, M.A.N. and S.R.; resources, M.A.N.; data curation, M.A.N.; writing—original draft preparation, M.A.N.; writing—review and editing, M.D. and S.R.; visualization, M.A.N.; supervision, M.D.; project administration, M.D.; funding acquisition, M.D. All authors have read and agreed to the published version of the manuscript.

Funding: This work was funded by the "Innovative Solution for Optimizing User Productivity through Multi-Modal Monitoring of Activity and Profiles – OPTIMIZE"/"Soluție Inovativă de Optimizare a Productivității Utilizatorilor prin Monitorizarea Multi-Modala a Activității și a Profilelor— OPTIMIZE" project, Contract Number 366/390042/27.09.2021, MySMIS code: 121491.

Institutional Review Board Statement: The study was conducted in accordance with the Declaration of Helsinki and approved by the Ethics Committee of the Faculty of Automated Control and Computers, University Politehnica of Bucharest.

Informed Consent Statement: Not applicable.

Data Availability Statement: The dataset for Romanian text summarization is freely available on HuggingFace (https://huggingface.co/datasets/readerbench/AlephNews; last accessed 20 October 2022); the models built on top of RoGPT-2 are available on HuggingFace (https://huggingface.co/readerbench/RoSummary-large; last accessed 20 October 2022); the corresponding code is released on GitHub (https://github.com/readerbench/RoSummary; last accessed 20 October 2022).

Acknowledgments: Special thanks to the TensorFlow Research Cloud (https://www.tensorflow.org/tfrc; last accessed on 20 October 2022) programs for providing us the Tensor Processing Unit (TPU) (https://cloud.google.com/tpu/; last accessed on 20 October 2022) that was used to train the models.

Conflicts of Interest: The authors declare no conflict of interest.

Abbreviations

The following abbreviations are used in this manuscript:

BERT	Bidirectional Encoder Representations from Transformers
GPT	Generative Pre-trained Transformer
ICC	Intraclass Correlation Coefficient
ROUGE	Recall Oriented Understudy for Gisting Evaluation
NLP	Natural Language Processing
MSE	Mean-Squared Error
MAE	Mean Absolute Error
NLG	Natural Language Generation
TPU	Tensor Processing Unit

Appendix A

Appendix A.1

News: "Zona Cheile Râșnoavei, sufocată de gunoaie Un telespectator Digi24 a trimis o sesizare la autoritățile locale, dar reprezentații primăriei ridică neputincioși din umeri: au încercat să curețe, dar romii din apropiere fac mizerie din nou, peste noapte. La câțiva metri de drumul care duce spre Cheile Râșnoavei, unul din cele mai frumoase locuri de vizitat din județ, frumusețea peisajului este umbrită de gunoaiele aruncate pe o rază de mai bine de o sută de metri. Profitând de faptul că zona este marcată ca fiind poligon de trageri, oamenii au aruncat aici nestingheriți saci întregi de gunoi, fără să se gândească la turiștii care trec pe aici sau la felul în care nepăsarea lor strică imaginea orașului. Cunoscut pentru cetatea țărănească și pentru peisajele de poveste de pe Cheile Râșnoavei, orașul Râșnov atrage la fiecare sfârșit de săptămână mii de turiști. Cei care ajung însă la periferie rămân dezamăgiți: mormane întregi de sticle, hârtii, gunoi menajer și chiar cărămizi s-au adunat aici. Iar în ultima perioadă, localnicii au început să ducă acolo chiar și gunoaiele din grajduri. Ovidiu Drăgunoiu locuiește în Brașov și este un împătimit al drumețiilor. Zilele trecute a vrut să meargă cu câinele la plimbare pe drumul spre Cheile Râșnoavei. A filmat mizeria și a anunțat autoritățile. Luați la întrebări, reprezentații primăriei au găsit rapid o scuză. „Am făcut ordine acolo, am curățat, am nivelat zona ca într-o săptămână zona să fie la loc. Vin cu căruțele, cu sacii, cu fel și Iel de modalități ei pun acolo din curte parcă intenționat parcă sfidător să arate zona din nou murdară și plină de mizerie", a declarat Marian Ilie, responsabil cu problemele de mediu la Primăria Râșnov. Locuitorii orașului sunt si ei afectați de mormanele de gunoaie. Nu de puține ori s-au îmbolnăvit animalele duse la păscut în zonă. Autoritățíe din Râșnov spun că toate gunoaiele vor fi adunate, iar cei care nu le depozitează corespunzător vor fi amendați. Deocamdată însă, nimeni nu a primit nicio sancțiune."

Summary: Zona Cheile Râșnoavei, sufocată de gunoaie Un telespectator Digi24 a trimis o sesizare la autoritățile locale, dar reprezentații primăriei ridică neputincioși din umeri: au încercat să curețe, dar romii din apropiere fac mizerie din nou, peste noapte. La câțiva metri de drumul care duce spre Cheile Râșnoavei, unul din cele mai frumoase locuri de vizitat din județ, frumusețea peisajului este umbrită de gunoaiele aruncate pe o rază de mai bine de o sută de metri. La câțiva metri de drumul care duce spre Cheile Râșnoavei, unul din cele mai frumoase locuri de vizitat din județ, frumusețea peisajului este umbrită de gunoaiele aruncate pe o rază de mai bine de o sută de metri.

Appendix A.2

News: "HOROSCOP. Leii pleacă într-o vacanță mult-așteptată PEȘTI Atenție la cheltuieli. Nu cedați tentațiilor. BERBEC Se anunță o zi dinamică. Sunt favorizate activitățile intelectuale. TAUR Vă puteți întâlni cu persoane care vă îndeamnă la comunicare. GEMENI Sunteți nemulțumit de ritmul în care se desfășoară un proiect. Lucrurile vor reveni la normal. RAC Este posibil să primiți niște bani din colaborări mai vechi. LEU Puteți pleca într-o călătorie pe care o așteptați de mult timp. FECIOARĂ Petreceți o seară specială cu cei dragi. Primiți vizita copiilor. BALANȚĂ Sunteți foarte solicitați la birou. Aveți o serie de responsabilități. SCORPION Foarte implicați în relația de iubire, Scorpionii petrec o seară specială alături de partener. SAGETĂTOR Nu cumpărați tot ce vă iese în cale. Mai mult de jumătate dintre achiziții se vor dovedi inutile. CAPRICORN În aceste zile veți vedea rezultate concrete ale muncii dumneavoastră și veți avea ocazia să vă exprimați ideile. VĂRSĂTOR Ați putea primi o veste importantă, care vă reține la birou. Nu neglijați totuși, familia."

Summary: Berbecii pleacă într-o vacanță mult-așteptată PEȘTI Atenție la cheltuieli. Nu cedați tentațiilor.

Appendix B. Results for Control Tokens

Appendix B.1. Simple Scenarios

Table A1. Results for NoSentences (bold marks the best results).

Model	Decode Method	Precision (%)	BERTScore Recall (%)	F_1 (%)	MSE	MAE
Base	Greedy	73.15	72.87	72.92	3.630	0.920
	Beam Search	73.69	73.53	73.54	0.857	**0.661**
	Top-p Sampling	72.52	72.24	72.32	1.554	1.026
Medium	Greedy	73.54	74.08	73.74	0.996	0.814
	Beam Search	73.49	74.42	73.89	**0.813**	0.702
	Top-p Sampling	72.72	73.04	72.83	0.955	0.852
Large	Greedy	**73.96**	73.97	73.90	1.141	0.987
	Beam Search	73.90	**74.78**	**74.27**	0.989	0.870
	Top-p Sampling	73.34	72.99	73.11	1.168	1.001

Table A2. Results for NoWords (bold marks the best results).

Model	Decode Method	Precision (%)	BERTScore Recall (%)	F_1 (%)	MSE	MAE
Base	Greedy	73.73	73.24	73.43	257.15	9.28
	Beam Search	74.17	73.67	73.88	114.31	7.55
	Top-p Sampling	72.84	72.56	72.67	397.93	9.14
Medium	Greedy	74.34	74.04	74.15	529.18	8.11
	Beam Search	74.71	74.45	74.55	67.42	5.44
	Top-p Sampling	73.43	73.07	73.23	110.34	6.53
Large	Greedy	74.58	74.33	74.42	147.61	6.73
	Beam Search	**74.90**	**74.67**	**0.7475**	**51.87**	**4.96**
	Top-p Sampling	73.53	73.27	73.37	77.69	6.10

Table A3. Results for RatioTokens (bold marks the best results).

Model	Decode Method	Precision (%)	BERTScore Recall (%)	F_1 (%)	Spearman (%)	Pearson (%)
Base	Greedy	74.46	71.98	73.10	51.88	30.36
	Beam Search	74.81	72.48	73.55	59.44	58.09
	Top-p Sampling	73.22	71.59	72.32	54.48	40.58
Medium	Greedy	**75.47**	73.41	74.34	54.26	38.19
	Beam Search	75.45	73.41	74.34	62.06	63.23
	Top-p Sampling	74.11	72.49	73.22	55.08	53.41
Large	Greedy	74.12	74.37	74.21	90.03	55.80
	Beam Search	74.35	**74.66**	**74.48**	**93.17**	**88.23**
	Top-p Sampling	73.22	73.37	73.26	90.63	84.81

Table A4. Results for LexOverlap (bold marks the best results).

Model	Decode Method	Precision (%)	BERTScore Recall (%)	F_1 (%)	Spearman (%)	Pearson (%)
Base	Greedy	75.13	73.59	74.28	77.68	78.93
	Beam Search	75.62	74.32	74.89	72.74	69.37
	Top-p Sampling	73.48	73.17	73.27	80.38	84.65
Medium	Greedy	75.59	74.55	75.01	77.79	0.8074
	Beam Search	75.90	**74.94**	75.36	76.77	74.62
	Top-p Sampling	73.95	73.88	73.87	81.78	86.68
Large	Greedy	75.83	74.44	75.07	79.72	83.46
	Beam Search	74.37	73.83	74.05	79.84	80.29
	Top-p Sampling	**76.30**	74.66	**75.42**	80.74	86.11

Appendix B.2. Complex Scenarios

Table A5. Results for RatioTokens-NoSentences (bold marks the best results).

Model	Decode Method	Precision (%)	BERTScore Recall (%)	F_1 (%)	MSE NoSentences	MAE NoSentences	Spearman (%) RatioTokens	Pearson (%) RatioTokens
Base	Greedy	73.22	73.44	73.25	1.641	1.019	62.19	42.57
	Beam Search	73.77	74.07	73.86	1.002	0.714	66.71	66.01
	Top-p Sampling	72.56	72.98	72.72	2.678	1.316	64.29	49.99
Medium	Greedy	74.39	74.11	74.19	0.974	0.759	74.57	69.14
	Beam Search	74.47	74.34	74.36	**0.677**	**0.549**	**77.70**	**78.03**
	Top-p Sampling	73.48	73.00	73.20	1.123	0.808	77.02	68.41
Large	Greedy	74.59	74.17	74.33	0.685	0.555	74.86	72.91
	Beam Search	**74.81**	**74.54**	**74.63**	0.919	0.757	77.02	74.00
	Top-p Sampling	73.77	73.18	73.43	1.027	0.811	74.70	72.85

Table A6. Results for NoSentences-RatioTokens (bold marks the best results).

Model	Decode Method	Precision (%)	BERTScore Recall (%)	F_1 (%)	MSE NoSentences	MAE NoSentences	Spearman (%) RatioTokens	Pearson (%) RatioTokens
Base	Greedy	73.88	73.41	73.58	1.188	0.829	74.60	45.64
	Beam Search	**74.23**	73.89	74.01	**0.834**	**0.599**	78.80	75.22
	Top-p Sampling	72.87	72.87	72.83	1.774	1.036	76.88	73.45
Medium	Greedy	72.22	74.83	73.46	3.707	1.414	82.59	71.82
	Beam Search	72.67	75.28	73.91	1.888	1.087	86.45	78.72
	Top-p Sampling	71.76	73.96	72.81	3.408	1.537	84.84	81.96
Large	Greedy	72.84	74.77	73.75	2.368	1.309	87.39	76.25
	Beam Search	73.25	**75.51**	**74.33**	1.670	1.077	89.52	**85.69**
	Top-p Sampling	72.48	73.99	73.19	2.629	1.415	**89.53**	85.21

Table A7. Results for NoWords-NoSentences (bold marks the best results).

Model	Decode Method	Precision (%)	BERTScore Recall (%)	F_1 (%)	MSE NoWords	MAE NoWords	Spearman (%) NoSentences	Pearson (%) NoSentences
Base	Greedy	73.99	72.82	73.35	291.70	10.80	1.323	0.791
	Beam Search	74.28	73.46	73.82	**190.02**	**9.66**	**0.715**	**0.532**
	Top-p Sampling	73.01	72.18	72.55	196.83	10.29	1.270	0.875
Medium	Greedy	73.86	74.36	74.05	414.65	12.50	1.519	1.023
	Beam Search	73.98	**74.71**	74.30	201.53	11.03	0.905	0.714
	Top-p Sampling	72.94	73.21	73.04	232.68	11.69	1.586	1.077
Large	Greedy	74.28	74.26	74.21	294.37	12.43	1.156	0.890
	Beam Search	**74.43**	**74.71**	**74.52**	239.29	11.55	84.85	69.37
	Top-p Sampling	73.66	73.47	73.52	245.23	11.76	1.178	0.925

Table A8. Results for NoSentences-NoWords (bold marks the best results).

Model	Decode Method	Precision (%)	BERTScore Recall (%)	F_1 (%)	MSE NoWords	MAE NoWords	MSE NoSentences	MAE NoSentences
Base	Greedy	72.93	73.51	73.17	238.36	11.28	1.794	1.063
	Beam Search	73.30	74.16	73.70	160.75	9.75	**1.156**	**0.773**
	Top-p Sampling	72.10	72.86	72.44	226.73	11.79	2.284	1.224
Medium	Greedy	73.46	74.72	74.05	290.49	11.53	2.083	1.170
	Beam Search	**73.91**	75.33	**74.58**	**148.71**	**9.42**	1.263	0.837
	Top-p Sampling	72.61	73.74	73.15	229.48	11.64	2.517	1.290
Large	Greedy	73.33	74.97	74.09	383.55	14.77	4.283	1.226
	Beam Search	73.46	**75.34**	74.35	308.95	13.88	1.530	0.985
	Top-p Sampling	72.73	74.11	73.38	338.57	13.82	2.529	1.284

Table A9. Results for LexOverlap-NoWords (bold marks the best results).

Model	Decode Method	Precision (%)	BERTScore Recall (%)	F_1 (%)	MSE NoWords	MAE NoWords	Spearman (%) LexOverlap	Pearson (%) LexOverlap
Base	Greedy	74.06	73.86	73.89	577.91	15.65	0.548	0.578
	Beam Search	73.98	74.28	74.06	470.63	15.35	0.417	0.439
	Top-p Sampling	72.99	73.07	72.97	464.38	15.25	57.83	64.11
Medium	Greedy	74.76	74.42	74.54	257.78	11.61	**68.33**	**72.44**
	Beam Search	**75.05**	**74.84**	**74.90**	**224.48**	1,0.99	64.09	65.60
	Top-p Sampling	73.49	73.52	73.46	245.16	11.70	66.07	72.41
Large	Greedy	74.34	74.18	74.21	321.30	12.29	64.58	68.29
	Beam Search	74.89	74.60	74.69	398.75	12.14	60.77	61.18
	Top-p Sampling	73.71	73.69	73.66	289.60	12.36	65.06	69.99

Table A10. Results for NoWords-LexOverlap (bold marks the best results).

Model	Decode Method	Precision (%)	BERTScore Recall (%)	F_1 (%)	MSE NoWords	MAE NoWords	Spearman (%) LexOverlap	Pearson (%) LexOverlap
Base	Greedy	74.12	73.83	73.90	690.47	15.70	57.18	60.38
	Beam Search	74.06	74.21	74.06	629.78	15.61	42.64	44.49
	Top-p Sampling	72.85	73.02	72.88	436.36	15.30	58.94	66.40
Medium	Greedy	74.77	74.44	74.56	263.85	11.78	67.68	71.77
	Beam Search	**75.08**	**74.92**	**74.95**	**245.22**	**11.43**	64.16	65.61
	Top-p Sampling	73.64	73.76	73.66	272.39	12.23	**68.80**	**74.56**
Large	Greedy	74.25	74.10	74.13	277.87	12.25	63.87	67.61
	Beam Search	74.81	74.59	74.65	408.00	12.55	59.81	60.23
	Top-p Sampling	73.53	73.56	73.50	282.77	12.42	61.51	65.75

Appendix C. Summaries Generated While Varying Values for Control Token(s)

Appendix C.1. Summaries Generated with <NoSentences>

News: "O româncă a vândut costume de baie de lux în valoare de 2 milioane de euro în 2020. Cine a fost puțin creativ anul trecut a făcut bani frumoși. Roxana Ispas este fondatoarea brandului Ronna Swimwear.A lucrat mai mulți ani în domeniul juridic, apoi a avut un business în domeniul consultanței, iar acum s-a reprofilat. Face costume de baie de lux. A profitat de faptul că multe românce au mers anul trecut în vacanțe exotice și a făcut haine de plajă, sutiene și chiloți. Și nu îi merge rău deloc. Are comenzi din toată lumea și cliente fidele mai ales în Germania, Franța sau Dubai. În 2020 Roxana a avut încasări de 2 milioane de euro.Roxana Ispas, fondatoare Ronna Swimwear: Profilul clientei–cea care vrea să arate ca un milion dollar baby. Așa am vândut bine și în Madrid și la Monte Carlo și la Paris și Dubai. Online am vândut prima oară cel mai bine, dar anul trecut a fost jumate-jumate chiar. În 2021 sper să se dea drumul să călătorim, să fie mult mai ok". Și deja stăm foarte ok la capitolul vacanțe exotice, România se află pe locul 5 în topul țărilor care au trimis cei mai mulți turiști în Maldive. Doar în primele 10 zile din ianuarie 2021 aproape 1500 de turiști români au preferat această destinație. I-am depășit pe nemți, francezi, elvețieni și chiar pe americani."

Original: "Pandemia le-a adus celor îndrăzneți vânzări uriașe în 2020. Roxana vinde costume de baie de lux în Franța, Germania sau Dubai. Roxana a avut vânzări de 2 milioane de euro în 2020. România a trimis mai mulți turiști în Maldive decât SUA, Germania sau Elveția."

Generate for <NoSentences>=2: "Roxana Ispas este fondatoarea brandului Ronna Swimwear. Roxana a vândut costume de baie de lux în valoare de 2 milioane de euro în 2020."

Generate for <NoSentences>=3: "Roxana Ispas este fondatoarea brandului Ronna Swimwear. Roxana a vândut costume de baie de lux în valoare de 2 milioane de euro în 2020. Roxana Ispas este fondatoarea brandului Ronna Swimwear."

Generate for <NoSentences>=4: "Roxana Ispas este fondatoarea brandului Ronna Swimwear. Roxana a vândut anul trecut costume de baie de lux în valoare de 2 milioane de euro. Roxana Ispas: "Profilul clientei–cea care vrea să arăte ca un milion dollar baby. Așa am vândut bine și în Madrid și la Monte Carlo și la Paris"."

Generate for <NoSentences>=5: "Roxana Ispas este fondatoarea brandului Ronna Swimwear. Roxana a lucrat mai mulți ani în domeniul juridic, apoi a avut un business în domeniul consultanței. Roxana a vândut costume de baie de lux în valoare de 2 milioane de euro în 2020. Roxana Ispas: "Profilul clientei – cea care vrea să arăte ca un milion dollar baby. Așa am vândut bine și în Madrid și la Monte Carlo și la Paris"."

Appendix C.2. Summaries Generated with the Combination <NoSentences>-<NoWords>

News: "Studenții de la UMF Craiova sunt voluntari în campania de vaccinare. Când se termină campania de vaccinare non-stop. Studenții de la Universitatea de Medicină și Farmacie din Craiova ajută la campania de vaccinare. Spun că doar așa se pot întoarce în sălile de curs.Ioana Deaconu e studentă în anul II. Vrea să devină chirurg, dar până acum n-a reușit deloc să facă practică în spital, din cauza restricțiilor anti pandemice. Acum, s-a înscris voluntar în campania de vaccinare non-stop. Împreună cu prietena ei, Amalia, îi ajută pe cei care vin la vaccinare să completeze formularele de triaj.Printre primii care au venit să se vaccineze au fost mai mulți străini. Ana este studentă în Spania, dar va locui o perioadă în România, unde a venit să lucreze ca voluntar la o organizație de luptă împotriva traficului de persoane. Spune că, atunci când a auzit că se poate vaccina fără programare, nu a stat pe gânduri.Peste 100 de studenți de la Medicină participă, timp de o săptămână, la campania de vaccinare non-stop de la stadionul Ion Oblemenco.Tudor Bălșanu, prodecanul Facultății de Medicină, spune că studenții nu sunt obligați să fie vaccinați pentru a putea participa la cursuri, dar riscurile scad atunci când sunt imunzați cât mai mulți.Campania de vaccinare non-stop din Craiova se va încheia pe 17 mai. Centrul are 10 fluxuri de vaccinare ziua și două noaptea."

Original: "Aproximativ 100 de studenți de la UMF Craiova sunt voluntari în campania de vaccinare. La Craiova, până în data de 17 mai, te poți vaccina non-stop, la stadionul Ion Oblemenco. Și străinii se pot vaccina, fără programare, la centrul deschis la stadionul Ion Oblemenco."

Generate for <NoSentences>=3 and <NoWords>-50%: "Studenții de la UMF Craiova ajută la campania de vaccinare non-stop. Ioana Deaconu este studentă în Spania, dar va locui o perioadă în România."

Generate for <NoSentences>=3 and <NoWords>-25%: "Studenții de la UMF Craiova sunt voluntari în campania de vaccinare non-stop. Ioana Deaconu este studentă în Spania, dar va locui o perioadă în România, unde a venit să lucreze ca voluntar la o organizație de luptă împotriva traficului de persoane."

Generate for <NoSentences>=3 and <NoWords> + 0%: "Studenții de la UMF Craiova sunt voluntari în campania de vaccinare non-stop. Ioana Deaconu, studentă în anul II, spune că doar așa se pot întoarce în sălile de curs. Peste 100 de studenți de la Medicină participă, timp de o săptămână, la campania de vaccinare non-stop de la stadionul Ion Oblemenco."

Generate for <NoSentences>=3 and <NoWords> + 25%: "Studenții de la UMF Craiova sunt voluntari în campania de vaccinare non-stop. Ioana Deaconu, studentă în anul II, spune că doar așa se pot întoarce în sălile de curs. Peste 100 de studenți de la Medicină participă, timp de o săptămână, la campania de vaccinare non-stop de la stadionul Ion Oblemenco. Campania de vaccinare non-stop din Craiova se va încheia pe 17 mai."

Generate for <NoSentences>=3 and <NoWords> + 50%: "Studenții de la Universitatea de Medicină și Farmacie din Craiova ajută la campania de vaccinare non-stop. Ioana Deaconu e studentă în anul II. Vrea să devină chirurg, dar până acum n-a reușit deloc să facă practică în spital, din cauza restricțiilor anti pandemice. Peste 100 de studenți de la Medicină participă, timp de o săptămână, la campania de vaccinare non-stop de la stadionul Ion Oblemenco."

References

1. Vaswani, A.; Shazeer, N.; Parmar, N.; Uszkoreit, J.; Jones, L.; Gomez, A.N.; Kaiser, Ł.; Polosukhin, I. Attention is all you need. In Proceedings of the Advances in Neural Information Processing Systems, Long Beach, CA, USA, 4–9 December 2017; pp. 5998–6008.
2. Radford, A.; Wu, J.; Amodei, D.; Amodei, D.; Clark, J.; Brundage, M.; Sutskever, I. Better language models and their implications. *OpenAI Blog* **2019**, *1*, 2. Available online: https://openai.com/blog/better-language-models (accessed on 14 October 2022).
3. Brown, T.B.; Mann, B.; Ryder, N.; Subbiah, M.; Kaplan, J.; Dhariwal, P.; Neelakantan, A.; Shyam, P.; Sastry, G.; Askell, A.; et al. Language models are few-shot learners. *arXiv* **2020**, arXiv:2005.14165.
4. Black, S.; Gao, L.; Wang, P.; Leahy, C.; Biderman, S. GPT-Neo: Large Scale Autoregressive Language Modeling with Mesh-Tensorflow. *arXiv* **2020**, arXiv:2101.00027.
5. Wang, B.; Komatsuzaki, A. GPT-J-6B: A 6 Billion Parameter Autoregressive Language Model. 2021. Available online: https://github.com/kingoflolz/mesh-transformer-jax (accessed on 14 October 2022).
6. Raffel, C.; Shazeer, N.; Roberts, A.; Lee, K.; Narang, S.; Matena, M.; Zhou, Y.; Li, W.; Liu, P.J. Exploring the limits of transfer learning with a unified text-to-text transformer. *J. Mach. Learn. Res.* **2020**, *21*, 1–67.
7. Masala, M.; Ruseti, S.; Dascalu, M. Robert–a romanian bert model. In Proceedings of the 28th International Conference on Computational Linguistics, Barcelona, Spain, 8–13 December 2020; pp. 6626–6637.
8. Dumitrescu, S.D.; Avram, A.M.; Pyysalo, S. The birth of Romanian BERT. *arXiv* **2020**, arXiv:2009.08712.
9. Avram, A.M.; Catrina, D.; Cercel, D.C.; Dascălu, M.; Rebedea, T.; Păiș, V.; Tufiș, D. Distilling the Knowledge of Romanian BERTs Using Multiple Teachers. *arXiv* **2021**, arXiv:2112.12650.
10. Niculescu, M.A.; Ruseti, S.; Dascalu, M. RoGPT2: Romanian GPT2 for Text Generation. In Proceedings of the 2021 IEEE 33rd International Conference on Tools with Artificial Intelligence (ICTAI), Washington, DC, USA, 1–3 November 2021; pp. 1154–1161.
11. Dumitrescu, S.D.; Rebeja, P.; Lorincz, B.; Gaman, M.; Avram, A.; Ilie, M.; Pruteanu, A.; Stan, A.; Rosia, L.; Iacobescu, C.; et al. Liro: Benchmark and leaderboard for Romanian language tasks. In Proceedings of the Thirty-fifth Conference on Neural Information Processing Systems Datasets and Benchmarks Track (Round 1), Online, 7–10 December 2021.
12. Nallapati, R.; Zhou, B.; Nogueira dos santos, C.; Gulcehre, C.; Xiang, B. Abstractive text summarization using sequence-to-sequence RNNs and beyond. *arXiv* **2016**, arXiv:1602.06023.
13. Scialom, T.; Dray, P.A.; Lamprier, S.; Piwowarski, B.; Staiano, J. MLSUM: The multilingual summarization corpus. *arXiv* **2020**, arXiv:2004.14900.
14. Narayan, S.; Cohen, S.B.; Lapata, M. Don't give me the details, just the summary! topic-aware convolutional neural networks for extreme summarization. *arXiv* **2018**, arXiv:1808.08745.
15. Völske, M.; Potthast, M.; Syed, S.; Stein, B. Tl; dr: Mining Reddit to learn automatic summarization. In Proceedings of the Workshop on New Frontiers in Summarization, Copenhagen, Denmark, 7 September 2017; pp. 59–63.
16. Cioaca, V.; Dascalu, M.; McNamara, D.S. Extractive Summarization using Cohesion Network Analysis and Submodular Set Functions. In Proceedings of the 22nd International Symposium on Symbolic and Numeric Algorithms for Scientific Computing (SYNASC 2020), Timisoara, Romania, 1–4 September 2020.
17. Dutulescu, A.; Ruseti, S.; Dascalu, M. Unsupervised Extractive Summarization with BERT. In Proceedings of the 24th International Symposium on Symbolic and Numeric Algorithms for Scientific Computing (SYNASC 2022), Linz, Austria, 12–15 September 2022.
18. Zhong, M.; Liu, P.; Chen, Y.; Wang, D.; Qiu, X.; Huang, X.J. Extractive Summarization as Text Matching. In Proceedings of the 58th Annual Meeting of the Association for Computational Linguistics, Online, 6–8 July 2020; pp. 6197–6208.
19. Liu, Y.; Lapata, M. Text Summarization with Pretrained Encoders. In Proceedings of the 2019 Conference on Empirical Methods in Natural Language Processing and the 9th International Joint Conference on Natural Language Processing (EMNLP-IJCNLP), Hong Kong, China, 3–7 November 2019; pp. 3730–3740.
20. Lewis, M.; Liu, Y.; Goyal, N.; Ghazvininejad, M.; Mohamed, A.; Levy, O.; Stoyanov, V.; Zettlemoyer, L. BART: Denoising Sequence-to-Sequence Pre-training for Natural Language Generation, Translation, and Comprehension. In Proceedings of the 58th Annual Meeting of the Association for Computational Linguistics, Online, 6–8 July 2020; pp. 7871–7880.
21. Liu, Y.; Liu, P.; Radev, D.; Neubig, G. BRIO: Bringing Order to Abstractive Summarization. In Proceedings of the 60th Annual Meeting of the Association for Computational Linguistics (Volume 1: Long Papers), Dublin, Ireland, 22–27 May 2022; pp. 2890–2903.
22. Qi, W.; Yan, Y.; Gong, Y.; Liu, D.; Duan, N.; Chen, J.; Zhang, R.; Zhou, M. ProphetNet: Predicting Future N-gram for Sequence-to-SequencePre-training. In Proceedings of the Findings of the Association for Computational Linguistics: EMNLP 2020, Online, 16–20 November 2020; pp. 2401–2410.
23. Zhang, J.; Zhao, Y.; Saleh, M.; Liu, P. Pegasus: Pre-training with extracted gap-sentences for abstractive summarization. *Proc. Int. Conf. Mach. Learn.* **2020**, *119*, 11328–11339.
24. Martin, L.; Fan, A.; de la Clergerie, É.; Bordes, A.; Sagot, B. MUSS: Multilingual unsupervised sentence simplification by mining paraphrases. *arXiv* **2020**, arXiv:2005.00352.
25. Clive, J.; Cao, K.; Rei, M. Control prefixes for text generation. *arXiv* **2021**, arXiv:2110.08329.
26. Kieuvongngam, V.; Tan, B.; Niu, Y. Automatic text summarization of COVID-19 medical research articles using BERT and GPT-2. *arXiv* **2020**, arXiv:2006.01997.

27. Papineni, K.; Roukos, S.; Ward, T.; Zhu, W.J. Bleu: A method for automatic evaluation of machine translation. In Proceedings of the 40th annual meeting of the Association for Computational Linguistics, Philadelphia, PE, USA, 7–12 July 2002; pp. 311–318.
28. Lin, C. Recall-oriented understudy for gisting evaluation (rouge). *Retrieved August* **2005**, *20*, 2005.
29. Banerjee, S.; Lavie, A. METEOR: An automatic metric for MT evaluation with improved correlation with human judgments. In Proceedings of the Acl Workshop on Intrinsic and Extrinsic Evaluation Measures for Machine Translation and/or Summarization, Ann Arbor, MI, USA, 25 June 2005; pp. 65–72.
30. Zhang, T.; Kishore, V.; Wu, F.; Weinberger, K.Q.; Artzi, Y. Bertscore: Evaluating text generation with BERT. *arXiv* **2019**, arXiv:1904.09675.
31. Yuan, W.; Neubig, G.; Liu, P. Bartscore: Evaluating generated text as text generation. *Adv. Neural Inf. Process. Syst.* **2021**, *34*, 27263–27277.
32. Sellam, T.; Das, D.; Parikh, A.P. BLEURT: Learning robust metrics for text generation. *arXiv* **2020**, arXiv:2004.04696.
33. Celikyilmaz, A.; Clark, E.; Gao, J. Evaluation of text generation: A survey. *arXiv* **2020**, arXiv:2006.14799.
34. Kingma, D.P.; Ba, J. Adam: A method for stochastic optimization. *arXiv* **2014**, arXiv:1412.6980.
35. Freitag, M.; Al-Onaizan, Y. Beam search strategies for neural machine translation. *arXiv* **2017**, arXiv:1702.01806.
36. Holtzman, A.; Buys, J.; Du, L.; Forbes, M.; Choi, Y. The curious case of neural text degeneration. *arXiv* **2019**, arXiv:1904.09751.
37. Devlin, J.; Chang, M.W.; Lee, K.; Toutanova, K. Bert: Pre-training of deep bidirectional transformers for language understanding. *arXiv* **2018**, arXiv:1810.04805.
38. Taylor, L. Assessing Reading-Into-Writing Skills for an Academic Context: Some Theoretical and Practical Considerations. 2013. Available online: https://github.com/kingoflolz/mesh-transformer-jax (accessed on 14 October 2022).
39. Westby, C.; Culatta, B.; Lawrence, B.; Hall-Kenyon, K. Summarizing expository texts. *Top. Lang. Disord.* **2010**, *30*, 275–287. [CrossRef]
40. Koo, T.K.; Li, M.Y. A guideline of selecting and reporting intraclass correlation coefficients for reliability research. *J. Chiropr. Med.* **2016**, *15*, 155–163. [CrossRef]

Article

Leverage Boosting and Transformer on Text-Image Matching for Cheap Fakes Detection [†]

Tuan-Vinh La [1,2,*], Minh-Son Dao [3,*], Duy-Dong Le [4], Kim-Phung Thai [4], Quoc-Hung Nguyen [4] and Thuy-Kieu Phan-Thi [4]

1. University of Information Technology, Ho Chi Minh City 700000, Vietnam
2. Vietnam National University, Ho Chi Minh City 700000, Vietnam
3. National Institute of Information and Communications Technology, Tokyo 184-8795, Japan
4. University of Economics, Ho Chi Minh City 700000, Vietnam
* Correspondence: vinhlt.16@grad.uit.edu.vn (T.-V.L.); dao@nict.go.jp (M.-S.D.)
† This paper is an extended version of our paper published in Proceedings of the 3rd ACM Workshop on Intelligent Cross-Data Analysis and Retrieval, Newark, NJ, USA, 27–30 June 2022 (https://dl.acm.org/doi/abs/10.1145/3512731.3534210).

Citation: La, T.-V.; Dao, M.-S.; Le, D.-D.; Thai, K.-P.; Nguyen, Q.-H.; Phan-Thi, T.-K. Leverage Boosting and Transformer on Text-Image Matching for Cheap Fakes Detection. *Algorithms* 2022, 15, 423. https://doi.org/10.3390/a15110423

Academic Editors: Xiang Zhang and Xiaoxiao Li

Received: 17 September 2022
Accepted: 11 October 2022
Published: 10 November 2022

Publisher's Note: MDPI stays neutral with regard to jurisdictional claims in published maps and institutional affiliations.

Copyright: © 2022 by the authors. Licensee MDPI, Basel, Switzerland. This article is an open access article distributed under the terms and conditions of the Creative Commons Attribution (CC BY) license (https://creativecommons.org/licenses/by/4.0/).

Abstract: The explosive growth of the social media community has increased many kinds of misinformation and is attracting tremendous attention from the research community. One of the most prevalent ways of misleading news is cheapfakes. Cheapfakes utilize non-AI techniques such as unaltered images with false context news to create false news, which makes it easy and "cheap" to create and leads to an abundant amount in the social media community. Moreover, the development of deep learning also opens and invents many domains relevant to news such as fake news detection, rumour detection, fact-checking, and verification of claimed images. Nevertheless, despite the impact on and harmfulness of cheapfakes for the social community and the real world, there is little research on detecting cheapfakes in the computer science domain. It is challenging to detect misused/false/out-of-context pairs of images and captions, even with human effort, because of the complex correlation between the attached image and the veracity of the caption content. Existing research focuses mostly on training and evaluating on given dataset, which makes the proposal limited in terms of categories, semantics and situations based on the characteristics of the dataset. In this paper, to address these issues, we aimed to leverage textual semantics understanding from the large corpus and integrated with different combinations of text-image matching and image captioning methods via ANN/Transformer boosting schema to classify a triple of (image, $caption_1$, $caption_2$) into OOC (out-of-context) and NOOC (no out-of-context) labels. We customized these combinations according to various exceptional cases that we observed during data analysis. We evaluate our approach using the dataset and evaluation metrics provided by the COSMOS baseline. Compared to other methods, including the baseline, our method achieves the highest Accuracy, Recall, and F1 scores.

Keywords: deep learning; computer vision; natural language processing; image-text matching; cheapfakes; misinformation; transformer encoder

1. Introduction

In recent years, the amount of information and news has dramatically increased due to the convenience and development of social media. However, besides the benefit of its growth, it also significantly increases the quantity and impact of misinformation on individuals and society, which is one of the most dangerous things that threaten democracy, journalism, and freedom of expression. Fake news disturbs the community on a multimedia platform and causes fatal consequences in many aspects of reality and for the ordinary lives of many people. For example, fake news affected the 2016 and 2020 U.S elections.

Besides the spread of the amount of false information, the way of spreading misleading information to the community has also changed and evolved in many types and formations, making it more effective at and convenient for deceiving humans. For example, the enlargement and popularity of microblogging platforms such as Twitter, Facebook and Instagram has also increased the speed of spreading rumours and fake news since social media platforms are becoming more and more usual and necessary things in ordinary life for many people. Furthermore, controlling the content and veracity of posts on microblogging platforms is difficult since there is a large number of users on the standard platforms such as Facebook, Twitter and Instagram.

The blossoming of deep learning has opened new domains and technology, one of which is deepfake [1,2]. Deepfake has received attention from the computer vision community and is a powerful technique that can manipulate images/videos with high quality and that are hard to discriminate from unaltered ones. However, despite the usefulness and effectiveness of deepfake in swaying people's beliefs, one of the most prevalent and frequent ways of spreading disinformation is out-of-context photos, which use unaltered images in news or posts with false context.

Cheapfakes are a type of fake news that utilizes both images and new context. The danger of cheapfakes is that they are easy and cheap to make. While deepfakes use deep learning, which takes high technology and complexity to create, cheapfakes make use of simple and non-AI techniques such as photoshop, manipulating video speed, or unaltered images/videos from different events with false context, which makes it simple to create and more common.

Based on the MIT technology review (https://www.technologyreview.com/2020/12/22/1015442/cheapfakes-more-political-damage-2020-election-than-deepfakes/, accessed on 7 October 2022), in the 2020 U.S presidential election, deepfakes did not disrupt the US election, but cheapfakes did. Fazio [3] also warned of the dangers and explained why out-of-context photos are compelling. First, photos are usually attached to news, and people are already used to them. Secondly, photos make people faster at retrieving an image-related event, making it feel more truthful. Lastly, by using photos, posts on social media platforms will receive more attention and help spread false information.

To meet the emerging requirements of having a good tool for cheapfakes detection and overcome the limitations of existing works, we propose several approaches that utilize multimodal representation learning techniques to overcome limitations. By combining several techniques, including text entailment, image text matching, and boosting algorithms, our methods have improved performance and assessed the performance of several methods in cheapfakes detection.

2. Related Work

This section briefly surveys fake news detection methods, including cheapfakes detection and other subdomain methods.

2.1. Fake News Detection

Fake news has existed for a long time, even before the internet appeared. Recently, fake news has been one of the most prevalent ways to spread disinformation to human society. There are many research and public datasets on this issue. Usually, the research topic and public dataset focus on the textual type of fake news. LIAR [4] and FEVER [5] are two famous public datasets where data are collected from the news website. Each consists of one statement and a given claim, with multiple grades to determine the relation and veracity. Classification news-based linguistic semantic features [6,7] and data mining [8,9] are two traditional methods for determining the veracity of the news based on the semantics of the given text. This approach relies on training and the given data, and cannot utilize external knowledge to verify the news. Based on the development in the data and methods of the knowledge graph, Refs. [10–12] make use of the knowledge graph as external knowledge. This approach is ideal in theory, but in reality the knowledge graph suffers from a lack of relation between entities and still has a long way to develop. Although the task usually focuses on textual fake news, there are many implications for the impact on detecting disinformation in both images and text.

2.2. Rumour Detection

Alongside fake news detection, rumour detection also has a long history. Rumours refer to information not confirmed by official sources that spreads on social media platforms. Unlike fake news, which consists primarily of textual information, rumours include many types of information such as reactions, comments, attached images, user profiles, and platforms. In rumor spreading, followers play an essential role when directly or directly contribute 86 exponential increments of rumors by forwarding news with or without their comments whose content could distort the original one. Hence, understanding the following (i.e., a series of comments tailored from original news), especially in social networks, can help filter out fake news. Because data collected from social networking services can contain more attributes than data collected from news websites, such as user profiles, attached relevant posts, reactions, and comments, the data are rich and have complex attributes. The following research also has various approaches compared to fake news detection. Tree structure, sequence network [13,14] and graph neural network [15,16] are common approaches for combining and extracting correlation features on sequence and time-series data from microblogging.

2.3. Fact Checking

Fact-checking is the task of classifying the veracity of a given claim. It is a time-consuming task to verify a given claim. People need to search and check the source website's reputation and impact. Some given claims even need several professionals and several days or hours. Many techniques have been researched and developed to reduce manual fact-checking to settle this issue. There are two popular dataset types for fact-checking: the first is to verify a given pair of claims and evidence [17]. Prior research has utilized text entailment [18] to compare semantic relations between claims and evidence. Liangming et al. [19] also utilized question-answering by generating questions from the given claim. The second utilizes data on a large scale, and processes based on the technique of the knowledge graph [20].

2.4. Verify Claim about Images

Besides fake news detection, rumour detection, and fact-checking, verifying claims about an image has also received attention in recent years. While the above task mainly verifies textual claims or posts, verifying the claim about the image focuses on the post/claim/caption with the attached image. This is a challenging task since verifying the veracity of the claim itself is hard, but verifying if the attached image is related or satisfactory for concluding the truth or not is even more challenging. Refs. [21–23] extract textual captions and attached images through corresponding pre-trained models then concatenate and infer through a linear layer for classifying. La et al. [24] utilized an image–text matching method to measure correlations between captions and images. Dimitrina et al. [25] also took advantage of Google image search to enrich information (website, categories of news, and images) and then made use of TF.IDF to predict veracity.

2.5. Multi/Cross-Modal Representation Learning

In the field of multimodal reasoning and matching, many techniques have been developed to resolve various challenging tasks such as Visual Question Answering (VQA) [26], Image Captioning [27], Text-to-Image [28], and Image–Text Matching [29]. Still, there is much research on the cross-modal between images and text. To verify claims about image tasks, many methods use the simple technique of extracting features of images through Convolution Neural Network and concatenating them with textual features to classify the truthfulness of news. This technique is simple yet depends on the training dataset, which cannot be generalized in reality and for other aspects and types of news.

3. Dataset

This section will briefly introduce the Out-of-Context Detection Dataset in COSMOS [30], which we used to assess and evaluate our proposal's performance. The dataset was collected from news websites (New York Times, CNN, Reuters, ABC, PBS, NBCLA, AP News, Sky News, Telegraph, Time, DenverPost, Washington Post, CBC News, Guardian, Herald Sun, Independent, CS Gazette, BBC) and fact-checking websites. The dataset consisted of the English language in 19 categories and did not consist of digitally-altered or fake images. The statistic is shown in Figure 1 and Table 1. We recommend readers read [31] for more details.

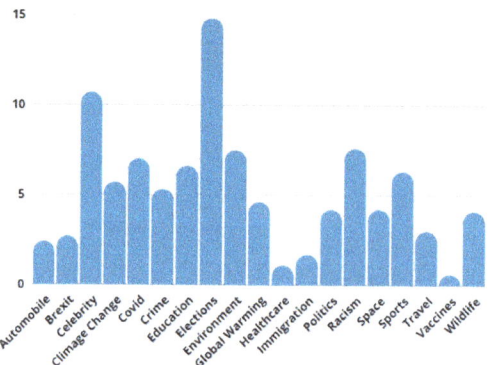

Figure 1. Distribution in categories and content of COSMOS dataset.

Table 1. COSMOS Dataset statistic.

Dataset	Images	Captions	Context Annotation
Training	161,752	360,749	✗
Validation	41,006	90,036	✗
Public Test	1000	2000	✓

Train/Validate Set: In the training set, captioned images were collected from the news website. Each captioned image consisted of one image, one or multiple attached captions, source URL, entity list in a caption, modified caption in which each entity is replaced by corresponding ontology, and location of 10 bounding boxes extracted by a pre-trained Mask-RCNN on MS COCO. Training data did not contain an out-of-context captioned image. Every captioned image was not-out-of-context and did not have a context label. Training data consisted of around 200,000 images with 450,000 matching textual captions. Furthermore, 20% of that was split for the validation set. The example of the captioned image of the training set is illustrated in Figure 2.

Figure 2. Example of the captioned image in the training set. Training data do not contain an out-of-context captioned image. Every captioned image is not-out-of-context and does not have a context label.

Test Set: In the test set, captioned images were collected from both news websites and fact-checking websites. Like the train set, each captioned image of the test set consisted of an image, captions, source URL, entity list, modified caption, and bounding box. However, each captioned image contained two corresponding captions in the test set. These captions always contained one caption not-out-of-context; the remaining caption could be out-of-context or not-out-of-context. Each captioned image also had context annotation to point out if that captioned image consisted of out-of-context captions or not. In summary, the test set contained 1000 captioned images, which included 1000 images and 2000 textual captions. The example of the captioned image of the test set is illustrated in Figure 3.

Figure 3. Example of the captioned image in the testing set. The captioned image contains one image and two corresponding captions. These captions always have one caption not-out-of-context; the remaining caption can be out-of-context or not-out-of-context.

4. Proposed Method

In this section, we will introduce COSMOS baseline [30], our motivation, and explain and describe our methods.

4.1. COSMOS Baseline

In prior research on image and news veracity classification, the method usually aims to utilize multi-modal by extracting features of text/captions and attached images through a pre-trained convolution neural network, LSTM [32] or BERT [33], layer and combine these features by concatenating or sum function with the appropriate objective function. This approach can take advantage of multiple datasets such as imagenet, MSCOCO, STS, and MNLI... for the basis of understanding and representing semantic information of data and fine-tuning other news datasets to improve performance.

Besides the advantage of prior research, it is also limited in terms of the dataset's attributes. Most of the prior work uses fine-tuning on the new dataset, which makes it limited in many respects, such as in categories and characteristics of news, and cannot cover all subjects or situations not included in the dataset.

In COSMOS, the author aims to match the caption with the most correlated object in the image by utilizing self-supervised learning. To do this, the author first uses Mask-RCNN [34] on MSCOCO [35] and selects the top 10 ROIs (Region of Interest) with the highest detection score and additional features of the entire image. For text pre-processing and processing, the author first makes use of NER (Named Entity Recognition) to generalize captions and then infers through USE (Universal Sentence Encoder) [36] to extract caption embedding. Next, the author infers the bounding box and caption embedding through a linear layer for mapping to the same dimension. The paper also uses max margin ranking loss [30] as objective/loss function using the equation:

$$\mathcal{L} = \frac{1}{N} \sum_{i}^{N} \max(0, (S_{IC}^r - S_{IC}^m) + \alpha), \quad (1)$$

where S_{IC}^r, S_{IC}^m is the measure of similarity between a random caption–image pair and a matching caption–image pair, and α is the margin parameter. This measure is calculated by the maximum dot function between 11 ROIs and matching/random caption. The similarity measure function is illustrated as Equation :

$$S_{IC} = \max_{i}^{N} (b_i^T c), \quad (2)$$

where b_i is the features of the proposal bounding box and c is the features of the caption.

At testing time, for each captioned image (caption$_1$,caption$_2$,image), the COSMOS method uses the simple if else rule to determine out-of-context captioned images:

$$\begin{cases} OOC, & \text{If } IoU(B_{IC_1}, B_{IC_2}) > t_i \text{ \& } S_{sim}(C_1, C_2) < t_c \\ NOOC, & \text{otherwise,} \end{cases} \quad (3)$$

where $IoU(B_{IC_1}, B_{IC_2})$ is the intersection-over-union of two bounding boxes having the largest value of similarity measure with the corresponding two captions; $S_{sim}(C_1, C_2)$ is the similarity measure defined in cosine space, and t_i, t_c is the fixed threshold of $IoU(B_{IC_1}, B_{IC_2})$ and $S_{sim}(C_1, C_2)$.

By matching and comparing two captions with the corresponding object, the author can assess if two captions mention a related subject/object or not (determined by $IoU(B_{IC_1}, B_{IC_2})$). If two captions mention a related subject/object and have uncorrelated semantic similarity (determined by $S_{sim}(C_1, C_2)$), then the given captioned image is out-of-context. The other situation is not-out-of-context.

4.2. Motivation

By training the model matching caption with the correlated object in the image and utilizing a pre-trained large-scale textual dataset, the method can utilize the semantic features and understanding of another large-scale dataset, which make it less prone to overfitting on other tasks or datasets of news or fact verification.

Besides the advantages of the COSMOS baseline, the weakness of this method is that by utilizing features of the entire image of Mask-RCNN on MSCOCO, it cannot optimize the express context of the entire image because the Mask-RCNN's task is object detection, not describing. Moreover, the caption usually mentions multiple objects and highly correlates with the context image.

Based on the insufficiency of the COSMOS method when comparing the image with the caption, in this paper, we propose and evaluate a method that utilizes a more optimized method to express content features of the image and better extracts the semantic relation between two captions. Furthermore, instead of defining a rule for determining out-of-context captioned images, we combined results from multiple methods by making use of boosting techniques to improve performance.

4.3. Methodology

This paper proposes two approaches to measuring the correlation between image and caption: image captioning and image–caption matching.

Image Captioning: For the image captioning approach, we aim to utilize [37] to generate the content description of an image. We can use a pre-trained large-scale dataset on the STS [38] task (Semantic Textual Similarity) to measure the correlation between caption and image by converting the image's content to textual form.

Image-Caption Matching: For the image-caption matching approach, we utilized a trained model of image–text matching on the MSCOCO dataset [35] to measure the correlation between caption and image. In this paper, we used the Visual Semantic Reasoning [39] method to measure the similarity between image and caption. See Figure 4 for illustration.

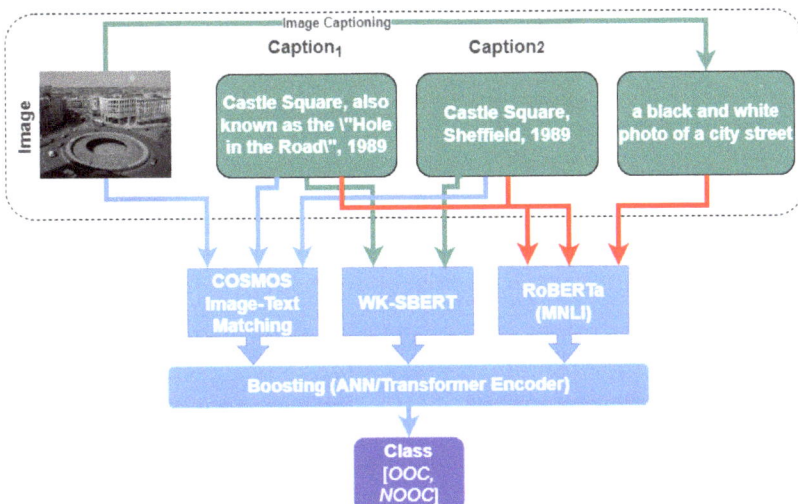

Figure 4. Illustration of boosting with image captioning method. First, the image will be inferred self-critically [37] to obtain a description of the image in textual form. Next, RoBERTa(MNLI) is utilized to extract the correlation between caption$_1$, caption$_2$, and image (NLI(caption$_1$, caption$_2$), NLI(caption$_1$, caption$_{image}$), NLI(caption$_2$, caption$_{image}$)).To overcome the difference between training data and testing data issues and improve performance, we take advantage of the boosting algorithm on the part of the testing data to combine results from our proposal and the COSMOS baseline.

The VSRN (Visual Semantic Reasoning) [39] method utilizes margin ranking loss as the objective function. The margin ranking loss objective is the correlation measurement of the matching caption–image, which is higher than the non-matching caption-image and not trying to make matching caption–image have a matching score higher than the threshold. As shown in Figure 5, the matching caption image's matching score has a different range of values. It can have a lower value compared with different captions and images that do not match each other. However, compared to the same image with another caption that is not matching, the correlation measurement of the matching caption image is higher than that of the non-matching caption image. Based on this attribute of the VSRN method and margin ranking loss, we normalized the matching score using Equation (4) to overcome this issue. See Figure 6 for illustration.

$$\hat{S}(I,C) = S(I,C) - \frac{1}{2N}\sum_{r}^{N}[S(I,C_r) + S(I_r,C)], \qquad (4)$$

where $\hat{S}$ defines the normalize matching score, and r defines the random index that satisfies $C_r \neq C$ and $I_r \neq I$. By subtracting the mean of the matching score from the N sample, the result can express the correlation degree of the given matching image caption compared with other non-matching image captions.

Figure 5. Example of the matching score between image and caption. Green expresses matching caption and red expresses non-matching caption. Based on the attribute of margin ranking loss, compared to one image, matching captions have a higher score than the non-matching caption. Not every matching caption always has a higher matching score than a non-matching caption.

Hence, to estimate the correlation between two captions better, instead of using only cosine similarity measures from other methods trained on the STS task [38], we also used other methods on the NLI task (Natural Language Inference) [40] to express the semantic relation between two captions. We chose SBERT-WK [41] and RoBERTa [42] to extract semantic relations between two captions.

One of the difficulties of the COSMOS dataset is that training/validation data have a different construct from testing data. In training data, each captioned image consists of only a not-out-of-context pair, and captions are always trustworthy news and match the image's context. While in testing data, data consist of out-of-context and not-out-of-context captioned images. The caption can be fake news, descriptions about the image, or match/mismatch with the image and other captions. Based on our experience, fine-tuning training data and evaluating directly on testing data gave poor results. We used boosting algorithms—which can utilize results from textual entailment (NLI, STS) and image–caption matching (image–text matching, image captioning) to increase the method's accuracy—on the part of the testing dataset to combine semantics understanding from multiple methods to improve performance and overcome the shift domain issue. We leveraged ANN and Transformer Encoder as boosting architecture. Six hundred captioned images were extracted as training data and 400 captioned images as evaluation data.

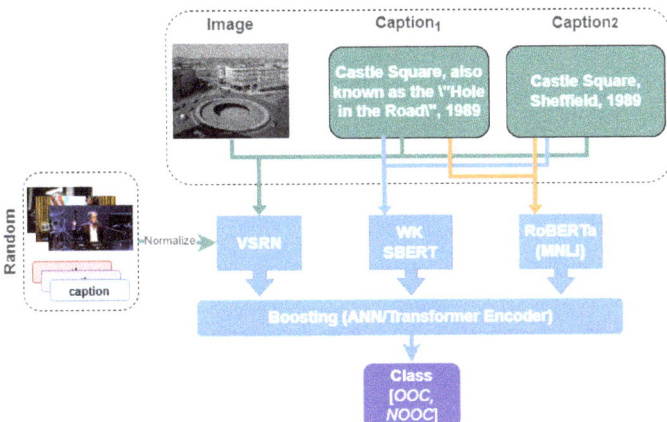

Figure 6. Illustration of boosting with image–caption matching method. First, image, caption$_1$, and caption$_2$ will be inferred through VSRN [39] and normalized by Equation (4) to obtain matching scores ($\hat{S}(I, C_1)$, $\hat{S}(I, C_2)$). In addition to enriching semantic correlation information between caption$_1$ and caption$_2$, we make use of RoBERTa(MNLI) to extract the relation between two captions. Similar to the image captioning method, we take advantage of the boosting algorithm on the part of testing data to combine results from our proposal and the COSMOS baseline.

We also used a boosting algorithms on a combination of mixed results to compare the effects of each component. In summary, we evaluated the performance of boosting algorithms on a set of components:

- Boosting combination of IoU(B_{IC_1}, B_{IC_2}) and $S_{sim}(C_1, C_2)$ using ANN;
- Boosting combination of IoU(B_{IC_1}, B_{IC_2}), $S_{sim}(C_1, C_2)$, $NLI(C_1, C_2, C_{image})$ using ANN [43];
- Boosting combination of IoU(B_{IC_1}, B_{IC_2}) and $S_{sim}(C_1, C_2)$ using Transformers Encoder;
- Boosting with IoU(B_{IC_1}, B_{IC_2}), $S_{sim}(C_1, C_2)$, $NLI(C_1, C_2, C_{image})$ using Transformers Encoder;
- Boosting combination of IoU(B_{IC_1}, B_{IC_2}), $S_{sim}(C_1, C_2)$, $\hat{S}(I, C_1)$, $\hat{S}(I, C_2)$, $NLI(C_1, C_2)$ using ANN;
- Boosting combination of IoU(B_{IC_1}, B_{IC_2}), $S_{sim}(C_1, C_2)$, $\hat{S}(I, C_1)$, $\hat{S}(I, C_2)$, $NLI(C_1, C_2)$ using Transformers Encoder,

where $NLI(C_1, C_2)$ and $NLI(C_1, C_2, C_{image})$ is the result of RoBERTa [42] on the NLI task given three pairs of sentences (C_1, C_2), (C_1, C_{image}), (C_2, C_{image}). The result contains three probabilities of three class that express the semantic relationship between two captions/sentences: entailment, neutral, and contradiction. We illustrated an example of boosting with image captioning and image–text matching in Figures 4 and 6.

5. Experimental & Results

This section introduces the dataset and metric used to evaluate our proposed method. We compare our method to others on the same dataset and metric. The thoughtful discussion also raises the advantages and disadvantages of our method.

5.1. Working Environment

All our experimental methods were implemented on three GPUs NVIDIA Tesla A100 40 GB, Intel Xeon Gold 5220R CPU, and 256 GB RAM. We extracted 600 captioned images of testing data for boosting and 400 captioned images for evaluating performance.

We used the same settings to make it easy to compare each method's performance. We used an Adam optimizer with a 1×10^{-3} learning rate, 4×10^{-5} weight decay, and cross-entropy loss for an updated model. We used simple ANN and a Transformers Encoder to boost the results.

We set the default target dimension for ANN to 64, fed-forward the activation layer (PReLU), and inferred through the linear layer to classify the captioned image.

For the Transformers Encoder, we set input features to 16 dimensions, two multi-head attention, and two layers to extract features. After that, we inferred through the linear layer to classify the captioned image.

5.2. Evaluation Metrics

To evaluate the effectiveness of our proposal, we used five metrics: accuracy, precision, recall, and F1-score with the following equation:

$$Accuracy = \frac{TP + TN}{TP + FP + FN + TN} \quad (5)$$

$$Precision = \frac{TP}{TP + FP} \quad (6)$$

$$Recall = \frac{TP}{TP + FN} \quad (7)$$

$$F1score = \frac{2 \times Recall \times Precision}{Recall \times Precision}, \quad (8)$$

where:

- True Positives (*TP*): Number of samples correctly identified as out-of-context;
- True Negatives (*TN*): Number of samples correctly identified as not-out-of-context;
- False Positives (*FP*): Number of samples incorrectly identified as out-of-context;
- False Negatives (*FN*): Number of samples incorrectly identified as not-out-of-context.

5.3. Datasets and Compared Methods

We evaluated our proposals and other methods on 400 captioned image testing datasets. Table 2 and Figure 7 summarize the result of our proposal compared with other methods.

Table 2. The Comparisons.

Method	Accuracy	Precision	Recall	F1-Score
Spotfake [21]	0.535	0.5252	0.5306	0.5279
EANN [21]	0.63	0.6025	0.6122	0.6185
SBERT-WK [41]	0.77	0.7241	0.8571	0.7850
COSMOS Baseline [30]	0.8325	0.8608	0.8067	0.8329
Tankut et al. [44]	**0.8975**	**0.8738**	0.9371	0.9044
Boosting with IoU(B_{IC_1}, B_{IC_2}) and $S_{sim}(C_1, C_2)$ with ANN	0.8375	0.8324	0.8367	0.8346
Boosting with IoU(B_{IC_1}, B_{IC_2}) and $S_{sim}(C_1, C_2)$ with Transformers Encoder	0.8425	0.8375	0.8418	0.8396
Boosting with IoU(B_{IC_1}, B_{IC_2}), $S_{sim}(C_1, C_2)$, $NLI(C_1, C_2, C_{image})$ with ANN [43]	0.865	0.8317	0.9081	0.8682
Boosting with IoU(B_{IC_1}, B_{IC_2}), $S_{sim}(C_1, C_2)$, $NLI(C_1, C_2, C_{image})$ with Transformers Encoder	0.8825	0.8669	0.8979	0.8822
Boosting with IoU(B_{IC_1}, B_{IC_2}), $S_{sim}(C_1, C_2)$, $\hat{S}(I, C_1), \hat{S}(I, C_2)$, & $NLI(C_1, C_2)$ with ANN	0.8875	0.8681	0.9227	0.8946
Boosting with IoU(B_{IC_1}, B_{IC_2}), $S_{sim}(C_1, C_2)$, $\hat{S}(I, C_1), \hat{S}(I, C_2)$ & $NLI(C_1, C_2)$ with Transformers Encoder	**0.8975**	0.8672	**0.9468**	**0.9053**

Bold factor meaning best evaluation score.

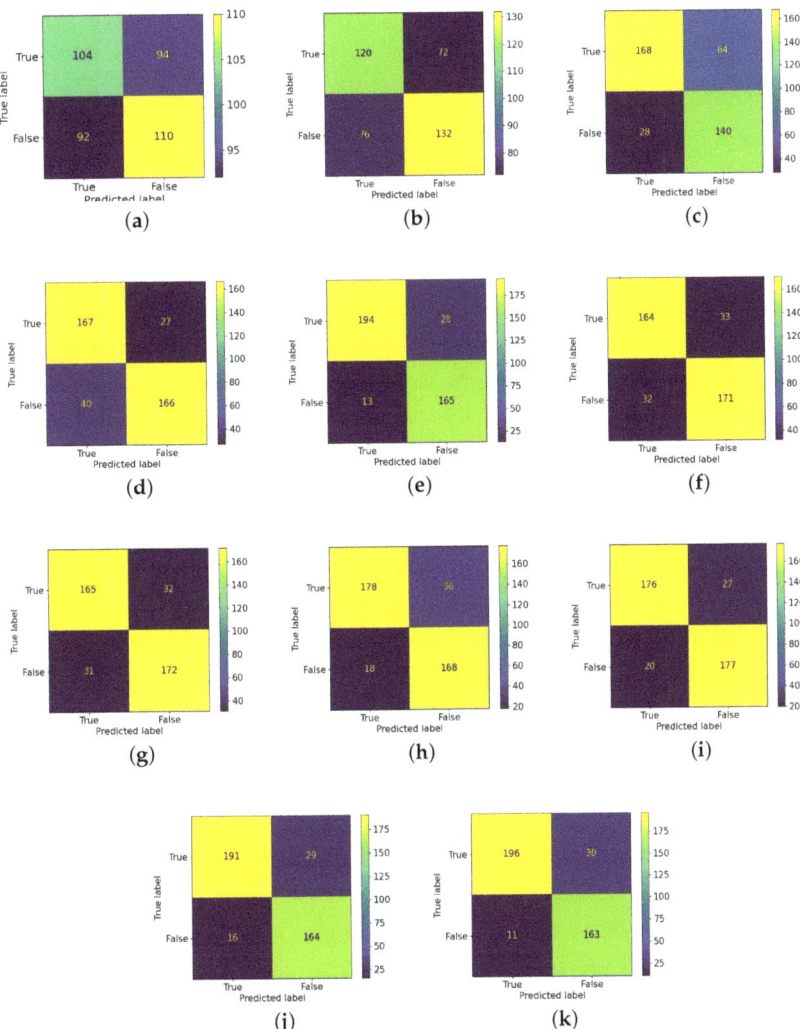

Figure 7. Confusion matrix of (**a**)Spotfake [23]; (**b**)EANN [21]; (**c**) SBERT-WK [41]; (**d**) COSMOS Baseline [30]; (**e**) COSMOS on Steroid [44]; (**f**) Boosting IoU(B_{IC_1}, B_{IC_2}) $S_{sim}(C_1, C_2)$ with ANN; (**g**) Boosting IoU(B_{IC_1}, B_{IC_2}) & $S_{sim}(C_1, C_2)$ with Transformers Encoder; (**h**) Boosting with IoU(B_{IC_1}, B_{IC_2}), $S_{sim}(C_1, C_2)$ & $NLI(C_1, C_2, C_{image})$ with ANN; (**i**) Boosting with IoU(B_{IC_1}, B_{IC_2}), $S_{sim}(C_1, C_2)$ & $NLI(C_1, C_2, C_{image})$ with Transformers Encoder; (**j**) Boosting with IoU(B_{IC_1}, B_{IC_2}), $S_{sim}(C_1, C_2)$ $\hat{S}(I, C_1)$, $\hat{S}(I, C_2)$ & $NLI(C_1, C_2)$ with ANN; (**k**) Boosting with IoU(B_{IC_1}, B_{IC_2}), $S_{sim}(C_1, C_2)$ $\hat{S}(I, C_1)$, $\hat{S}(I, C_2)$ & $NLI(C_1, C_2)$ with Transformers Encoder.

5.4. Discussions

First, we made use of Spotfake [23] as a training baseline approach based on its simplicity—fine-tuning and concatenating visual and textual embedding to classify the veracity of the news. We leveraged Spotfake architecture on the given training and testing data of COSMOS. In particular, when training, we created out-of-context content by selecting captions and images from different sources' captioned images and not-out-of-context content from the same source captioned images. When evaluating, we classified both (caption$_1$, image) and (caption$_2$, image). If both the captions were not-out-of-context, the triplet (caption$_1$, caption$_2$, image) was not-of-context, and the other was out-of-context. The method gave poor results based on the different attributes between training and testing data, and the method could not overcome and generalize the issue.

Next, downstream from another dataset approach, we chose EANN. We used the same method from Spotfake to evaluate the performance—classify both (caption$_1$, image) and (caption$_2$, image). On the MediaEval2015 dataset [45], EANN could achieve a 71.5% accuracy point. However, when downstream of COSMOS, the method produced unqualified results, even though MediaEval2015 consists of a large corpus of textual news and various cases of misused images, similar to the COSMOS dataset. The current training and downstream approach to a given news dataset is limited in categories, domains, and types of news and may not perform well in reality.

Compared to the baseline, our methods improved the 6.5% accuracy score. Furthermore, in relation to Tankut et al.'s [44] research, our method has equal accuracy and has a higher recall and F1-score. Tankut et al. [44] took advantage of handcraft features by matching the most relevant fake news keywords (fake, hoax, fabrication, supposedly, falsification, propaganda, deflection, deception, contradiction, defamation, lie, misleading, deceive, fraud, concocted, bluffing, made up, double meaning, alternative facts, tricks, half-truths, untruth, falsehoods, inaccurate, disinformation, misconception) and alternated captions in testing datasets with fake words ("was true" and "was not true") to compare semantic features. Our methods used various semantic understandings in computer vision and natural language processing on large-scale datasets to assess the correlation between the original image and caption. The impact of each image-text matching method is also present in our paper.

In Figures 8 and 9 we show a few examples of our false negative (FP) and our false positive (FN) predictions. As we can see in the false negative cases, the content of news and the abstract relation with the corresponding image are hard to distinguish, even by humans, and much news needs an expert or time with search tools to determine. For false positive cases, our method failed to distinguish between the image description (generated by humans) and false news.

Figure 8. False negative cases. Out-of-context captioned image is classified as not-out-of-context.

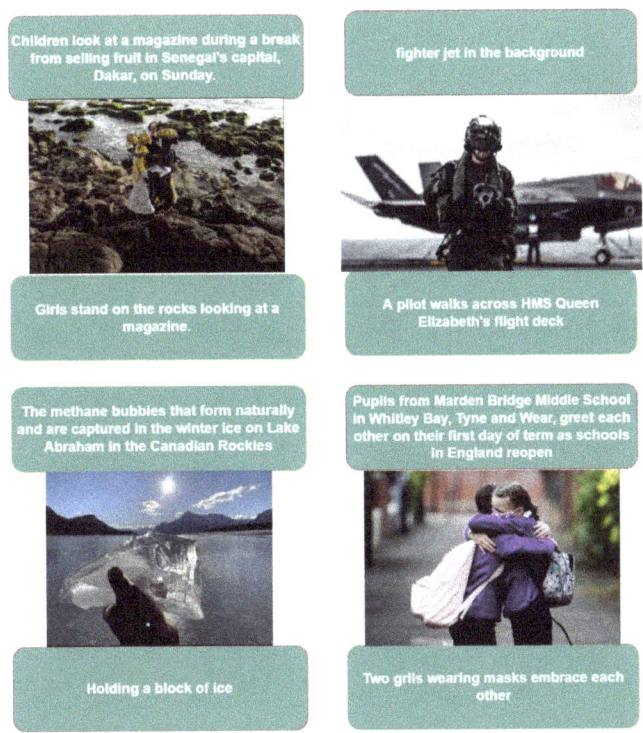

Figure 9. False positive cases. Not-out-of-context captioned image is classified as out-of-context.

6. Conclusions

We have presented and evaluated multiple approaches to the cheapfakes detection problem and conducted experiments on the COSMOS dataset. Our work evaluates the effectiveness of different image–text matching methods, which can leverage semantic features from large-scale datasets instead of fine-tuning and concatenating features from text and images, which makes methods limited in the attribute of a given dataset. Compared to the existing method for cheapfakes detection, we have proposed a method that takes advantage of attributes from the testing dataset instead of directly alternating and defines handcraft patterns based on human effort. Moreover, we have extended experiments of the same theoretical results previously described [43]. Compared to another approach, our methods achieve competitive results, which achieve equal accuracy and higher recall and F1-score. Overall, we believe that our method makes a valuable contribution towards addressing misinformation in news and social media.

In the future, we will consider abstract images that cannot explain or understand with popular image understanding methods without specific knowledge, such as a photo of an art painter, a personal event, a snapshot from a film, or a photo of a book cover. We also consider mapping images and captions into the third coordinator, where additional knowledge can bridge the semantic/knowledge gap between them. Not but not least, extending captions using domain knowledge (e.g., hugging face) to enrich the semantic content of captions and utilize content graphs extracted from images can be another promising research direction.

Author Contributions: Project administration, M.-S.D.; conceptualization, M.-S.D.; writing—review and editing, T.-V.L.; writing—original draft preparation, T.-V.L.; methodology, T.-V.L.; formal analysis, T.-V.L.; validation, T.-V.L.; software, T.-V.L.; funding acquisition, D.-D.L.; data curation, D.-D.L., K.-P.T., Q.-H.N. and T.-K.P.-T.; resource D.-D.L., K.-P.T., Q.-H.N. and T.-K.P.-T. All authors have read and agreed to the published version of the manuscript.

Funding: This research is funded by the University of Economic Ho Chi Minh City (UEH) Vietnam grant number 2022-09-09-1144.

Data Availability Statement: The authors will make the data used in this research available on request.

Acknowledgments: We acknowledge the University of Economic Ho Chi Minh City (UEH) for funding this research.

Conflicts of Interest: The authors declare no conflict of interest. The funders had no role in the design of the study; in the collection, analyses, or interpretation of data; in the writing of the manuscript; or in the decision to publish the results.

References

1. Westerlund, M. The emergence of deepfake technology: A review. *Technol. Innov. Manag. Rev.* **2019**, *9*, 40–53. [CrossRef]
2. Collins, A. *Forged Authenticity: Governing Deepfake Risks*; Technical Report; EPFL International Risk Governance Center (IRGC): Lausanne, Switzerland, 2019.
3. Fazio, L. Out-of-Context Photos Are a Powerful Low-Tech Form of Misinformation. Available online: https://mat.miracosta.edu/mat210_cotnoir/instructor/pdfs-for-class/Out-of-context-photos-are-a-powerful-low-tech-form-of-misinformation.pdf (accessed on 7 October 2022).
4. Thorne, J.; Vlachos, A.; Christodoulopoulos, C.; Mittal, A. Fever: A large-scale dataset for fact extraction and verification. *arXiv* **2018**, arXiv:1803.05355.
5. Wang, W.Y. " liar, liar pants on fire": A new benchmark dataset for fake news detection. *arXiv* **2017**, arXiv:1705.00648.
6. Choudhary, A.; Arora, A. Linguistic feature based learning model for fake news detection and classification. *Expert Syst. Appl.* **2021**, *169*, 114171. [CrossRef]
7. Singh, V.; Dasgupta, R.; Sonagra, D.; Raman, K.; Ghosh, I. Automated fake news detection using linguistic analysis and machine learning. In Proceedings of the International Conference on Social Computing, Behavioral-Cultural Modeling, & Prediction and Behavior Representation in Modeling and Simulation (SBP-BRiMS), Washington, DC, USA, 5–8 July 2017; pp. 1–3.
8. Shu, K.; Sliva, A.; Wang, S.; Tang, J.; Liu, H. Fake news detection on social media: A data mining perspective. *ACM SIGKDD Explor. Newsl.* **2017**, *19*, 22–36. [CrossRef]
9. Bharadwaj, P.; Shao, Z. Fake news detection with semantic features and text mining. *Int. J. Nat. Lang. Comput. (IJNLC)* **2019**, *8*, 17–22. [CrossRef]
10. Pan, J.Z.; Pavlova, S.; Li, C.; Li, N.; Li, Y.; Liu, J. Content based fake news detection using knowledge graphs. In Proceedings of the International Semantic Web Conference, Monterey, CA, USA, 8–12 October 2018; pp. 669–683.
11. Hu, L.; Yang, T.; Zhang, L.; Zhong, W.; Tang, D.; Shi, C.; Duan, N.; Zhou, M. Compare to the knowledge: Graph neural fake news detection with external knowledge. In Proceedings of the 59th Annual Meeting of the Association for Computational Linguistics and the 11th International Joint Conference on Natural Language Processing (Volume 1: Long Papers), Online, 1–6 August 2021; pp. 754–763.
12. Wang, Y.; Qian, S.; Hu, J.; Fang, Q.; Xu, C. Fake news detection via knowledge-driven multimodal graph convolutional networks. In Proceedings of the 2020 International Conference on Multimedia Retrieval, Dublin, Ireland, 26–29 October 2020; pp. 540–547.
13. Ma, J.; Gao, W.; Mitra, P.; Kwon, S.; Jansen, B.J.; Wong, K.F.; Cha, M. Detecting rumors from microblogs with recurrent neural networks. In Proceedings of the Twenty-Fifth International Joint Conference on Artificial Intelligence, New York, NY, USA, 9–15 July 2016.
14. Ma, J.; Gao, W.; Wong, K.F. *Rumor Detection on Twitter with Tree-Structured Recursive Neural Networks*; Association for Computational Linguistics: Stroudsburg, PA, USA, 2018.
15. Wu, Z.; Pi, D.; Chen, J.; Xie, M.; Cao, J. Rumor detection based on propagation graph neural network with attention mechanism. *Expert Syst. Appl.* **2020**, *158*, 113595. [CrossRef]
16. Bian, T.; Xiao, X.; Xu, T.; Zhao, P.; Huang, W.; Rong, Y.; Huang, J. Rumor detection on social media with bi-directional graph convolutional networks. In Proceedings of the AAAI Conference on Artificial Intelligence, New York, NY, USA, 7–12 February 2020; Volume 34, pp. 549–556.
17. Mishra, S.; Suryavardan, S.; Bhaskar, A.; Chopra, P.; Reganti, A.; Patwa, P.; Das, A.; Chakraborty, T.; Sheth, A.; Ekbal, A.; et al. Factify: A multi-modal fact verification dataset. In Proceedings of the First Workshop on Multimodal Fact-Checking and Hate Speech Detection (DE-FACTIFY), Vancouver, BC, Canada, 22 February–1 March 2022.
18. Gao, J.; Hoffmann, H.F.; Oikonomou, S.; Kiskovski, D.; Bandhakavi, A. Logically at the factify 2022: Multimodal fact verification. *arXiv* **2021**, arXiv:2112.09253.
19. Pan, L.; Chen, W.; Xiong, W.; Kan, M.Y.; Wang, W.Y. Zero-shot fact verification by claim generation. *arXiv* **2021**, arXiv:2105.14682.
20. Ciampaglia, G.L.; Shiralkar, P.; Rocha, L.M.; Bollen, J.; Menczer, F.; Flammini, A. Computational fact checking from knowledge networks. *PLoS ONE* **2015**, *10*, e0128193.
21. Wang, Y.; Ma, F.; Jin, Z.; Yuan, Y.; Xun, G.; Jha, K.; Su, L.; Gao, J. Eann: Event adversarial neural networks for multi-modal fake news detection. In Proceedings of the 24th ACM Sigkdd International Conference on Knowledge Discovery & Data Mining, London, UK, 19–23 August 2018; pp. 849–857.

22. Khattar, D.; Goud, J.S.; Gupta, M.; Varma, V. Mvae: Multimodal variational autoencoder for fake news detection. In Proceedings of the World Wide Web Conference, San Francisco, CA, USA, 13 May–17 May 2019; pp. 2915–2921.
23. Singhal, S.; Shah, R.R.; Chakraborty, T.; Kumaraguru, P.; Satoh, S. Spotfake: A multi-modal framework for fake news detection. In Proceedings of the 2019 IEEE Fifth International Conference on Multimedia Big Data (BigMM), Singapore, 11–13 September 2019; pp. 39–47.
24. La, T.V.; Dao, M.S.; Tran, Q.T.; Tran, T.P.; Tran, A.D.; Nguyen, D.T.D. A Combination of Visual-Semantic Reasoning and Text Entailment-based Boosting Algorithm for Cheapfake Detection. In Proceedings of the ACM MM 2022, Lisbon, Portugal, 10–14 October 2022.
25. Zlatkova, D.; Nakov, P.; Koychev, I. Fact-checking meets fauxtography: Verifying claims about images. *arXiv* **2019**, arXiv:1908.11722.
26. Antol, S.; Agrawal, A.; Lu, J.; Mitchell, M.; Batra, D.; Zitnick, C.L.; Parikh, D. Vqa: Visual question answering. In Proceedings of the IEEE International Conference on Computer Vision, Santiago, Chile, 7–13 December 2015; pp. 2425–2433.
27. Li, X.; Yin, X.; Li, C.; Zhang, P.; Hu, X.; Zhang, L.; Wang, L.; Hu, H.; Dong, L.; Wei, F.; et al. Oscar: Object-semantics aligned pre-training for vision-language tasks. In Proceedings of the European Conference on Computer Vision, Glasgow, UK, 23–28 August 2020; pp. 121–137.
28. Ramesh, A.; Pavlov, M.; Goh, G.; Gray, S.; Voss, C.; Radford, A.; Chen, M.; Sutskever, I. Zero-shot text-to-image generation. In Proceedings of the International Conference on Machine Learning, PMLR, Virtual Event, 18–24 July 2021; pp. 8821–8831.
29. Lee, K.H.; Chen, X.; Hua, G.; Hu, H.; He, X. Stacked cross attention for image-text matching. In Proceedings of the European Conference on Computer Vision (ECCV), Munich, Germany, 8–14 September 2018; pp. 201–216.
30. Aneja, S.; Bregler, C.; Nießner, M. Cosmos: Catching out-of-context misinformation with self-supervised learning. *arXiv* **2021**, arXiv:2101.06278.
31. Aneja, S.; Midoglu, C.; Dang-Nguyen, D.T.; Khan, S.A.; Riegler, M.; Halvorsen, P.; Bregler, C.; Adsumilli, B. ACM Multimedia Grand Challenge on Detecting Cheapfakes. *arXiv* **2022**, arXiv:2207.14534.
32. Hochreiter, S.; Schmidhuber, J. Long short-term memory. *Neural Comput.* **1997**, *9*, 1735–1780. [CrossRef] [PubMed]
33. Devlin, J.; Chang, M.W.; Lee, K.; Toutanova, K. Bert: Pre-training of deep bidirectional transformers for language understanding. *arXiv* **2018**, arXiv:1810.04805.
34. He, K.; Gkioxari, G.; Dollár, P.; Girshick, R. Mask r-cnn. In Proceedings of the IEEE International Conference on Computer Vision, Venice, Italy, 22–29 October 2017; pp. 2961–2969.
35. Lin, T.Y.; Maire, M.; Belongie, S.; Hays, J.; Perona, P.; Ramanan, D.; Dollár, P.; Zitnick, C.L. Microsoft coco: Common objects in context. In Proceedings of the European Conference on Computer Vision, Zurich, Switzerland, 6–12 September 2014; pp. 740–755.
36. Cer, D.; Yang, Y.; Kong, S.y.; Hua, N.; Limtiaco, N.; John, R.S.; Constant, N.; Guajardo-Cespedes, M.; Yuan, S.; Tar, C.; et al. Universal sentence encoder. *arXiv* **2018**, arXiv:1803.11175.
37. Rennie, S.J.; Marcheret, E.; Mroueh, Y.; Ross, J.; Goel, V. Self-critical sequence training for image captioning. In Proceedings of the IEEE Conference on Computer Vision and Pattern Recognition, Honolulu, HI, USA, 21–26 July 2017; pp. 7008–7024.
38. Cer, D.; Diab, M.; Agirre, E.; Lopez-Gazpio, I.; Specia, L. Semeval-2017 task 1: Semantic textual similarity-multilingual and cross-lingual focused evaluation. *arXiv* **2017**, arXiv:1708.00055.
39. Li, K.; Zhang, Y.; Li, K.; Li, Y.; Fu, Y. Visual semantic reasoning for image-text matching. In Proceedings of the IEEE/CVF International Conference on Computer Vision, Seoul, Korea, 27 October–2 November 2019; pp. 4654–4662.
40. Williams, A.; Nangia, N.; Bowman, S.R. A broad-coverage challenge corpus for sentence understanding through inference. *arXiv* **2017**, arXiv:1704.05426.
41. Wang, B.; Kuo, C.C.J. Sbert-wk: A sentence embedding method by dissecting bert-based word models. *IEEE/ACM Trans. Audio Speech Lang. Process.* **2020**, *28*, 2146–2157. [CrossRef]
42. Liu, Y.; Ott, M.; Goyal, N.; Du, J.; Joshi, M.; Chen, D.; Levy, O.; Lewis, M.; Zettlemoyer, L.; Stoyanov, V. Roberta: A robustly optimized bert pretraining approach. *arXiv* **2019**, arXiv:1907.11692.
43. La, T.V.; Tran, Q.T.; Tran, T.P.; Tran, A.D.; Dang-Nguyen, D.T.; Dao, M.S. Multimodal Cheapfakes Detection by Utilizing Image Captioning for Global Context. In Proceedings of the 3rd ACM Workshop on Intelligent Cross-Data Analysis and Retrieval, Newark, NJ, USA, 27–30 June 2022; pp. 9–16.
44. Akgul, T.; Civelek, T.E.; Ugur, D.; Begen, A.C. COSMOS on Steroids: A Cheap Detector for Cheapfakes. In Proceedings of the 12th ACM Multimedia Systems Conference, Istanbul, Turkey, 28 September–1 October 2021; pp. 327–331.
45. Boididou, C.; Andreadou, K.; Papadopoulos, S.; Dang-Nguyen, D.T.; Boato, G.; Riegler, M.; Kompatsiaris, Y. Verifying multimedia use at mediaeval 2015. *MediaEval* **2015**, *3*, 7.

Article

Image-to-Image Translation-Based Data Augmentation for Improving Crop/Weed Classification Models for Precision Agriculture Applications

L. G. Divyanth [1,2], D. S. Guru [3], Peeyush Soni [1], Rajendra Machavaram [1], Mohammad Nadimi [2] and Jitendra Paliwal [2,*]

[1] Department of Agricultural and Food Engineering, Indian Institute of Technology Kharagpur, Kharagpur 721302, India
[2] Department of Biosystems Engineering, University of Manitoba, Winnipeg, MB R3T 5V6, Canada
[3] Department of Studies in Computer Science, University of Mysore, Mysore 570006, India
* Correspondence: j.paliwal@umanitoba.ca

Abstract: Applications of deep-learning models in machine visions for crop/weed identification have remarkably upgraded the authenticity of precise weed management. However, compelling data are required to obtain the desired result from this highly data-driven operation. This study aims to curtail the effort needed to prepare very large image datasets by creating artificial images of maize (*Zea mays*) and four common weeds (i.e., Charlock, Fat Hen, Shepherd's Purse, and small-flowered Cranesbill) through conditional Generative Adversarial Networks (cGANs). The fidelity of these synthetic images was tested through t-distributed stochastic neighbor embedding (t-SNE) visualization plots of real and artificial images of each class. The reliability of this method as a data augmentation technique was validated through classification results based on the transfer learning of a pre-defined convolutional neural network (CNN) architecture—the *AlexNet*; the feature extraction method came from the deepest pooling layer of the same network. Machine learning models based on a support vector machine (SVM) and linear discriminant analysis (LDA) were trained using these feature vectors. The $F1$ scores of the transfer learning model increased from 0.97 to 0.99, when additionally supported by an artificial dataset. Similarly, in the case of the feature extraction technique, the classification $F1$-scores increased from 0.93 to 0.96 for SVM and from 0.94 to 0.96 for the LDA model. The results show that image augmentation using generative adversarial networks (GANs) can improve the performance of crop/weed classification models with the added advantage of reduced time and manpower. Furthermore, it has demonstrated that generative networks could be a great tool for deep-learning applications in agriculture.

Keywords: generative adversarial networks; deep-learning; crop/weed classification; transfer learning; feature extraction

1. Introduction

The potential of deep-learning algorithms has been demonstrated in almost all stages of agricultural activities, paving the way for efficient handling and non-destructive evaluation. One of the agricultural domains that could benefit from these algorithms is weed management. It is well-known that efficient weed control is one of the inevitable contributing factors towards sustainable agriculture as it can positively contribute to plant growth, yield, and quality while minimizing the need for weedicides. However, manual and traditional weed removal methods have been labor-intensive and inefficient. In this regard, scholars have developed numerous deep-learning models based on convolutional neural networks (CNNs) to classify various crops and weed species [8–11]. Moreover, machinery based on machine vision has been developed to provide profound solutions for weed management [12–15].

Although deep-learning networks have enhanced the authenticity of automated crop/weed classification algorithms, the technique suffers from mining large amounts of data that are collected from various geographic conditions. Furthermore, a majority of in-field weed identification tasks require pixel-level annotations [16–18]. Overall, acquiring huge amounts of data and the preparation of ground truth is a tedious task, especially for precision agriculture applications [19].

Though many open-source agriculture datasets have been available in recent years, the quality and amount of data do not meet the requirements of researchers [19,20]. In addition, models trained with such data fail to generalize and are not robust enough to be used in diverse practical environments [21]. One way to overcome these difficulties is by adopting image geometric- and intensity-based data augmentation [22]. In addition, when CNNs are employed for machine vision tasks, transfer learning is preferred [23,24], where a pre-trained deep-learning model is fine-tuned with an available dataset for a particular task [25]. This approach has seen a lot of utilization for in-field weed identification [26–28]. For instance, Espejo-Garcia et al. developed a solution based on feature extraction from deep layers of various transfer-learned CNN models for automated crop and weed identification [26]. Chen et al. performed a similar study based on transfer learning for identifying weeds in cotton production systems [27]. Both of the above studies recorded classification accuracies greater than 95%. However, such traditional image augmentation techniques and transfer learning provide highly correlated images and only little additional information to the deep-learning model. This not only reduces the ability of the model to generalize but leads to over-fitting problems.

In recent years, another advancement in deep learning, in the form of generative adversarial networks (GANs), has proven to be very efficient for data augmentation and image enhancement [29]. GANs can generate artificial-realistic images using existing image data. The combination of these artificial and original images could enhance the development of subsequent models. GANs have been effectively applied to various tasks, such as human identification [30], organ segmentation [31], and emotion classification [32]. These models have also been used for machine-vision applications in agriculture, such as generating images of specific plants [33,34], plant disease recognition [35], grain quality analysis [4], and for synthesizing images of plant seedlings [36]. A few studies have also utilized GANs to assist in deep-learning-based operations in precision weed management (Table 1). With numerous architectures of GANs available, a performance comparison study was performed on the different combinations of a GAN model and a CNN-based classification model for designing a crop/weed classification pipeline tested on images of tomato crops and black nightshade [37]. The authors obtained the highest accuracy of 99.07% and firmly concluded that GANs improve the classification performance of CNN networks. A few other studies used GANs to generate multi-spectral images of crops and weeds [38]. In all the discussed works, GANs were used to synthesize the entire crop/weed/agricultural field image without any attention to the location and shape of the desired object in the image. It was observed that the generalizability of such networks over the texture and morphology-based features of the target classes was sub-optimal.

Henceforth as an improvement, in this study, we performed image generation using a conditional GAN (cGAN) based on the image-to-image translation concept [40]. The primary objective here was to synthesize the images by preserving (conditioning) the original footprint of the objects in the real image, such as the shape of the plants. The real images of a particular class, along with their pixel-wise labels, were combinedly and fed into the GAN model to train it and, eventually, to obtain the artificial images of the respective classes. The image synthesis network exploited here is similar to the *pix2pix* conditional adversarial network, a very commonly used model for image translation tasks [40]. Secondly, the validity of a classification task using the newly derived dataset was assessed for the two commonly adopted techniques, i.e., transfer learning [26,28] and the feature extraction method [41–44]. For the above tasks, a pre-defined, state-of-the-art CNN architecture, the *AlexNet* [45], was employed. In the feature extraction technique, features from deep layers of the *AlexNet* were extracted to develop machine learning models using the support vector machines (SVM) and linear discriminant analysis (LDA) classifiers. Hence, the major objectives of this work are (i) the implementation of cGAN as a data augmentation approach to synthesize realistic plant images and analyze cGAN performance and (ii) to study the combination of cGANs and the classification algorithms for improving crop/weed species identification.

Table 1. Summary of previous studies on the application of GANs for crop/weeds identification tasks.

Purpose	Crop Production System	Image Synthesis Technique	Results/Conclusion	Reference
Synthetic RGB images of individual tomato and black night-shade plants were generated for improving classification performance.	Tomato	Conventional GANs	F1-score of 0.86 was obtained when GAN-based augmentation was performed, compared to 0.84 without the artificial dataset.	[37]
Generation of multi-spectral images of agricultural fields for semantic segmentation of crop/weeds.	Sugarbeet	Conditional GAN (cGAN)	Intersection over union (mIoU) value was improved to 0.98 from 0.94 for background class and to 0.89 from 0.76 for vegetation.	[38]
Artificial data were generated using UAV-acquired images for supporting crop/weed species identification at an early stage.	Strawberry and peas	Semi-supervised GAN (SGAN)	Classification accuracy of 90% was achieved using only 20% of labelled dataset.	[39]

2. Materials and Methods

2.1. Dataset and Pre-Processing

The dataset consisted of five classes, including maize (*Zea mays*) and four weed species commonly identified in maize production systems, namely, Charlock (*Sinapis arvensis*), Fat Hen (*Chenopodium album*), Shepherd's purse (*Capsella bursa-pastoris*), and Small-flowered Cranesbill (*Geranium pusillum*). The dataset was derived from Kaggle's image data of the crop and weed seedlings at different growth stages, a public image dataset offered by Giselsson et al. [46]. Each class contained 200 RGB images at various growth stages (5–8 weeks) and illumination effects. These images were manually and binary segmented at pixel level using the Image Segmenter app of *MATLAB R2020a* and the Image Processing toolbox to distinguish the vegetation from the background. These semantic-segmented images were arranged in class-wise folders, as such so that the sequence of images matched the corresponding real image folder. This allowed for the easier pairing of real and segmented images, which was necessary during the cGAN training process. Figure 1 shows some sample images from the dataset along with their binary-segmented counterparts. The images were resized to a size of 256 × 256 pixels.

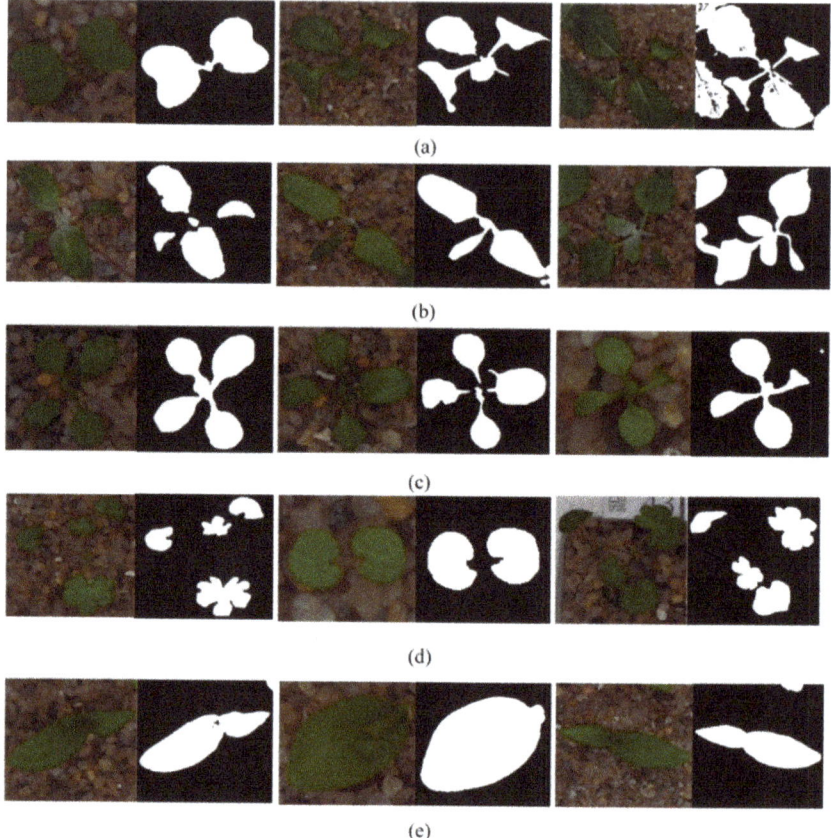

Figure 1. Sample images of (**a**) Charlock, (**b**) Fat Hen, (**c**) Shepherd's purse, (**d**) Small-flowered Cranesbill, and (**e**) Maize.

2.2. Image Synthesis through GAN

The size of the dataset used here is small when compared to the ones generally employed in learning-based machine-vision tasks. Hence, augmentation through the adversarial networks was performed to increase the size of the dataset. Typically, a GAN architecture comprises a generator network that generates artificial images and a discriminator that aims to differentiate these artificial images from the real images [29]. Both components are simultaneously trained in an adversarial manner, in which the generator aims to entrap the discriminator using its artificial images. The first proposed GAN models did not have control over any auxiliary information on the data that were being synthesized. Later, researchers introduced a conditional variable into the network's objective functions that contained the network over a particular attribute to synthesize images with the desired features [47]. For instance, GANs were conditioned on text descriptions for text-to-image synthesis and on class labels to generate MNIST dataset digits [48]. Image conditional GAN was first studied by Isola et al. [40] for image-to-image translations.

In cGANs, the generator and discriminator networks are conditioned on the class label y, i.e., mapping to y is learned from the input image (or source image) x and the random vector z. The objective function can be given as:

$$\mathcal{L}_{cGAN}(G, D) = E_{x,y}[\log D(x,y)] + E_{x,z}[\log(1 - D(x, G(x,z)))] \tag{1}$$

The cGAN architecture employed here is very similar to the model proposed in its original work for image-to-image translation, called the *pix2pix* GAN [40]. The model is trained with paired images, i.e., the real and binary analog, in order to learn to map the features of these images. The attributes of the output image are conditioned by the source images (here, the binary images act as the source images). Suppose $T \in \epsilon^{w \times h}$ is the binary mask of an image with width w and height h pixels, the network's goal is to make the model learn a mapping function that converts I into a photo-realistic image. Figure 2 shows the image generation workflow. The generator follows the U-Net framework [49], and the discriminator classifier is based on the PatchGAN [50]. The U-Net is an encoder-decoder network where the input is first down-sampled to a bottleneck layer and then up-sampled from this point. Moreover, skip connections (which concatenate the channels for the two layers) are added between the i-th and $n − i$-th layers (n is the total number of layers). The PatchGAN discriminator classifies every *patch* in the image as real or artificial and the final output is determined by the average response. Overall, the generator model used here is a set of convolutional down-sampling layers and transpose convolutional up-sampling layers that are blended through a bottle-neck layer. The discriminator consists of six convolutional layers, such as an 8 × 8 pixel patch, which is obtained at the end. From this patch, the binary classification result (real image or generated image) is acquired.

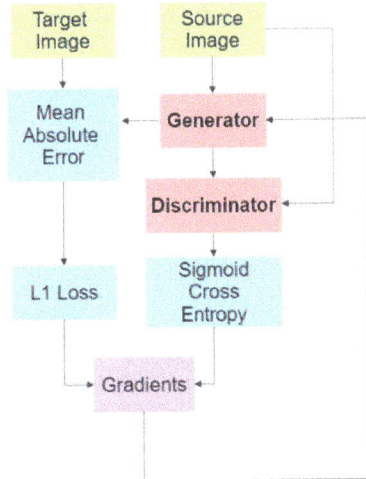

Figure 2. Training procedure for image generator through L1 and GAN loss functions.

To monitor the fidelity of the generated images after each iteration, the t-distributed stochastic neighbor embedding (t-SNE) visualization is used. The t-SNE algorithm presents the similarities between the samples by iteratively comparing the probability distribution of the different data points in high- and low-dimensional spaces [51]. By applying t-SNE to the real and generated images, the similarities and variances of the images can be further analyzed. Once the training is complete, new images are generated and amassed to analyze through the classifiers (see Sections 2.3 and 2.4). An Acer Nitro 5 Intel Core i5 9th Generation Laptop (32GB/1 TB HDD/Windows 10 Home/GTX 1650 Graphics) was used to run the *MATLAB* application.

2.3. Classification through Transfer Learning

In this study, we focus on a popular CNN architecture—AlexNet [45], which was designed in the context of the "Large Scale Visual Recognition Challenge" (ILSVRC) [52] for the ImageNet dataset [53]. AlexNet effectively comprises five convolution layers, three fully connected (FC) layers, and a Softmax layer. The first, second, and fifth convolution layers are followed by a max-pooling layer with a pool size of 3 × 3 and strides of 2 × 2.

The convolution layers were furnished with half-padding and ReLU activation function layers. The details on the number of filters and the layer-wise operations are presented in Figure 3. To implement transfer learning, the last three layers of the network—an FC layer configured for 1000 classes; a Softmax layer; and the final classification layer were all replaced with an FC layer for 5 classes, followed by a Softmax layer and a classification layer, with their weights initialized through the Glorot normal method.

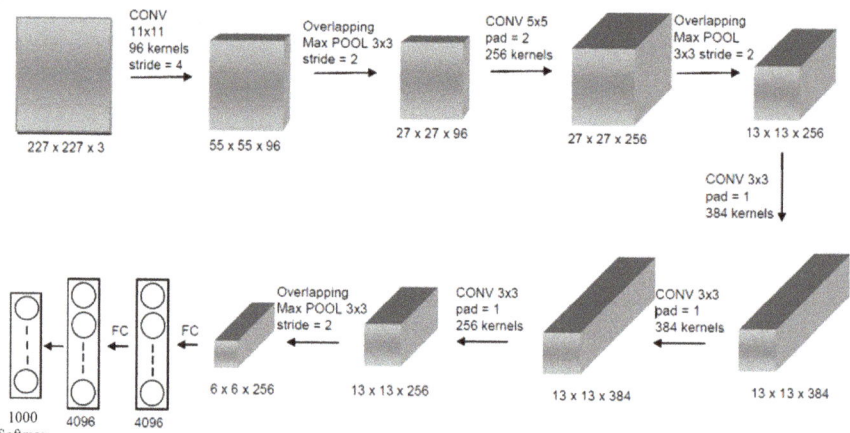

Figure 3. Illustration of the original *AlexNet* [45] architecture.

In order to fit *AlexNet*'s input size, the images were resized to a dimension of 227 × 227 pixels. The evaluation was performed in two steps: firstly, the model was trained only with the real images, and then the real and artificial images were simultaneously used for training. Additional augmentations, such as image rotations, translations, and reflections along the x- and y- axes were specified for both cases. Regarding the training options, the gradient descent with momentum (*sgdm*) was chosen as the optimizer with an initial learning rate set to 0.001, a momentum of 0.9, and a weight decay factor of 0.0001. The training was limited to a maximum of 1000 epochs, with a mini-batch size of 32. The results of this transfer-learning model on the training and test sets are presented in Section 3.2.

2.4. Classification through Feature Extraction Technique

The convolutional layers in CNN summarize the features associated with each class through a set of filters, carrying the aspects of the input image to the subsequent layers [54]. In the feature extraction method, the features were derived from the deep layers of a CNN, and a machine learning-based model was developed based on these features [55]. An activation map was derived from the first convolution layer of the CNN and is represented in Figure 4. In this study, the features from the global pooling layer of *AlexNet* (*pool5* layer) were extracted, which provided a vector of 9216 features. Due to a very high-dimensional feature map, the principal component analysis was applied to select only the components that explained 97% of the total variance.

Figure 4. Visualization of activations of the first Conv-layer of *Alexnet*.

The entire workflow is depicted in Figure 5. After deriving these features, two classifiers, namely, SVM and LDA, were adopted for classification purposes. These classifiers were chosen due to their exceptional performances in many agricultural datasets over other machine learning algorithms [42,56]. The performance of the developed models was analyzed using precision, recall, and F1-score metrics, given by:

$$Precision = \frac{True\ positives}{Number\ of\ predicted\ samples} \quad (2)$$

$$Recall = \frac{True\ positives}{Actual\ number\ of\ samples} \quad (3)$$

$$F1 - score = 2\frac{Precision \cdot Recall}{Precision + Recall} \quad (4)$$

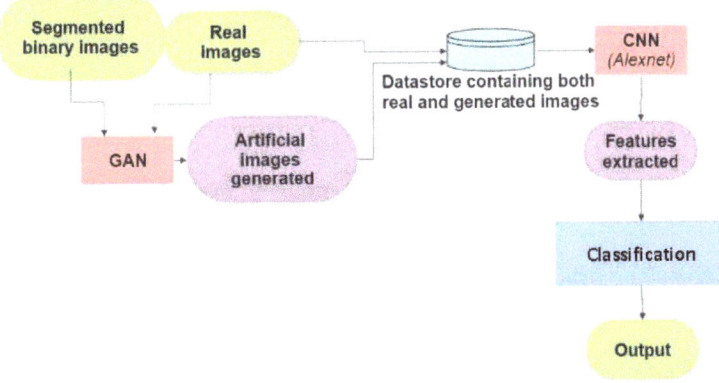

Figure 5. Workflow for the artificial image synthesis through adversarial network and crop/weeds classification.

2.4.1. Support Vector Classification

Support vector machines (SVMs) have been widely used as a classifier for weed identification. Wu and Wen [57] performed crop/weed classification on a dataset of maize crops and four weed species images using SVM on image color and texture features. Later, they also included shape features in the SVM model and tested their performance using three different kernel functions (polynomial, sigmoid, and RBF) [58]. According to Wong et al. [59], multi-class classification using SVMs generates the best probabilistic output. They trained an SVM model to differentiate the monocotyledon weeds, *Ageratum conyzoides*, and *Amaranthus palmeri* weeds from other weeds for selective spraying. Many other studies have also utilized the different versions of SVMs and discussed their advantages [60,61].

In SVM, the classification is performed by identifying a hyper-plane that differentiates the classes very well. The algorithm aims to maximize the minimum distance between a point and the discriminating hyper-plane [57]. In this study, the radial basis function (RBF) was used to transform the feature space. This function computes the element (i, j) of the Gram matrix G as:

$$G(x_i, x_j) = \exp\left(-||x_i - x_j||^2\right) \quad (5)$$

where, x_i and x_j are the i-th and j-th observations of the training set.

2.4.2. Linear Discriminant Analysis

Discriminant analysis is based on the principle that different classes generate data based on various Gaussian distributions (multi-dimensional and normal distributions). Being a supervised technique, it collects information from all the variables and plots a new margin so that the classification outcome is at its best. In LDA, the attributes are assumed to be a Gaussian mixture distribution with different means but with a common covariance matrix. To recall, this matrix contains the variance of the data along the diagonal and covariance along with the corresponding off-diagonal elements. The center of the distribution is determined by the mean, and the shape is determined by the covariance matrix. Once the distributions are fitted, the boundaries are estimated by determining the points around them where the probabilities are similar.

Assuming there are C classes (all having a multivariate normal distribution), let Σ and μ_c ($c = 1, 2, \ldots, C$) be the covariance matrix and the mean vector of the distribution of the samples in the c classes. Say, $x_{i,c}$ is the i-th sample in class c, the objective of LDA is to assign this observation to class $\hat{c}$, minimizing the function h given by

$$h = (x_{c,i} - \mu_{\hat{c}})^T \Sigma^{-1} (x_{c,i} - \mu_{\hat{c}}) \quad (6)$$

The mathematics and computations behind the discriminant analysis and its regularized version can be further explored in [62] and [63]. These classifiers have also been extensively used for classification tasks in precision agriculture applications [56,64,65].

3. Results and Discussions

3.1. Evaluation of Generated Images

Before evaluating the results of the classification task, we assessed the fidelity of the generated images. The real and generated images for each class are shown in Figure 6. One can see that after around 60 iterations, the model started producing plausible artificial images. To give a fair insight into the image impression, a t-SNE method of visualization was adopted for 100 real and generated images for each class (see Figure 7). The dimension-reduction technique was used to plot the data points in a two-dimensional plot. Some outliers were identified in the t-SNE plot for Charlock. However, the synthetic Charlock images closely exhibit the shape and color features of the original images. For other classes, a similar distribution of the points corresponding to the actual and artificial images denoted that pertinent features are adequately learned and produced through the GAN. The artificial images preserved the key features of the real images and widened the coverage of the training dataset.

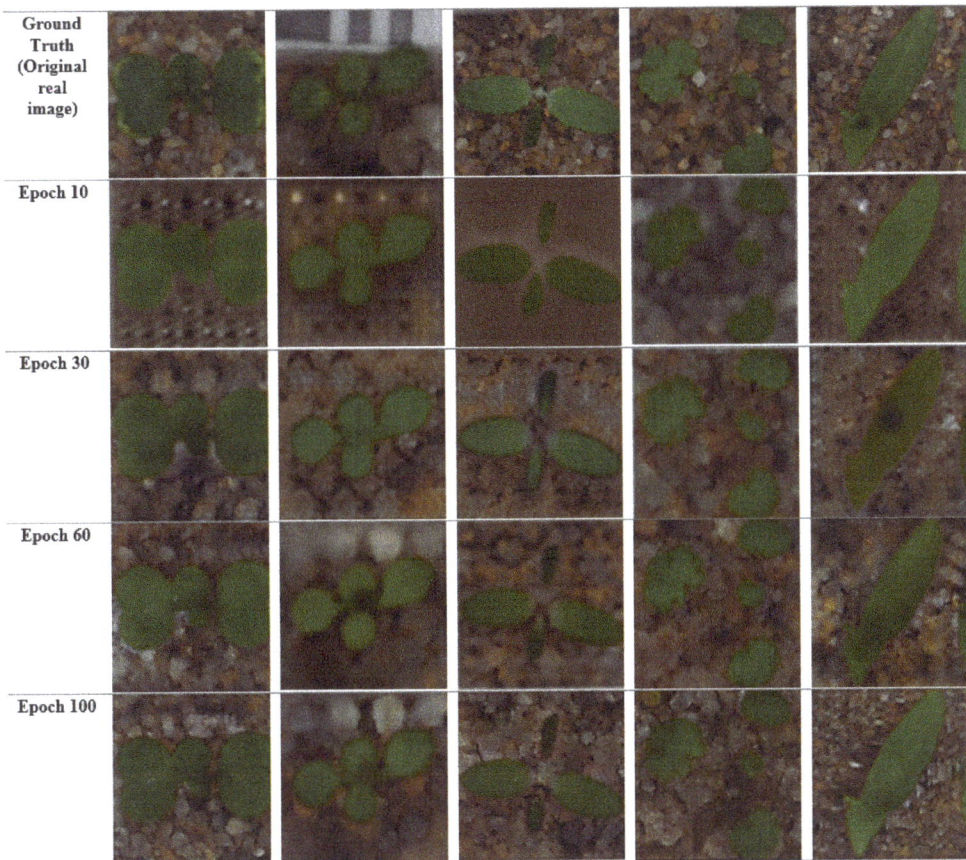

Figure 6. Sample ground truth images and generated images at different epochs during GAN training. Column-wise from left to right: Charlock, Fat Hen, Shepherd's purse, Small-flowered Cranesbill, Maize.

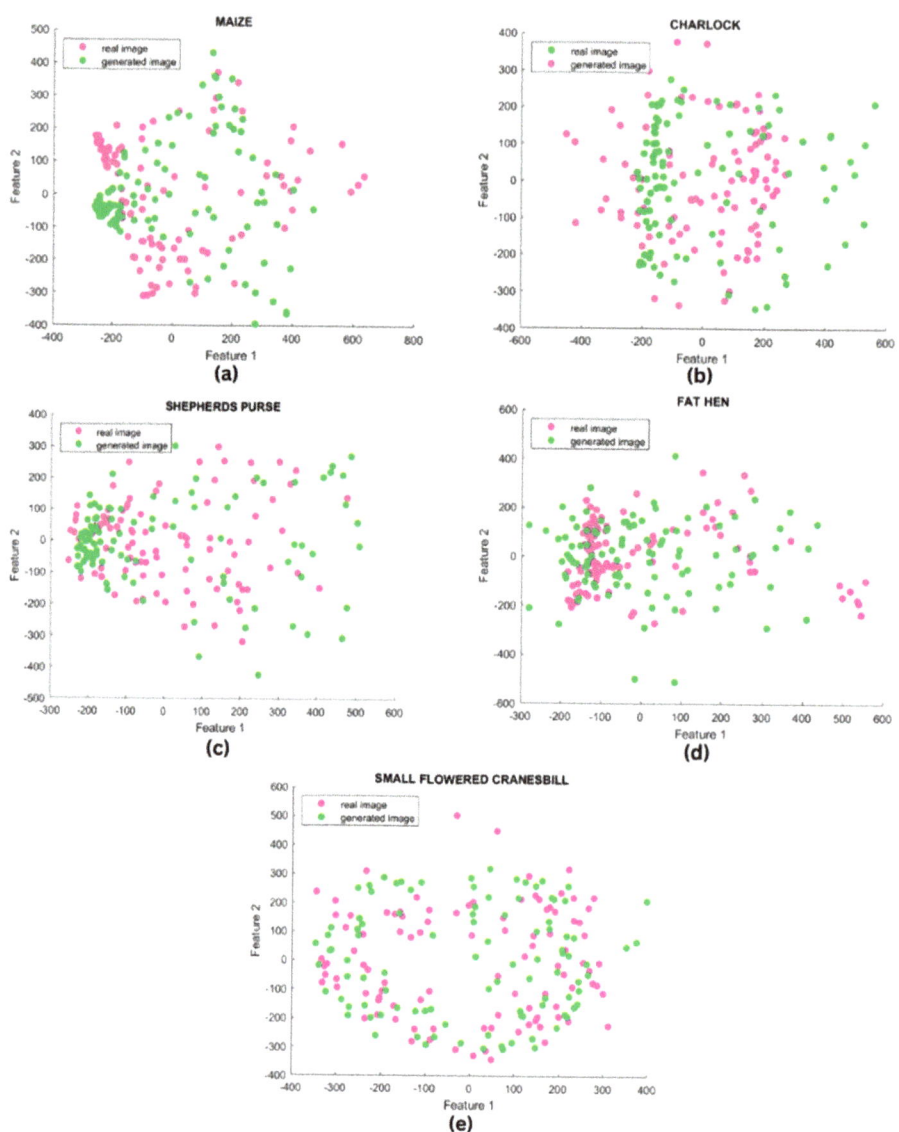

Figure 7. t-SNE visualization plots for real (green points) and synthetic (red) images for all five classes—(**a**) Maize, (**b**) Charlock, (**c**) Shepherd's purse, (**d**) Fat Hen, and (**e**) Small-flowered Cranesbill.

Hence, realistic images were generated with the help of GAN, which could augment the existing crop/weed dataset. The advantage of GAN-based augmentation includes a reduced annotation workload since the generated images can be associated with the same segmentation mask created earlier. Moreover, the classification model can generalize better when trained with a dataset comprising GAN-generated images, especially on shape-based features. Apart from this, GANs can also be used to enhance image clarity, which was observed in the case of some real images, especially of the maize crop. The GAN-synthesized images have the potential to replace erroneous and ill-advised real data. In addition, some real images contained irrelevant objects (such as the labels, referring to the image of Fat Hen in Figure 6) in the background, and the model was successful in replacing them with the ground appearance, thus exhibiting its potential to create a variety of environmental and background conditions.

One drawback to this GAN model is its inability to learn and reproduce textural features, though it performs exceptionally well in acquiring the shape and color attributes. Notably, in the images of Shepherd's purse, where the textural appearance of the weed was quite imperative, the model could not fabricate them into artificial images. This might pose a problem for classification when the crops and weeds have a similar physical appearance. For further operations, 200 images were generated for each class through the developed GAN to boost the training dataset.

3.2. Classification Results and Evaluation

3.2.1. Performance Analysis of Transfer Learning Method

As a means of performance comparison to the transfer learning approach with and without GAN-based data augmentation, the results of the *AlexNet* model that was trained using the real images were initially compiled. The dataset was geometrically augmented by random rotations, translations, and reflections. Later, the model was trained again from the initial condition with both the real and generated images to analyze the potency of image data augmentation through GAN. Henceforth, 200 new images were generated for each class to support the training set. Briefly, the combined dataset utilized for the final model had 2000 images in total (400 images per class), out of which 75 real images from each class were reserved for testing purposes. Table 2 clearly summarizes the image distribution for the training and testing.

Table 2. Summary of data distribution for each class.

Dataset	Charlock	Fat Hen	Shepherd's Purse	Cranesbill	Maize
Real images	200	200	200	200	200
Artificial images	200	200	200	200	200
Total	400	400	400	400	400
Training images	325	325	325	325	325
Test images	75	75	75	75	75

After training with the original (real) dataset, the CNN model produced a classification F1-score of 0.970. After adding artificial images, the F1-score of the CNN (denoted as GAN-TL) improved remarkably and reached a value of 0.986. The statistical classification results on the test set have been recorded in Table 3. In addition, the accuracy improved to 98.40% from the previously attained 97.07% (without GAN augmentation) in the test data. A remarkable increment in the performance metrics was observed for Shepherd's Purse and Fat Hen, while the results remained unchanged for the maize and Cranesbill classes (Table 3). Overall, image augmentation with the help of a conditional GAN resulted in an improved classification result through the transfer learning method.

Table 3. Analysis of the classification results based on the transfer learning method. TL and GAN-TL refer to the models trained with the real image data, and combined real and artificial datasets, respectively.

Class Name	Precision		Recall		F1-Score	
	TL	GAN-TL	TL	GAN-TL	TL	GAN-TL
Charlock	0.9493	0.9615	1.0000	1.0000	0.9739	0.9804
Fat Hen	0.9136	0.9868	0.9867	1.0000	0.9487	0.9934

Table 3. *Cont.*

Class Name	Precision		Recall		F1-Score	
	TL	GAN-TL	TL	GAN-TL	TL	GAN-TL
Shepherd's Purse	1.0000	1.0000	0.8801	0.9333	0.9362	0.9655
Cranesbill	1.0000	1.0000	1.0000	1.0000	1.0000	1.0000
Maize	1.0000	1.0000	0.9867	0.9867	0.9933	0.9933

3.2.2. Performance Analysis of Feature Extraction Technique

The feature extraction-based classification models were developed using the activations derived from the global pooling layer of the CNN. Again, the models were developed in two stages, first on the dataset of real images and then on the combined dataset. Since the feature vector obtained from *AlexNet* had 9216 activations, it offered a wide range of features for classification. The important reason behind choosing *AlexNet* over other state-of-the-art models was its small convolution kernel sizes and network architecture, which supported the extraction of fine-grain details in the images. The performance of the models trained through SVM and LDA classifiers were compared.

The classification results on the test data have been recorded in Tables 4 and 5, containing the mean precision, recall, and *F*1 scores for the five independent runs. The overall accuracy registered by LDA (GAN-LDA) and SVM classifiers (GAN-SVM) was 96.0%. In the training data, LDA performed slightly better than SVM (94.3% and 92.4%). As anticipated, the synthetic images enhanced the performance of both classifiers. The *F*1-score of the SVM model increased from 0.935 to 0.960, and that of the LDA model increased from 0.943 to 0.959.

Table 4. Analysis of classification results of SVM on deep features of *AlexNet*. The SVM and GAN-SVM refer to the SVM models trained with the real image data, and combined real and artificial datasets, respectively.

Class Name	Precision		Recall		F1-Score	
	TL	SVM-TL	TL	SVM-TL	TL	SVM-TL
Charlock	0.8537	0.9012	0.9333	0.9733	0.8975	0.9358
Fat Hen	0.9571	0.9722	0.8933	0.9333	0.9241	0.9523
Shepherd's Purse	0.9589	0.9863	0.9333	0.9333	0.9459	0.9591
Cranesbill	0.9726	0.9740	0.9467	0.9600	0.9594	0.9669
Maize	0.9351	0.9722	0.9600	1.0000	0.9474	0.9859

Table 5. Analysis of classification results of LDA on deep features of *AlexNet*. The LDA and GAN-LDA refer to the LDA models trained with the real image data, and combined real and artificial datasets, respectively.

Class Name	Precision		Recall		F1-Score	
	TL	LDA-TL	TL	LDA-TL	TL	LDA-TL
Charlock	0.9853	0.9857	0.8933	0.9200	0.9370	0.9517
Fat Hen	0.9324	0.9589	0.9200	0.9333	0.9261	0.9459
Shepherd's Purse	0.9452	0.9474	0.9200	0.9600	0.9324	0.9537
Cranesbill	0.9242	0.9615	1.0000	1.0000	0.9606	0.9804
Maize	0.9367	0.9487	0.9867	0.9867	0.9611	0.9673

Tables 4 and 5 demonstrate that the GAN-based augmentation method can provide an excellent performance boost to different classifiers, especially when developed using a limited dataset. Furthermore, Figure 8 presents the best testing confusion matrices upon using the original and GAN-augmented images. In the case of LDA, the performance of certain classes, such as maize and Charlock did not change much on applying GAN-based augmentation. However, the results of classes, such as Cranesbill and Fat Hen, improved significantly. This is because Cranesbill and Fat Hen are relatively more complicated in shape, requiring more data by the network to learn the features. In contrast, the features of maize and charlock are simple and distinct; hence, they are easier for the classifiers to perform the classification task. From the $F1$ scores of all the classes, it can be observed that the GAN-based image augmentation provided more information and enhanced the performance of transfer learning, as well as the feature extraction techniques for the crop/weed classifications.

In previous works, classification accuracies greater than 90% have been achieved using SVM and LDA classifiers, especially for crop/weed classifications. Accuracies between 92 and 95% were achieved using SVM on the color and texture features for identifying four common weed seedlings in the maize production systems [57]. When morphological features were added to the feature space, an improved accuracy of 96.5% was obtained using RBF-SVM [58]. In another study, local binary pattern-based texture features yielded a 98.5% accuracy with RBF as the kernel function [66]. Siddiqi et al. used the stepwise LDA to classify weeds into three classes: broad weed, narrow weed, and other weed species [67]. Their method accorded 98.1% overall accuracy on a database of 1200 images. In the case of deep-learning-based classifications, most studies used a transfer learning approach rather than training the CNN from scratch. For identifying weeds in cotton and tomato fields, the performances of seven state-of-the-art CNNs were evaluated [26]. All the models registered classification $F1$-scores greater than 88%.

Moreover, the fine-tuning method was compared with a feature-extraction approach for all the adopted CNNs [26]. They observed that most of the networks gave better results through the feature-extraction approach—a similar inference from this study as well. Similarly, the Alexnet CNN architecture was transfer-learned with potato and sugar beet plant image datasets for binary classification [68]. The model's accuracy was 98.0%, with an average prediction time of fewer than 0.1 s, supporting real-time applications. As an improvement, Chen et al. evaluated 35 CNN architectures for classifying 15 weed species in cotton production systems, for which ten of them achieved an $F1$ score greater than 95% [27]. These results show that the classification models in this study have provided performances comparable to those previously developed.

Overall, the results indicate that data augmentation through GANs can increase the training resources needed for classifiers, enabling researchers to develop better imaging-based predictors. The authors believe that the proposed methodology can revolutionize intelligent crop/weed classifiers. An interesting topic for future work could be to examine the capability of the proposed approach on other machine vision-based applications, such as fruit maturity detection [69,70], fruit grading [71], agri-food product microstructural evaluation [65,72,73], crop disease identification [74], and crop growth and yield monitoring [75–77].

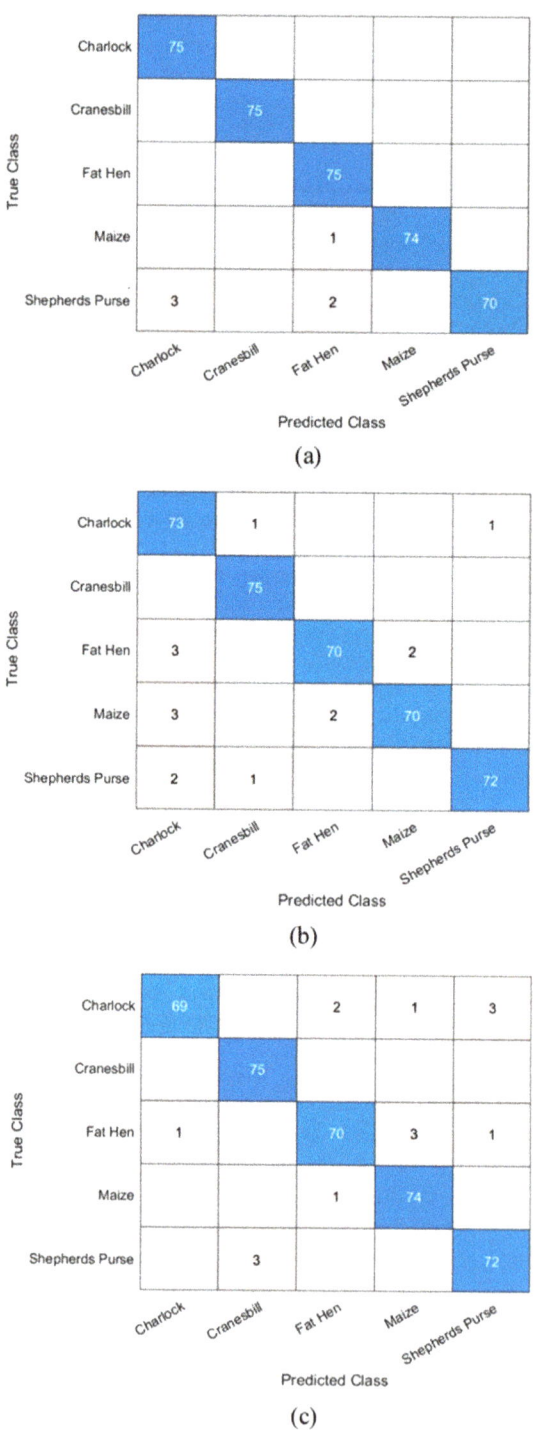

Figure 8. Best testing confusion matrices based on—(**a**) Transfer learning (GAN-TL), (**b**) Feature extraction—SVM (GAN-SVM), and (**c**) Feature extraction—LDA (GAN-LDA), using both real and GAN-synthesized datasets.

4. Conclusions

This study explored the potential of cGAN-based data augmentation techniques for improving imaging-based crop/weed classification. Using cGAN, artificial images were generated to double the training data of the available classes. The t-SNE method was used for the fidelity inspection of the new images, and the t-SNE plots showed high similarities between the feature distributions of real and artificial images. The performance of crop/weed classification with and without the artificial images was examined via two approaches viz. transfer learning and feature extraction. The obtained results confirmed the capability of the cGAN-based technique to improve the performance of crop/weed classifiers. Overall, this study opens a new pathway for implementing GANs, not only for crop/weed classification but also for the development of other machine vision-based precision agriculture systems.

Author Contributions: Conceptualization, L.G.D., D.S.G., R.M. and P.S.; methodology, L.G.D.; validation, L.G.D.; formal analysis, L.G.D.; investigation, L.G.D., D.S.G. and P.S.; resources, L.G.D., P.S., M.N. and J.P.; writing—original draft preparation, L.G.D.; writing—review and editing, D.S.G., R.M., P.S., M.N. and J.P.; supervision, P.S. and J.P.; project administration, P.S. All authors have read and agreed to the published version of the manuscript.

Funding: This research was funded by the Canada Foundation for Innovation (CFI) grant number 33090 and the Natural Sciences and Engineering Council of Canada (NSERC) grant number RGPIN2021-03350. The authors would also like to thank the financial support provided by Mitacs.

Institutional Review Board Statement: Not applicable.

Informed Consent Statement: Not applicable.

Data Availability Statement: The data that support the findings of this study are available from the corresponding authors, upon reasonable request.

Conflicts of Interest: The authors declare no conflict of interest.

References

1. Zhang, Q.; Liu, Y.; Gong, C.; Chen, Y.; Yu, H. Applications of Deep Learning for Dense Scenes Analysis in Agriculture: A Review. *Sensors* **2020**, *20*, 1520. [CrossRef] [PubMed]
2. Divyanth, L.G.; Ahmad, A.; Saraswat, D. A Two-Stage Deep-Learning Based Segmentation Model for Crop Disease Quantification Based on Corn Field Imagery. *Smart Agric. Technol.* **2022**, *3*, 100108. [CrossRef]
3. Liakos, K.G.; Busato, P.; Moshou, D.; Pearson, S.; Bochtis, D. Machine Learning in Agriculture: A Review. *Sensors* **2018**, *18*, 2674. [CrossRef] [PubMed]
4. Divyanth, L.G.; Chelladurai, V.; Loganathan, M.; Jayas, D.S.; Soni, P. Identification of Green Gram (Vigna Radiata) Grains Infested by Callosobruchus Maculatus Through X-Ray Imaging and GAN-Based Image Augmentation. *J. Biosyst. Eng.* **2022**, *47*, 302–317. [CrossRef]
5. Wani, J.A.; Sharma, S.; Muzamil, M.; Ahmed, S.; Sharma, S.; Singh, S. Machine Learning and Deep Learning Based Computational Techniques in Automatic Agricultural Diseases Detection: Methodologies, Applications, and Challenges. *Arch. Comput. Methods Eng.* **2021**, *29*, 641–677. [CrossRef]
6. Sivakumar, C.; Chaudhry, M.M.A.; Nadimi, M.; Paliwal, J.; Courcelles, J. Characterization of Roller and Ferkar-Milled Pulse Flours Using Laser Diffraction and Scanning Electron Microscopy. *Powder Technol.* **2022**, *409*, 117803. [CrossRef]
7. Erkinbaev, C.; Nadimi, M.; Paliwal, J. A Unified Heuristic Approach to Simultaneously Detect Fusarium and Ergot Damage in Wheat. *Meas. Food* **2022**, *7*, 100043. [CrossRef]
8. Pantazi, X.E.; Moshou, D.; Bravo, C. Active Learning System for Weed Species Recognition Based on Hyperspectral Sensing. *Biosyst. Eng.* **2016**, *146*, 193–202. [CrossRef]
9. Tang, J.L.; Chen, X.Q.; Miao, R.H.; Wang, D. Weed Detection Using Image Processing under Different Illumination for Site-Specific Areas Spraying. *Comput. Electron. Agric.* **2016**, *122*, 103–111. [CrossRef]
10. Raja, R.; Nguyen, T.T.; Slaughter, D.C.; Fennimore, S.A. Real-Time Weed-Crop Classification and Localisation Technique for Robotic Weed Control in Lettuce. *Biosyst. Eng.* **2020**, *192*, 257–274. [CrossRef]
11. Sabzi, S.; Abbaspour-Gilandeh, Y.; Arribas, J.I. An Automatic Visible-Range Video Weed Detection, Segmentation and Classification Prototype in Potato Field. *Heliyon* **2020**, *6*, e03685. [CrossRef] [PubMed]
12. Lee, W.S.; Slaughter, D.C.; Giles, D.K. Robotic Weed Control System for Tomatoes. *Precis. Agric.* **1999**, *1*, 95–113. [CrossRef]
13. Utstumo, T.; Urdal, F.; Brevik, A.; Dørum, J.; Netland, J.; Overskeid, Ø.; Berge, T.W.; Gravdahl, J.T. Robotic In-Row Weed Control in Vegetables. *Comput. Electron. Agric.* **2018**, *154*, 36–45. [CrossRef]

14. Chang, C.L.; Lin, K.M. Smart Agricultural Machine with a Computer Vision-Based Weeding and Variable-Rate Irrigation Scheme. *Robotics* **2018**, *7*, 38. [CrossRef]
15. Grimstad, L.; From, P.J. The Thorvald II Agricultural Robotic System. *Robotics* **2017**, *6*, 24. [CrossRef]
16. Yu, H.; Men, Z.; Bi, C.; Liu, H. Research on Field Soybean Weed Identification Based on an Improved UNet Model Combined With a Channel Attention Mechanism. *Front. Plant Sci.* **2022**, *13*, 1881. [CrossRef]
17. Kamath, R.; Balachandra, M.; Vardhan, A.; Maheshwari, U. Classification of Paddy Crop and Weeds Using Semantic Segmentation. *Cogent Eng.* **2022**, *9*, 2018791. [CrossRef]
18. Sodjinou, S.G.; Mohammadi, V.; Sanda Mahama, A.T.; Gouton, P. A Deep Semantic Segmentation-Based Algorithm to Segment Crops and Weeds in Agronomic Color Images. *Inf. Process. Agric.* **2022**, *9*, 355–364. [CrossRef]
19. Lu, Y.; Young, S. A Survey of Public Datasets for Computer Vision Tasks in Precision Agriculture. *Comput. Electron. Agric.* **2020**, *178*, 105760. [CrossRef]
20. Zheng, Y.Y.; Kong, J.L.; Jin, X.B.; Wang, X.Y.; Su, T.L.; Zuo, M. CropDeep: The Crop Vision Dataset for Deep-Learning-Based Classification and Detection in Precision Agriculture. *Sensors* **2019**, *19*, 1058. [CrossRef]
21. Espejo-Garcia, B.; Mylonas, N.; Athanasakos, L.; Fountas, S. Improving Weeds Identification with a Repository of Agricultural Pre-Trained Deep Neural Networks. *Comput. Electron. Agric.* **2020**, *175*, 105593. [CrossRef]
22. Moazzam, S.I.; Khan, U.S.; Tiwana, M.I.; Iqbal, J.; Qureshi, W.S.; Shah, S.I. A Review of Application of Deep Learning for Weeds and Crops Classification in Agriculture. In Proceedings of the 2019 International Conference on Robotics and Automation in Industry (ICRAI), Rawalpindi, Pakistan, 21–22 October 2019. [CrossRef]
23. Chen, J.; Chen, J.; Zhang, D.; Sun, Y.; Nanehkaran, Y.A. Using Deep Transfer Learning for Image-Based Plant Disease Identification. *Comput. Electron. Agric.* **2020**, *173*, 105393. [CrossRef]
24. Too, E.C.; Yujian, L.; Njuki, S.; Yingchun, L. A Comparative Study of Fine-Tuning Deep Learning Models for Plant Disease Identification. *Comput. Electron. Agric.* **2019**, *161*, 272–279. [CrossRef]
25. Pan, S.J.; Yang, Q. A Survey on Transfer Learning. *IEEE Trans. Knowl. Data Eng.* **2010**, *22*, 1345–1359. [CrossRef]
26. Espejo-Garcia, B.; Mylonas, N.; Athanasakos, L.; Fountas, S.; Vasilakoglou, I. Towards Weeds Identification Assistance through Transfer Learning. *Comput. Electron. Agric.* **2020**, *171*, 105306. [CrossRef]
27. Chen, D.; Lu, Y.; Li, Z.; Young, S. Performance Evaluation of Deep Transfer Learning on Multi-Class Identification of Common Weed Species in Cotton Production Systems. *Comput. Electron. Agric.* **2022**, *198*, 107091. [CrossRef]
28. Xu, Y.; Zhai, Y.; Zhao, B.; Jiao, Y.; Kong, S.; Zhou, Y.; Gao, Z. Weed Recognition for Depthwise Separable Network Based on Transfer Learning. *Intell. Autom. Soft Comput.* **2021**, *27*, 669–682. [CrossRef]
29. Goodfellow, I.J.; Pouget-Abadie, J.; Mirza, M.; Xu, B.; Warde-Farley, D.; Ozair, S.; Courville, A.; Bengio, Y. Generative Adversarial Nets. *Adv. Neural Inf. Process. Syst.* **2014**, *27*, 139–144.
30. Zheng, Z.; Zheng, L.; Yang, Y. Unlabeled Samples Generated by GAN Improve the Person Re-Identification Baseline in vitro. In Proceedings of the 2017 International Conference on Computer Vision, Venice, Italy, 22–29 October 2017; pp. 3774–3782. [CrossRef]
31. Frid-Adar, M.; Klang, E.; Amitai, M.; Goldberger, J.; Greenspan, H. Synthetic Data Augmentation Using GAN for Improved Liver Lesion Classification. In Proceedings of the 2018 IEEE 15th International Symposium on Biomedical Imaging (ISBI 2018), Washington, DC, USA, 4–7 April 2018; pp. 289–293. [CrossRef]
32. Zhu, X.; Liu, Y.; Li, J.; Wan, T.; Qin, Z. Emotion Classification with Data Augmentation Using Generative Adversarial Networks. In *Advances in Knowledge Discovery and Data Mining*; Lecture Notes in Computer Science; Springer: Cham, Switzerland, 2018; Volume 10939 LNAI, pp. 349–360. [CrossRef]
33. Giuffrida, M.V.; Scharr, H.; Tsaftaris, S.A. ARIGAN: Synthetic Arabidopsis Plants Using Generative Adversarial Network. In Proceedings of the 2017 International Conference on Computer Vision, Venice, Italy, 22–29 October 2017; pp. 2064–2071. [CrossRef]
34. Divyanth, L.G.; Marzougui, A.; González-Bernal, M.J.; McGee, R.J.; Rubiales, D.; Sankaran, S. Evaluation of Effective Class-Balancing Techniques for CNN-Based Assessment of Aphanomyces Root Rot Resistance in Pea (*Pisum sativum* L.). *Sensors* **2022**, *22*, 7237. [CrossRef]
35. Arsenovic, M.; Karanovic, M.; Sladojevic, S.; Anderla, A.; Stefanovic, D. Solving Current Limitations of Deep Learning Based Approaches for Plant Disease Detection. *Symmetry* **2019**, *11*, 939. [CrossRef]
36. Madsen, S.L.; Dyrmann, M.; Jørgensen, R.N.; Karstoft, H. Generating Artificial Images of Plant Seedlings Using Generative Adversarial Networks. *Biosyst. Eng.* **2019**, *187*, 147–159. [CrossRef]
37. Espejo-Garcia, B.; Mylonas, N.; Athanasakos, L.; Vali, E.; Fountas, S. Combining Generative Adversarial Networks and Agricultural Transfer Learning for Weeds Identification. *Biosyst. Eng.* **2021**, *204*, 79–89. [CrossRef]
38. Fawakherji, M.; Potena, C.; Pretto, A.; Bloisi, D.D.; Nardi, D. Multi-Spectral Image Synthesis for Crop/Weed Segmentation in Precision Farming. *Rob. Auton. Syst.* **2021**, *146*, 103861. [CrossRef]
39. Khan, S.; Tufail, M.; Khan, M.T.; Khan, Z.A.; Iqbal, J.; Alam, M. A Novel Semi-Supervised Framework for UAV Based Crop/Weed Classification. *PLoS ONE* **2021**, *16*, e0251008. [CrossRef] [PubMed]
40. Isola, P.; Zhu, J.Y.; Zhou, T.; Efros, A.A. Image-to-Image Translation with Conditional Adversarial Networks. In Proceedings of the IEEE Conference on Computer Vision and Pattern Recognition, Honolulu, HI, USA, 21–26 July 2017; pp. 5967–5976. [CrossRef]
41. Khurana, G.; Bawa, N.K. Weed Detection Approach Using Feature Extraction and KNN Classification. In *Advances in Electromechanical Technologies*; Lecture Notes in Mechanical Engineering; Springer: Singapore, 2021; pp. 671–679. [CrossRef]

42. Jin, X.; Che, J.; Chen, Y. Weed Identification Using Deep Learning and Image Processing in Vegetable Plantation. *IEEE Access* **2021**, *9*, 10940–10950. [CrossRef]
43. Wang, A.; Zhang, W.; Wei, X. A Review on Weed Detection Using Ground-Based Machine Vision and Image Processing Techniques. *Comput. Electron. Agric.* **2019**, *158*, 226–240. [CrossRef]
44. Sunil, G.C.; Zhang, Y.; Koparan, C.; Ahmed, M.R.; Howatt, K.; Sun, X. Weed and Crop Species Classification Using Computer Vision and Deep Learning Technologies in Greenhouse Conditions. *J. Agric. Food Res.* **2022**, *9*, 100325. [CrossRef]
45. Krizhevsky, A.; Sutskever, I.; Hinton, G.E. ImageNet Classification with Deep Convolutional Neural Networks. *Adv. Neural Inf. Process. Syst.* **2012**, *60*, 84–90. [CrossRef]
46. Giselsson, T.M.; Jørgensen, R.N.; Jensen, P.K.; Dyrmann, M.; Midtiby, H.S. A Public Image Database for Benchmark of Plant Seedling Classification Algorithms. *arXiv* **2017**, arXiv:1711.05458. [CrossRef]
47. Mirza, M.; Osindero, S. Conditional Generative Adversarial Nets. *arXiv* **2014**, arXiv:1411.1784. [CrossRef]
48. Reed, S.; Akata, Z.; Yan, X.; Logeswaran Reedscot, L.; Schiele, B.; Lee Schiele, H. Generative Adversarial Text to Image Synthesis. In Proceedings of the International Conference on Machine Learning (ICML 2016), New York, NY, USA, 19–24 June 2016; pp. 1060–1069.
49. Ronneberger, O.; Fischer, P.; Brox, T. U-Net: Convolutional Networks for Biomedical Image Segmentation. In Proceedings of the International Conference on Medical Image Computing and Computer-Assisted Intervention 2015, Munich, Germany, 5–9 October 2015; Volume 9351, pp. 234–241. [CrossRef]
50. Li, C.; Wand, M. Precomputed Real-Time Texture Synthesis with Markovian Generative Adversarial Networks. In Proceedings of the European Conference on Computer Vision 2016, Amsterdam, The Netherlands, 11–14 October 2016; Volume 9907 LNCS, pp. 702–716. [CrossRef]
51. van der Maaten, L.; Hinton, G. Visualizing Data Using T-SNE. *J. Mach. Learn. Res.* **2008**, *9*, 2579–2605.
52. Russakovsky, O.; Deng, J.; Su, H.; Krause, J.; Satheesh, S.; Ma, S.; Huang, Z.; Karpathy, A.; Khosla, A.; Bernstein, M.; et al. ImageNet Large Scale Visual Recognition Challenge. *Int. J. Comput. Vis.* **2015**, *115*, 211–252. [CrossRef]
53. Deng, J.; Dong, W.; Socher, R.; Li, L.J.; Li, K.; Fei-Fei, L. ImageNet: A Large-Scale Hierarchical Image Database. In Proceedings of the 2009 IEEE Conference on Computer Vision and Pattern Recognition, Miami, FL, USA, 20–25 June 2010; pp. 248–255. [CrossRef]
54. Szegedy, C.; Liu, W.; Jia, Y.; Sermanet, P.; Reed, S.; Anguelov, D.; Erhan, D.; Vanhoucke, V.; Rabinovich, A. Going Deeper with Convolutions. In Proceedings of the IEEE Conference on Computer Vision and Pattern Recognition 2015, Boston, MA, USA, 7–12 June 2015; pp. 1–9. [CrossRef]
55. Wiatowski, T.; Bolcskei, H. A Mathematical Theory of Deep Convolutional Neural Networks for Feature Extraction. *IEEE Trans. Inf. Theory* **2018**, *64*, 1845–1866. [CrossRef]
56. Nanehkaran, Y.A.; Zhang, D.; Chen, J.; Tian, Y.; Al-Nabhan, N. Recognition of Plant Leaf Diseases Based on Computer Vision. *J. Ambient Intell. Humaniz. Comput.* **2020**, *1*, 1–18. [CrossRef]
57. Wu, L.; Wen, Y. Weed/Corn Seedling Recognition by Support Vector Machine Using Texture Features. *African J. Agric. Res.* **2009**, *4*, 840–846.
58. Wu, L.; Wen, Y. Application of Support Vector Machine for Identifying Single Corn/Weed Seedling in Fields Using Shape Parameters. In Proceedings of the 2nd International Conference on Information Science and Engineering, Hangzhou, China, 4–6 December 2010. [CrossRef]
59. Wong, W.K.; Chekima, A.; Mariappan, M.; Khoo, B.; Nadarajan, M. Probabilistic Multi SVM Weed Species Classification for Weed Scouting and Selective Spot Weeding. In Proceedings of the 2014 IEEE International Symposium on Robotics and Manufacturing Automation (ROMA), Kuala Lumpur, Malaysia, 15–16 December 2014; pp. 63–68. [CrossRef]
60. Karimi, Y.; Prasher, S.O.; Patel, R.M.; Kim, S.H. Application of Support Vector Machine Technology for Weed and Nitrogen Stress Detection in Corn. *Comput. Electron. Agric.* **2006**, *51*, 99–109. [CrossRef]
61. Venkataraju, A.; Arumugam, D.; Stepan, C.; Kiran, R.; Peters, T. A Review of Machine Learning Techniques for Identifying Weeds in Corn. *Smart Agric. Technol.* **2022**, *3*, 100102. [CrossRef]
62. Friedman, J.H. Regularized Discriminant Analysis. *J. Am. Stat. Assoc.* **1989**, *84*, 165–175. [CrossRef]
63. Guo, Y.; Hastie, T.; Tibshirani, R. Regularized Linear Discriminant Analysis and Its Application in Microarrays. *Biostatistics* **2007**, *8*, 86–100. [CrossRef]
64. Qadri, S.; Khan, D.M.; Ahmad, F.; Qadri, S.F.; Babar, M.E.; Shahid, M.; Ul-Rehman, M.; Razzaq, A.; Shah Muhammad, S.; Fahad, M.; et al. A Comparative Study of Land Cover Classification by Using Multispectral and Texture Data. *Biomed Res. Int.* **2016**, *2016*, 8797438. [CrossRef]
65. Nadimi, M.; Loewen, G.; Paliwal, J. Assessment of Mechanical Damage to Flaxseeds Using Radiographic Imaging and Tomography. *Smart Agric. Technol.* **2022**, *2*, 100057. [CrossRef]
66. Ahmed, F.; Bari, A.S.M.H.; Shihavuddin, A.S.M.; Al-Mamun, H.A.; Kwan, P. A Study on Local Binary Pattern for Automated Weed Classification Using Template Matching and Support Vector Machine. In Proceedings of the 2011 IEEE 12th International Symposium on Computational Intelligence and Informatics (CINTI), Budapest, Hungary, 21–22 November 2011; pp. 329–334. [CrossRef]
67. Siddiqi, M.H.; Lee, S.-W.; Khan, A.M. Weed Image Classification Using Wavelet Transform, Stepwise Linear Discriminant Analysis, and Support Vector Machines for an Automatic Spray Control System. *J. Inf. Sci. Eng.* **2014**, *30*, 1227–1244. [CrossRef]

68. Suh, H.K.; IJsselmuiden, J.; Hofstee, J.W.; van Henten, E.J. Transfer Learning for the Classification of Sugar Beet and Volunteer Potato under Field Conditions. *Biosyst. Eng.* **2018**, *174*, 50–65. [CrossRef]
69. Sabzi, S.; Abbaspour, Y.; Nadimi, M.; Paliwal, J. Non-destructive estimation of physicochemical properties and detection of ripeness level of apples using machine vision. *Int. J. Fruit Sci.* **2022**, *22*, 628–645. [CrossRef]
70. Kheiralipour, K.; Nadimi, M.; Paliwal, J. Development of an Intelligent Imaging System for Ripeness Determination of Wild Pistachios. *Sensors* **2022**, *22*, 7134. [CrossRef] [PubMed]
71. Hosainpour, A.; Kheiralipour, K.; Nadimi, M.; Paliwal, J. Quality assessment of dried white mulberry (*Morus alba* L.) using machine vision. *Horticulturae*, 2022; In press.
72. Li, X.; Guillermic, R.M.; Nadimi, M.; Paliwal, J.; Koksel, F. Physical and microstructural quality of extruded snacks made from blends of barley and green lentil flours. *Cereal Chem.* **2022**, *99*, 1112–1123. [CrossRef]
73. Nadimi, M.; Divyanth, L.G.; Paliwal, J. Automated detection of mechanical damage in flaxseeds using radiographic imaging and machine learning. *Foods Bioprocess Technol.* **2022**, In press.
74. Nadimi, M.; Brown, J.M.; Morrison, J.; Paliwal, J. Examination of wheat kernels for the presence of *Fusarium* damage and mycotoxins using near-infrared hyperspectral imaging. *Meas. Food* **2021**, *4*, 100011. [CrossRef]
75. Nadimi, M.; Loewen, G.; Bhowmik, P.; Paliwal, J. Effect of laser biostimulation on germination of sub-optimally stored flaxseeds (*Linum usitatissimum*). *Sustainability* **2022**, *14*, 12183. [CrossRef]
76. Nadimi, M.; Sun, D.W.; Paliwal, J. Effect of laser biostimulation on germination of wheat. *ASABE Appl. Eng. Agric.* **2022**, *38*, 77–84. [CrossRef]
77. Nadimi, M.; Sun, D.W.; Paliwal, J. Recent applications of novel laser techniques for enhancing agricultural production. *Laser Phys.* **2021**, *31*, 053001. [CrossRef]

Article

Lithium-Ion Battery Prognostics through Reinforcement Learning Based on Entropy Measures

Alireza Namdari [1], Maryam Asad Samani [2] and Tariq S. Durrani [3,*]

[1] Department of Industrial Engineering and Engineering Management, Western New England University, Springfield, MA 01119, USA
[2] Department of Electrical Engineering, Iran University of Science and Technology, Tehran 13114-16846, Iran
[3] Department of Electronic and Electrical Engineering, University of Strathclyde, Glasgow G1 1XW, UK
* Correspondence: t.durrani@strath.ac.uk; Tel.: +44-(0)-141-548-2540

Abstract: Lithium-ion is a progressive battery technology that has been used in vastly different electrical systems. Failure of the battery can lead to failure in the entire system where the battery is embedded and cause irreversible damage. To avoid probable damages, research is actively conducted, and data-driven methods are proposed, based on prognostics and health management (PHM) systems. PHM can use multiple time-scale data and stored information from battery capacities over several cycles to determine the battery state of health (SOH) and its remaining useful life (RUL). This results in battery safety, stability, reliability, and longer lifetime. In this paper, we propose different data-driven approaches to battery prognostics that rely on: Long Short-Term Memory (LSTM), Autoregressive Integrated Moving Average (ARIMA), and Reinforcement Learning (RL) based on the permutation entropy of battery voltage sequences at each cycle, since they take into account vital information from past data and result in high accuracy.

Keywords: lithium-ion battery; prognostics; long short-term memory; ARIMA; reinforcement learning

Citation: Namdari, A.; Samani, M.A.; Durrani, T.S. Lithium-Ion Battery Prognostics through Reinforcement Learning Based on Entropy Measures. *Algorithms* **2022**, *15*, 393. https://doi.org/10.3390/a15110393

Academic Editor: Frank Werner

Received: 28 August 2022
Accepted: 20 October 2022
Published: 24 October 2022

Publisher's Note: MDPI stays neutral with regard to jurisdictional claims in published maps and institutional affiliations.

Copyright: © 2022 by the authors. Licensee MDPI, Basel, Switzerland. This article is an open access article distributed under the terms and conditions of the Creative Commons Attribution (CC BY) license (https://creativecommons.org/licenses/by/4.0/).

1. Introduction

1.1. Lithium-Ion Batteries

Lithium-ion batteries, as the primary power source in electric vehicles, have attracted significant attention recently and have become a focus of research. It is assumed that lithium-ion batteries have the inherent potential for building future power sources for environmentally friendly vehicles [1].

Lithium-ion batteries are the best option for electrical vehicles due to their high-quality performance, capacity, small volume, light weight, low pollution, and rechargeability with no memory effect [2]. However, battery performance degrades when facing poor pavement conditions, temperature, and load changes. This leads to leakage, insulation damage, and partial short-circuits. Consequential situations can arise if these failures are not detected timeously [3,4]. As an example, several Boeing 787 aircraft caught fire because of lithium-ion battery failure in 2013, causing the airliners to be grounded [5]. Hence, it is necessary to detect performance degradations timeously and estimate future battery performance. This is where battery prognostics and health management (PHM) plays an important and vital role. PHM determines the battery state of health prediction (SOH) and battery remaining useful life prediction (RUL) of the product using possible failure information in the system, thus yielding improved system reliability and stability in the actual life-cycle of the battery.

Battery PHM and a battery management system (BMS) are important to ensure the reliable and safe functionality of energy storage units [6]. Battery RUL prediction, battery SOH prediction, and battery capacity fade prediction are among the topics which have drawn more attention from researchers in the recent decade [7]. However, these tasks are very difficult, as battery degradation has a complex nature and numerous factors must be taken into consideration [8,9].

1.2. Entropy Measures

Entropy is a measurement metric for irregularities in time series data, and is used to quantify the stochastic process in data analyses [10]. It was first introduced in classical thermodynamics, and has applications in diverse fields such as chemistry and physics, biological systems, cosmology, economics, sociology, weather science, climate change research, and information systems. Entropy has expanded to far-ranging fields and systems. Shannon, Permutation, Renyi, Tsallis, Approximate, and Sample entropy measures are some of the conceptions of entropy regularly in use [11].

From the afore-mentioned entropies, permutation entropy (PE) is a simple and robust approach to calculating the complexity of a non-linear system using the order relations between values of a time series and assigning a probability to the ordinal patterns. The permutation entropy measure technique works flexibly; it is computationally efficient, and has a range of several thousand parameter values similar to Lyapunov exponents. PE is discussed in more detail in Reference [12]. In this study, PE of the discharge battery voltage sequences is calculated and used as an input to the proposed models.

1.3. ML and DL Techniques

Recently, Machine Learning (ML) and Deep Learning (DL) algorithms have found very significant and useful applications in research and practice. These concepts have been used to develop various models for predicting different characteristics in diverse fields. In general, ML and DL algorithms aim to capture information from past data, learn from that data, and apply what they have learned to make informed decisions. Therefore, the associated systems are not required to be broadly programmed in all aspects.

ML is used to synthesize the fundamental relationships between large amount of data to solve real-time problems such as big-data analytics and evolution of information [13]. DL, in turn, is able to process a large number of features and, hence, is preferred when computing huge datasets and unstructured data. DL facilitates analysis and extraction of important information from raw data by using computer systems. [14]. Different types of parameters with various quantities can be applied to the developed models as the input to obtain expected predictive variables as the output.

Deep Learning techniques, including Long Short-Term Memory (LSTM) [15] and Reinforcement Learning (RL) [16], can fit numerical dependent variables and have great generalization ability, and therefore, are applicable to battery data. The LSTM algorithm, a Deep Learning algorithm with multiple gates, performs on the basis of updating and storing key information in the time series data [15], and is applicable to battery prognostics. The RL algorithm, on the other hand—as one of the latest Deep Learning methods and tools—has the capability of creating a simulation of the whole system and making intelligent decisions (i.e., charge, replace, repair, etc.) after it is utilized to predict the battery RUL and SOH for the purpose of battery PHM and BMS [16].

1.4. Research Objective

In this study, the objective is to progress the study of lithium-ion battery performance based on battery SOH and RUL prognostics. To do so, we propose an entropy-based Reinforcement Learning model, predict the next-cycle battery capacity, and compare the numerical results from the proposed entropy-based RL models to those from two other data-driven methods—namely, ARIMA and LSTM—which are both constructed based on the same input variable (i.e., permutation entropy of voltage sequences at each cycle). Permutation entropy of the battery discharge voltage, as well as the previous battery capacities, are given to these models as input variables. Finally, evaluation metrics such as MSE, MAE, and RMSE are applied to the proposed methods to compare the observed and predicted battery capacities.

Based on Figure 1, the remainder of this work consists of the following sections. First, battery data is prepared and provided for the study. The data is then analyzed from different points of view. Based on the data analysis, various models are proposed for lithium-ion battery performance using ML and DL techniques. We evaluate and compare the models in detail in the next sections. Finally, conclusions are presented in the last section.

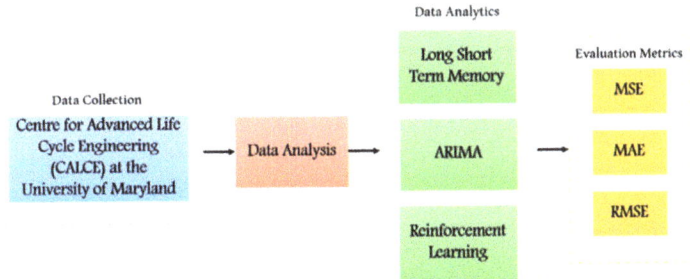

Figure 1. Prediction system for the lithium-ion batteries.

2. Related Work

In the current literature, entropy-based predictive models for battery prognostics, as well as other predictive models, have been researched and tested. Table 1 illustrates a brief overview of some of the most relevant and recently published papers that use data-driven methods for lithium-ion battery prognostics.

Table 1. An overview of different approaches to lithium-ion battery prognostics.

Ref.	Data	Methods	Results
[17]	NASA Ames Prognostics Center of Excellence (PCoE) database	Deep neural networks (DNN)	The proposed model successfully predicts the SOH and RUL of the lithium-ion battery but is less effective when real-time processing comes into play.
[18]	Center for Advanced Life Cycle Engineering (CALCE) at the University of Maryland	Deep neural networks (DNN)	The ANN predicts the battery State of Charge values with accuracy using only voltage, current, and charge/discharge time as inputs and achieves an MSE of 3.11×10^{-6}.
[19]	NASA Ames	Long short-term memory (LSTM)	The proposed model has a better performance for the time series problem of li-ion battery prognostics and a stronger learning ability of the degradation process when compared to other ANN algorithms.
[20]	NASA lithium-ion battery dataset	Long short-term memory (LSTM)	The method produces exceptional performances for RUL prediction under different loading and operating conditions.
[21]	Data repository of the NASA Ames Prognostics Center of Excellence (PCoE)	Autoregressive integrated moving average (ARIMA)	The RMSE of the model for the RUL prognostics varies in the range of 0.0026 to 0.1065.
[22]	Lithium-ion battery packs from forklifts in commercial operations	Autoregressive integrated moving average (ARIMA)	The ARIMA method can be used for SOH prognostics, but the loss function indicates further enhancement is needed for the environmental conditions.
[23]	NASA prognostic model library	Reinforcement Learning (RL)	RL model enables accurate calibration of the battery prognostics but has only been tested on simulated data and sim-to-real transfer needs to be made to test the proposed algorithm on real data.
[24]	SPMeT	Reinforcement Learning (RL)	The proposed method can extend the battery life effectively and ensure end-user convenience. However, experimental validation needs to be implemented for the optimal charging strategy.

Table 1. *Cont.*

Ref.	Data	Methods	Results
[25]	Simulated datasets	Ensemble Learning	A data-driven method known as Ensemble Learning is presented for predicting degradation in a time-varying environment.
[26]	Experimental data from multiple lithium-ion battery cells at three different temperatures	Sparse Bayesian	The authors present a Sparse Bayesian model based on sample entropy of voltages for estimating SOH and RUL. It is shown that the Sparse Bayesian model outperforms the Polynomial model with the same input and target data.
[27]	Collected data through an experimental study	Unscented Particle Filter and Support Vector Regression	A hybrid model based on a combination of a data-driven method and a model-based approach is presented, which results in higher accuracy compared to each model individually.

The literature review reveals a research gap, which can be summarized as follows. Most of the research undertaken so far has relied on traditional Machine Learning and Deep Learning methods. However, the RL method is recognized as an area with room for exploration. Based on these findings, this paper is devoted to filling this gap in the research. LSTM and ARIMA methods are also studied as state-of-the-art models, which can be developed based on the entropy measures and compared with the RL method.

The main contribution of our study is the proposal of a Reinforcement Learning model based on the permutation entropy of the voltage sequences for predicting the next-cycle battery capacity. To the best of our knowledge, an RL model for lithium-ion battery prognostics, using entropy measures as the input, has not been previously tested in the literature. Additionally, we compare the numerical results from our proposed entropy-based RL model with the results from the state-of-the-art models (i.e., ARIMA and LSMT), which are built based on entropy measures for a fair and reliable comparison.

3. Data and Battery Specifications

The datasets used in this study were retrieved from the Center for Advanced Life Cycle Engineering (CALCE) at the University of Maryland [28]. The studied batteries are graphite/LiCoO2 pouch cells with a capacity rating of 1500 mAh, weight of 30.3 gm, and dimensions of 3.4 × 84.8 × 50.1 mm, labeled as PL19, PL11, and PL09. Table 2 shows the number of cycles in each dataset.

Table 2. Battery Cycles.

Batteries	# of Cycles
PL19	526
PL11	702
PL09	528

Figure 2 illustrates the battery capacities over the number of cycles and indicates the decrease in capacities as the number of cycles increases. It can also be observed that in PL09 and PL19 capacities are discrete, while in PL11, they differ continuously.

Since the battery capacity and entropy were not observed in all cycles, we have estimated each unrecorded capacity value and its related entropy using the average of its previous and next known capacity and entropy value. By doing so, we have increased the number of data, and hence, the proposed models can be trained and tested more accurately.

Figures 3–5 indicate the resultant capacities and entropies after filling the missing data.

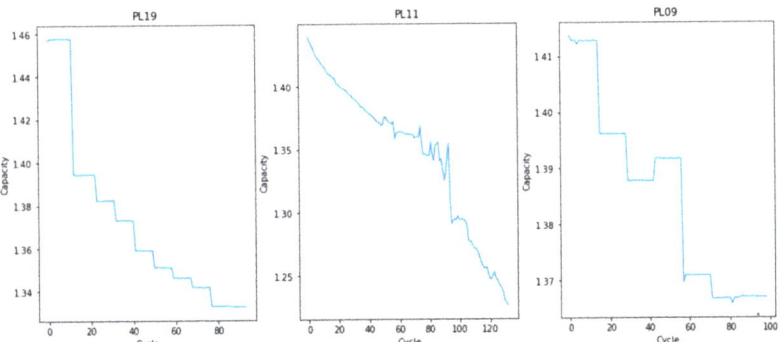

Figure 2. Capacity vs. Cycle for PL11, PL19, and PL09.

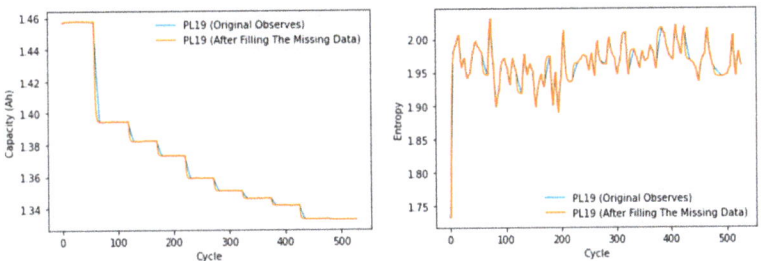

Figure 3. Capacity vs. Cycle (**left**) and Entropy vs. Cycle (**right**) for PL19.

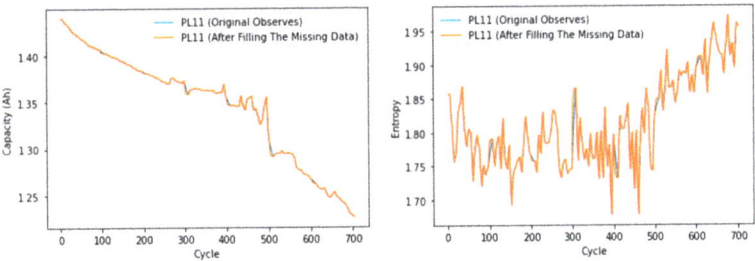

Figure 4. Capacity vs. Cycle (**left**) and Entropy vs. Cycle (**right**) for PL11.

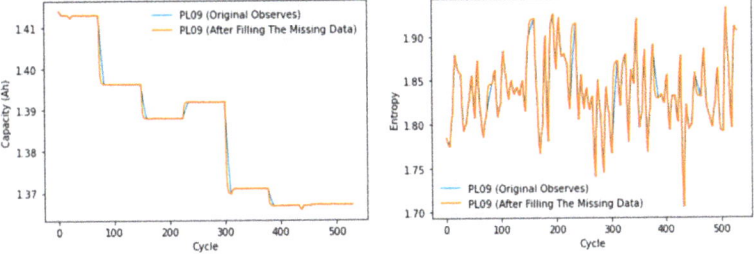

Figure 5. Capacity vs. Cycle (**left**) and Entropy vs. Cycle (**right**) for PL09.

4. Methodology

The mathematical notations used throughout this paper are summarized in Table 3.

Table 3. Glossary.

Indices	
n	Number of time series data
T	Number of times the permutation is found in time series data
Variables	
x_t	Input variable (permutation entropy of battery voltage) at step t
y_t	Observed battery capacity at step t
$\hat{y}_t$	Output variable (predicted battery capacity) at step t
h_t	Previous state at step t
c_t	Current state at step t
$\tilde{c}_t$	Intermediate cell state at step t
i_t	Input gate at step t
f_t	Forget gate at step t
o_t	Output gate at step t
p	Order of auto-regression
d	Order of difference
q	Order of moving average
s_t	State at step t
a_t	Action at step t
r_t	Reward at step t
R	Sum of the rewards
α	Learning rate
γ	Discount factor
Q_{s_t, a_t}	Q Table for states and actions at step t
Parameters	
PE	Permutation entropy
D	Order of permutation entropy
τ	Time delay in data series
V	Time series data matrix
l_i	Columns in V
π	Permutation pattern
P	Relative probability of each permutation
$W_i, W_f, W_o, W_c, U_i, U_f, U_o, U_c$	Weights in LSTM cells
b_i, b_f, b_o, b_c	bias vectors in LSTM cells
$\theta, \varnothing$	ARIMA coefficients
ε_t	Normal white noise with zero mean

In the following subsections, permutation entropy calculation and the proposed models will be discussed.

4.1. Permutation Entropy

To compute a D order permutation entropy for a one-dimensional set of time series data with n data points, the following steps are taken [29]. First, the data is partitioned into a matrix with D rows and $n - (D - 1)\tau$ columns, where τ is the delay time.

$$V = \begin{bmatrix} v(1) & v(1+\tau) & \cdots & v(1+(D-1)\tau) \\ v(2) & v(2+\tau) & \cdots & v(2+(D-1)\tau) \\ \vdots & \vdots & & \vdots \\ v(n) & v(n+\tau) & \cdots & v(n+(D-1)\tau) \end{bmatrix} \quad (1)$$

After rebuilding the data, π is defined as the permutation pattern for V columns:

$$\pi = \{l_0, l_1, \ldots, l_{D-1}\} = \{0, 1, \ldots, D-1\} \quad (2)$$

The relative probability of each permutation in π is calculated as below:

$$P(\pi) = \frac{T}{n - D + 1} \qquad (3)$$

where T is the number of times the permutation is found in the time series. Finally, the relative probabilities are used to compute the permutation entropy:

$$PE = -\sum_{i=1}^{D!} P(\pi) \log_2 P(\pi) \qquad (4)$$

An algorithm for the permutation entropy computation is presented below.

Algorithm 1: Permutation Entropy

Step1 Reshape the data series into a matrix as in Equation (1)
Step2 Find the permutation patterns π
Step3 Calculate the probability of each permutation in π
Step4 Compute PE as in Equation (4)

Permutation entropy of the coarse-grained battery voltage is extracted, as in Figure 6. Despite the noise affecting the entropies, in PL11, the differences in the entropies are relatively small compared to the earlier cycles, while the deviations increase as the number of cycles increases. In PL19, the range of entropy is approximately constant over a different number of cycles; however, in PL09, they are completely random.

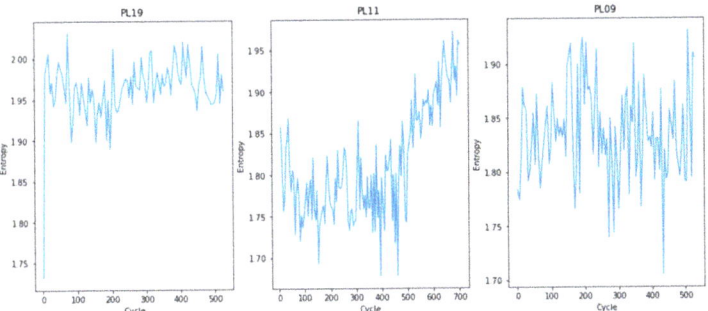

Figure 6. Entropy vs. Cycles for PL11, PL19, and PL09.

After data analysis, we split the data into train and test subsets. The proposed models utilize approximately 90% of the data for training purposes and take the rest for evaluation, as in Figure 7. The mechanism through which the training/test ration is selected is explained in the following sections.

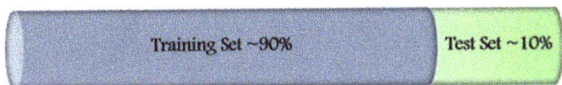

Figure 7. Train–Test split schematic.

4.2. Predictive Models

The predictive models are presented in this section as follows.

4.2.1. LSTM

Long Short-Term Memory, known simply as LSTM, is a framework for a recurrent neural network (RNN) which avoids the problem of long-term dependency. Unlike standard feedforward neural networks, LSTM has feedback connections, and hence, it can update and store necessary information. It has been widely utilized in time series forecasting in different fields of science in recent years [30].

A unit LSTM cell consists of an input gate i_t, forget gate f_t, and an output gate o_t. Each gate receives the current input x_t, the previous state h_{t-1}, and the state c_{t-1} of the cell's internal memory. x_t, h_{t-1}, and c_{t-1} are passed through non-linear functions, which yield the updated c_t and h_t [31]. Considering W_i, W_f, W_o, W_c and U_i, U_f, U_o, U_c as the correspondig weights matrices and b_i, b_f, b_o, b_c as the bias vectors, each LSTM cell operates based on the following Equations.

$$i_t = \sigma(x_t U_i + h_{t-1} W_i + b_i) \tag{5}$$

$$\tilde{c}_t = \tan h(x_t U_c + h_{t-1} W_c + b_c) \tag{6}$$

$$f_t = \sigma\left(x_t U_f + h_{t-1} W_f + b_f\right) \tag{7}$$

$$c_t = f_t * C_{t-1} + i_t * \tilde{c}_t \tag{8}$$

$$o_t = \sigma(x_t U_o + h_{t-1} W_o + b_o) \tag{9}$$

$$h_t = \tan h(c_t) * o_t \tag{10}$$

In this study, all three gates take permutation entropy of the battery voltage at cycle t and the battery capacity at cycle $t - 1$ as their input variables, x_t and c_{t-1}, and output the estimated battery capacity, $\hat{y}$, for the given inputs as shown in Figure 8. Furthermore, an algorithm is presented for the proposed LSTM model.

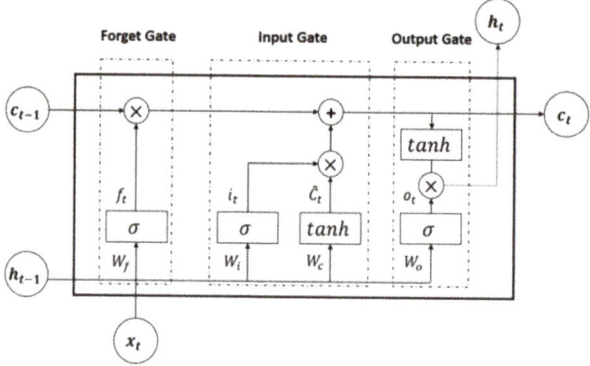

Figure 8. Schematic of a unit LSTM cell.

Algorithm 2: LSTM

Input: $x = \{PE_1. PE_2. ....PE_n\}$: Permutation Entropy of Battery Voltage and c_{t-1};
Output: $\hat{y} = \{Capacity_1.Capacity_2. ..... Capacity_n\}$: Battery Capacity;
for t in range(epoch) do
Step1 Calculate i_t
Step2 Determine $\tilde{c}_t$
Step3 Calculate f_t
Step4 Update c_t
Step5 Calculate o_t
Step6 Update h_t
Step7 Determine the output $\hat{y} = \text{LSTM}_{\text{forward}}(x)$
Step8 Compute the loss function as Equations (20)–(22)
end

4.2.2. ARIMA

The Autoregressive Integrated Moving Average (ARIMA) method is proposed as a technique for statistical analysis in time series data. An ARIMA model is a combination of the autoregressive (AR) and moving average (MA) models. The ARIMA model can be explained according to three notations—p, d, and q—which define the type of the ARIMA model:

- p : order of auto-regression
- d : order of difference
- q : order of moving average

For AR (p), we have:

$$\hat{y}_t = \varnothing_1 y_{t-1} + \varnothing_2 y_{t-2} + \cdots + \varnothing_p y_{t-p} + \varepsilon_t \tag{11}$$

MA (q) can be described as follows:

$$\hat{y}_t = \varepsilon_t - \theta_1 \varepsilon_{t-1} - \theta_2 \varepsilon_{t-2} - \cdots - \theta_q \varepsilon_{t-q} \tag{12}$$

ARMA $(p.q)$ is a combination of AR (p) and MA (q), and is described as below:

$$\hat{y}_t = \varnothing_1 y_{t-1} + \cdots + \varnothing_p y_{t-p} + \varepsilon_t - \theta_1 \varepsilon_{t-1} - \cdots - \theta_q \varepsilon_{t-q} \tag{13}$$

where y_t and $\hat{y}_t$, respectively, are the observed and estimated values; $\varnothing$ and θ, respectively, are coefficients; and ε_t is a normal white noise process with zero mean.

ARIMA is an advanced version of ARMA, which also works well for non-stationary time series data. To convert the non-stationary to stationary data, a data transformation is needed using a d-order difference equation [32]. Consequently, ARIMA $(p.d.q)$ can be described as Equation (14).

$$\hat{w}_t = \varnothing_1 w_{t-1} + \cdots + \varnothing_p w_{t-p} + \varepsilon_t - \theta_1 \varepsilon_{t-1} \cdots - \theta_q \varepsilon_{t-q} \tag{14}$$

where $w_t = \nabla^d y_t$ and ∇ is the gradient operator. When $d = 0$, Equation (14) is the same as Equation (13) and, thus, ARIMA acts the same as ARMA. p and q are initialized using the autocorrelation function (ACF) and partial autocorrelation function (PAFC).

AFC measures the average correlation between data points in a time series and previous values of the series measured for different lag lengths. PACF is the same as ACF, except that each correlation controls for any correlation between observations of a shorter lag length [32].

Figure 9 demonstrates the ARIMA framework from the input data stage through the prediction stage.

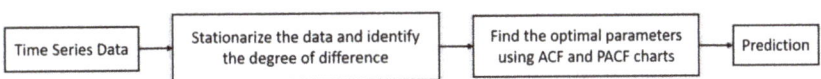

Figure 9. ARIMA framework.

In this study, an ARIMA model is proposed to predict future battery capacities. Since we are working with a non-stationary time series, we have made a data transformation with $d = 1$. p and q, respectively, are set to 5 and 0, and thus, predictions were made with ARIMA (5.1.0). The rationale behind choosing the order of the ARIMA model is as follows. We compare the results from a range of non-negative integers, $p = [1, 10]$ (extracted from the existing literature), and select the optimal number of time lags for the autoregressive model, which results in minimal errors compared to other orders in that range. The results from the optimal model are displayed and reported here.

There is a battery voltage sequence at each cycle (i.e., a time series of voltages at each cycle). We first compute the permutation entropy of each voltage sequence according to the corresponding algorithm; then, we use the time series of the permutation entropy measures (i.e., one entropy measure at each cycle) as an input in the ARIMA model, compare them with the deviations in the battery capacities, and predict the next-cycle battery capacity as an output of the model.

An algorithm for the ARIMA model is presented as follows.

Algorithm 3: ARIMA

Input: $x = \{PE_1.PE_2.\ldots.PE_n\}$: Permutation Entropy of Battery Voltage Sequences at each Cycle;
Output: $\hat{y} = \{Capacity_1.Capacity_2\ldots.Capacity_n\}$: Battery Capacity;

- Make time series data stationary with appropriate d;
- Initialize p and q using ACP and PACF;
- Fit ARIMA $(p.d.q)$ to data;
- Predict the next-cycle capacity as Equation (14);
- Calculate the loss function using Equations (20)–(22).

4.2.3. Reinforcement Learning

Reinforcement Learning (RL) is a type of multi-layered neural network, and has become a focus of research in modern artificial intelligence. The concept is based on rewarding or punishing an agent's performance in a specific environment. A state is a description of the environment made to provide the necessary information for the agent to decide at each time step. For each and every state s, the agent has a number of selecting actions a to make decisions from. A policy is required, based on a cost function, to map each state to the optimal action with the consideration of maximizing its reward function during the episode [33].

Reinforcement Learning has real-life applications in various fields such as driving cars, landing rockets, trading and finance, diagnosing patients, and so on. This Deep Learning technique differs from supervised learning, as it does not require correct sets of actions and labeled input/output pairs [34]. Instead, the goal is to find a balance between exploration and exploitation. Figure 10 illustrates the schematic of a general Reinforcement Learning structure and its Equations are described as follows.

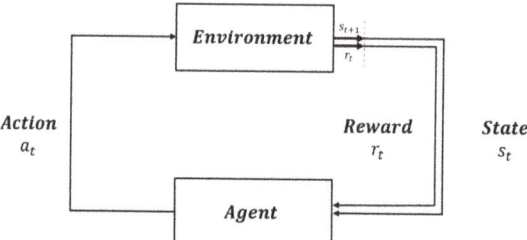

Figure 10. Reinforcement Learning Schematic.

$$a_t \sim \pi(a_t|s_t) \tag{15}$$

$$s_{t+1} \sim f_{state}(s_{t+1}|s_t.a_t) \tag{16}$$

$$r_{t+1} = f_{reward}(s_t.a_t.s_{t+1}) \tag{17}$$

$$R = \sum_{t=0}^{\infty} \gamma^t r_{t+1} \tag{18}$$

$$Q^{new}_{s_t.a_t} = Q^{old}_{s.a_t} + \alpha \left(\overbrace{r_t + \gamma max Q^{next\ s-a}_{s_{t+1}.a}}^{Target} - \overbrace{Q^{Q}_{s_t.a_t}}^{Prediction} \right) \tag{19}$$

In this study, we have considered the permutation entropy of the battery voltage as the states and the capacities as the actions, which should be taken at each state based on the given entropy. An algorithm for the RL model is presented in the following.

Algorithm 4: Reinforcement Learning

States: $s = \{PE_1. PE_2. \ldots .PE_n\}$: Permutation Entropy of Battery Voltage;
Actions: $a = \{Capacity_1 . Capacity_2. \ldots . Capacity_n\}$: Battery Capacity;
Define the optimal policy;
Initialize the parameters α and γ;
for t in range (epoch) **do**
Calculate a_t using the optimal policy
Determine s_{t+1} as a function of the state and the previous state and action
Compute r_{t+1} and R
Update Q_{s_t, a_t} using Equation (19)
Evaluate the estimation using the following loss function as in Equations (20)–(22)
end

The hyperparameters of the proposed models define how they are structured. Optimal hyperparameters are approximated so that the loss is reduced. In other words, we explore various model architectures and search for the optimal values in the hyperparameter space to minimize the resulting performance metrics; for instance, Mean Squared Error. For this purpose, in the three models, grid search is used for tuning the hyperparameters and achieving reliable comparisons between the numerical results from the models. A model is built for each possible combination of all of the hyperparameter values; next, the models are evaluated based on the performance metrics, and then the architecture which produces the best results is selected. The results and findings are reported in the following section.

5. Results and Findings

The numerical results and findings are presented in this section as follows.

5.1. Performance Measures

To evaluate the performance of the proposed models, we present the observed and predicted battery capacities for ARIMA and LSTM models and the reward and loss functions obtained from the RL model. Furthermore, we compare the observed and predicted battery capacities gained from each of these models using three performance metrics [35] as shown below:

Mean Squared Error (MSE):

$$\text{MSE} = \frac{1}{n}\sum_{t=1}^{n}(y_t - \hat{y}_t)^2 \qquad (20)$$

Mean Absolute Error (MAE):

$$\text{MAE} = \frac{1}{n}\sum_{t=1}^{n}|y_t - \hat{y}_t| \qquad (21)$$

Root Mean Squared Error (RMSE):

$$\text{RMSE} = \sqrt{\text{MSE}} = \sqrt{\frac{1}{n}\sum_{t=1}^{n}(y_t - \hat{y}_t)^2} \qquad (22)$$

where y_t and $\hat{y}_t$, respectively, are the observed and predicted capacity at cycle t, and n is the number of test data.

5.2. Numerical Results

The observed and predicted battery capacities results from ARIMA and LSTM models are shown in Figures 11–13. Based on the graphs obtained, it can be seen that in all three datasets the ARIMA model predictions are following the trends in the test data, and so, yields better results as compared to the LSTM model for predicting the time series of battery capacities.

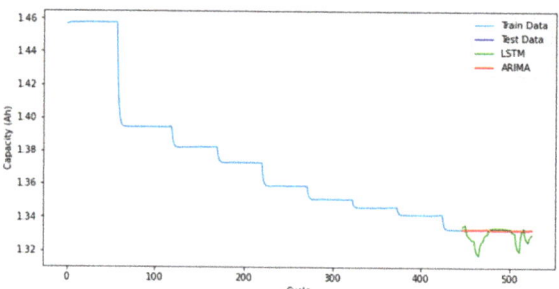

Figure 11. Train, test, and predicted data results from ARIMA and LSTM models for PL19.

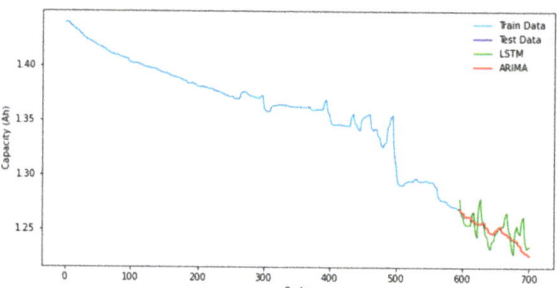

Figure 12. Train, test, and predicted data results from ARIMA and LSTM models for PL11.

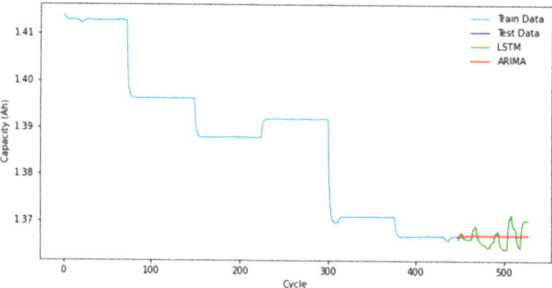

Figure 13. Train, test, and predicted data results from ARIMA and LSTM models for PL09.

The early battery-life prediction, which includes a prediction of the battery cycles at earlier cycles, is performed, and the results are displayed in Figures 14–16. It is observed that the deviation between the predicted capacities and the actual capacities are not significant, indicating that the proposed ARIMA and LSTM models are capable of predicting battery capacities at earlier cycles.

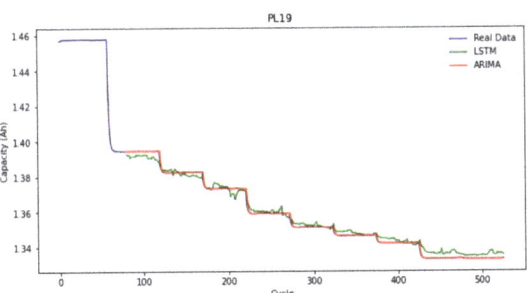

Figure 14. Train, test, and predicted data results from ARIMA and LSTM models for PL19.

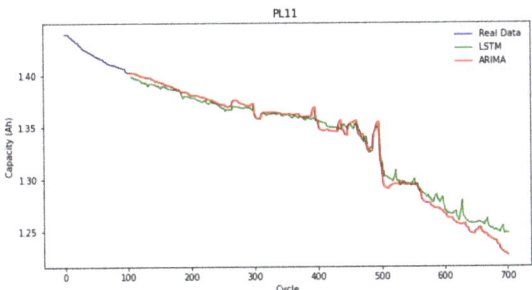

Figure 15. Train, test, and predicted data results from ARIMA and LSTM models for PL11.

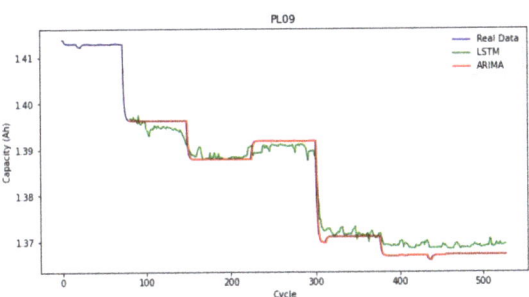

Figure 16. Train, test, and predicted data results from ARIMA and LSTM models for PL09.

In the RL model, as demonstrated in Figure 17, the reward values have an impressive increase and immediately become stable with some noise. The loss values increase at first; however, after approximately 250 epochs, they decline to 0, which verifies the procedure of Reinforcement Learning.

To find the best data split ratio, our proposed RL approach is initially trained using shuffled datasets with five different training ratios (70%, 75%, 80%, 85%, and 90%). Afterwards, Mean Squared Error (MSE) is utilized as a loss function to evaluate the obtained results. Based on Table 4, the best accuracy is gained by using 90% of each dataset for training purposes and using the rest for the testing process (Figure 18). Finally, this ratio is applied to training the other two models (LSTM and ARIMA). To save space, the results from the LSTM and ARIMA models are not reported here. The results from the other two models are consistent with those from RL (i.e., the best training ratio of 10%).

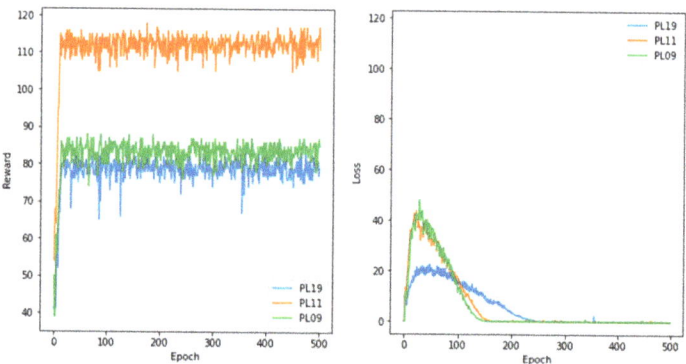

Figure 17. Reward and Loss Function (RL model).

Table 4. MSE Value for Different Training Ratios for the RL model.

Battery	Training Ratio				
	70%	75%	80%	85%	90%
PL19	0.0422	0.0618	0.0179	0.0008	0.0002
PL11	0.0718	0.0465	0.0153	0.0156	0.0084
PL09	0.0209	0.0007	0.0006	0.0003	0.0003

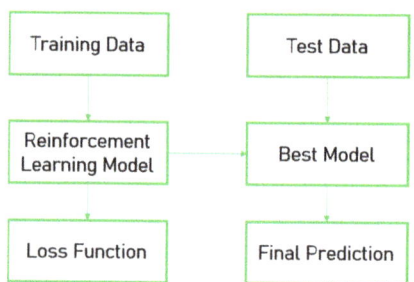

Figure 18. Finding the best Train–Test Split.

5.3. Comparisons

Tables 5–7 represent a snapshot comparison of the aforesaid models for the PL19, PL11, and PL09 datasets, respectively. As the results show, in all datasets, ARIMA slightly surpasses the LSTM and RL models since it results in the smallest MSE, MAE, and RMSE values. However, the differences are not significant, and for PL19 and PL11, ARIMA and RL yield approximately the same values of performance measures. It is concluded that LSTM and RL also result in minor errors.

Table 5. MSE, MAE, and RMSE values for the predictive models (PL19).

Evaluation Metric	LSTM	ARIMA	RL
MSE	0.00003	0.00001	0.0002
MAE	0.00417	0.00001	0.00005
RMSE	0.00580	0.00003	0.00009

Table 6. MSE, MAE, and RMSE values for the predictive models (PL11).

Evaluation Metric	LSTM	ARIMA	RL
MSE	0.00011	0.00001	0.0084
MAE	0.00012	0.00026	0.00054
RMSE	0.01095	0.00066	0.00090

Table 7. MSE, MAE, and RMSE values for the predictive models (PL09).

Evaluation Metric	LSTM	ARIMA	RL
MSE	0.00001	0.00001	0.0003
MAE	0.00171	0.00001	0.03997
RMSE	0.00200	0.00002	0.05751

From Tables 5–7, it is observed that the ARIMA model yields smaller errors compared to the LSTM model. ARIMA, which is a mean-reverting process, has the ability to predict battery capacities with smaller deviations. However, the LSTM model—which is a recurrent network—attempts to avoid the long-term dependency by storing only necessary information, and thus, it is unable to probabilistically exclude the input (i.e., previous permutation entropy of battery voltage sequences) and the recurrent connections to the units of the network from the activation and weight updates while the model is being trained. Consequently, the deviations between the actual battery capacities and the predicted capacities resulting from the LSTM model are greater than those resulting from the ARIMA model. The results displayed on Figures 11–13 are consistent with the Tables.

6. Conclusions

In lithium-ion battery applications, failures in the system can be minimized by performing prognostics and health management. Data-driven methods are one way of doing so, and identify the optimal replacement intervals or the optimal time for changing the battery in an appropriate manner. This paper presents three different models (LSTM, ARIMA, and RL), which all are built based on the permutation entropies of the battery voltage sequences, for next-cycle battery capacity prediction using the status of the previous states. In various data conditions, different models may be required; having a collection of models, even for the same purpose, can be useful. In addition to accurate prediction of battery capacities based on the ARIMA model, it is shown that the LSTM and the proposed entropy-based RL models have similar performance and both result in small errors.

Author Contributions: Conceptualization, A.N.; methodology, A.N.; software and coding, M.A.S. and A.N.; validation, A.N. and M.A.S.; formal analysis, M.A.S. and A.N.; model and algorithm design, M.A.S. and A.N.; investigation, A.N.; resources, A.N.; data curation, A.N.; writing—original draft preparation, M.A.S. and A.N.; writing—review and editing, A.N. and M.A.S.; visualization, M.A.S. and A.N.; supervision, A.N. and T.S.D.; project administration, A.N. and T.S.D. All authors have read and agreed to the published version of the manuscript.

Funding: This research received no external funding.

Institutional Review Board Statement: Not applicable.

Informed Consent Statement: Not applicable.

Data Availability Statement: The data presented in this study are available on request from Dr. Alireza Namdari.

Conflicts of Interest: The authors declare no conflict of interest.

References

1. Shimamura, O.; Abe, T.; Watanabe, K.; Ohsawa, Y.; Horie, H. Research and development work on lithium-ion batteries for environmental vehicles. *World Electr. Veh. J.* **2007**, *1*, 251–257. [CrossRef]
2. Jaguemont, J.; Boulon, L.; Dubé, Y. A comprehensive review of lithium-ion batteries used in hybrid and electric vehicles at cold temperatures. *Appl. Energy* **2016**, *164*, 99–114. [CrossRef]
3. Han, X.; Lu, L.; Zheng, Y.; Feng, X.; Li, Z.; Li, J.; Ouyang, M. A review on the key issues of the lithium ion battery degradation among the whole life cycle. *eTransportation* **2019**, *1*, 100005. [CrossRef]
4. Wu, L.; Fu, X.; Guan, Y. Review of the remaining useful life prognostics of vehicle lithium-ion batteries using data-driven methodologies. *Appl. Sci.* **2016**, *6*, 166. [CrossRef]
5. Williard, N.; He, W.; Hendricks, C.; Pecht, M. Lessons learned from the 787 dreamliner issue on lithium-ion battery reliability. *Energies* **2013**, *6*, 4682–4695. [CrossRef]
6. Ge, M.F.; Liu, Y.; Jiang, X.; Liu, J. A review on state of health estimations and remaining useful life prognostics of lithium-ion batteries. *Measurement* **2021**, *174*, 109057. [CrossRef]
7. Li, X.; Zhang, L.; Wang, Z.; Dong, P. Remaining useful life prediction for lithium-ion batteries based on a hybrid model combining the long short-term memory and Elman neural networks. *J. Energy Storage* **2019**, *21*, 510–518. [CrossRef]
8. Li, P.; Zhang, Z.; Xiong, Q.; Ding, B.; Hou, J.; Luo, D.; Rong, Y.; Li, S. State-of-health estimation and remaining useful life prediction for the lithium-ion battery based on a variant long short term memory neural network. *J. Power Sources* **2020**, *459*, 228069. [CrossRef]
9. Tran, M.K.; Panchal, S.; Khang, T.D.; Panchal, K.; Fraser, R.; Fowler, M. Concept review of a cloud-based smart battery management system for lithium-ion batteries: Feasibility, logistics, and functionality. *Batteries* **2022**, *8*, 19. [CrossRef]
10. Atkins, P. *The Laws of Thermodynamics: A Very Short Introduction*; Oxford University Press (OUP): Oxford, UK, 2010.
11. Namdari, A.; Li, Z.S. A Multiscale Entropy-Based Long Short Term Memory Model for Lithium-Ion Battery Prognostics. In Proceedings of the 2021 IEEE International Conference on Prognostics and Health Management (ICPHM), Detroit, MI, USA, 7–9 June 2021; pp. 1–6.
12. Bandt, C.; Pompe, B. Permutation entropy: A natural complexity measure for time series. *Phys. Rev. Lett.* **2002**, *88*, 174102. [CrossRef]
13. Awad, M.; Khanna, R. *Efficient Learning Machines: Theories, Concepts, and Applications for Engineers and System Designers*; Springer Nature: Berlin/Heidelberg, Germany, 2015.
14. Singh, B.; Desai, R.; Ashar, H.; Tank, P.; Katre, N. A Trade-off between ML and DL Techniques in Natural Language Processing. In *Journal of Physics: Conference Series*; IOP Publishing: Bristol, UK, 2021; Volume 1831, p. 0120025.
15. Zhang, Y.; Xiong, R.; He, H.; Pecht, M.G. Long short-term memory recurrent neural network for remaining useful life prediction of lithium-ion batteries. *IEEE Trans. Veh. Technol.* **2018**, *67*, 5695–5705. [CrossRef]
16. Li, W.; Cui, H.; Nemeth, T.; Jansen, J.; Uenluebayir, C.; Wei, Z.; Zhang, L.; Wang, Z.; Ruan, J.; Dai, H.; et al. Deep reinforcement learning-based energy management of hybrid battery systems in electric vehicles. *J. Energy Storage* **2021**, *36*, 102355. [CrossRef]
17. Khumprom, P.; Yodo, N. A data-driven predictive prognostic model for lithium-ion batteries based on a deep learning algorithm. *Energies* **2019**, *12*, 660. [CrossRef]
18. Almeida, G.; Souza, A.C.; Ribeiro, P.F. A Neural Network Application for a Lithium-Ion Battery Pack State-of-Charge Estimator with Enhanced Accuracy. In Multidisciplinary Digital Publishing Institute Proceedings. *Proceedings* **2020**, *58*, 33. [CrossRef]
19. Long, B.; Li, X.; Gao, X.; Liu, Z. Prognostics comparison of lithium-ion battery based on the shallow and deep neural networks model. *Energies* **2019**, *12*, 3271. [CrossRef]
20. Hinchi, A.Z.; Tkiouat, M. A deep long-short-term-memory neural network for lithium-ion battery prognostics. In Proceedings of the International Conference on Industrial Engineering and Operations Management, Paris, France, 26–27 July 2018; pp. 2162–2168.
21. Chen, L.; Xu, L.; Zhou, Y. Novel approach for lithium-ion battery on-line remaining useful life prediction based on permutation entropy. *Energies* **2018**, *11*, 820. [CrossRef]
22. Huotari, M.; Arora, S.; Malhi, A.; Främling, K. A Dynamic Battery State-of-Health Forecasting Model for Electric Trucks: Li-Ion Batteries Case-Study. In Proceedings of the ASME International Mechanical Engineering Congress and Exposition, Portland, OR, USA, 16–19 November 2020; Volume 84560, p. V008T08A021.
23. Unagar, A.; Tian, Y.; Chao, M.A.; Fink, O. Learning to Calibrate Battery Models in Real-Time with Deep Reinforcement Learning. *Energies* **2021**, *14*, 1361. [CrossRef]
24. Kim, M.; Baek, J.; Han, S. Optimal Charging Method for Effective Li-ion Battery Life Extension Based on Reinforcement Learning. *arXiv* **2020**, arXiv:2005.08770.
25. Wang, L.; Lu, D.; Wang, X.; Pan, R.; Wang, Z. Ensemble learning for predicting degradation under time-varying environment. *Qual. Reliab. Eng. Int.* **2020**, *36*, 1205–1223. [CrossRef]
26. Hu, X.; Jiang, J.; Cao, D.; Egardt, B. Battery health prognosis for electric vehicles using sample entropy and sparse Bayesian predictive modeling. *IEEE Trans. Ind. Electron.* **2015**, *63*, 2645–2656. [CrossRef]
27. Peng, X.; Zhang, C.; Yu, Y.; Zhou, Y. Battery remaining useful life prediction algorithm based on support vector regression and unscented particle filter. In Proceedings of the 2016 IEEE International Conference on Prognostics and Health Management (ICPHM), Ottawa, ON, Canada, 20–22 June 2016; pp. 1–6.

28. He, W.; Williard, N.; Osterman, M.; Pecht, M. Prognostics of lithium-ion batteries based on Dempster–Shafer theory and the Bayesian Monte Carlo method. *J. Power Sources* **2011**, *196*, 10314–10321. [CrossRef]
29. Namdari, A.; Li, Z. A review of entropy measures for uncertainty quantification of stochastic processes. *Adv. Mech. Eng.* **2019**, *11*, 1687814019857350. [CrossRef]
30. Sak, H.; Senior, A.; Beaufays, F. Long short-term memory based recurrent neural network architectures for large vocabulary speech recognition. *arXiv* **2014**, arXiv:1402.1128.
31. Elsaraiti, M.; Merabet, A. Application of Long-Short-Term-Memory Recurrent Neural Networks to Forecast Wind Speed. *Appl. Sci.* **2021**, *11*, 2387. [CrossRef]
32. Box, G.E.; Jenkins, G.M.; Reinsel, G.C.; Ljung, G.M. *Time Series Analysis: Forecasting and Control*; John Wiley & Sons: Hoboken, NJ, USA, 2015.
33. Abedi, S.; Yoon, S.W.; Kwon, S. Battery energy storage control using a reinforcement learning approach with cyclic time-dependent Markov process. *Int. J. Electr. Power Energy Syst.* **2022**, *134*, 107368. [CrossRef]
34. Haney, B. Reinforcement Learning Patents: A Transatlantic Review. In *Transatlantic Technology Law Forum*; Working Paper Series; Stanford Law School: Stanford, CA, USA, 2020.
35. Namdari, A.; Li, Z.S. An Entropy-based Approach for Modeling Lithium-Ion Battery Capacity Fade. In Proceedings of the 2020 Annual Reliability and Maintainability Symposium (RAMS), Palm Springs, CA, USA, 27–30 January 2020; pp. 1–7.

Article

Convolutional Neural Networks: A Roundup and Benchmark of Their Pooling Layer Variants

Nikolaos-Ioannis Galanis, Panagiotis Vafiadis, Kostas-Gkouram Mirzaev and George A. Papakostas *

MLV Research Group, Department of Computer Science, International Hellenic University, 65404 Kavala, Greece
* Correspondence: gpapak@cs.ihu.gr

Abstract: One of the essential layers in most Convolutional Neural Networks (CNNs) is the pooling layer, which is placed right after the convolution layer, effectively downsampling the input and reducing the computational power required. Different pooling methods have been proposed over the years, each with its own advantages and disadvantages, rendering them a better fit for different applications. We introduce a benchmark between many of these methods that highlights an optimal choice for different scenarios depending on each project's individual needs, whether it is detail retention, performance, or overall computational speed requirements.

Keywords: Convolutional Neural Network (CNN); pooling; deep learning; computer vision; image analysis; benchmark

Citation: Galanis, N.-I.; Vafiadis, P.; Mirzaev, K.-G.; Papakostas, G.A. Convolutional Neural Networks: A Roundup and Benchmark of Their Pooling Layer Variants. *Algorithms* **2022**, *15*, 391. https://doi.org/10.3390/a15110391

Academic Editor: Frank Werner

Received: 9 September 2022
Accepted: 18 October 2022
Published: 23 October 2022

Publisher's Note: MDPI stays neutral with regard to jurisdictional claims in published maps and institutional affiliations.

Copyright: © 2022 by the authors. Licensee MDPI, Basel, Switzerland. This article is an open access article distributed under the terms and conditions of the Creative Commons Attribution (CC BY) license (https://creativecommons.org/licenses/by/4.0/).

1. Introduction

Computer vision can be described as the way machines interpret images and is a field of AI that trains computers to comprehend the visual world [1]. During the last 20 years, computer vision has evolved rapidly, with deep learning and especially Deep Convolutional Neural Networks (D-CNNs) standing out among other methodologies. The accuracy rates for object classification and identification have increased to the point of being comparable to that of humans, enabling quick automated image detection and reactions to optical inputs.

CNNs are considered unquestionably the most significant artificial neural network architecture for any computer vision and image analysis project at the moment. Making an appearance in the 1950s with simple and complex cell biological experiments [2,3] and officially introduced in the 1980s [4] as a neural network model for a mechanism of visual pattern recognition, they have progressed greatly over the last years until today's complex pre-trained computer vision models. One of the main applications of deep learning and CNN's is that of image classification where the system tries to identify a scene or an object inside it. CNNs can also be taken a step further, by using one or more bounding boxes to recognize and locate multiple objects inside an image.

Many traditional machine learning models such as Support Vector Machine (SVM) [5] or K-Nearest Neighbor (KNN) [6] were used for image classification before CNNs, where each individual pixel was considered a feature. With CNNs, the convolution layer was introduced, breaking down the image into multiple features, which are used for predicting the output values. However, since convolution itself is a demanding computation, pooling was introduced to make the overall process less resource intensive along the network. This method reduces the overall amount of computations required, essentially downsampling the input every time it is applied while trying to maintain the most important information.

In this review, we attempt to summarize many of the pooling variants along with the advantages and disadvantages of each individual method, while also comparing their performance in a classification scenario with three different datasets.

Initially, the pooling methods are presented one by one, providing an overview of each approach. In the end, we summarize the models and datasets that each method uses in a table, as a preamble to the testing methodology, which is explained right after. Finally, we present and analyze our benchmark results, focusing on the performance and ability to retain the details of the original input.

2. Materials and Methods

2.1. Related Work

The following content is separated into two sections: a roundup of pooling methods summarizing each approach and a benchmark of their performance taking into account multiple factors, focusing on 2D image applications. There have been some review papers on this subject in the past, mostly summarizing the theory behind individual proposals.

Some of them are quite extensive [7,8] and may reference the test results from various external sources [8], though this type of compilation is not ideal for a direct comparison since each experiment is performed under different conditions (model, hardware, etc.). Others focus on deep architectures or neural networks in general, including only some of the pooling methods along with their main research subject [9,10]. In some cases, there are even small-scale tests, but they are targeted at very specific use cases, such as medical data [11].

To our best knowledge, though the subject is similar—which may cause some overlapping content—there has not been an extended benchmark implementation using the same environment so that there can be a direct comparison between the methods' performances.

2.2. Pooling the Literature

The publications that this review was based on were located by searching for a combination of the terms "Pooling" and "CNN" or "Convolution" (and their derivatives, such as "convolutional") in the title, keywords, and abstract. After shortlisting some of the results, further literature was added by extensively searching through references and related publications of the initially selected papers, focusing on the applications of CNNs and not the generic subject. While there are some references in 1990 when Yamaguchi introduced the concept of Max pooling [12], most pooling proposals and ideas appear to be chronologically placed in the last decade. Figure 1 shows a steady interest in the general subject of pooling for the last decade, perhaps with small increases or decreases per year.

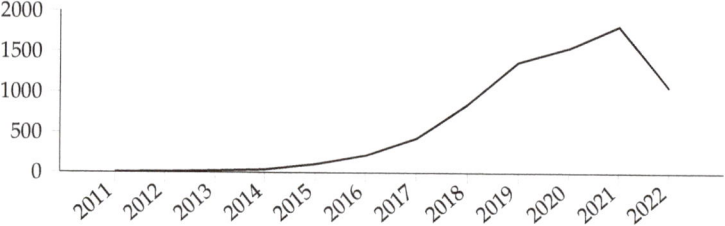

Figure 1. Publications for total results about pooling for CNNs in Scopus.

2.3. Let the Pooling Begin

Three of the most common pooling methods are Max pooling, Min pooling, and Average pooling. As their names suggest, for every area of the input where the sliding window focuses, the maximum, minimum, or average value is calculated accordingly.

Average pooling (also referred to as Mean pooling) has the drawback that it takes into consideration all values regardless of their magnitude, and even worse, in some cases (depending on the activation function that is used), strong positive and negative activations can cancel each other out completely.

On the other hand, Max pooling captures the strongest activations while ignoring other weaker activations that might be equally important, thus erasing input data, while also tending to overfit frequently and not generalizing very well. While most of the other methods try to either improve, combine, or even completely replace these "basics", they still tend to be widely used due to their efficiency, ease of use, and low computational power required. Let us explore each of the available methods in detail.

2.3.1. Max and Min Pooling

Max pooling is one of the most-common pooling methods, which selects the maximum element from the area of the feature map covered by the kernel applied, as seen in Figure 2. Depending on the filter and stride, the outcome is a feature map having the most distinguished features of the input [13]. On the other hand, Min pooling does the exact opposite, selecting the minimum element from the selected area. As expected, Max pooling tends to retain the lighter parts of the input when it comes to images, while Min pooling does the same with the darker parts.

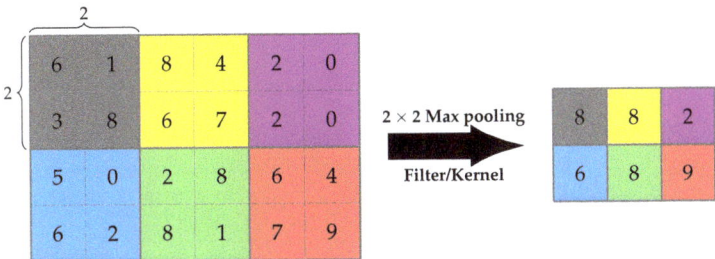

Figure 2. An example of Max pooling's functionality [14].

2.3.2. Fractional Max Pooling

Fractional Max Pooling (FMP) [15] is, as its name suggests, a variant of Max pooling, but the reduction ratio can be a fraction as well, instead of an integer. The most important parameter is the scaling factor a by which the input image will be downscaled, with $1 < a < 2$. Considering an input of size $N_{in} \times N_{in}$, we select two sequences of integers a_i, b_i that start at 1, and they are incremented by 1 or 2 and end at N_{in}. These sequences can be either completely random or pseudorandom when they follow the equation $a_i = ceil(a*(i+u))$, where a is the scaling factor and u is a number in the range (0, 1). Then, the input is split into pooling regions, either disjoint or overlapping using the respective variant of Formula (1), and the Max value for each region is retained.

$$P_{i,j} = [a_{i-1}, a_i - 1] \times [b_{j-1}, b_j - 1] \text{ or } P_{i,j} = [a_{i-1}, a_i] \times [b_{j-1}, b_j] \qquad (1)$$

where

P : the pooling region
a_i, b_i : integer sequences according to the FMP algorithm

According to the writers' experiments, overlapping FMP seems to have better results than the disjoint alternative, while a random choice of the sequences a_i, b_i distorts the image, in contrast with the pseudorandom ones. Overall, FMP's performance appears to be better than that of Max pooling.

2.3.3. Row-Wise Max-Pooling

Row-wise Max pooling is referred to alongside a deep panoramic representation for 3D shape classification and recognition called DeepPano [16]. A panoramic view is created from the projection of the 3D model as a cylinder to its principle axis. The pooling layer is placed after the last convolution layer and uses the highest value of each row in the input map. The suggested methodology appears to be rotation-invariant according to the experiments, since its output is not affected by the rotation of the 3D shape input.

2.3.4. Average Pooling

Average pooling has a similar function as Max pooling, but it calculates the average value of the pooled area [17], as seen in Figure 3.

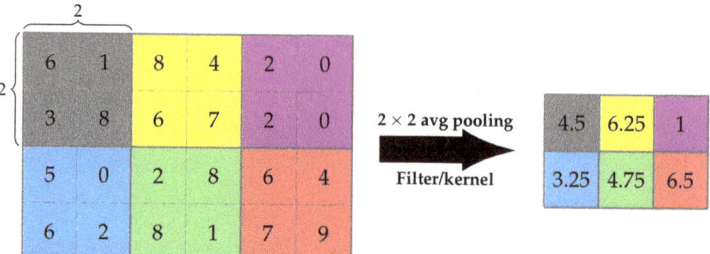

Figure 3. An example of Average pooling's functionality [14].

Average pooling, in contrast to Max pooling, which seeks the top features, extracts a patch of features, makes some calculations based on them, and returns a smoother result. This may lead to lower accuracy. In general, it depends on the density of the features (pixels) and the use of the output product.

2.3.5. Rank-Based Pooling

The rank-based pooling methods [18] are an alternative to Max pooling, with three variants: rank-based Average pooling (RAP), rank-based weighted pooling (RWP), and rank-based stochastic pooling (RSP). The most-important characteristics of these methods are:

- The top features can be easily identified by their ranks.
- Ranks remain slightly unchanged from the activation values.
- Ranking can avoid scaling across value-based methods.

Before applying any of the three methods, the ranking process takes place, where an activation function is applied to the individual elements, and they are sorted in descending order according to that function's value.

RAP attempts to resolve the main issues of Max and Average pooling, which are the information loss of non-Max values in Max pooling and the information being downgraded due to near-zero negative activations in Average pooling. It does so by using an average of the top t important features, where t is a predefined downsizing threshold—if we want to downsize, for instance, by a factor of 2 and the kernel has a size of 2 × 2, t will have the value of 2 as well. Then, we set weights for all the elements within the kernel, with the top t having a weight of 1/t, whereas all other weights are set to 0, and the output is calculated from Equation (2).

$$s_j = \frac{1}{t} \sum_{i \in R_j, r_i \leq t} a_i \qquad (2)$$

where a is the activation function value and t is the rank threshold that determines which activation affects the averaging.

RWP takes into consideration that each region in an image might not be equally important, thus setting rank-based weights for each activation. Thus, the pooling output now changes to Equation (3).

$$s_j = \frac{1}{t} \sum_{i \in R_j} p_i a_i \qquad (3)$$

where a is the activation value and the probability p that is used for each weight is given by the ranking Equation (4) where b is a hyper-parameter, r is the rank of activations, and n is the size of the pooling area.

$$p_r = b(1-b)^{r-1}, r = 1, \ldots n \tag{4}$$

Lastly, Equation (5) is used for RSP in a very similar way to RWP.

$$s_j = \alpha_i, \text{where } i \sim Multinomial(p_1, \ldots, p_n) \tag{5}$$

where α is the activation value for each element in the pooled region. Then, the final activation values are sampled based on probabilities p calculated by a multinomial distribution, based on Formula (4).

2.3.6. Mixed, Gated, and Tree Pooling

Mixed pooling [19] combines Max and Average pooling, selecting one of these two methods, outperforming both of them when used separately. Lee et al. proposed two different variants along with the base one: mixed Max–Average pooling, and gated Max–Average pooling, along with an alternative method for tree pooling. An overview of the three methods can be seen in Figure 4.

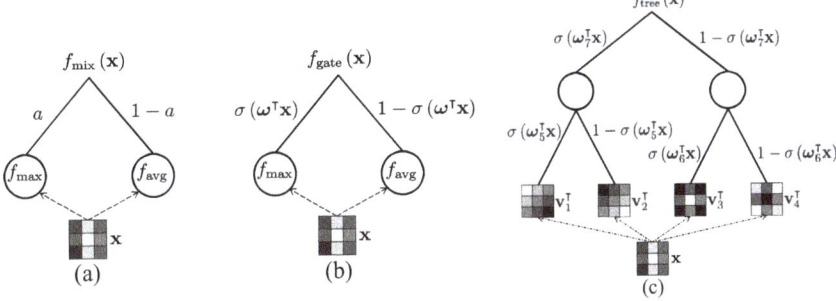

Figure 4. A schematic comparison of the three proposed operations in [19]: (**a**) mixed Max–Average pooling, (**b**) gated Max–Average pooling and (**c**) tree pooling with 3-level binary tree.

In **mixed Max–Average pooling**, a parameter a is learned and can be different per the whole network, per layer, or per pooling region. Then, the output of the pooling layer is computed by Equation (6):

$$f_{\text{mix}}(x) = a f_{\text{Max}}(x) + (1-a) f_{\text{avg}}(x) \tag{6}$$

where:

- x : the input to be pooled;
- a : a learned parameter;
- $\sigma(w^T x)$: a sigmoid function, $1/(1 + exp(-w^T x))$.

In **gated Max–Average pooling**, a mask of weights is learned and the inner product of that mask with the pooled region passed through a sigmoid function is used to decide whether to use Max or Average pooling. This mask can differ per network, layer, or region. The output is then calculated as described in Equation (7). According to the method's paper [19], in a comparison between this method and mixed Max–Average pooling, it appears that the gated variant performs consistently better.

$$f_{\text{gate}}(x) = \sigma(w^T x) f_{\text{Max}}(x) + (1 - \sigma(w^T x)) f_{\text{avg}}(x) \tag{7}$$

where:

x	: the input to be pooled;
w	: the learned mask of weights;
T	: the transpose operator;
$\sigma(w^T x)$	: a sigmoid function, $1/(1 + exp(-w^T x))$.

A third alternative was proposed in the same paper for **tree pooling**, where a binary tree is used and the pooling filters are learned. The tree level is a pre-defined parameter, and each node holds a learned pooling filter. Furthermore, gating masks are used in a similar way as described for gated pooling previously. Thus, the pooling result for each node is described by the function (8), and the output of the pooling method is the calculated output for the root node.

$$f_m(x) = \begin{cases} v_m^T & \text{if leaf node} \\ \sigma(w_m^T x) f_{m,left}(x) + (1 - \sigma(w_m^T x)) f_{m,right}(x) & \text{if internal node} \end{cases} \quad (8)$$

where:

v	: the learned filter for each node;
w	: the learned mask of weights;
m	: the tree node index;
T	: the transpose operator;
$\sigma(w_m^T x)$	: a sigmoid function, $1/(1 + exp(-w_m^T x))$.

2.3.7. LP Pooling

Sermanet et al. [20] proposed LP pooling as part of an architecture to recognize house numbers. It is essentially another alternative to the Average and Max pooling methods, closer to the one or the other depending on the value of P, a predefined parameter chosen during the setup of the layer. This method is a sort of weighted function ending up with higher weights for more important features and lower for the lesser ones, which can be applied by using Formula (9).

$$O = \left(\sum \sum I(i,j)^P \times G(i,j)\right)^{1/P} \quad (9)$$

where O is the output, I is the input, and G is a Gaussian kernel. We should also note that when $P = 1$, it is essentially Gaussian averaging, while when $P = \infty$, it is similar to Max pooling. Using this type of pooling, the authors managed to achieve an average of about 4% better accuracy than Average pooling for the Street View House Numbers (SVHN) dataset.

2.3.8. Weighted Pooling

Weighted pooling [21] is a pooling strategy that aims to use the weighted average number of matches in a particular match. This is achieved by assigning different weights to different activation methods based on common information. Three main features of weighted pooling are, firstly, the amount of information of the pooling area is quantified by information theory for the first time. Second, each activation's benefaction is quantified for the first time, and these contributions reduce the uncertainty of the pooling area in which it is placed. Last, for selecting a senator in this pooling area, the weight of each activation clearly overtakes the value of activation.

2.3.9. Stochastic Pooling

Stochastic pooling [22] attempts to improve the commonly used Max and Average pooling and their previously mentioned drawbacks, by selecting the pooled values of the input based on probabilities. According to this suggestion, a probability p_i is calculated for each of the elements inside the pooling region using Formula (10), and then, one of the elements with a probability greater than zero is chosen randomly. This method though does appear to have a drawback similar to that of Max pooling, since important parts of the input might be ignored in favor of other parts with non-zero probabilities. The stochastic pooling strategy can be joined with any other forms of regulation such as dropout, data augmentation, weight decay, and others to avoid overfitting in deep convolutional network training.

$$p_{i}, j = \frac{a_i}{\sum_{k \in R_j} a_k} \qquad (10)$$

where:

a : the applied activation function;
R : the pooled region;
j : the index of the pooled region.

2.3.10. Spatial Pyramid Pooling

Spatial Pyramid Pooling (SPP) was inspired by the bag-of-words model [23], which is one of the best-known representation algorithms for object categorization. The fully connected layers at the end of the CNNs require a fixed length input. Spatial pyramid pooling [24] attempts to fix that by converting the input of any size into a predefined fixed length, essentially removing that fixed-size constraint, which might be problematic. Basically, a fixed-size window with a constant stride makes the output be relative to the input. On SPP layers the stride, and the pooling window are proportional to the input image, so the output can be a fixed size. The name came from the ability of the layers to apply more than one pooling operation and combining the outcome prior to moving on to the next layer, as described in Figure 5.

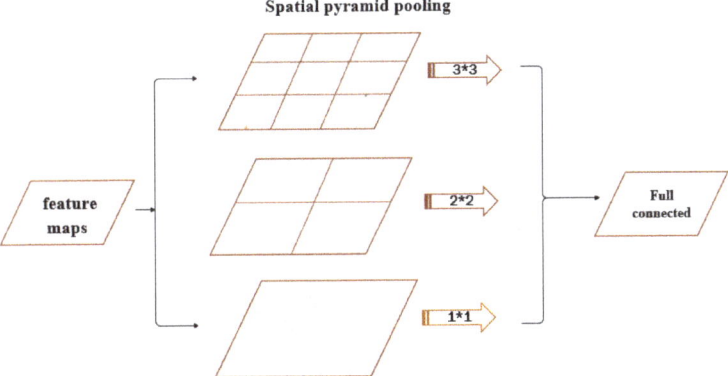

Figure 5. A network structure with a spatial pyramid pooling layer [25].

2.3.11. Per-Pixel Pyramid Pooling

The largest pooling window used in per-pixel pyramid pooling [26] differs from the original spatial pyramid pooling method, in order to manage obtaining the desired size of the receptive field. This may have as a result the loss of some of the finer details. For that reason, more than one pooling layer with different window sizes is applied, and the outputs are combined to create new feature maps. This pooling task is executed for every pixel without strides. The output is calculated by Equation (11).

$$P^{4P}(\mathbf{F}, s) = [P(\mathbf{F}, s_1), \ldots, P(\mathbf{F}, s_M)] \qquad (11)$$

where s is a vector with M elements, $\mathbf{F}$ is the pooling function applied, and $P(\mathbf{F}, s_i)$ is the pooling operation with an s_i-sized kernel and stride 1.

2.3.12. Fuzzy Pooling

The Type-1 fuzzy pooling [27] is achieved by combining the fuzzification, aggregation, and defuzzification of feature map neighborhoods. The method is applied using the following steps:

1. The input of depth n is sampled with a kernel of size $k \times k$ and a specific stride σ to obtain a set of patches p.
2. For each patch, we apply a set of v membership functions μ_v, obtaining a set of fuzzy patches $\pi_v^n = \mu_v(p^n)$.
3. Each fuzzy patch is summed, resulting in a sum $s_{\pi_v}^n$.
4. For each patch, the fuzzy patch with the highest sum of the previous step is selected out of the total set of v fuzzy patches (π').
5. Finally, the dimensionality is reduced using Equation (12):

$$p'^n = \frac{\sum_{i=1}^{k} \sum_{j=1}^{k} (\pi'^n_{i,j} \cdot p^n_{i,j})}{\sum_{i=1}^{k} \sum_{j=1}^{k} \pi'^n_{i,j}} \qquad (12)$$

2.3.13. Overlapping Pooling

Overlapping pooling was proposed as part of a paper with the suggestion of an architecture that classifies the ImageNet LSVRC-2010 dataset [28]. The idea behind it that can be applied to most—if not all—pooling methods is setting a smaller stride than the kernel size, so that there is overlap between neighboring pooled regions. The experiments with the proposed architecture showed that the top 1 and top 5 error rates were reduced by 0.4% and 0.3%, respectively for the case of Max pooling, while the model seemed to overfit slightly less when using overlapping—while that was rather an observation, and no specific evidence was presented.

2.3.14. Superpixel Pooling

Superpixel is a term for 2D image segments. Essentially, superpixel pooling [29], just like overlapping pooling, is not a pooling method itself, but a method of applying a pooling function such as the Max or Average. The difference is that, instead of using a standard square sliding kernel as in other methods, the 2D image is already segmented—usually based on edges. Then, the selected pooling function is applied in each segment. This process reduces the computational cost significantly, while preserving a high accuracy in the models used.

2.3.15. Spectral Pooling

While most other methods process the input in the spatial domain, spectral pooling [30] takes it to the frequency domain, pools the input, and then, returns the output back to the spatial domain. One of the main advantages is that information is preserved better—compared to other common methods such as Max pooling—since lower frequencies tend to contain that information and higher frequencies usually contain noise.

The application of this type of pooling is rather straightforward, applying a Discrete Fourier Transform (DFT) to the input, cropping a predefined size window from the center, and returning it back to the spatial domain by using the inverse DFT.

Obviously, a significant issue is the computational cost, since the DFT is required—both forward and inverse. That overhead though can be minimized when the FFT is used for the calculation of the convolution in the previous layer, thus limiting its use only to such scenarios. Zhang et al. [31] suggested an alternative implementation based on the Hartley transform, which might require less computational power while retaining the same amount of information.

2.3.16. Wavelet Pooling

The wavelet pooling method [32] features a completely different approach compared to the previously mentioned ones that use neighboring inputs, attempting to minimize the artifacts produced during the process of pooling. It is based on the Fast Wavelet Transform (FWT), a transformation that is applied twice on the input, once on the rows, and once again on the columns. Then, the input features are reconstructed using only the second-order wavelet sub-bands by applying the Inverse FWT (IFWT), reducing by half the total image features.

Unfortunately, though on the MNIST dataset, the wavelet pooling managed to outperform other competitors, on other datasets (CFAR-10, SHVN, KDEF), simpler methods such as Average or Max pooling performed better. Furthermore, as one can see in Table 1, the computational power required appears to be 110 K mathematical operations for the simpler MNIST dataset, which goes up to a tremendous total of 6.2 M for the KDEF dataset, compared to 3.5 K and 29 K—200-times less—operations required by the much simpler-to-apply Average pooling.

Table 1. A comparison of the total mathematical operations required per method [32].

	MNIST	CIFAR-10	SHVN	KDEF
Max	6.2 K	13 K	26 K	50 K
Avg	3.5 K	7.4 K	15 K	29 K
Mixed	4.8 K	10 K	20 K	40 K
Stochastic	10.6 K	22 K	45 K	86 K
Wavelet	110 K	405 K	810 K	6.2 M

2.3.17. Intermap Pooling

To achieve an increase in robustness for spectral variations of audio signals and acoustic features, Intermap Pooling (IMP) was introduced [33]. This was accomplished by the addition of a convolution maxout layer (IMP), which groups the feature maps, and then the Max activation function at each position is chosen.

2.3.18. Strided Convolution Pooling

Ayachi et al. [34] proposed strided convolution as a drop-in replacement for Max pooling layers with the same stride and kernel size, attempting to make the CNNs more memory efficient. The convolution function that is applied is:

$$c_{i,j,n}(f) = \sigma(\sum_{h=0}^{k} \sum_{w=0}^{k} \sum_{u=0}^{m} \theta_{h,w,u,n} f_g(h,w,i,j,u)) \tag{13}$$

where σ is the activation function, $n \in [0, m]$ is the total number of output feature maps of the previous convolution layer, k is the kernel size, (w, h, n) are the width, height, and number of channels, and finally, θ is the kernel of the convolution weights, and it is $\theta = 1$ if $n = u$, or $\theta = 0$ otherwise.

In Table 2, one can easily see that the replacement of the pooling layer with the strided convolution does seem promising, since it actually reduces the total memory required by each model while also increasing the overall accuracy.

Table 2. Model size and top 5 error reduction before and after replacing the Max pooling layer with strided convolution for the ILSVRC2012 classification challenge [34].

	VGG Net	Google Net	Squeeze Net
Original	528 MB	51.1 MB	4.7 MB
Strided Conv	493 MB	42.6 MB	3.2 MB
Original top 5 error (%)	8.1	9.2	19.7
Strided Conv top 5 error (%)	6.6	8.7	17.8

2.3.19. Center Pooling

Center pooling [35] is a pooling method used for object detection and intends to identify distinct and more recognizable visual patterns. In an output feature map, we obtain the maximum values for a pixel in it is vertical and horizontal axis and add them—which will show us if that pixel is a center keypoint, which is the center of a detected object within an image.

2.3.20. Corner Pooling

On the other hand, corners usually are located outside the objects, which do not have local relative features. Therefore, corner pooling [36] was introduced to solve this problem. Corner pooling finds the maximum values on the boundary directions and, in this way, identifies the corners. This has an effect on making the corners sensitiveto the edges. Addressing this issue, in order to let corners identify the visual patterns of the objects if needed, we use the cascade corner pooling method. Detecting the corners of an object can help define the edges of an object itself better.

2.3.21. Cascade Corner Pooling

Cascade corner pooling [37] looks like a combination of center and corner pooling, by taking the maximum values in both the boundary directions and internal directions of the objects. Initially, from each boundary, it finds a boundary maximum value, then proceeds to look inside the location of the boundary maximum value to obtain an internal maximum value, and finally, it adds them together. As a result, the corners obtain both the boundary information and the visual patterns of objects.

2.3.22. Adaptive Feature Pooling

Adaptive feature pooling [38] is used to gather features from all layers for each object detection proposition and merges them for the upcoming prediction. For each one, they are mapped at other feature levels. It is usually used to pool grids of features from each level. A fusion function (maximum or sum of elements) is then used to secure the grids of features from different levels.

2.3.23. Local-Importance-Based Pooling

Local-Importance-based Pooling (LIP) [39] is a pooling layer that can increase discreet features during the downsampling process by learning adaptive weightings based on inputs. Using this kind of didactic network, the importance function now is not limited to manual forms and has the ability to recognize the criterion for the discriminativeness of features. Furthermore, the size of the LIP window is limited to a minimum dimension, so that it is not less than the step of making full use of the feature map and avoiding the issue of a defined sampling interval. More specifically, the importance function in LIP is implemented by a tiny fully convergent network, which learns to generate the importance map based on end-to-end inputs [40].

2.3.24. Soft Pooling

Soft Pooling (SoftPool) [41] is a quick and effective kernel-based process that aggregates exponentially weighted activations, as described in Formula (14). In comparison with a number of other methods, SoftPool holds more information in the downsampled activation maps, so by having a more sophisticated downsampling process, the result returns better classification accuracy. It can be used to downsample 2D images and 3D video activation maps.

$$w_i = \frac{e^{a_i}}{\sum_{j \in R} e^{a_j}} \quad (14)$$

where:

a : the activation value;
i, j : the pooled region index.

3. Putting the Methods to the Test

3.1. The Benchmark Setup

In order to choose the optimal architecture and datasets to use for our benchmark, Table 3 was compiled. which summarizes what was used for each method in the corresponding paper.

Table 3. A cumulative table of models and datasets used in each method's publication.

Method	Model(s)	Datasets
Fractional Max [15]	Custom CNN	CIFAR-10, CIFAR-100, MNIST, CASIA-OLHWDB1.1
Row-wise Max [16]	Custom CNN	ModelNet-10, ModelNet-40
Rank-based [18]	Custom CNN	MNIST, CIFAR-10, CIFAR-100, NORB
Mixed [19]	Custom CNN	MNIST, CIFAR-10, CIFAR-100, SVHN
Gated [19]	Custom CNN	MNIST, CIFAR-10, CIFAR-100, SVHN
Tree [19]	Custom CNN	MNIST, CIFAR-10, CIFAR-100, SVHN
LP [20]	Custom CNN	SVHN
Stochastic [22]	Custom CNN	MNIST, CIFAR-10, CIFAR-100, SVHN
Spatial pyramid [24]	ZF-5, Convnet-5, Overfeat-5/7	VOC 2007, Caltech 101, ILSVRC 2014, ImageNet 2012
Per-pixel pyramid [26]	Custom CNN	Middlebury benchmark "training dense" [42]
Fuzzy [27]	LeNet	MNIST, Fashion-MNIST, CIFAR-10
Overlapping [28]	Custom CNN	ILSVRC 2010, ILSVRC 2012/2013, ImageNet2012
Super-pixel [29]	VoxResNet	IBSR, Cityscapes
Spectral [30]	Custom CNN	CIFAR-10, CIFAR-100
Wavelet [32]	MatConvNet [43]	MNIST, CIFAR-10, SVHN, KDEF
Weighted [21]	Custom CNN	CIFAR-10, MNIST, PASCAL VOC 2007
Intermap [33]	Custom CNN	Switchboard-I Release 2
Strided convolution [34]	VGG11-19, GoogleNet, SqueezeNet	ILSVRC 2014, ILSVRC 2012
Center [35]	CenterNet	MS-COCO
Corner [36]	CornerNet	MS-COCO
Cascade corner [35]	Cascade R-CNN	MS-COCO
Adaptive feature [38]	Mask R-CNN (/w Caffe)	MS-COCO, Cityscapes, MVD
Local-importance-based [39]	ResNet, DenseNet	MS-COCO, ImageNet 1K
Soft [41]	ResNet, DenseNet, ResNeXt, InceptionV1	ImageNet 1K, DIV2K, Urban 100, Manga 109, Flicker 2K, ImageNet 1K, HACS, Kinetics-700, UCF-101

It seems that less-potent architectures are preferred in most cases. This is probably because they usually achieve a lower overall performance, but that also means that the impact of changing the pooling layer will be better highlighted. Thus, a similar model was chosen, a LeNet5 architecture with 2 convolution layers, 2 respective interchangeable pooling layers, and 2 fully connected layers, as shown in Figure 6.

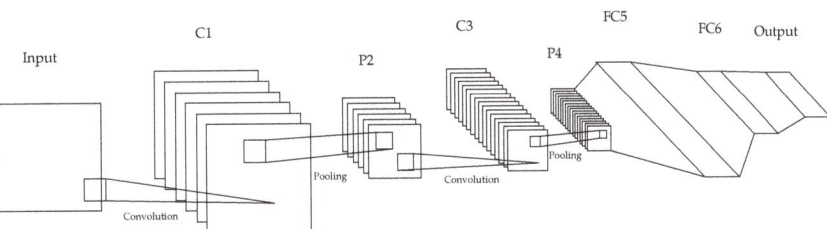

Figure 6. The CNN architecture used for the tests.

Regarding the datasets, the MNIST, CIFAR10, and CIFAR100 were used, since it seems from Table 3 that these are commonly used in the reviewed papers. They are also ideal since we had to make sure they were interchangeable for the exact same architecture without changes to the fully connected layer(s), just by modifying the total output class parameter.

Lastly, we focused on testing pooling methods that can be used as a direct drop-in replacement for the Max pooling layer, with a kernel size and stride of size 2, in order to reduce each dimension by half—applying parameters that would provide similar results wherever required (like a 0.5 scaling factor, for instance, for the spectral pooling layer). Stochastic gradient descent was used as an optimizer, with a learning rate of 0.01 and momentum of 0.9 over 300 epochs.

3.2. Performance Evaluation

For the performance comparison, we used the standard top 1 and top 5 testing accuracy (higher is better); for the computational complexity, we used the time required per epoch (lower is better), while also including three indicators, which can provide better insight into how well the details of the original image are maintained—for all three (higher values are better):

Root-Mean-Squared Contrast (RMSC) [44], as defined in Formula (15) for a $M \times N$ image:

$$RMSC = \sqrt{\frac{1}{M \times N} \sum_{i=0}^{M-1} \sum_{j=0}^{N-1} (x_{ij} - \bar{x})^2} \tag{15}$$

where
x_{ij} : each pixel of the image;
$\bar{x}$: $(\sum_{i=0}^{M-1} \sum_{j=0}^{N-1} x_{ij})/(M \times N)$.

Peak-Noise-to-Signal Ratio (PSNR) [45], as defined in Formula (16) for a $M \times N$ image:

$$PSNR = 20 log_{10} \left(\frac{MAX_f}{\sqrt{MSE}} \right) \tag{16}$$

where:

MSE : (Mean-Squared Error) = $(\sum_{i=0}^{M-1} \sum_{j=0}^{N-1} \|f(i,j) - g(i,j)\|^2)/(M \times N)$;
f : the data of the original image;
g : the data of the pooled image;
MAX_f : the maximum signal value of the original image.

Structural Similarity Index (SSIM) [46], which is defined by three combined metrics for luminance, contrast, and structure and can be simplified for two signals x, y in the form seen in Formula (17):

$$SSIM(x,y) = \frac{(2\mu_x \mu_y + C_1)(2\sigma_{xy} + C_2)}{(\mu_x^2 + \mu_y^2)(\sigma_x^2 + \sigma_y^2 + C_2)} \tag{17}$$

where:
μ_x, μ_y : the pixel mean $\mu_x = \sum_{i=1}^{N} x_i / N$;
σ_x, σ_y : standard deviation $\sigma_x = \sqrt{\sum_{i=1}^{N} (x_i - \mu_x)^2 / (N-1)}$;
σ_{xy} : $\sum_{i=1}^{N} (x_i - \mu_x)(y_i - \mu_y)/(N-1)$;
C_1 : $(k_1 L)^2$;
C_2 : $(k_2 L)^2$;
L : the dynamic range of pixels, 255 for 8-bit grayscale images;
k_1 : A small constant <1, 0.01 used in the paper experiments;
k_2 : A small constant <1, 0.03 used in the paper experiments.

All tests were performed using a PyTorch implementation of the methods, on an Nvidia GTX1080 GPU.

4. Results

4.1. Details Retention

As previously described, three metrics were used as a means of comparison for how well details are preserved after pooling the original input. The first one is the Root-Mean-Squared Contrast (RMSC) [44], which is the standard deviation of the pixel intensities, which indicates how well the contrast levels are maintained between the input and output. The second, the Peak-Noise-to-Signal Ratio (PSNR) [45], shows how strong the original image signal is compared to the introduced noise due to pooling. Lastly, the Structural Similarity Index (SSIM) [46] can range from −1 to 1 and shows the actual similarity between the input and output of the pooling layer.

In Table 4, Average pooling appears to be the best choice, since it shows the best SSIM values across all dataset tests. Furthermore, it achieved a top ranking PSNR as well for two out of the three datasets—which can be interpreted as a low level of introduced noise. When it comes to the RMSC, though other methods achieved better values, Average pooling kept up, and as we can see in the pooling layers' output examples, higher contrast is not always good, at least when it comes to comparing similarities with the original image.

Table 4. The details' retention indicators of our benchmark. The best value for each metric in each separate dataset is highlighted.

	MNIST			CIFAR10			CIFAR100		
	RMSC	PSNR	SSIM	RMSC	PSNR	SSIM	RMSC	PSNR	SSIM
Max	0.35	65.66	0.76	0.17	68.69	0.82	0.26	66.84	0.80
Adaptive Max	0.35	65.66	0.76	0.17	68.69	0.82	0.26	66.84	0.80
Fractional Max	0.35	65.66	0.76	0.17	68.69	0.82	0.26	66.84	0.80
Average	0.28	69.47	**0.89**	0.15	**75.52**	**0.86**	0.26	**70.80**	**0.84**
Mixed	0.16	70.54	0.85	0.16	70.54	0.85	0.26	69.03	0.82
Gated	0.30	68.49	0.83	0.14	72.24	0.85	0.26	69.22	0.82
Tree (Level 2)	0.53	60.57	0.69	**0.33**	53.74	0.62	0.46	54.84	0.73
LP (L2)	**0.57**	58.66	0.61	0.29	55.02	0.66	0.52	52.43	0.66
Stochastic	0.15	**70.67**	0.83	0.15	70.66	0.83	0.26	68.91	0.81
Fuzzy	0.55	59.95	0.68	0.29	55.20	0.67	0.52	52.58	0.66
Overlapping Max	0.40	60.46	0.56	0.18	64.92	0.70	0.25	62.01	0.58
Spectral	0.58	58.72	0.66	0.30	55.08	0.61	**0.53**	52.53	0.57
Wavelet	0.26	69.47	0.89	0.15	72.52	**0.86**	0.26	**70.80**	**0.84**
Local Importance	0.31	67.76	0.81	0.15	71.51	**0.86**	0.26	70.01	**0.84**
Soft	0.29	62.92	0.65	0.15	67.87	0.67	0.27	65.91	0.63

In Figures 7–9, a sample input of each dataset is presented, as well as the respective output for each pooling layer. Each method might have a tendency to favor higher or lower values of the input pixels, while some increase the contrast significantly.

Combined with the results of Table 4, it seems that Average pooling indeed achieved a result that was very close to the original image. On the other hand, tree, l2, fuzzy, and spectral pooling introduced a much higher contrast to the image, generating an output that was very different from the original input.

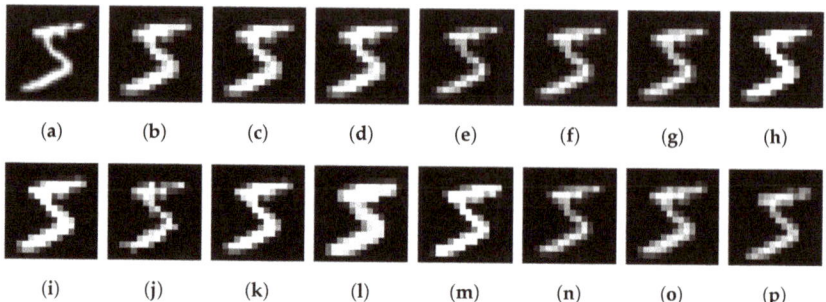

Figure 7. The MNIST "5" original image (**a**) and the respective results of the first pass of pooling for the methods Max (**b**), adaptive Max (**c**), fractional (**d**), Average (**e**), mixed (**f**), gated (**g**), tree (**h**), l2 (**i**), stochastic (**j**), fuzzy (**k**), overlapping Max (**l**), spectral (**m**), wavelet (**n**), LIP (**o**), and SoftPool (**p**).

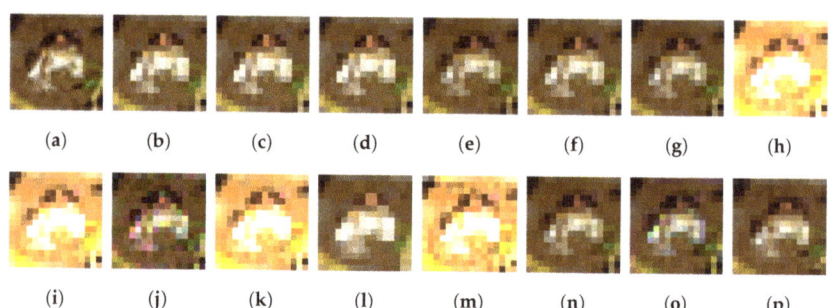

Figure 8. The CIFAR10 frog original image (**a**) and the respective results of the first pass of pooling for the methods Max (**b**), adaptive Max (**c**), fractional (**d**), Average (**e**), mixed (**f**), gated (**g**), tree (**h**), l2 (**i**), stochastic (**j**), fuzzy (**k**), overlapping Max (**l**), spectral (**m**), wavelet (**n**), LIP (**o**), and SoftPool (**p**).

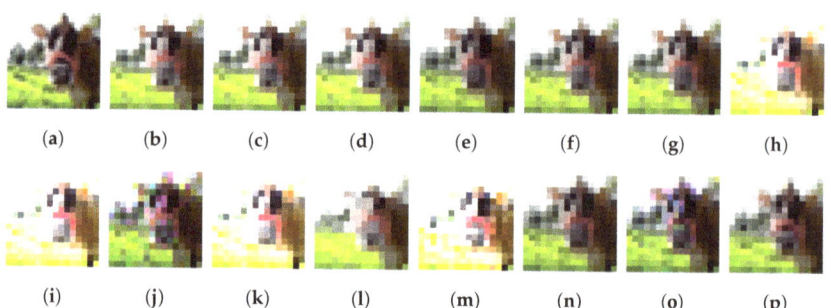

Figure 9. The CIFAR100 horse original image (**a**) and the respective results of the first pass of pooling for the methods Max (**b**), adaptive Max (**c**), fractional (**d**), Average (**e**), mixed (**f**), gated (**g**), tree (**h**), l2 (**i**), stochastic (**j**), fuzzy (**k**), overlapping Max (**l**), spectral (**m**), wavelet (**n**), LIP (**o**) and SoftPool (**p**).

4.2. Model Performance

In Table 5, the accuracy of the individual pooling methods is presented, along with the time required per epoch. It appears that for the MNIST, perhaps due to the ease of the dataset, the results were almost identical. Though, in the previous section, Average pooling appeared to "win the battle" of details' retention, here, it is obvious that Max pooling and its variants—especially overlapping Max pooling—seemed to perform much better.

Table 5. The top 1/top 5 validation accuracy and time required per epoch for each model.

	MNIST			CIFAR10			CIFAR100		
	TOP-1	TOP-5	Time	TOP-1	TOP-5	Time	TOP-1	TOP-5	Time
Max	0.99	1.00	8 s	0.60	0.95	8 s	0.31	0.60	8 s
Adaptive Max	0.99	1.00	7 s	**0.65**	**0.97**	8 s	0.31	0.59	8 s
Fractional Max	0.99	1.00	8 s	0.64	**0.97**	8 s	0.32	0.61	8 s
Average	0.99	1.00	8 s	0.59	0.95	8 s	0.27	0.55	8 s
Mixed	0.99	1.00	8 s	0.61	0.96	8 s	0.30	0.58	8 s
Gated	0.99	1.00	10 s	0.61	0.96	10 s	0.31	0.60	10 s
Tree (Level 2)	0.99	1.00	11 s	0.58	0.95	11 s	0.28	0.56	11 s
LP (L2)	0.99	1.00	8 s	0.63	0.96	8 s	0.30	0.59	8 s
Stochastic	0.99	1.00	9 s	0.60	0.95	9 s	0.31	0.59	9 s
Fuzzy	0.97	1.00	14 s	0.57	0.95	13 s	0.19	0.44	13 s
Overlapping Max	0.99	1.00	8 s	**0.65**	**0.97**	8 s	**0.34**	**0.63**	8s
Spectral	0.99	1.00	8 s	0.60	0.95	8 s	0.29	0.57	8 s
Wavelet	0.99	1.00	10 s	0.59	0.95	10 s	0.29	0.56	10 s
Local Importance	0.99	1.00	10 s	0.58	0.95	9 s	0.28	0.56	9 s
Soft	0.99	1.00	8 s	0.57	0.95	8 s	0.28	0.57	8 s

Figures 10–12 show the top 1 accuracy of the model over the 300 training epochs of the benchmark. In Figure 12, it is clear that overlapping Max pooling is the overall better-performing method for CIFAR100, significantly outperforming the rest—though the difference is not that obvious for the other two datasets.

When it comes to complexity, most methods required about 8 s per epoch, with some requiring a much increased time—which might perhaps perform much better with a C++ implementation. Overlapping Max pooling had one of the lowest times required per epoch, giving it yet another advantage. On the other hand, some methods managed to converge much more quickly. For instance, tree, l2, spectral, and Average pooling seemed to require far less than 100 epochs to obtain the highest possible accuracy. Thus, l2 might be a better choice after all, since it achieved a high accuracy in fewer epochs and one of the lowest processing times per epoch.

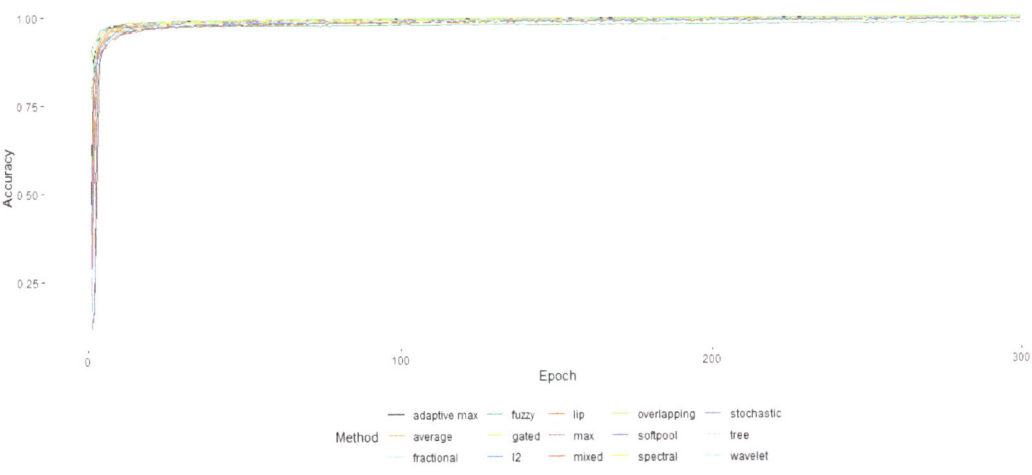

Figure 10. The top 1 accuracy of the models for the MNIST dataset over the epochs.

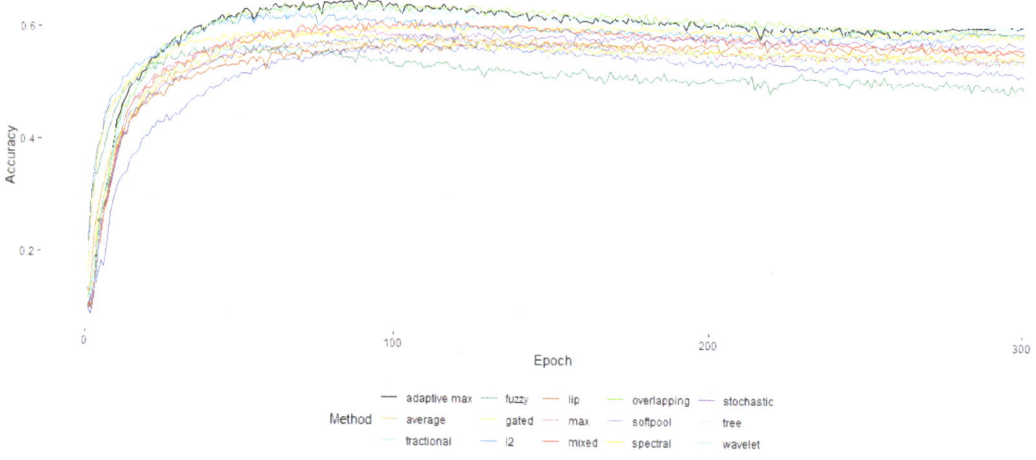

Figure 11. The top 1 accuracy of the models for the CIFAR10 dataset over the epochs.

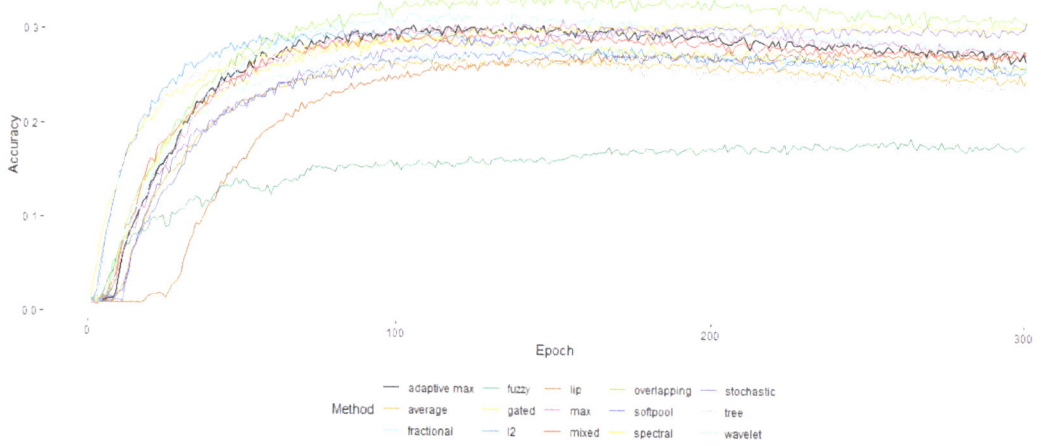

Figure 12. The top 1 accuracy of the models for the CIFAR100 dataset over the epochs.

On a closing note, the overall selected amount of 300 epochs might be a bit higher than required since most methods achieved their peak accuracy at less than 100–150 epochs. The high amount of epochs though did make sure that there were enough for each method to achieve the best performance possible.

5. Discussion

As expected, there is no "absolute best" for the pooling layer—one that may work great for one application might not even be viable for another. Though overlapping Max pooling seemed to be the "winner" of this benchmark, there may be different scenarios where other commonly used methods may be more suitable—such as, for instance, when detail retention is important, Average pooling is a better choice and easy to implement and has similar performance. Therefore, the choice of the proper pooling layer is not always that simple and straightforward.

One of the most important factors is probably the overall computational power required. Since the convolution layer itself is resource-heavy and the pooling layer's role is to "relieve" part of that load, it would be expected for the added overhead to be as minimal as possible.

Other factors that one should keep in mind are the level of invariance required—usually when the input is a video or highly variable images of similar objects—and the overall detail retention that is required. Of course, a combination of two or even more pooling methods could be applied to further improve the overall accuracy of the output. Some might even prefer simpler methods due to their ease of implementation—in the case where a rapid prototype would be adequate as a proof of concept. Taking into consideration all the model's requirements and even the personal favorites of the development team is what usually drives the final selection of the pooling layer.

6. Conclusions

CNNs are an important part of computer vision, and pooling can significantly reduce their overall processing, allowing the implementation of models and architectures with far fewer resources than would normally be required. We created a roundup of many of the pooling methods that have been proposed so far—though it might not be exhaustive—summarizing each approach and a benchmark for a practical comparison.

Overlapping Max pooling appeared to perform better than the rest, at least for the selected datasets. Even though it might be next to impossible to pinpoint and test every single variation for all existing pooling methods, hopefully, it will be more than enough to function as a starting point for every researcher and machine learning scientist in order to help choose the one that is more appropriate or even inspire new approaches or improvements for current implementations.

Author Contributions: Conceptualization, G.A.P.; methodology, N.-I.G., P.V. and K.-G.M; software N.-I.G., P.V. and K.-G.M; validation N.-I.G.; formal analysis, N.-I.G., P.V. and K.-G.M; investigation, N.-I.G., P.V. and K.-G.M; resources, N.-I.G., P.V. and K.-G.M; data curation, N.-I.G.; writing—original draft preparation, N.-I.G., P.V. and K.-G.M; writing—review and editing, N.-I.G.; visualization, N.-I.G., P.V.; supervision, G.A.P.; project administration, N.-I.G.; funding acquisition, G.A.P. All authors have read and agreed to the published version of the manuscript.

Funding: This research received no external funding.

Data Availability Statement: The source code of this study is available via https://github.com/MLV-RG/cnn-pooling-layers-benchmark/, (accessed on 8 September 2022).

Acknowledgments: This work was supported by the MPhil program "Advanced Technologies in Informatics and Computers", hosted by the Department of Computer Science, International Hellenic University, Kavala, Greece.

Conflicts of Interest: The authors declare no conflict of interest.

References

1. Forsyth, D.A.; Ponce, J. *Computer Vision: A Modern Approach*; Prentice Hall: Upper Saddle River, NJ, USA, 2002
2. Carandini, M. What simple and complex cells compute. *J. Physiol.* **2006**, *577*, 463–466. [CrossRef]
3. Movshon, J.A.; Thompson, I.D.; Tolhurst, D.J. Spatial summation in the receptive fields of simple cells in the cat's striate cortex. *J. Physiol.* **1978**, *283*, 53–77. [CrossRef] [PubMed]
4. Fukushima, K.; Miyake, S. Neocognitron: A self-organizing neural network model for a mechanism of visual pattern recognition. In *Competition and Cooperation in Neural Nets*; Springer: Berlin/Heidelberg, Germany, 1982; pp. 267–285.
5. Lin, Y.; Lv, F.; Zhu, S.; Yang, M.; Cour, T.; Yu, K.; Cao, L.; Huang, T. Large-scale image classification: Fast feature extraction and svm training. In Proceedings of the CVPR 2011, Colorado Springs, CO, USA, 20–25 June 2011; pp. 1689–1696.
6. Zhang, H.; Berg, A.C.; Maire, M.; Malik, J. SVM-KNN: Discriminative nearest neighbor classification for visual category recognition. In Proceedings of the 2006 IEEE Computer Society Conference on Computer Vision and Pattern Recognition (CVPR'06), New York, NY, USA, 17–22 June 2006; Volume 2, pp. 2126–2136.
7. Akhtar, N.; Ragavendran, U. Interpretation of intelligence in CNN-pooling processes: A methodological survey. *Neural Comput. Appl.* **2020**, *32*, 879–898. [CrossRef]

8. Sharma, S.; Mehra, R. Implications of pooling strategies in convolutional neural networks: A deep insight. *Found. Comput. Decis. Sci.* **2019**, *44*, 303–330. [CrossRef]
9. Khan, A.; Sohail, A.; Zahoora, U.; Qureshi, A.S. A survey of the recent architectures of deep convolutional neural networks. *Artif. Intell. Rev.* **2020**, *53*, 5455–5516. [CrossRef]
10. Gholamalinezhad, H.; Khosravi, H. Pooling Methods in Deep Neural Networks, a Review. *arXiv* **2020**, arXiv:2009.07485.
11. Nirthika, R.; Manivannan, S.; Ramanan, A.; Wang, R. Pooling in convolutional neural networks for medical image analysis: A survey and an empirical study. *Neural Comput. Appl.* **2022**, *34*, 5321–5347. [CrossRef] [PubMed]
12. Yamaguchi, K.; Sakamoto, K.; Akabane, T.; Fujimoto, Y. A neural network for speaker-independent isolated word recognition. In Proceedings of the First International Conference on Spoken Language Processing, Kobe, Japan, 18–22 November 1990.
13. Murray, N.; Perronnin, F. Generalized Max pooling. In Proceedings of the IEEE Conference on Computer Vision and Pattern Recognition, Columbus, OH, USA, 23–28 June 2014; pp. 2473–2480.
14. Thoma, M. LaTeX Examples. 2012. Available online: https://github.com/MartinThoma/LaTeX-examples (accessed on 8 September 2022).
15. Graham, B. Fractional Max-pooling. *arXiv* **2014**, arXiv:1412.6071.
16. Shi, B.; Bai, S.; Zhou, Z.; Bai, X. Deeppano: Deep panoramic representation for 3-d shape recognition. *IEEE Signal Process. Lett.* **2015**, *22*, 2339–2343. [CrossRef]
17. Zubair, S.; Yan, F.; Wang, W. Dictionary learning based sparse coefficients for audio classification with Max and Average pooling. *Digit. Signal Process.* **2013**, *23*, 960–970.
18. Shi, Z.; Ye, Y.; Wu, Y. Rank-based pooling for deep convolutional neural networks. *Neural Netw.* **2016**, *83*, 21–31. [CrossRef] [PubMed]
19. Lee, C.Y.; Gallagher, P.W.; Tu, Z. Generalizing pooling functions in convolutional neural networks: Mixed, gated, and tree. In Proceedings of the Artificial Intelligence and Statistics, Cadiz, Spain, 9–11 May 2016; pp. 464–472.
20. Sermanet, P.; Chintala, S.; LeCun, Y. Convolutional neural networks applied to house numbers digit classification. In Proceedings of the 21st International Conference on Pattern Recognition (ICPR2012), Tsukuba, Japan, 11–15 November 2012; pp. 3288–3291.
21. Zhu, X.; Meng, Q.; Ding, B.; Gu, L.; Yang, Y. Weighted pooling for image recognition of deep convolutional neural networks. *Clust. Comput.* **2019**, *22*, 9371–9383. [CrossRef]
22. Zeiler, M.D.; Fergus, R. Stochastic pooling for regularization of deep convolutional neural networks. *arXiv* **2013**, arXiv:1301.3557.
23. Zhang, Y.; Jin, R.; Zhou, Z.H. Understanding bag-of-words model: A statistical framework. *Int. J. Mach. Learn. Cybern.* **2010**, *1*, 43–52. [CrossRef]
24. He, K.; Zhang, X.; Ren, S.; Sun, J. Spatial pyramid pooling in deep convolutional networks for visual recognition. *IEEE Trans. Pattern Anal. Mach. Intell.* **2015**, *37*, 1904–1916. [CrossRef] [PubMed]
25. ResearchGate. Available online: https://tinyurl.com/researchgateSPPfigure (accessed on 14 May 2021).
26. Park, H.; Lee, K.M. Look wider to match image patches with convolutional neural networks. *IEEE Signal Process. Lett.* **2016**, *24*, 1788–1792. [CrossRef]
27. Diamantis, D.; Iakovidis, D. Fuzzy Pooling. *IEEE Trans. Fuzzy Syst.* **2020**, *29*, 3481–3488. [CrossRef]
28. Krizhevsky, A.; Sutskever, I.; Hinton, G.E. ImageNet classification with deep convolutional neural networks. *Commun. ACM* **2017**, *60*, 84–90. [CrossRef]
29. Schuurmans, M.; Berman, M.; Blaschko, M.B. Efficient semantic image segmentation with superpixel pooling. *arXiv* **2018**, arXiv:cs.CV/1806.02705.
30. Rippel, O.; Snoek, J.; Adams, R.P. Spectral representations for convolutional neural networks. *arXiv* **2015**, arXiv:1506.03767.
31. Zhang, H.; Ma, J. Hartley Spectral Pooling for Deep Learning. *arXiv* **2018**, arXiv:1810.04028.
32. Williams, T.; Li, R. Wavelet pooling for convolutional neural networks. In Proceedings of the International Conference on Learning Representations, Vancouver, BC, Canada, 30 April–3 May 2018.
33. Lee, H.; Kim, G.; Kim, H.G.; Oh, S.H.; Lee, S.Y. Deep CNNs Along the Time Axis with Intermap Pooling for Robustness to Spectral Variations. *IEEE Signal Process. Lett.* **2016**, *23*, 1310–1314. [CrossRef]
34. Ayachi, R.; Afif, M.; Said, Y.; Atri, M. Strided convolution instead of Max pooling for memory efficiency of convolutional neural networks. In Proceedings of the International Conference on the Sciences of Electronics, Technologies of Information and Telecommunications, Genoa, Italy and Hammammet, Tunisia, 18–20 December 2018; Springer: Berlin/Heidelberg, Germany, 2018; pp. 234–243.
35. Duan, K.; Bai, S.; Xie, L.; Qi, H.; Huang, Q.; Tian, Q. Centernet: Keypoint triplets for object detection. In Proceedings of the IEEE/CVF International Conference on Computer Vision, Seoul, Korea, 27 October–2 November 2019; pp. 6569–6578.
36. Law, H.; Deng, J. Cornernet: Detecting objects as paired keypoints. In Proceedings of the European Conference on Computer Vision (ECCV), Munich, Germany, 8–14 September 2018; pp. 734–750.
37. Wang, J.; Sun, K.; Cheng, T.; Jiang, B.; Deng, C.; Zhao, Y.; Liu, D.; Mu, Y.; Tan, M.; Wang, X.; et al. Deep high-resolution representation learning for visual recognition. *IEEE Trans. Pattern Anal. Mach. Intell.* **2020**, *43*, 3349–3364. [CrossRef] [PubMed]
38. Liu, S.; Qi, L.; Qin, H.; Shi, J.; Jia, J. Path aggregation network for instance segmentation. In Proceedings of the IEEE Conference on Computer Vision and Pattern Recognition, Salt Lake City, UT, USA, 18–22 June 2018; pp. 8759–8768.
39. Gao, Z.; Wang, L.; Wu, G. Lip: Local importance-based pooling. In Proceedings of the IEEE/CVF International Conference on Computer Vision, Seoul, Korea, 27 October–2 November 2019; pp. 3355–3364.

40. Hyun, J.; Seong, H.; Kim, E. Universal pooling—A new pooling method for convolutional neural networks. *Expert Syst. Appl.* **2021**, *180*, 115084. [CrossRef]
41. Stergiou, A.; Poppe, R.; Kalliatakis, G. Refining activation downsampling with SoftPool. *arXiv* **2021**, arXiv:2101.00440.
42. Scharstein, D.; Szeliski, R. A taxonomy and evaluation of dense two-frame stereo correspondence algorithms. *Int. J. Comput. Vis.* **2002**, *47*, 7–42. [CrossRef]
43. Vedaldi, A.; Lenc, K. Matconvnet: Convolutional neural networks for matlab. In Proceedings of the 23rd ACM International Conference on Multimedia, Brisbane, Australia, 26–30 October 2015; pp. 689–692.
44. Peli, E. Contrast in complex images. *JOSA A* **1990**, *7*, 2032–2040. [CrossRef]
45. Instruments, N. Peak Signal-To-Noise Ratio as an Image Quality Metric. 2013. Available online: https://www.ni.com/en-us/innovations/white-papers/11/peak-signal-to-noise-ratio-as-an-image-quality-metric.html (accessed on 8 September 2022).
46. Wang, Z.; Bovik, A.C.; Sheikh, H.R.; Simoncelli, E.P. Image quality assessment: From error visibility to structural similarity. *IEEE Trans. Image Process.* **2004**, *13*, 600–612. [CrossRef]

Review

Defect Detection Methods for Industrial Products Using Deep Learning Techniques: A Review

Alireza Saberironaghi [1], Jing Ren [1] and Moustafa El-Gindy [2,*]

[1] Department of Electrical, Computer and Software Engineering, Ontario Tech University, Oshawa, ON L1G 0C5, Canada
[2] Department of Automotive and Mechatronics Engineering, Ontario Tech University, Oshawa, ON L1G 0C5, Canada
* Correspondence: moustafa.el-gindy@ontariotechu.ca; Tel.: +1-905-721-8668 (ext. 5718)

Abstract: Over the last few decades, detecting surface defects has attracted significant attention as a challenging task. There are specific classes of problems that can be solved using traditional image processing techniques. However, these techniques struggle with complex textures in backgrounds, noise, and differences in lighting conditions. As a solution to this problem, deep learning has recently emerged, motivated by two main factors: accessibility to computing power and the rapid digitization of society, which enables the creation of large databases of labeled samples. This review paper aims to briefly summarize and analyze the current state of research on detecting defects using machine learning methods. First, deep learning-based detection of surface defects on industrial products is discussed from three perspectives: supervised, semi-supervised, and unsupervised. Secondly, the current research status of deep learning defect detection methods for X-ray images is discussed. Finally, we summarize the most common challenges and their potential solutions in surface defect detection, such as unbalanced sample identification, limited sample size, and real-time processing.

Keywords: defect detection; surface defect detection; defect detection for X-ray images; defect recognition; deep learning

1. Terminology

- Support Vector Machine (SVM): an algorithm used in supervised learning for classifying and performing regression tasks.
- Region of Interest (ROI): an area within an image or video that is deemed particularly significant or relevant.
- Local Binary Patterns (LBP): a technique used in computer vision for extracting features and analyzing images.
- Reduced Coordinate Cluster Representation (RCCR): a method for representing and processing image data for object recognition that is efficient.
- Convolutional Neural Network (CNN): a neural network architecture commonly used for image and video processing tasks.
- Zero Defect Manufacturing (ZDM): a strategy to eliminate defects in the manufacturing process and improve quality.
- Deep Neural Network (DNN): a neural network architecture with multiple layers, commonly used for image recognition and natural language processing tasks.
- MobileNet Single Shot MultiBox Detector (MobileNet-SSD): a lightweight convolutional neural network that is designed for real-time object detection on mobile and embedded devices.
- Fully Convolutional Network (FCN): a neural network architecture used for semantic segmentation tasks.
- Region-based Convolutional Neural Network (RCNN): a neural network architecture used for object detection tasks.

- Autoencoders (AEs): a neural network architecture used for unsupervised learning tasks such as dimensionality reduction and anomaly detection.
- Generative Adversarial Networks (GANs): a neural network architecture used for generative tasks such as image synthesis and image-to-image translation.
- Self-Organizing Map based (SOM-based): an unsupervised learning algorithm that organizes data into a 2D grid of clusters.
- General-purpose Annotation of Photos and Replica (GAPR) datasets: created by the German Pattern Recognition Association, is a collection of images specifically designed for the detection of texture defects.
- German Association for Pattern Recognition (DAGM) datasets: a collection of images specifically designed for the detection of textured surfaces.
- Northeastern University (NEU) datasets: created by Northeastern University, a collection of images of surface defects that includes six different types of defects.
- Convolutional Denoising AutoEncoder (CDAE): a type of autoencoder designed to remove noise from images.
- Non-Destructive Testing (NDT): a method of evaluating the properties of a material, component, or system without causing damage.
- VGG: VGG is a pioneering object-recognition model that can have up to 19 layers. Created as a deep CNN, it surpasses other models on many tasks and datasets apart from ImageNet. VGG is still a widely used architecture for image recognition today.
- Mean Average Precision (mAP): a metric used to evaluate the performance of object detection models, that calculates the average precision across different classes and object instances.

2. Introduction

Several factors affect the quality of manufactured products during the manufacturing process, including poor working conditions, inadequate technology, and various other factors. Among product defects, poor product quality is most visible in surface defects. Therefore, detecting product surface defects [1] ensures a high qualification ratio and reliable quality.

A defect is generally defined as an absence or area that differs from a normal sample. Figure 1 compares normal samples with defective samples of industrial products.

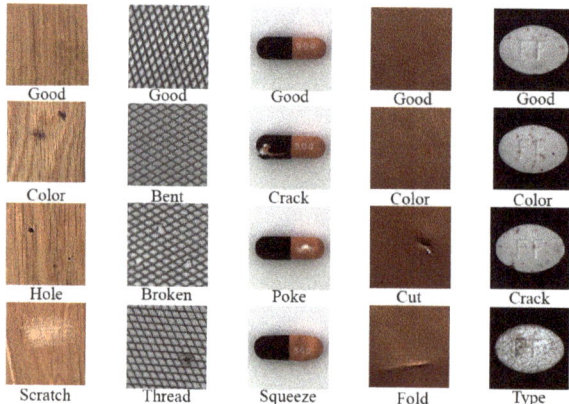

Figure 1. Normal samples of industrial products are compared to defective samples. The first row contains good samples, and the second, third, and fourth rows contain defective samples. The first, second, third, fourth, and fifth columns display wood, grid, capsule, leather, and bill, respectively, and there are three types of defects listed below the image.

In the past, identifying defects was carried out by experts, but this process was not efficient. One major reason for this was that human subjectivity greatly affected the detection results. Additionally, human inspection alone cannot meet the need for real-time detection, and thus, it is not able to fulfill all the necessary requirements.

A significant amount of time has been dedicated to using traditional methods to detect surface defects. When differentiation exists between the defect color and the background, traditional image processing methods can perform well. Traditional methods in terms of the product's features can be categorized into three types: texture-based features, color-based features, and shape-based features.

Several studies have used specialized techniques for detecting surface defects. In color-based feature, for instance, literature [2] proposed a technique involving the use of a percentage of the feature of color histogram and a vector texture feature to classify image blocks to detect surface defects on wood; this method has been proven effective by experiments, especially with defects involving junctions. In Figure 2, the method results are shown.

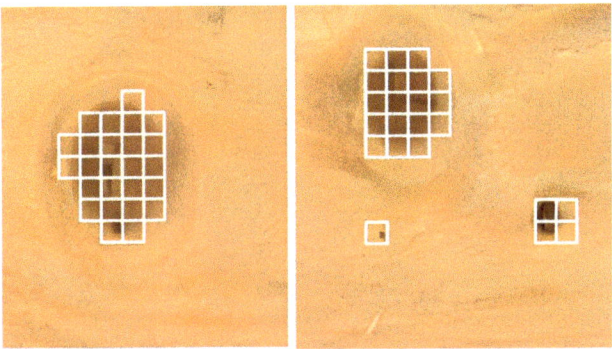

Figure 2. An example of the result of wood defect detection using the presented technique in [2].

Research conducted in literature [3] employed cosine similarity to verify the validity of the periodic law in magneto-optical images by utilizing the color moment feature. This method was successful in identifying the appropriate magneto-optical image for detecting and locating welding defects. Literature [4] describes a two-step technological process for SVM-based and color histogram-based defect detection in particle boards, followed by localization of defects using smoothing and thresholding. According to literature [5], color moment features and FSIFT features were merged based on their magnitude of influence for the purpose of resolving the tile surface defect problem not being adequately described by a single feature.

In terms of shape-based feature methods, literature [6] proposed a method of detecting cutting defects on magnetic surfaces. In this method, the image of the magnetic surface is reconstructed using the Fourier transform and Hough transform, and, in order to obtain defect information, the gray difference between the original image and the reconstructed image is compared. A method for identifying defects on bottle surfaces was presented in reference [7]. This method includes a step for extracting regions of interest, where the boundary line of the light source is determined using a fast Hough transform algorithm. In [8], global Fourier image reconstruction and template matching were proposed as a method for detecting and locating small defects in aperiodic images. Literature [9] described how to detect surface defects on small camera lenses using Hough transforms, polar coordinate transforms, weighted Sobel filters, and SVM algorithms. Different types of defects were detected in several test images. In Figure 3, red highlights are used to indicate defects such as stains, scratches, and dots.

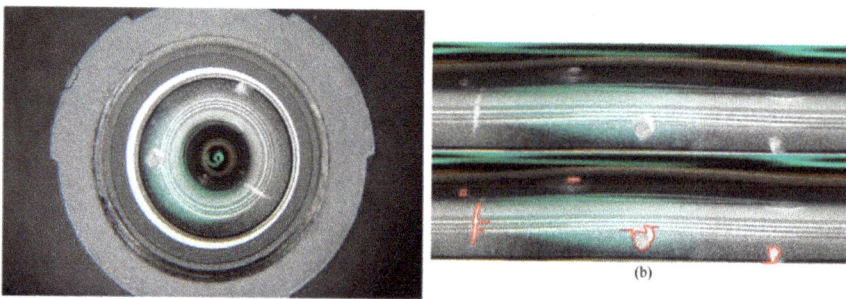

Figure 3. A camera lens with several defects: (**a**) original image and (**b**) converted result based on inspection result and polar coordinate transformation [9].

In the texture-based feature method, for example in [10], a multi-block local binary pattern (LBP) algorithm has been improved. In addition to having the simplicity and efficiency of LBP, this algorithm ensures high recognition accuracy by varying the block size to describe defect features. According to the experiment, the method has the speed to meet online real-time detection requirements (63 milliseconds/image), outperform the widely used scale-invariant feature transform (SIFT), speed up robust features (SURF), and gray-level co-occurrence matrix (GLCM) algorithms for recognition accuracy (94.30%), demonstrating that MB-LBP can be used to detect images in real time online. Literature [11] used a fuzzy model that was based on extracting GLCM features and processed it using MATLAB. The model took in three variables as inputs: autocorrelation, square root of variance, and the number of objects. Using fuzzy logic on ceramic defects, the accuracy of the ceramic inspection process with a light intensity of 300 lx, camera distance of 50 cm, and a 1.3 MP or 640 × 480 pixel image size was determined using the training data of 96.87%, and the accuracy of the real-time system was 92.31%. According to literature [12], features such as Reduced Coordinated Cluster Representation (RCCR) are used to form a one-class classifier. An algorithm based on texture periodicity estimates the primitive unit size of defect-free fabrics during the training phase. After splitting the fabrics into samples of one unit, RCCR features are used in a one-class classifier to learn their local structure. In [13], morphological filters are used to detect defects on billet surfaces in order to distinguish them from scales. With the help of morphological erosion and dilation techniques with repetition, the image is converted into a binary image by using morphological top-hat filtering and thresholding. The detection efficiency of the proposed algorithm is evaluated using real billet images to evaluate its performance. The proposed algorithm is found to be effective and suitable for analyzing billet images with scales in experiments. According to literature [14], the GLCM is defined as the fabric image's characteristic matrix. To distinguish defect-free from defective images, Euclidean distance is used and, in order to determine the pattern period, the autocorrelation function is used. In this paper, the authors discussed two GLCM parameters in relation to Euclidean distances. Furthermore, in addition to being concise and objective, Euclidean distances have the advantage of being reliable and objective for defect detection. According to the algorithm's tests, it is not only accurate, but also more adaptable to yarn-dyed fabrics with short organization cycles. Table 1 summarizes recent applications of machine learning algorithms for surface defect detection in industrial products, categorized by texture, color, and shape features. Table 2 compares the strengths and weaknesses of feature-based methods for detecting surface defects, including accuracy, computational efficiency, and robustness. These tables provide an overview of the diversity of approaches and key factors affecting performance in the field of surface defect detection.

Table 1. Recent applications using machine-learning-based vision algorithms for detecting surface defects in industrial products, categorized into three categories based on texture, color, and shape features.

Approach	Reference	Feature	Target	Performance
Texture-based	[11]	Gray level co-occurrence matrix	Ceramic	Recognition rate: 92.31%
	[13]	Mathematical morphological	Billet	Accuracy: 87.5%
	[15]	Fractal model	Steel	Accuracy: 88.33%
	[16]	Gabor filter	Steel billet	Thin crack: 91.9% and corner crack: 93.5%
Color-based	[3]	Bivariate color histogram	Particleboards	Can effectively detect and localize defect
	[17]	Color coherence vectors combined with texture features as a basis	NWPU-RESISC45 data sets	Accuracy: 96.66%
	[18]	Color histogram	Cementitious materials	ERT can be efficient for situ monitoring and defect detection of cement mortar
Shape-based	[6]	Fourier image	Magnet	Can automatically detect surface-cutting defects in magnets
	[8]	Comparison of the whole Fourier spectra between the template and the inspection image	Non-periodical pattern images	Can detect various types of non-repeating patterns in the electronic industry, even those as small as one pixel wide, making it useful for identifying defects
	[9]	A circle Hough transformation, weighted Sobel filter, and polar transformation	Compact camera lens	Able to identify defects in complicated circular inspection areas and has been proven to be highly effective

Table 2. An overview of the strengths and weaknesses of various feature-based methods for detecting surface defects in industrial products.

Approach	Reference	Method	Strengths	Weaknesses
Texture-based	[10]	Multi-block local binary pattern (LBP) algorithm	High recognition accuracy and meets online real-time detection requirements; robust to rotation and scaling; fast processing time	Does not perform well with defects that do not involve texture changes; may not be able to detect defects with low contrast;
	[11]	Fuzzy model based on GLCM extraction	Can be useful for detecting defects in images with low contrast or noise, where other methods may fail	Not as good at detecting defects that have a very different texture than the one used to train the model; may not be as accurate as deep learning-based methods, which can learn from data and adapt to new types of defects
	[12]	Reduced Coordinated Cluster Representation (RCCR)	Good at detecting defects with high precision, as it is able to extract features of the defects and identify them; good at detecting defects in images with low contrast or noise, as it is able to extract features that are robust to these challenges	It is limited to detecting specific types of defects (based on the specific clustering method and feature extraction technique used), which can make it less suitable for more complex or varied defects

Table 2. Cont.

Approach	Reference	Method	Strengths	Weaknesses
Color-based	[2]	Color histogram and vector texture feature	Proven to be effective with defects involving junctions; able to handle multiple input features	Not be suitable for detecting defects in textures with complex patterns; may not work well for defects that do not involve changes in color
	[3]	Cosine similarity and color moment feature	A robust method for comparing similarity between images, which can be useful for detecting small defects that are difficult to see with the naked eye; are able to identify different types of defects with high precision, as they are able to extract features of the defects and identify them	May require additional preprocessing steps, such as image enhancement techniques, to improve their performance; do not have the ability to learn from data as compared to deep learning based methods, which can make them less adaptable to new types of defects or variations in the data
	[4]	SVM-based and color histogram-based	High accuracy rate; able to extract useful information from the color of an image, which can be useful for detecting defects that are based on color variations, such as stains or discolorations	May not perform well with other types of materials; may not be able to detect defects with low contrast
	[5]	Color moment features and FSIFT features	Successful in resolving tile surface defect problem not being adequately described by a single feature	May not perform well with defects that do not involve color changes; not be able to detect defects with low contrast
Shape-based	[6]	Fourier transform and Hough transform	Good at detecting periodic patterns, which can be useful for detecting defects in materials with repeating patterns, such as in fabrics or metals	Do not have the ability to learn from data as compared to deep learning based methods, which can make them less adaptable to new types of defects or variations in the data
	[7]	Fast Hough transform	Good at detecting linear features, such as cracks or scratches, in an image; good at detecting defects with high precision, as it is able to extract features of the defects and identify them.	Is not as good at detecting defects in images with low contrast or noise, which can make it less effective in some industrial applications; does not have the ability to learn from data as compared to deep learning based methods, which can make it less adaptable to new types of defects or variations in the data
	[8]	Global Fourier image reconstruction and template matching	Good at detecting small defects, such as scratches or cracks, in an image by reconstructing the original image from the Fourier domain	Limited to detecting specific types of defects (based on the specific templates or reconstruction of the Fourier domain), which can make them less suitable for more complex or varied defects

Using only one feature or one class of features on industrial products is rarely sufficient because their surfaces typically contain a variety of information. Consequently, many features are used in combination in practical applications, making it difficult to detect defects. Additionally, feature-based approaches are highly effective when they detect defects in images with little or no variation, and when defects appear on surfaces in a consistent pattern. Considering the wide range of uncertainties in industrial settings, it is important to develop methods that are adaptable to such wide ranges of variations in defect intensity, shape, and size.

Deep learning models based on convolutional neural networks (CNN) have had a lot of success in various computer vision fields, such as recognizing faces, identifying pedestrians, detecting text in images, and tracking targets. Additionally, these models are used in a wide range of industrial settings for defect detection. This includes both commercial and industrial applications, such as in the automotive industry for detecting defects in cars. The deep-learning-based surface defect detection software is employed in these settings to improve the efficiency and accuracy of the defect detection process.

Recently, several papers covering the latest techniques, applications, and other aspects have been published on deep learning in defect detection [19]. Literature [12] describes the different types of defects and compares mainstream and deep learning methods for defect detection. Various defect detection techniques are discussed in literature [20], including ultrasonic inspection, machine vision, and deep learning. Literature [21] focuses on the use of AI-enhanced metrology, computer vision, and quality assessment in the Zero Defect Manufacturing (ZDM) process. The study also highlights the use of IoT/IIoT technology as a means of supporting these tools and implementing AI algorithms for data processing and sharing. Literature [22] discusses deep learning methods for detecting surface defects, then discusses three critical issues related to small samples and real-time defects detection. In [23,24], the authors analyze and compare the benefits and drawbacks of the above methods. There are also defect detection surveys in several application domains, including fabric defects [25], corrosion detection [26], pavement defects [27], metal defect detection [28], and industrial applications [29]. The investigation shows that, in the field of surface defect detection of industrial products, there is currently a limited literature review on machine learning methods, and while some papers summarize the challenges and problems, the mentioned solutions are not systematic. The first section of this paper addresses the above issues by summarizing the research status on the detection of surface defects on industrial products using deep learning algorithms and then discusses the issues in the process of industrial surface defect detection, such as unbalanced sample identification problems, small sample problems, and real-time problems.

This paper is organized as follows. Section 3 provides an overview of deep learning methods for surface defect detection in industrial products from three perspectives, along with a common dataset for surface defect detection. In Section 4, we summarize the recent research status of deep learning methods for X-ray image defect detection. A discussion of the main problems and their solutions is provided in Section 5. In Section 6, a brief description of future research directions is provided and Section 7 concludes the paper with a conclusion.

3. Deep Learning Surface Defect Detection Methods for Industrial Products

Deep learning has become increasingly popular in the field of defect detection due to its rapid development. This section summarizes the state of research on inspection of industrial products for detecting surface defects. Learning-based approaches are classified as supervised, semi-supervised, and unsupervised. The performance of learning-based methods is best optimized when large datasets are provided. In particular, supervised techniques perform well when there are sufficient examples of each class in the dataset.

3.1. Supervised

Supervised detection requires large datasets of defect-free and defective samples labeled in a training set. Since all the training data is labeled, detection rates can be very high. It must be noted, however, that supervised detection may not always the most effective approach due to the imbalance of classes in the datasets. There are a number of datasets that supervised learning methods use, including the fabric dataset [30], rail defect dataset [31], and railroad dataset [32].

Deep neural networks and feature extraction and classification methods used in supervised methods differ in their structures. For example, detecting cross-category defects without retraining was proposed using a two-layer neural network in the literature [33]. Based on structural similarities between image pairs, the method learns differential features, which may result in some structural similarities among different classification objects. This method has been shown to be able to detect defects in different types of factories based on experiments in real factory datasets. Literature [34] suggests that the composition of kernels is more important than the number of layers when it comes to detection results. To detect small defects and textures in surface images, it is necessary to use a sample image that is large enough for computational accuracy and reducing the cost of the network. ShuffleNet uses convolution of pointwise groups and channel shuffle as two new techniques to achieve this goal. Literature [35] proposes a novel in-line inspection system for plastic containers based on ShuffleNet V2. The system can be used to inspect images on complex backgrounds as well. In [36], they proposed ShuffleDefectNet, a deep-learning-based defect detection system that achieved 99.75% accuracy on the NEU dataset.

Reference [37] suggested that shallow CNN networks can be used to identify anomalies. To train the model, only negative images are used and the research employs full-size images. The argument is that it is not necessary to have full-size examples of both defective and defect-free samples, as the negative samples already have pixels that correspond to the defect-free regions. Based on the Fast R-CNN model, Faster R-CNN introduces a region proposal network (RPN), which enables an end-to-end learning algorithm. This leads to a near-costless regional recommendation algorithm that significantly improves the speed of target detection. Faster R-CNN was used in [38] to detect PCB surface defects, a new network was proposed combining ResNet50, GRAPN residual units, and ShuffleNetV2. Using a cascaded RCNN structure, as described in literature [39], the defect detection problem of power line insulators can be changed into a two-level target detection problem; the results are shown in Figure 4.

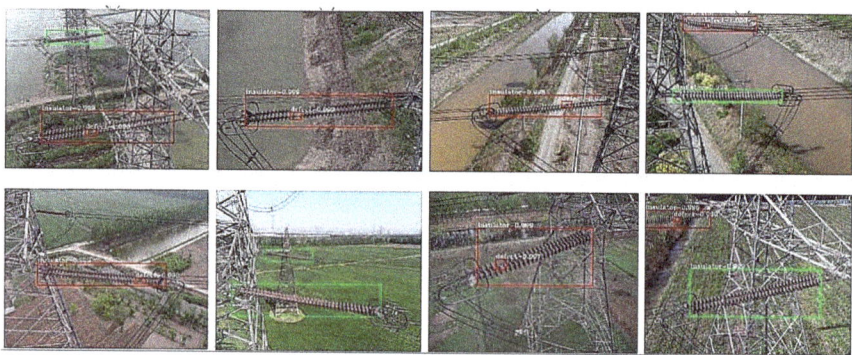

Figure 4. The results of insulator defect detection. The green box represents the non-defective insulator, and the red box represents the defective insulator [39].

In limited hardware configurations, MobileNet-SSD [9] improves real-time object detection performance. There is no need to sacrifice accuracy for the reduction of parameters in this network. An SSD network classifies regression and boundary box regression using various convolution layers. Translation invariance and variability are resolved in this model, resulting in good detection precision and speed. Object detection is effective when defects have regular or predictable shapes [40]. Additional preprocessing steps can be applied to more complex defect types. Fully Convolutional Networks (FCNs) use all convolutional layers as network layers; label maps can be directly derived using pixel-level prediction. To achieve accurate results, a deconvolution layer with larger data sizes is used. In literature [41], FCN and Faster R-CNN were combined to develop a deep learning model that could detect stains, leaks, and pipeline blockages in tunnels. A method for segmenting defects in solar cell electroluminescence pictures was presented in [42]. A defect segmentation map was obtained in one step by combining FCN with a specific U-net architecture.

3.2. Unsupervised

Research has begun to explore unsupervised methods to overcome the disadvantages of supervised methods. By learning the inherent characteristics of the input training data, the machine can learn some of its own characteristics and connections when there is no label information and automatically classifies the input training data based on the pattern of these unlabeled data [43]. It automatically classifies these unlabeled data based on inherent characteristics and connections between the data. Methods based on reconstruction and embedding similarity are the most commonly used to detect surface defects among unsupervised learning methods. Reconstruction-based methods such as autoencoders (AEs) and Generative Adversarial Networks (GANs) are most commonly used. Popular algorithms include PaDIM [44], SPADE [45] PatchCore [46], etc. In [47], an algorithm based on DBN was proposed for detecting defects in solar cells. Both training and reconstructed images were used as supervision data by the fine-tuning network of the BP algorithm. Literature [48] proposed a multi-scale convolutional denoising autoencoder with high accuracy and robustness that synthesizes the results of multiple pyramid levels.

A SOM-based detection method was proposed in [49] for determining the difference between normal and defective wood. The first stage involves detecting suspected defect areas, and the second stage involves separately inspecting each defect area. A detection method that uses GANs was proposed in reference [50]. The method is divided into two stages: first, a generative network and a learning mechanism based on statistical representation are used to detect new areas. In the second stage, defects and normal samples are directly distinguished using the Frechet distance. The solar panel dataset was used to test the method, and it achieved 93.75% accuracy.

A multiscale AE with fully convolutional neural networks has been proposed [51], in which each FCAE sub-network directly obtains the original feature image from the input image and performs feature clustering. Utilizing a fully convolutional neural network, the residual images were combined to create the defect image. PatchCore, introduced in literature [46], is a technique for identifying and isolating abnormal data in scenarios where only normal examples are available. It balances the need to retain normal context through memory banks of patch-level features extracted from pre-trained ImageNet networks and minimize computational time via coreset subsampling to create a leading system for cold-start image anomaly detection and localization that is efficient on industrial benchmarks. On MVTec, the algorithm demonstrated an AUROC of over 99%, while also being highly efficient in small training set scenarios. Literature [52] presented a GAN-based surface vision detection framework that uses OTSU to segment fusion feature response maps and fuses the responses of the three layers of the GAN discriminator. The framework has been proven effective on datasets of wood cracks and road cracks. As shown in Figure 5, ref. [53] proposed a GAN-based method for detecting strip steel surface defects, in which the generator G uses encoding and the hidden space features in the penultimate layer are fed into a SVM to detect defects. The test results on images provided by the Handan Iron and Steel Plant indicated good accuracy. It is more effective at detecting texture images; however, its accuracy still needs to be improved.

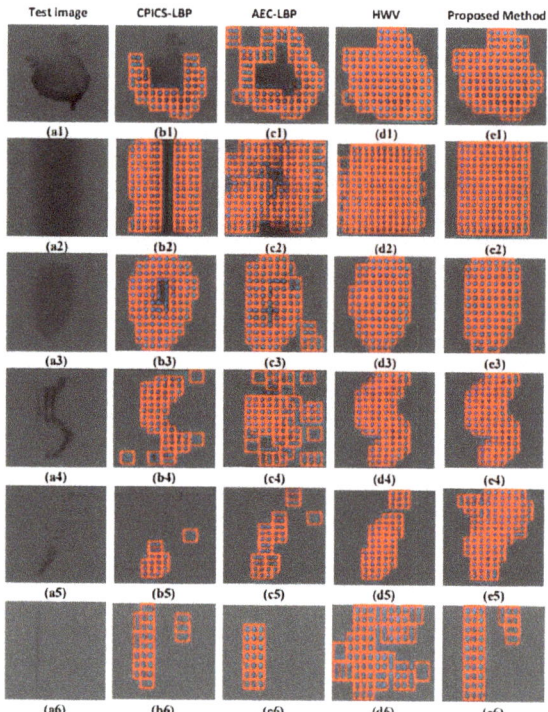

Figure 5. Presenting the results of experiments on six defect samples using four methods. The defect types are listed in the first column and include drops tar, shadow, floating, crush, pitted surface and scratch. The results from traditional manual feature extraction methods (CPICS-LBP, AEC-LBP, HWV and the proposed method in [53]) are shown in columns 2–5. The experiment compares the proposed method with current state-of-the-art methods in detecting strip steel surface defects.

3.3. Semi-Supervised

As a result of combining the properties of supervised and unsupervised methods, semi-supervised methods are developed. Only normal samples are used as training data for semi-supervised defect detection and a defect-free boundary is learned and set, and any samples outside the boundary are considered anomalous. Since there are few defective samples to be obtained, the method is extremely useful. Nevertheless, this method has lower accuracy in defect detection compared to supervised methods. Unlabeled sample data can be automatically generated by semi-supervised methods without manual intervention.

A framework for identifying defects in PCB solder joints was proposed in literature [54], which utilizes a combination of active learning and self-training through a sample query suggestion algorithm for classification. The framework has been demonstrated to improve classification accuracy while reducing the need for manual annotations. A semi-supervised model of convolutional autoencoder (CAE) and generative adversarial network is proposed in [55]. After training with unlabeled data, the stacked CAE's encoder network is retained and input into the SoftMax layer as a GAN discriminator. Using GAN, false images of steel surface defects were generated to train the discriminator. For the detection of steel surface defects, literature [56] developed a WSL framework combining localization networks (LNets) and decision networks (DNets), with LNets trained by image level labels and outputs a heat map of potential defects as input to DNets. Through the use of the RSAM algorithm to weight the regions identified by LNet, the proposed framework has been demonstrated to be effective on real industrial datasets. The application prospects for weakly supervised methods are also wide because the methods simultaneously combine advantages of both supervised and unsupervised methods. There are few weakly supervised methods for detecting surface defects in industrial products. The literature [57] proposed a deep learning algorithm to learn defects from a variety of defect types with an unbalanced training sample pool for PCBA manufacturing products. In this method, an overall defect recognition accuracy of 98% is achieved in PBCA images using a novel batch sampling method and the sample weighted cost function.

A semi-supervised learning system that generates samples to detect surface defects was proposed according to the literature [58]. As part of the semi-supervised learning part, two CDCGAN and ResNet18 classifiers were used, and the NEU-CLS dataset was used to compare the two classifiers. In this way, supervised learning and transfer learning are both shown to be inferior to the method. A convolutional neural network structure based on residual network structures was proposed in [59] by stacking two layers of residual building modules together, resulting in a 43-layer convolutional neural network, while at the same time by appropriately increasing the network width; a more balanced network depth and network width can be obtained and accuracy can be improved. The network structure shows good performance on the DAGM, NEU steel, and copper clad plate datasets. Table 3 provides an overview of recent research in surface defect detection, including classifications of targets and Table 4 evaluates the strengths and weaknesses of deep learning techniques for detecting surface defects in industrial products, including accuracy, computational efficiency, and robustness. These tables give a comprehensive understanding of current research and the considerations for using deep learning in surface defect detection. Table 5 lists a selection of commonly used datasets for training and testing algorithms for detecting surface defects in industrial products. The datasets are classified based on the type of industrial products they are intended for. This information is useful for researchers and practitioners looking for suitable datasets for their work in the field of surface defect detection.

Table 3. An overview of recent research publications as well as classifications based on targets.

Reference	Year	Method	Target	Performance
[46]	2022	PatchCore	MVTec benchmark datasets, the ShanghaiTech Campus dataset (STC), and the Magnetic Tile Defects dataset (MTD)	Demonstrated a high level of performance on the MVTec dataset with an AUROC of over 99% and a particularly strong ability to perform well with small training sets
[60]	2019	CNN	Steel	This method achieves significantly higher recognition accuracy for steel surface defects than state-of-the-art classifiers
[55]	2019	GAN	Steel	CAESGAN achieves the best classification rate compared to traditional methods, especially for hot rolled plates
[61]	2019	SDD and ResNet	Steel	Steel surface defect detection can be performed with high speed and accuracy
[62]	2019	Faster-RCNN	Steel	Achieved higher detection accuracy and more accurate location of defects, especially for tiny and slender defects
[63]	2018	CNN	DAGM dataset	Can achieve a 99.8% accuracy rate in detecting defects
[64]	2016	CNN	DAGM dataset	This method demonstrates a low false alarm rate and excellent defect detection results

Table 3. Cont.

Reference	Year	Method	Target	Performance
[65]	2019	FCN	DAGM dataset	A defect image (512 × 512) can be processed each second, with more than 99% of pixel accuracy
[66]	2017	2-stage FCN framework	DAGM dataset	Able to achieve meaningful results in terms of performance and speed
[34]	2016	CNN	Texture	In comparison to traditional manual inspection systems, this method offers several advantages in time and cost savings
[67]	2018	AutoEncoder	Various materials	Compared to traditional hand-engineered feature extraction methods, this approach is more generic
[68]	2020	CNN		On the datasets, it is possible to achieve 100% recall and high precision
[69]	2021	YOLOv5	PCB	Can achieve a 0.7% mAP promotion on HRIPCB dataset
[70]	2021	YOLOv3	PCB	The detection rate increases to 63 frames per second due to an increase in mAP of 92.13%. As a result, PCB surface defect detection has increased application prospects
[71]	2021	CNN	Flexible printed circuit boards (FPCBs)	Achieves 94.15% mean average precision (mAP) in comparison with existing surface defect detection networks
[72]	2022	CNN	Rails	Detected 98.2% of defects at the image level and 97.42% at the pixel level, respectively
[73]	2021	YOLOv3	RailwayHub	High-speed rail wheels can be detected more accurately and many defects can be located with greater accuracy with this system
[74]	2019	Faster R-CNN	Railway insulator	Algorithms superior to others
[75]	2017	CNN and SVM	Metal surface	In classification, this method outperforms both state-of-the-art traditional handcrafted features and other deep ConvNet features extracted from a preselected best layer based on several anomaly and texture datasets
[76]	2021	CNN	Metal Workpiece	It has strong adaptability and is capable of automatically extracting and detecting defects
[77]	2021	YOLOv5	Insulator	It reduces unsafe manual detection and increases detection efficiency by effectively identifying and locating insulator defects across transmission lines
[78]	2021	Mask R-CNN	Insulator	Detection accuracy: 87.5%
[79]	2021	SE-YOLOv5	Fabric	As compared to the original YOLOv5, the improved SE-YOLOv5 has a higher accuracy, generalization ability, and robustness for detecting fabric defects

Table 3. Cont.

Reference	Year	Method	Target	Performance
[80]	2021	YOLOv4	Fabric	Can quickly and accurately locate defects, and can also be used in other defect detection industries
[81]	2022	UNet	Fabric	Detection accuracy rate: 99%
[82]	2022	SVM	Non-woven fabric	It is highly accurate and performs well in real time
[83]	2021	Faster R-CNN	Aluminum	In comparison with the original algorithm, this algorithm achieved 78.8% mean average accuracy (mAP), which is 2.2% higher
[84]	2018	CNN	Copper clad lamination surface	Accuracy rate: 98.2%
[85]	2019	Faster-RCNN and feature fusion	(GAPR) texture defect dataset	Performs well under various conditions and has good adaptability
[86]	2022	Autoencoder and morphological operation	Textile	Superior performance to other prevailing models
[87]	2019	Faster R-CNN	Weel hub	It is simpler, faster, and more accurate than both R-CNN and YOLOv3 methods for wheel hub defects
[88]	2022	YOLOv3	Polarizer	There is a slight increase in its mAP over YOLOv3, and it has a detect speed increase of 44% to 121 frames per second
[89]	2021	Faster R-CNN	Belt Layer of Radial Tire	False negatives and false positives decrease by 7.79%, 3.4%, and 5%, respectively, compared with the vanilla Faster R-CNN
[90]	2017	CNN	Pavement crack analysis	Accurately detects pavement cracks and evaluates their types
[91]	2022	YOLO v5	Solar Cell	Solar cell EL images were used to train the model, which achieved 89.64% mAP
[92]	2017	CNN	Mangosteen	Recognition accuracy: 97%
[93]	2017	CrackNet	Crack detection on 3D asphalt surfaces	With 200 3D images, CrackNet achieved high precision
[94]	2021	R-CNN	Textile fabric	Defect detection accuracy improved by 4.09% to 95.43%
[95]	2020	CNN	AigleRN and DAGM2007	Can achieve high detection accuracy and efficiency
[96]	2019	Faster R-CNN	Aluminum profile	With regard to the multiscale defect-detection network, it achieved a 75.8% mAP over Faster R-CNN
[97]	2022	MobileNetV3	Sanitary ceramics	With the Faster R-CNN method, detection speed is improved by 22.9%, precision is improved by 35.0%, and memory consumption is reduced by 8.4% compared to the SSD, YOLO V3, and one-stage SSD methods
[98]	2017	CNN	Welding	Recognition accuracy rate: 95.83%

Table 3. *Cont.*

Reference	Year	Method	Target	Performance
[99]	2017	CNN	Concrete cracks	The CNN is trained on 40,000 images with a resolution of 256 × 256 pixels and achieves an accuracy rate of approximately 98%
[100]	2022	YOLOv5	Plastic	Superior performance to other prevailing models
[101]	2019	SDD-CNN	Roller subtle	Accuracy rate: 99.56%
[102]	2018	GAN	MPCG (Mobile Phone Cover Glass)	MPCG defects can be detected with high accuracy of 98%
[103]	2022	YOLOv5	Ceramic ring	Accuracy rate: 89.9%
[104]	2018	CNN	Solar cell	Recognition rate: 94.30%
[105]	2022	Wavelet Decomposition and CNN	Automobile Pipe Joints	Reduces the impact of uneven illumination, random noises, and texture processing on defect classification accuracy, and the SVM classification method demonstrates an accuracy of approximately 83% for identifying the presence of no defects, pits, and scratches in a given set of data
[106]	2021	Multi-Feature Fusion and PSO-SVM	Lithium Battery Pole Piece	Average recognition rate: 98.3%
[107]	2018	CNN	Shinny surfaces	Classification rate: around 89%
[108]	2017	DL-based ASI	NEU, Weld, and wood defect database	Can improve the accuracy by 0.66% to 25.50% for datasets
[109]	2022	SCED-Net	Steel Coil	As compared to recent networks used in steel coil end face detection and some classical object detection networks, this method offers better performance
[110]	2021	FFCNN consists of (feature extraction module, feature fusion module, and decision-making module)	Magnetic Tile	The performance of a combination of mean fusion and Resnet-50 with CBAM is 97.0%, while the combination of max fusion and Resnet-50 with CBAM has an accuracy rate of 95.0%
[111]	2018	AlexNet and SVM	Custom dataset	Detection Accuracy: 99.201%
[112]	2021	YOLOv3	Chip	mAP REACHES 86.36%
[113]	2017	CNN and a voting mechanism	Metallic gasket, DAGM defects, and screw image	Performs well in arbitrary textured images as well as in images with special structures, proving that it is superior to traditional detection algorithms
[114]	2022	CNN	High Voltage Circuit Breaker	The network model has been shown to be able to accurately detect four different levels of rust through experimental results, with a success rate of 94.25%

Table 4. Strengths and weaknesses of different techniques for detecting surface defects on industrial products using deep learning.

Approach	Reference	Method	Strengths	Weaknesses
Supervised	[33]	Two-layer neural network	Able to detect cross-category defects without retraining; simplicity of the structure of the model allows for faster training and inference	Limited to only two layers; may not be able to extract complex features; the simplicity of the model may make it less robust to noise and other variations in the input data
	[34]	Composition of kernels	Efficient network architecture for detecting small defects and textures in surface images	Lack of emphasis on the number of layers may lead to suboptimal results
	[35,36]	ShuffleNet	Can only be trained with negative images	May not perform well on larger, more complex datasets
	[37]	Shallow CNN	Significantly improves detection speed and can be used for end-to-end learning	Limited to identifying anomalies and may not perform well on more complex defects
	[38]	Faster RCNN	Requires a separate region proposal network; significantly improves the speed of target detection; can detect objects of different scales.	Might not perform well on highly cluttered scenes with many overlapping objects.
	[39]	Cascaded RCNN	Can effectively solve the defect detection problem for specific applications such as power line insulators	May not perform well on defects with irregular or unpredictable shapes
	[9]	MobileNet-SSD	Highly efficient and capable of real-time object detection in limited hardware configurations	May not perform as well as other models on larger, more complex datasets
	[42]	FCN	Can achieve high accuracy and directly output label maps at the pixel-level	Can be computationally expensive, especially when used with large datasets
Unsupervised	[46]	PatchCore	Identifies and isolates abnormal data in scenarios where only normal examples are available	May not perform as well as other models on larger and more complex datasets
	[47]	DBN	Utilizes both training and reconstructed images as supervision data for fine-tuning; can learn useful features from the data without the need for manual feature extraction, which can save time and resources	May not have the capacity to identify more complex features in the images
	[48]	Multi-scale convolutional denoising autoencoder	High precision and robustness by combining results from multiple pyramid levels; can effectively remove noise from the input data, which can improve the performance of defect detection in noisy images	May not be able to generalize well to new unseen data, especially if the data is vastly different from the training data; computationally expensive to train, especially when the input data is high-dimensional, which can be a limitation in real-time applications
	[49]	SOM-based detection	Can effectively cluster and classify high-dimensional data, which can be useful for detecting defects in images and other types of data	Can be sensitive to the initial conditions of the map and the choice of parameters, which can make it challenging to obtain accurate and consistent results
	[50]	GANs	Two-stage process for detecting new areas and directly distinguishing defects and normal samples	GANs can be difficult to train and may require a large amount of data

Table 4. Cont.

Approach	Reference	Method	Strengths	Weaknesses
	[51]	Multiscale AE with fully convolutional neural networks	Obtains the original feature image and performs feature clustering through each FCAE sub-network; can effectively learn spatial relationships between pixels, which can be useful for detecting defects in images	May struggle with detecting small or subtle defects, which may not be easily distinguished from normal patterns in the input data
	[52]	GAN-based surface vision detection framework	Proven effective on datasets of wood cracks and road cracks; can be used to generate images that can be used to improve the interpretability of the model and help identify the specific features that are used to detect defects	May struggle to generate high-quality images if the training dataset is small or of poor quality; may face mode collapse problem, where the generator produces only a small subset of all possible outputs
	[53]	GAN-based method for detecting strip steel surface defects	Tailored for detecting strip steel surface defects, it could be more effective and accurate than general-purpose models	Performance may be limited to the specific application of detecting strip steel surface defects and may not generalize well to other types of defects or materials
Semi-Supervised	[54]	Active learning and self-training	Improves classification accuracy while reducing the need for manual annotations	Can be limited by the quality of the unlabeled data, which may contain a large number of examples that are not relevant to the task at hand
	[55]	Convolutional Autoencoder and Generative Adversarial Network	Allows the model to effectively extract high-level features from the input data, which can be useful for detecting defects	May struggle to generate high-quality images if the training dataset is small or of poor quality
	[56]	WSL framework	Combines localization networks and decision networks for effective detection of real industrial datasets	May not perform well on images with intricate backgrounds
	[58]	Semi-supervised learning system	Generates samples to detect surface defects with improved accuracy compared to supervised and transfer learning methods	May not perform well on images with intricate backgrounds
	[59]	Residual network structures	Shows good performance on DAGM, NEU steel, and copper clad plate datasets with a balanced network depth and width	May require more computational resources to train

Table 5. A list of common surface defect datasets with classifications for industrial products.

Name and Reference	Target	Link
MVTec AD [115]	Various materials	http://mvtec.com/company/research/datasets (accessed on 2 February 2023)
Steel Defect Detection	Steel	https://kaggle.com/c/severstal-steel-defect-detection/data (accessed on 2 February 2023)
GC10–Det [116]	Metal	https://kaggle.com/alex000kim/gc10det (accessed on 2 February 2023)
Industrial Metallic Surface Dataset	Metal	https://kaggle.com/datasets/ujik132016/industrial-metallic-surface-dataset (accessed on 2 February 2023)
Bridge Cracks [117]	Bridge	https://github.com/Iskysir/Bridge_Crack_Image_Data (accessed on 2 February 2023)
Fabric defect dataset	Fabric	https://kaggle.com/datasets/rmshashi/fabric-defect-dataset (accessed on 2 February 2023)

Table 5. Cont.

Name and Reference	Target	Link
DeepPCB dataset [118]	PCB	https://github.com/tangsanli5201/DeepPCB (accessed on 2 February 2023)
PCB Defects	PCB	https://kaggle.com/datasets/akhatova/pcb-defects (accessed on 2 February 2023)
PCB DSLR DATASET	PCB	https://zenodo.org/record/3886553#.Y1dNl3bMKUk (accessed on 2 February 2023)
Structural Defects Network (SDNET) 2018 [119]	Concrete	https://kaggle.com/datasets/aniruddhsharma/structural-defects-network-concrete-crack-images (accessed on 2 February 2023)
COncrete DEfect BRidge IMage Dataset	Concrete	https://zenodo.org/record/2620293#.Y1dPO3bMKUk (accessed on 2 February 2023)
Surface Crack Detection Dataset [120]	Concrete	https://kaggle.com/arunrk7/surface-crack-detection (accessed on 2 February 2023)
Pavement crack dataset	Pavement	https://github.com/fyangneil/pavement-crack-detection (accessed on 2 February 2023)
Cracks and Potholes in Road Images Dataset	Road	https://biankatpas.github.io/Cracks-and-Potholes-in-Road-Images-Dataset (accessed on 2 February 2023)
Crack Forest Datasets [121]	Road	https://github.com/cuilimeng/CrackForest-dataset (accessed on 2 February 2023)
Tianchi aluminum profile surface defect dataset	Aluminum	https://tianchi.aliyun.com/competition/entrance/231682/information (accessed on 2 February 2023)
Solar cell EL image defect detection	Solar panel	https://ieee-dataport.org/documents/photovoltaic-cell-anomaly-detection-dataset (accessed on 2 February 2023)
Elpv-dataset [122]	Solar panel	https://github.com/zae-bayern/elpv-dataset (accessed on 2 February 2023)
Magnetic tile surface defects [123]	Tile	https://github.com/abin24/Magnetic-tile-defect-datasets (accessed on 2 February 2023)
Dataset for Rail Surface Defects Detection	Rail	https://arxiv.org/abs/2106.14366 (accessed on 2 February 2023)
Railway Track Fault Detection	Rail	https://kaggle.com/datasets/salmaneunus/railway-track-fault-detection (accessed on 2 February 2023)

4. Deep Learning Defect Detection Methods for X-ray Images for Industrial Products

Non-destructive testing (NDT) is a method that uses radiography or ultrasound technologies to discover faults without causing damage to the detected objects. It is widely used in engineering industries to detect and evaluate defects in materials of all types.

An important technique in non-destructive testing is radiographic testing, which uses X-rays to identify and evaluate flaws or defects, such as cracks or porosities. Defects can appear in X-ray images in many shapes and sizes, making detection difficult. The images are often low contrast and noisy, making identification of defects difficult.

The traditional approach for identifying defects in industrial products is for human operators or experts to visually inspect radiographs. However, this method can be subjective and prone to errors. Additionally, the process of examining a large number of images can be time-consuming and may lead to misinterpretations. However, there have been significant advancements in the field of defect detection in recent years, thanks to the emergence of deep learning techniques. As a result, a number of methods for detecting defects have been proposed, which are more efficient and reliable than the conventional approach. This section aims to provide a summary of current research on industrial product defect detection methods using X-ray images. Specifically, it covers the use of deep learning techniques such as convolutional neural networks and generative adversarial networks to analyze radiographic images and identify defects with a high degree of accuracy. These methods have the potential to reduce the subjectivity and human errors associated with the traditional approach, as well as the time required for inspection. Additionally, they can be trained to improve over time with more data, making them more robust and reliable.

A proposed system in literature [124] aimed to automate the process of inspecting and monitoring the condition of machines in the hard metal industry by analyzing defects in real production samples. Three models were created to analyze different types of data, a method called stacked generalization ensemble was applied and a random forest classifier was utilized to combine and analyze the results of the microprofilometer and ultrasound models. The fusion model was found to have improved performance and higher classification accuracy (88.24%) as compared to the individual models. Additionally, the shop floor model was able to effectively identify breakdowns during the manufacturing process and the ultrasound model was found to have better classification scores compared to the VGG-19 model. According to literature [125], a three-stage deep learning algorithm was proposed for detecting bubble patterns in engines. The algorithm consisted of training an autoencoder using normal images, fixing the coefficients of the encoder, and training a fully-connected network using both normal and defective images. To improve the performance of the network, the entire system was fine-tuned. According to [126], a CNN model was designed with ten layers that belong to six grades for detecting defects in X-ray welding images. It was possible to achieve 98.8% classification accuracy using CNN if the ReLU activation function was used for X-ray welding image recognition. A real-time X-ray image analysis method using Support Vector Machines (SVMs) was presented in [127]. Using a background subtraction algorithm, all potential defects were segmented, and three features were extracted, including the defect area, the grayscale average difference, and the grayscale standard deviation. In order to distinguish non-defects from defects, the extracted features were input into an SVM classifier. A real-time X-ray image defect detection method based on the proposed method reduced undetected defects and false alarms. Another SVM-based method for detecting weld defects was described in [128]. The training SVM is trained by extracting three feature vectors from potential weld defects using grey-level profile analysis. In the last step, the SVM is trained to differentiate between defects that are real and those that are potential. A high percentage of correct detections could be achieved using the proposed method. For detecting insert molding in automotive electronics, ref. [129] proposed a Yolov5-based DR image defect detection algorithm. Width and a window level are adjusted in the preprocessing stage of the acquired data, and fast guided filtering is used for edge retention. Using the overlap, tiny anomalies are detected, and a multi-task dataset is constructed. Using Ghost, which replaces the standard convolutional network with the backbone network with enhanced features, the number of parameters can be further reduced. Moreover, CSP-modules are embedded in the neck and backbone of the network to enhance feature extraction. As a result of adding the transformer attention module after spatial pyramid pooling, over-fitting can be avoided while computational effort can be reduced. DR data-based Yolo series target detection algorithms are used as a final step to conduct consistent experiments. For detecting bead toe errors, ref. [130] proposed a lightweight semantic segmentation network. An encoder extracts the texture features of different regions of the tire in the network first. Then, to fuse the encoder's output feature, a decoder is introduced. A reduction in the dimension of the feature maps has allowed the positions of the bead toe to be recorded in the X-ray image. An index of local mIoU (L-mIoU) is proposed to evaluate the final segmentation effect. YOLOv3_EfficientNet is used as the backbone of the methodology instead of YOLOv3_darknet53. It results in a substantial improvement in YOLOv3 mean average precision, as well as a substantial reduction in inference time and storage space. DR image features are then used to enhance the data, thereby increasing the diversity of the clarity and shape of defects. With depth separable convolution, models can be deployed on embedded devices with acceptable accuracy loss ranges. A method was presented in [131] that utilizes deep learning with X-ray images to detect defects in aluminum casting parts used in automobiles, with the goal of improving the accuracy of both the algorithm and data augmentation. The study found that using Feature Pyramid Networks (FPNs) resulted in a 40.9% increase in Mean of Average Precision (mAP) value, making it the most effective modification. Additionally, using RoIAlign instead of RoI pooling in Faster R-CNN improved the accuracy of bounding box location. The study also proposed various data augmentation methods to compensate for the limited availability of X-ray image datasets for defect detection. The results showed that the mAP values for each data augmentation method reached an optimal value and did not continue to increase as the number of datasets increased. Overall, the proposed improvements to the Faster R-CNN algorithm resulted in better performance for X-ray image defect detection of automobile aluminum casting parts. Using the Faster R-CNN detection model with X-ray preprocessing was applied to the detection of tire defects in [132] to improve curve fitting performance. Faster R-CNN precision and recall of defects were improved by adjusting its feature extractor, proposal generator, and box classifier. According to literature [133], triplet deep neural networks can be used to detect weld defects. X-ray images are first preprocessed into relief images to make defects easier to identify. Following that, a deep network is constructed based on triplets, and a feature vector is obtained by mapping the triplets. The distance between similar defect feature vectors and the distance between different types of defect feature vectors must be closer. The SVM is also used for automatic detection and classification of weld defects. Based on the results of two experiments, the proposed method is capable of effectively detecting multiple defects. Tables 6 and 7 together provide a comprehensive overview of the current state of research and practices in the field of deep learning for defect detection in X-ray images. Table 6 summarizes recent research publications, and Table 7 compares the strengths and weaknesses of different techniques. This information can be valuable for anyone interested in the advancement of this field.

Table 6. Recent publications on deep learning defects detection in X-ray images.

Reference	Method	Target	Performance
[125]	Three-Stage Deep Learning Algorithm	Engines	Accuracy rate: above 90%
[126]	Convolutional Neural Network (CNN)	Welding	Recognition accuracy can be more than 90%
[127]	Support Vector Machine (SVM)	Welding	Accuracy rate: 99.4%
[128]	Support Vector Machine (SVM)	Welding	Rate of detection is approximately 99.1%
[129]	Yolov5	Insert Molding	Recognition accuracy: 93.6%
[130]	Lightweight semantic segmentation network	Tire	Achieved 97.1% mIoU and 92.4% L-mIoU for 512 × 512 input images
[131]	Faster R-CNN	Automobile casting aluminum parts	RoIAlign showed a significant improvement in the accuracy of bounding box location compared to RoI pooling, resulting in an increase of 23.6% accuracy under Faster R-CNN
[132]	Faster R-CNN	Tire	Compared with other methods, this method is capable of achieving a higher level of detection accuracy
[133]	Triplet Deep Neural Network	Welding	Can be more effective than traditional methods.
[134]	Deep Convolution Neutral Networks	Aluminum Conductor Composite Core (ACCC)	Can be effective in recognizing small and inconspicuous defects, with a 3.5% improvement in mean Average Precision compared to RetinaNet
[135]	Unsupervised Learning with Generative Adversarial Network	Tire	A tire X-ray dataset achieves 0.873 Area Under Curve (AUC)

Table 6. Cont.

Reference	Method	Target	Performance
[136]	R-CNN	Metal	Can eliminate time-consuming and inconsistent criteria while making judgments more efficient and accurate
[124]	Deep Neural Networks (DNNs)	Actual samples from the hard metal production industry	Indicates that the fusion model outperforms the separate models in terms of recall (100%), precision (60%), F-score (75%), and accuracy (88.24%)

Table 7. Strengths and weaknesses of different deep-learning techniques for identifying defects in X-ray images.

Reference	Method	Strengths	Weaknesses
[125]	Three-stage Deep Learning Algorithm	Ability to adapt to different types of patterns; the three-stage approach allows for more accurate and efficient detection of defects	The accuracy of the model can depend on the specific models used in each stage, if the models are not well-suited for the task, the performance may suffer
[126]	CNN model with 10 layers	Ability to achieve high classification accuracy	May not work well with other types of images
[127]	SVM-based method	Achieved real-time X-ray image analysis and reduced undetected defects and false alarms; can work well with small datasets	SVM's can be sensitive to the choice of kernel and parameters
[129]	Yolov5-based DR image defect detection algorithm	Ability to detect tiny anomalies and improve edge retention by using fast guided filtering	May not work well with other types of images or industries
[130]	Lightweight semantic segmentation network	The dimension reduction allows for accurate recording of bead toe positions in X-ray images; can be trained to work with different types of x-ray images, such as mammograms or chest x-rays	The model may not generalize well to different types of images
[131]	Deep learning with X-ray images and Feature Pyramid Networks (FPNs)	40.9% increase in Mean of Average Precision (mAP) value, can effectively detect objects at different scales, which is important for defect detection in X-ray images as defects can be small and difficult to spot	May have a high false positive rate as X-ray images can have many benign structures that could be mislabeled as defects
[132]	Faster R-CNN detection model with X-ray preprocessing	Improved curve fitting performance; able to handle multiple defect classes; can handle images of different scales, which is important for defect detection in X-ray images, as defects can be small and difficult to spot	Limited to specific type of image and specific type of defect; may have a high false positive rate as X-ray images can have many benign structures that could be mislabeled as defects
[133]	Triplet deep neural network	Effective at detecting multiple defects, it works well with X-ray images, by preprocessing them into relief images to make defects easier to identify	It may not generalize well to different types of images
[124]	Stacked Generalization Ensemble	Improved performance and higher classification accuracy compared to individual models; ability to effectively identify breakdowns during manufacturing process; the ensemble approach can improve the robustness of the model by combining the strengths of multiple models	May not work well with other industries or types of defects

5. Problems and Solutions

5.1. Unbalanced Sample Identification Problem

In industrial products, surface defects can also be detected with deep learning using unbalanced sample sets [137,138]. To train the deep learning model, it is usually necessary to have a balanced sample set of samples of different categories. This ideal situation, however, almost never occurs in the real world. More often than not, the majority of data in the dataset comes from "normal" samples, while "defective" or "abnormal" samples only make up a small portion. Supervised learning is one of the main tasks that suffers from unbalanced sample identification. The algorithm will therefore pay more attention to categories with larger data volumes and underestimate categories with smaller data volumes, affecting the model's generalization and prediction abilities. The data-level process methods aim to maintain a consistent number of samples for all types within the training set. Resolving the unbalanced sample identification issue at the data level can be broken down into five categories: data resampling, data augmentation, class equalization sampling, data source, and synthetic sampling. It is necessary to collect more samples in fewer categories from the data source. By horizontally or vertically flipping, rotating, zooming, cropping, and other operations, we can purposefully increase the number of sample data in each category.

Regarding data resampling [139,140], it is good to resample a sample set to change the proportion of samples in each category, including oversampling and undersampling. Class equalization sampling groups samples by categories and generates sample lists for each category. To ensure that each category has an equal chance of participating in training, a random category is selected during training, and samples are randomly selected from the corresponding sample list. Synthetic samples [141] are generated by combining various characteristics of an existing sample to create a new sample. Using this method, you can create a new sample by randomly selecting a value from the feature.

5.2. Small Sample Problem

As a result of continuous optimization of industrial processes, the number of defective samples has decreased. This makes it difficult to use deep learning methods to detect surface defects in industrial products, since there are fewer and fewer defect images available for deep learning. Overfitting problems in training can easily occur with small samples [142]. Transfer learning applies knowledge gained from one task to a different but related task when there is insufficient data to complete the target task. Consequently, transfer learning is also a critical method for solving the small sample problem. For surface defect detection, literature [143,144] used VGG networks and transfer learning to detect emulsion pump bodies, printed circuit boards, transmission line components, steel plates, and wood surfaces. Fabric surface defect detection using DenseNet and transfer learning was described in [145]. The combination of transfer learning and AlexNet was used to detect surface defects on solar panels and fabrics in [146,147]. Solving the small sample problem can also be achieved by optimizing the network structure. For the first time, GAN was used for image anomaly detection with the AnoGAN model [148] in 2017. A continuous iterative optimization process is used to find an image that matches the test image closest in the latent space, and then DCGAN is used to detect anomalies in that image. The f-AnoGAN model was introduced in [149]. This model proposes a method of encoding an image so that latent points can be quickly mapped, and then using WGAN to detect anomalies. As a result of the introduction of an encoder, the AnoGAN's iterative optimization process is much faster and less time-consuming. Additionally, the GANomaly model was proposed in [150] in 2018. It detects abnormal samples by comparing latent variables obtained by coding with latent variables obtained by reconstructing. There is no requirement for training with negative samples in any of the above models. It is also possible to obtain many sample images by enlarging the data. Using synthetic defects [151], the decorated plastic part dataset is expanded by adding synthetic defects to the defect-free image. Literature [152] described a technique for generating defect representations that combine hand-made and unsupervised learning features.

5.3. Real-Time Problem

It is essential to consider real-time problems when performing surface defect detection in real industrial environments. Real-time detection problems involve reducing detection time and improving detection efficiency to maintain roughly the same accuracy. Research has been conducted on real-time problems by some scholars. To detect surface defects on printed circuit boards, literature [153] suggested combining SSIM and MobileNet. Comparing the proposed algorithm with Faster R-CNN, it maintained high accuracy while being at least 12 times quicker than the existing algorithm. Literature [154] developed a novel 11-layer CNN model for detecting welding defects in robotic welding manufacturing. The proposed method was capable of detecting metal additive manufacturing in real time, which meets specific requirements for online detection.

6. Discussion

Deep learning technology has revolutionized the field of defect detection in industrial products. However, finding a suitable deep learning model for solving the defect detection problem is very difficult due to the particularities of industrial scenarios. In the coming years, deep learning will encounter challenges and trends as it becomes more widely used in industrial fields. A brief description of recent trends and future research directions is provided in this section.

- Integrating deep learning with other methods:

By incorporating other techniques such as traditional image processing, the robustness and performance of the defect detection system in challenging conditions can be enhanced. For instance, using traditional image processing techniques to preprocess the images before inputting them into a deep learning model can improve the quality of the data and make it easier for the model to effectively detect defects. Additionally, integrating deep learning with other techniques, such as physics-based simulations, can provide better understanding of the underlying physical causes of defects and lead to the development of more efficient and effective defect detection methods.

- Adjustment to various lighting scenarios:

Examining industrial products frequently occurs under diverse lighting conditions, which can make it hard to identify defects. Research in this field could concentrate on developing techniques for adapting to various lighting conditions and using them to enhance the precision of defect detection. This could include methods such as image enhancement techniques, color constancy techniques, and multiple exposure fusion techniques, to improve the visibility of defects in different lighting conditions. Additionally, research could also focus on developing deep learning models that are robust to changes in lighting conditions, such as using adversarial training methodologies, to improve the robustness of the model. This may lead to a more accurate and reliable defect detection system that can function in a wide range of lighting scenarios.

- Transparent AI:

To be implemented in industrial environments, defect detection systems need to be transparent and explainable. Research in this field could focus on developing techniques to make deep-learning-based defect detection systems more understandable, so that users can comprehend why a defect was missed or incorrectly identified.

- All aspects need to be taken into account:

In order for a defect detection system to perform well, it must take into account various factors. There are many factors that can influence the accurate detection of defects, such as defect size, shape, the technique for image acquisition, alignment and distortion of images, resolution of images, and algorithmic speed, among others. It is important to consider all of these factors when creating a mature and successful method.

- Limited number of defect samples:

In many industrial applications, deep learning methods require a large training dataset and have high computational costs, and the number of defect samples is often insufficient to detect defects. Additionally, as the product line is frequently updated, new defect types are introduced and the detection process becomes more challenging. When training on normal samples, a simple defect detection method does not have any issues dealing with a small defect dataset, but, when it comes to defect localization and classification, the size of the dataset containing defects can be a challenge.

- Utilizing transfer learning:

Defect patterns may be shared between two different application domains. There may be similarities in the morphology of cracks in two different materials, but they may be different in their sizes and colors. It is currently necessary to train two different networks in order to use current approaches. A well-trained, tested network can transfer its knowledge to a new network to speed up the training process. Currently, transfer learning is not effectively utilized in most approaches.

- Multi-modal sensor integration:

Defect detection in industrial products often relies on visual inspections using cameras or other imaging devices. However, incorporating other types of sensors, such as thermal, acoustic, or vibration sensors, can provide additional information that can aid in the detection of defects. Research in this area could focus on developing methods for integrating data from multiple sensors and using it to improve the accuracy of defect detection. This could include techniques such as sensor fusion, where data from multiple sensors is combined to provide a more comprehensive view of the product, or methods for combining deep learning with other types of sensor data, such as sensor data from IoT devices.

- Continuous learning:

In industrial environments, the product line is frequently updated, and new defect types are introduced. Research in this area could focus on developing methods for continuous online learning, which can be used to adapt the defect detection system as new data is acquired and new defects are introduced. This could include online learning techniques, where the system can continuously update its knowledge as new data is acquired, or active learning methods, where the system can actively select the most informative images for annotation. This would allow the system to adapt to changes in the product line and improve its performance over time.

- Real-time detection:

There are only a few existing defect detection methods that are implemented in real time. In order to apply these methods to real-time inspection scenarios in the future, computationally efficient methods must be developed among these methods in order to achieve detection success rates in real time.

- Reducing the complexity:

Users of defect detection methods are interested in understanding why a defect has been missed or incorrectly identified in an acceptable part when such a method fails to find the defect. The majority of deep learning methods follow a complex architecture, so humans have difficulty understanding the decision-making process and providing a rationale for failure. When it comes to deploying and improving the performance of a system, this can be a challenge. Moreover, in industrial applications, lightweight deep learning networks will be easier to deploy. Often, the processing resources used to support artificial intelligence computations are valuable in quality inspections on production lines and industrial maintenance monitoring. By using lightweight networks, the prediction system's workload can be effectively reduced, which is extremely beneficial for simple terminal deployments and can also reduce costs and performance.

- A common reference database:

Testing can be conducted on different databases, though several studies have failed to provide satisfactory results due to inconsistency in such databases and a lack of testing samples. Additionally, most of the studies presented in this review have their own databases with varying sizes and quality. To evaluate and compare performance in the future, a common reference database would be helpful.

7. Conclusions

Deep learning is rapidly gaining momentum as a powerful tool in the field of defect detection on industrial products. In this paper, we conducted a comprehensive review of the current state-of-the-art in the use of machine learning methods for detecting defects in industrial products. We specifically focused on deep learning methods for detecting surface defects and defects from X-ray images, and provided a detailed overview of the different techniques and algorithms that have been proposed in these areas. We also discussed some of the key challenges and limitations of these methods, and highlighted potential solutions to these problems. The goal of this review was to provide researchers with a clear understanding of the current state-of-the-art in the field of surface defect detection for industrial products, and to serve as a reference for future research in this area.

Author Contributions: Authors contributed as follows: Conceptualization, A.S. and J.R.; methodology, J.R. and M.E.-G.; funding acquisition, J.R. and M.E.-G.; investigation, A.S., J.R. and M.E.-G.; writing original draft preparation, A.S. and J.R.; writing—review and editing, A.S., J.R. and M.E.-G.; supervision, J.R. and M.E.-G. All authors have read and agreed to the published version of the manuscript.

Funding: This research was funded by Natural Sciences and Engineering Research Council of Canada (NSERC), grant number 210471.

Data Availability Statement: In the manuscript, you will find a list of the corresponding websites.

Conflicts of Interest: There are no conflicts of interest between the authors.

References

1. Rasheed, A.; Zafar, B.; Rasheed, A.; Ail, N.; Sajid, M.; Dar, S.H.; Habib, U.; Shehryar, T.; Mahmood, M.T. Fabric Defect Detection Using Computer Vision Techniques: A Comprehensive Review. *Math. Probl. Eng.* **2020**, *2020*, 8189403. [CrossRef]
2. Song, W.; Chen, T.; Gu, Z.; Gai, W.; Huang, W.; Wang, B. Wood Materials Defects Detection Using Image Block Percentile Color Histogram and Eigenvector Texture Feature. In Proceedings of the First International Conference on Information Sciences, Machinery, Materials and Energy, Chongqing China, 11–13 April 2015.
3. Ma, N.; Gao, X.; Wang, C.; Zhang, Y.; You, D.; Zhang, N. Influence of Hysteresis Effect on Contrast of Welding Defects Profile in Magneto-Optical Image. *IEEE Sens. J.* **2020**, *20*, 15034–15042. [CrossRef]
4. Prasitmeeboon, P.; Yau, H. Defect Detection of Particleboards by Visual Analysis and Machine Learning. In Proceedings of the 2019 5th International Conference on Engineering, Applied Sciences and Technology (ICEAST), Luang Prabang, Laos, 2–5 July 2019; pp. 1–4. [CrossRef]
5. Li, J.H.; Quan, X.X.; Wang, Y.L. Research on Defect Detection Algorithm of Ceramic Tile Surface with Multi-feature Fusion. *Comput. Eng. Appl.* **2020**, *56*, 191–198.
6. Wang, F.l.; Zuo, B. Detection of surface cutting defect on magnet using Fourier image reconstruction. *J. Cent. South Univ.* **2016**, *23*, 1123–1131. [CrossRef]
7. Wang, J.; Fu, P.; Gao, R.X. Machine vision intelligence for product defect inspection based on deep learning and Hough transform. *J. Manuf. Syst.* **2019**, *51*, 52–60. [CrossRef]
8. Tsai, D.M.; Huang, C.K. Defect Detection in Electronic Surfaces Using Template-Based Fourier Image Reconstruction. *IEEE Trans. Compon. Packag. Manuf. Technol.* **2019**, *9*, 163–172. [CrossRef]
9. Chang, C.-F.; Wu, J.-L.; Chen, K.-J.; Hsu, M.-C. A hybrid defect detection method for compact camera lens. *Adv. Mech. Eng.* **2017**, *9*, 1687814017722949. [CrossRef]
10. Liu, Y.; Xu, K.; Xu, J. An Improved MB-LBP Defect Recognition Approach for the Surface of Steel Plates. *Appl. Sci.* **2019**, *9*, 4222. [CrossRef]
11. Putri, A.P.; Rachmat, H.; Atmaja, D.S.E. Design of Automation System for Ceramic Surface Quality Control Using Fuzzy Logic Method at Balai Besar Keramik (BBK). *MATEC Web. Conf.* **2017**, *135*, 53. [CrossRef]

12. Yang, J.; Li, S.; Wang, Z.; Dong, H.; Wang, J.; Tang, S. Using Deep Learning to Detect Defects in Manufacturing: A Comprehensive Survey and Current Challenges. *Materials* **2020**, *13*, 5755. [CrossRef]
13. Lee, D.; Kang, Y.; Park, C.; Won, S. Defect Detection Algorithm in Steel Billets Using Morphological Top-Hat filter. *IFAC Proc. Vol.* **2009**, *42*, 209–212. [CrossRef]
14. Zhu, D.; Pan, R.; Gao, W.; Zhang, J. Yarn-Dyed Fabric Defect Detection Based On Autocorrelation Function And GLCM. *Autex Res. J.* **2015**, *15*, 226–232. [CrossRef]
15. Gao, X.; Xie, Y.; Chen, Z.; You, D. Fractal feature detection of high-strength steel weld defects by magneto optical imaging. *Trans. China Weld. Inst.* **2017**, *38*, 1–4. [CrossRef]
16. Yun, J.P.; Choi, S.H.; Kim, J.W.; Kim, S.W. Automatic detection of cracks in raw steel block using Gabor filter optimized by univariate dynamic encoding algorithm for searches (uDEAS). *NDT E. Int.* **2009**, *42*, 389–397. [CrossRef]
17. Li, Y.; Liu, M. Aerial Image Classification Using Color Coherence Vectors and Rotation & Uniform Invariant LBP Descriptors. In Proceedings of the 2018 IEEE 3rd Advanced Information Technology, Electronic and Automation Control Conference (IAEAC), Chongqing China, 12–14 October 2018; pp. 653–656. [CrossRef]
18. Ren, H.; Tian, K.; Hong, S.; Dong, B.; Xing, F.; Qin, L. Visualized investigation of defect in cementitious materials with electrical resistance tomography. *Constr. Build. Mater.* **2019**, *196*, 428–436. [CrossRef]
19. Ma, Y.; Li, Q.; He, F.; Liu, Y.; Xi, S. Adaptive segmentation algorithm for metal surface defects. *Chin. J. Sci. Instrum.* **2017**, *38*, 245–251.
20. Li, S.; Yang, J.; Wang, Z.; Zhu, S.; Yang, G. Review of Development and Application of Defect Detection Technology. *Acta Autom. Sin.* **2020**, *46*, 2319–2336.
21. Papageorgiou, E.I.; Theodosiou, T.; Margetis, G.; Dimitriou, N.; Charalampous, P.; Tzovaras, D.; Samakovlis, I. Short Survey of Artificial Intelligent Technologies for Defect Detection in Manufacturing. In Proceedings of the 2021 12th International Conference on Information, Intelligence, Systems & Applications (IISA), Chania Crete, Greece, 12–14 July 2021; pp. 1–7. [CrossRef]
22. Tao, X.; Hou, W.; Xu, D. A Survey of Surface Defect Detection Methods Based on Deep Learning. *Acta Autom. Sin.* **2020**, *47*, 1017–1034.
23. Zhang, Z.; Pang, W.; Xie, W.; Lv, M.; Wang, Y. Deep Learning for Real-time Applications: A Survey. *J. Softw.* **2020**, *31*, 2654–2677.
24. Ma, S.; Wu, N.; Li, X. Deep learning with big data: State of the art and development. *CAAI Trans. Intell. Syst.* **2016**, *11*, 728–742.
25. Kumar, A. Computer-Vision-Based Fabric Defect Detection: A Survey. *IEEE Trans. Ind. Electron.* **2008**, *55*, 348–363. [CrossRef]
26. Ahuja, S.K.; Shukla, M.K. A survey of computer vision based corrosion detection approaches. In *International Conference on Information and Communication Technology for Intelligent Systems*; Springer: Berlin/Heidelberg, Germany, 2017; pp. 55–63.
27. Cao, W.; Liu, Q.; He, Z. Review of Pavement Defect Detection Methods. *IEEE Access* **2020**, *8*, 14531–14544. [CrossRef]
28. Fouzia, M.T.; Nirmala, K. A literature survey on various methods used for metal defects detection using image segmentation. *Evaluation* **2010**, *5*, 8.
29. Czimmermann, T.; Ciuti, G.; Milazzo, M.; Chiurazzi, M.; Roccella, S.; Oddo, C.M.; Dario, P. Visual-Based Defect Detection and Classification Approaches for Industrial Applications—A SURVEY. *Sensors* **2020**, *20*, 1459. [CrossRef] [PubMed]
30. Silvestre-Blanes, J.; Albero-Albero, T.; Miralles, I.; Pérez-Llorens, R.; Moreno, J. A Public Fabric Database for Defect Detection Methods and Results. *Autex Res. J.* **2019**, *19*, 363–374. [CrossRef]
31. Faghih-Roohi, S.; Hajizadeh, S.; Núñez, A.; Babuska, R.; De Schutter, B. Deep convolutional neural networks for detection of rail surface defects. In Proceedings of the 2016 International Joint Conference on Neural Networks (IJCNN), Vancouver, BC, Canada, 24–29 July 2016; pp. 2584–2589. [CrossRef]
32. Gan, J.; Li, Q.; Wang, J.; Yu, H. A Hierarchical Extractor-Based Visual Rail Surface Inspection System. *IEEE Sens. J.* **2017**, *17*, 7935–7944. [CrossRef]
33. Luan, C.; Cui, R.; Sun, L.; Lin, Z. A Siamese Network Utilizing Image Structural Differences For Cross-Category Defect Detection. In Proceedings of the 2020 IEEE International Conference on Image Processing (ICIP), Abu Dhabi, United Arab Emirates, 25–28 October 2020; pp. 778–782. [CrossRef]
34. Park, J.-K.; Kwon, B.-K.; Park, J.-H.; Kang, D.-J. Machine learning-based imaging system for surface defect inspection. *Int. J. Precis. Eng. Manuf.-Green Technol.* **2006**, *3*, 303–310. [CrossRef]
35. Liang, Q.; Zhu, W.; Sun, W.; Yu, Z.; Wang, Y.; Zhang, D. In-line inspection solution for codes on complex backgrounds for the plastic container industry. *Measurement* **2019**, *148*, 106965. [CrossRef]
36. Anvar, A.; Cho, Y.I. Automatic Metallic Surface Defect Detection using ShuffleDefectNet. *J. Korea Soc. Comput. Inf.* **2020**, *25*, 19–26.
37. Racki, D.; Tomazevic, D.; Skocaj, D. Towards surface anomaly detection with deep learning. *Procedia CIRP* **2019**, *79*, 484–489.
38. Hu, B.; Wang, J. Detection of PCB Surface Defects With Improved Faster-RCNN and Feature Pyramid Network. *IEEE Access* **2020**, *8*, 108335–108345. [CrossRef]
39. Tao, X.; Zhang, D.; Wang, Z.; Liu, X.; Zhang, H.; Xu, D. Detection of Power Line Insulator Defects Using Aerial Images Analyzed With Convolutional Neural Networks. *IEEE Trans. Syst. Man Cybern. Syst.* **2020**, *50*, 1486–1498. [CrossRef]
40. Song, L.; Li, X.; Yang, Y.; Zhu, X.; Guo, Q.; Yang, H. Detection of Micro-Defects on Metal Screw Surfaces Based on Deep Convolutional Neural Networks. *Sensors* **2018**, *18*, 3709. [CrossRef]
41. Gao, X.; Jian, M.; Hu, M.; Tanniru, M.; Li, S. Faster multi-defect detection system in shield tunnel using combination of FCN and faster RCNN. *Adv. Struct. Eng.* **2019**, *22*, 2907–2921. [CrossRef]

42. Balzategui, J.; Eciolaza, L.; Arana-Arexolaleiba, N. Defect detection on Polycrystalline solar cells using Electroluminescence and Fully Convolutional Neural Networks. In Proceedings of the 2020 IEEE/SICE International Symposium on System Integration (SII), Honolulu, HI, USA, 12–15 January 2020; pp. 949–953. [CrossRef]
43. Dike, H.U.; Zhou, Y.; Deveerasetty, K.K.; Wu, Q. Unsupervised Learning Based On Artificial Neural Network: A Review. In Proceedings of the 2018 IEEE International Conference on Cyborg and Bionic Systems (CBS), Shenzhen, China, 25–27 October 2018; pp. 322–327. [CrossRef]
44. Defard, T.; Setkov, A.; Loesch, A.; Audigier, R. PaDiM: A Patch Distribution Modeling Framework for Anomaly Detection and Localization. *arXiv* **2020**, arXiv:2011.08785.
45. Cohen, N.; Hoshen, Y. Sub-Image Anomaly Detection with Deep Pyramid Correspondences. *arXiv* **2020**, arXiv:2005.02357.
46. Roth, K.; Pemula, L.; Zepeda, J.; Schölkopf, B.; Brox, T.; Gehler, P. Towards Total Recall in Industrial Anomaly Detection. *arXiv* **2021**, arXiv:2106.08265.
47. Wang, X.; Li, J.; Yao, M.; He, W.; Qian, Y. Solar Cells Surface Defects Detection Based on Deep Learning. *Pattern Recognit. Artif. Intell.* **2014**, *27*, 517–523.
48. Mei, S.; Yang, H.; Yin, Z. An Unsupervised-Learning-Based Approach for Automated Defect Inspection on Textured Surfaces. *IEEE Trans. Instrum. Meas.* **2018**, *67*, 1266–1277. [CrossRef]
49. Silvén, O.; Niskanen, M.; Kauppine, H. Wood inspection with non-supervised clustering. *Mach. Vis. Appl.* **2003**, *13*, 275–285. [CrossRef]
50. Lai, Y.T.K.; Hu, J.S. A Texture Generation Approach for Detection of Novel Surface Defects. In Proceedings of the 2018 IEEE International Conference on Systems, Man, and Cybernetics (SMC), Miyazaki, Japan, 7–10 October 2018; pp. 4357–4362. [CrossRef]
51. Yang, H.; Chen, Y.; Song, K.; Yin, Z. Multiscale Feature-Clustering-Based Fully Convolutional Autoencoder for Fast Accurate Visual Inspection of Texture Surface Defects. *IEEE Trans. Autom. Sci. Eng.* **2019**, *16*, 1450–1467. [CrossRef]
52. Zhai, W.; Zhu, J.; Cao, Y.; Wang, Z. A Generative Adversarial Network Based Framework for Unsupervised Visual Surface Inspection. In Proceedings of the 2018 IEEE International Conference on Acoustics, Speech and Signal Processing (ICASSP), Calgary, AB, Canada, 15–20 April 2018; pp. 1283–1287. [CrossRef]
53. Liu, K.; Li, A.; Wen, X.; Chen, H.; Yang, P. Steel Surface Defect Detection Using GAN and One-Class Classifier. In Proceedings of the 2019 25th International Conference on Automation and Computing (ICAC), Lancaster, UK, 5–7 September 2019; pp. 1–6. [CrossRef]
54. Dai, W.; Mujeeb, A.; Erdt, M.; Sourin, A. Soldering defect detection in automatic optical inspection. *Adv. Eng. Inform.* **2020**, *43*, 101004. [CrossRef]
55. Di, H.; Ke, X.; Peng, Z.; Dongdong, Z. Surface defect classification of steels with a new semi-supervised learning method. *Opt. Lasers Eng.* **2019**, *117*, 40–48. [CrossRef]
56. Xu, L.; Lv, S.; Deng, Y.; Li, X. A Weakly Supervised Surface Defect Detection Based on Convolutional Neural Network. *IEEE Access* **2020**, *8*, 42285–42296. [CrossRef]
57. Ren, J.; Gabbar, H.A.; Huang, X.; Saberironaghi, A. Defect Detection for Printed Circuit Board Assembly Using Deep Learning. In Proceedings of the International Conference Control Science and System Engineering (ICCSSE), Guangzhou, China, 14–16 July 2022.
58. He, Y.; Song, K.; Dong, H.; Yan, Y. Semi-supervised defect classification of steel surface based on multi-training and generative adversarial network. *Opt. Lasers Eng.* **2019**, *122*, 294–302. [CrossRef]
59. Zheng, X.; Wang, H.; Chen, J.; Kong, Y.; Zheng, S. A Generic Semi-Supervised Deep Learning-Based Approach for Automated Surface Inspection. *IEEE Access* **2020**, *8*, 114088–114099. [CrossRef]
60. Fu, G.; Sun, P.; Zhu, W.; Yang, J.; Cao, Y.; Yang, M.Y.; Cao, Y. A deep-learning-based approach for fast and robust steel surface defects classification. *Opt. Lasers Eng.* **2019**, *121*, 397–405. [CrossRef]
61. Akhyar, F.; Lin, C.Y.; Muchtar, K.; Wu, T.Y.; Ng, H.F. High Efficient Single-stage Steel Surface Defect Detection. In Proceedings of the 2019 16th IEEE International Conference on Advanced Video and Signal Based Surveillance (AVSS), Taipei, Taiwan, 18–21 September 2019; pp. 1–4. [CrossRef]
62. Li, K.; Wang, X.; Ji, L. Application of Multi-Scale Feature Fusion and Deep Learning in Detection of Steel Strip Surface Defect. In Proceedings of the 2019 International Conference on Artificial Intelligence and Advanced Manufacturing (AIAM), Dublin, Ireland, 17–19 October 2019; pp. 656–661. [CrossRef]
63. Wang, T.; Chen, Y.; Qiao, M.; Snoussi, H. A fast and robust convolutional neural network-based defect detection model in product quality control. *Int. J. Adv. Manuf. Technol.* **2018**, *94*, 3465–3471. [CrossRef]
64. Weimer, D.; Scholz-Reiter, B.; Shpitalni, M. Design of deep convolutional neural network architectures for automated feature extraction in industrial inspection. *CIRP Ann.* **2016**, *65*, 417–420. [CrossRef]
65. Qiu, L.; Wu, X.; Yu, Z. A High-Efficiency Fully Convolutional Networks for Pixel-Wise Surface Defect Detection. *IEEE Access* **2019**, *7*, 15884–15893. [CrossRef]
66. Yu, Z.; Wu, X.; Gu, X. Fully convolutional networks for surface defect inspection in industrial environment. In *International Conference on Computer Vision Systems*; Springer: Berlin/Heidelberg, Germany, 2017; pp. 417–426.
67. Mujeeb, A.; Dai, W.; Erdt, M.; Sourin, A. Unsupervised Surface Defect Detection Using Deep Autoencoders and Data Augmentation. In Proceedings of the 2018 International Conference on Cyberworlds (CW), Singapore, 3–5 October 2018; pp. 391–398. [CrossRef]

68. Deng, Z.; Yan, X.; Liu, X. Extremal Region Analysis based Deep Learning Framework for Defects Detection. In Proceedings of the 2020 IEEE International Conference on Information Technology, Big Data and Artificial Intelligence (ICIBA), Chongqing, China, 6–8 November 2020; pp. 142–145. [CrossRef]
69. Wang, X.; Zhang, X.; Zhou, N. Improved YOLOv5 with BiFPN on PCB Defect Detection. In Proceedings of the 2021 2nd International Conference on Artificial Intelligence and Computer Engineering (ICAICE), Hangzhou, China, 5–7 November 2021; pp. 196–199. [CrossRef]
70. Lan, Z.; Hong, Y.; Li, Y. An improved YOLOv3 method for PCB surface defect detection. In Proceedings of the 2021 IEEE International Conference on Power Electronics, Computer Applications (ICPECA), Shenyang, China, 22–24 January 2021; pp. 1009–1015. [CrossRef]
71. Luo, J.; Yang, Z.; Li, S.; Wu, Y. FPCB Surface Defect Detection: A Decoupled Two-Stage Object Detection Framework. *IEEE Trans. Instrum. Meas.* **2021**, *70*, 1–11. [CrossRef]
72. Zhang, Q.; Wu, B.; Shao, Y.; Ye, Z. Surface Defect Detection of Rails Based on Convolutional Neural Network Multi-Scale-Cross FastFlow. In Proceedings of the 2022 5th International Conference on Pattern Recognition and Artificial Intelligence (PRAI), Chengdu, China, 19–21 August 2022; pp. 405–411. [CrossRef]
73. Yu, Y.; Wang, M.; Wang, Z.; Zhou, P. Surface Defect Detection of Hight-speed Railway Hub Based on Improved YOLOv3 Algorithm. In Proceedings of the 2021 IEEE 4th Advanced Information Management, Communicates, Electronic and Automation Control Conference (IMCEC), Xi'an, China, 25–27 May 2021; pp. 1386–1390. [CrossRef]
74. Kang, G.; Gao, S.; Yu, L.; Zhang, D. Deep Architecture for High-Speed Railway Insulator Surface Defect Detection: Denoising Autoencoder With Multitask Learning. *IEEE Trans. Instrum. Meas.* **2019**, *68*, 2679–2690. [CrossRef]
75. Natarajan, V.; Hung, T.Y.; Vaikundam, S.; Chia, L.T. Convolutional networks for voting-based anomaly classification in metal surface inspection. In Proceedings of the 2017 IEEE International Conference on Industrial Technology (ICIT), Toronto, ON, Canada, 22–25 March 2017; pp. 986–991. [CrossRef]
76. He, H.; Yuan, M.; Liu, X. Research on Surface Defect Detection Method of Metal Workpiece Based on Machine Learning. In Proceedings of the 2021 6th International Conference on Intelligent Computing and Signal Processing (ICSP), Xi'an, China, 9–11 April 2021; pp. 881–884. [CrossRef]
77. Feng, Z.; Guo, L.; Huang, D.; Li, R. Electrical Insulator Defects Detection Method Based on YOLOv5. In Proceedings of the 2021 IEEE 10th Data Driven Control and Learning Systems Conference (DDCLS), Suzhou, China, 14–16 May 2021; pp. 979–984. [CrossRef]
78. Hu, M.; Ju, X. Two-stage insulator self-explosion defect detection method based on Mask R-CNN. In Proceedings of the 2021 2nd International Conference on Intelligent Computing and Human-Computer Interaction (ICHCI), Shenyang, China, 17–19 December 2021; pp. 13–18. [CrossRef]
79. Zheng, L.; Wang, X.; Wang, Q.; Wang, S.; Liu, X. A Fabric Defect Detection Method Based on Improved YOLOv5. In Proceedings of the 2021 7th International Conference on Computer and Communications (ICCC), Chengdu, China, 10–13 December 2021; pp. 620–624. [CrossRef]
80. Liu, Q.; Wang, C.; Li, Y.; Gao, M.; Li, J. A Fabric Defect Detection Method Based on Deep Learning. *IEEE Access* **2022**, *10*, 4284–4296. [CrossRef]
81. Liu, K.H.; Chen, S.J.; Liu, T.J. Unsupervised UNet for Fabric Defect Detection. In Proceedings of the 2022 IEEE International Conference on Consumer Electronics—Taiwan, Taipei, Taiwan, 6–8 July 2022; pp. 205–206. [CrossRef]
82. Huang, Y.; Yi, M.; Yang, W.; Yang, M. Research on surface defect intelligent detection technology of non-woven fabric based on support vector machine. In Proceedings of the 2022 IEEE International Conference on Electrical Engineering, Big Data and Algorithms (EEBDA), Changchun, China, 24–26 February 2022; pp. 895–898. [CrossRef]
83. Li, L.; Jiang, Z.; Li, Y. Surface Defect Detection Algorithm of Aluminum Based on Improved Faster RCNN. In Proceedings of the 2021 IEEE 9th International Conference on Information, Communication and Networks (ICICN), Xi'an, China, 19–21 August 2021; pp. 527–531. [CrossRef]
84. Sison, H.; Konghuayrob, P.; Kaitwanidvilai, S. A Convolutional Neural Network for Segmentation of Background Texture and Defect on Copper Clad Lamination Surface. In Proceedings of the 2018 International Conference on Engineering, Applied Sciences, and Technology (ICEAST), Phuket, Thailand, 4–7 July 2018; pp. 1–4. [CrossRef]
85. Lin, Z.; Guo, Z.; Yang, J. Research on texture defect detection based on faster-rcnn and feature fusion. In Proceedings of the 2019 11th International Conference on Machine Learning and Computing, Zhuhai, China, 22–24 February 2019; pp. 429–433.
86. Wang, D.; Yu, W.; Lian, P.; Zhang, M. Textile Defect Detection Algorithm Based on Unsupervised Learning. In Proceedings of the 2022 7th International Conference on Image, Vision and Computing (ICIVC), Xi'an, China, 26–28 July 2022; pp. 81–86. [CrossRef]
87. Sun, X.; Gu, J.; Huang, R.; Zou, R.; Giron Palomares, B. Surface Defects Recognition of Wheel Hub Based on Improved Faster R-CNN. *Electronics* **2019**, *8*, 481. [CrossRef]
88. Chen, L.; Zhou, Y.; Zhou, H.; Zu, J. Detection of Polarizer Surface Defects Based on an Improved Lightweight YOLOv3 Model. In Proceedings of the 2022 4th International Conference on Intelligent Control, Measurement and Signal Processing (ICMSP), Hangzhou, China, 8–10 July 2022; pp. 138–142. [CrossRef]
89. Li, P.; Dong, Z.; Shi, J.; Pang, Z.; Li, J. Detection of Small Size Defects in Belt Layer of Radial Tire Based on Improved Faster R-CNN. In Proceedings of the 2021 11th International Conference on Information Science and Technology (ICIST), Chengdu, China, 21–23 May 2021; pp. 531–538. [CrossRef]

90. Wang, X.; Hu, Z. Grid-based pavement crack analysis using deep learning. In Proceedings of the 2017 4th International Conference on Transportation Information and Safety (ICTIS), Banff, AB, Canada, 8–10 August 2017; pp. 917–924. [CrossRef]
91. Zhang, M.; Yin, L. Solar Cell Surface Defect Detection Based on Improved YOLO v5. *IEEE Access* **2022**, *10*, 80804–80815. [CrossRef]
92. Azizah, L.M.; Umayah, S.F.; Riyadi, S.; Damarjati, C.; Utama, N.A. Deep learning implementation using convolutional neural network in mangosteen surface defect detection. In Proceedings of the 2017 7th IEEE International Conference on Control System, Computing and Engineering (ICCSCE), Penang, Malaysia, 24–26 November 2017; pp. 242–246. [CrossRef]
93. Zhang, A.; Wang, K.C.; Li, B.; Yang, E.; Dai, X.; Peng, Y.; Fei, Y.; Liu, Y.; Li, J.Q.; Chen, C. Automated pixel-level pavement crack detection on 3d asphalt surfaces using a deep-learning network. *Comput.-Aided Civ. Infrastruct. Eng.* **2017**, *32*, 805–819. [CrossRef]
94. Li, Y.; Wang, Z. Research on Textile Defect Detection Based on Improved Cascade R-CNN. In Proceedings of the 2021 International Conference on Artificial Intelligence and Electromechanical Automation (AIEA), Guangzhou, China, 14–16 May 2021; pp. 43–46. [CrossRef]
95. He, Z.; Liu, Q. Deep Regression Neural Network for Industrial Surface Defect Detection. *IEEE Access* **2020**, *8*, 35583–35591. [CrossRef]
96. Wei, R.; Bi, Y. Research on Recognition Technology of Aluminum Profile Surface Defects Based on Deep Learning. *Materials* **2019**, *12*, 1681, PMCID:PMC6566656. [CrossRef]
97. Hang, J.; Sun, H.; Yu, X.; Rodríguez-Andina, J.J.; Yang, X. Surface Defect Detection in Sanitary Ceramics Based on Lightweight Object Detection Network. *IEEE Open J. Ind. Electron. Soc.* **2022**, *3*, 473–483. [CrossRef]
98. Khumaidi, A.; Yuniarno, E.M.; Purnomo, M.H. Welding defect classification based on convolution neural network (CNN) and Gaussian kernel. In Proceedings of the 2017 International Seminar on Intelligent Technology and Its Applications (ISITIA), Surabaya, Indonesia, 28–29 August 2017; pp. 261–265. [CrossRef]
99. Cha, Y.-J.; Choi, W.; Buyukozturk, O. Deep learning-based crack damage detection using convolutional neural networks. *Comput.-Aided Civ. Infrastruct. Eng.* **2017**, *32*, 361–378. [CrossRef]
100. Roslan, M.I.B.; Ibrahim, Z.; Aziz, Z.A. Real-Time Plastic Surface Defect Detection Using Deep Learning. In Proceedings of the 2022 IEEE 12th Symposium on Computer Applications & Industrial Electronics (ISCAIE), Penang, Malaysia, 21–22 May 2022; pp. 111–116. [CrossRef]
101. Xu, X.; Zheng, H.; Guo, Z.; Wu, X.; Zheng, Z. SDD-CNN: Small Data-Driven Convolution Neural Networks for Subtle Roller Defect Inspection. *Appl. Sci.* **2019**, *9*, 1364. [CrossRef]
102. Yuan, Z.-C.; Zhang, Z.-T.; Su, H.; Zhang, L.; Shen, F.; Zhang, F. Vision-based defect detection for mobile phone cover glass using deep neural networks. *Int. J. Precis. Eng. Manuf.-Green Technol.* **2018**, *19*, 801–810. [CrossRef]
103. Guan, S.; Wang, X.; Wang, J.; Yu, Z.; Wang, X.; Zhang, C.; Liu, T.; Liu, D.; Wang, J.; Zhang, L. Ceramic ring defect detection based on improved YOLOv5. In Proceedings of the 2022 3rd International Conference on Computer Vision, Image and Deep Learning & International Conference on Computer Engineering and Applications (CVIDL & ICCEA), Changchun, China, 20–22 May 2022; pp. 115–118. [CrossRef]
104. Chen, H.; Pang, Y.; Hu, Q.; Liu, K. Solar cell surface defect inspection based on multispectral convolutional neural network. *J. Intell. Manuf.* **2018**, *31*, 453–468. [CrossRef]
105. Yang, Z.; Zhang, M.; Li, C.; Meng, Z.; Li, Y.; Chen, Y.; Liu, L. Image Classification for Automobile Pipe Joints Surface Defect Detection Using Wavelet Decomposition and Convolutional Neural Network. *IEEE Access* **2022**, *10*, 77191–77204. [CrossRef]
106. Xu, C.; Li, L.; Li, J.; Wen, C. Surface Defects Detection and Identification of Lithium Battery Pole Piece Based on Multi-Feature Fusion and PSO-SVM. *IEEE Access* **2021**, *9*, 85232–85239. [CrossRef]
107. Maestro-Watson, D.; Balzategui, J.; Eciolaza, L.; Arana-Arexolaleiba, N. Deep learning for deflectometric inspection of specular surfaces. In *The 13th International Conference on Soft Computing Models in Industrial and Environmental Applications*; Springer: Berlin/Heidelberg, Germany, 2018; pp. 280–289.
108. Ren, R.; Hung, T.; Tan, K.C. A Generic Deep-Learning-Based Approach for Automated Surface Inspection. *IEEE Trans. Cybern.* **2018**, *48*, 929–940. [CrossRef]
109. Li, Y.; Lin, S.; Liu, C.; Kong, Q. The Defects Detection in Steel Coil End Face Based on SCED-Net. In Proceedings of the 2022 International Joint Conference on Neural Networks (IJCNN), Padua, Italy, 18–23 July 2022; pp. 1–6. [CrossRef]
110. Xie, L.; Xiang, X.; Xu, H.; Wang, L.; Lin, L.; Yin, G. FFCNN: A Deep Neural Network for Surface Defect Detection of Magnetic Tile. *IEEE Trans. Ind. Electron.* **2021**, *68*, 3506–3516. [CrossRef]
111. PLien, C.; Zhao, Q. Product Surface Defect Detection Based on Deep Learning. In Proceedings of the 2018 IEEE 16th Intl Conf on Dependable, Autonomic and Secure Computing, 16th Intl Conf on Pervasive Intelligence and Computing, 4th Intl Conf on Big Data Intelligence and Computing and Cyber Science and Technology Congress (DASC/PiCom/DataCom/CyberSciTech), Athens, Greece, 12–15 August 2018; pp. 250–255. [CrossRef]
112. Yang, X.; Dong, F.; Liang, F.; Zhang, G. Chip defect detection based on deep learning method. In Proceedings of the 2021 IEEE International Conference on Power Electronics, Computer Applications (ICPECA), Shenyang, China, 22–24 January 2021; pp. 215–219. [CrossRef]
113. Wu, X.; Cao, K.; Gu, X. A surface defect detection based on convolutional neural network. In *International Conference on Computer Vision Systems*; Springer: Berlin/Heidelberg, Germany, 2017; pp. 185–194.

114. Lei, S.; Guo, Y.; Liu, Y.; Li, F.; Zhang, G.; Yang, D. Detection of Mechanical Defects of High Voltage Circuit Breaker based on Improved Edge Detection and Deep Learning Algorithms. In Proceedings of the 2022 6th International Conference on Electric Power Equipment-Switching Technology (ICEPE-ST), Seoul, Republic of Korea, 15–18 March 2022; pp. 372–375. [CrossRef]
115. Bergmann, P.; Fauser, M.; Sattlegger, D.; Steger, C. MVTec AD—A Comprehensive Real-World Dataset for Unsupervised Anomaly Detection. In Proceedings of the 2019 IEEE/CVF Conference on Computer Vision and Pattern Recognition (CVPR), Long Beach, CA, USA, 15–20 June 2019; pp. 9584–9592. [CrossRef]
116. Lv, X.; Duan, F.; Jiang, J.-j.; Fu, X.; Gan, L. Deep Metallic Surface Defect Detection: The New Benchmark and Detection Network. *Sensors* **2020**, *20*, 1562. [CrossRef]
117. Li, L.; Ma, W.; Li, L.; Lu, C. Research on Detection Algorithm for Bridge Cracks Based on Deep Learning. *Acta Autom. Sin.* **2019**, *45*, 1727–1742.
118. Tang, S.; He, F.; Huang, X.; Yang, J. Online PCB Defect Detector on A New PCB Defect Dataset. *arXiv* **2019**, arXiv:1902.06197.
119. Dorafsha, S.; Thomas, R.J.; Maguire, M. SDNET2018: An annotated image dataset for non-contact concrete crack detection using deep convolutional neural networks. *Data Brief.* **2018**, *21*, 1664–1668. [CrossRef]
120. Zhang, L.; Yang, F.; Zhang, Y.D.; Zhu, Y.J. Road crack detection using deep convolutional neural network. In Proceedings of the 2016 IEEE International Conference on Image Processing (ICIP), Phoenix, AZ, USA, 25–28 September 2016; pp. 3708–3712. [CrossRef]
121. Cui, L.; Qi, Z.; Chen, Z.; Meng, F.; Shi, Y. *Pavement Distress Detection Using Random Decision Forests*; Springer: Sydney, NSW, Australia, 2015; pp. 95–102.
122. Deitsch, S.; Christlein, V.; Berger, S.; Buerhop-Lutz, C.; Maier, A.; Gallwitz, F.; Riess, C. Automatic classification of defective photovoltaic module cells in electroluminescence images. *Sol. Energy* **2019**, *185*, 455–468. [CrossRef]
123. Huang, Y.; Qiu, C.; Guo, Y.; Wang, X.; Yuan, K. Surface Defect Saliency of Magnetic Tile. In Proceedings of the 2018 IEEE 14th International Conference on Automation Science and Engineering (CASE), Munich, Germany, 20–24 August 2018; pp. 612–617. [CrossRef]
124. Kotsiopoulos, T.; Leontaris, L.; Dimitriou, N.; Ioannidis, D.; Oliveira, F.; Sacramento, J.; Amanatiadis, S.; Karagiannis, G.; Votis, K.; Tzovaras, D.; et al. Deep multi-sensorial data analysis for production monitoring in hard metal industry. *Int. J. Adv. Manuf. Technol.* **2021**, *115*, 823–836. [CrossRef]
125. Ren, J.; Ren, R.; Green, M.; Huang, X. Defect Detection from X-Ray Images Using A Three-Stage Deep Learning Algorithm. In Proceedings of the 2019 IEEE Canadian Conference of Electrical and Computer Engineering (CCECE), Edmonton, AB, Canada, 5–8 May 2019; pp. 1–4. [CrossRef]
126. Li, Y.; Gao, W. Research on X-ray welding image defect detection based on convolution neural network. *J. Phys. Conf. Ser.* **2019**, *1237*, 032005. [CrossRef]
127. Shao, J.; Shi, H.; Du, D.; Wang, L.; Cao, H. Automatic weld defect detection in real-time X-ray images based on support vector machine. In Proceedings of the 2011 4th International Congress on Image and Signal Processing, Shanghai, China, 15–17 October 2011; pp. 1842–1846. [CrossRef]
128. Wang, Y.; Guo, H. Weld Defect Detection of X-ray Images Based on Support Vector Machine. *IETE Tech. Rev.* **2014**, *31*, 137–142. [CrossRef]
129. Wang, B.; Huang, F. A Lightweight Deep Network for Defect Detection of Insert Molding Based on X-ray Imaging. *Sensors* **2021**, *21*, 5612. [CrossRef]
130. Yi, X.; Peng, C.; Zhang, Z.; Xiao, L. The defect detection for X-ray images based on a new lightweight semantic segmentation network. *Math. Biosci. Eng.* **2022**, *19*, 4178–4195. [CrossRef] [PubMed]
131. Du, W.; Shen, H.; Fu, J.; Zhang, G.; He, Q. Approaches for improvement of the X-ray image defect detection of automobile casting aluminum parts based on deep learning. *NDT E Int.* **2019**, *107*, 102144, ISSN 0963-8695. [CrossRef]
132. Chen, J.; Li, Y.; Zhao, J. X-ray of Tire Defects Detection via Modified Faster R-CNN. In Proceedings of the 2019 2nd International Conference on Safety Produce Informatization (IICSPI), Chongqing, China, 28–30 November 2019; pp. 257–260. [CrossRef]
133. Liu, X.; Liu, J.; Qu, F.; Zhu, H.; Lu, D. A Weld Defect Detection Method Based on Triplet Deep Neural Network. In Proceedings of the 2020 Chinese Control And Decision Conference (CCDC), Hefei, China, 22–24 August 2020; pp. 649–653. [CrossRef]
134. Hu, Y.; Wang, J.; Zhu, Y.; Wang, Z.; Chen, D.; Zhang, J.; Ding, H. Automatic defect detection from X-ray Scans for Aluminum Conductor Composite Core Wire Based on Classification Neutral Network. *NDT E Int.* **2021**, *124*, 102549, ISSN 0963-8695. [CrossRef]
135. Wang, Y.; Zhang, Y.; Zheng, L.; Yin, L.; Chen, J.; Lu, J. Unsupervised Learning with Generative Adversarial Network for Automatic Tire Defect Detection from X-ray Images. *Sensors* **2021**, *21*, 6773. [CrossRef]
136. Lin, C.H.; Ho, C.W.; Hu, G.H.; Kuo, P.C.; Hu, C.Y. Alloy Cast Product Defect Detection Based on Object Detection. In Proceedings of the 2021 International Symposium on Intelligent Signal Processing and Communication Systems (ISPACS), Hualien City, Taiwan, 16–19 November 2021; pp. 1–2. [CrossRef]
137. Tao, X.; Li, Q.; Ren, C.; Guo, W.; He, Q.; Liu, R.; Zou, J. Affinity and class probability-based fuzzy support vector machine for imbalanced data sets. *Neural. Netw.* **2020**, *122*, 289–307. [CrossRef] [PubMed]
138. Ali-Gombe, A.; Elyan, E. MFC-GAN: Class-imbalanced dataset classification using Multiple Fake Class Generative Adversarial Network. *Neurocomputing* **2019**, *361*, 212–221. [CrossRef]

139. Bennin, K.E.; Keung, J.W.; Monden, A. On the relative value of data resampling approaches for software defect prediction. *Empir. Softw. Eng.* **2019**, *24*, 602–636. [CrossRef]
140. Li, M.; Xiong, A.; Wang, L.; Deng, S.; Ye, J. ACO Resampling: Enhancing the performance of oversampling methods for class imbalance classification. *Knowl. Based Syst.* **2020**, *196*, 105818. [CrossRef]
141. Potharaju, S.P.; Sreedevi, M.; Ande, V.K.; Tirandasu, R.K. Data mining approach for accelerating the classification accuracy of cardiotocography. *Clin. Epidemiol. Glob. Health* **2019**, *7*, 160–164. [CrossRef]
142. Lv, Y.; Ma, L.; Jiang, H. A Mobile Phone Screen Cover Glass Defect Detection MODEL Based on Small Samples Learning. In Proceedings of the 2019 IEEE 4th International Conference on Signal and Image Processing (ICSIP), Wuxi, China, 19–21 July 2019; pp. 1055–1059. [CrossRef]
143. Zhu, C.; Zhou, W.; Yu, H.; Xiao, S. Defect Detection of Emulsion Pump Body Based on Improved Convolutional Neural Network. In Proceedings of the 2019 International Conference on Advanced Mechatronic Systems (ICAMechS), Shiga, Japan, 26–28 August 2019; pp. 349–352. [CrossRef]
144. He, T.; Liu, Y.; Xu, C.; Zhou, X.; Hu, Z.; Fan, J. A Fully Convolutional Neural Network for Wood Defect Location and Identification. *IEEE Access* **2019**, *7*, 123453–123462. [CrossRef]
145. Dafu, Y. Classification of Fabric Defects Based on Deep Adaptive Transfer Learning. In Proceedings of the 2019 Chinese Automation Congress (CAC), Hangzhou, China, 22–24 November 2019; pp. 5730–5733. [CrossRef]
146. Şeker, A. Evaluation of Fabric Defect Detection Based on Transfer Learning with Pre-trained AlexNet. In Proceedings of the 2018 International Conference on Artificial Intelligence and Data Processing (IDAP), Malatya, Turkey, 28–30 September 2018; pp. 1–4. [CrossRef]
147. Zyout, I.; Oatawneh, A. Detection of PV Solar Panel Surface Defects using Transfer Learning of the Deep Convolutional Neural Networks. In Proceedings of the 2020 Advances in Science and Engineering Technology International Conferences (ASET), Dubai, United Arab Emirates, 4 February–9 April 2020; pp. 1–4. [CrossRef]
148. Schlegl, T.; Seeböck, P.; Waldstein, S.M.; Schmidt-Erfurth, U.; Langs, G. Unsupervised Anomaly Detection with Generative Adversarial Networks to Guide Marker Discovery. In *International Conference on Information Processing in Medical Imaging*; Springer: Philadelphia, PA, USA, 2017; pp. 146–157.
149. Schlegl, T.; Seeböck, P.; Waldstein, S.M.; Langs, G.; Schmidt-Erfurth, U. f-AnoGAN: Fast unsupervised anomaly detection with generative adversarial networks. *Med. Images Anal.* **2019**, *54*, 30–44. [CrossRef]
150. Akcay, S.; Atapour-Abarghouei, A.; Breckon, T.P. GANomaly: Semi-Supervised Anomaly Detection via Adversarial Training. In *Asian Conference on Computer Vision*; Springer: Berlin/Heidelberg, Germany, 2018; pp. 622–637.
151. Haselmann, M.; Gruber, D.P. Pixel-Wise Defect Detection by CNNs without Manually Labeled Training Data. *Appl. Artif. Intell.* **2019**, *33*, 548–566. [CrossRef]
152. Mei, S.; Yang, H.; Yin, Z. Unsupervised-Learning-Based Feature-Level Fusion Method for Mura Defect Recognition. *IEEE Trans. Semicond. Manuf.* **2017**, *30*, 105–113. [CrossRef]
153. Xia, B.; Cao, J.; Wang, C. SSIM-NET: Real-Time PCB Defect Detection Based on SSIM and MobileNet-V3. In Proceedings of the 2019 2nd World Conference on Mechanical Engineering and Intelligent Manufacturing (WCMEIM), Shanghai, China, 22–24 November 2019; pp. 756–759. [CrossRef]
154. Zhang, Z.; Wen, G.; Chen, S. Weld image deep learning-based on-line defects detection using convolutional neural networks for Al alloy in robotic arc welding. *J. Manuf. Process.* **2019**, *45*, 208–216. [CrossRef]

Disclaimer/Publisher's Note: The statements, opinions and data contained in all publications are solely those of the individual author(s) and contributor(s) and not of MDPI and/or the editor(s). MDPI and/or the editor(s) disclaim responsibility for any injury to people or property resulting from any ideas, methods, instructions or products referred to in the content.

MDPI
St. Alban-Anlage 66
4052 Basel
Switzerland
www.mdpi.com

Algorithms Editorial Office
E-mail: algorithms@mdpi.com
www.mdpi.com/journal/algorithms

Disclaimer/Publisher's Note: The statements, opinions and data contained in all publications are solely those of the individual author(s) and contributor(s) and not of MDPI and/or the editor(s). MDPI and/or the editor(s) disclaim responsibility for any injury to people or property resulting from any ideas, methods, instructions or products referred to in the content.

www.ingramcontent.com/pod-product-compliance
Lightning Source LLC
LaVergne TN
LVHW070250100526
838202LV00015B/2200